# A History of
# Modern Economic
# Analysis

# A History of Modern Economic Analysis

ROGER BACKHOUSE

Basil Blackwell

© Roger Backhouse, 1985

First published, 1985

Basil Blackwell Ltd
108 Cowley Road,
Oxford, OX4 1JF, UK

Basil Blackwell Inc.
432 Park Avenue South,
Suite 1505,
New York, NY 10016, USA

*British Library Cataloguing in Publication Data*

Backhouse, Roger
    A history of modern economic analysis.
    1. Economics—Methodology
    I. Title
    330.    HB131

    ISBN 0–631–14314–9


*Library of Congress Cataloging in Publication Data*

Backhouse, Roger.
    A history of modern economic analysis.

    Includes index.
    1. Economics—History    I. Title.
    HB87.B23  1985    330′.09    85–4054
    ISBN 0–631–14314–9


Typeset by Photo Graphics, Honiton, Devon
Printed in Great Britain by T. J. Press Ltd., Padstow

# Contents

# List of Figures

# Preface

The aim of this book is to tell the story of how economic analysis has reached its present state. To do this it is necessary to devote most of the available space to developments which have taken place since the 1870s. One disadvantage of such an approach is that the coverage of eighteenth and early nineteenth century economics, which has traditionally taken pride of place in many treatments of the history of economic thought, must inevitably be compressed. If we wish to understand the nature of the discipline of economics as it exists today, however, this is a price worth paying.

Concentrating on twentieth century developments also creates two further problems. The first is that because both the number of economists and the quantity of economic literature have increased so rapidly during the twentieth century, especially since the war, it has been necessary to rely more heavily on surveys and on secondary literature than is the case with earlier periods. Thus, though I have attempted to refer back to the original sources as much as possible, this is a book which could not have been written but for the large quantity of secondary material on the subject.

The second problem is posed by the very technical nature of much twentieth century economics. When considering, for example, classical economics, it is reasonable to assume that students know enough economic theory, and enough mathematics, to understand many of the technical issues involved. When we consider on the other hand, topics such as post-war general equilibrium theory, or social choice theory, as we must do if we are to provide a broad perspective on modern economics, technical issues cannot be discussed in the same way. It is therefore necessary to try to explain what economists have done, or are doing, without getting into technical details any more than is necessary.

In considering twentieth century economics, a thematic treatment is essential, for it is the only way to show how ideas have evolved over time. This is particularly true of the period since 1945: the number of economists involved makes it inappropriate to tell the story in terms of a few leading individuals. This approach, though necessary, has the drawback that it becomes harder to get a picture of the work of individual economists who have contributed to a variety of fields. Samuelson's work, for example, is discussed in virtually every chapter in Part IV.

Though I have attempted to adopt a cosmopolitan outlook, the emphasis is, with notable exceptions, on English-speaking economics. This reflects, to some extent, the fact that whilst the "leadership" of the economics profession was, at the turn of the century, shared amongst many countries, it has increasingly become located in the United States. The exception to this attempt to adopt a cosmopolitan attitude is the two chapters on Economics and Policy, where I have confined my attention to Britain. The dependence of economic policy-making on the economic and political environment, in a way not true of economic theory, makes it necessary to concentrate on a particular country, and I have chosen to cover the one most familiar to me.

The emphasis of this book is on developments within the "neoclassical" mainstream of economic theorizing, dominant since the time of Marshall. This approach to economics, however, has not gone unchallenged, and so two chapters are devoted to alternative approaches. This organization of the material should not, however, be taken as implying that what lies outside these two chapters constitutes a monolithic orthodoxy. Not only are the boundaries of "mainstream" economics almost impossible to define satis-factorily, but even within them there has been enormous variety. Although I use the terms "mainstream economics" and "alternative approaches", this is to make the story easier to tell, rather than because any definite dividing lines exist.

In writing this book I have received an enormous amount of assistance. Published work to which I am indebted is, I hope, acknowledged in footnotes, or in the Bibliographical Note at the end of the book. In addition, numerous colleagues have suggested references for me to use, or explained various points for me. Thanks are due in particular to those who have read and commented on drafts of particular chapters: Peter Cain, John Cantwell, Mark Casson, George Catephores, Bob Coats, David Collard, John Creedy, Les Fishman, Rick Garside, Paul Grout, Stephen Hannah, Geoffrey Harcourt, Terence Hutchison, Jan Kregel, Stephen Littlechild, Prasanta Pattanaik, Douglas Rimmer, Somnath Sen. They have provided me with many ideas, and helped me remove many errors and ambiguities. The person who must be singled out, however, is Denis O'Brien, who read a draft of the entire book, and whose comments have enabled me to improve virtually every chapter. Neither he, nor any of the others, however, is responsible for any errors or inadequacies which may remain. Though others may be responsible for many of the book's good points, I alone am responsible for its shortcomings.

Finally, thanks are due to my wife, Merida, and my son, Robert, for putting up with my seeming to prefer my word processor's company to theirs.

# 1

## Introduction

### 1.1 THE HISTORY OF ECONOMIC ANALYSIS

Schumpeter, in what must be regarded as the classic work on the history of economic analysis (1954), defined his subject matter as

the history of the intellectual efforts that men have made in order to *understand* economic phenomena or, which comes to the same thing, the history of the analytic or scientific aspects of economic thought.[1]

Though this defines a subject matter somewhat narrower than the history of all economic thought, it is wider than simply the history of economic theory: historical and statistical work, for example, are also included.

The history of economic analysis is important for several reasons, some applicable to any science, others specific to economics. Amongst the former there is what Schumpeter described as the highest claim that could be made for the history of any subject, "that it teaches us much about the ways of the human mind".[2] Of more direct relevance, however, is the need to place contemporary economics in perspective. Like most other disciplines, the structure of economics was neither planned nor rationally thought out. It simply grew and developed as economists pursued new lines of inquiry, dropped or modified old ones, developed new techniques, and so on. Even within particular branches of the subject we find different, and not always compatible approaches coexisting with each other (within microeconomics, for example, the theory of the firm and the theory of general competitive equilibrium). Studying the history of these ideas, seeing how and why they developed as they did, puts them into perspective.

The history of their subject is particularly important for economists, for two reasons. The first is that, unlike the situation in the natural sciences, the subject matter of economics is constantly changing. Not only are the issues with which economists are concerned changing in response to political and social changes, but the economy is itself changing. The structure of the British economy, for example, is very different now from the way it was at the time Adam Smith was writing. In addition, human behaviour itself cannot necessarily be assumed to be unchanging: as people become aware of new possibilities, (for example, when a new statistical regularity is discovered) they may alter their behaviour. Because of all these changes a historical perspective is more important in economics than in the natural sciences.

The second reason why the history of economics is so important concerns methodology. One of the characteristics of economics, *vis-à-vis* the other social sciences, is the large body of formal, abstract theory, much of it formulated mathematically. Despite this body of theory, however, there is substantial disagreement over its interpretation, and over the criteria which are to be used in deciding which parts of it to accept, and which parts to reject. Though most economists would subscribe to some notion of empirical testing, interpretations of this vary widely. The history of economic theorizing can be used to pursue some of these methodological issues. It is because of the importance of these methodological issues that some philosophical issues are considered next.


## 1.2   SOME CONCEPTS FROM THE PHILOSOPHY OF SCIENCE

### *Falsificationism and the growth of knowledge*

Perhaps the most important question in the philosophy of science concerns the relationship between scientific theories and empirical evidence: how can empirical evidence be used to appraise a scientific theory? Here the most important contribution, as far as most economists are concerned, has been that of Popper.[3] Central to Popper's approach to science is the concept of *falsification*. His argument is that empirical observation can *never* establish that a scientific generalization is true, for, however much evidence we obtain in support of a theory, we can never be sure that the next observation will not turn out to be inconsistent with the theory. All that successful testing of a theory can do is fail to refute the theory. Such successful testing of a theory may be regarded as "confirming" the theory, in the sense that it increases our confidence in it, but this is not the same as proving the theory to be true. This impossibility of verifying a theory through collecting empirical evidence is the so-called *problem of induction*.

Popper's solution to the problem of induction involves arguing that although empirical observation cannot be used to verify a theory, it can be used to refute it. He thus argues that the crucial characteristic of a scientific theory is not verifiability, for finding evidence to confirm a theory is easy, but *falsifiability*. He thus uses falsifiability as the criterion with which to distinguish between science and non-science. Scientific statements, for Popper, are, at least in principle, falsifiable: there are certain events which, if they occurred, would be inconsistent with the theory. Non-scientific statements, on the other hand, are unfalsifiable, in that they do not rule out the occurrence of anything. Marxism is thus, for Popper, unscientific, for its adherents can always reconcile whatever happens with the theory.

In addition to providing a "demarcation criterion" for distinguishing science from non-science, Popper's emphasis on falsification leads him to stress the growth of scientific knowledge. Scientific knowledge, according to Popper, is not knowledge that has been established as true, but simply generalizations which have, so far, survived attempts to refute them. Science progresses by progressively eliminating false hypotheses, a point of view which stresses the growth of knowledge. Popper's contribution has been aptly summed up as being to replace

the central problem of classical rationality, *the old problem of foundations*, [how we can know our knowledge is true] with *the new problem of fallible–critical growth*.[4]

The situation is, however, more complicated than the above account suggests, for falsification is always problematic. To see why, consider an example from economics: the hypothesis that the demand curve for bananas slopes downwards. If someone has produced empirical data to suggest that it slopes upwards, there would be many reasons why economists might refuse to accept that the theory had been refuted. (1) Doubts could be raised about the data – were price and quantity measured correctly? (2) The statistical procedures might be questioned – had a supply curve, rather than a demand curve been estimated? (3) Questions could be raised about the *ceteris paribus* condition – perhaps incomes changed, or tastes shifted for some reason? (4) Finally, there would be the question of whether or not the theory was correctly formulated. These details are less important than the general lesson that because it is *always* possible, in Popper's words, to "immunize" any theory against criticism, rejection of a theory becomes a matter of decision.[5]

From here the argument can be taken in several directions, two of which are relevant here. One direction is that taken by Popper, who suggested that scientists should adopt the methodological rule of refusing to adopt *ad hoc* strategems to save their theories. At the same time, however, he recognized that such a rule would have to be applied carefully, for if no one were protective towards theories, a new theory might be abandoned too soon, before it had had time to make its contribution to science.[6] The other line of argument is to investigate more closely the circumstances under which theories are rejected or accepted. If this approach is adopted, a much wider range of factors becomes relevant. For example, unanimity concerning refutation of a theory could be reached simply by "expelling" all those who disagree, by declaring them "cranks", whose opinion does not count for anything. The sociology of the scientific community is thus relevant. This approach underlies the work of Kuhn, whose ideas will be considered next.

### Normal science and scientific revolutions

*Normal science* is the fundamental concept in Thomas Kuhn's account of the growth of scientific knowledge. He defined it to mean "research based upon one or more past scientific achievements that some particular scientific community acknowledges for a time as supplying the foundation for further practice."[7] As examples of such *exemplars* or *paradigms* he cites Aristotle's *Physica*, Newton's *Principles* and Lavoisier's *Chemistry*. For a scientific achievement to form the basis for further research in this way, it must have two characteristics: it must be sufficiently unprecedented to attract an enduring group of adherents; and it must be sufficiently open-ended to leave all sorts of problems for scientists to solve.

Normal science has several important characteristics, the main one being the abandoning of critical discourse in the sense that there is a set of assumptions which are not questioned, and a set of procedures which are followed. This is the *disciplinary matrix* within which normal science is carried on. In undertaking normal science, scientists are not following a series of explicit rules, but they are following an example. Provided the initial scientific achievement, and the results obtained, are accepted without question, rules are not needed.[8] Even if they were desired, suitable rules to govern the conduct of research might prove hard, if not impossible, to articulate.[9]

Far from such an uncritical attitude being a problem, as might be inferred from Popper's theory, it is only such an uncritical attitude which, according to Kuhn, permits the application of the theory to a large number of problems, enabling a large number of detailed aspects of the world to be investigated. If scientists spent all their time arguing over fundamentals, they would never manage to investigate many "small" phenomena. Within normal science, therefore, most research takes the form of "puzzle-solving". Puzzle-solving is research where the results are generally known beforehand, where it is known that there is a solution, and which operates within certain rules.[10] Kuhn divides such puzzles into three main areas: establishing facts (these being required either because they are interesting in their own right, or in order to help confirm the superiority of the paradigm involved over another); applying the paradigm to new areas; and reformulating the ideas involved in the paradigm, the first articulation of which may well have been clumsy, or difficult to apply to certain problems.

Such normal science has implications for the nature of the scientific community. Acceptance of a particular form of normal science leads to a more rigid definition of a field of research, those who do not accept its basic assumptions being excluded from the relevant scientific community.[11] Education in the subject becomes learning to solve the puzzles produced by the paradigm, and because of the shared assumptions within the group, textbooks can become important.[12] At the same time, professional competence is judged in terms of ability at solving the research puzzles produced by the paradigm, for failure to solve a puzzle does not discredit the paradigm so much as the scientist who fails.[13]

For much of the time normal science can, according to Kuhn, progress satisfactorily along these lines, but from time to time *crises* arise. The main element in a crisis is the discovery of *anomalies*: awkward facts which cannot be explained in terms of the paradigm.[14] Much of the time anomalies can be ignored: they are simply facts that the theory cannot yet explain. An anomaly produces a crisis either when it concerns something that is fundamental to the paradigm, or when it is particularly important for external reasons – it may be, for example, that scientists are failing to explain something that the public expects them to explain. This failure of a paradigm may, Kuhn argues, produce bewilderment amongst the scientists concerned, for they do not know how to put it right: they can no longer be guided by the paradigm.[15]

Alternatively, a crisis may arise, not because a paradigm cannot explain some awkward fact, but because the modifications required to the theory render it transparently unsatisfactory. The classic example of this is pre-Copernican astronomy, in which the movements of the planets could be explained, but only through introducing more and more complicated systems. The problem was that the complexity of the system was increasing much more rapidly than the accuracy of its predictions, thus making it clear that something was fundamentally wrong with the whole system[16] Finally, an anomaly may provoke a crisis simply because it has persisted for a sufficiently long time.[17]

The result of a crisis is a large number of *ad hoc* modifications to the theory concerned, and of divergent articulations of the paradigm.[18] There may be confusion as the basis for the subject is undermined. Scientists search apparently randomly for answers, even turning to philosophy, something for which there is little place in normal science.[19] Eventually, from these new articulations of the paradigm, a new exemplar emerges. This involves a reconstruction of the field from fundamentals, and a new period of normal science emerges.[20] For Kuhn, therefore, it is only in such periods of *revolutionary science* when the fundamentals of the science are questioned, that the Popperian idea of theories being tested through confrontation with empirical evidence is applicable.

A scientific revolution in Kuhn's sense involves the replacement of one paradigm with another. There is continuity in that it is the unanticipated novelty produced by one paradigm which provides the basis for the new theory and the new paradigm.[21] At the same time, there is a break with the past, a break which, Kuhn argues, involves more than simply the replacement of one theory by another. Not only does a change of paradigm involve a change of world view,[22] but it also involves decisions which cannot be made on the basis of logic and evidence alone.[23] The reason for this is the "nonsubstantive differences between paradigms".[24] Because normal science cannot provide the information needed to make a purely rational choice between two paradigms, crises in normal science "are terminated, not by deliberation and interpretation, but by a relatively sudden and unstructured event like the gestalt switch".[25] Because of the non-rational elements involved in the switch from one paradigm to another, it becomes difficult to speak of scientific progress except within a single paradigm.[26]

## Scientific research programmes

Kuhn's response to the problem of determining the circumstances under which the incompatibility of a theory with empirical evidence led to the theory's being rejected led him to investigate the way scientists actually behave. Though he finds reasons for liking the pattern of scientific activity described by his term normal science, he is moving away from Popper's search for a normative theory, of how scientific activity ought to be conducted, into an investigation of how it is conducted. A different approach is to pursue Popper's approach, and to seek to explain the circumstances under which theories come to be rejected by looking more carefully at the structure of scientific theories. This is the approach which led Lakatos to his concept of *scientific research programmes*.[27]

Lakatos's first modification to Popper's scheme is to argue that the unit of appraisal should be the *research programme* rather than an individual theory, or even succession of theories. A research programme, according to Lakatos, has two main components: a *hard core* of provisionally accepted assumptions which, as long as the research programme continues, are treated as irrefutable; and a *positive heuristic*, defined as "a powerful problem-solving machinery [which] defines problems, foresees anomalies and turns them victoriously into examples according to a preconceived plan".[28] This hard core of a research programme is protected by a *protective belt* of auxiliary hypotheses. An example is Newtonian science which, in addition to its hard core comprising Newton's laws of dynamics and gravitation, contains the machinery for coping with anomalies.

For instance, if a planet does not move as it should, the Newtonian scientist checks his conjectures concerning atmospheric refraction, concerning propagation of light in magnetic storms, and hundreds of other conjectures which are all part of the programme. He may even invent a hitherto unknown planet and calculate its position, mass and velocity in order to explain the anomaly.[29]

In addition to changing the unit of appraisal in this way, Lakatos altered the criterion for appraisal. A research programme, Lakatos argued, will be rejected if there is a better one to replace it. A "better" one is one which has excess empirical content over its rival. This means that it must explain everything that its rival can explain, as well as predicting some novel facts that its rival cannot predict. In this context a newly interpreted fact might be viewed as a new fact, though a theory would be expected eventually to predict genuinely novel facts.[30]

In that this criterion allows for *ad hoc* modifications to a theory, and for minor inconsistencies, it is more tolerant than Popper's criterion of falsification. It allows a research programme time to develop. On the other hand, it is stricter than Popper's criterion in that it requires a research programme to produce better predictions than its rival. What the criterion does is to separate falsification from rejection: if a better research programme appears, a research programme may be rejected without being falsified; or one may be retained after anomalies have become apparent, simply because no better programme is available. Lakatos's methodology recognizes that many theories are falsified, in the sense of being inconsistent with some facts, right from the start, but that this does not render them unscientific.

If falsifiability cannot be used as a demarcation criterion to distinguish science from non-science, what can be put in its place? Lakatos suggests using the distinction between *progressive* and *degenerating* research programmes. With any research programme, anomalies will arise, and modifications (which may be thought *ad hoc*) will have to be made to account for them.

The crucial distinction is not between theories which are so modified and those which are not, but between cases where such *ad hoc* modifications result in the prediction of novel facts, and those which do not. A research programme is *theoretically progressive* if it predicts novel, hitherto unexpected facts. It is *empirically progressive* if these predictions are corroborated. The *ad hoc* modifications introduced into the Newtonian research programme, for example, resulted in the prediction of planets the existence of which had previously been unknown. These predictions were confirmed. In contrast, the modifications introduced into Marxism have served merely to explain events already known.[31] Lakatos's demarcation criterion is thus a historical one, involving the way a theory evolves over time.

Another implication of Lakatos's approach is that in a research programme methodological rules will suggest lines for further research, which accounts for the relative autonomy of theoretical research[32] The order in which Kuhnian puzzles are solved is determined not by current anomalies, but by theoretical considerations. It is mathematical problems, rather than anomalies, which determine the path pursued by science.[33] It may take decades before such theoretical research results in interestingly testable theory, or in the prediction of novel facts.[34]

## Multiple discoveries

The final concept to be considered is Merton's one of a *multiple discovery*:

The pages of the history of science record thousands of instances of similar discoveries having been made by scientists working independently of one another. Sometimes the discoveries are simultaneous or almost so; sometimes a scientist will make anew a discovery which, unknown to him, somebody else had made years before. Such occurrences suggest that discoveries become virtually inevitable when prerequisite kinds of knowledge and tools accumulate in man's cultural store and when the attention of an appreciable number of investigators becomes focussed on a problem, by emerging social needs, by developments internal to the science, or by both.[35]

Merton provides the hypothesis that we should *expect* multiple discoveries to be common:

far from being odd or curious or remarkable, the pattern of independent multiple discoveries in science is in principle the dominant pattern. ... It is the singletons – discoveries made only once in the history of science – that are the residual cases requiring explanation.[36]

The reason for this is that science is a social activity. Scientists are linked to the past by the knowledge they inherit; and to their contemporaries, both by interaction with other scientists, and by having their attention drawn to particular ideas and problems.[37] Multiple discoveries, therefore, arise through scientists "responding to much the same social and intellectual forces that impinge upon them all".[38]

Merton draws attention to the fact that discoveries are often made, only to be neglected for years until they are rediscovered: it is only on being rediscovered, perhaps by several scientists working independently, that they are incorporated into the science. This, Merton argues, is because multiple discoveries have a greater chance of being heard.[39]

Apart from its use in analysing specific events in the history of economics, Merton's ideas are useful to counteract the idea that the history of economic thought is concerned simply, or even primarily, with who first invented particular concepts. It is of course important to be as accurate as possible in ascribing priority in the development of economic ideas, but because economics, like any science, is a social activity, the date when an idea came into general circulation may be more important than the date of the earliest document in which the idea can be found. When forgotten precursors of later ideas are found, the main interest is often in why they were neglected, as much as in the ideas themselves.

## 1.3   THE APPROACH TO BE FOLLOWED

*The philosophy of science and the history of economic analysis*

One approach to the history of economic analysis would be to appraise economic ideas in terms of a particular methodology, taken from the philosophy of science. Kuhnian paradigms, or Lakatosian research programmes, could be identified and the story told in these terms. Such an approach is not without value, but it begs the question of how far the methodology chosen is appropriate for economics. Suppose, for example, that it turned out that little of the history of economic analysis could be fitted into Lakatos's methodology of scientific research programmes. One possible conclusion would be that the history of economics should be judged adversely. Alternatively, it would be possible to draw the conclusion that the methodology was simply inappropriate for economics.

There would be problems, too, should the methodology explain everything. Would some other methodology, such as Kuhn's paradigms, have performed equally well? Were the criteria for testing the applicability of the methodology sufficiently stringent for the results to mean anything? For example, if economics is divided up into chunks, each of which is to be tried out as a Kuhnian paradigm, or as a Lakatosian research programme, there are many ways in which we might divide it up. We might take the whole of economics inquiry since Adam Smith as one unit. We might separate classical economics, marginalist economics and Keynesian economics. Dividing still further we might consider episodes such as the post-Marshallian theory of the firm, or neoclassical growth theory. "Verification" of a methodology ought to be easy, as there are so many possible ways of applying it.

Why not, then, abandon the philosophy of science altogether? Firstly, the philosophy of science does provide useful concepts and ideas, and it suggests questions which are worth asking. Even though we may conclude that, for example, the marginal revolution was not a scientific revolution in Kuhn's sense, we may learn something in the process of coming to this conclusion. Secondly, though extreme caution must be applied in doing this, the history of economic analysis is useful for evaluating alternative methodologies. If economists have not followed what appear to be sound methodological principles, there may be a good reason why not (there may, of course be less respectable reasons too).

## The following chapters

In this book the main emphasis will be on what Schumpeter called "the Filiation of Scientific Ideas", "the process by which men's efforts to understand economic phenomena produce, improve, and pull down analytic structures in an unending sequence".[40] Though the history of economic analysis will not, in what follows, be analysed simply in terms of a single methodology, it will nonetheless be critical. Using Blaug's words, "Criticism implies standards of judgement, and my standards are those of modern economic theory."[41] This statement, though fundamental, must be subject to two very important qualifications.[42] (1) Economic theory involves not only logic, but also a set of assumptions. Thus to appraise past theories it is not enough, important as this is, simply to look at their logical coherence. It is necessary also to examine the assumptions economists have made, and here modern economic theory can provide less guidance. This is particularly important if we are to be critical of contemporary theory itself. It is important to be open to the possibility that what may at first sight appear to be logical inconsistency, may be the result of making assumptions at variance with the assumptions made in modern economics.

(2) In addition, there is more to economic theories than simply a formal, logical structure. Two economists may, for example, take a particular set of equations and interpret them in different ways. It is for this reason that a lot of attention will be paid to the way economists viewed what they were doing: to their "systems", considered as wholes. To stress this is not "relativism",[43] for it is not being claimed that a particular philosophy or particular circumstances in any way "justify" defective economic theories. It is rather that examining economists' systems as wholes, distinguishing philosophical attitudes from what we might think of as pure economic logic, is valuable in helping to distinguish those claims which depend for their validity on certain philosophic presuppositions, from those which depend on economic logic alone.

In the following chapters the emphasis is on modern economic analysis, in particular developments which took place from around the 1870s. Any dividing lines are arbitrary, but in important respects the best dividing lines appear to be the 1870s, or shortly thereafter, and the late 1930s.[44] Because the aim of the book is to illuminate contemporary economics, as much weight is given to the period after 1939 as to the one before. At the other end, whilst the 1870s do mark a turning point, it is impossible to understand many subsequent developments without going further back. This is the rationale for covering, albeit very briefly, the period of English classical economics. Because so much of Classical economics stems from him, Adam Smith is taken as the starting point.

# I

## BACKGROUND: POLITICAL ECONOMY BEFORE 1870

# 2

## Adam Smith

### 2.1 POLITICAL ECONOMY AS A SMITHIAN CREATION

To understand the economics from which modern economics arose in the 1870s we have to go back to Adam Smith, whose importance has been described as being "without any real parallel in the entire development of economics"[1] His influence on English classical political economy, from James Mill, Ricardo and Malthus to J. S. Mill and Cairnes, is obvious, for although these economists revised Smith's ideas their political economy remained within the Smithian mould. But Smith also had an influence outside England with which none of his English successors could compete. Ricardo's *Principles* (1817) never matched the success of the *Wealth of Nations* (1776), whilst Mill's *Principles* (1848) was explicitly an attempt to re-work and bring up to date the *Wealth of Nations*. In addition Smith's influence outlasted the classical period, many late nineteenth and twentieth century economists owing much to Smith.[2]

The *Wealth of Nations* was important for containing many of the components from which classical political economy was made up: it contained both the main elements of the classical theory of value and distribution, and the main classical policy prescriptions. But far more important than this was the fact that Smith provided the vision of the economic system which permeated the whole of classical economics. This was of a system based on the "notion of a natural, effective self-adjusting mechanism as being usually at work throughout competitive economies or markets."[3] Provided that the government maintained a framework of law, justice and security of property, the individual pursuit of self-interest would cause the wealth of a nation to increase more effectively than would a system of government intervention.

However, whilst it is correct to emphasize Smith's overwhelming importance in the history of economic thought, it would be wrong to see him, as did some of the classical economists (especially McCulloch and Mill), as the founder of economics.[4] By the mid eighteenth century when Smith formed his ideas there was an extensive literature dealing with all aspects of economics: a subjective theory of value, associated with Galiani, Pufendorf and Hutcheson; the origins of the labour theory of value had been put forward by Petty and Locke; there was an extensive literature on money, from that of the pamphleteers of the mid seventeenth century (such as Misselden and Mun) to the writings of Locke, Law and Cantillon; and even the idea of self-equilibrating mechanisms was present in the literature of the seventeenth century. In addition, Smith owed much to his contemporaries, especially Hume and the Physiocrats such as Quesnay and Turgot. Indeed, Smith's debts were so extensive that Schumpeter felt able to describe the *Wealth of Nations* as containing "no really novel ideas."[5]

## 2.2 SMITH'S SYSTEM

*Philosophy*

Although many economists of the eighteenth and nineteenth centuries were philosophers, the most notable, apart from Smith, being Mill and Sidgwick, their economics can, on the whole, be understood independently of the rest of their philosophy. This is not the case with Smith, however, whose system of political economy formed merely a part of a wider philosophical system covering ethics, law, politics and economics.[6] Two features of this are relevant to his economics. Firstly, Smith's stress on the beneficent results of the pursuit of self-interest arose from a much more general, teleological view of the universe, in which the action of guiding Providence could be seen. For example, the phrase "the invisible hand" is only one of several phrases for guiding Providence in *The Theory of Moral Sentiments* (1759), the main work in which Smith developed his ethical system.[7] More important than this, however, is the fact that in *The Theory of Moral Sentiments* Smith developed a theory of natural justice based on "sympathy": the ability of men to see things from someone else's point of view. Ideas of justice derived in this way formed the basis for both law and individual behaviour. It was only within such a framework of justice that Smith claimed beneficent effects for the pursuit of self-interest. For him self-interest was a self-interest permeated with ideas of justice, self-interest being pursued as much for vanity as for its own sake:

> It is the vanity, not the ease, or the pleasure, which interests us. But vanity is always founded on the belief of our being the object of attention and approbation.[5]

For example, natural justice precluded employers from colluding in order to depress wages; if they did this then competition could not be relied upon to produce a harmony of interests.

*Concern with growth*

As the full title, *An Inquiry into the Nature and Causes of the Wealth of Nations*, indicates, Smith was concerned above all with economic growth, this concern underlying both his theory of the invisible hand and his advocacy of economic liberty. Thus although Smith's stress on interdependence and the invisible hand may remind us of modern, static general equilibrium theory, it would be wrong to interpret Smith within this context.[9] For Smith, competition is not perfect competition as we understand it, but something much more dynamic: it eliminates excess profits, widens markets, increases productivity and causes capital to move into the most profitable ventures. Similarly, his theory of the invisible hand was not concerned with an optimal, static allocation of resources, but with producing conditions conducive to growth.

Smith's concern with growth, and his advocacy of a policy of *laissez faire*, have led some historians to see him as the prophet of the industrial revolution, linking Smithian and classical economics with the interests of the rising industrial class.[10] Such an argument is, however, *extremely* misleading. Although the *Wealth of Nations* was published in 1776, and revised in 1784, the main ideas were developed much earlier, going back to the 1750s. At this time the "industrial revolution" had hardly begun. Furthermore, Smith nowhere refers, even in the revised edition, either to the application of steam power or to the inventions which were on the verge of revolutionizing the cotton industry.[11] On the other hand, it would be wrong to go to the other extreme and to portray Smith as concerned with a purely agricultural economy: though agriculture was still dominant, industry was growing throughout the eighteenth century. It is this early phase of industrial development, not the "industrial revolution" itself, which forms the background to the *Wealth of Nations*: hence Smith's stress on division of labour rather than mechanization as the source of increased productivity, and his emphasis on circulating capital rather than investment in machinery.[12]

## 2.3   THE THEORY OF GROWTH

### Definitions

Smith's concern was with the wealth of nations, which he defines in terms of per capita income: the proportion of "the necessaries and conveniences of life" annually consumed to the number of consumers.[13] This per capita income is determined by two factors:

First, by the skill, dexterity and judgement with which its labour is generally applied; and secondly, by the proportion between the number of those who are employed in useful labour, and those who are not so employed.[14]

Obvious though this might seem at first sight, it immediately raises questions about Smith's system of national income accounting, for Smith is referring to the division of the labour force, not between employment and unemployment, but between productive and unproductive labour. The criterion for this distinction is whether or not the labour leaves behind "any trace or value ... for which an equal quantity of service could afterwards be procured."[15] Unproductive labour thus covered many workers, ranging from domestic servants to the armed forces and the sovereign himself.[16] This is a distinction that does not make sense in modern economics, for such services would be included in national output, valued at their cost of production. As Smith did not include these services in national income his distinction between productive and unproductive labour did make sense.

This definition of national output is linked to Smith's view of capital. He views capital as the stock of goods that must be held owing to the fact that production takes time:

A weaver cannot apply himself entirely to his peculiar business, unless there is before hand stored up somewhere, either in his own possession or that of some other person, a stock sufficient to maintain him, and to supply him with the tools of his work, till he has not only completed but sold his web.[17]

"Stock", as Smith calls this accumulated wealth, includes consumer goods (those needed to maintain labourers), fixed capital (useful machines, profitable buildings, improvements of land and "acquired and useful abilities" of members of society) and circulating capital (intermediate goods).[18] The point of the definition of productive labour is that it is productive labour alone whose activity serves to increase the amount of this stock, and hence the potential for further production. Tangibility is not the sole criterion for the distinction between productive and unproductive labour, the production of tangible goods being unproductive if, for example, the goods are luxury goods not needed to sustain labour. These definitions are linked to Smith's view of accumulation and growth, but before turning to that we have to consider his views on the division of labour.

### Division of labour

Of the two factors influencing per capita income, Smith believed on the basis of empirical observation that it was the former, "the productive powers of labour", that was the more important.[19] He argued that the most important reason for the increases in the productive powers of labour which had occurred was the division of labour.[20] The aspect of the division of labour with which we are most familiar is the division of labour within a single plant, but of far more importance to Smith was the division of labour permitted by exchange. Men could specialize on producing one thing, obtaining other goods they required by exchange. The scope for the division of labour depended on the extent of the market.[21] Thus growth of the market contributed to productivity. It was only at this point that Smith introduced the phenomena associated with exchange – value, prices, money and so on.

### Accumulation and growth

Smith analysed the process of capital accumulation, so closely bound up with the extension of the market and division of labour, in terms of a simple aggregative model. The economy starts with a given, previously accumulated stock. This is used to support productive labourers who produce output. This output can be used in one of two ways: it can be consumed by unproductive labourers, perhaps producing luxury goods, or it can be added to the stock available to support productive labourers in the following period. This is illustrated in Figure 2.1. Through this process the stock may be increased and the economy grow. The growth rate will depend on two factors: the productivity of productive labour, and the ratio of productive to unproductive labour.[22] The last of these, which corresponds to the division of the produce between consumption and saving, requires some comment.

(i) The concepts used do not correspond exactly to modern concepts. Consumption necessary to maintain labourers comes out of stock, and is provided for by saving. Modern national income accounting would include it within consumption. A further reason for not identifying Smith's second factor with, for example, Keynes' propensity to consume, is that Smith's definition of produce, as mentioned above, excludes the "produce" of unproductive labour, something that would be included in modern calculations of income.

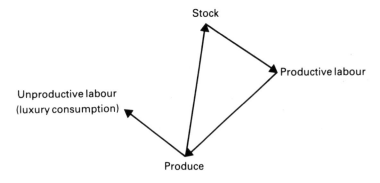

FIGURE 2.1 *Smith's Theory of Growth*

(ii) It is on the basis of this model that Smith reaches his conclusions that (a) "Parsimony, and not industry, is the immediate cause of the increase of capital", and (b) "What is annually saved is as regularly consumed as what is actually spent."[23] He was assuming that savings would not be hoarded, for this was something which did not make sense. This meant that the only role for money in Smith's system was that of being a medium of exchange. As such it was an element of the capital stock which, like any other element, contributed to productivity. There would be, at any time, a definite requirement for money, and supply would accommodate to this, silver flowing into or out of the country as necessary. If paper currency were used as a medium of exchange, this would reduce the need for silver: an increase in paper currency would produce an equivalent reduction in the quantity of silver circulating (if silver and paper have different velocities of circulation the increase in paper need not equal the decline in silver). As for the price of silver, this was determined by the cost of producing it.

*International trade*

Smith's theory of international trade forms part of his theory of economic growth, for he saw international trade as a means of extending the market and hence the scope for division of labour. He adopted an "absolute advantage" theory, assuming that commodities would be produced wherever they could be produced most cheaply. This approach is one which makes sense only if capital and labour are assumed to be mobile between countries as well as within them. Differences in production costs are assumed to arise because different countries have different endowments of land and natural resources. International trade is thus assumed to be fundamentally the same as inter-regional trade.

If production does take place wherever goods can be produced most cheaply, there is no reason why a country should not find itself producing more than its domestic market can absorb. This gives rise to the view that international trade should be regarded as a means of disposing of surplus produce – the so-called "vent for surplus" theory.

*Wider issues*

The model described here forms only a part of Smith's theory of growth. It presumes the existence of a stable institutional framework, in particular a system of law and security of property. In addition there are microeconomic aspects to the process of growth, for resources, both capital and labour, must be allocated efficiently. To understand this, however, we need to know something of his theory of value, a part of which is concerned with the distribution of income between classes, an issue which in turn will bring us back to growth.

## 2.4   VALUE AND DISTRIBUTION

*Value*

The importance of the theory of value contained in the *Wealth of Nations* lies in its being the source from which all classical discussions of the subject were derived. This is significant because Smith consciously and explicitly rejected the subjective value theory he inherited from his predecessors (in particular Hutcheson and Pufendorf) in favour of a cost of production theory. The crucial paragraph is the following:

The word VALUE, it is to be observed, has two different meanings, and sometimes expresses the utility of some particular object, and sometimes the power of purchasing other goods which the possession of that object conveys. The one may be called "value in use"; the other "value in exchange". The things which have the greatest value in use frequently have little or no value in exchange; and on the contrary, *those which have the greatest value in exchange have frequently little or no value in use*. Nothing is more useful than water; but it will purchase scarce anything; scarce anything can be had in exchange for it. A diamond, on the contrary, has scarce any value in use; but a very great quantity of other goods may frequently be had in exchange for it.[24]

Both his predecessors and his successors defined utility subjectively, as the property of giving satisfaction, but Smith defined it as objective usefulness, making it easy for him to dismiss any connection between value and utility.

Smith starts by making it clear that he is concerned to explain the rules governing *relative* prices, which he does in three stages: looking for the "real measure" of exchange value; dividing this "real price" into its component parts; and examining the relationship between market price and this price.

*The real measure of exchange value* Smith starts by arguing that the value of a commodity is what it really costs, namely the "toil and trouble" that its owner is spared through having the commodity. This leads Smith to define the value of a commodity to its owner as "the quantity of labour which it enables him to purchase or command".[25] However, whilst the value of a commodity is its "real cost" it is impracticable to estimate value this way, for real cost depends not just on hours of work but also on the hardship endured and the ingenuity used in making the commodity. It is practicable to measure value only in terms of other commodities, money (gold and silver) and corn (the necessaries of life) being the obvious choices. Smith argues that over long periods corn is the better measure of value, whilst for short periods silver is better. His criterion here is that of which better approximates changes in real costs: in the short run it is silver that has the more stable value; in the long run, corn. This discussion is important, for it makes clear the purpose of Smith's theory of value. Labour commanded was not used by Smith as a theory of exchange value, but as a measure of changes in welfare over time.

*The components of price* However, whilst labour commanded measures the real cost of commodities, this will not be equal to the labour required to produce the commodities concerned. Where capital is employed an element of profit must be included as well, otherwise the employer would have no incentive to supply the necessary capital. In addition the use of land requires, for similar reasons, that rent be paid. Value thus comprises three parts – wages, profit and rent – each being the supply price of a particular factor of production.[26] To explain this Smith started with the "earliest and rudest" state of society, in which, because there was no capital and land was not privately owned, the whole produce belonged to the labourer.[27] In such a society the value (labour commanded) of a commodity would be equal to the labour required to produce it: the labour theory of value. But although these passages in Smith's writings were taken up by later advocates of the labour theory of value, above all by Marx, Smith was not advocating a labour theory of value. Indeed, by showing that it applied only to a state in which capital was absent and land free he was attacking the labour theory of value. His own labour commanded theory was very different from a theory of exchange value.[28]

*Market price and natural price*   The natural price of a commodity was defined as the price just sufficient to pay the ordinary wages of labour, the ordinary rent of land and the ordinary rate of profit on the capital employed.[29] But the actual, or market price of a commodity would not always be equal to the natural price, for it depended on the quantity brought to the market compared with what Smith called the effectual demand for the commodity. When market price was above the natural price some factor must be receiving more than the normal remuneration, so there would be an incentive to produce more of the commodity; similarly less would be produced when market price was below the natural price. Smith reached the conclusion that "the natural price, therefore, is, as it were, the central price, to which the prices of all commodities are continually gravitating."[30] When market price equals natural price supply will equal demand.

## Wages

Having given an account of value in terms of costs of production Smith then explained how these costs were determined, starting with wages. His theory was one in which supply and demand for labour determined real wages, the quantity of necessaries and conveniences of life received by the labourer. Demand depended on "the funds which are destined for the payment of wages".[31] This fund was not taken as constant, for it increased with national wealth (high profits increased it) and it responded to prices (if corn were cheap farmers would employ servants rather than sell corn, thus increasing the wage-fund).[32] Supply, on the other hand, depended on real wages, for prosperity would cause the population to increase, whilst poverty would reduce it.[33] The money wage is determined simply by multiplying the real wage, determined by supply and demand for labour, by the price of provisions.[34]

The operation of supply and demand led to a situation in which the average level of wages depended, above all, on whether society was advancing or declining. In a progressive society profits, the wage-fund and demand for labour would be high. The result was that competition would result in high real wages and an increasing population. In a stationary or declining society, on the other hand, the pressure of labour supply would lower real wages, causing distress and a declining population. Comparison of Britain with China was used to support this.

## Profits

The rise and fall in the profits of stock depend upon the same causes with the rise and fall in the wages of labour, the increasing or declining state of society; but those causes affect the one and the other very differently.[35]

The competition resulting from an increase in stock (capital) raises wages and decreases profits. Thus the progress of the British economy since Henry VIII's time, involving as it did a secular rise in the stock of capital, had led to a fall in the rate of profit. The latter was something Smith had deduced from the secular decline he observed in the rate of interest, this, though not the same as the profit rate, being a proxy for it. The reason suggested for this fall in the rate of profit was simply that shortage of labour results in the bidding up of wages at the expense of profits, though later in *The Wealth of Nations* he offers an alternative explanation in terms of limited opportunities for investment.[34]

The close parallel between Smith's theories of wages and profits is emphasized by the fact that when he comes to consider differences between wage and profit rates in different occupations, he treats the two together.[37] In a situation of perfect liberty,

The whole of the advantages and disadvantages of the different employments of labour and stock must, in the same neighbourhood, be either perfectly equal or continuously tending to equality.[38]

In applying this to wages he brings in the agreeableness of different occupations, training costs, variability of employment, the degree of trust involved and the probability of success. Of these, only the last is relevant to profits, from which Smith concludes that profit rates will be more nearly uniform than wage rates.

Of a different nature, but applying to both profits and wages, are inequalities brought about by restrictions on liberty, restrictions of which Smith was very critical.

## Rent

For Smith, rent is a residual, the revenue left after deducting from the value of the produce the supply price of inputs other than land:

Rent ... is naturally the highest which the tenant can afford to pay in the actual circumstances of the land. In adjusting the terms of the lease, the landlord endeavours to leave him no greater share of the produce than what is sufficient to keep up the stock for which he furnishes the seed, pays the labour, and purchases and maintains the cattle and other instruments of husbandry, together with the ordinary profits of farming stock in the neighbourhood.[39]

He described this as a monopoly rent determined not by "what the landlord may have laid out upon the improvement of the land" (its supply price) but by "what the farmer can afford to give".[40] As such rent varied with the fertility of the land and with its location.

In developing his theory of rent Smith drew a sharp distinction between corn and other commodities produced by using land (in particular meat and mining products). The basis for this distinction was that land producing food was considered always to produce enough to yield a rent.[41] At the same time, food production created its own demand, for population would grow in proportion to the quantity of food.[42] This meant that land could always be used to produce food. If land were to be used to produce other things the rent paid would have to be as great as the rent paid on corn-producing lands, which meant that the rent paid on corn-producing land regulated other rents. If other rents were higher this was due to the scarcity of the appropriate land.

### Progress and distribution

Progress, according to Smith, would increase both wages and rents at the expense of profits, a vision of the long term which came to dominate classical economics. But the route by which Smith reached this conclusion was very different from that of his successors, for they reached it *without* postulating diminishing returns in agriculture.[43] Smith implicitly assumed constant returns in the production of corn, for he argued that the value of corn, on average, remained constant: on the one hand improvements were raising the productivity of labour, but on the other hand the price of cattle, "the principal instruments of agriculture", was increasing, these two effects offsetting each other.[44] The landlord's share rose because (a) the rise in the total value of the produce resulting from improvement raised it, and (b) the rise in the price of cattle, caused by the rising price of fodder, raised rents. At the same time improvements in industry reduced the prices of manufactures, raising the real value of rents. Competition of capitals led to an increase in wages and to a fall in profits. It was the competition of capitals which caused the secular changes in distribution, not developments in agriculture. This was very different from the picture painted by later classical economists.

## 2.5   ECONOMIC POLICY

As is well known, Smith advocated a policy of *laissez faire*, arguing for the removal of artificial barriers to trade, internal as well as external. He advocated what he called a system of natural liberty, which he contrasted with the "mercantile system" and the "system of agriculture" (Physiocracy). One argument for this was in terms of allocative efficiency. He argued that capital should move to whichever branches of trade offered the greatest prospects of profit, something that would happen as a matter of course in the absence of artificial barriers to trade.[45] Similar arguments were applied to labour. Thus Smith could argue that interference, whether duties on foreign trade or restrictions on the mobility of labour, were undesirable.[46] Further arguments followed from Smith's model of capital accumulation and growth. Artificial stimulation of industry would be counterproductive, for by encouraging capital to move away from agriculture it would reduce the surplus from which net additions to stock had to come. Growth required net additions to stock, not merely its redistribution, and agriculture was important for this. In addition it was a waste of resources for a country to attempt to accumulate money beyond the level needed for circulation. Smith thus berated the mercantile system for mistakenly confusing money with wealth.

On the other hand, Smith did not advocate *laissez faire* in the sense of the unrestricted pursuit of self-interest. As mentioned above, Smith presupposed a framework of justice, which had two implications. One was that the pursuit of self-interest was the pursuit of a self-interest permeated with ideas of justice resulting from sympathy with fellow human beings: competition would be restricted to certain forms of expression. In addition the framework of justice implied a role for the state much greater than simply that of maintaining a legal and institutional framework. Extensive regulation and intervention in the economy, ranging from regulating monopolies and the provision of roads, bridges and canals to laws to check the engrossing of land in the colonies, was required.

## 2.6 SMITH'S LEGACY

### Method

The account of Smith's theory given above gives no idea of Smith's comprehensive approach to economics, for it details only the theoretical part of his work. A characteristic of *The Wealth of Nations* was its combination of this theory with a wealth of empirical detail, not only on the contemporary British economy, but also on other parts of the world. This emphasis is important for three reasons. Firstly, it was a major reason for the success and for the lasting value of the book. Many people read it who would never have read a more abstract work. Secondly, it tells us about Smith's own attitude to method: impressive though the theoretical system may be, his method was not purely deductive. He never gets very far from concrete facts. Finally, the approach of *The Wealth of Nations* is important in explaining why such a variety of economists, from Ricardo to Jones in the classical period, and from Wicksell to Cunningham in a later one, could find in Smith a predecessor. Economists with historical leanings could view his approach as inductive, whilst others could see it as primarily deductive.

### Theory

Smith's main contribution in the field of economic theory was to provide a system in which pricing, production and distribution were interdependent. Although it would be very misleading to view it in Walrasian terms, it was, in certain respects, a system of general equilibrium: the cost of production theory of value brought out the connection between distribution and prices; whilst the terms "natural" and "ordinary" clearly defined equilibrium values. Smith was sometimes accused of circular reasoning – prices determine costs, and costs determine values – but this was the result of his attempting to portray a system of general equilibrium without using the apparatus of simultaneous equations.

Smith's theme, of a link between distribution and growth, was taken up by his successors, in particular Ricardo. But Smith's handling of it did not determine the manner in which his theory was developed, for he brought in an enormous variety of ideas. Although the exposition above has concentrated on presenting a consistent theory, the *Wealth of Nations* contained many hints at other explanations of value and distribution: though in our view Smith clearly did not advocate a labour theory of value, there is enough material for economists to find the basis of a labour theory of value in his writing; and although he rejected utility as an explanation of value, the advocates of a utility theory could find enough in his writing to claim him as a predecessor. With distribution too there were hints at a large number of theories: for example, he describes a wage fund theory of wages, a productivity theory and a subsistence theory. These ideas were not necessarily inconsistent with each other, but they provided a variety of ways in which the *Wealth of Nations* could be developed. The same was true of his writing on profits and rent. Furthermore, in addition to the aspects of his theory considered here there was his trade theory. It was in the area of money where he contributed least, his work here being in some way inferior to Hume's. But even here his doctrine that saving constitutes spending was extremely influential, whilst the real bills doctrine fuelled later controversy.

Thus in the same way that his comprehensiveness as regards method enabled a variety of economists to acknowledge him, his comprehensiveness in theory provided enormous scope for development. These developments were encouraged by Smith's use of theory to advance policy prescriptions that came to catch the imagination.

# 3

# Ricardo's Theory of Value and Distribution

## 3.1 INTRODUCTION

Classical economics certainly originated with Smith, his *Wealth of Nations* being probably the most widely read treatment of the subject until J. S. Mill's *Principles* appeared in 1848. Classical economics was, however, much more than merely a reworking of Smithian ideas. Though Smith's concern with capital accumulation and growth remained, the theories in which this vision was embodied changed greatly, and the vision itself also changed significantly. These changes were the result both of new assumptions, some of which were adopted in response to changes in the economic environment, and of new methods. Amongst the new assumptions, those underlying the theories of population and rent were most fundamental, for whilst traces of both the Malthusian theory of population and diminishing marginal productivity in agriculture can be found in the *Wealth of Nations* their importance in Smith's theory was insignificant in comparison with their role in classical theories. In the field of method, the crucial change was Ricardo's introduction of abstract, purely deductive theorizing.

*Population and rent*

One of the two main elements of the classical theory of distribution and economic growth was the Malthusian theory of population, first published in 1798, and later revised in successive editions of Malthus' *Essay on Population*. The central theme of this theory was the pressure of population on resources. If the birth rate were not lowered by "preventive checks", then "positive checks" would come into operation, raising the death rate. This theory carried the implication that wages could never depart very far, or for very long, from the level required for subsistence. If wages rose, then population would grow faster, the resulting increase in labour supply pushing wages back towards subsistence. If wages fell below subsistence then the population would fall until wages could rise back towards subsistence. Though the interpretation of this theory, and in particular the interpretation attached to "subsistence", varied greatly both in Malthus' writings and in classical economics generally, some version of the Malthusian theory underlay most classical writings on economics.

Malthus' theory of population, together with the shortage of cultivable land during the Napoleonic wars, when, due to wartime demands and to Napoleon's blockade of England, corn prices and rents rose dramatically, provided the background to the other main element of classical economics, the theory of differential rent. Though first put forward by Anderson (1777) this came into prominence only when discovered by Malthus and West, in two pamphlets published in 1815.

### Ricardo's method

Though the main elements of the classical theory of growth, value and distribution can be found in the works of Smith, Malthus, West and others, the integration of these elements into a coherent logical system was the achievement of Ricardo, after Smith the greatest system builder in classical economics. Though working within the general framework established by Smith, Ricardo constructed a radically different system. A major reason for the difference between the Smithian and the Ricardian systems was Ricardo's use of long, purely deductive arguments where Smith had used short chains of reasoning interspersed with empirical observation. Here Ricardo's mentor was James Mill, with his desire to derive economic propositions as certain as the propositions of Euclidian geometry. The use of deductive reasoning was not, however, the sole reason for the abstract nature of Ricardo's theorizing, for he also adopted the technique of using "strong cases", much of his theorizing dealing with conditions of long run equilibrium under highly simplified assumptions.

Though there is a sense in which Ricardo can be seen as having embodied the Smithian vision of the process of economic growth in a new theory, there is an equally important sense in which the vision itself changed. Where Smith's emphasis was overwhelmingly on the possibilities for growth through increased division of labour and capital accumulation, Ricardo and, following him, many of the later classical economists, focussed on the obstacles to growth. In part this changed vision can be blamed on the different economic environments in which Smith and Ricardo were work-ing: this certainly explains some of the new assumptions. But it is arguable that Ricardo's new abstract methods were also, to a certain extent, to blame, for division of labour and the possibilities for technical progress are much less amenable to Ricardian deductive techniques than are the more mechanical relationships between income distribution, savings and capital accumulation.

## 3.2   THE CORN MODEL

### Income distribution

Though Ricardo was not the originator of what is usually called the Ricardian theory of rent, it was Ricardo who first made it the basis of a coherent system. Central to this system is the so-called "corn model", first used by Ricardo in his *Essay on Profits* (1815),[1] written shortly after Malthus' pamphlet on rent.[2] To derive Ricardo's model we start by assuming that demand for food (agricultural output) is completely inelastic, given by the size of the population, and that capital and labour are used in fixed proportions in agriculture. Capital can be thought of as circulating capital, comprising the stock of food needed to sustain the labourers until the harvest is available. It is further assumed that the application of capital and labour to the land is subject to diminishing returns, as shown in Figure 3.1.[3] Given the size of the labour force, ON, we can read off average output, OQ, and total output, the rectangle OQXN. Rent, according to Ricardo, was the surplus earned by owners of land more productive than the least productive land under cultivation, which means that total rent is the rectangle PQXY. In other words, labour and capital together receive their joint marginal product, OP. This leaves the question of how the output not received as rent is divided between wages and profits. Here we can bring in the Malthusian theory to argue that wages will be determined by the subsistence requirements of the workers, OW. Total wages will be the rectangle OWZN, leaving profits as the residual, WPYZ.

This theory determines profits in agriculture, but according to Ricardo this will determine the rate of profit in industry, for should profit rates differ capitalists will move capital from agriculture to industry or vice versa as they seek to increase their profits. This leads Ricardo to the conclusion which was central to Ricardian economics, that "The general profits of stock depend wholly on the profits of that last portion of capital employed on the land."[4]

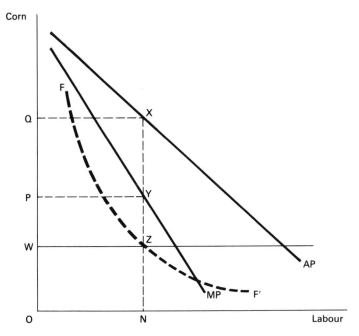

FIGURE 3.1   *Ricardo's Theory of Distribution*

For Ricardo diminishing returns in agriculture regulated the rate of profit in the economy as a whole. Two implications follow from this. The first is that if the employment of capital and labour increases (remember that they are assumed to be used in fixed proportions) profits must fall, for not only does the average product of capital and labour fall, but the share taken by rents increases. The second is that if the wage rate increases the only effect of this is to lower profits. There is an inverse relationship between profits and wages.

### Capital accumulation and growth

This model of distribution can easily be turned into a model of growth by adding assumptions about the savings behaviour of the different classes. Ricardo assumed that workers and landlords consumed all their income, whilst capitalists saved all theirs. This means that as long as profits are positive, as at ON in Figure 3.1, the capital stock is increasing. As the capital stock increases so too does employment, labour supply being completely elastic at the subsistence wage. As employment of capital and labour increase their average product falls, and rents rise. Because the wage rate cannot fall, the rise in rents must be at the expense of profits, which fall. This process continues until profits are reduced to zero, at which point accumulation ceases. Accumulation of capital benefits merely the landlords.

### The corn model

This theory, however, depends on a critical assumption not yet mentioned, namely that a single commodity – corn, or wheat – serves as both input and output in agriculture. In particular, the real wage is in terms of corn, and capital comprises a stock of corn.[5] To see the importance of this, suppose that an increase in manufacturing productivity lowers the price of manufactured goods relative to that of agricultural output (corn). If Ricardo's theory is to hold, this rise in manufacturing productivity must not affect the rate of profit. However, if, for example, wages depend on the price of manufactured goods as well as on the price of corn (the workers' subsistence, for example, may comprise clothing as well as food) the wage rate in terms of corn will fall. This will raise the rate of profit. Thus it is only if wages are fixed in terms of corn that the Ricardian theory works. Hence Ricardo's need for a "corn model": the assumption that corn constitutes the only input and the only output is more than just a convenient simplification, for it is critical for the Ricardian theorem that profits depend solely on the rate of return in agriculture.

### 3.3  THE LABOUR THEORY OF VALUE

### Value in Ricardo's system

In comparing the Ricardian and Smithian theories of value it is easy to see that Ricardo was looking for a theory with greater logical rigour than was

Smith. This, however, explains only part of the difference between their theories of value. In Smith's system the theory of value is used to show the interdependence of the various parts of the economy, as part of his "general equilibrium system". In so far as Smith was concerned to find an absolute standard of value it was because he wanted to estimate changes in welfare over time: corn was chosen as a better measure of value for long periods; money for short periods. Ricardo's use of value theory was very different, arising from the problems encountered when he tried to relax the assumptions of the corn model. He wanted a theory of value in order to be able to aggregate, so as to obtain a model which, though describing a multi-commodity economy, behaved like the corn model. To find such a theory he turned to the labour theory of value, defining value in a very un-Smithian way:

The value of a commodity, or the quantity of any other commodity for which it will exchange, depends on the relative quantity of labour which is necessary for its production.[6]

Before going on to consider in more detail Ricardo's value theory we need to turn to its relation to his theory of rent. In deriving his theory of value Ricardo's first step was to get rid of rent by assuming "that the price of corn is regulated by the quantity of labour necessary to produce it, with that portion of capital which pays no rent".[7]

Value can thus be reduced to two components – wages and profits. The problem with this approach is that it requires that all rent is a price-determined surplus. In Ricardo's theory, where demand for wage goods is totally inelastic, workers consuming goods in fixed proportions, this causes no problem: land has no alternative uses, and so its supply price is zero. In general, however, land will have other uses, which means that cost of production will include the rent that land could obtain in alternative uses – its supply price.

## The invariable measure of value

Two theorems were central to Ricardian economics: the inverse relationship between wages and profits; and the theorem that the rate of profit in agriculture determined the rate of profit in industry. The problem with generalizing these results to a multi-commodity economy was that as the distribution of income changed, relative values, and hence the value of total output, might change. The reason for this is to do with capital, and the fact that capital and labour are combined in different proportions in different industries. Suppose the wage rate were to rise and the profit rate were to fall. For commodities produced using a sufficiently high capital–labour ratio the fall in the profit rate would outweigh the rise in the wage rate, and their value would fall. For labour-intensive commodities, on the other hand, value would rise.

Ricardo's problem was to find a commodity such that when the distribution of income changed the value of this commodity did not change. If he found such a commodity he would have found an absolute measure of value, for measured in terms of this commodity the value of output would be independent of the distribution of income. The result would be that if the real wage rate, measured in terms of this invariable measure, rose, profits must fall, for from the definition of the invariable measure the value of output could not change. The implication of this was that if values were measured in terms of an invariable measure of value, the predictions of the corn model would translate into a multi-commodity model.

Ricardo recognized that such an invariable measure would have to be produced with the average capital–labour ratio for the economy as a whole. Though he tried using, at various times, both corn and gold, there was no reason why either of these, or any other commodity for that matter, should be produced using the average capital–labour ratio. Ricardo thus never found the invariable standard of value so important for his model. The problem was solved only by Sraffa (1960), who constructed an imaginary "standard commodity", comprising an appropriately constructed bundle of goods produced by the economy.[8]

### Capital

Because of its importance in the post-Ricardian history of economic thought it is worth digressing slightly at this point to consider in a little more detail Ricardo's view of capital and its relationship to the problem of value. Ricardo argued that the value of a commodity comprised not only the labour applied immediately to its production, but also "the labour bestowed on the implements tools and buildings with which such labour is assisted".[9] There are two ways production and capital can be viewed, and hence two ways in which the value of a commodity, as just defined, can be expressed. One way is to regard capital as being the value of the capital and intermediate goods used in production. Price or value is then given by an equation such as

$$p_0 = l_w + (l + r)(p_1 k_1 + p_2 k_2 + ...)$$

where $p_0$ is the price of the output, $l$ the quantity of labour used, $w$ the wage rate, $r$ the rate of profit, and $p_i$ and $k_i$ the prices and quantities of the capital goods used in production. In other words, we consider production as involving different goods all available at the same date.

The alternative approach, also used by Ricardo, is to reduce commodities to "dated labour". For example, to produce a loaf of bread requires labour to be applied in the bakery; but before this can be done labour must be applied in milling the flour; and before this can be done labour must be used to produce the wheat; before the wheat can be grown a plough must be built, and so on. The value of a commodity is, on this view of production, the sum of all the labour required to produce it. However, the labour theory of value is subject to the same problems when this view of production is adopted, for we need to distinguish the various dates at which labour is applied in order to calculate the appropriate interest charges. The price of a commodity is given by an equation such as

$$p_0 = w\{l_0 + (l + r)l_{-1} + (l + r)^2 l_{-2} + \ldots\},$$

where $l_0, l_1, l_2, \ldots$ represent the labour applied now, last period, two periods ago and so on.

The problems which arise when different commodities are produced using different capital–labour ratios re-emerges in the form of different time structures of production. The price of a commodity requiring only current labour for its production will be unaffected by a rise in the interest rate. By contrast, the price of a commodity which requires labour to be expended many years in advance of the output being produced, will be very dependent on the rate of interest. Though Ricardo's problems centred on the labour theory of value, he raised issues which have confronted all economists who have since tried to deal with the question of capital.[10]

## 3.4 THE WAGES FUND AND MACHINERY

The problem with using the Malthusian, subsistence theory as an explanation of the wage rate is that it is a long run theory. To explain wages in the short run the device used was the wages fund, a doctrine which, though traceable, as are many other theories of wages, to Smith, is probably best ascribed to Ricardo. Ricardo did not use the term wages fund, but the concept was there, the term circulating capital being used to denote that part of the capital stock used to employ labour. The context in which the wage fund is most clearly defined is that of an agricultural economy in which capital comprises food saved from the previous year's harvest in order to provide workers with their subsistence until the new harvest is available. If we assume that the fund destined for payment of wages is fixed (that capitalists do not alter their consumption) the demand curve for labour will be a rectangular hyperbola, $w = F/N$, where $F$ is the wages fund. Such a demand curve is shown by FF' in Figure 3.1. Given the supply of labour, inelastic in the short run, we can derive a wage rate which can be used to determine the distribution of income between profits and wages.

Though the wages fund was widely used in classical economics to argue that wages could be increased only by capital accumulation (something which required high profits) and not by combinations of workmen, one of the more interesting applications of the doctrine was Ricardo's use of the concept to show how mechanization might, in the short run at least, be against the interests of the working class.[11] His argument was that the introduction of machinery might come about through the conversion of circulating capital into fixed capital. Instead of using labour to produce food, the capitalist might use a part of the labour force to produce machinery. The result, in the following period, would be that, because output of food had been lower in the previous period, the fund of food available to employ labour would be smaller. The result would be either lower employment, or a lower wage rate. It would be only in subsequent periods, when the new machinery came into use, raising productivity, that the stock of circulating capital would be replenished.

## 3.5   CONCLUSIONS

### Ricardo and Smith

Smith's influence on Ricardo was enormous. Not only was the overall approach, of analysing the link between savings, capital accumulation and growth, inspired by Smith, but many of Ricardo's specific assumptions can be traced back to Smith. Many of these assumptions, however, were ones to which Smith attached much less importance than did Ricardo: the link between real wages and population growth; the link between circulating capital and employment; diminishing returns in agriculture. The effect of taking certain features out of Smith's system and constructing from them a model emphasizing only those relationships which were amenable to treatment in terms of simple functional relationships was to transform Smith's theory into something very different. Thus where Smith assumed, most of the time at least, increasing returns in industry and constant returns in agriculture, Ricardo assumed constant and diminishing returns respectively. Furthermore, where Smith explained growth in terms of both capital accumulation and technical progress, with Ricardo the emphasis was overwhelmingly on capital accumulation. The result was not only a different model, but a very different, much more pessimistic vision of the nature of economic progress.

### Ricardo's importance

Ricardo is undoubtedly one of the most important figures in the history of economic thought, but there is no unanimity as to the nature of his influence. Schumpeter wrote of the "Ricardian vice" in economic theorizing:

The comprehensive vision of universal interdependence which haunted Thünen probably never cost Ricardo so much as an hour's sleep. His interest was in the clear-cut result of practical significance. In order to get this he cut that general system to pieces, bundled up as large parts of it as possible, and put them in cold storage – so that as many things as possible should be frozen and "given". He then piled one simplifying assumption upon another until, having really settled everything by these assumptions, he was left with only a few aggregative variables between which, given these assumptions, he set up simple one-way relations so that, in the end, the desired results emerged almost as tautologies.[12]

He goes on to cite Ricardo's theorem that profits depend solely on the price of wheat, arguing that it is true simply because everything else is assumed given. Another good example would be the discussion of machinery outlined above, in which there is an enormous number of extremely restrictive, and in some ways very arbitrary, assumptions, all of which are crucial to the result.

Whilst there is undoubtedly a very great deal of truth in this criticism, it is undoubtedly excessively harsh given the state of economics at the beginning of the nineteenth century.[13] There are many ways in which Smith's economics could have been developed, and it was above all Ricardo who ensured that, in England at least, the route leading towards deductive theorizing, of using logical analysis to work out as precisely as possible the implications of various assumptions. In Blaug's words, "if economics is essentially an engine of analysis, a method of thinking rather than a body of substantial results, Ricardo literally invented the technique of economics".[14] This explains why many of the nineteenth century's outstanding economic theorists, including some whose approach to economics was very different from Ricardo's, acknowledged his pre-eminence. Examples of such economists include Marx, Walras, Marshall and Wicksell.

Although it might seem paradoxical to claim this, both Schumpeter and Blaug are substantially correct. The two views can be reconciled by asserting that the problems with Ricardo's economics lay not in his use of abstract methods, or even in his use of simplifying assumptions, for given the state of economics when he wrote it is hard to see how rigorous deductive theorizing could have been done any other way; but rather in the excessive confidence which was attached to the predictions derived from such simplified models. Ricardo and his followers did not claim merely to be working out implications of certain hypothetical assumptions, but to be describing the laws by which economies actually worked. When comparisons were made with Euclidian geometry and Newtonian mechanics, the implication was not merely that economics followed similar methods, but also that the theorems of political economy were established with a degree of certainty similar to that attached to the theorems of Euclid and Newton. It can be argued that it is this aspect of Ricardo's theorizing which lays him open to Schumpeter's charge, and which explains why Ricardian economics has been the subject of so much controversy. In the words of a recent writer,

his tremendous intellectual vitality had burnt deep scars on to the Classical-economic consciousness. *It is simply not possible to read the Classical economic literature and understand it unless we know the system in which those scars originated.*[15]

The same is true of the period after 1870, for although the Ricardian system was abandoned, Ricardo's influence was pervasive right up to the end of the century and beyond.[16]

# 4

## Alternatives to Ricardian Economics

### 4.1 THE FRENCH SCHOOL

*J. B. Say*

One of Say's main contributions was to expound Smith's *Wealth of Nations*, a book many found full of stimulating ideas, but badly organized, to a European audience.[1] His *Traité d'Economique Politique* went through several editions between 1803 and 1826. Say was, however, more than merely a popularizer of Smith. In addition to the law of markets for which he is best known,[2] he developed a utility theory of value, and associated with this, a view of production very different from that of Ricardo.

Say argued that value depended not on cost, but on utility and scarcity. Cost influenced value only through imposing a lower limit to price, and through affecting supply. Say was able to use this theory that value depended on utility to argue that the essence of production was the creation of utilities, not the creation of commodities. Commodities were desired only because they yielded utility. Say thus opposed both the Physiocratic and the Smithian notions of productive labour, arguing that services, just as much as manufacturing or agriculture, were productive, for they too yielded utilities.

Associated with this was a different view of the role of factors in production. Production, according to Say, was a co-operative process in which three types of factor, namely human industry, nature and capital, worked together to produce output. These three factors each have value because of their role in production. Because of this view of production Say saw an important and distinctive role for the entrepreneur, the man who brings the various factors together and organizes production.[3]

Say did not, however, adopt a completely subjective view of value, for he was viewing value as something inherent in an object when he distinguished between two types of value. These were "natural riches", value given by nature, and "social riches", value created by the work of capital and labour. Because, Say argued, only social riches had to be paid for, it was only social riches which gave a commodity exchange value. Natural riches were not reflected in exchange value (price). It was for this reason that Say, criticizing Smith, argued that the distinction between value in use and value in exchange was irrelevant to economics.[4]

Thus although Say had a utility theory of value, and although he used it to attack Ricardo,[5] he failed to tackle the problem in such a way as to solve the paradox of value. Indeed, his theory of utility was formulated in such a way as to rule out the line of inquiry which led to marginal utility theory.[6]

His challenge to the Ricardian doctrine that utility was merely a precondition for a commodity to have value, and not a cause of value, was ineffective. Having said this, however, Say did establish a tradition in French economics very different from the Ricardian tradition in England, the labour theory of value never taking root in France. His stress on scarcity as the determinant of value, his view of production as involving the co-operation of different factors, and his emphasis on the role of the entrepreneur remained characteristic of French economics right up to Walras's work in the 1870s.

## Cournot

One of the most remarkable works on economics to appear in the first half of the nineteenth century was Cournot's *Researches into the Mathematical Principles of the Theory of Wealth* (1838). Cournot rejected Say's notions of utility and scarcity as too vague and ill-defined for use in economics. Value was for him purely relative. "We can only assign value to a commodity by reference to other commodities. In this sense there are only relative values."[7] An arbitrarily chosen numeraire is used to measure value. Deciding "not to accompany most speculative writers back to the cradle of the human race", Cournot took as his starting point a downward-sloping demand curve, $D = F(p)$. Given such a demand curve, he argued that sellers would seek to maximize the revenue obtained from their produce. Where there was a single seller the profit-maximizing condition was found by Cournot to be given by

$$D + (dD/dp) [p - d \{\Phi(D)\} / dD] = 0,$$

where $\Phi(D)$ denotes costs as a function of output. This is equivalent to the condition that marginal cost equal marginal revenue.[8]

Had Cournot stopped here he would have anticipated much that later economists were laboriously to rediscover.[9] But Cournot went much further, adopting a distinctive approach to the analysis of competition. After analysing monopoly Cournot went on to study duopoly, making the assumption that each duopolist takes his rival's output as given. Cournot then increased the number of producers, arguing that when this became sufficiently large the equilibrium price would be given by

$$p - \Phi'_k(D_k) = 0.$$

This states that for firm $k$, price must equal marginal cost. He used this result to derive, using both algebra and supply and demand curves, comparative static results, such as the effect of an increase in cost on price. In doing so he derived some of the results often associated with Marshall.

Thus Cournot, unlike most of his contemporaries, did not see monopoly and competition as separate phenomena to be analysed differently. Monopoly and competition were, for Cournot, seen as limiting cases of oligopoly. In addition, Cournot perceived the idea of general equilibrium, in which all prices and quantities were interdependent, described by a set of equations. He considered the analysis of such interdependence, however, beyond the powers of mathematical analysis.

### Dupuit

Dupuit was one of a long line of French engineers who contributed to economics.[10] Concerned with the problem of estimating the value of public works projects, such as roads and bridges, Dupuit arrived at the concept of marginal utility and related it to the demand curve. Though contemporaries, he and Cournot appear to have been ignorant of each other's work. In trying to solve the problem of the value of public investment projects, Dupuit decided that Say had been wrong to dismiss Smith's distinction between use-value and exchange-value. According to Say's logic, if costs fell then the utility derived from an object would also fall. Dupuit argued instead that utility was *at least* as great as price, not equal to it. Furthermore, different increments of a commodity have different utilities. Using these ideas he arrived at the concept of consumers' surplus, which he called "the utility remaining to consumers", as the area under the demand curve.

In addition to deriving the concept of consumers' surplus, Dupuit addressed problems of monopoly. He used the demand curve and his measures of utility to investigate the effects of cost changes on monopoly price, the costs of monopoly to consumers, and price discrimination.

## 4.2   ENGLISH CRITICS OF THE LABOUR THEORY OF VALUE

### Bailey

Ricardo's *Principles* was the subject of immediate discussion. Ricardian ideas were presented in a more accessible form in Mrs. Marcet's immensely successful *Conversations on Political Economy* (1817)[11] and in James Mill's *Elements of Political Economy* (1821).[12] McCulloch advanced Ricardian ideas in the *Edinburgh Review* and the *Encyclopaedia Britannica*. From the start, however, Ricardian economics was subject to criticism, but most of the early critics could be, and were, ignored. Malthus never managed to make his case effectively. Prinsep, the translator of Say's *Traité*, which might have provided a focus for opposition to Ricardo, stressed the areas of agreement rather than those of difference. The leading followers of Ricardo, moreover, deliberately tried to work for unity amongst the leading exponents of political economy in order to increase the subject's authority. Torrens expressed a widely held hope when, in 1821, he wrote that

with respect to Political Economy, the period of controversy is passing away, and that of unanimity rapidly approaching. Twenty years hence there will scarcely exist a doubt respecting any of its fundamental principles.[13]

The work which shattered such hopes appeared in 1825: Samuel Bailey's *A Critical Dissertation on the Nature, Measure and Causes of Value: Chiefly in Reference to the Writings of Mr. Ricardo and his Followers*. In this Bailey attacked the leading writers on value – Ricardo, Malthus and James Mill – for having failed to give sufficient attention to the meaning of the terms they used. The result, according to Bailey, was confusion and obscurity:

The confusion and obscurity, which mark the work of some of the most celebrated writers in these momentous topics, are sufficient to make the student abandon his inquiries on the very threshold of the science. Words used without determinate ideas, terms introduced without proper explanations, definitions abandoned almost as soon as enunciated, principles without first being examined, verbal instead of real simplifications – such are the obstacles which everywhere meet him.[14]

Bailey opens his argument by claiming that "Value, in its ultimate sense, appears to mean the esteem in which an object is held."[15] From this starting point he goes on, not to a concept of utility, but to the conclusion that

It is only when objects are considered together as subjects of preference or exchange that the specific feeling of value can arise... . Value denotes nothing positive or intrinsic, but merely the relation in which two objects stand to each other as exchangeable commodities.[16]

Since value is a relation between commodities, and is not intrinsic to them, it follows that the search for an invariable measure of value is illusory.

When Bailey came to expound the causes of value he did so by dividing commodities into three categories.

1  Commodities which are monopolized, or protected from competition by natural or adventitious circumstances.
2  Commodities, in the production of which some persons possess greater facilities than the rest of the community, and which therefore the competition of the latter cannot increase, except at a greater cost.
3  Commodities, in the production of which competition operates without restraint.[17]

It is important to note that under monopoly Bailey included not only "true" monopoly, where there is a single supplier, but also situations in which there is a limited supply of commodities, even if this supply is owned by several people. His second and third categories are those of competition with increasing and constant costs respectively.

The causes of value, Bailey argued, were different in each case. The novelty of his argument lay not in his claim that the values of different types of commodity were determined by different factors, for Ricardo had conceded at the outset of his *Principles* that the value of some commodities depended on scarcity. Ricardo, however, confined the effects of scarcity to commodities of which "No labour can increase the quantity",[18] the value of most commodities being dependent on the labour required to produce them. Bailey's contribution was rather to show that scarcity was the general case:

Instead of scarcity, or, in other words, monopoly, or protection from competition being an unimportant source of value, ... we have seen that it is a most extensive source of value, and that the value of many of the most important articles of interchange must be referred to this as its origin.[17]

Rent, for example, could be explained in terms of scarcity. What was for Ricardo a special case was subsumed within Bailey's more general theory.

### Senior

Despite the substantial impact made by Bailey's attack, Ricardian economics survived, many economists paying tribute to Bailey, but finding reasons to continue with the Ricardian approach.[20] A common reaction was that Bailey was attempting to destroy political economy without putting anything in its place. One economist, however, who did see the significance of Bailey's ideas, was Nassau Senior.

Senior can be seen as attempting to reconcile the apparently divergent lines of thought represented by the Ricardians on the one hand, and Say and Bailey on the other. Value, for Senior, depended on goods possessing utility, on their being transferable from one individual to another, and on their being limited in supply. He followed Bailey in arguing that value depended on causes which limited the supply of commodities, this giving them their utility. On the side of demand he developed Say's ideas on utility, providing a clear statement of diminishing marginal utility.

It is obvious, however, that our desires do not aim so much at quantity as at diversity. Not only are there limits to the pleasure which commodities of any given class can afford, but the pleasure diminishes in a rapidly diminishing ratio long before those limits are reached. Two articles of the same kind will seldom afford twice the pleasure of one, and still less will ten give five times the pleasure of two.[21]

Senior failed, however, to relate this to the demand curve.

On the supply side of the market, Senior investigated the link between cost and supply, analysing clearly the link between scarcity and rising cost of production. Costs of production provided the limits between which prices would settle: the costs of existing producers set a lower limit to price; the costs of potential producers set an upper limit. Thus in the case of constant costs, where these two costs are the same, cost and price must coincide. Like Bailey, Senior used monopoly to refer to situations where supply was inelastic, whether the cause of this was rising costs or the existence of a single producer. In analysing the various cases in a classification of commodities influenced by Bailey's, Senior stressed the importance of demand. For example, with rising costs price coincides with cost at the margin, the position of this margin being determined by demand.

### Longfield

Another economist to provide an alternative to the Ricardian theory was Longfield (1834), who related utility and cost of production through supply and demand:

the value of every article depends on the demand and the supply, and ... indirectly the cost of production of any commodity, as well as its utility, has an effect on its price. The cost of production, by its influence on supply, since men will not produce commodities unless with a reasonable expectation of selling them for more than the cost of producing them. And the utility has some effect, although not so easily calculated, since it is to utility, in the more extended sense of the word, that the demand is to be entirely attributed.[22]

Longfield clearly separated utility and price, arguing that an individual will exchange a commodity only for something "which is, *relative to him*, of more utility".[23] Exchange was seen, more clearly than in the writings of Longfield's contemporaries, as a process of maximizing utility through exchange.[24] When he analysed demand, however, he turned to Malthus' concept of the "intensity of demand".[25] Intensity of demand was the maximum price someone was willing to pay for a unit of a commodity. Longfield used this to explain clearly the negative relationship between price and quantity demanded. He even argued, though in different language, that a rich man's demand curve would be less elastic than that of a poor man.[26] Thus Longfield used Malthus' concept of intensity of demand

as a way round the difficulty of discovering the effect of utility on price, because although he, like so many others, observed the phenomena of diminishing marginal utility, he was unable to draw conclusions from it in such a way which demonstrated the precise influence of utility on exchange value.[27]

All the main elements of exchange value were there, but they were not put together.

## 4.3  WAGES AND PROFITS

*Senior*

Alongside these attacks on the labour theory of value were attempts to provide alternatives to the Ricardian theory of distribution. The background to this was that by the 1830s the Malthusian theory appeared, especially in view of the results of the census of 1831, as of less relevance. A result of this was that economists tried to develop theories of wages, and hence of profits, which did not rely on population pressure keeping wages at subsistence level. Two such attempts were those of Senior and Longfield.

In line with his value theory, Senior recognized that scarcity would affect the value of factors of production. Thus land would command rent provided it were scarce, even if it were all equally productive.[28] Furthermore, similar arguments could be extended to other factors, such as capital goods.[29] Land was no longer seen as unique amongst factors of production. To explain profits Senior introduced the term "abstinence" to denote

that agent, distinct from labour and the agency of nature, the concurrence of which is necessary to capital, and which stands in the same relation to profit as labour does to wages.[30]

Abstinence underlay the supply of capital, demand being influenced by its productivity.[31]

### Longfield

Longfield, too, integrated the theories of rent, profits and wages, through his framework of supply and demand. He arrived at a marginal productivity theory of capital:

The profits which the capitalist or owner of this instrument will reap, will be the difference between the quantity of work which the labourer can do with and without its assistance.[32]

As the quantity of capital increased, capitalists had to resort to using "inferior" labourers:

the rate of profits must be determined by those cases in which the efficiency of capital is the least... . [T]he profits of a single tool will be equal to the difference of the qualities of work which the feeblest labourer could execute with and without its assistance.[33]

Later Longfield introduced two further factors which caused the productivity of capital to fall as its quantity increased: to find employment for the increased quantity of capital, the degree of mechanization had to increase, the cost of capital rising faster than its efficiency; and as production increases, the price of the product will fall. Though it was incomplete, for he simply assumed a given, limited, supply of capital, Longfield thus derived a supply and demand theory of profits, in which demand for capital was dependent on marginal productivity, this diminishing as the stock of capital increased.[34]

Longfield's theory of wages was similarly based on supply and demand, with demand dependent on productivity.[35] Supply of labour was taken as given – "the present existing race of labourers" – Malthusian concerns being cast aside.[36] His innovation was to postulate that wages depended on the discounted productivity of labour:

the ultimate value of [the labourer's] labour is, as it were, discounted for him by his employer... . [The capitalist] receives profits only proportional to the length of time which has elapsed between his payment of the labourer's wages and his receiving the price of the article in the state in which he disposes of it.[37]

Longfield had therefore reversed the Ricardian procedure: wages were now the residual, obtained by deducting profit from the productivity of labour.

## 4.4   SOME GERMAN CONTRIBUTIONS

Important contributions to both utility and productivity theories of demand were also made by a series of German economists, in particular Hermann, Mangoldt, Thünen and Gossen. Two works are especially significant in view of later developments: those of Thünen and Gossen.

In *The Isolated State*, various parts of which were published between 1826 and 1863, Thünen developed what Schumpeter describes as a brilliantly original economic theory.[38] As suggested by his title, the problem he tackled was that of location, his starting point being an isolated region, containing uniformly fertile land, free of obstacles to mobility, and with a town at its centre. From this starting point, as abstract as that of Ricardo, he proceeded to use differential calculus to derive a marginal productivity theory of profits and wages. Furthermore, like Cournot, he saw the interdependence of all economic quantities, and the necessity of representing this by a system of equations.

Gossen's contribution was to publish, in 1854, a mathematical theory of utility maximization, anticipating much of Jevons' later work. His first law was that of diminishing marginal utility, a law which he stated algebraically and graphically. His second law was the first order condition for utility maximization: that a good must be distributed between various uses in such a way that its marginal utility is equal in all uses. His work, however, was completely neglected until discovered by Jevons in 1878, several years after Jevons, Menger and Walras had all arrived at similar conclusions.

## 4.5 J. S. MILL

### Mill's "half-way house"

The final, and most important work to be considered in this chapter is that of John Stuart Mill; for though it was Mill who was instrumental in keeping the Ricardian tradition alive, in doing so he brought in so many other ideas that he transformed Ricardian theory, almost beyond recognition. Schumpeter justifiably described Mill's *Principles* (1848) as a "half-way house" between the economics of Ricardo and that of Marshall.[39]

Value, for Mill, was, as for Bailey and Senior, a relative concept, its determinants being analysed in terms of supply and demand.[40] Though using neither algebra nor geometry, Mill clearly analysed supply and demand in terms of schedules, thus clearing up much of the confusion present in earlier controversies. Though he continued to regard utility merely as a condition of value, not as a cause of value, adhering to a cost of production theory, Mill recognized the influence, through demand, of scarcity on value.

In analysing the effects of scarcity on value Mill distinguished, following Smith, between market value, dependent simply on supply and demand, and natural value, about which market value fluctuates. Whether natural value corresponds to cost of production or depends on scarcity depends on conditions of supply. Thus though Mill retained vestiges of the Ricardian theory, they were so heavily qualified as almost to deprive them of significance. Thus rent was not a part of cost of production, except either where it represented a scarcity value (where land had alternative uses within agriculture) or where the land could be applied to some use other than agriculture. Similarly, though the quantity of labour required for production was the most important element in cost, all the other elements were significant.

### Production and distribution

It is in the sphere of production and distribution that the Ricardian influence remained strongest, though even here Mill introduced changes. His discussion is still set in the Smithian framework of growth, and he upholds the distinction between productive and unproductive labour as crucial to an explanation of capital accumulation. The rate of capital accumulation, for Mill as for Smith, depended on the proportion of the labour force employed productively. Because Mill claimed that productive labour was productive of wealth rather than merely of commodities, the crucial character of the product being its permanence rather than its material nature, he broadened the concept to include the acquisition of skills. The utilities resulting from productive labour might be embodied either in natural objects or in human beings. On the other hand, he did claim that little harm was done by defining productive labour as productive of material objects.

On distribution Mill took over Senior's abstinence theory of interest, defining the abstinence involved as abstinence from present consumption. Abstinence thus covered not only decisions not to consume out of current income, but also decisions to refrain from consuming inherited capital. Time preference was brought in to explain why such abstinence needed to be rewarded. This adoption of Senior's view is consistent with Mill's emphasis on cost of production rather than simply labour as the cause of value. The aspect of Mill's theory, however, which attracted most attention was his theory of wages. Though the emphasis was very different, the Malthusian stress on population growth was very much present in Mill's writing. The wages fund was used as an argument for limiting family size, for if population were to grow this would reduce wages. This was despite the emphasis on the possibilities for improvement, rather than on the reduction of wages to subsistence, in the classical tradition.

Mill did, however, introduce what turned out to be a significant weakening of the Ricardian theory of wages: the doctrine of non-competing groups. Non-competing groups were groups of workers such that within each group there was competition, but between groups competition was absent, due to the inability of workers to move from one group to another. Though this doctrine was a very minor point in Mill's *Principles*, it was given much more prominence by Cairnes (1874) who used it in an attempt to defend the Ricardian system against later attacks. Its significance arose because the assumption of homogeneous labour (or at least the assumption that wage differentials were given exogenously) was crucial to the Ricardian approach to value and distribution. The wages fund provided a theory of the average rate of wages. The labour theory of value made sense only if there was a homogeneous factor called labour. Thus when the assumption of homogeneous labour was abandoned, the whole Ricardian approach to value and distribution, not simply the theory of wages, was laid open to attacks such as those of Jevons.[41]

## 4.6 CONCLUSIONS: POLITICAL ECONOMY IN 1870

The most important lesson to be learnt from this chapter is that, even in England, Ricardian economics did not go unchallenged. Under the influence of Bailey and Senior, significant changes had been introduced into the Ricardian system. Though Ricardian in inspiration, Mill's *Principles* was *much* more than Ricardian economics. Outside England, Ricardian economics gained no hold at all. But although the success of Ricardian economics was thus limited, no coherent alternative emerged, the nearest to this being the French tradition inspired by Say. The barrier to an alternative, utility-based theory of value was posed by the failure to resolve Smith's paradox of value. Apart from some isolated economists, the problems involved in relating utility to value were not solved. Partly this can be attributed to technical limitations, but Say's approach to utility and value, dismissing the paradox of value as irrelevant to economics, cannot have helped.

Another major conclusion to be drawn concerning Classical political economy is the importance of Smith. Say's political economy was a development from the *Wealth of Nations* just as much as was Ricardo's. Many of the ideas about value and distribution discussed in the classical period could be found, albeit only in embryo, in the *Wealth of Nations*. Mill's statement of the theory of value shows very clearly how much more classical economics owed to Smith than to Ricardo. For all Mill's debts to Ricardo, Mill's *Principles* was based more on the model of Smith's *Wealth of Nations* than on that of Ricardo's *Principles*. In the words of one commentator,

in the last resort, classical economics *is* conceivable without Ricardo, whose influence progressively waned from 1830 if not before; it is quite inconceivable without Adam Smith and *The Wealth of Nations*.[42]

Though parts of the structure were modified beyond recognition, the Ricardian system survived into the 1860s. To a substantial extent this is to be attributed to Mill's influence, his *Principles* being the first book to rival the success of Smith's *Wealth of Nations*. But equally important was the enormous prestige attached to political economy at this time. For all their differences on technical questions, the representatives of English classical political economy shared the same liberal values, and similar general attitudes towards economic policy. In the absence of any simple, cogent alternative, political economy and Ricardian economics were to a certain extent identified, the latter benefiting from the prestige attached to the former.

In the 1860s and 1870s, however, the situation changed. Political economy came under attack from a variety of sources.[43] Political economy had become, rightly or wrongly,[44] associated with doctrinaire *laissez faire*, but with the increasing concern with social questions, and the increasing calls for state intervention, such an attitude seemed less appropriate. There were also attacks on deductive theory, of which Ricardian economics was the pre-eminent example, from writers advocating a more historical approach.[45] Against this background theoretical criticisms, which a decade or so earlier might have been brushed aside, assumed a greater importance. This accounts for the significance which came to be attached to Mill's so-called recantation on the wages fund in 1869. The arguments to which Mill was responding were no more cogent than many offered in previous decades. Similarly, Mill's concessions were in themselves less important than many of the concessions made to non-Ricardian writers in his *Principles* over 20 years before. In the changed environment, however, Mill's concessions on the wages fund were seized upon. Classical political economy had become an anachronism.

# 5

# Money and Commercial Crises

## 5.1 BACKGROUND

*Hume and Smith*

In the second half of the eighteenth century the important figure in monetary economics is not Smith but Hume (1752). Two aspects of Hume's monetary theory need mentioning. Most important is the price-specie-flow mechanism. The way this works is that a trade imbalance causes specie (gold or silver) to flow either into or out of a country. This causes a change in the price level which alters the country's competitiveness in trade, which in turn corrects the initial trade imbalance. It followed that "mercantilist" policies designed to produce a trade surplus would be self-defeating; if a surplus were to be produced this would be only temporary, for the resulting bullion inflows would raise the domestic price level, reducing exports and increasing imports, thus eliminating the surplus. The second important aspect of Hume's work is that, following a long tradition amongst writers on monetary questions,[1] he argued that monetary changes might have very different effects in the short and the long run. In the short term an increase in the money supply might stimulate industry, for prices would rise faster than costs; but in the long run, when the relationship between prices and costs had returned to normal, the only effect of a monetary expansion would be to raise the price level.

Smith was aware of Hume's monetary theory, but made little use of it in the *Wealth of Nations*. Indeed, Smith emphasized the so-called real bills doctrine – the doctrine that provided money was lent only for genuine commercial purposes, the effect would not be inflationary, for money would be created only to meet the genuine needs of trade. In other words, money would be lent only if the goods it was to purchase were already in existence. As important as Smith's advocacy of the real bills doctrine was his dictum that savings are spent just as much as is consumption: that savings are translated into investment and not hoarded. This formed the background not only to the classical emphasis on saving as the cause of capital accumulation, but also to the denial of the possibility of general overproduction, important in discussions of the trade cycle and commercial crises.

*Events*

In the first decade of the nineteenth century there occurred a ferment of thinking on monetary questions, the stimulus to this coming from the monetary problems with which Britain was confronted as a result of the war with France which followed the French revolution. Of particular importance was the suspension, in 1797, of cash payments: sterling was no longer convertible into gold at a fixed price. The price of bullion remained above par (i.e. sterling remained below its nominal value in terms of gold) for most of the next 20 years. These years were also years of inflation, though it is important to note that although people were sure that the value of money in terms of goods was falling, and although index numbers were available, these were not used to measure inflation.

These events provoked intensive debate concerning the nature of the relationships between the price of bullion, the quantity of currency issued by the Bank of England, the balance of payments, bad harvests and government expenditure on the war. There was also the policy question of whether or not there should be an attempt to restore the convertibility of sterling, and if so how? These issues were the subject of the so-called Bullion debates in the years around 1810.

The war ended in 1815 and from 1818 to 1821 sterling's convertibility was restored. Although this came to be accepted remarkably quickly, debate on monetary questions did not disappear, for there was the question of how a convertible currency should be run: on what principles should the Bank of England operate if convertibility was to be maintained? The outcome of these discussions was the Bank Charter Act of 1844.

These discussions may seem a long way removed from any current concerns, but they are important for two reasons. The first is that they form the background to later discussions of monetary economics. There is an enormous degree of continuity in monetary theory, the most important example of this being the so-called indirect mechanism linking money and prices, worked out by Thornton (1802), and central to many of the most important contributions to nineteenth and twentieth century monetary theory. Though the formulation of the theory has changed its essentials have remained the same. The second reason for the importance of these discussions was that they influenced the monetary framework within which economic activity took place, not just for Britain, but for much of the world. Britain's role in the world monetary system up to 1914 was such that the policies of the Bank of England affected many countries.

## 5.2   THE BULLION CONTROVERSIES

*Thornton*

The greatest performance in the field of monetary economics was that of Henry Thornton. In his *Essay on the Nature of the Paper Credit of Great Britain* (1802) he presented an analysis of the operation of a paper currency unequalled till Wicksell's work nearly a century later. His starting point was that he regarded paper credit (notes and bills of exchange) as one item in a balance sheet. Both notes and bills circulate, bills circulating more slowly because they bear interest, but the velocity of circulation of both bills and notes depends on confidence: in a "season of distrust", for example, demand for notes will increase. Hicks' judgement is that "All in all, there is as much Liquidity Preference [in Thornton's work] as anyone could have got – as anyone ought to have got – in 1802."[2] Thus although Thornton was a bullionist in that he regarded the price of bullion as the test of whether or not the Bank of England had over-issued currency, he recognized that this did not apply in the short run. Fluctuations in confidence might cause fluctuations in the demand for money, and hence in the price of bullion, irrespective of the Bank of England's actions. Another factor which might, according to Thornton, affect the price of bullion independently of any changes in the money supply was the balance of payments. Currency might flow abroad, depressing the exchanges (raising the price of bullion) as the result of exceptional remittances abroad. The import of grain following a harvest failure, and subsidies paid to foreign governments fighting Napoleon, were important causes of such remittances in the 15 years after 1800. The possibility of an "external drain" of gold, due to an adverse balance of payments, together with the possibility of an "internal drain", caused by a loss of confidence in paper currency, either of which might alter the price of bullion, meant that Thornton did not adhere rigidly to the argument that a high price of bullion implied an over-issue of currency. Over-issue was simply one possible cause of a high price of bullion.

Thornton's main contribution, however, did not lie here but in his analysis of the so-called indirect mechanism whereby monetary changes affected the economy. The argument is that a monetary expansion comes about through the banking system's reducing the cost of borrowing below the rate of profit that can be earned on capital. The increased availability of bank loans raises demand for goods and the price level rises. This process continues for as long as the rate of interest on loans remains below the rate of profit on capital, but once the rate of interest returns to equality with the rate of profit, the process will stop. The economy will have a higher stock of money and a higher price level.[3]

This account assumes that a rise in demand for commodities will produce a rise in prices. Whilst this may be true in the long run, Thornton recognized that in the short run a monetary change might lead to changes in the level of activity.

The tendency, however, of a very great and sudden reduction of the accustomed number of bank notes, is to create an *unusual* and *temporary* distress, and a fall in price resulting from that distress. But a fall arising from a temporary distress will be attended probably with no correspondent fall in the rate of wages; for the fall of price, and the distress, will be understood to be temporary, and the rate of wages, we know, is not so variable as the price of goods.[4]

It was for this reason that Thornton argued that under some circumstances inflation, not deflation, might be the appropriate response to a crisis: a drain of currency, either into domestic hoards or abroad, might need to be met by increasing the issue of currency in order to prevent distress.[5]

It was this moderate bullionist position which underlay the Bullion Report of 1810, of which Thornton was one of the principal authors. Though the report recommended the resumption of cash payments, it recognized that a variety of factors, not simply the quantity of currency in circulation, influenced the value of sterling.

### Ricardo

A much more rigid bullionist position was taken by Ricardo who, in *The High Price of Bullion* (1810), argued that the sole cause of an unfavourable balance of trade, and of a high price of bullion, was the over-issue of currency. This was based on the Humean notion that gold and silver move, through the price-specie-flow mechanism, from one country to another so as to equalize price levels in different countries. The situation in England, Ricardo argued, was that over-issue had reduced the value of paper currency. The effect of an increase in the circulation of paper currency was to reduce the amount of specie in circulation, adding to the quantity of bullion on the market, thus reducing the price of bullion.

As with his work on value and distribution Ricardo saw the problem in very simple terms, many of Thornton's qualifications to the bullionist position being swept aside. Thus although Ricardo made use of Thornton's indirect mechanism he focussed on the long run where the rate of interest depends on "the abundance or scarcity of that part of capital not consisting of money".[6] The rate of interest, according to Ricardo, could be kept low only by increasing the supply of capital, not by monetary expansion: "Profits can only be lowered by a competition of capitals not consisting of circulating medium."[7] Ricardo was assuming that Thornton's indirect mechanism worked itself out very quickly. Though he argued that the monetary contraction involved needed to be brought about gradually, Ricardo argued strongly for the resumption of cash payments. His reason was that he saw deflation as a means of defrauding the public through reducing the value of debts. It was wrong, Ricardo argued, for the directors of the Bank of England to have the power of regulating the price of a certain type of property (i.e. debts expressed in terms of money) thus rendering it insecure.

### The anti-bullionists

The anti-bullionists contributed little. The links between foreign remittances and the exchange rate which they stressed were analysed just as effectively by moderate bullionists such as Thornton. Smith's real bills doctrine was used, but ineffectively, not least because times had changed. The currency was no longer convertible, as assumed by Smith, and much lending was not against real bills but against government debt. More fundamentally, however, the opponents of the quantity theory never provided an explanation either of how the price level was to be determined, or of the rate of interest at which bills were to be discounted. The problem with the real bills doctrine is that if the money supply depends on the quantity of real bills, the price level is indeterminate. Suppose, for example, that the price level were to double. The value of every transaction would double, and hence the value of "real" bills available for discount would also double, thus doubling the increase in the money supply. Whatever the price level, a sufficient quantity of money will be issued to support it. As Thornton had argued, if the discount rate were kept too low, the demand for loans and credit expansion would increase indefinitely, for credit expansion would raise prices, increasing the demand for loans, thus expanding the level of credit still further.

## 5.3   THE BANKING CONTROVERSIES

*The bank charter debate*

The second stage in the establishment of the nineteenth century British monetary orthodoxy was the debates, after the resumption of cash payments, as to how the currency ought to be managed. This was an issue brought into prominence by the problems faced by the Bank of England in its attempts to maintain convertibility in the face of a series of crises in the 1820s and 1830s, the controversy coming to a head in the debates prior to the Bank Charter Act of 1844. One solution was that proposed by the so-called currency school, the leading members of this group being Robert Torrens, James Pennington and Lord Overstone. Though the details of the schemes put forward varied, the underlying idea was the "currency principle", the notion that the quantity of bank notes in circulation should be made to behave like a metallic currency would behave in similar circumstances. Rules had to be established to link the supply of currency to the stock of gold, removing the Bank of England's discretion, thus forcing the Bank of England to respond promptly to changes in flows of gold.

Two aspects of this theory are worth emphasizing. The first is that it rested on the view that reducing fluctuations in the volume of currency would reduce fluctuations in economic activity, the over-extension of credit which occurred in a boom being one of causing fluctuations to be larger than they would otherwise be.[8] By making the currency respond more quickly to gold losses, and by making it behave more like a metallic one, this source of fluctuations could be removed. It was assumed that the fluctuations to which a metallic currency was subject were ones which had to be accepted. The second point is that the linking of the note issue to gold flows, and hence to the balance of payments, was entirely deliberate. As Overstone argued, "The amount of the import or export of precious metals is a pretty sure measure of what would have been the increase or decrease of the amount of a metallic currency."[9]

Against this were the arguments of the banking school, of which Thomas Tooke was the leading member. Tooke criticized the currency principle on several grounds. The first was that they overemphasized the role of notes and coin in the economy, many transactions being effected entirely without either notes or coin. More important was the argument that note-issuing banks could not directly alter the amount of money in circulation. Banknotes, Tooke argued, "are issued to those only who, being entitled to demand gold, desire to have notes in preference.... . The quantity, therefore, is an effect and not a cause of demand."[10] If a bank issued an excessive number of notes, they would return to it as people exchanged them for cash, or for assets they did want. There was an enormous difference, Tooke argued, between a convertible currency, where notes would be held only because people preferred them to gold, and an inconvertible one where the government forced the public to accept pieces of paper they would rather not have. Though the banking school made much of the "doctrine of reflux", the notion that issues of currency beyond what the public wished to hold would return to the issuing bank, it was no more than a restatement of the real bills doctrine, and was subject to the same objections.

Related to this was a stress on incomes, not money, as the determinant of expenditure. In addition, spending was argued to be interest inelastic, so that expenditures would be largely independent of the supply of money, even if this altered the rate of interest.[11] But Tooke's main argument against the view that low rates of interest were a cause of inflation was that they were inconsistent with empirical observation: he argued that the theory was "the reverse of the truth", prices falling in times of low interest rates, a phenomenon he attributed to the effect of low interest rates on costs.[12]

The outcome of these discussions was the Bank Charter Act, introduced by Peel in 1844, which enshrined the currency principle. The separation of the Banking and Issue departments of the Bank, together with the stipulation that any note issues in excess of a fixed amount had to be backed by gold, was intended to ensure that an outflow of gold was met by an immediate reduction in the note issue. This will be considered further in the light of discussions of the trade cycle.

## 5.4   SAY'S LAW

*A distinction*

There are two senses in which the term Say's Law can be used. Walras's Law states that, by definition, the sum of all excess demands must be zero. From this we can deduce that excess demand for money must equal excess supply of all other commodities added together. One interpretation of Say's Law (sometimes called Say's identity) is that it means that excess demand for money is zero *all the time*: that general over-production (an excess supply of all goods) is impossible. A weaker version (sometimes called Say's equality) holds that, whilst general over-production may occur temporarily, there is a tendency towards equilibrium in which excess demand for money is zero.

*Say and James Mill*

Though, as with so much of classical economics, the essentials of the idea can be traced back to Smith's *Wealth of Nations*, credit for formulating what is now known as Say's Law is due to Jean Baptiste Say (1803) and James Mill (1808). Say's argument was that production by itself creates a demand for other products, because the reason producers wish to sell their output is that they wish to buy other goods. They do not wish to get money for its own sake. Thus when we look at transactions as a whole, it is as if goods were being exchanged directly for each other.[13] It is not clear which of the two senses described above Say intends, some remarks suggesting that excess supply of goods is thought to be equal to zero all the time, other remarks suggesting that he thought of this as an equilibrium condition.[14]

In contrast to Say's ambiguous formulation of his law of markets, James Mill's version was much more clear cut. The basis for Mill's claim that general over-production was *impossible* was the argument that demand for goods comes from income, and that when production increases, so too does income.

But wherein consist the collective means of payment of the whole nation? Do they not consist in its annual produce, in the annual revenue of the general mass of its inhabitants? But if a nation's power of purchasing is exactly measured by its annual produce, as it undoubtedly is, the more you increase the annual produce, the more by that very act you extend the national market, the power of purchasing and the actual purchases of the nation.[15]

He goes on to suggest that general excess demand is *impossible*:

Whatever the additional quantity of goods therefore which is at any time created in any country, an additional power of purchasing, exactly equivalent, is *at the same instant* created; so that a nation can never be naturally overstocked either with capital or with commodities.[16]

Over-production of one commodity, for Mill, implied under-production of another; an imbalance in production rather than a failure of demand.[17]

Mill's version of Say's Law shows that, though he formulated it as an identity, the context in which he used it was that of long run growth. Say's Law could be used to show that demand did not constitute a barrier to growth. Mill was thus able to argue that continuous growth did not depend on the expansion of foreign markets: the process of growth would of itself expand demand in the home market. Trade was undertaken not in order to get surplus produce,[18] but in order to obtain different commodities from those produced at home.

*Malthus and Ricardo*

Malthus' views on under-consumption came into prominence when, in the *General Theory*, Keynes claimed Malthus as a precursor, bemoaning the success of Ricardo.[19] Malthus' arguments, however, were very different from those of Keynes. One argument he used was the fallacious one that because workers receive less than the value of their product, luxury consumption will be necessary to maintain demand. It can be argued that it is only *because of* spending on investment and on capitalists' consumption that demand is sufficient to keep the value of the product above wages. More important, however, was Malthus' argument about the difficulties involved in maintaining balanced growth. If savings were too high, capital would accumulate too quickly, and supply would grow faster than demand. As a result, profits would be depressed below the rate necessary to justify the accumulation going on. One reason for this fall in profits was that if the supply of labour were inelastic, expansion might raise wages. Malthus wanted an increase in unproductive consumption not in order to stimulate demand so much as to reduce investment, so as to reduce the rate of accumulation to a sustainable level. Thus the problem Malthus was tackling was closer to that of the Harrod–Domar growth model than to that of Keynes' *General Theory*.

Ricardo's use of Say's Law was very different. Central to his system was the inverse relationship between the rate of profits and the real wage rate. This was the basis for his claim that the *only* cause of decline in the profit rate was the rising cost of corn. Ricardo thus used Say's Law to argue against Smith's doctrine that competition of capitals lowered the rate of profit. Because production creates its own demand, Ricardo argued,

It follows ... that there is no limit to demand – to the employment of capital while it yields any profit, and that however abundant capital may become, there is no other adequate reason for a fall of profit but a rise of wages, and ... that the only adequate and permanent cause for the rise of wages is the increased difficulty of providing food and necessaries for the increased number of workmen.[20]

## J. S. Mill

As in many other branches of classical economics, Ricardo's views were not representative of classical economics as a whole, for most of the classical economists understood the difference between Say's Law as a long run equilibrium condition, and as a short run identity. Much more representative of classical attitudes towards Say's Law is J. S. Mill. In his *Essays on Some Unsettled Questions of Political Economy* (1844) J. S. Mill clearly stated the equilibrium version of Say's Law. Considering the argument that the sum of effective demands for goods must of necessity be zero, he argues,

This argument is evidently founded on the supposition of a state of barter; and on that supposition it is perfectly incontestable.... . If, however, we suppose that money is used, these propositions cease to be exactly true.[21]

After conceding that money is desired simply in order to purchase commodities, he argues,

Now the effect of the employment of money, and even the utility of it, is, that it enables this one act of interchange [barter] to be divided into two separate acts or operations; one of which may be performed now, and the other a year hence, or whenever it shall be most convenient.

Thus it may happen that there may be

at some time, a very general inclination to sell with as little delay as possible, accompanied with an equally general inclination to defer all purchases as long as possible.[22]

For Mill, as for all the classical economists, Say's Law was concerned with arguing against the doctrine that "a country may accumulate capital too fast".[23] He was not using it to argue that general over-production could never occur.

## 5.5  COMMERCIAL CRISES

*Overstone and Tooke*

Commercial crises had long been familiar, but it was only from the 1820s that crises were seen as phases in a wavelike, or cyclical, movement. Two economists who noticed this and attempted an explanation are Lord Overstone and Thomas Tooke. Overstone (1837a) distinguished 10 stages of a cycle:

We find [the state of trade] subject to various conditions which are periodically returning; it revolves apparently in an established cycle. First we find it in a state of quiescence, – next improvement, – growing confidence, – prosperity, – excitement, – overtrading, – convulsion, – pressure, – stagnation, – distress, – ending again in quiescence.[24]

He argued that real, not monetary, factors were the original cause of fluctuations:

Fluctuations in the amount of currency are seldom, if ever, the original and exciting cause of fluctuations in prices and in the state of trade. The buoyant and sanguine character of the human mind; miscalculations as to the relative extent of supply and demand; fluctuations of the seasons; changes in taste and fashion; legislative enactments and political events; excitement or depression in the condition of other countries connected with us by active trading intercourse; an endless variety of casualties acting upon those sympathies by which masses of men are often urged into a state of excitement or depression; – these, all or some of them, are generally the original exciting cause of ... variations in the state of trade.[25]

On the other hand, whilst monetary factors were not the original cause of fluctuations, fluctuations in credit were a major factor linking the various phases of the cycle. Credit expansion raised prices, causing a drain of currency and threatening convertibility. The result was a rise in interest rates and a contraction of credit.[26] Fluctuations in credit, according to Overstone, accentuated the cycle, which led him to the conclusion that although currency was a "subordinate agent", seldom originating fluctuations, "it may, and often does, exert a considerable influence in restraining or augmenting the violence of commercial oscillations".[27] Overstone likened fluctuations in business activity to "the waves of the ocean swelling into fearful magnitude", arguing that monetary reform according to currency principles (i.e. acting counter-cyclically, by regulating the issue of notes according to the state of the balance of payments) could keep these fluctuations within bounds, limiting, though not completely eliminating, the damage they did.[28] Management according to banking principles (meeting the "needs of trade") would not achieve this.

A distinctive view of the cycle was also offered by Tooke, in the course of his *History of Prices* (1838). Tooke emphasized the importance of the relationship of supply to demand, and changes in stocks:

> But as a state of rising markets, and eventually a high range of them, in consequence of supplies having for some length of time fallen short of expectations, or of the estimated rate of consumption, is usually followed, first by stagnation, and then by reverses; so a long course of falling markets is eventually followed by a reduction of stocks, while the consumption is extended; and this state of things is the precursor of improved markets, and of a period of prosperity in the branches of trade to which the previous distress from low prices had applied.[29]

Though the language is different, and though much of the argument may appear imprecise, many of the themes contained in later discussions of the cycle can be found in these works, written in the 1830s.[30]

## J. S. Mill

The nearest to a synthesis of classical views on the cycle is to be found in Mill's *Principles* (1848).[31] Mill's theory is primarily a speculative theory of the cycle, in which expectations of profit lead people to use credit to increase their purchases of commodities. This in turn raises prices, justifying the original expectations of profit, and spending rises still further. Following Thornton, Mill distinguishes clearly the rate of interest on loans and the expected rate of profit on investment, seeing investment as responding to a discrepancy between these rates. There were usually, according to Mill, grounds for the original rise in prices, but this speculative process would usually lead to prices rising excessively. The downturn comes when investors realize that prices have risen too high, and start to sell rather than buy. Prices fall and businesses find themselves in difficulties.

Mill argues that an extension of credit underlies the price rise, but he places far less emphasis on the quantity of banknotes in circulation than does Overstone. Cash and banknotes are merely one form of credit, not even the largest. On the other hand, Mill does not go as far as Tooke in arguing that money cannot affect prices. Rather he argues that the link between money and prices depends on the state of expectations. In a quiescent state of the market, Tooke's argument about increases in the note issue returning to the banks was justified: people already had the facility to spend, but were choosing not to use it.[32] When markets were in a speculative state, on the other hand, Mill considered that an increase in the note issue could cause prices to rise further than they would otherwise have done.[33]

On policy Mill saw the one real purpose of the Bank Charter Act as being to mitigate commercial crises by preventing excessive monetary expansion. Having said this, however, he argued that not all crises involved speculative activity. He saw the crisis of 1847, for example, as stemming from the withdrawal from the loan market of a considerable portion of the capital which usually supplied it, this being due to a high price of cotton, and to unprecedented imports of food.[34] In addition, Mill was critical of the Bank Charter Act, claiming that an expansion of credit was appropriate in a recession. Mill quotes Tooke's argument that it is only after prices have started to fall

that an increased demand for capital takes place, the market rate of interest rises, and increasing applications are made to the Bank of England for discount.[35]

He concluded that

the multiplication of bank notes and other transferable paper does not, for the most part, accompany and facilitate the speculation; but comes into play chiefly when the tide is turning, and difficulties begin to be felt.[36]

Thus it was because Mill believed that an expansion of the note issue could reduce the extent of the contraction, and that linking the note issue to gold would not permit this, that he considered the advantages brought by the Bank Charter Act to have been "purchased by still greater disadvantages".[37]

The proponents of the currency principle had won, in the sense that the Bank Charter Act of 1844 was based on their views, the arrangements set up by the Act lasting until 1914. This conclusion, however, has to be subject to two qualifications. Firstly, there were occasions, albeit very few, when the Act had to be suspended in order to cope with a crisis: on one such occasion the note issue had to be expanded beyond the limits set by the Act, whilst on the other the possibility of doing this was enough to restore confidence. Secondly, two factors made the provisions of the Act far less restrictive than they might otherwise have been. The mid-century gold discoveries resulted in an increase in the supply of currency, and the enormous increase in the use of cheques made restrictions on the supply of currency far less significant than they might otherwise have been. Thus though the Act survived, its critics, such as Mill, were not proved completely wrong.

# 6

# International Trade and Economic Policy

## 6.1 THE THEORY OF TRADE

*Classical trade theory*

Three aspects of classical trade theory will be discussed here: the Ricardian theory of comparative advantage; Mill's theory of reciprocal demand; and the two main viewpoints on the mechanism whereby international transfers are effected. It is, however, important to note that these aspects of classical theory, though they are the ones most relevant to an understanding of later controversies, do not constitute the whole of classical thought on the subject. The classical discussions of international trade were wide ranging.[1] McCulloch, for example, followed the Smithian approach[2] of analysing trade in the context of growth, assuming international factor mobility and explaining trade in terms of absolute advantage. Malthus stressed, against the Ricardian criterion of productive efficiency, the utility gains that could result from trade. In addition, discussions of trade were frequently linked with controversies over policy, these ranging from the monetary controversies of the wartime years to issues of commercial policy and the empire.

*Comparative advantage*

The starting point for classical discussions of the pure theory of trade is chapter VII of Ricardo's *Principles*, for though the theory of comparative advantage on which it is based was first propounded by Torrens,[3] it was Ricardo who was responsible for its wide acceptance. The crucial assumption in the Ricardian theory, differentiating it from Smith's, is that factors of production are mobile within countries, but immobile between them.[4] This means that the relative prices of goods traded between countries are determined by a different rule from that determining relative values within a country.[5] The perspective from which Ricardo's theory is developed is that of a barter economy, in which there are two ways of obtaining commodities; one is to produce them directly; the other to produce goods for export, and to exchange these for the commodities required. A country will choose to obtain goods through trade when a unit of labour applied to exports will produce more goods for home use than will result from the application of labour to produce these goods domestically. This will be the case whenever the relative labour costs involved in the production of different commodities differ from one country to another.

This point is best illustrated with Ricardo's well-known example, in which production costs were assumed to be the following:[6]

| | England | Portugal |
|---|---|---|
| Wine | 120 man-years | 80 man-years |
| Cloth | 100 man-years | 90 man-years |

In this example Portugal is more efficient in producing both commodities than is England, but she will, provided the terms of trade are such that wine is valued at anything more than 8/9 units of cloth, wish to obtain cloth through trade instead of producing it domestically. Suppose the terms of trade settle at a ratio of one unit of cloth for one unit of wine (this figure being chosen solely for simplicity). 90 man-years of Portuguese labour could produce one unit of cloth directly; but applied to producing wine for export the same amount of labour would produce 90/80=1.125 units of wine which can be traded for 1.125 units of cloth. At this price ratio England too gains from the trade, for England can obtain a unit of wine by trade at a lower labour cost than by producing it in England.

In a barter economy the above arguments can be applied directly, but in a monetary economy trade will be determined by money prices, not by relative labour costs. Ricardo's argument here involved the specie-flow mechanism. Suppose, in the above example, that the gold price of labour were the same in England and Portugal. Merchants would buy both cloth and wine in Portugal, where the prices of both goods would be below English prices, in order to ship them to England. These goods would have to be paid for with gold, the result being a flow of specie from England to Portugal, this in turn raising Portuguese prices and lowering English prices. Such gold flows and price changes would continue until trade balanced, something which will occur only when cloth is cheaper in England, and wine cheaper in Portugal. In other words, the specie-flow mechanism will ensure that goods in which a country has a comparative advantage will sell for less than the equivalent foreign commodities, and those in which it has a comparative disadvantage will sell for more. In Ricardo's words, "the money of each country is apportioned to it in such quantities only as may be necessary to regulate a profitable trade of barter".[7] Trade in a monetary economy could thus be analysed in the same way as that in a barter economy.

*Reciprocal demand*

The second strand in classical trade theory relevant to later developments is Mill's theory of reciprocal demand, first published in his *Essays on Some Unsettled Questions of Political Economy*,[8] and later in what Edgeworth described as Mill's "great chapter"[7] in the *Principles*. Mill's starting point is the Ricardian framework in which "all trade is in reality barter",[10] and where factors of production are immobile between countries. He points out that though the Ricardian theory can explain why countries will wish to trade, it cannot explain the values at which goods are actually traded: relative values could be anywhere in the range set by the two countries' comparative costs. Mill's remedy for this situation is to fall back on what he calls the "antecedent law" of supply and demand.[11] He derived the result that

> when two countries trade together in two commodities, the exchange value of these commodities relatively to each other will adjust itself to the inclinations and circumstances of the consumers on both sides, in such measure that the quantities required by each country, of the articles which it imports from its neighbour, shall be exactly sufficient to pay for one another.[12]

Because no country will be prepared to trade on terms worse than those given by its own costs of production, this mechanism will result in relative values lying in between the limits set by comparative costs.

Having reached this conclusion for the 2-country 2-commodity case, Mill went on to extend the theory, bringing in transport costs, a larger number of countries and a greater variety of commodities, finding that the same law, which he christened the "Equation of International Demand",[1] still applied. Of particular importance is his analysis of changes in demand and cost conditions. He finds that an increase in the demand for a country's exports will improve the terms of trade, whilst an increase in its demand for imports will worsen them.[14] The extreme case is where one country wishes to export more goods than its neighbour wishes to import, whatever the price, in which case relative values will equal that country's relative costs: all the gains from trade will accrue to its neighbour. Changes in costs of production proved more complicated, for their effects depended on how demand changed when relative values changed.[15] Mill analysed three cases, corresponding to elastic, inelastic and unit elastic demand, finding the effects of cost reductions different in each.[16]

*List and the case for protection*

An alternative to the classical theory of trade was provided by Friedrich List in his *National System of Political Economy* (1841). His criticism of the classical theory was that it was ahistorical, failing to recognize that different countries were at different stages of development. List defended protection as a means whereby a country could develop its "productive forces". He saw a country's "productive forces" as more important than its current wealth, arguing that it was more important to increase these than to increase current consumption.

Though List was a critic of classical political economy, his case for protection was not inconsistent with the classical theory of trade, J. S. Mill, for example, accepted the infant industry argument for trade, though he attached much less importance to it than did List.

*The transfer mechanism*

Classical discussions of the transfer mechanism arose out of the bullion debates, for economists were concerned with the effects of unilateral transfers on the price of bullion.[17] The most well-known classical theory of the transfer mechanism was Hume's price-specie-flow mechanism, used by Thornton as an argument against a strict bullionist position. A unilateral payment would, according to this view, cause an outflow of specie. This would cause a fall in prices in the paying country, and a rise in prices in the receiving country. As a result of these price changes, the paying country would achieve a balance of payments surplus sufficient to pay for the transfer.

Hume's price-specie-flow theory, however, was not the only transfer mechanism present in classical discussions. Also present was the notion that unilateral transfers result directly in a transfer of demand from the paying to the receiving country, independently of any specie flow. In the wartime discussions of the currency, this demand transfer mechanism was present in the work of both Thornton and Wheatley.[18] The issue, however, which produced the most thorough analysis of the demand-transfer mechanism was Ireland, where substantial rents were paid by the Irish to absentee English landlords.

An early treatment of this subject was by Foster (1804).[17] His argument was that absentee remittances caused a shift of demand from domestic to foreign markets, without any gold flows or exchange rate changes. Referring to absentee landlords, he argued,

Perhaps the most correct mode of considering the effect of the absentees in the abstract would be that, had they continued in Ireland, they would have given birth to a quantity of produce equal in value to their rent, and *consumed it in Ireland*; but that, living in England, they give birth to an equal amount of Irish produce, *but consume it in England.* The produce of Irish industry, and the consumption of it, are equal in both cases.[20]

Though the same quantity of Irish produce is consumed in either case, the consumers are different. When he lives in England, instead of the landlord consuming Irish produce himself, "he is the cause that others become consumers of Irish produce of another description".[21] Though the mechanism was worked out for Ireland, Foster went on to apply the same logic to war expenditures and foreign loans. All these diverted demand, and caused an equal rise in exports, independently of specie flows or exchange rate changes.

This treatment of absentee remissions and foreign loans was reiterated by some of the most important of the classical economists, including J. S. Mill, McCulloch, Senior and Cairnes.[22]

It is important to note that though these discussions of the transfer mechanism focus on the shift of demand caused by the transfer, they are not the same as the Keynesian income-adjustment mechanism. The stress is on the transfer of demand represented by the loan or remittance itself. The Keynesian idea that changes in income will be larger than the required change in the balance of trade is missing. However, because the classical economists did not have the concept of the multiplier, it is difficult to distinguish any income-adjustment mechanism from a straightforward transfer of demand.

Throughout this account, no mention has been made of Ricardo.[23] His arguments in defence of a strict bullionist position have sometimes been taken as supporting the demand transfer mechanism. An alternative interpretation, much more consistent with the rest of Ricardian economics, is that his arguments are irrelevant to the issue of the transfer mechanism. The transfer mechanism is a short run problem: the mechanism through which adjustment to equilibrium takes place. Ricardo, in contrast, was dealing with the long run. For example, he argues that bullion will not be exported in response to a harvest failure because people will know it is only temporary: if they wait long enough the situation will sort itself out and bullion movements will not be necessary. Similarly, Ricardo treats of foreign debts (the stock) rather than foreign loans (the flow). It is Ricardo's habit of telescoping the long and short run which creates the misleading impression that his arguments are relevant to the transfer question.

## 6.2   THE EMPIRE[24]

The empire needs mentioning here for two reasons. It was a major area of policy, where classical theories were applied – in particular the theories of trade distribution and growth. Secondly, it raises the classical economists' view of the development of the non–European world, important as a background to later developments in the theory of imperialism and economic development.

### Smith and Bentham

In the period from 1776 until the 1820s economists in Britain, together with radical opinion more generally, were critical of the empire and the government's attempts to reconstruct the old colonial system, disrupted by the loss of the American colonies. The dominant influence on such thinking was Smith's *Wealth of Nations*, in which the colonial system was criticized on two main lines. Firstly, the doctrine of absolute advantage implied that countries gained most from trade when they imported goods from the cheapest source of supply. The protective duties and restrictions on trade involved in the colonial system meant that goods were purchased not from the cheapest source but from more expensive suppliers within the empire. Secondly, the monopoly created by the colonial system artificially raised the rate of profit earned in colonial trade, attracting capital away from other activities. By diverting trade into less profitable channels,

The industry of the country ... is ... turned away from a more, to a less advantageous employment, and the exchange value of its annual produce, instead of being increased, according to the intention of the lawgiver, must necessarily be diminished by every such regulation.[25]

This was not to say that the opening of colonies had not increased the wealth of European nations. Smith argued that by increasing the extent of the market the expansion of trade with the colonies had produced beneficial effects. It was rather that, due to the monopolies created, the gains from colonial ventures had been less than would otherwise have been the case.[26] Without mercantilist restrictions on trade, the structure of the domestic economy would have been different, for domestic and European trade would have been much greater.

Though Smith remained very critical of colonial ventures, and of the colonial system as it then operated, he did argue that the acquisition of new colonies might help sustain the rate of profit. Capital accumulation could, according to Smith, increase the competition of capitals, lowering prices, raising wages, thus lowering the rate of profit.[27] By providing an outlet for some of this capital, colonial expansion could help prevent the rate of profit from falling. To place too much emphasis on this, however, would be misleading, for two reasons. Firstly, Smith was not alarmed by the prospect of a falling rate of profit. Secondly, he believed that the desire for betterment, combined with the division of labour, meant that any stationary state was still a long way off.

The leading exponent of anti-imperialism after Smith was Bentham,[28] whose case, whilst owing much to Smith, contained several distinctive arguments. On the economic side Bentham introduced a version of Say's Law[29] to argue that capital employed in colonies could have been employed equally profitably at home.[30] He disagreed, therefore, with Smith's conclusion that colonies could provide an outlet for surplus capital. By stressing the capital stock, rather than Smith's more general notion of the extent of the market, as determining the level of economic activity, Bentham was moving towards a more restrictive view of the role for trade.[31] In addition, Bentham stressed political factors, claiming, as part of his plan for universal peace, that emancipation of colonies would reduce international conflicts.[32]

Over his lifetime, however, Bentham was not consistent in upholding an anti-colonial position. His strict interpretation of Say's Law gave way to a view which recognized that capital accumulation might run ahead of domestic investment opportunities.[33] Capital export was seen as a possible remedy for a falling rate of profit.

Ricardo and his followers too were opposed to colonies, though on different grounds. Ricardo, holding different theories of both trade and the rate of profit,[34] denied that colonial outlets for capital could affect the overall rate of profit. In addition, whilst he opposed restraints on trade, Ricardo did admit the possibility that, through creating a monopoly of colonial trade, a country might be able to gain at the expense of a colony by moving the terms of trade in its own favour. McCulloch's reaction, that though right in principle, Ricardo's argument was inapplicable to the British situation, reflected the changing economic situation.[35] Where prior to the French revolution Britain had been merely one amongst many colonial powers, British commercial supremacy was unchallenged after 1815. In addition the enormous growth of trade with the United States since the latter's independence had shown that colonial rule was not necessary for trade to flourish.[36] It became less common for economists to argue against restrictions on colonial trade, for they became less relevant.

### Horton and systematic emigration

In the 1820s hostility to the maintenance of colonies waned, discussion of the colonies turning to various schemes for emigration, in particular that of Horton.[37] Emigration to the colonies was proposed as a means of alleviating distress, and reducing the cost of poor relief. Horton's scheme involved financing the emigration of paupers, and setting them up as farmers in Canada. He argued that the cost of such emigration, even after allowing for the cost of providing them with sufficient capital to survive until they could support themselves, would be paid for within a few years from the savings in poor relief. Any strengthening of the empire would be a by-product.

Discussion of Horton's scheme concentrated on the wage fund, and on the likely response of population growth to any rise in the standard of living it might produce. Horton's defence was in terms of the wage fund: if the scheme could be made self-financing, paupers could be removed without reducing the wage fund, and real wages could be raised. Critics argued that the scheme would not be self-financing, and that the wage fund would be reduced, possibly making the situation worse. Even if the wage fund were not reduced it could be argued that it would be better to use resources in providing paupers with productive employment at home, rather than in sending them to the colonies. In addition, there lay behind all these discussions of the wage fund the Malthusian objection, that population increase would fill any vacuum left by emigration.

### Wakefield and systematic colonization

Although it too involved emigration to the colonies, the colonization scheme advocated in the 1830s by Wakefield and the Colonial Reform Movement was very different from that of Horton, for it was concerned with the colonies themselves, not simply with the effects of the scheme on the colonizing country. Out of this different concern arose a perspective on economic development much closer to that of Smith than to that of Ricardo and his followers. Central to Wakefield's argument was Smith's argument that progress was associated with specialization, in particular with what Wakefield called "general combination", a process involving capital accumulation, the extension of the market, and division of labour.[38] Wakefield argued that the chief problem facing many colonies was the dispersion of the population over large areas of land, the result of this being that markets did not develop sufficiently to promote the division of labour.[39] The limited degree of specialization meant that the productive powers of labour were less developed than in Europe, this offsetting the favourable effects of more fertile land. In addition Wakefield revived Smith's supply and demand theory of profits, and his idea that trade provided a vent for surplus produce. Wakefield's key concept was the "field of production", a somewhat elastic term describing the scope for employment of capital and labour. Though the availability of suitable land was an important factor determining the field of production,[40] the latter was something which could be extended: provided that the field of production were continually extended capital and labour could increase without alteration in the rate of profit or wages.[41]

Wakefield's plan for colonization involved two things.[42] Firstly, the government had to set a "sufficient" price for land in the colony. The purpose of this was to create the optimal ratio of land to labour: it would deter excessive use of land, and it would force new migrants to work as hired labourers for a number of years before setting themselves up as landowners. Secondly, the revenues raised from selling land should be used to finance emigration to the colony. This link between land sales and migration was intended to make the scheme "self-regulating", causing a balanced expansion of the population and the land in use, the result of this being specialization and the use of more efficient techniques than if land were abundant relative to labour.[43]

Although Wakefield's scheme had a justification in terms of economic development, it had another aspect. Its aim was to transplant European, hierarchical society to the colonies: Wakefield wished to make it attractive for the European middle classes, as well as the working classes, to emigrate. He saw the egalitarian society produced in a country where land was cheap as culturally backward.[44] Wakefield was not an admirer of American society.

Wakefield's schemes were supported by most of the classical economists, including J. S. Mill. The only major economist consistently to oppose Wakefield's schemes was McCulloch.[45] McCulloch argued that, though a certain degree of concentration was desirable, Wakefield's scheme would produce excessive concentration. Sufficient concentration would be produced by granting land only in proportion to a settler's capital; and by stipulating that the land reverted to the state if the settler did not develop it. It was important, furthermore, that land was cheap, for cheap land was one of the major advantages possessed by colonies. To impose a high price on land would reduce colonies to the state of an old country.

In contrast to Wakefield, McCulloch believed that settlers did know what was in their own interests. They were right in wanting cheap land. It was in accordance with this view that McCulloch advocated the setting up of new colonies, but not of retaining control over them.[46] He was very critical of colonies controlled by Britain, such as India. These produced a loss, not only because of military spending, but because they distorted trade. The gains from colonial trade could be obtained without the costs of maintaining colonies.

## 6.3   ECONOMIC POLICY

The period of English classical political economy is sometimes thought of as
the age of *laissez faire*, when, under the influence of Smith and Ricardo,
governments removed mercantilist restrictions on the economy, keeping
intervention to a minimum. Smith, for example, was widely read, and
several prime ministers, from North to Pitt, turned to him for advice.
Protective duties were removed, in particular from the 1820s, the culmination of this movement being the repeal of the Corn Laws in 1846. There
followed a period in which a series of commercial treaties extended the
system of free trade throughout Europe. For this movement, and for the
prosperity which went with it, political economists claimed credit.

Smith's influence on attitudes towards economic policy was indeed
profound, and it is true that he did advocate commercial freedom, but it is
wrong to portray him as having advocated pure, or dogmatic *laissez faire*.[47]
Smith saw that competition had to work within definite limits if its results
were to be beneficent. The government had to uphold these restraints on
competition, a view which carried over into classical political economy,
there being wide recognition of the fact that there were certain activities
which, if not undertaken by government, would be undertaken by nobody.
Areas where important economists advocated state intervention included
not only the obvious ones of defence, justice and the enforcement of
contracts, but also public health, education, regulation of the quality of
food, and of trading standards, the provision of medical treatment, the
provision of roads, harbours, bridges, lighthouses, and the organization of
the Post Office.[48]

Whilst acknowledging Smith's influence, it is important to recognize that
he was not alone in determining attitudes to public policy. Particularly
important was Bentham, who, though he did advocate *laissez faire*,
provided more exceptions to this general rule than did Smith or Ricardo.
Furthermore, Bentham's utilitarian criterion of the greatest happiness of the
greatest number, together with his reforming zeal, could be regarded as
providing an intellectual basis for the transformation of the machinery of
government which occurred in the mid nineteenth century, a change
without which it would have been impossible to contemplate the enormous
expansion in the role of the state which took place in the century which
followed.

Why then does the view of the early nineteenth century as the age of
*laissez faire* have such currency? Several reasons can be offered. Firstly, there
is Smith's trenchant criticism of mercantilism, of systematic attempts by
governments to control the pattern of trade and of economic activity. This
was an attitude shared by his followers. Even here, however, the picture is
more complicated than might appear at first sight. Smith, for example,
defended certain mercantilist restrictions: Usury Laws (imposing a maximum to the rate of interest) on the grounds that they prevented prodigal
borrowers from bidding funds away from productive investments; the
Navigation Acts, on the grounds that maintaining the supply of seamen was

important for defence. But more important was the fact that these mercantilist restrictions were opposed not so much because of a doctrinaire commitment to *laissez faire* as because they favoured one section of the community at the expense of others.

Secondly, there is the exaggerated importance sometimes attached to Ricardo. Ricardo, to an extent unmatched by any of the other major classical economists, was prepared to draw policy conclusions directly from highly simplified models. He favoured a rigid monetary rule and was against the Poor Laws on straightforward Malthusian grounds, though on both issues he was in favour of introducing change gradually. More typical of classical political economy were men such as Senior, McCulloch and J. S. Mill, whose use of simple theoretical models was much more restrained. Ricardo's importance in the history of economic theory does not mean that he should be taken as representative of classical attitudes to policy.

A third reason why the age is associated with *laissez faire* is that there were people and organizations that were less restrained in their attitudes towards *laissez faire*. There was, for example, the strongly individualist philosophy of Herbert Spencer. There were also Evangelical Christians who used moral arguments to condemn governmental attempts to mitigate the effects of competition. These people, however, were often not economists at all, and if they were they could hardly be considered major ones. The major economists, such as Senior and McCulloch, were much more circumspect. The presence of these doctrinaire advocates of *laissez faire*, however, meant that Cairnes was attacking more than a straw man when he warned against the dangers of associating political economy with specific policy recommendations.

A fourth reason is the anti-Corn Law agitation, and the Manchester School, led by Cobden, which dominated discussions of trade policy in the middle of the century. When foreign economists attacked free trade, for example, they often referred to it as "Manchesterism". This movement, however, was not led by economists. Indeed, whilst many economists were sympathetic to the removal of the Corn Laws, it was the economists who were more reserved in their pronouncements. The advocacy of free trade was based on more than simply economic issues. This is particularly true of Cobden, whose advocacy of free trade owed as much to his pacifism as to purely economic arguments: for Cobden free trade was a means towards increasing peace, and towards reducing militarism.

Perhaps the main reason, however, for the problems involved in interpreting the attitudes of the classical economists towards *laissez faire* is the length of time over which they wrote. From Smith's *Wealth of Nations* (1776) to Cairnes' *Leading Principles* (1874) is virtually a century. This was a century, moreover, when unprecedented changes were occurring. The economic and social problems with which the policy-makers of Smith's time were faced were as nothing to those created by the rapid industrialization and urbanization of the first half of the nineteenth century. Much of the legislation with which economists were concerned was introduced in an attempt to deal with the newly emerging problems associated with urbanization. On these issues economists were subject to the same influences as educated opinion more generally, and this opinion moved with the times. Thus when seemingly contradictory statements with regard to *laissez faire* are produced, the explanation is sometimes simply that times had changed. This is illustrated by the economists' attitudes towards factory legislation.[49] It has been shown that whilst economists generally favoured regulation of the hours worked by children and women, and whilst they favoured regulations on conditions of work, they were not in favour of regulating adult male hours, this being something established by contract between people responsible for their own actions. Even on this, however, economists were far from dogmatic. On factory legislation, as on so much else, economists adopted a fairly pragmatic attitude, moving with the times and responding to the new circumstances with which they were confronted.

# II

## THE NEW SYSTEMS, 1870–1890

# 7

# Jevons

## 7.1 INTRODUCTION

Modern economics is often argued to stem from what has variously been described as the "marginal", "marginal utility" or "subjectivist" revolution of the 1970s, when classical cost-based theories were supplanted by theories based on utility maximization.[1] Marginal utility as an explanation of value, however, emerged almost simultaneously from the work of three men, Jevons, Menger and Walras, each working against a very different background. Thus whilst their work did share important features, it is in some respects important to consider them as creating three different systems, rather than as proposing three variants on the same system.

Although marginalist economics, or whatever we wish to call it, stems form the work of Jevons, Menger and Walras, there were important aspects of the economic ideas which emerged towards the end of the nineteenth century that are not traceable to this triumvirate. It is for this reason that Marshall's economics is considered as a separate system: though Marshall probably got his ideas on marginal utility from Jevons, there are important features of Marshallian economics without which developments over the following half century would be incomprehensible. The situation is similar with J. B. Clark, for even if his theory of marginal utility was subjectively original, it was over a decade too late. Clark is important not only for introducing some important ideas into economics, but also for his role in American economics, for it is from the late nineteenth century that US economists began to play an increasingly important role in the development of the subject. Finally, there is Marx, whose work, for obvious reasons, requires separate treatment.

## 7.2 JEVONS' SYSTEM

William Stanley Jevons was described by Keynes as exhibiting the "many sidedness" necessary for an economist.[2] Whilst he is most widely known, on account of his marginal utility theory of value, as one of the originators of the so-called "marginal revolution", he was known to his contemporaries primarily as a statistician, his most well known work being on the question of exhaustible resources (coal) and the effects of gold discoveries on the price level, both of these being topical issues in the 1860s. Yet despite the diversity of his interests (he was also a qualified chemist, a meteorologist, and the author of a widely read book on scientific method) there is a system underlying his work. The unity of his work is provided by two themes: his views on scientific method and his Benthamite utilitarianism.[3]

In the second half of the nineteenth century there was a deep division between the deductive approach of the classical economists and the inductive methods of the historical school.[4] Jevons denied that induction and deduction were opposed to each other – "induction is simply an inverse employment of deduction".[5] He argued that the great triumphs of science were due to "the Newtonian method of deductive reasoning combined with empirical verification"[6] and that such methods were also appropriate for economics. It was his philosophy of science, not mere eclecticism, that led him to the view that economics should comprise a diversity of subjects. Its central core is the abstract, deductive science which deals with general, universal laws analogous to the laws of motion in physics. Equally important, however, is the empirical, inductive science which tests these laws through examining their concrete applications. Jevons considered the knowledge resulting from either type of inquiry to be uncertain, the only way to reduce this uncertainty being to accumulate exact, statistical data which could be used to quantify economic laws. This stress on quantification makes Jevons seem much closer to modern economics than to the classical economists.

The other unifying strand in Jevons' work is Bentham's utilitarianism. The utilitarian criterion is used to judge proposals for social reform in a way which leads Jevons away from *laissez faire* towards a pragmatic interventionism. But also, and this is very important, Jevons views the central core of economics, pure theory, as comprising "the mechanics of utility and self interest".[7] Utility maximization is to economics what the laws of motion are to physics. This view results in a new perspective, in which problems of resource allocation become primary. Jevons did not completely neglect the issues which concerned the classical economists, his work on coal, for example, dealing with the implications of a scarce resource for long term growth, but he saw these issues as primarily empirical questions. Associated with this view of utility as being central to economics was Jevons' view that, because it deals with quantities, economics was inherently mathematical, a view which distinguished him from the English classical orthodoxy as represented by Mill and Cairnes.

### 7.3  ECONOMIC THEORY: THE MECHANICS OF UTILITY AND SELF-INTEREST

In the Benthamite scheme, pleasures and pains are the basic motives underlying human action, comprising "all the forces which drive us to action",[8] but although the problem of economics was seen as being to maximize pleasure, Jevons argued that it was more convenient to focus on utility, the ability of objects to increase pleasure or to reduce pain. The utility, or usefulness, of an object depends not only on the object itself, but also on circumstances, and it is something that can be determined only by the individual concerned, and only in relation to the utility of other objects. He explicitly rejects the possibility of any objective inter-personal comparisons of utility.

In *The Theory of Political Economy* (1871) Jevons makes considerable use of mathematics to distinguish very carefully between total and marginal utility, calling the latter "the degree of utility",[9] before going on to examine the mechanics of utility maximization. His starting point is to show that the marginal utility of a commodity will diminish as consumption of that commodity increases, from which it follows that an individual who can use a commodity in two ways will allocate it between two uses in such a way that the final degree of utility in the two uses is the same. But of more interest are the ways in which individuals can increase their utilities: through exchange, through labour and through the use of capital.

Jevons argues that exchange will always increase utility, for if any party's utility were reduced they could opt out. Where a commodity is indivisible (say a house) exchange will take place whenever, for both parties, the utility of the good received exceeds that of the good exchanged for it. The problem of exchange where the quantity that can be exchanged is variable is more complicated, and to solve it Jevons brings in what he calls "the law of indifference": the assumption that all units of a commodity must exchange for the same price. Using this he derives the condition for equilibrium in exchange. In more modern notation this can be written as

$$MU^A_X/MU^A_Y = MU^B_Y/MU^B_Y = y/x$$

where agents are exchanging commodities $X$ and $Y$, the quantities exchanged being $x$ and $y$.[10] Notice that prices are not used, $y/x$ being the relative price or, as Jevons puts it, "the ratio of exchange of the two goods". He used this approach in order to avoid the confusion surrounding the term value in the classical literature, where it was used in a wide variety of senses.

Despite deriving the above, very familiar, relationship between prices and marginal utilities, Jevons' theory is subject to a serious weakness. In order to be able to represent all exchange as bilateral, he examined exchange between two "trading bodies", arguing that these trading bodies could be either individuals or groups of individuals. He failed to make clear the crucial difference between bilateral monopoly, where the outcome is indeterminate, and competition.

The use of labour to increase utility is analysed in a similar way, to show that in equilibrium, the marginal disutility of labour must equal the marginal utility of the produce obtained by the work:

$$dl/dt = (du/dx)(dx/dt)$$

where $l$ is the disutility of labour, $t$ the number of hours worked, $x$ the output produced and $u$ the utility of this output.[10] Note that Jevons defines labour unconventionally, not as the number of hours worked, but as the disutility of work. This equation simply states that the marginal disutility of work equals the marginal utility of output multiplied by the marginal productivity of work. After generalizing this theory to cover the production of more than one commodity it is combined with the theory of exchange. The result is a general equilibrium system incorporating marginal utility and marginal productivity, though the latter is not made very explicit. Ratios of exchange (relative prices) are shown to "depend upon a general balance of producing power and of demand as measured by the final degree of utility".[12] This is summarized by the condition, here expressed in modern terminology, that

$$MPL_Y/MPL_X = MC_X/MC_Y = P_X/P_Y = MU_X/MU_Y$$

where the notation should be self-explanatory.[13] From this, comparative statics results are derived. Jevons points out the similarity of his results to the classical theory of rent, expounding the latter along similar lines.

The third means of increasing utility is to employ capital. For Jevons, capital comprises "those commodities which are required for sustaining labourers of any kind or class employed in work",[14] its importance being that it allows production to take time. Capital thus has two dimensions, the amount of capital invested and the time for which it is invested. Longer production processes are assumed to be more productive than shorter ones. Thus if we write output as a function $F(t)$ of $t$, the time for which capital is invested, the derivative $F'(t)$ is assumed to be positive. In other words, if production processes are chosen such that capital is invested for a longer period, output will be higher. Jevons gives as examples the growing of a forest, and the maturing of wine.[15] There are, however, limits to the extent to which output can be increased by increasing the period for which capital is invested, for as $t$ increases $F'(t)$ will, Jevons assumes, decline to zero.

From this Jevons arrives at a marginal productivity theory of interest, the rate of interest being given by

$$r = F'(t)/F(t).[16]$$

The right hand side is the percentage increase in output resulting from increasing the time for which capital is invested by one period, which is the marginal return to increasing $t$. As the interest rate is the marginal cost of increasing $t$, this equation is simply marginal cost equals marginal revenue, applied to Jevons' model.

## 7.4   STATISTICAL WORK

### *The coal question*

As mentioned above, it was not Jevons' work on utility theory that was responsible for his reputation amongst his contemporaries, but his statistical work. Of this, the work to gain him the widest reputation was *The Coal*

*Question* (1865), published at a time when Britain's prosperity was at its height due, in Jevons' words, to "the unprecedented commercial reforms of the last twenty years".[17] In this book he questions Britain's ability to sustain this progress, the problem being that prosperity was founded on supplies of coal which were rapidly becoming exhausted.

The argument he used was a development of the Malthusian one: "living beings of the same nature and in the same circumstances multiply in the same geometrical ratio".[18] With the repeal of the corn laws food would continue to be available through trade and coal would become the limiting factor. Not only would coal continue to be needed in large quantities, but it would be needed in even larger quantities: "the new applications of coal are of an unlimited character".[19] His conclusion was, "So far, then, as our wealth and progress depend on the superior command of coal, we must not only stop – we must go back."[20] This argument was supported with detailed statistical evidence showing that up until then British industry had been expanding unchecked, at a constant proportional rate. Reserves of coal were calculated, and their lifetime worked out.

A natural response to such an argument was that trade could provide a way out. Jevons, however, argued strongly that it could not: "Take away that resource [coal] and our expectations from free trade must be of a very minor character".[21] The reason for this was that trade depended upon comparative costs (the Ricardo–J. S. Mill view). Britain could benefit from free trade through importing corn because cheap coal provided a comparative advantage in the export of manufactured goods. The cost of transporting coal meant that when indigenous coal was used up this advantage must disappear. Jevons argued that the appropriate response to the prospect of vanishing coal reserves was to pay off the National Debt, a move which would add to the country's productive capacity, check the country's too rapid progress and lessen future difficulties.

Jevons' discussion of the coal question is interesting because it shows that, even though he did not regard it as part of the theoretical core of economics, and even though his approach was different from that of the classical economists, Jevons was concerned with the classical problem of growth. The Malthusian argument was taken as an empirical law to be tested statistically, and to be modified to take account of changing circumstances. The failure to appreciate the possibilities for technical progress, and of the development of substitutes for coal, mean that his conclusions have not been borne out, but as a piece of applied economics blending theoretical and statistical work the book is remarkable.

## Money

Although not attracting so much publicity as his work on coal, Jevons' pamphlet, "A serious fall in the value of gold ascertained, and its social effects set forth" (1863) was an even more remarkable statistical contribution. In this Jevons addressed himself to the question of whether the recent

Californian gold discoveries had lowered the value of gold. Four aspects of his argument need to be distinguished:
(1) defining a fall in the value of gold;
(2) establishing, statistically, that this had taken place;
(3) examining its causes;
(4) examining its consequences.
Today the first two questions would be routine ones: a fall in the value of gold would be seen as equivalent to a rise in the price level, standard techniques being available to calculate the appropriate index number. But for Jevons this was not the case.

Answering the first of these questions, Jevons argued, in terms which today might seem self evident, "If prices on the average have risen ever so little, *this constitutes a fall in the value of gold*",[22] yet even this was controversial. Cairnes argued that value should be defined in relation to cost, not as a relative term.[23] This difference of opinion reflected their views on value theory. In quantifying the rise in prices Jevons created index numbers for various lists of commodities, analysing a variety of indices, showing that they all indicated a rise in prices. In order to determine the effect of the gold discoveries he also took averages over several years, taking the average for the years 1845–1850, a complete cycle, as his base. He concluded that gold had fallen in value by about 10%, though there was some ambiguity, this arising from uncertainty as to which index number to use.[24]

*Fluctuations*

The third area in which Jevons undertook statistical work was that of fluctuations. Here he followed an inductive approach, analysing and measuring seasonal fluctuations as well as the trade cycle. His sunspot theory of the latter is a more worthwhile piece of work than it is sometimes taken to be, for at the time it was generally thought that sunspots were linked to the weather. Jevons attempted to test the hypothesis that variations in the weather were linked, through harvests, to the trade cycle. After finding some evidence for the theory, he tried to test the theory more thoroughly by considering a longer period. When it did not work for European harvests he looked at Indian harvests, and their effect, through trade flows, on economic acitvity in Europe.[25] Whilst we may feel that Jevons clung to his theory rather too tenaciously in the face of contrary evidence, he was nonetheless following a method that many contemporary economists would advocate.

## 7.5  SOCIAL REFORM

Jevons' approach to economic policy was utilitarian. In *The State in Relation to Labour* (1882) he wrote, "The state is justified in passing any law, or even in doing any single act which, without ulterior consequences, adds to the sum total of human happiness."[26] However, as mentioned above, for him the utilitarian criterion was not simply an objective, scientific one: "We cannot expect to agree in utilitarian estimates, at least without much debate."[27] Thus Jevons' utilitarianism provided the justification for an increasingly pragmatic approach to state intervention. His earlier writings reveal a strong individualism. He saw "freedom for *all* commercial transactions [as] the spirit of improved legislation",[28] and he was critical of charities, including "the whole of our medical charities", on the grounds that they undermined self-help. He viewed the Poor Law of 1832 as "one of the wisest measures ever concerted by any government", and was concerned "lest any mistaken feelings of humanity should lead us to relax the rigour of its application".[29] In contrast, in his last book, he argued that the principle of maximizing liberty of action

fails to give a sure guiding light. So intricate are the ways, industrial, sanitary, or political, in which one class or section of the people affect other classes or sections, that there is *hardly any limit to the interference of the legislator.*[30]

So numerous were the cases requiring intervention that a new branch of economics was required, to show the limits to *laissez faire.*

This change of attitude arose as Jevons discovered more and more cases for intervention, his views being dominated by his cautious, empirical approach stressing the need for accurate, detailed information, and advocating piecemeal social experimentation to obtain this. His views on nationalization illustrate his approach of treating each case on its merits: he favoured nationalization of the Post Office, approved the Russian State railways, but thought nationalization of the British railway system would lead to disaster.

Monopoly was not a reason used by Jevons to justify intervention, his proposals for reform covering instead areas where individual choice proved inadequate: cases of ignorance, paternalism, public goods and externalities. Trade union monopolies were, however, something that concerned Jevons, for he argued that the only way a union could raise wages was through monopoly power, effectively taxing the rest of the community for the benefit of a small group. Yet he had no desire to suppress trade unions, for he believed that "legislation with regard to labour has almost always been class-legislation ... the effort of some dominant body to keep down a lower class".[31] He valued the other functions of trade unions, such as providing insurance, and was encouraged by the debates on industrial legislation which took place at the Trades Union Congress in 1881. He encouraged co-operatives and other forms of industrial partnership.

Two areas where Jevons remained in the classical tradition, despite his movement towards collectivism, were those of trade and taxation. He remained a supporter of free trade, and he continued to support proportional taxation, perhaps surprisingly in view of his utilitarianism.

## 7.6   JEVONS AND ENGLISH CLASSICAL ECONOMICS

The preface to the second edition of *The Theory of Political Economy* ends with Jevons' widely quoted criticism of Ricardo and Mill.

When at length a true system of economics comes to be established it will be seen that that able but wrong-headed man, David Ricardo, shunted the car of economic science on to a wrong line – a line, however, on which it was further urged towards confusion by his equally able and wrong-headed admirer, John Stuart Mill. There were economists, such as Malthus and Senior, who had a far better comprehension of the true doctrines (though not free from Ricardian errors), but they were driven out of the field by the unity and influence of the Ricardo–Mill school.[31]

Ignoring the question of how far this description of classical economics was justified,[33] it raises the question of exactly how Jevons differed from Ricardo and Mill.

The economics contained in *The Theory of Political Economy* was sharply at variance with both the classical labour, or cost-of-production theory of value, and with the aggregative theory of wages contained in the wage fund theory. Crucial to both elements of the classical system was the simplification that various types of labour could be reduced to a common, homogeneous "labour", the relationship between different types of labour remaining constant. With the changes that took place in the economy during the nineteenth century, such an assumption was no longer tenable, and its removal undermined the whole of the classical system. It was no longer possible to use either a labour cost theory of value, or a theory of a general average wage rate if the value of labour was essentially variable. So Jevons' alternative theory, in which the value of labour was determined by the value of the produce, should be seen as an attempt to replace a system acknowledged to be theoretically inadequate, not as an attempt to replace the classical theory with one more acceptable, ideologically or politically.

Although Jevons' differences from the classical economists over economic theory, both as regards the theory of value and distribution, and as regards the use of mathematics, were real enough,[34] it is important to note two things. Firstly, there was much less unanimity within classical economics than the above quotation from Jevons implies. Secondly, there was much less disagreement in other areas of economics. *The Coal Question* was a book consistent with the classical approach, whilst Jevons' work on money and prices was greatly appreciated by Cairnes, who disagreed with him so strongly over the theory of value. Similarly Jevons had great respect for Cairnes' empirical work. Thus, though important changes were taking place in both economic theory and economic policy, there was also a substantial degree of continuity.[35]

# 8

# Walras

## 8.1 WALRAS'S SYSTEM

Like his contemporary, Jevons, Walras saw as lying at the centre of economics a core of abstract, deductive theory, analogous to the laws of motion in physics. Although this Pure Economics, as he called it, turned out to have much in common with Jevons' theory, its origins were very different: it was based not on Benthamite utilitarianism, but on a desire to explain price determination "under a hypothetical regime of free competition".[1] He regarded the assumption of free competition as a first step towards describing how the real world operated; as an approximation in the same way that the assumption of frictionless machines is used in mechanics.[2] In justifying this procedure he asked what physicist would pick cloudy weather for observing the stars.[3]

On the other hand, whilst Walras was concerned to construct a model of how a capitalist economy worked, he had another motive for analysing the case of free competition: he was trying to describe an economy that worked in conformity with certain principles of justice. In natural law philosophy, two types of justice were distinguished: distributive justice, referring to the distribution of wealth between persons; and commutative justice, or justice in exchange. For justice in exchange, the value of the goods exchanged had to be equal, otherwise one party to the exchange would gain, and the other lose. Thus if there was to be justice in exchange, two conditions had to be fulfilled: (1) any commodity had to have a uniform price at all places and at all times; and (2) the price of a commodity had to equal its cost of production. This double condition would be satisfied only under free competition. Thus if Walras could show how an economy could operate under free competition, he would have shown how one form of injustice, that arising from unequal exchange, could be eliminated. In other words, Walras was trying to create a "realistic utopia"; realistic in that it was subject to the same constraints as was an actual economic system; a utopia in that it was based on justice.[4]

This was Walras's pure economics, found in his *Elements of Pure Economics*, published in instalments between 1874 and 1877. The other branches of economics that he distinguished were applied and social economics. Applied economics dealt with relations between men as producers, with departures from the competitive ideal; whilst social economics considered questions of property, distribution and justice. These branches of economics were examined by Walras in his *Etudes d'Economie Politique Appliqué* (1896), and *Etudes d'Economie Sociale* (1898), collections of essays he published in lieu of the second and third volumes of the *Elements* he never managed to write.

Both the philosophical basis for his system and much of the terminology he used came from his father, Auguste Walras, Jaffe claiming that Leon Walras departed "not one iota" from his father's philosophy.[5] The stress on scarcity (or *rareté*) as the source of value came from him, though it had roots in a long French tradition.[6] Despite providing Walras with his starting point, however, it can be argued that his faithfulness to his father's terminology was to some extent a disadvantage. It accounts, for example, for the convolutions in his discussions of utility[7]

An equally important aspect of Walras's system was his use of mathematics, for his method was to proceed by constructing a set of equations. He saw the economist as reaching the same set of prices through solving the appropriate set of simultaneous equations as the real economy achieved through a different process. The main example here was that of Cournot.[8] In addition to analysing monopoly, Cournot had discussed perfect competition and the exchange of two commodities for each other. Walras extended this in two ways. He explained the demand curve, which Cournot had taken as given, in terms of marginal utility; and he extended the analysis to cover an equilibrium with an indefinite number of markets, these covering consumers' goods, factor services and money. This task, of constructing a general equilibrium system for many markets, was something Cournot had avoided attempting, considering it mathematically too difficult.[9]

These changes were more than minor technicalities, for they led Walras to the conclusion, also reached by Jevons and Menger, albeit by different routes, that

the theory of exchange based on the proportionality of prices to *intensities of the last wants satisfied* [marginal utilities] ... constitutes the very foundation of the whole edifice of economics.[10]

It was marginal utilities that determined the prices of products and, indirectly, the prices of factors of production. Marginal utilities held everything together.

## 8.2   THE PURE ECONOMICS

Walras builds up his general equilibrium system in several stages. In successive parts of the *Elements* he constructs systems of equations to analyse, first, two-commodity exchange, and then the exchange of several commodities. After this he introduced production, capitalization and credit, and, finally, circulation and money. After building this system of equations, he then proceeds to analyse economic progress, monopoly and taxation.

*Exchange and commodity prices*

In considering the first stage, the theory of exchange, Walras reached the same conclusion as his father, that utility depended on the *rareté*, or scarcity, of a commodity. However, whereas Auguste Walras had stopped here, producing a rather unhelpful doctrine, Leon Walras went on to equate *rareté* with "the intensity of the last need satisfied"; in other words, with marginal utility. He showed that in equilibrium relative prices would equal the ratios of the corresponding *raretés*. He thus transformed his father's ideas into something resembling the theory of Jevons. However, there are several aspects of his theory, even at the level of two commodities, which mark it apart from that of Jevons. Firstly, he used marginal utility to derive demand curves, something that Jevons failed to do. In this respect his theory is closer to Marshall's. Secondly, no doubt due to Cournot's influence, he provided a much clearer account of competition. Lastly, he provided a much more detailed account of how equilibrium was reached: the theory of *tâtonnement*, or groping. Starting from arbitrarily given prices this involved raising the prices of commodities in excess demand, and lowering those of commodities in excess supply, this process eventually resulting in equilibrium of supply and demand being reached. He referred to this *tâtonnement* process as the "realistic" solution to the problem of determining prices: it was the process through which the market would reach the same set of prices as the economist reached through solving sets of supply and demand equations.

## Production and the prices of factor services

The theory of exchange, even when extended to many commodities, was still only a first step, the next being to incorporate production. Crucial to Walras's theory of production is the distinction between durable resources (capital goods, land, human capital) and the *services* they yield. The prices of the services of productive resources are the first to be determined. The key here is entrepreneurs, who purchase factor services, produce and sell commodities. Production of any commodity the price of which exceeds its cost of production will be increased as entrepreneurs respond to opportunities to make a profit. Similarly, production of loss-making commodities will be reduced. Entrepreneurs thus link the product and factor services markets. For example, a rise in the demand for a product means that its price will rise, causing entrepreneurs to increase its production; this will raise demand for the factors used in producing the product, raising their prices. Walras argued that a *tâtonnement* process, operating simultaneously in product and factor service markets, would result in an equilibrium being reached in which (1) supply and demand were equal in all markets, and (2) the price of every commodity equalled its cost of production, entrepreneurs, *qua* entrepreneurs, making neither profit nor loss. As did Jevons, Walras argued that factor prices were inherently variable, being determined by the value (*rareté*) of the product they were being used to produce.

## The interest rate and the prices of fixed capital goods

The price of the *service* of a factor of production is the income, or rental, accruing to its owner. Walras defined the *net income* from a capital good as this rental, less insurance charges and depreciation allowances. The *rate of return* on the asset is then the net income from the asset, divided by the purchase price of the asset.[11] If there is competition, the rates of return on all assets must be the same. Calling this common rate of return the rate of interest, it follows that the price of a capital good must equal its net income (rental less depreciation and insurance charges), determined in the market for factor services, divided by the interest rate.[12] Production of new capital goods will then depend on the relationship of their prices, determined in this way, to costs of production. The value of land is determined in the same way, the only difference being that its quantity is fixed, not variable.

This account of how the prices of capital goods are determined leaves the rate of interest unexplained. The rate of interest, he argued, would depend on supply and demand for new capital goods. Demand for capital goods came from savers, savings being defined as the excess of income over consumption, something Walras believed would increase when the rate of interest rose. In bringing savings into the model, Walras deliberately avoided the Austrian route[13] of bringing in time preference, preferring instead to incorporate an imaginary commodity, an annuity or bond, comprising a stream of perpetual net income. Consumers were assumed to demand, not individual capital goods, but entitlements to perpetual net income, the price of which was the reciprocal of the interest rate.[14] The supply of new capital goods was the quantity produced, the value of this being assumed to decrease when the interest rate rose. The equilibrium value of the interest rate would thus be determined by supply and demand, simultaneously with the other prices in the system.

### Maximum satisfaction

In the course of developing his general equilibrium system Walras developed, again in several stages, a doctrine of maximum satisfaction. His doctrine is that in a situation of free competition, consumers will obtain "the greatest possible satisfacton of their wants" consistent with the "double condition" that (1) each service and each product has a single price in the market, and (2) the selling price of each product equals its cost of production.[15] This result extends not only to the production and consumption of consumers' goods, but also the production and use of new capital goods, the rate of return on which has to be equalized for satisfaction to be maximized.

Care has to be taken in interpreting this doctrine, for Walras did not mean by maximum satisfaction the same thing as Marshall.[16] Walras's natural law philosophy is crucial here, for the "double condition" he mentions is the condition for commutative justice. Walras's doctrine does *not* deny the possibility of increasing welfare through an appropriate redistribution of wealth. Though it would be going too far to credit Walras with the idea of Pareto-optimality,[17] his doctrine is far closer to this than to the Marshallian doctrine of maximum satisfaction. Economists who have tried to interpret Walras's doctrine in Marshallian terms have, not surprisingly, found fault with it.[18]

*Circulating capital and money*

Walras modelled the need to hold money in the same way as the need to hold stocks of circulating capital goods. He assumed that they yielded their holders "services of availability", producers and consumers alike deriving a benefit from having money available. From this, demand functions could be derived, these being incorporated without difficulty into the overall system of supply and demand equations.

Because money is of special interest, it is worth considering Walras's treatment of it in more detail. In the first edition of the *Elements* he used an equation of exchange similar to Fisher's,[19] in which demand for money was related to the needs of circulation. But from the second edition, he replaced this with the concept of *encaisse desirée*, desired cash balances, deriving an equation identical to the cash balance equation later used by Keynes.[20] It was in the third edition that he saw how to integrate this with the rest of his system, by treating money as circulating capital, yielding a service of availability, or as yielding utility. Walras thus anticipated several concepts in monetary economics which economists, ignoring his work, developed in the twentieth century.[21] Having brought money into his system in this way, Walras then went on to consider the implications of having two commodities which served as money (bimetallism) and of having a paper currency. Of his treatment of bimetallism, Schumpeter wrote of it, in 1910, that it was "nothing short of classic", and that it would be "definitive for a long time to come".[22]

*Economic progress*

With the introduction of money, Walras's static general equilibrium system was complete. The next step in the *Elements* was to use it to analyse economic progress, namely the effects of capital accumulation and population growth.[23] To do this he assumed that the economy was continuously in equilibrium, but that capital accumulation and population growth were continuously altering this equilibrium. In addition to its significance for interpreting Walras's economics as a whole, this section is interesting for several reasons. Firstly, it is here that Walras, in later editions of the *Elements*, introduces a marginal productivity theory of factor prices.[24] With capital accumulation, Walras argued, technical coefficients may change as capital is substituted for land, entrepreneurs choosing the cost minimizing methods of production, from which proportionality of factor prices to marginal products follows.[25] Secondly, Walras carefully defines progress in terms of diminishing *raretés*, thus clearly defining it in terms as an increasing standard of living.[26] Diminishing *raretés* are clearly distinguished from prices (relative *raretés*), which may move in any direction. Thirdly, and most importantly, Walras is, in this section, closest to English classical economics. His main conclusion has been described by Harrod as "pure Ricardo":[27]

In a progressive economy, the price of labour [wages] remaining substantially unchanged, the price of land services [rent] will rise appreciably and the price of capital services [the interest charge] will fall appreciably.[28]

However, despite reaching this conclusion, he did not accept the theories of Ricardo and Mill, the following two "lessons" containing refutations of "the English theories" of rent, wages and interest. His hostility to their theories is shown even more clearly in a letter to Jevons, in which he wrote that if only Jevons had revised his *Theory of Political Economy* more thoroughly, Jevons would have been able to destroy the Ricardo–Mill system.[29] His criticisms of this theory are similar to those of Jevons: he dismisses the wage fund as a truism; he argues that the English school attempt to determine two variables with a single equation; and that the value of labour is determined by the value of the product, not the other way round.[30]

## 8.3    SOCIAL REFORM AND THE ROLE OF THE STATE

Walras was a social reformer, a socialist in the nineteenth century sense of being someone who believed in the rational reform of society. He accepted neither the individualism of the orthodox French school of economists, nor the collectivism of the Marxists, but he argued for a synthesis of collectivism and individualism. The basis for this synthesis was his theory of justice, summarized, according to Jaffe, by his father's maxim, "égalité de conditions, intégalité de positions".[31] Justice requires that no-one be allowed to infringe on the rights of others to pursue unequal positions; but for these unequal positions in society to be just, the conditions under which they are reached must be the same for everyone.

Equality of conditions requires commutative justice, justice in exchange, which in turn requires free competition, the working of which had been expounded in Walras's pure economics. But Walras did not associate free competition with *laissez faire*, for he saw the maintenance of free competition as requiring state intervention, something he recognized to be a "very complicated task".[32] One area requiring intervention was that of natural monopolies, where the state had to ensure that goods were sold at cost price. Another area was that caused by consumers' being ignorant, or being liable to be misled: hence he made proposals for controlling advertising, and for controlling speculative activities on the stock exchange. A similar area was that of public goods ("services et produits d'intérêt public"), goods for which everyone had the same need, and for which the sole consumer was the state. Such goods, needing to be produced by the state, included security, justice, education and communications.[33]

To these areas for state intervention Walras added another, not usually grouped with them: the regulation of the price level. This too followed from the requirement of commutative justice, for if the price level varied, consumers would lose or gain through exchange. To achieve price level stability Walras advocated a state monopoly of coinage, or, if this were not practicable, the issue of cupro-nickel coins ("billon d'argent regulateur") in order to ensure that the coins in circulation were adjusted to demand and that the price level remained constant.[34]

Equality of conditions, however, also required distributive justice, and it is here that Walras's views stand out from those of the other major economists of the period. Walras shared his father's views, their common view stemming from their natural law philosophy. Walras argued that individuals have a right to the produce of their own labour, differences in wealth arising from differences in personal faculties being perfectly just. He argued, however, that the other source of wealth, land, was by rights the property of all mankind. As the institution representing the community, the state had a right to the revenues arising from the land. Linked to this was the question of taxation, which Walras saw as synonymous with the question of property.[35] Taxation of income from labour was an incursion on an individual's property, and hence unjust. The only just taxation was thus taxation on land, or on the revenue from it. State ownership of the land, whether through nationalization of land, or simply the taxation of rents, would thus solve two problems. It would permit the replacement of existing, unjust, taxes with a form of revenue to which the state was entitled. In addition, it would eliminate what, along with monopoly, Walras saw as the major source of inequality in the France of his day.

State ownership of land revenues should not, however, be achieved immediately, for this would penalize the present owners of land, some of whom had purchased land with the fruits of their own labour, this objection applying to both confiscation of land and to taxation. Instead he proposed what amounted to a tax on the increase in land values in order to "put a stop to *further* usurpations of land".[36] Furthermore, as Walras believed that economic progress was accompanied by rising rents, he believed that this source of revenue would rise continually, the state gradually appropriating a greater and greater proportion of rents.

In conclusion, it can be seen that Walras sought to provide a synthesis of collectivism and individualism through ascribing, on the basis of his natural law philosophy, certain rights to individuals, and others to the state. Though he rejected the extreme solutions of the advocates of *laissez faire* on the one hand, and those of the Marxists on the other, he was averse to neither individualism nor collectivism in principle. However, whilst the role Walras saw for the state had much in common with that envisaged by Jevons or Marshall, the philosophy on which it was based was becoming unfashionable. This factor, together with his complete inability to furnish succinct, practical policy advice, accounts for his complete failure to get his ideas on policy taken seriously.[37]

## 8.4 ASSESSMENT

Walras's main contribution to economics was his theory of general equilibrium. Although he has to be credited with developing the theory of marginal utility independently of Jevons and Menger, it was in seeing the general interdependence of all prices, *and in developing this idea into a comprehensive model of a competitive economy* that Walras achieved so much more than his contemporaries. Perhaps because of his fidelity to his father's ideas, his theory of utility was at best only the equal of those of Jevons and Menger.[38] Many of the concepts Walras used in developing his system, such as those of the *numéraire*, *tâtonnement* and the distinction between factor services and stocks of factors, are still used; and although his proofs of the existence of equilibrium (through counting equations) and of stability (the *tâtonnement*) have quite correctly been criticized, the problems he saw are ones which many more recent economists have tried to solve. To quote Blaug, "nearly all economics nowadays *is* Walrasian economics".[39]

Even if there is widespread agreement on the importance of Walras's general equilibrium theory, there is still room for disagreement over its interpretations: was it positive or normative in its aim? Morishima has argued the former: "Walras' aim is to obtain a scientific description of the real world."[40] For him, the crucial part of the *Elements* is part VII, on economic progress, where Walras uses the static model to examine how an economy develops over time. Morishima thus sees Walras as close to Ricardo, placing him alongside Marx as one of Ricardo's "greatest disciples – or critics". In contrast, Jaffe has argued that the normative aim was paramount. Because of his desire to examine a system, albeit one subject to the same constraints as operate in the real world, in which commutative justice prevailed, Walras was concerned only to examine how an imaginary system might work, not to discover laws governing the behaviour of real economies. Jaffe thus sees part VII as a "coda", written simply to show the uses to which the model could be put.

The problem with both these interpretations is that they separate the positive and normative aspects of Walras's system, whereas both were important, for both were crucial to the schemes of social reform to which he attached so much importance. The importance Walras attached to his schemes of social reform clearly makes the normative aspects of his system important, for it is his view of social justice which provides their rationale. On the other hand, if the Walrasian system did not describe, at least to a substantial extent, how contemporary economies actually worked, the justification for many of Walras's schemes, in particular his schemes of land nationalization, would disappear: for if the world was not described, at least approximately, by the competitive model, Walras would have no basis for claiming that a tax on the increase in land values would eliminate private landownership. In other words, it is *because of* Walras's normative economics and the importance he attached to his land nationalization scheme, that his Ricardo-like conclusion on economic progress is important.

# 9

# Menger and the Austrian School

## 9.1 INTRODUCTION

Menger's Austrian background is relevant to an understanding of his economics, for it made the situation in which he was writing very different from that facing either Jevons or Walras. Due in part to the different political climate, the movement towards *laissez faire*, characteristic of mid nineteenth century England and France, was not evident in Austria.[1] There were German economists who had made important contributions to economic theory, but German-speaking economics was characterized, on the whole, by the absence of any theoretical system. Though Smith was widely read, the Ricardian strand in classical economics, and with it the labour theory of value, never took root.[2] In Germany the Historical School was dominant, but this was not the case in Austria.[3] As for the positive influences on Menger, he had a background in law, economics being taught to students training in law, and he was very much influenced by Aristotelian philosophy, something still widely taught in Austria.

## 9.2 THE THEORY OF VALUE

*Goods and the structure of production*

Menger's contribution to economic theory is contained almost entirely within one book, the *Principles of Economics* (1871). In it his starting point is the satisfaction of human needs, his whole theory being built up on this. The first stage in his argument is to define *goods*, which he does in the following way.

If a thing is to become a good ... all four of the following prerequisites must be simultaneously present:
1 A human need.
2 Such properties as render the thing capable of being brought into a causal connection with the satisfaction of this need. [i.e. the power to satisfy human needs.[4]]
3 Human knowledge of this causal connection.
4 Command over the thing sufficient to direct it to the satisfaction of the need.[5]

Menger stressed that all four of these were required.

But if it is human needs that give things their "goods character", what about things which apparently satisfy no human need? Menger's answer is that in addition to goods which satisfy our needs directly (which he calls goods of the 1st order) there are goods which satisfy human needs indirectly (called goods of higher order). For example, to satisfy hunger, we need bread (1st order); to make bread we need flour and yeast (2nd order); to make flour we need wheat and millstones (3rd order) and so on. Menger thus assumes a complex structure of production, causal connections running back from wants to goods of higher and higher order. The goods character of higher-order goods is derived from that of lower-order goods and, ultimately, from human needs.[6]

This approach to economic theory led Menger to stress issues neglected by Jevons and Walras. (1) He integrated factors of production and intermediate goods into a general economic theory, rather than explaining them separately. (2) He stressed complementarity between higher order goods (e.g. wheat *and* millstones needed). (3) Uncertainty and the importance of knowledge were brought in at the start, for they are covered by the third of the prerequisites for goods character listed above.

### Economic goods and value

Having defined goods in this way, the concept of *economic goods* follows naturally: these are goods for which requirements exceed the available quantity. When men recognize that certain goods are scarce they will try to maintain at their disposal as much of these goods as possible, the sum of such goods constituting an individual's wealth; and they will use such goods as they do control to satisfy their needs as fully as possible, this phenomenon being described by Menger as *economizing*.

It is at this stage that Menger introduces the concept of *value*:

Value is thus the importance that individual goods or quantities of goods attain for us because we are conscious of being dependent on command of them for the satisfaction of our needs.[7]

Value is thus purely subjective, being the satisfaction an individual obtains from command over the good concerned. The satisfaction obtained from a unit of a good is assumed to diminish as the amount of the good consumed increases, something Menger illustrated with a table, shown below as Table 9.1. In this table he designates the most important satisfaction, on which life depends, with 10, and the least important with 1, other satisfactions being given numbers in between. Although Menger does not use the term, what he is describing here is, clearly, diminishing marginal utility.[8] Menger then derives a crucial proposition.

The value to this person of any portion of the whole available quantity of the good is equal to the importance to him of the satisfactions of least importance among those assured by the whole quantity and achieved with an equal portion.[9]

Thus if a consumer has 4 units of commodity I and 2 units of commodity III, these two units are of equal value.[10]

As a marginal utility theory of value this hardly goes any further than the theories of Jevons or Walras. Where Menger does go beyond them is in extending his theory to explain the value of higher-order goods, for he makes it very clear that the value of higher-order goods (including factors of

Table 9.1

| | Goods consumed | | | | |
|---|---|---|---|---|---|
| | I | II | III | ... | X |
| Satisfaction obtained | 10 | 9 | 8 | ... | 1 |
| from an extra unit of the | 9 | 8 | 7 | ... | 0 |
| good | 8 | 7 | 6 | ... | |
| | . | . | . | | |
| | . | . | . | | |
| | 1 | 0 | | | |
| | 0 | | | | |

production such as land and labour) is imputed from the value of lower-order goods, the value of which is in turn imputed from the satisfactions they allow to be satisfied: "the value of goods of higher order is dependent on the expected value of lower order goods they serve to produce".[11] Menger thus completely rejects the idea that the value of a good depends on the value of the goods used to produce it.[12]

Menger's theory contains the essentials of a marginal productivity theory of distribution:

The value of a given quantity of a particular good of higher order ... is equal to the importance of the satisfactions provided for by the portion of the product that would remain unproduced if we were not in a position to command the given quantity of the good of higher order.[13]

Where higher-order goods are complementary, their economic character may depend on quantities of the relevant other goods being available, otherwise they may be unusable. In general, however, Menger, sees the possibility of varying "over a wide range" the proportions in which higher-order goods are used.[14] Being able to use higher-order goods in variable proportions means that the removal of a unit of one higher-order good will not reduce the value of complementary goods to zero: the value of this unit of the higher-order good can then be calculated by subtracting from the value of the produce obtained with it, the value of the produce that can be obtained without it.[15]

These rules apply to all higher-order goods, including land, labour and capital. Indeed, Menger argues that it is *crucial* to the theory that it is applicable to all goods. Of these three factors, Menger views capital as associated with the fact that production takes time, for time permits the use of higher-order goods, thus increasing production. "Wherever economic goods are to be produced, *command of the services of capital is necessary* for a certain period of time."[16] The value of the services of capital needs to be deducted from the value of the produce in order to obtain the value of higher-order goods used. In other words, the present value of the technical factors of production by themselves is not equal to the full prospective value of the product, but always behaves in such a way that a margin for the services of capital and entrepreneurial activity remains.[17]

### Exchange and price

So far, and this is over half-way through the *Principles*, neither exchange nor price has been mentioned. Exchange is explained on the grounds that it occurs if both parties to a possible exchange benefit from it. There are limits to the possibility of exchange, these being imposed by the fact that when either of the parties to a bargain can no longer gain from further exchange, no more can take place. This feature of exchange, that it permits greater satisfaction of individual needs, is seen as fundamental. Prices, on the other hand, "are only incidental manifestations of these activities".[18]

What determines prices? In the case of bargains between isolated individuals all we can say is that prices will lie in between the limits set by the two individuals' valuations of the goods, their exact levels being decided by the individuals' bargaining strengths. Where a good is monopolized, the monopolist will set its price so as to maximize its profit, holding back part of the supply where the resulting higher price will increase its profit. Competitors, on the other hand, will not have the incentive to do this, and they will market a greater quantity of their produce than will a monopolist, something Menger illustrates with the case of a monopoly that is divided into two parts.

### 9.3   MENGER'S SYSTEM

### Knowledge

An aspect of Menger's system to which some economists have attached great significance is his emphasis on time and uncertainty.[19] Consumers need knowledge of the satisfactions they can acquire from things, if these things are to have goods character. Similarly, the goods character of higher-order goods depends on there being an entrepreneur who recognizes that they can be used to produce lower-order goods. The whole process of production takes time, and because knowledge is inevitably limited, is subject to much uncertainty. Related to this is Menger's view of competition, which has a dynamic element. If we were to consider only the formal, static theory discussed above, Menger's theory of competition would compare unfavourably with that of Walras, and possibly even with that of Jevons. Where Menger goes beyond either is in his description of competition as a dynamic process, in which monopolies are progressively eliminated: "the need for competition itself calls forth competition, provided there are no social or other barriers in the way".[20]

*Institutions*

This argument that the need for competition calls forth competition, provides one example of another feature of Menger's system, differentiating it from that of either Jevons or Walras: his stress on the endogeneity of economic institutions. Of economic institutions, the most fundamental is perhaps that of property itself. Menger sees property as arising from the economic nature of goods.

> Property ... is not an arbitrary invention, but rather the only practically possible solution of the problem that is, in the nature of things, imposed upon us by the disparity between requirements for, and available quantities of, all economic goods.[21]

Menger thus discovers an economic origin of the legal order, in particular the protection of ownership.

Exchange institutions arise similarly, as the *unintended* consequences of individuals' actions. Of particular importance is money. Menger argues that individuals come to recognize that it is in their own interests, whenever they cannot immediately obtain the goods they wish to consume, to exchange commodities for more saleable commodities. Money emrges unplanned, without any compulsion, without any agreement, and without regard for the public interest, out of the economizing behaviour of individuals.[22]

*Economic progress*

These views on the importance of knowledge and on the evolution of economic institutions in response to individuals' economizing actions, form part of Menger's view of economic progress: economic progress is accompanied by an increase in competition, and by the development of exchange institutions, reducing the cost of exchange. In addition to this, consumers learn more and more about the ability of things to satisfy their needs, and so the number of goods is increased. At the same time, the number of "imaginary goods", goods which people mistakenly view as satisfying their wants, is reduced.[23] Thus Menger viewed technical progress as occurring through the growth of knowledge: individuals learn about how higher-order goods can be used to produce lower-order goods more efficiently, and about how other things can become goods. As more and more things become goods, more of them become scarce and become economic goods, possessing value. Because it increases the ways in which wants are satisfied, this increase in knowledge increases welfare.

Associated with this growth of knowledge is the increased use of higher-order goods and the use of goods of higher and higher order. This involves lengthening the time period over which men's provident activity is extended: men have to undertake activities that will contribute to the satisfaction of human needs only after decades. Although this will, according to Menger, eventually increase the available quantity of commodities available for consumption, it requires an increase in the amount of capital available. As this process of capital accumulation continues, so more and more goods, previously non-economic, neither scarce nor valuable, come to acquire an economic character.[24]

From this discussion we can see that not only did Menger's theory of economic activity as centred on the satisfaction of human needs provide the basis for an explanation of prices, but it also provided the basis for a view of economic progress rivalling Smith's in its comprehensiveness. Central to this view of economic progress was not the concept of price, but that of subjective value, this reflecting the availability of goods in relation to their ability to satisfy human needs. All economic activity had to be explained in terms of this.

## 9.4  METHOD

The background to Menger's writings on method is the neglect of his *Principles* in Germany, where the dominant, Historical School attached little value to theoretical work.[25] Thus instead of developing the economic ideas put forward in the *Principles*, Menger turned to a defence of theoretical work, and to a critique of the methodology of the Historical School.[26]

Menger defended theoretical economics as a subject distinct from historical or statistical economics. This was not so much an argument about method (inductive versus deductive) as one about the aims of the subject. Following his Aristotelian training, Menger was concerned to explain the *essence* of economic phenomena, something he found in subjective value. He argued that general theoretical inquiry gave *exact laws* – laws of nature – which were in principle unfalsifiable, as opposed to *empirical laws*, which are subject to exceptions.[27] These exact laws concern the essence, or true nature, of economic phenomena.

Menger's Aristotelian background also explains his emphasis on causal chains, rather than simultaneous determination. The opening sentences of the *Principles* are: "All things are subject to the law of cause and effect. This great principle knows no exception."[28] The whole of the first paragraph is then concerned with elaborating on this. It is in this context that he introduces goods, things which can be placed in a "causal connection" with human needs.[29] That this is more than a mere rhetorical flourish is suggested by the close correspondence between Menger's four prerequisites for a thing to have goods-character, and Aristotle's four causes: the material, the efficient, the formal and the final causes.[30] Menger is arguing that the satisfaction of human needs is the purpose of economic activity, and that the true nature of economic phenomena is to be understood only in terms of the relationship of these phenomena to this purpose. The exact laws of economics are thus those derived from considering human activity in relation to its ultimate purpose.

It can thus be argued that to see the controversy with Schmoller and the Historical School in terms of a conflict between deduction and induction is to miss the point. Menger's disagreement with Schmoller was as much about aims as about methods of achieving those aims. His stress, in the controversy, on "methodological individualism" (his insistence on analysing aggregates in terms of the behaviour of individuals), and his criticism of the inductive laws of historical development put forward by the Historical School, are quite consistent with this.

This interpretation of Menger's aims also explains his disagreements with Walras. These were twofold. He objected to the use of mathematics as a tool of economic research, on the grounds that it could not help establish the essence of economic phenomena.[31] In addition, it was because of his teleological viewpoint that he objected to Walras's stress on simultaneous determination, for this negated the purposive nature of economic activity.

However, for all Menger's claims as to the exact nature of his theoretical results, he was very much aware of their limitations when it came to explaining observed economic phenomena. These limitations arose from the fact that his exact laws were applicable only to the special kind of human behaviour where ignorance and error were absent. Thus his exact laws explain only "economic" reality, not the "real, in part extremely uneconomic, phenomena of human economy".[32] Thus despite his claims for the organic, spontaneous evolution of social phenomena in response to economic needs, Menger did not make the claim that existing institutions were in any sense optimal, for it could not be assumed that individuals never erred.

## 9.5   THE AUSTRIAN SCHOOL

*Wieser*

Menger, because of his concentration on methodology, failed to develop the economic ideas contained in the *Principles*, this task falling to his followers, in particular Wieser and Böhm-Bawerk. The establishment of what became known as the Austrian School owed as much to these two as to Menger himself. Wieser developed Menger's ideas in three main ways. (1) He shared Menger's view of economic theory as investigating the essences of economic phenomena, arguing that these could be discovered through introspection. (2) He extended Menger's subjective value theory to allow for costs, these being interpreted as subjective opportunity costs. (3) He developed Menger's theory of factor pricing, using the theory of imputation.

An important aspect of this work was his application of subjective value theory to the problem of a communist state. Fundamental to Wieser's approach was his concept of "natural value", the value imputed to goods by virtue of their ability either to satisfy human needs directly, or to produce goods which in turn would satisfy human needs. This natural value was not something artificial, but was something which arose "from the social relation between amount of goods and utility".[33] It followed that "Natural value shall be that which would be recognised by a completely organic and most highly rational community."[34] It is the measure of value appropriate to an ideal, communist state.

Exchange value, on the other hand, is something different, for it depends not only on natural value, but on other factors. In addition to "human imperfection, ... error, fraud, force [and] chance" the existence of private property affects exchange value.

In natural value goods are estimated simply according to their marginal utility; in exchange value according to a combination of marginal utility and purchasing power. In the former, luxuries are estimated far lower, and necessaries, comparatively, much higher than in the latter. Exchange value, even when considered as perfect, is, if we may so call it, a caricature of natural value; it disturbs its economic symmetry, magnifying the small and reducing the great.[35]

Wieser was able to use his concept of natural value to discuss socialism. On the one hand, his argument that exchange value did not correspond to natural value could be used, in much the same way as Pigou's later distinction between private and social cost,[36] as an argument against the existing economic order. On the other hand it provided the basis from which he could criticize the Marxian labour theory of value. He believed that, "In the socialist theory of value pretty nearly everything is wrong."[37] Socialists attributed value to labour, not to utility; they overlooked the value of productive land and capital; and they overlooked the role of value in the material control of the economy:

in the natural order of economy, labour is valued according to its utility, value attaches to land and capital, and land rent, as well as interest on capital, is calculated among costs. If this were to be neglected production would become chaos.[38]

This theme, that values are vital to the organization of production, is one to which later Austrians have returned.[39]

### Böhm-Bawerk

The other important disciple of Menger was Böhm-Bawerk, described by Schumpeter as "one of the greatest architects of economic science" on account of his model of the economic process as a whole.[40] Böhm-Bawerk provided an exposition of the subjective theory of value which, because his work was translated into English very quickly, was the route via which Austrian ideas reached English-speaking economists. Because of this, together with the fact that he was a great controversialist, Böhm-Bawerk was seen, by the 1890s, as the main representative of Austrian economics. It was Böhm-Bawerk who, in *Karl Marx and the Close of His System* (1896) provided what has often been regarded as the classic critique of Marxian economics.[41]

Böhm-Bawerk's theory of the economic process was centred on his theory of capital and the rate of interest. In this theory he built upon Menger's view of capital, attempting to measure the capital stock with his concept of the period of production.[42] Though this work clearly followed on from Menger's, there were important differences, notably Böhm-

Bawerk's greater willingness to use aggregates. Böhm-Bawerk's use of an aggregative wage fund gives part of his work a classical flavour.

*Other Austrians*

In the hands of Wieser and Böhm-Bawerk, the Austrian tradition had already developed in different directions, and in the hands of their successors these divergences developed still further.[43] At one extreme, Mises took Menger's and Wieser's stress on methodological individualism, and on the difference between economics and the natural sciences, even further.[44] Though his aggressive critique of socialism received a lot of attention,[45] Mises' dogmatic views placed him outside the mainstream of economic ideas. Possibly more important than Mises was Hayek, who, though he increasingly differed from Mises' views on method, shared his views on the nature of the competitive process.[46] Using the view of the structure of production associated with Menger and Böhm-Bawerk, Hayek contributed to the theory of capital, using this to develop a theory of the trade cycle which, in the early 1930s, rivalled that of Keynes.[47] Very different from either of these was the approach of Schumpeter, who combined Austrian ideas with Walrasian general equilibrium theory. Schumpeter's view of the entrepreneur, and the nature of the competitive process, however, remained very Austrian. It was these which underlay his theory of the rate of profit and the process of economic development.[48]

Equally important, however, was the absorption of Austrian ideas outside Austria. Marshall read Menger's *Principles* and was influenced by it. But above all, Böhm-Bawerk's ideas inspired Wicksell, who could be seen as integrating Böhm-Bawerk's theory of capital with Walras's general equilibrium theory, to obtain a theory of the economic process free of many of the blemishes which marred Böhm-Bawerk's development of his own theory. It could be argued that, at the level of pure theory, Wicksell's contribution was unequalled until Hicks's *Value and Capital* (1939).

# 10

## Marshall

### 10.1 INTRODUCTION

The inclusion of Marshall's work in a list of new systems emerging from the 1870s requires some explanation. Apart from an elementary textbook published in 1879, Marshall's major works cover the period from 1890 to 1923. This, together with the synthetic character of Marshall's economics, which brings together the insights of both Jevons and the English Classical economists in a framework involving both marginal utility and marginal productivity, would seem to place him alongside Pareto, Fisher and Wicksell, rather than Jevons, Menger and Walras. However, there are several reasons why it is more appropriate to consider Marshall alongside the latter group. The first is that although the *Principles of Economics* was not published until 1890, much of the work on which it was based was done much earlier. Marshall himself claimed to have worked out his views on value and distribution between 1867 and 1870, independently of his contemporaries.[1] Furthermore, these views were being propagated sufficiently widely for his reputation to be well established, even before his *Principles* appeared: his lecturing influenced his pupils, an influence which was much more important when the number of economists in England was still very small; his diagrammatic treatment of foreign trade and of supply and demand was privately printed and circulated in 1879; and *The Economics of Industry* (1879) was much more than the introduction to Mill's economics that it purported to be. When we allow for the delay in the publication of his ideas, Marshall belongs, chronologically, with Jevons, Walras and Menger.

Although he arrived at his theory of value and distribution at about the same time as Jevons, Menger and Walras, and although his theory shared many features with theirs, Marshall was the only one to reach this position through developing the ideas of the English Classical School.[2] Marshall arrived at his system through attempting, in the late 1860s, to formulate Mill's theories mathematically, using ideas taken from Cournot and von Thünen. These origins help explain several distinctive features of his system.

One feature of Marshall's system is that although he gives a lot of attention to the microeconomics of resource allocation, his main concern is with distribution and growth. The *Principles* is very much in the tradition of Smith's *Wealth of Nations*. Smith's influence goes even further, for in the same way that Smith, in his theory of growth, laid enormous stress on the division of labour, so Marshall's economics is dominated by economies of scale and increasing returns.

Another feature of Marshall's economics is that whereas utility was fundamental to the systems of Jevons, Walras and Menger, it played a subsidiary role, possibly no more than an expository one, for Marshall. In his early work Marshall, following Cournot, started with the demand curve rather than utility.[3] It is unclear whether he introduced utility before or after reading Jevons' *Theory of Political Economy* (1871), but in any case utility played a subordinate role as Marshall was never prepared to take wants as exogenously given. Even the idea of consumers' surplus was not intended to represent utility, but was intended as a rough and ready measure analogous to the rent of land (in early writing it was called "consumers' rent"). Corresponding to this minor role for utility was a major role for costs of production and supply. Once again Marshall was following the English Classical tradition. Although he came to respect Jevons' work, he regarded Jevons' claim that utility determined value, as even more misleading than Ricardo's claim that it was costs of production which did so.[4]

Before looking at the details of Marshall's economics there is a further aspect to consider: his stress on evolution. The 1860s were a time when evolutionary ideas were being widely discussed in England, and Marshall was influenced by them to an extent that made him describe evolutionary ideas such as those of Spencer and Hegel as having been the main influence on the substance of the ideas expressed in the *Principles*. The main effect of these evolutionary ideas was that he saw the notion of continuous, gradual change as central to economics, and he wanted, continually, to use dynamic, biological analogies rather than static, mechanical ones. However, because of the complexity of the forces to be dealt with it was necessary to deal with them a few at a time: in other words to use partial equilibrium analysis, much of it static. It is thus important to stress that although much of Marshall's work is about static, partial equilibrium analysis, it was the dynamic, evolutionary theory, theory which does not fit into the conventional "neoclassical" mould, to which Marshall attached most importance.[5]

## 10.2 THE THEORY OF VALUE AND DISTRIBUTION

### General equilibrium

In a letter to J. B. Clark,[6] Marshall wrote that his whole life had been given to "presenting in realistic form" as much as he could of Note XXI of the Mathematical Appendix to the *Principles*.[7] In this note Marshall takes a "bird's eye view" of the problem of supply and demand in the economy as a whole. His concern is to show that he has exactly the right number of equations to determine the values of all the unknowns, these being the prices and quantities of the $n$ commodities and the $m$ factors of production. Starting with a simple case, and adding complications later, he shows that he has $2m + 2n$ equations comprising:

(1) demand equations, relating the price and quantity of each commodity;

(2) equations connecting the price of each commodity with the prices of the factors used in producing it;

(3) equations relating inputs of factors to outputs of commodities;

(4) supply equations, linking the supply of each factor to its price.

The middle two sets of equations (2 and 3) describe the behaviour of firms, and can be used to obtain demands for factors and supplies of commodities.

Marshall's attitude to this note shows the importance he attached to simultaneous determination: to find the value of one variable it is necessary to solve all the equations together. This means that to find the price of a commodity, not only do supply and demand *both* have to be considered, but also the prices of commodities and the prices of factors have to be considered together, the problem of factor pricing being a part of the general theory of value.

### Commodity prices

Although commodity prices are part of the general equilibrium problem described above, Marshall argued that in practice it was possible to use partial equilibrium analysis. For one commodity, provided it accounts for only a small part of consumers' expenditure, supply and demand could be treated as if they were independent of each other. Thus for a single commodity, price and output could be analysed using supply and demand curves. But supply and demand curves are static, whereas the problem which obsessed Marshall was that of adjustment to equilibrium over time. He analysed this through considering various time periods.

(a) In the shortest possible time period there is a certain quantity of goods on the market, and there is no time to produce more. If the commodity is perishable, such as fish, it will be sold for whatever it will fetch, the situation being as in Figure 10.1a.[8] If it is storable, on the other hand, sellers will have the opportunity of storing it in the hope of obtaining a higher price in following periods; the supply curve may thus be very elastic, as in Figure 10.1b, its position depending not on production costs but on sellers' expectations of future prices. Thus in the very short period, whether or not the good is perishable, production costs will have no direct influence on price. Any influence will only be indirect, via expectations of future costs and prices.

(b) If we allow a slightly longer period we enter the *short run*, in which firms are assumed to be able to vary their production, but cannot vary their inputs of skilled labour, the stock of machinery they use, or their methods of production. Supply will depend on short run marginal costs, these being increasing, as in Figure 10.1c. Marginal cost and demand jointly determine prices.

(c) When we consider a still longer time period we enter Marshall's *long run*, where not only can production be varied, but also the firm can change its use of skilled labour, its equipment and its organization. Because all inputs and the methods of production employed can be varied, increasing returns become a strong possibility. The long run

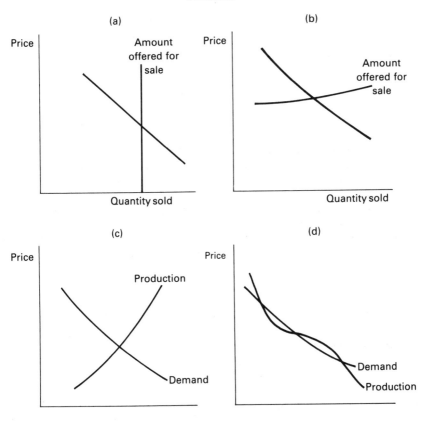

FIGURE 10.1 *Marshall's Theory of Value*

supply price, which Marshall describes as "the whole expenses (including insurance, and gross earnings of management) of a marginal increment in the aggregate *process of production and marketing*",[9] may well fall with output, as in Figure 10.1d, and may cut the demand curve a number of times.

It is at this point, at least for someone used to the modern theory of the firm, that the difficulties begin, for it is natural to regard long run equilibrium as a static equilibrium in which *everything* has had time to adjust. Furthermore, problems arise in reconciling perfect competition with increasing returns to scale. The now conventional response is to argue that the two are compatible only if the economies of scale that lead to increasing returns are internal to the industry, but external to the firm, a category not very important in practice. Marshall accepted this argument, but far more important was the fact that his concept of the long run was not static, and did not involve perfect competition. In Marshall's long run there was still change going on, even in "equilibrium": new firms were coming into the market and old firms leaving it, and any individual firm's costs were constantly changing. Costs were calculated for a "representative firm [, one with] normal access to the economies, both external and internal, which belong to the aggregate volume of production".[10] Also, he recognized that some firms would have their own "special market" and would face falling demand curves.[11] A further complication arises in that Marshall took many economies of scale to be irreversible – once gained they would not be lost, even if output were to fall.

At the beginning of this section Marshall was quoted as wanting to express *in a realistic form* his general equilibrium equations. This is the key to his value theory. His aim was to explain normal values: in other words to explain the prices that could be expected to prevail on average, over long and short periods, in an economy such as that of late nineteenth century Britain. To do this it would be grossly misleading simply to work out results from a formal, simplified model: the complications involved in dealing with an evolving economy have to be brought in.

### Income distribution

Though he was sceptical as to its significance, Marshall's theory of distribution was based on marginal productivity, or the "principle of substitution" between factors. The notion of quasi-rents was used to generalize the notion of rent to all factors, all factor prices being governed by the same general principles. However, his system remained "classical" in two respects. One is that he devoted much attention to long run changes – population growth and capital accumulation. These will be considered later. The other is that he had an aggregative theory of distribution. In considering distribution Marshall was not prepared to make the assumption, made in analysing commodity prices, that demand and supply are independent of each other, for each factor is the source of demand for all the others: "the national dividend which is the joint product of all, and which increases with the supply of each of them, is also the sole source of demand for each of them".[12] Marshall's criticism of the wage fund was that it linked "the *stock* of capital and the *flow* of wages, instead of the true correlation between the *flow* of the products of labour aided by capital and the flow of wages".[13] By reformulating the classical wage fund in this way Marshall reached the idea of the circular flow of income which, *with hindsight*, does not seem far from the Keynesian notion of aggregate demand.

### International values and money

The sphere of foreign trade is another area where Marshall used an aggregative approach. Supply and demand curves, which would be dependent on each other, were not helpful. Marshall's theory is very close to Mill's, his main contributions being to formulate Mill's theory of reciprocal demand geometrically, and to use the concept of elasticity of demand to analyse the results more thoroughly.[14]

The traditional theory of the value of money was the quantity theory. Marshall's contribution here was to integrate the theory of money with the general theory of value, by formulating the quantity theory in terms of the demand for cash balances (determined by the marginal costs of holding money) and showing that this approach is equivalent to the traditional, velocity of circulation approach, whilst being more fruitful.[15]

## 10.3  ECONOMIC PROGRESS

Although it is the theory discussed in section 10.2 for which Marshall is best known, his main concern was with economic progress, something he saw as bound up with the all-important issue of the human character. In the opening section of the *Principles* he wrote that, whilst on one side economics was the study of wealth, it was, "on the other and more important side, a study of man. For man's character has been moulded by his every-day work, and the material resources which he thereby procures".[16] This was much more than a moralizing aside, for it was an important part of his theory of progress.[17]

Marshall saw growth as depending on capital accumulation, needed to achieve improved organization and greater division of labour with the resulting economies of scale, and on increases in the size and the efficiency of the labour force. Capital accumulation depended on a variety of factors, including the level of output, the rate of profit, and the share of profits in national income. More unusual was Marshall's view of the labour force, for he distinguished between two types of consumption, or wants. Most important are those wants associated with what Marshall termed "the standard of life".

The term *standard of life* is here taken to mean the standard of activities adjusted to wants. Thus a rise in the standard of life implies an increase in intelligence and energy and self-respect; leading to more care and judgement in expenditure, and to an avoidance of food and drink that gratify the appetite but afford no strength, and of ways of living that are unwholesome physically and morally.[18]

Such an increase in consumption was associated with increased productivity. The *standard of comfort*, on the other hand, included not only these wants, but also "artificial wants", which do nothing to improve either efficiency or character.

It was through simultaneously developing new activities and new wants that men could rise out of the Malthusian trap, for with new sources of imported food now available the constraint imposed on wages by agricultural production was no longer a problem. Increased wants meant that increases in wages need not simply cause the population to expand, but permitted a rise in the standard of life. If this occurred, the rise in the standard of life would raise efficiency, thus making it possible for the increased level of wages to be sustained. If a wage rise were not accompanied by increased efficiency, then profits would be reduced and capital would flow abroad. Thus the growth of new wants, and the improvement in man's character associated with it, were inextricably linked to the process of capital accumulation and economic progress.

## 10.4  FREE ENTERPRISE AND THE STATE

The combination of marginalist arguments about resource allocation and a more classical concern with economic growth also underlies Marshall's views on free enterprise and the role of the state. The marginalist component of his work on free enterprise is found in his use of consumers' surplus to analyse the doctrine of maximum satisfaction, namely, "the doctrine according to which every position of demand and supply may fairly be regarded as a position of maximum satisfaction.".[19] After clearly stating the basis for the doctrine in a single paragraph, however, his main concern is with exceptions to it. Firstly there is the argument, taken up more vigorously by Edgeworth,[20] that redistribution of property from the rich to the poor may raise aggregate satisfaction because of diminishing marginal utility of income. Secondly, there is the possibility that a system of taxation which increases production in industries facing increasing returns, at the expense of production in those with decreasing returns, may raise welfare. This is a distinctively Marshallian idea, but one with severe technical limitations. Finally, there is the problem of monopoly, which may reduce aggregate demand below its maximum level.

However, whilst these arguments suggest imperfections in a system of free enterprise, Marshall saw other factors which would work to render the scope for government intervention less than it might seem at first sight to be. Of particular importance are the sense of duty and the desire for approbation, for Marshall objected strenuously to the basing of economic theory on the postulate of economic man, if by economic man is understood an agent who mechanically and selfishly pursues economic gain.[21] Instances of altruism were those of parents bringing up their children, and firms educating their employees, even though the benefits of such education are as much external effects as benefits specific to the firm concerned. In discussing monopoly, Marshall considered the case of a monopolist balancing monopoly profits against gains in consumers' surplus, a clear case of altruism.

Marshall was prepared to recommend intervention by the state in the economy, but was extremely cautious in doing so. One reason for this was his concern to promote growth, an issue not allowed for in static models of resource allocation. The importance he attached to growth was more than merely the remains of the classical tradition, being fostered by a strong awareness of Britain's changing economic position in relation to her rivals, notably Germany and the US. Measures that would reduce enterprise and initiative were to be avoided. For this reason, whilst he accepted the merits of regulation to prevent monopoly power, he opposed "administrative socialism", the state regulation of production, as in nationalization.

It was economic growth that Marshall saw as the key to what he claimed was the dominant issue in his whole life's work – the problem of poverty. Despite this, his attitude was radically different from that of his classical predecessors, the main difference being the absence of the Malthusian obstacle to raising the level of real wages. Because of his view that an improved "standard of life" (note the definition given above) would raise efficiency, he argued that redistribution of income towards wages could improve productivity, whilst the welfare benefits of which he most approved were those which would most improve character and hence efficiency (such as education). Marshall came out in favour of progressive taxation provided that it was not imposed in such a way as to impair enterprise. For most of the population his view was that, given a certain amount of altruism ("economic chivalry"),[22] growth would provide a remedy, but he recognized the existence of a "residuum", not capable of self-help, for whom government support was a necessity.[23]

This account of Marshall's views on free enterprise has concentrated on its economic effects, but of perhaps greater significance for him was the effect of free enterprise on character. Marshall viewed the improvement of character as of supreme importance, the virtues he admired, such as frugality, rationality, industry and honour, being those associated with the "ideal" businessman in the mid-Victorian world of owner-managed firms. Marshall's Appendix A, the material which came right at the beginning of the earlier editions of the *Principles*, on the growth of free industry and enterprise, is as much about moral and social progress as economic. Thus, even if purely economic arguments did not support free enterprise, any economic arguments would need to outweigh these moral arguments in favour of free enterprise.

## 10.5   MARSHALL'S METHOD

Marshall's views on method are of particular importance, for, in Hutchison's words, Marshall

was mainly responsible for the shaping of economic science in England and elsewhere for a generation, formulating the approach and the questions to be asked, and also, by implication, the questions not to be asked.[24]

The aspect of methodology over which controversy was most intense in the 1870s concerned the roles of deduction and induction, or of history and theory.[25] Marshall, throughout his career, was dominated by a concern for realism, and sought a synthesis of theory and history. This concern to blend deduction and induction was something Marshall shared with Jevons, but their ways of achieving it were very different. Whereas Jevons put a mathematical, deductive theory at the centre of economics, to be supplemented with empirical and, above all, statistical investigation, Marshall not only wished to keep the theoretical core of the subject, and *a fortiori* its mathematics, in as subordinate a role as possible. In addition, his use of empirical material was very different from Jevons' use of statistics. Marshall's attempts to blend the fruits of empirical observation, not usually expressed statistically, with his theory, are in some ways closer to Smith's method than to that of Jevons.

Marshall stressed that it was "the central scheme of economic reasoning", not any particular doctrine, that was central to the subject:

That part of economic doctrine, which alone can claim universality, has no dogmas. It is not a body of concrete truth, but an engine for the discovery of concrete truth, similar to, say, the theory of mechanics.[26]

However, whilst he saw theory as essential to understanding economic problems, he distrusted intensely the isolated pursuit of pure theory. "But I conceive no more calamitous notion than that abstract, or general, or 'theoretical' economics was economics 'proper'."[27]

Corresponding to this almost ambivalent attitude towards pure theory is an apparent paradox in Marshall's attitude towards mathematics. On the one hand, on his own admission, he owed his theoretical system to his attempts to translate the doctrines of Mill into mathematics; but on the other hand he disparaged its use in economics. One reason for the latter was his "evolution mindedness", with his preference for biological analogies, less amenable to mathematical treament, rather than mechanical ones.[28] The same obstacles to the use of mathematics were present in economics as in biology: the complexity of the systems involved, and their changing and irreversible nature. Thus Marshall wanted mathematical arguments to be kept short and simple, with the results always being translated back into English. He was unwilling to let economic arguments lose touch with reality.

A counterpart to this minor role for theory, and above all for mathematical theory, was a major one for empirical work, in particular economic history. Although less and less emphasis was placed on economic history in successive editions of the *Principles*, his early work included much history, whilst his last book, *Industry and Trade* (1923) contains an enormous amount of factual information on the organisation of industry. This emphasis on history was linked to Marshall's awareness, to an extent exceeding that of most other "neoclassical" economists, of the historical relativity of economic institutions. More important, however, is the effect of his emphasis on history on the nature of his economics, for even in the *Principles* factual material is mixed in with economic theory in a manner reminiscent of Smith's *Wealth of Nations*. In defending the *Principles* he argued that the word "theory" applied only to book V, on the general relations of supply, demand and value.[29] Together with his great interest in the details of industrial organization, acquired over many years spent looking around industrial premises, this desire to keep theory and reality close together all the time affected the nature of the empirical evidence he used. Much of it appears anecdotal, rather than statistical, and illustrative rather than essential. His practice of using empirical data in this way contrasts with some of his methodological pronouncements on the need for quantitative and statistical methods.[30]

The main price to be paid for this stress on realism, and for the desire to keep theory and fact so close together, was ambiguity. Because Marshall's aim was not to construct a logically precise, abstract model, he would not always commit himself to precise assumptions. One commentator has described him as having the "habit of leaving the context to explain his meaning".[31] For example, in his partial equilibrium analysis the *ceteris paribus* clauses were not always adequately specified. More important is his use of the term "economic freedom" rather than competition, this being linked to his refusal to specify exactly what degree of competition was being considered.[32] His whole construction of "normal value", involving neither perfect competition nor complete equilibrium, was shrouded in ambiguity.

A clue to Marshall's methodology can be found in the motto appearing on the title page of *Industry and Trade*, "The many in the one, and the one in the many." Though he realized that there were common causes underlying diverse economic phenomena, in order to arrive at a unified explanation it was necessary to work through the multifarious details of the real world, the central doctrines of economics being incapable of being made simple. In 1899 he wrote, "In my view the *Many* is the ground of study; the *One* is the Holy Grail to be sought by the pious and laborious pilgrim."[33]

Because of these ambiguities, the merits of Marshall's "realistic" approach are less clear cut then they might at first seem. To illustrate the problems which arise, consider the judgement of perhaps the leading post-war economic theorist, Samuelson:

The ambiguities of Alfred Marshall paralyzed the best brains of the Anglo-Saxon branch of our profession for three decades. By 1930 the profession had just about reattained the understanding of the pure theory of monopoly that Cournot had achieved in 1838 ... where Marshall threw off two generations of scholars was in his insistence on having his cake and eating it too. ... Marshall was so afraid of being unrealistic that he merely ends up being fuzzy and confusing – and confused.[34]

From the point of view of Austrian or Walrasian general equilibrium theory, concerned with working out the implications of maximizing behaviour under carefully specified assumptions, there is an element of truth in this.[35] Marshall, however, was concerned with much more than this, for he believed that the analysis of static equilibrium conditions left out some of the most important aspects of reality. Thus although Marshall's development of partial equilibrium analysis, his distinction between the long and short run, his emphasis on irreversibilities in the production process and so on may seem, from one point of view, very imprecise, and even confusing, it is only through such concepts that formal equilibrium theory can be given any meaning. From this point of view, therefore, it can be argued that Marshall, far from confusing the issues, made Cournot's more formal analysis usable for analysing real problems.[36]

The final aspect of Marshall's method that must be considered, on account of its importance, is his attitude towards the positive–normative distinction. Though his view of economic progress might suggest that his practice did not always live up to it, he consistently argued that economic science must be kept free from ethical judgements. Although inspired by strong moral and social ideals, he was equally concerned to be scientific. For Marshall, "scientific" was no hollow, tendentious prestige term. It means "observing and respecting ... crucial distinctions and demarcations".[37] He thus argued that when they made recommendations as to the best policies to pursue, economists spoke only with their own authority, not with the voice of their science.[38] This desire to create a science, respecting the positive–normative distinction, was reflected in Marshall's advocacy of the term "economics" rather than "political economy".

## 10.6   CONCLUSIONS

On Marshall's death Taussig, with considerable justification, wrote that

In the death of Alfred Marshall, economic science has lost its most distinguished representative. None among the English-speaking will question his primacy; and I doubt whether on the Continent or elsewhere a name could be mentioned that would dispute his title. For a generation his position of leadership was secure.[39]

Despite his acknowledged pre-eminence, however, Marshall occupies a peculiar position in the history of economic analysis. On the one hand, he appears as a bastion of orthodoxy, the champion of marginalist analysis. There was, however, another side to his thought, by virtue of which he should be placed alongside dissenters such as Veblen, rather than alongside economists such as Wicksell, Fisher or Pareto. Marshall's thought was permeated with evolutionary ideas, and as a result he was never satisfied with the restrictive framework of marginalist analysis. Like Veblen and the American institutionalists, he refused to take wants as given, and he concerned himself with historical processes. However, whilst Marshall managed to keep these two divergent strands together, few of his successors even attempted the task.

# 11

## Clark

### 11.1   INTRODUCTION

John Bates Clark[1] merits attention here not as an independent discoverer of marginal utility (he did develop the concept independently of Jevons, Walras and Menger, though he attributes the idea to Knies, who would have been familiar with, if unsympathetic towards, Menger's work[2]) but because he produced a distinctive system based on marginal utility, one very different from those of his European counterparts, and which was very influential in the US. In evaluating Clark's work it is important to bear in mind his background, that of an American who, along with many others of his generation, went to Germany to learn economics.[3] Due to the work of Henry George amongst others,[4] distribution was a burning issue in the US, and Clark concentrated on this. His theory of distribution provided an alternative to socialist theories being discussed at the time. The influence of his teachers, especially Knies, is marked in his first book, *The Philosophy of Wealth* (1886),[5] though it is less apparent in the later *Distribution of Wealth* (1899).

### 11.2   THE PHILOSOPHY OF WEALTH

*Criticisms of existing theories*

Like Jevons, Clark was concerned to reconstruct economics, which he believed to be based on false premises, but his objections were very different: (1) "The better elements of human nature" were ignored, actions being less mechanical and selfish than economic theory's "degraded conception of human nature allowed". (2) Utility and its role in exchange were misconceived, no account being taken of the fact that "society is an organism, to be treated as a unit in the discussion of many processes affecting wealth".[6] The purpose of Clark's work was thus

to broaden the conception of wealth, as the subject of the science, to find a place in the system for the better motives of human nature, to construct a new theory of value, to apply at all points the organic conception of society, and to suggest other corrections.[7]

*Utility and wealth*

The basis of Clark's theory was the idea that wealth comprised those elements of the material environment that served to increase well being.

This led to utility being defined in the following way: "The want-satisfying power created by labour is a 'utility', and if the attribute of appropriability be also conferred, wealth is created".[8] The utilities created by labour were then divided into four categories: elementary utility (the production of new material); form utility (the reshaping of material); place utility, and time utility. But more important than this was his demonstration that value, "the quantitative measure of utility",[9] depended on effective utility, Clark's term for marginal utility.

The similarity with Menger's theory goes further, for Clark goes on to argue that the desire for an object creates a desire for the objects used to create it. Clark's terminology, referring to "secondary" utilities and consumption, is reminiscent of Menger's higher-order goods. Like Menger, Clark argues that exchange and distribution have to be seen as part of the process of production and consumption. However, it is important to note that although Clark has a theory of imputation, and although he refers to demand and supply dividing the produce into rent, gross profits and wages,[10] nowhere in *The Philosophy of Wealth* does he come close to the idea of marginal productivity.

*Ethics and the social organism*

Although Clark's theory of marginal utility is similar to Menger's, he diverges sharply from his European contemporaries in his interpretation of marginal utility, for he argues that market value measures the value "society" places on a commodity.[11] The issue of how it is possible to make the transition from the individual to society is not faced. Within a society comprising a group of individuals linked by altruism and various ethical requirements, Clark views competition as a mechanism through which society as a whole determines the values it places on things, and through which it distributes the produce to its members. Ethical considerations are crucial here, for Clark draws a sharp distinction between "conservative competition", competition in which competitors try to provide a better or cheaper service than each other, and "cut-throat" competition, where ethical constraints on behaviour are abandoned.[12] He argues that the idea of competition without moral restraints is absurd: to find it we would have to go back to "the isolated troglodyte, the companion of the cave bear".[13] But although Clark makes it abundantly clear that for him "society" is much more than a rhetorical device,[14] nowhere does he justify the term in more than an intuitive way.

The idea of some sort of social contract is implicit in his view of the provision of what he calls inappropriable utilities, provided free of charge by society for its own benefit. Such inappropriable utilities ranged from those provided by railroads, to those derived from the preaching of the church.

Ethical requirements were similarly crucial to Clark's analysis of what he saw as the dominant problem facing society in his own day: the increase in "competition", both of employers and employees, with the resulting breakdown of competition. In proposing a remedy, Clark argued the virtues of co-operative enterprises and profit-sharing, with arbitration being available until these were more fully developed. He saw such institutions as a means of enabling society to impose the requirements of justice, arguing that once imposed they would become generally accepted.

## 11.3  THE DISTRIBUTION OF WEALTH

*Method*

Although Clark did not abandon his conception of society as a single organism,[15] it played a much less prominent role in the work which contains his major analytical contribution: *The Distribution of Wealth*. Central to this book is his distinction between statics and dynamics.[16] A static state was one free of the disturbances caused by progress (capital accumulation, population growth, technical progress and the growth of wants); the significance of the "static" or "stationary state" rates of wages, interest and profit being that it was about these that the actual rates would fluctuate.[17] He argued that the "natural" rates used by the classical economists were, in fact, static. Clark credited Ricardo with adopting a static method, but criticized him for doing so only unconsciously; a result of this being that he failed to distinguish sufficiently clearly between statics and dynamics.[18]

Clark's static state was similar to Ricardo's in that he assumed capital and labour to be completely mobile. He differed from Ricardo in making it explicit that he was dealing with an imaginary situation, abstracting from dynamic forces in order to isolate the most important elements in the economic system. For Clark, economics was very much a deductive science. When it came to dynamics, his method was still deductive, Clark providing a very clear description of the method of comparative statics.[19]

*Marginal productivity and capital*

The main contribution of *The Distribution of Wealth* was to provide a thoroughly worked out marginal productivity theory of distribution, something Clark arrived at through generalizing the Ricardian doctrine of rent. Distinguishing carefully between the intensive and extensive margins (i.e. using more labour on the same land, and bringing more land into cultivation) Clark reached the conclusion that wages were determined by the effective product of labour: the amount an employer would lose when a worker left, assuming that he could reallocate the remaining workforce optimally.[20] If labourers were identical, the effective product of each labourer would be equal to the product of the marginal labourer, this being in turn equal to the product of labour on no-rent land.

What distinguishes Clark's marginal productivity theory from others is his theory of capital. His starting point was to emphasize the distinction between individual *capital goods* and *capital* as a fund. Capital goods have a fixed life, but capital itself is permanent, new capital goods covering depreciation. Although individual capital goods are continually disappearing, the fund of social capital remains. Thus Clark attempted to provide an alternative to Böhm-Bawerk's theory of capital based on the period of production.[21] In other words, Clark advocated *synchronization* economics, analysing production in terms of the factors in use at any one moment, as opposed to Böhm-Bawerk's *advance* economics, which concentrated on the time structure of production.

Within this fund of capital, Clark included land, arguing that there was no fundamental difference between rents and interest payments: one stresses the return to something physical, the other the return to the fund of social capital, without there being any essential difference between the two.[22] As with labour, the earnings of capital (call it rent or interest) were determined by marginal productivity – the interest rate generally conforms to the earnings of the final increment of social capital.

The distinction between social capital and capital goods has implications for wages, for in calculating the marginal product of labour it makes a difference whether it is assumed that it is the fund of social capital (the *value* of the capital stock) or the stock of specific capital goods that is held constant. If it is the former, then there is much more flexibility in how labour is employed, for the stock of equipment cn be altered to suit the number of labourers being employed. In explaining the wage rate Clark used the effective (or marginal) product of labour, found by keeping the *fund* of social capital constant.

## Dynamics

For Clark, the study of statics was a vital prerequisite to any study of dynamics. He used the analogy of the ocean:

A static ocean is imaginary, for there never was such a thing; but there has never been a moment in the history of the stormiest seas, when the dominant forces that controlled them were not those which, if left entirely alone, would reduce their waters to a static condition. Gravity, fluidity, pressure, and nothing else, would have the effect of making the sea level and motionless. ... If we take a bird's eye view of the ocean, we are tempted to say that a static philosophy of it is sufficient and that we may treat waves and currents as minor aberrations due to "disturbing influences".[23]

Dynamics had, according to Clark, two tasks. (1) To explain deviations of value, wages and interest from their static standards (explaining the waves on the sea); and (2) to explain changes in the static standards themselves (changes in the average level of the sea).[24] Of these, he argued that the latter were in practice by far the most important.

Clark's treatment of dynamic changes can best be illustrated by his treatment of innovation. Initially, he argues, an innovation will create entrepreneurial profits: the economy will be moved out of equilibrium. At the same time the static equilibrium will have been changed, for an innovation will raise the equilibrium rate of wages.[25] Over time, therefore, wages will rise and entrepreneurial profits will be eroded. Given sufficient time they would be reduced to zero, but in practice this rarely happens, for innovations are continually occurring. Clark thus sees the economy as continuously moving towards an equilibrium which is itself changing. Entrepreneurial profits are a subject for economic dynamics, a feature of disequilibrium, not equilibrium.[26] This does not make them unimportant, for profits are the lure which stimulates innovation.

Thus although, like the oceans, economies are never in static equilibrium, static models are invaluable as indicating the direction in which an economy is moving. The relevance of static theory is, according to Clark, further increased by two other factors. The first is that disturbances will often offset each other. For example, an increase in the labour force tends to depress wages, and an increase in capital to raise them. If both capital and labour increase, however, wages will be affected less than if either changed on its own.[27] The second is that although in principle the economy comprises all humanity,[28] it is possible to isolate parts of it within which adjustments take place relatively quickly. Economic changes which, from the point of view of the world as a whole, are adjustments towards a static equilibrium, can from the point of view of an individual country be regarded as exogenous, shifting the economy from one static equilibrium to another.[29]

### Ethical implications of marginal productivity

Although far less prominent than in Clark's earlier work, ethical considerations were nonetheless present in *The Distribution of Wealth*. These took the form of the argument that with competition each agent gets what it produces: anything else would be "institutional robbery", the principle of property being that men are entitled to the wealth which they themselves create.[30] This argument was clearly intended as a counter to socialist claims that, under capitalism, capitalists necessarily took a share of the produce rightfully belonging to labour.

### 11.4  EVALUATION

Clark's economics, more than that of any of the other economists considered above, has been the subject of great controversy. More than any of the others, he saw marginal productivity theory as a counter to socialism, rendering him liable to criticism on grounds of ideology. His ethical interpretation of marginal productivity theory laid him open to attack from economists such as Veblen,[31] who attacked him for this and for his view of human nature. His theory of capital, on which much depended, has been attacked from a variety of standpoints. In addition, there are problems in interpreting his work which arise from the contrast between his earlier and his later writings. Though it became much less prominent, his stress on the organic nature of society remained in his later work. What did happen was that the technical aspects of his theory improved enormously, becoming more important.

The portrayal of Clark as having switched dramatically from being a supporter of co-operation and Christian socialism, to being a supporter of competition, though in a sense correct, is an exaggeration. More important is the change in his attitude towards monopoly. When he wrote *The Philosophy of Wealth* he was alarmed, as were many of his contemporaries, by the growth of monopoly: the problem to which he proposed co-operative solutions was not competition, but its breakdown. In *The Distribution of Wealth*, and even more in his later work, he was far less concerned about the breakdown of competition, even coming to welcome monopoly on the grounds that it led to greater accumulation of capital. Limits on prices could be provided by "latent" competition, whilst the growth of capital kept competition alive.[32] The loss which the public experiences as a result of higher profits is offset by the continual increase in firms' capital accumulation. Several reasons for this change have been offered: the move from the mid-west, with its environment of populism, to the "establishment" of the eastern seaboard; or the irresistible analytical beauty of the competitive system.[33] Alternatively, it could simply be that whilst combination was still new and unknown, it was feared, but that experience suggested that these fears were unfounded.

# 12
## Marx[1]

### 12.1 INTRODUCTION

*Marx's system*

Marx's main ideas were the product of the 1840s. In this sense he is the contemporary of J. S. Mill. *Capital*, Marx's main work, however, was written much later, volume I and parts of later volumes being written in the mid 1860s. Though volume I was published in 1867, volumes II and III were published, posthumously, much later, in 1885 and 1894. It is for this reason that Marx is most appropriately considered alongside Jevons, Menger, Walras and Marshall, rather than as a predecessor.

Unlike the other economists just mentioned, Marx made no claim to scientific detachment. He was deeply involved in socialist and workers' movements, and his work on economics was very much a part of this political activity. He did, nonetheless, see himself as a scientist in a very real sense. He saw his work as revealing the true nature of capitalist society, that of his "bourgeois" contemporaries amounting to no more than apologetics. The basis for his attempts to combine scientific inquiries with political activity was his view of knowledge as having a practical character. For Marx, according to Kolakowski, knowledge "can never free itself from the practical, situational manner in which it is acquired. We cannot contemplate the subject itself, free from historical involvement; the cogito is an impossibility."[2]

Marx was much more than merely an economist, not simply because of his political commitment, but because he was concerned with much wider issues. His thought dealt with all aspects of human activity, of which economic activity was an integral part. What gave Marx's philosophy its distinctive character was his "materialist conception of history", the notion that the ultimate determinants of social relations were the material conditions of production. To understand the significance Marx attached to this it is necessary to consider his debt to Hegel.[3]

Hegel had tried to demonstrate the existence of predetermined, evolutionary processes operating in the fields of philosophy, law and history. Central to all such evolutionary processes was his "dialectic" philosophy, for he argued that the rules of reasoning were the same as the laws underlying the behaviour of the universe. Every concept, according to Hegel, was composed of a "thesis" out of which arose its partial negation, its "antithesis". Over time the contradictions this implied were assumed to grow, the result being that concepts were modified until, eventually, a "synthesis" emerged. The process then repeated itself on the basis of the new "synthesis".

For Hegel, historical evolution depended on intellectual developments, each stage of history being dominated by its "*Zeitgeist*", the spirit of the time. Whilst Marx retained the Hegelian dialectic, he reversed the relationship of spiritual and material evolution. For Marx it was material evolution that determined the evolution of ideas, the character of each stage in history being determined by the prevailing mode of production, which was itself part of a dialectic process. The process contained internal contradictions, and the contradictions within a mode of production would lead eventually to its replacement by a new mode of production.

The dominant mode of production at the time he was writing was, according to Marx, capitalism. Its defining feature was that one class owned the means of production, thus enabling it to extract a surplus from the class responsible for producing wealth. The contradictions within the capitalist mode of production were the contradictions arising from this asymmetric relationship between the capitalist class and the working class. The purpose of Marx's economics, therefore, was to provide an analysis of these contradictions, contradictions which would eventually lead to the downfall of the capitalist mode of production.

### Marx's economics

Marx's earliest writings on economics were written in the course of his work as a journalist having to comment on economic issues, and it is in this role that he conceived, in the early 1840s, some of the ideas that he later developed as central to his work. Completely missing from this early work, however, was the labour theory of value, for it was only through an article of Engels, published in 1844, that Marx was introduced to classical political economy, "an already existing rigorous science which had attempted to formulate laws of private property".[4] Between 1844 and 1847 he discovered how he could use Ricardian political economy to provide a rigorous theoretical foundation for views about capitalism which he had already developed. For example, Marx's view of value and exploitation changed substantially. In his earliest writings he described the notion of surplus value as "an economic fantasy". In 1844, shortly after reading Engels' article, he explained exploitation in terms of capitalists' being able to sell dearer than they bought. Finally, from 1847, he dismissed the ability of capitalists to make a profit through selling goods at more than their value as an accidental, not a fundamental, feature of capitalism, arguing that exploitation could occur even when goods were selling at their values.[5] Behind all these changes, however, and behind the very substantial changes which occurred in his philosophical position and in his attitude towards the state, Marx retained the same underlying vision of capitalism: one in which value was closely connected with the institution of private property. Marx thus took over Ricardian political economy, using and developing it to articulate a pre-existing vision of the economic system.[6]

It is this background which explains why Marxian economics can be viewed from such different perspectives. On the one hand it can be viewed as part of his Hegelian philosophy: it can be related to his view of history, of philosophy and of society as a whole. On the other hand, it is possible, because so much of his purely economic analysis was taken from Ricardo, to consider the economic aspects of his thought in the context of developments in "bourgeois" economics. This is the approach that will be followed here, though in doing this it is important not to forget the broader historical perspective which, for Marx, gave his economic analysis its significance.

## 12.2 EXPLOITATION AND VALUE

*Some definitions*

The notion of value, fundamental to the whole Marxian system, is the first thing Marx discusses in *Capital*. After discussing the difference between use-value and exchange-value, Marx defines exchange value as the human labour embodied in a commodity, or the amount of "socially necessary" labour required to produce a commodity.[7] The labour embodied in commodities can be divided into two parts: the "living" labour directly used in producing the commodity, and the stored up labour embodied in the intermediate goods used up in the production process. It is this distinction which forms the basis for Marx's important distinction between constant and variable capital. Variable capital, $v$, is the capital used to employ labour, which corresponds to the amount of living labour used in production. Constant capital, $c$, on the other hand, represents the stock of dead labour embodied in the commodities produced: the material inputs, comprising both the depreciation of fixed capital and inputs of intermediate goods. As we shall see, an important term in Marx's system is the *organic composition of capital*, $k$, defined as the ratio of constant capital to total capital, $c/(c+v)$. Though defined in a slightly different way, Marx's organic composition of capital is clearly analogous to the capital–labour ratio.[8]

The significance of the distinction between constant and variable capital is that Marx *assumes* that it is only living labour, and hence variable capital, which produces a surplus, this surplus, $s$, constituting the capitalist's profits. Two ratios are defined in relation to this surplus: the rate of exploitation, $e = s/v$, relating surplus value to variable capital; and the rate of profit, relating surplus value to total capital, $r = s/(c+v)$.

*Exploitation*

Marx's theory of exploitation, central to his whole system, is based on the idea that surplus value arises through the relationship between capitalists and workers. Surplus arises because the capitalist buys labour power at its value: that is at its cost of production, or the value of the worker's subsistence, this being socially, rather than biologically, determined. Because the value of the commodities produced by the worker is greater than the value of the labour power, the capitalist is left with a surplus. Thus one definition of the rate of exploitation is the ratio of paid to unpaid labour: if the worker is forced to work for 12 hours, and if it takes only 4 hours' labour to produce his subsistence, then he is working 8 hours "unpaid" labour, which constitutes the capitalist's surplus. In aggregate terms this definition of the rate of exploitation becomes the ratio of the amount of surplus value to the value of labour power, or the ratio of surplus to necessary labour. For Marx, therefore, exploitation arose because the capitalist class had a monopoly of the means of production. He argued that exploitation was the source of the surplus, and that surplus was the source of profits.

## The transformation problem

A problem which concerned Ricardo was the problem that if the capital–labour ratio was not the same in all industries, then relative prices would not equal relative labour values. The related problem in the Marxian scheme is that if the organic composition of capital varies across industries, it is not possible to have at the same time a uniform rate of exploitation and a uniform rate of profit. From the definitions given above it follows that,

$$r = (1 - k)e,$$

from which this conclusion immediately follows.

Marx's solution to this problem is to argue that there are two, parallel systems: a system of values, in which the rate of exploitation is uniform, and a system of prices in which the rate of profit is uniform.[9] There are thus three stages in the process of determining prices. (1) The rate of exploitation can be used to calculate values and the total amount of surplus value received by the capitalist class. (2) Total surplus value is *assumed* to equal total profits. Given the value of the capital stock this determines the average rate of profit. (3) Competition establishes prices such that all capitalists earn this average rate of profit. Marx thus solves the *transformation problem*, the problem of how values are transformed into prices, by having what can be described as a labour theory of *profits*. It is based on the arbitrary assumption that total profits equal total surplus value. He has abandoned the labour theory of value in the sense that, for Marx, relative labour values no longer determine relative prices in any simple way.[10]

To make this clearer, consider a simplified version of one of Marx's examples.[11] Five sectors are given (Table 12.1), each with a different organic composition of capital, and employing a total capital of 100. Constant and variable capital are shown in column 1. Assuming a rate of exploitation of 100% we can derive the amounts of surplus value shown in column 2, and the *value* of each sector's output shown in column 3. We now have to add up the total quantity of surplus value, adding all the items in column 2 to get 110. As the total capital is 500, the average rate of profit is 22%. Because the example is simplified and each sector has a capital of 100, this means that each sector must earn profits equal to 22, and that the selling

Table 12.1

| Sector | (1)<br>$c + v$ | (2)<br>$s = v$ | (3)<br>$o =$<br>$c + v + s$ | (4)<br>Profits | (5)<br>Selling<br>price | (6)<br>(3)–(5) |
|--------|------|------|------|------|------|------|
| I      | 80 + 20 | 20 | 120 | 22 | 122 | 2 |
| II     | 70 + 30 | 30 | 130 | 22 | 122 | −8 |
| III    | 60 + 40 | 40 | 140 | 22 | 122 | −18 |
| IV     | 85 + 15 | 15 | 115 | 22 | 122 | 7 |
| V      | 95 +  5 | 5  | 105 | 22 | 122 | 17 |
| Totals | 500 | 110 | 610 | 110 | 610 | 0 |

*price* of each sector's output is 122. It is clear that relative values are not the same as relative prices, but there is still a sense in which exploitation is the "ultimate determinant" of relative prices.

## 12.3  REPRODUCTION SCHEMES

*Digression: Quesnay's* tableau

Marx was one of the few nineteenth century economists to appreciate Quesnay's *Tableau Economique*, a remarkable idea described in 1758–1760 by one of the leading representatives of the French economists of the period known as the Physiocrats.[12] The *tableau* was a diagram illustrating the circular flow of income within an economy, and the movement of goods between landlords, agriculture and the manufacturing sector. In this Quesnay started out with given stocks of food and money and he showed how the landlords' expenditure of their rents would generate, through what we would now call a multiplier process, enough income to buy all the produce of agriculture and the manufacturing sector, leaving each of the sectors with the same stocks at the end of the period as at its beginning.

Quesnay's *tableau* was constructed on the basis of the following set of assumptions:[13]

(1) There is a productive class (farmers) which uses advances of £1000 to employ labour. This labour is used on the land to produce a net output of agricultural output worth £2000,[14] yielding a return of 100% on the initial advance of £1000. Farmers are thus able to pay the landlords (or the sovereign) a rent of £1000, and still be left with £1000 to form the next period's advances.

2 The unproductive class (artisans) starts with a stock of 500 units (£s worth) of raw materials previously purchased from the farmers. Using 500 units (again £s worth) of labour the artisans produce manufactured output worth £1000. It is because this class produces no surplus, the value

of the output being equal to the value of the inputs, that it is called the sterile, or unproductive, class.

3 Landlords and the workers in the productive sector are assumed each to spend half their income on food, purchased from the farmers, and half on manufactured consumption goods purchased from the artisans.

4 Workers in the unproductive sector are assumed to spend all their income on food purchased from the farmers.[15]

From these assumptions can be constructed a model of the circular flow of income. Rather than use Quesnay's own diagram, it is simpler to analyse this using a flow of funds table (Table 12.2). This shows each sector's income and expenditure. It is easy to check that the entries in it follow from the assumptions listed above. Several features of this table are worth pointing out. (1) Each sector's expenditure equals its income, which means that each sector ends up with exactly the same money balances as it started with. The landlords end up with £1000 which constitutes the following period's advances, and the landlords have £1000 with which to purchase consumption goods. (2) Consumption of manufactured goods equals production. Thus all the sterile class is doing is using labour to transform raw materials into a form suitable for consumption. It does not contribute to the production of a surplus. (3) Of the 2000 units of food produced, 1500 are consumed as food, with 500 being purchased by the sterile class to constitute the raw materials for the following period's production. The economy ends up in exactly the same state as that in which it started.

Note that for Quesnay's system to work, a particular set of numbers is required, this including not merely the propensities to consume and the

Table 12.2

| Receipts | Payments | | | | | Incomes |
|---|---|---|---|---|---|---|
| | F | PW | L | A | UW | |
| F | $-$[16] | 500 (food) | 500 (food) | 500 (food) | 500 (raw materials) | 2000 |
| PW | 1000 (rent) | – | – | – | – | 1000 |
| L | 1000 (wages) | – | – | – | – | 1000 |
| A | – | 500 (manufactured goods) | 500 (manufactured goods) | | | 1000 |
| UW | – | – | – | 500 (wages) | – | 500 |
| Total expenditures | 2000 | 1000 | 1000 | 1000 | 500 | |

input–output coefficients, but also the relative sizes of the two sectors. Quesnay, for example, has assumed that the productive sector is twice the size (in terms of employment) of the unproductive sector. It can thus be argued that the *tableau* describes a static equilibrium: it does not explain how it comes about.

### Simple reproduction[17]

Marx's schemes of simple reproduction deal with the same situation as the version of Quesnay's *tableau* described above, for before investigating the accumulation of capital he analysed an economy which was reproducing itself exactly from year to year. Adopting the simplifying assumption that products exchange at their values, Marx tried to answer the question,

How is the *capital* consumed in production replaced in value out of the annual product and how does the movement of this replacement intertwine with the consumption of the surplus-value by the capitalists and of the wages of the labourer?[18]

He divides the economy into two "departments", or sectors, one (department I) producing investment goods, and the other (department II) producing consumption goods. Assuming a rate of exploitation of 100% Marx considers the following scheme.

Dept. I: $4000c + 1000v + 1000s \rightarrow 6000$
Dept. II: $2000c + 500v + 500s \rightarrow 3000$

The amounts on the right hand side are the values of the outputs produced by the two sectors. To complete the model Marx has to specify how wages (variable capital) and profits (surplus value) are spent. For this scheme of simple reproduction he assumes that all wages and profits are consumed. Total demand for consumer goods is thus 3000, the same as the supply. Similarly, demand for constant capital will, if the economy continues on the same scale in the next period, be 6000, exactly equal to the supply.

To see how much is going on, even in this simple model, consider Table 12.3, which shows the expenditure flows between capitalists and workers in

Table 12.3

| Payees | Payers | | | | Incomes |
|---|---|---|---|---|---|
| | Cap. I | Wor. I | Cap. II | Wor. II | |
| Cap. I | 4000 | – | 2000 | – | 6000 |
| Wor. I | 1000 | – | – | – | 1000 |
| Cap. II | 1000 | 1000 | 500 | 500 | 3000 |
| Wor. II | – | – | 500 | – | 500 |
| Expenditures | 6000 | 1000 | 3000 | 500 | |

the two sectors. Consider first the capitalists in department I. These pay out 1000 to their own workers, they spend 1000 on consumption goods, purchased from department II's capitalists, and they purchase 4000 on investment goods bought from each other. This gives column 1. The workers in each sector are simpler: they simply spend all their wages on consumption goods purchased from department II's capitalists (columns 2 and 4). Finally department II's capitalists spend 2000 on investment goods bought from department I, 500 on wages and 500 on consumption goods bought from each other. It can be seen that incomes and expenditures are equal for all four groups.

It is worth noticing that if we applied modern national income accounting methods, only the output of department II would be included in Net National Product: because there is no net investment, the entire output of department I comprises intermediate goods and replacement investment.

The model can be represented algebraically, using the following equations.

$$O_I = C_I + V_I + S_I$$
$$O_{II} = C_{II} + V_{II} + S_{II}$$

If the economy is to reproduce itself exactly, output of capital goods must equal the quantity of capital goods used up in production, which gives

$$O_I = C_I + C_{II},$$

from which we can obtain the condition that

$$C_{II} = V_I + S_I.$$

This states that if the economy is reproducing itself exactly, the consumption sector's demand for investment goods must equal the investment sector's demand for consumption goods.[19] Marx's example works because he has chosen sectors which are the right size relative to each other for this to be the case.[20] To see this, suppose that the rate of exploitation were to rise. Surplus value would increase, which means that given the existing sizes of the two sectors, demand for consumption goods would rise, requiring an expansion of the consumption goods sector to keep supply and demand equal.

### Extended reproduction[21]

Simple reproduction was for Marx only the prelude to analysis of the more important case where capital was being accumulated: reproduction on an extended scale.[22] To get extended reproduction Marx dropped the assumption that the surplus was entirely consumed, assuming instead that a part was consumed and a part used to accumulate capital. He made the further assumption that the labour force could be expanded as fast as required: that the supply of labour was completely elastic. Consider one of Marx's numerical examples, noting that not only is the size of department II different from that of the above example, but also that he has changed his assumption about the organic composition of capital (i.e. the assumption that capitalists accumulate part of their surplus is not the only assumption he has changed).

### Year 1

Dept. I:    $4000c + 1000v + 1000s$    $\rightarrow 6000$
Dept. II:    $1500c + 750v + 750s$    $\rightarrow 3000$

The first assumption we add is that capitalists in department I consume half their profits, and accumulate the other half. Of the 500 they accumulate they will wish to invest 400 in constant capital and 100 in variable capital, maintaining the same organic composition of capital. Marx now introduces the rather peculiar assumption that the capitalists in department II invest an amount sufficient to keep supply and demand for capital goods in balance. As output of capital goods is 6000, and as department I demands 4400, this means that the capitalists of department II must purchase 1600 units of constant capital: in other words that they invest 100 of their surplus in constant capital. Because their organic composition of capital is 2, they will invest 50 in variable capital, which leaves 600 to be consumed. This means that in the next period the situation will be as follows.

### Year 2

Dept. I:    $4400c + 1100v + 1100s$    $\rightarrow 6600$
Dept. II:    $1600c + 800v + 800s$    $\rightarrow 3200$

In the following period the process is repeated, but from the new starting point.

### Year 3

Dept. I:    $4840c + 1210v + 1210s$    $\rightarrow 7280$
Dept. II:    $1760c + 880v + 880s$    $\rightarrow 3520$

In these schemes of reproduction Marx is providing what we would now call a growth model: a model of how a simple economy with two sectors, in equilibrium with supply and demand equal in both sectors, can grow. In his example the growth rates for the two sectors are 10% and 6.7% in the first year, but in the second year both sectors grow at a rate of 10%, a rate which continues thereafter. In other words, Marx has shown that the economy will reach a balanced growth path on which both sectors are growing at the same rate, with the relative size of the two sectors remaining unchanged. Strong objections may be raised concerning several of the assumptions made in these reproduction schemes, in particular the assumptions that goods exchange at their values, that the rate of surplus value is the same in both departments, and concerning the peculiar investment function used.[23] Despite this, however, it is important to recognize that Marx was tackling a problem not widely tackled by non-Marxist economists until much later.[24]

## 12.4   THE FUTURE OF CAPITALISM

The reproduction schemes discussed above simply show how balanced growth could occur in a capitalist economy. Although he used these schemes to show how capital reproduced itself under capitalism, his view of how a capitalist economy actually grew was very different from this. Crucial to all his predictions about the future of capitalism was the prediction that the organic composition of capital would steadily increase: that capital would increasingly be substituted for labour. Perhaps the main effect of this was the tendency towards a declining rate of profit, which follows from the equation $r(1 - k) = e$. If $k$ is rising, then unless the rate of exploitation rises by an equivalent amount, the rate of profit must fall. Acting against this tendency are a number of factors which raise the rate of exploitation. Capitalists try to increase the length of the working day; they introduce innovations which raise productivity without requiring increases in constant capital; they try to depress wages below the value of labour power, something which is easier when unemployment is high; and they use foreign trade to try to reduce the cost of constant capital and the means of subsistence.[25] These factors, however, can, according to Marx, do no more than temporarily offset the tendency of the rate of profit to fall. For example, there are obvious physical limits to the ability of capitalists to increase the length of the working day.

Increased mechanization and the accumulation of capital have, according to Marx, dire implications for the working class. The substitution of constant for variable capital throws people out of work, creating what Marx called the industrial reserve army of the unemployed. The pressure on capitalists to increase exploitation in order to maintain their profit rates may result in lower real wage rates. Even if this does not occur, however, the working class will nonetheless become pauperized, for mechanization will destroy the demand for skills, reducing work to mere mechanical activity, and causing a deterioration in working conditions. It is as well to remember that the background to Marx's writing was the 1840s, the decade when the effects of the industrial revolution in England were probably at their worst, just before the steady rise in the standard of living which occurred from about mid-century began to be evident.

Marx suggested a variety of reasons why the pace of capital accumulation would be uneven. Technical change and innovations occurred at irregular intervals; the industrial reserve army might temporarily become depleted; or imbalances between sectors might develop, the result being physical shortages. Any of these might cause the rate of profits to fall below its normal rate, the result being a fall in investment and a crisis of over-production. In such a crisis surplus value would still be produced, but capitalists would be unable to realize all this surplus value, goods remaining unsold. The over-production which occurred was not over-production relative to the needs of society, but simply over-production relative to the needs of capitalist production. The desire to accumulate capital in the face of a falling rate of profit would result in crises becoming more and more severe, and in a tendency towards permanent depression, the reserve army of the unemployed becoming ever larger. It was in response to this that the proletariat would, Marx predicted, unite, and capitalism would be overthrown.

## 12.5 CONCLUSIONS

There is a sense in which Marx was the last, and one of the greatest, of the classical economists.[26] Though Marx's theory ranged *far* beyond the concerns of most of the English classical economists, he shared their theoretical framework: a labour, or cost theory of value; a class analysis of income distribution; and a theory of growth based on a distinction between factors which did and did not yield a surplus. Behind all the differences are strong affinities between Marx's economics and the economics of Ricardo.

Where Marx went beyond the English classical tradition was in his use of classical political economy as a part of his theory of history. In this chapter we have concentrated on Marx's formal economic logic, whereas Marx applied this to a vision of the world in which capitalism was only a passing stage. It can be argued, moreover, that many of the most striking predictions of Marxian economics derive not from his formal economic logic, but from the setting in which this is placed. His doctrines of the immiseration of the proletariat, and the tendency towards worse and worse crises, for example, depend not so much on his reproduction schemes or his theory of value, as on the auxiliary hypotheses brought in from outside concerning the nature of technical change, the response of capitalists to falling profit rates and so on. One commentator has argued that Marx's predictions either follow from the tendency of the rate of profit to fall, or are ad hoc.[27] The formal model is, on the whole, the vehicle for Marx's predictions rather than their source.

For all his work on the labour theory of value Marx failed to solve the problems confronting the Ricardian theory of value. Some of the technical problems with Marx's theory can be corrected, but there are fundamental flaws which cannot be. The defects in the labour theory of value which caused Jevons to react against Ricardo were also present in Marx's work, which meant that economists of Marshall's generation could justifiably reject it on the same grounds that they rejected Ricardo. Price theory could manage without value theory, for values and surplus value were unobservable, and the labour theory of profits was totally arbitrary. Was the reason for this, as Hilferding later argued,[28] that Marx, unlike the marginal utility theorists, saw the task of economics as being to explain, not the determination of relative prices, but the evolution of capitalism? Though there is undoubtedly some truth in this, it has to be pointed out that Marx needed, if he was to explain how the surplus was distributed amongst capitalists, to explain prices. But it would seem plausible that the main explanation of Marx's commitment to the labour theory of value lay in its ideological implications. Marx was doing much more than simply measuring value in terms of labour time, for surplus value carried with it the ethical implication that profits constituted the fruits of exploitation. Marx's problem was that he wished to prove this scientifically, whereas no scientific justification of such a proposition is possible.

# 13

# The 1870s as a Turning Point

## 13.1 THE MARGINAL REVOLUTION?

*The revolution that wasn't*[1]

Though the work of Jevons, Menger and Walras does, in the light of subsequent developments, mark an important turning point in the history of economic analysis, it is important not to exaggerate the change which occurred. The theory of marginal utility was discovered in the 1830s, and its significance was seen by several economists in the 1850s. In addition there were many economists who stressed demand as a determinant of value, even in England, the home of Ricardian economics. Longfield and Senior, for example, both argued the case for a subjective value theory. The stress on demand as well as on costs in Mill's theory of value marked a significant departure from the abstractions of Ricardian theory. It is, therefore, in some ways misleading to refer to a revolution in the theory of value occurring in 1870.

An even stronger case can be made as regards other branches of economics. In the theory of trade, not only has Mill's theory of reciprocal demand remained an important part of the pure theory of trade, but so too has the Ricardian theory of comparative advantage. Though the application of marginal analysis and the use of mathematics contributed to the theory's being stated more precisely, and enabled it to be developed more fully, there was no discontinuity in the development of trade theory. Similar remarks can be made concerning monetary economics and the theory of the cycle. For example, when allowance has been made for changes in circumstances and for improved technique, the monetary economics of Marshall and Wicksell would be hard to distinguish from that of Thornton.

*Marginalism*

For all the continuity, and this was *very* substantial, the 1870s can be seen, in retrospect, as marking a decisive turning point in the development of economic analysis. Since the late nineteenth century a theory of resource allocation based on marginal analysis has remained at the centre of economic theory. Though there have been important critics, from Thorstein Veblen to Herbert Simon and Joan Robinson, the dominant theme in twentieth century economic theory has been the development and use of a system of economic equilibrium, in which maximizing behaviour on the part of individuals is brought into some sort of equilibrium through markets. In addition, the increased use of mathematics in economics has been associated above all else with marginal analysis. This line of inquiry clearly dates from the contributions of Jevons, Menger and Walras. This is not to imply that such a development could not have taken place on the basis of, say, Gossen's work: merely that it did not.

From this perspective, the contributions of Jevons, Menger and Walras should, despite the enormous differences between them, be grouped together. It would, however, be misleading to see their work as a multiple discovery in the sense in which Merton uses the term. A multiple discovery, for Merton, arises because scientists are working in a common environment: they share the same background, and are subject to similar pressures and influences. This was not the case with Jevons, Menger and Walras: they were writing against three very different backgrounds. Before the 1870s there was not the widespread international exchange of ideas which developed later in the century[2]

It is this insularity, probably most marked in Britain, which makes it inappropriate to see the developments of the 1870s in Kuhnian terms: Kuhn's theory of paradigms and scientific revolutions presumes the existence of a scientific community. Such a scientific community began to develop on an international basis only after 1870. It was only after Walras and Jevons discovered that they had independently developed similar theories, that economic theory began to become more cosmopolitan, and even then this was a slow process.

### The Jevonian revolution

The country where the term "revolution" seems most applicable is Britain. British political economy, in the 1860s, exhibited some of the symptoms of a Kuhnian crisis. Confidence in the classical system of political economy collapsed, and there was little agreement even on how economic inquiry should be conducted. Economists bemoaned the lack of any consensus on fundamental doctrines.[3] Hutchison has described this collapse of confidence in English classical political economy as

a case almost unparalleled in the history of economic theory, of the comparatively sudden abandonment of a very central theoretical core, which had long and authoritatively prevailed as an established orthodoxy. The over-worked term "revolution" does not seem far fetched in describing this process in England in the late 1860s and early 1870s.[4]

Although the emergence of a new orthodoxy to replace classical political economy was a slow process, Jevons' ideas taking a long time to gain acceptance, it seems reasonable to refer to the change as revolutionary.

The situation in Austria and France was very different. Walras was working in a long French tradition which stressed the role of demand and utility. Neither was Menger rebelling against any established orthodoxy. In Hutchison's words, "Menger's *Grundsatze* marks an important beginning, but does not mark an end, as does Jevons' *Theory*, which can be said to mark both an end and a beginning."[5] Hutchison thus uses the term

"Jevonian" revolution to indicate: (1) that it was only in England that "any drastically 'revolutionary' processes" took place; and (2) that it was Jevons who played the most distinguished role, both in the attack on the classical regime, and in laying the foundations of what was, eventually, to become a new system of thought.[6]

## 13.2 THE ECONOMICS PROFESSION

*The emergence of an economics profession*

It was in the closing decades of the nineteenth century that economics became professionalized. Of the important economists writing after 1870, the vast majority were professors and also specialists in economics. This was not true earlier in the century: Smith, for example, was a professor of moral philosophy; Ricardo a stockbroker; Malthus a clergyman. The American Economic Association was founded in 1885, the British Economics Association (later the Royal Economic Society) in 1891. It was at this time, too, that important contributions to economics came to be published in specialized journals: the *Journal of Political Economy* (founded in 1893); the *Quarterly Journal of Economics* (1886); the *Economic Journal* (1891).

As the economics profession developed, it became more international. Hutchison has attached particular importance to the preface to the second (1979) edition of Jevons' *Theory of Political Economy*. The novelty of this preface lay in its providing an international documentation of a new idea (marginal utility theory), the purpose of which was "to create a contemporary international market of ideas and to make advances in the subject to some extent a process of international co-operation".[7] It is also arguable that the mathematical nature of the new theory of value and distribution assisted the international flow of ideas. This international exchange of ideas, at its peak in the late 1880s and 1890s, meant that the ideas of that period were worked out in a setting very different from the comparative isolation in which Jevons, Menger and Walras had developed their ideas:

Edgeworth, Wicksteed, Auspitz and Lieben, Wieser, Böhm-Bawerk, Wicksell, Walras, Pareto, Barone and Fisher all drew on a broad, internationally known literature, made up to a large extent of their own writings. Works like Wicksell's *Value, Capital and Rent* [1893] and Pareto's *Cours* [1896], though they contain their own particular original ideas, are constructed essentially on the basis of a wide, eclectic, cosmopolitan reading of their contemporaries and immediate predecesors.[8]

*English insularity*

This movement towards greater cosmopolitanism in economic theorizing was not, however, unimpeded. Of particular importance was the Marshallian school, which came to dominate English economics from the 1890s. It was as a result of the Marshallian influence that English economics once again became very insular, some of the most important developments in European and American economics going almost un-noticed in England until the 1920s and 1930s.[9] Indicative of this lack of interest in foreign ideas is the paucity of foreign contributions appearing the *Economic Journal*.

One of the reasons for the insularity of English economics was Marshall's dislike of criticism. In his desire to establish economics as a science: he feared that the prestige of the subject would be undermined by dissent amongst economists. In addition, Marshall's stress on respect for the authority of the past served to strengthen his own position, for, as Hutchison has argued,

Marshall was to become for a generation the great father figure of English economics, firmly upholding the virtue of respect for one's elders and betters in the family of economists. After the middle eighties there were in England patently no betters than Marshall himself, and, of course, fewer and fewer comparable elders.[10]

Marshall's dominance of English economics was made possible by the absence of any centre on which opposition to Marshall could be focussed. For various reasons, Oxford failed to provide such an alternative.[11] Thus when Continental ideas did at last begin to gain a wide audience amongst English economists, they came through the London School of Economics, founded in 1895.[12]

Perhaps the main problem with academic schools such as the Marshallian or the Austrian, was that they rested on a set of presuppositions that was never fully articulated: "indoctrination into the subtle connotations of economic terms ... could hardly be acquired except by personal contact with the fount of knowledge".[13] Because the assumptions underlying a school's work could not be learnt simply by reading published work, discussion with outsiders was relatively difficult.

### Economics in the United States

The most significant aspect of the emergence of the economics profession in the late nineteenth century has been left until last: the emergence of American economics. Prior to the third quarter of the nineteenth century the contribution of American economists to the development of economic analysis had been minimal, a situation which had changed radically by the end of the century. The American economics profession was important, not merely because of its rapidly growing size, but because American economics differed from English economics in several important respects.

American economics never came to be dominated by a single centre, in the way that English economics came, for a while, to be dominated by Cambridge. This was not simply because of the size of the United States, but was also a result of the very different nature of American society. There was much more competition between institutions and individuals:

During the late-nineteenth and early-twentieth centuries the spirit of academic entrepreneurship flourished as never before among presidents, administrators, and professors, and the ideals of productivity and efficiency emerged as the source of the now familiar requirement to publish or perish. Within the academic community there was a marked but protracted, shift of emphasis from teaching to research.[14]

It was this background which accounted for the very rapid professionalization of American economics.[15]

Why did this professionalization of American economics come so rapidly? One reason was that professionalization, for all professions, not simply economics, provided "an important avenue to elite status and increased influence in an undeferential society lacking a clear-cut social stratification".[16] There were other reasons too. Of particular importance was the conflict between two pressures to which American academics were subject. On the one hand there was the need to demonstrate the relevance of their work to contemporary life. On the other hand, if they did comment on topical issues (of which there were plenty – silver, the tariff, trusts, unions) they were liable to offend some vested interest, and might endanger their reputation or their academic post.[17] The result was a *professional* conservatism: there emerged a consensus about professional standards, in which moderation tended to be associated with scholarly merit. A discipline-centred approach was also encouraged by the increasing stress on research rather than teaching.

Finally, it is important to point out the strong connections between American and European (non-British) economics. The economists of J. B. Clark's generation went to Europe, particularly to Germany, for their training. The result was that ideas were borrowed from English, German and Austrian sources, and new theories and textbooks proliferated.[18] These new theories did not, however, develop into doctrinal schools such as were to be found in Europe.

## 13.3  CONCLUSIONS

The professionalization of economics, together with the emergence of a system of economic equilibrium based on maximizing behaviour, have given twentieth century economics a character very different indeed from that of classical economics. The rise of American economics, with all its distinctive features, was one of the most important developments. Though the use of the word "revolution" is probably inappropriate outside the British context, it is reasonable to see this change as constituting a major turning point in the development of the subject. Though it would be *very* misleading to see the adoption of marginalist ideas in terms of the need to defend an ideology, let alone as a counter to Marxism, the professionalization of the subject and the rise of marginalism were probably not unrelated. The slight narrowing of perspective and the increased scope for formal analysis, were consistent with the desire to establish a scientific basis for economics.

# III

## THE NEOCLASSICAL PERIOD, 1890–1939

# 14

# Equilibrium Analysis

## 14.1 INTRODUCTION

The new systems proposed by Jevons, Menger, Walras and Marshall were all systems of static equilibrium, in which prices were determined by the interaction, in competitive markets, of the maximizing behaviour of economic agents. The emphasis was thus very different from that of the classical economists for whom a static system of price determination, though present, was in the background *vis à vis* the theory of growth and capital accumulation. It is the development of this system of static equilibrium, which though propounded in the 1870s, was far from fully worked out, that forms the subject of this chapter. It can be argued that the working out of this system was the greatest achievement of the period leading up to 1914.

There were a variety of ways in which this development could proceed, for static equilibrium theory was formulated in widely differing ways, each having its adherents. There were differences of opinion with regard to utility, the nature of costs, the usefulness of mathematics and the issue of simultaneous determination versus one-way causation. In addition, there were still, in the years after 1870, many economists who retained older approaches to the theory of value. Furthermore, despite isolated attempts, the problem of income distribution had not, before the 1890s, been systematically reformulated in the same way as the theory of commodity pricing. Though their nature changed markedly, discussions of the nature of utility, the way in which economic equilibrium should be handled, and controversies over the theory of distribution continued throughout the period.

## 14.2 THE CONSUMER AND DEMAND

In a sense the theory of the consumer was fundamental to all the new systems, for values were derived from the values of final consumption goods, these in turn being derived from the ability of goods to satisfy wants. Although the way in which consumer theory was expounded varied from Jevons' Benthamite utilitarianism to Menger's stress on the ability of goods to satify human needs, all these writers analysed consumer behaviour in terms of utility. It was marginal utility which determined the value of a commodity. In addition, for all of them, the utility of a commodity was assumed to depend solely on consumption of that commodity.

There were several ways in which these investigations could be developed. One was to investigate the nature of utility: could it be measured, and if so how? What was its connection with hedonism? The second way was to introduce technical improvements into utility analysis, permitting a more thorough analysis of demand. Finally, there was the approach of abandoning utility analysis in favour of alternative ways of representing consumer behaviour. In the period from 1880 to 1939 all three of these approaches were pursued.

### The meaning of the term utility[1]

For economists wishing to investigate further the nature of utility, one recourse was to psychology. The only major economist of the period to follow Jevons[2] in adopting this approach was Edgeworth. Edgeworth made use of the Weber–Fechner laws of sensation, dating from the 1860s, taking as his unit of measurement the "just perceivable increment", something applicable to both the intensity and the duration of pleasure. This "equation to each other of indistinguishable events or cases" he regarded as axiomatic, incapable of proof.[3]

Edgeworth was, however, atypical, the main reason for this being that amongst psychologists interest in hedonism was waning. Several writers, of whom the first was Bonar (1888),[4] warned economists of this, raising the question of whether utility analysis had to fall with hedonism. Reactions to this amongst more orthodox economists were varied. At one extreme we have Marshall. In the first edition of the *Principles* (1890) the utilitarian basis of the theory was explicit, but in later editions, though the issue was never explicitly discussed, references to "pleasure" and "pain" were replaced with more innocuous words such as "satisfaction" and "detriment". The substance of the theory was unaffected. At the other extreme we have Veblen's attacks (1898, 1899), not only on hedonism but on the notion of rational choice itself.[5]

But of greater importance than either of these extremes were the attempts of economists to provide accounts of consumer behaviour free of hedonism, the most important contributions being those of Fisher and Pareto. Fisher (1892) described the foisting of psychology on economics by Gossen, Jevons and Edgeworth as "inappropriate and vicious", arguing that it was possible to base economics on the much simpler postulate, "each individual acts as he desires".[6] Though Fisher continued to use the word "utility" it was merely as a means of describing behaviour: to say that the utility of A exceeded that of B meant no more than that the individual preferred A to B. Referring to Bentham, Fisher argued that "his *word* [utility] is the more acceptable, the less it is entangled with his *theory*".[7] The distance between Fisher's conception of utility and that of Bentham and Jevons is shown by the following paragraph.

Thus if we seek only the causation of the *objective facts of prices and commodity distribution* four attributes of utility as a quantity are entirely unessential, (1) that one man's utility can be compared to another's, (2) that for the same individual the marginal utilities at one consumption-combination can be compared with those at another, or at one time with another, (3) even if they could, total utility and gain might not be integrable, (4) even if they were, there would be no need of determining the constants of integration.[8]

A similar position was taken by Pareto who, apparently independently of Fisher, noticed that a utility function might not exist. He approached this problem in the following way. Slopes of indifference curves (which will equal the slopes of the appropriate price lines) can be obtained from budgetary data. To obtain utility functions from these, two further steps are necessary: (i) to integrate equations for the slopes of the indifference curves to obtain the indifference curves themselves; and (ii) to integrate these equations to obtain utility functions. Pareto observed that whilst the first step might be possible under certain conditions, there was no way of going from the indifference curves to a unique utility function. Like Fisher, Pareto was clearly taking observed behaviour as the datum, utility functions being no more than a way of representing this. It was for this reason that he advocated the term *ophélimité* for utility. Pareto was, however, slow to see the implications of these arguments. He noted the problem as early as 1892,[9] but in the *Cours* (1896) he not only used utilities, but assumed that the utilities of different individuals could be compared. Even the *Manual* is not entirely consistent in its attitude to utility measurement. Despite this, however, Pareto must, along with Fisher, be regarded as one of the main architects of modern, ordinal, utility theory.

Pareto was in a minority amongst leading economists of the late nineteenth century in rejecting the measurability of utility. Wicksell, Wicksteed and Edgeworth all advocated measurable utility, and Marshall considered utility to be measurable under certain special circumstances. In the period after 1900, however, significant contributions were made towards developing a non-utilitarian consumer theory: Johnson (1913), apparently independently of Pareto, analysed consumer choice in terms of the ratios of marginal utilities, arguing that economics did not need to know the marginal utility of any commodity[10]; and Slutsky (1915), referring to Pareto but not Johnson, attempted to provide a completely empirical concept of utility. Their contributions were, however, neglected, and it was not until the 1930s that the concept of purely ordinal utility became generally accepted.[11] Hicks and Allen were the main proponents of this approach, whilst Lange was responsible for pointing out exactly what assumptions were involved in the various types of utility. But to understand these developments we need to consider other aspects of consumer theory, to which we now turn.

### Utility and demand

When shorn of its utilitarian associations the function of utility theory was to provide a theory of demand. Both Walras and Marshall used utility maximization to derive their demand curves, but they did so only for the case where the utility of each good depended on the consumption of that good alone, i.e. for an additively separable utility function.[12] The problem with this was that, although easy to understand, it ruled out the issue of complementarity: for the essence of complementarity is that the utility of one good depends on how much of another good is being consumed. Thus an important step was the replacement of the additively separable utility function with a more general one. The first economist to do this was Edgeworth (1881). He, however, did not pursue the link between complementarity and the form of the utility function.

The first formal definition of complementarity was provided by Auspitz and Lieben (1889) who defined it in terms of the second derivative of the utility function: if an increase in consumption of one good increases the marginal utility of another, then they are complementary; if it reduces it they are competing goods. Despite their rejection of measurable utility, on which this definition depends, both Fisher and Pareto took over this definition. It was not until Johnson's article in 1913 that a definition of complementarity that did not depend on utility measurement was provided. This defined complementarity in terms of the slope of the indifference curve. The modern definition, in terms of the sign of cross substitution effects (i.e. according to whether a rise in the price of one good increases or reduces the demand for another), was provided by Hicks and Allen in 1934.

Complementarity was not, however, the only reason why the form of the utility function mattered. It was because they assumed utility functions to be additively separable that Marshall and Walras were able to deduce that demand curves sloped downwards. When Fisher and Pareto analysed this problem using more general utility functions they found that in general demand functions might slope either way. Here again it was Johnson and Slutsky who solved the problem, the most thorough treatment being that of Slutsky. Slutsky distinguished between what we now call normal and inferior goods, calling them "relatively indispensable" and "relatively dispensable". Demand curves for the former necessarily sloped downwards; those for the latter probably sloped downwards, but did not necessarily do so. Because of the neglect of Johnson's and Slutsky's work, however, Marshall's analysis of demand continued to be used, despite its limitations. It was only when Hicks and Allen derived these results, independently of Johnson and Slutsky, though they later acknowledged them fully naming the fundamental equation after Slutsky, that the generally held theory of demand changed.

*Indifference curves*

These developments in consumer theory required a means of analysing consumer choice without using utility, and this was found in indifference curves. However, despite the use of indifference curves by Fisher, Pareto, Johnson, Hicks and Allen as a means of avoiding reliance on utility, indifference curves were first used by a committed utilitarian – Edgeworth. Because Edgeworth used his indifference curves to analyse bargaining, they sloped upwards, relating an individual's consumption of one good to the amount of the other good he had to give up. It was Fisher and Pareto who saw in indifference curves the possibility of developing a non-utilitarian analysis of consumer behaviour, and who used the now conventional downward-sloping indifference curves. Fisher combined these with a budget line,[13] whilst Pareto combined them with constraints which might, or might not be straight. It was Johnson who used indifference curves and budget lines to derive the now familiar income- and price-consumption curves.[14]

As with other aspects of consumer theory, Hicks and Allen re-worked much of this, taking the analysis further. One key to their treatment was the concept of the elasticity of substitution, developed by Hicks, Robinson and Lerner to analyse the production function, but used by Hicks and Allen to measure the curvature of indifference curves.[15] Their contribution, no doubt a major reason for the success of their work, was to show that indifference curves provided a way of analysing demand without making any assumptions about the effects of income on demand. One of the problems with Marshall's theory of demand was that he had had to assume that the marginal utility of money was constant. It was this assumption which had enabled Marshall to measure marginal utility in terms of money, and to infer a downward-sloping demand curve from the hypothesis of diminishing marginal utility.[16] Fisher and Pareto had shown that indifference curves could be used to analyse demand but without showing that this made it possible to dispense with the Marshallian assumption. It was Hicks and Allen who did this.

*More radical approaches*

The use of indifference curves and ordinal utility indices enabled economists to dispense with utilitarianism. There were, however, economists who wished to go even further than this. One such was Cassel (1899, 1918a) who advocated a return to Cournot's approach of starting with demand functions. He argued that it was sufficient to assume "that the demand for each of the articles in question is settled as soon as the prices of these articles are fixed."[17] To analyse economic problems utility is superfluous, demand functions telling us all we need to know. A similar attitude was taken both by Barone (1908) and Moore (1914). In all his work on statistical demand curves, Moore found no help from utility theory.

The most significant exponent of this approach was, however, Samuelson (1938a) with his theory of revealed preference. Arguing that the hypothesis of a diminishing marginal rate of substitution introduced by Hicks and Allen was just as empty a concept as utility, Samuelson proposed to base consumer theory on a different set of assumptions, more directly related to observable behaviour. To do this he started from the same assumption as Cassel, Barone and Moore: that given the set of prices individuals choose to purchase certain commodities. Where Samuelson went further was in making the further assumption (the axiom of consistency) that when a consumer chooses a certain bundle of goods it can be inferred that he or she prefers this bundle to all other bundles which could have been chosen instead. This enabled Samuelson to derive all Hicks and Allen's results without using even indifference curves. With Samuelson's work, the movement towards stripping consumer theory of all inessentials, reducing it to a theory of choice, could be said to have reached its conclusion.

## 14.3   ECONOMIC EQUILIBRIUM

*1870–1914*

There is a sense in which the concept of an economic equilibrium, in which the prices and quantities are determined by the balancing of various forces, permeates the whole of classical economics, from Smith to Ricardo, Mill and Cairnes. This is not, however, the whole story, for two reasons. (1) The classical economists never gave a significant role to demand in determining equilibrium prices.[18] (2) From its origins in Smith's *Wealth of Nations* classical economics was permeated by a concern with growth and development, the result being that the development of a theory of static equilibrium was a subsidiary theme. It was only in the period after 1870 that a thoroughly worked out system of statics did emerge.[19]

The clearest statement of the nature of economic equilibrium was undoubtedly that of Walras. Though important aspects of it were perceived by both Jevons and Menger, neither developed the concept so thoroughly: Jevons was more concerned with the principle of utility; Menger with explaining the essence of value. Walras, on the other hand, was concerend above all with the interdependence of various markets, a concern which led naturally into an analysis of general equilibrium. Though Walras, like the classical economists, analysed the evolution of an economy over time he made it clear that such analysis was dependent on a prior analysis of static equilibrium.

More clearly than either his predecessors or his contemporaries, Walras provided a theory of general competitive equilibrium: firms were price takers, and in equilibrium earned only the normal rate of return on capital. Equilibrium prices were determined by on the one hand consumers' maximization of utility, and on the other by the technical coefficients describing the ability of firms to transform inputs into outputs. Although neglected in England, Walras obtained influential followers in Europe, the most important being Pareto and Wicksell. It was Pareto who removed the theory's dependence on utility, arguing that the essence of the problem of economic equilibrium was "the opposition between men's tastes and the obstacles to satisfying them".[20] Wicksell, on the other hand, integrated Walras's theory of equilibrium with Böhm-Bawerk's theory of capital, extending it to provide a marginal productivity theory of distribution.

Very different was the Marshallian approach, not so much because of Marshall's preference for partial as opposed to general equilibrium analysis, as because of his preference for a more realistic form of analysis. Being wary of excessive abstraction, Marshall's equilibrium was not the static, perfectly competitive equilibrium of Walras, Pareto and Wicksell: in it firms were continually evolving, old firms gradually being replaced by new; there were imperfections of competition; and some of the changes which occurred when firms moved along their supply curves were irreversible. Though not too much should be read into this, Marshall's use of the term "normal profit" rather than "zero profit" as his condition for market equilibrium is symptomatic of his approach. Furthermore, his preference for short chains of reasoning and his desire for realism worked against his analysing the logic of a general competitive equilibrium in the same way as his European contemporaries. His description of a full competitive equilibrium is brief, and in an appendix, not in the main text of the *Principles*.

Although changes were taking place even in Marshall's long period, there was in the background the notion of a full, stationary equilibrium, one in which events can be correctly anticipated an indefinite time beforehand. This was, however, a concept of which he was very critical, arguing

it is to this cause more than any other that we must attribute that simplicity and sharpness of outline, from which the economic doctrines in favour in the first half of this century derive some of their seductive charms as well as most of whatever tendency they may have to lead to false practical conclusions.[21]

Despite being critical of the assumption of a stationary state Marshall did generalize the concept to cover balanced growth, a lead taken up by Cassel. On the whole, however, the problem of dynamics was set aside.

There was also a third approach to the question of competitive equilibrium, one which though not influential at the time, became important in the 1950s. This was Edgeworth's analysis of competition in terms of bargaining. Starting with a bargain between two individuals he derived the contract curve, showing that the competitive equilibrium was one point on this curve. By gradually increasing the number of individuals involved in the bargain Edgeworth was able to show that as the size of the economy increased so the contract curve shrank towards the competitive equilibrium. Competitive equilibrium could thus be interpreted as the only feasible outcome in a bargain between an infinitely large number of individuals.

Despite the tendency to assume some sort of competition, whether the Walrasian "free competition" or the Marshallian "economic freedom", problems of monopoly and oligopoly were not neglected. Cournot's influence was pervasive. His theory of monopoly was taken over by Marshall, who extended it by a more thorough analysis of the structure of costs, and a recognition of the fact that static optimization may be inadequate to describe a monopolist's behaviour. In Schumpeter's words, Marshall

added little, if anything, to Cournot's analytic skeleton, but ... he developed from it ... an *economic analysis* that almost dwarfed both that skeleton and the technically superior performance of a later age.[22]

Cournot also influenced the period's discussion of oligopoly. His solution, involving the assumption that each of a pair of duopolists takes his rival's output as given, was criticized by many economists, in particular by Bertrand, Marshall and Edgeworth. Edgeworth's contribution is the most important here, for he showed that equilibrium would be indeterminate, a result which held not only when two firms produced the same good, but also when demands for their two, different, products were related.

These discussions of monopoly were never, however, integrated into the discussions of general economic equilibrium. Pareto rejected Walras's confining of pure economics to the study of perfect competition, aiming at greater generality. Despite this, however, he was unsuccessful in incorporating monopolistic elements into his general equilibrium analysis, this relating only to a competitive economy. Superficially, Marshall was more successful in dispensing with the over-simplification of perfect competition. This success was, however, to some extent more apparent than real, for it was only through his being imprecise about his exact assumptions that he was able to do this. The *formal skeleton* of his general equilibrium analysis was as reliant of the assumption of perfect competition as those of his contemporaries.

### Chamberlin's monopolistic competition

In the 1920s and 1930s considerable progress was made in the analysis of economic equilibrium, the most notable developments being those sometimes described by the phrase "the monopolistic competition revolution". Two works were particularly influential: Chamberlin's *Theory of Monopolistic Competition* (1933) and Robinson's *Economics of Imperfect Competition* (1933a). Common to both theories, although derived independently, were the use of marginal revenue curves and the so called "tangency condition": if there is free entry to a market, but firms face downward–sloping demand curves for their own products, equilibrium will be attained where each firm's demand curve is tangent to its average cost curve. This implies that in equilibrium there will typically be excess capacity, with firms operating below the output at which average cost is minimized. But despite these similarities, and despite the concern of both Chamberlin and Robinson with the general theory of value, their approaches were fundamentally *very* different.

Chamberlin's central concern was to extend Marshall's work to deal with market structures characterized by advertising and product differentiation. For Chamberlin, firms controlled not only the price of their product, but also its quality and the amount of effort they put into advertising and selling it. Chamberlin was led, therefore, to classify markets not merely according to the number of sellers, but *also* according to the degree to which firms' products were differentiated.[23] Product differentiation implied that each firm, however great the number of its competitors, would have a certain amount of monopoly power. In such a world of differentiated products the theory of monopoly, Chamberlin argued, will seem appropriate to explain the market for each firm's product. Competition, however, is not eliminated, for the behaviour of firms producing substitutes will affect demand for a monopolist's product.[24] Because each firm's product is different, there is no reason to expect that competition could ever eliminate monopoly altogether.

Several features of Chamberlin's approach are worth emphasizing. The first is the attention he paid to oligopoly. After arguing that competition and monopoly should not be separated, he turns, on the first page, to the theory of oligopoly.[25] In his discussion of oligopoly, the mutual dependence of oligopolists is emphasized. Monopolistic competition arises where the number of sellers is sufficiently large that such interdependence can be neglected. Secondly, the "tangency condition", to which so much attention has been paid, was, for Chamberlin, merely a special case. To obtain this special case it was necessary to make what he described as "certain heroic assumptions": in particular that each member of the group of firms being considered faced the same demand curve and the same cost conditions as other members of the group.[26] For Chamberlin, therefore, the tangency condition was used "mainly as an expositional device, of only limited direct applicability".[27] Thirdly, Chamberlin assumed that firms produce products which are genuinely different from the products of other firms. Thus monopolistic elements are not simply the result of irrational behaviour on the part of consumers. This meant that it was not possible to infer that monopolistic competition implied waste: perfect competition was not available in such a situation.

Chamberlin's work succeeded in showing that economists had to analyse a variety of market structures, not simply perfect competition and monopoly. It is on account of his destroying "the bold generalizations of Marshallian price theory" that Blaug concludes that "we are justified in speaking of a Chamberlinian Revolution in modern microeconomics in just the same way that we speak of a Keynesian Revolution in macroeconomics".[28] Chamberlin, however, never succeeded in providing a more general theory of value to supplant the competitive theory, for his theory remained at the level of partial equilibrium analysis. This point comes across most clearly if we consider Triffin's *Monopolistic Competition and General Equilibrium Theory* (1940) where he sees monopolistic competition theory as bridging the gap between the particular equilibrium analysis of Marshall, which focussed on the industry, and the Walrasian analysis, starting with the firm. Triffin claimed that monopolistic competition had abolished the "inner boundary" between the firm and the industry, going beyond Chamberlin in arguing that the concept of the industry, or "group" of firms, had to be dropped from value theory. There was, however, an inconsistency in this, for when, by abolishing the industry, the transition is made to a general equilibrium analysis, the macroeconomic implications of any changes have to be considered, something neither Chamberlin nor Triffin achieved.

*Robinson's imperfect competition*

Very different were the scope and purpose of Robinson's *Economics of Imperfect Competition*, as is evident from its opening words:

"Among persons interested in economic analysis, there are tool-makers and tool-users." This book is presented to the analytical economist as a box of tools. It is an essay in the technique of economic analysis and can make only an indirect contribution to our knowledge of the actual world.[29]

Thus where Chamberlin had been concerned with realism, his geometry being in a sense incidental to his main inquiry, geometric techniques were prominent in Robinson's book. Robinson, however, did not confine herself to providing a box of tools: she drew conclusions about the real world. Where she did this her approach bore no resemblance to Chamberlin's. Product differentiation made no appearance in her book. Instead she used her techniques to draw conclusions about welfare. Thus when she came to consider monopsony in the labour market she admitted that despite her professed concern to be providing no more than a box of tools, "The temptation to stray from the path of analysis and to offer reflections of a moral character is here too strong to be resisted."[30] This shift of emphasis was complete in her final chapter in which, as she put it, "we are no longer occupied with the theory of Value, and have stepped over into the province of the Economics of Welfare".[31] She linked her work explicitly to Pigou's welfare economics.

In complete contrast to Chamberlin, Robinson emphasized the inefficiencies which resulted under imperfect competition, and on the exploitation of labour, this being defined as the difference between the real wage rate and the value of the marginal product of labour. Either monopoly in the product market, or monopsony in the labour market, would result in exploitation.[32]

The immediate context out of which Robinson's work emerged was discussions of Marshall's theory which took place in the late 1920s. These discussions were not concerned with the realism of Marshall's construct so much as with its internal logical consistency. The major contributors to the destruction of Marshallian theory which took place were Sraffa (1926), Robbins (1928) and Pigou (1928b).

Sraffa's argument was that in the long run, neither increasing nor decreasing returns to scale were compatible with partial equilibrium analysis of competitive industry. If there were economies of scale, these must be internal to the industry (otherwise they would not affect the supply curve) but external to the firm (otherwise a firm could expand indefinitely until it dominated the market). Since this category of economies was, according to Sraffa, hardly ever encountered, there was no way increasing returns could be compatible with competition. As for decreasing returns, these could arise, in the long run, only through increasing factor costs. But if factor costs rose when output increased, this would raise costs in other industries, and through affecting prices in other industries would affect demand. This, however, would violate the assumption, central to Marshall's partial equilibrium analysis, that supply and demand were independent. So Sraffa concluded that returns to scale had to be constant, in which case a firm's output would be indeterminate. His solution to this problem was that economists needed to turn to the theory of monopoly.

Robbins' attack was on the concept of the representative firm. This was a device Marshall had used to deal with two types of problem: those arising from his supply curve not being a purely static construction (movements along the supply curve involved irreversible technical progress); and those arising from his assumption that each industry contained a variety of firms. The representative firm was a device used to ascertain how the industry would respond to a change in demand. It was not the average firm, but one judged to be typical in the relevant context. Robbins argued that not only was it difficult to recognize such a firm, for it was not an average which could be established statistically; but, more fundamentally, it contributed nothing to an understanding of economic equilibrium.

Why then, when we come to deal with long period profit doctrine and the differences of managerial and business ability, should we find it necessary to consider a firm, an entrepreneur of average or typical efficiency? Just as units of a given supply may be produced on lands of varying efficiency, so their production may be supervised by businessmen of varying ability. What is normal profit for one will not be normal profit for another, that is all. *There is no more need for us to assume a representative firm or representative producer, than there is for us to assume a representative piece of land, a representative machine, or a representative worker.* All that is necessary for equilibrium to prevail is that each factor shall get as much in one line of production as it could get in any other: as much, of course, including all advantages and disadvantages of work, hiring or investment.[33]

The crucial aspect of this argument is that Robbins is interpreting Marshallian economics in the context of a theory of static equilibrium. Such a change was apparent also in Pigou (1928), where Marshall's representative firm was replaced with the very different one of the "equilibrium firm". The equilibrium firm, for Pigou, was a firm such that if it were in equilibrium, the industry too would be in equilibrium. Although Pigou put this forward as a different way of describing Marshall's representative firm, it was a different concept.[34] From Pigou's equilibrium firm it was but a short step to replace Marshall's notion of the industry, comprising a spectrum of different firms, with the simpler concept of an industry made up of a set of identical firms.

The final attack on Marshallian theory came from Harrod and Robinson. Harrod (1930) distinguished between the firm's demand curve and the market demand curve, something necessary under neither monopoly nor perfect competition, after which he derived the marginal revenue curve, relating it to price by the formula: $MR = P (1 - 1/e)$ where $e$ is the elasticity of demand.[35] Harrod noted [36] that this implies the breakdown of supply and demand analysis, for if the firm produces an output such that marginal revenue equals marginal cost, supply will depend not simply on price but also on the elasticity of demand. This point was taken up by Robinson (1932, 1933a) who argued that there was no way of salvaging the notion of a supply curve for an industry. The effect of a shift in demand on output would depend on how it affected the elasticity of demand for each firm in the industry.[37] The basis of Marshallian economics, namely the concept of a long period normal price dependent on supply and demand, was undermined.

Important though these results were, it can be argued that far more significant was Robinson's method. As were the articles of Robbins (1928) and Pigou (1928), *The Economics of Imperfect Competition* was an exercise in the theory of static equilibrium, premised on the assumption that "each individual acts in a sensible manner ... from the point of view of his economic interests".[38] Where Marshall had found a place for other motives, even altruism, Robinson postulated simple profit maximization:

It is the assumption that any individual, in his economic life, will never undertake an action that adds more to his losses than to his gains, and will always undertake an action which adds more to his gains than to his losses, *which makes the analysis of value possible.* ... With bricks of this *one simple pattern* the whole structure of analysis is built up.[39]

This approach is closer to Austrian equilibrium analysis than to Marshall's "realistic" approach.

Robinson's simplifying assumptions simply cast aside many of the problems dear to Marshall, her analysis being conducted at a much higher level of abstraction. By way of explanation she pointed out that, though she did sometimes stray from this narrow path, her purpose was not to tackle real world problems, but to provide a "box of tools" for economists to use. In this she succeeded, her tools being the standard fare of contemporary microeconomics textbooks. The contrast between the old and the new methods is clearly revealed in an exchange between Shove and Robinson in the 1933 *Economic Journal*. Shove writes:

So long as we are content with a rough and ready indication of the forces at work, we can keep fairly near to the facts: but any attempt to make our treatment exact is apt to lead either to a degree of abstraction which renders the analysis inapplicable to the actual phenomena we set out to explain or to a degree of complication which makes it cumbrous to use.[40]

Robinson's reply acknowledges the fundamental difference in approach:

Indeed it is obvious that his realistic method of analysis and my highly formalised method do not operate in the same *terrain*, and any argument which turns upon the *results* obtained from such different sets of assumptions must in the nature of the case be idle[41]

Although this change in method had far reaching implications for the development of economic theory, it can be viewed in sharply contrasting ways. One interpretation[42] stresses the failure of the "new establishment" to deal with the vitally important problems of time, information and uncertainty with which Marshall had at least tried to grapple. The limitations of his approach can be put down to "methodological difficulties which could not be solved, only lived with".[43] Concern with an internally consistent model of economic equilibrium is potentially dangerous, since the conditions under which it will be possible to make generalizations about the factors determining equilibrium will never be met. Economists, on the other hand, whose first priority is the internal consistency of a theory, even if this implies making assumptions which go against empirical observation, view the change in method rather differently. Samuelson, for example, though he criticizes those economists who made such a fuss about "discovering" marginal revenue in the 1930s, has written scathingly about Marshall's approach.[44]

## Oligopoly

The attention which has been paid to imperfect competition should not be allowed to obscure the fact that in the 1920s and 1930s oligopoly received considerable attention. Chamberlin's interest in oligopoly has already been noted. The starting point for most discussions of oligopoly, as for that of Chamberlin, noted above, was the duopoly models of Cournot, Bertrand and Edgeworth.[45] A concept which helped to clarify the differences between various models was that of "conjectural variation": the amount by which a duopolist conjectures that his rival will alter her output should he increase his own output by one unit.[46] Cournot had assumed conjectural variations to be zero, but other assumptions can be made to give an immense variety of results. Of particular interest is Stackelberg's model (1933), in which one duopolist (the follower) has a conjectural variation of zero, whilst the other (the leader) takes as her conjectural variation the amount by which the follower will actually change his output.

The theory which gained the widest support was that of the kinked demand curve. This was implicit in Chamberlin's analysis, for he had distinguished two demand curves, one in which the industry's output was held constant when a firm changed its price, the other in which other firms varied their output. It was not far from these two, intersecting, demand curves to the kinked demand curve. The kinked demand curve was explicit in Robinson's *Economics of Imperfect Competition* (1933a).[47] The theory, however, received wide attention only with its appearance in 1939 in the work of Sweezy (in the US) and Hall and Hitch (in the UK),[48] even though their interpretation of it was no different from that of Robinson. In 1947 Stigler was able to claim that this theory had gained wide acceptance, some economists making it *the* theory of oligopoly price.[49]

The crucial assumption is that oligopolists expect competitors to match price cuts, but not price rises, which means that firms' demand curves will be less elastic for a fall in price than for a rise, the demand curve being kinked at the current price. Apart from its simplicity the theory had several features in its favour. (1) Through causing the marginal revenue curve to be discontinuous at the current price it explained why oligopolists' prices would be insensitive to changes in demand or costs. Sweezy went further, using the theory to explain why prices would be more likely to rise in response to an increase in demand, than to fall in response to a fall. (2) It was possible to relate the theory to evidence which Hall and Hitch obtained from a survey of businessmen's pricing policies. This showed that business-men neither understood the concept of the elasticity of demand, nor considered it relevant to their pricing decisions. On the other hand, there was a belief that price cuts, but not price rises, would be matched by competitors.

### Perfect competition

In contrast with the theory of imperfect competition, the theory of competitive equilibrium was comparatively well worked out by 1914. Several important developments nonetheless occurred in the period up to 1939.

One development was work on the conditions required for the existence of a competitive equilibrium. The stimulus here came from Cassel's (1918a) reformulation of Walras's system of equations describing a general competi-tive equilibrium. It can be argued that Cassel's system of equations contributed little in itself, its significance resting solely in the research it stimulated. Three papers appearing in 1932–1933 showed that the problem of the existence of an equilibrium required more than the counting of equations.[50] Neisser (1932) showed that equilibrium prices might be negative; whilst Stackelberg (1933) showed that if there were fewer commodities than factors there might be no set of outputs such that all factors were fully employed. But arguably more important was the contribution of Zeuthen (1933) who pointed out the necessity of modifying the supply = demand equilibrium condition by allowing for the possibility that the supply of a commodity might exceed the demand in equilibrium, provided that the price of the commodity was zero. Once this modification was introduced Neisser's and Stackelberg's problems vanished. It was at the same time that the first steps were taken towards the more rigorous treatment of the problem of existence characteristic of modern theory. The need for this was perceived by Schlesinger (1933), the proofs of existence being supplied by a mathematician, Wald, who analysed the problem for a variety of models, including Cassel's model, and a model of pure exchange.

Although, however, the concept of competitive equilibrium was widely used, the notion of *perfect* competition arose only in the 1920s and 1930s, for it was only as economists tackled imperfect competition that perfect competition was properly defined.[51] It was Pigou (1928b) who first drew the now familiar U-shaped average cost curve with its associated marginal revenue curve, and who defined perfect competition in terms of equality of price with both marginal and average costs. The concept of perfect competition arose naturally out of the theory of imperfect competition: if an industry is made up of firms with identical cost conditions, and if the number of firms is sufficiently large for firms' demand curves to be completely elastic, the result is perfect competition. Perfect competition was thus a limiting case of imperfect competition. In Chamberlin's world where firms all produce different outputs, the concept of perfect competi-tion arises less easily.

Although the concept of perfect competition, with its set of identical firms in equilibrium with horizontal demand curves tangential to identical U-shaped average cost curves, originated only with Chamberlin and Robinson, it can be argued that the essentials of this model were implicit, as was so much else, in the work of Cournot (1838). Of the economists considered in section II above, the one who was interested in the relation of firms to markets was Marshall. Marshall, however, chose to go in a different direction. His contemporaries, on the other hand, though they developed the theory of competitive equilibrium, were interested in issues other than that of the relationship of the firm to the industry. Thus, although it is correct to speak of a well-developed theory of competitive equilibrium before 1914, it is less correct to describe this as a theory of perfect competition in the modern sense.

Finally we come to Hicks's *Value and Capital* (1939a), a work which did much to revive interest in general equilibrium theory, not least because it explained general equilibrium theory in terms accessible to the non-mathematician. In this book Hicks concentrated on the case of perfect competition. His reasons for this were stated exceptionally clearly. After considering the equilibrium of a monopolist, he writes:

So far, so good; yet it has to be recognised that a general abandonment of the assumption of perfect competition, a universal adoption of the assumption of monopoly, must have very destructive consequences for economic theory. Under monopoly the stability conditions become indeterminate; and the basis on which economic laws can be constructed is therefore shorn away. ... It is, I believe, only possible to save anything from this wreck – and it must be remembered that the threatened wreckage is the greater part of general equilibrium theory – if we can assume that the markets confronting most of the firms with which we shall be dealing do not differ very greatly from perfectly competitive markets. ... We must be aware, however, that we are taking a dangerous step. ... Personally, however, I doubt if most of the problems we shall have to exclude for this reason are capable of much useful analysis by the methods of economic theory.[52]

Hicks saw the main contribution of *Value and Capital* as lying in its attempt to combine the static analysis of Pareto with the dynamics of the Swedish economists, in particular Myrdal and Lindahl, whose influence on him was strong.[53] The first part of the book was concerned with presenting the theory of static equilibrium, reworking the Paretian theory of equilibrium in terms of the new consumer theory he had developed with Allen. Of particular importance was his analysis of stability, which related stability to the amount of complementarity in the economy. When it came to dynamics, Hicks adopted Lindahl's approach of studying a temporary equilibrium, one in which the stock of capital and the state of expectations were given. Any one period was linked to the past by the capital stock it inherited, and to the future by expectations. In this context Hicks was able to bring in problems of capital, interest and money, and was able to analyse the stability of the economic system as a whole.

Although Hicks saw the link between statics and dynamics as crucial, it was his interpretation of Keynes' *General Theory* as a miniature, aggregative general equilibrium model that attracted more attention. In his review of the *General Theory* (1936) Hicks singled out Keynes' "method of expectations", comparing it with the method of Myrdal and Lindahl, whilst in his famous article "Mr. Keynes and the classics" (1937) he expounded the *General Theory* as a general equilibrium model with four markets: those for goods, money, bonds and labour. These ideas were taken further in *Value and Capital*, parts of which were strongly influenced by Keynes.

## 14.4 PRODUCTION AND DISTRIBUTION

*Marginal productivity*

It can legitimately be argued that marginal productivity theory as it is now understood dates from the last two decades of the nineteenth century. The idea of marginal productivity was not in itself new: the Ricardian theory of rent was a marginal productivity theory; and important aspects of marginal productivity theory can be found in Mill and, above all, Thünen. In addition, the work of both Jevons and Menger contains several important elements of marginal productivity. But several important developments occurred in the 1880s and 1890s, developments which served to transform marginal productivity theory into something qualitatively different from previous versions: (i) the concept of the production function emerged out of the classical laws of returns; (ii) marginal productivity became generalized to apply to all factors; and (iii) these developments permitted the production function to be set alongside the utility function, with factor prices being determined in substantially the same manner as prices of products. It was as a result of the extension and generalization of marginal ideas in this way that marginal analysis became generally accepted. Until the 1890s, despite the work of Jevons, Menger and Walras, classical influence was still strong.

*The controversy over wages*

"The great social question" concerning the relationship of capital and labour was a burning issue in the second half of the nineteenth century, in both England and the United States. The classical economists had used the wages fund theory to argue that wages were determined irrespective of the actions of either capitalists or trades unions, this providing the wage fund theory with a practical significance exceeding its significance in classical theory as a whole. It was because of this that Mill's "recantation" in 1869 caused such a stir. But the wage fund survived even Mill's recantation for not only did Cairnes, amongst others, continue to support it, but there was no agreed doctrine to replace it.

It was through the controversy which took place over the wages fund in the 1880s and 1890s that many of the most important contributions to marginal productivity theory emerged. The starting point for this debate was Walker's writings on the wages fund in the mid 1870s. Sidgwick, in a review (1879) of Walker's *The Wages Question* (1876) challenged Walker to produce a positive theory to replace the wage fund theory, to which Walker responded in 1887, this setting off an extensive debate, in particular in the pages of the *Quarterly Journal of Economics*, a debate in which both American and British economists took part.[54] Many aspects of the debate are no longer interesting, but two aspects are, for they illustrate the changes which took place at this time in the theory of static equilibrium.

It came to be accepted that the time element was crucial, for defence of the wages fund involved assuming a lag in the production process analogous to the lag between input (sowing) and output (harvest) in an agricultural economy. A variety of economists defended the wages fund on the ground that this time dimension to the economic process could not be neglected. Indeed, only two economists denied such a lag and rejected the wages fund theory altogether: Clark and Marshall, and of these Marshall took a long time to emancipate himself from the concept.[55] Despite the enormous influence of Clark and Marshall, however, few economists in the 1880s and early 1890s went along with their rejection of the time element in production. Yet by the mid 1890s the wages fund was a dead issue. How did this come about? One explanation is the growth of marginal productivity theory, which enabled the problem of wage determination to be treated as a problem in statics. The other was Böhm-Bawerk's theory of capital, as a result of which the problem of time came to be seen as a problem in capital theory rather than the economics of wages. Discussions of time simply dropped out of the discussion of wages.

But perhaps the most important aspect of this controversy is that it is out of it that important contributions to marginal productivity theory emerged. Three papers are of particular importance. Wood (1888, 1889), in arguing that demand for labour was, like anything else, a function of price, worked out the essence of a marginal productivity theory of distribution, but was largely neglected.[56] And in 1891 Hobson and Clark, as the titles of their articles, "The law of the three rents" and "Distribution as determined by a law of rent", suggest, explicitly generalized the theory of rent to apply to all factors, not simply land.

Although outside the mainstream of academic discussion, there is a side to the discussion of distribution that cannot be neglected – Henry George's *Progress and Poverty* (1879). George was concerned to argue that the problem of rent, and the unearned increment of land value, was the principal social problem of the time. To deal with it he advocated the use of a single tax – a tax on rents. Although he contributed little, if anything, to economic analysis,[57] his ideas stirred up a ferment of popular discussion, not only in the US, his home, but also in Britain.[58] It is partly due to George's influence that discussions of rent were so widespread at this time.

*Marginal productivity and the production function*

Though English economists were active and important participants in the debates over the wages fund this was primarily an American controversy, in that not only was it conducted primarily in American journals, but also in that most of the participants were American. Overlapping these discussions, however, was another debate, involving primarily European economists, one which examined marginal productivity theory in rather a different way.

In the same way that the first American statement of marginal productivity theory, that of Wood, was neglected, so too were the earliest European statements: those of Berry (1891) and Edgeworth (1889). Berry's contribution is worth summarizing in some detail. He writes down a production function, $f(g_1, g_2, \ldots l_1, l_2, \ldots c)$ giving a firm's output as a function of the inputs of different types of land ($g_k$), different types of labour ($l_j$) and capital. This is then used to derive marginal productivity equations for each factor:

$$p_i df_i/dg_k = r_k$$
$$p_i df_i/dl_j = w_j$$
$$p_i df_i/dc = i$$

$p_i$, $r_k$, $w_j$, and $i$ being the prices of output, rents of land, wage rates and the interest rate. These equations are then supplemented by demand equations for goods, supply equations for factors and the condition that all factors are fully used. The result of this was a general equilibrium system with as many equations as unknowns. Capital, labour and land were treated symmetrically, leading to the following, anti-Ricardian conclusion:

There is no more justification for assuming wages to be measured by the produce of the labourer working on the margin *without capital* than for assuming interest to be measured by an amount of capital *without labour*.[59]

In view of subsequent discussion it is worth noting Berry's method of ensuring exhaustion of the product: any difference between the value of the output and the value of the inputs constituted a surplus, appropriated by the entrepreneur. Competition would equalize the surplus received by entrepreneurs of equal ability.

Two features of Berry's work, his symmetric treatment of factors, and his treatment of marginal productivity as part of the general theory of value, are even more explicit in the book which aroused the greatest controversy in the 1890s: Wicksteed's *Essay on the Co-ordination of the laws of Distribution* (1984). After a preface in which he extolled the virtues of a mathematical approach making the production function explicit, he states his case very clearly:

In investigating the laws of distribution it has been usual to take each of the great factors of production such as Land, Capital and Labour, severally, to enquire into the special circumstances under which that factor co-operates in production, the special considerations which act upon the persons that have control of it, and from all these considerations to deduce a special law regulating the share of the product that will fall in distribution to that particular factor.

Now as long as this method is pursued it seems impossible to co-ordinate the laws of distribution and ascertain whether or not the shares which the theory assigns to the several factors cover the product and are covered by it. ... As long as the law of rent, for example, is based on the objective standard of the fertility of land, while the law of interest is based on the subjective standard of estimate of the future as compared with the present, it is difficult even to conceive any calculus by which the share of land and the share of capital could be added together and an investigation then instituted as to whether the residual share will coincide with what the theory assigns as the share of wages. But it is obvious that such a co-ordination must be within the purview of economic theory.[60]

As for the method used, he points out that "the modern investigations into the theory of value" provide this, "the law of exchange value [being itself] the law of distribution of the general resources of society".[61]

Where Wicksteed went beyond other authors, and where controversy arose, was in his attempt to show that factor shares determined by marginal productivity would completely and exactly exhaust the product if the production function exhibited constant returns to scale, or linear homogeneity.[62] His proof of this was rather clumsy, but was improved upon by a reviewer, Flux (1894) who, for the first time, used Euler's theorem to analyse the problem, an approach which has now become standard.

Reaction to Wicksteed's theory was mixed. Amongst continental economists Barone, Pareto and Walras were very hostile, attacking the assumptions of linear homogeneity, and full substitutability of factors of production. These criticisms were echoed by Edgeworth. Many of their criticisms were misconceived, but some progress was made. In particular Barone derived a product exhaustion theorem from the assumptions that (i) firms minimize cost, and (ii) cost and selling price are equal.[63] Marshall too was critical, but in a more guarded manner. He had been using marginal productivity ideas since his *Economics of Industry* in 1879, but he warned against thinking that marginal productivity could provide more than a part of a theory of wages because it analysed only factor demand. Despite this apparent hostility, however, successive editions of the *Principles* conceded more and more to the marginal productivity theory. For example, Wicksteed's theory about product exhaustion was incorporated into the third edition. The main contribution towards developing the marginal productivity theory came, however, not from Wicksteed's critics, but from his most consistent supporter, Wicksell.[64] Wicksell approached the problem by asking whether it mattered whether the landowner was the entrepreneur, hiring the workers, or whether the workers were the entrepreneurs, renting the land. But his main contributions were twofold: (i) he saw increasing, decreasing and constant returns not as alternatives but as applying to different regions of the production function. Thus Wicksteed's theory applied not because returns were constant throughout, but because firms moved to the portion of the production function exhibiting constant returns to scale. (ii) He argued that product exhaustion was an equilibrium condition rather than a condition which would be satisfied all the time. This interpretation was later endorsed by Hicks in his *Theory of Wages* (1932).

It was out of these discussions that the concept of the production function emerged, its derivatives describing the classical laws of returns. Nowadays these ideas may seem obvious, but this was not the case at the time, as is evidenced by the confusions abounding in many of the contributions made by otherwise distinguished economists. One reason, perhaps, for the controversy was Wicksteed's attempt to explain too much in terms of a single property of the production function. This accounts for Edgeworth's comment,

There is a magnificence in this generalization which recalls the youth of philosophy. Justice is a perfect cube, said the ancient sage; and rational conduct is a homogeneous function, adds the modern *savant*.[6]

Wicksteed did not have a proper theory of the firm and, as Wicksell later showed, an understanding of the theory of the firm was crucial to an understanding of Wicksteed's product exhaustion theorem.

So far the term production function has been used as though it referred to a single concept, but this is not the case. A production function can, at one extreme, refer to the function relating a single firm's output to a detailed list of all the inputs it uses. At the other extreme the concept relates to a whole economy, relating total social production to broad aggregates of land, labour and capital. The aggregation involved in the latter, both across firms and across factors, makes it a very different, and much more problematic, concept than the non-aggregative micro production function. We have seen Berry's use of the production function to describe the firm's production possibilities, a usage shared by Marshall and Walras, the only major economists of the period, according to Schumpeter, who were entirely free of the notion of an aggregate production function. Of the other authors discussed above, Clark, Wicksteed, and Wicksell argued explicitly in terms of an aggregate production function.

The classic statements of a marginal productivity theory of distribution based explicitly on an aggregative social production function came in the 1930s: Hicks' *Theory of Wages* (1932) and Douglas's *Theory of Wages* (1934). Using an aggregate production function Hicks analysed distributive shares in terms of the newly-developed concept of the elasticity of substitution. The elasticity or substitution, which measures the curvature of an isoquant at any point, determines whether an increase in, for example, labour will increase or reduce the share of labour in national income. As was also the case with Douglas's theory, this theory provided a very clear account of a static, aggregative marginal productivity theory of distribution. Douglas, along with his collaborator, Cobb, used the specific form of production function that has come to be named after them: $Y = AK^\alpha L^{1-\alpha}$.[66] Because the Cobb–Douglas production function has an elasticity of substitution equal to one, factor shares will be determined solely by the parameter $\alpha$ of the production function. This function formed the basis for Douglas's extensive econometric research on the distribution of income.

## 14.5   CAPITAL AND INTEREST

In the theories of distribution discussed above the share of capital is determined by its marginal product, but this makes no sense until we have defined what we mean by capital, and how it enters the production function. This was the subject of enormous controversy, especially in the closing decades of the nineteenth century when Böhm-Bawerk and Clark advocated diametrically opposed conceptions of capital, and in the 1930s when the main protagonists were Hayek and Knight. In both periods controversy centred on whether production should be viewed as a process in which inputs were applied at different dates, capital being measured by the average period for which resources were invested in the production process; or whether production should be viewed as a synchronous process, the current stock of capital and the current stock of labour determining the current level of output. Böhm-Bawerk and Wicksell were the outstanding advocates of the former view; Clark of the latter.

### Böhm-Bawerk and Wicksell

The idea of looking at production as a process involving time has a long history. We find in Ricardo the idea that the value of a commodity is made up of the value of labour input (this comprising both labour used directly and labour used indirectly, the latter being "stored up" in capital), plus an interest charge proportional to the time between the application of the inputs and the production of the output. Indeed, this, together with the fact that production processes for different goods were of different lengths, was one of the reasons why the labour theory of value would not work. It was a view of capital even more clearly specified by Jevons, who went so far as to write down a function relating output to the average period of production (the average time for which labour is invested), obtaining the rate of interest as the derivative of this function: the rate of interest was the marginal product of a lengthening of the period of production. The economist who, above all others, is associated with this theory is, however, Böhm-Bawerk, who advocated it in two widely read books: *History and Critique of Interest Theories* (1884) and, above all, *Positive Theory of Capital* (1889), both translated into English soon after publication (1890 and 1891 respectively).

There were two reasons, apart from the nature of the theory itself, why Böhm-Bawerk's work was so extensively criticized. One was that the quality of his insights far exceeded the quality of his technique. He made technical blunders onto which his critics could fasten. Schumpeter claimed that when all the necessary corrections were introduced into Böhm-Bawerk's theory nothing was left of it except the essential idea.[67] The other reason for criticism of Böhm-Bawerk was that he mixed together two rather different objectives: to provide a causal explanation of interest; and to provide a model in which, given the supply of labour and the stock of the means of subsistence, the rate of interest, wage rates and the period of production were simultaneously determined. These two parts of his theory will be considered in turn, but before that we need to examine his concept of the period of production.

Though Böhm-Bawerk held to a physical concept of capital (the stock of intermediate, including subsistence, goods) he did not regard capital as a third factor to be placed alongside labour and land, the two "original" factors, the stocks of which were determined by non-economic factors. Capital was, for Böhm-Bawerk, productive because it permitted the adoption of more roundabout methods of production, which increased the output from the "original" factors. He assumed that the adoption of more roundabout methods involved an increase in the average time for which capital was invested. Because it leads to more roundabout methods being used, an increase in the period of production, which Böhm-Bawerk used as his measure of the capital stock, would raise the productivity of the two original factors, labour and land, but it would do so at a diminishing rate. The function of capital was to increase the productivity of the other fasctors of production. Competition would ensure that these received not their marginal products, but the discounted values of their marginal products, the remainder constituting interest.

This raises the question of why, if capital is productive, and if its supply is not fixed by non-economic factors, the period of production should not be extended indefinitely, to the point where interest disappeared. Böhm-Bawerk adduced three reasons – his "reasons for interest":

(i)   different circumstances of want and provision in the present and the future (if people expect to be better off in the future they will value present consumption more highly than future consumption);

(ii)  undervaluation of the future (myopia, limited will power or the uncertainty of life);

(iii) the technical superiority of present over future goods (the greater productivity of longer production processes).

Though Böhm-Bawerk claimed that these were three independent reasons for interest, it can be argued, as did Fisher,[68] that the third is not: the rate of interest depends on supply and demand for loans, but Böhm-Bawerk's third reason affects only demand. Together, however, the three reasons do provide an explanation of interest.

Finally we come to Böhm-Bawerk's explanation of how the interest rate is determined. His starting point is the assertion that "The exchange of present goods for future goods, which constitutes the source of the phenomena of interest, is merely one special case under the rubric of exchange of goods in general."[69] So he starts, following Menger, with isolated exchange, where the price of a loan will be set somewhere between its value to each of the two individuals involved. But of more interest is his explanation of interest under market conditions. The main points here are illustrated by his simplest case, which is worth examining in some detail. He makes the assumption that capitalists are the sole suppliers and demanders of funds, and that workers are the only consumers. Thus the sole function of the subsistence fund is to provide for wages. Rather than use his numerical examples, however, we will use Figure 14.1 which

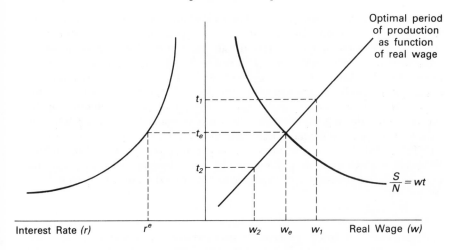

FIGURE 14.1 *Böhm-Bawerk's Theory of Interest*

represents graphically the relationships Böhm-Bawerk assumed. Three curves need to be considered. (i) As the real wage increases, so the optimal (profit maximizing) period of production will increase: at higher real wage rates firms will wish to use more capital-intensive methods. (ii) Corresponding to this is an inverse relationship between the interest rate and the period of production: as the production becomes more capital-intensive, so the marginal product of capital falls. (iii) Finally there is the condition that the stock of subsistence goods should equal the number of workers multiplied by the real wage rate times the period of production. Suppose the real wage were too high, say $w_1$.[70] The optimal period of production will rise to $t_1$, implying a low rate of interest (not marked). Given this long period of production, however, a stock of subsistence amounting to $w_1 t_1 N$ would be required. This is greater than $S$ (i.e. the point $t_1$, $w_1$ is to the right of $S/N=wt$). This means that capitalists will be unable to employ the whole labour force, and so the real wage rate will be bid down. Given the fixed subsistence fund employment will then be less than the supply of labour, so the real wage will be bid down. Similarly if the real wage were too low, say $w_2$, only a part ($w_2 t_2 N$) of the subsistence fund would be employed, so the real wage would be bid up. Three factors, therefore, determine the rate of interest:

1) The magnitude of the subsistence fund [$S$];
2) The number of workers the fund must support [$N$];
3) The gradation in the scale of increasing productivity that accompanies prolongation of the production period [the shape of the curves relating $r$, $w$ and $t$][71]

The staunchest defender of this theory was Wicksell, who did more than clear up technical blemishes and provide a more elegant exposition, true as both of these are. His main achievement was to integrate Böhm-Bawerk's theory with the Walrasian theory of general equilibrium, and to incorporate land as well as labour into the theory of capital and interest. But even Wicksell did not manage to clear up all the technical problems involved with this view of capital. Indeed, through his discovery of what is now called the "Wicksell effect" he opened up a path for later generations of critics of Böhm-Bawerk's and other theories of capital. Wicksell used this effect, whereby a change in the supply of capital causes a revaluation of the capital stock, altering the units in which it is measured, to explain why the marginal product of capital would usually be less than the rate of interest. The full significance of this, however, was not appreciated until the 1950s. Wicksell, for example, despite his good formal theory, ended up assuming that the marginal product of capital was equal to the rate of interest.[72]

## Clark

Fundamental to Clark's criticism of Böhm-Bawerk, as well as to his own view of capital, is the distinction between capital as a fund of value, and capital goods. Capital is, according to Clark, "a permanent fund of productive wealth, expressible in money" but embodied in capital goods. In a stationary economy there will be a constant fund of capital, but the concrete capital goods in which this is embodied are continually changing: capital goods are wearing out and being replaced by others. He uses the analogy of a waterfall:

A water-fall consists in particles of water. Can one say the same things of the fall that he does of the water? The water moves; the fall stays where it is. The water appears in globules condensed in the atmosphere, and it ultimately merges itself in the sea. The fall does not appear nor disappear. Capital goods are, like particles of water, vanishing elements. True capital is like the fall; it is an abiding element, owing its continuance to the constant wasting and replenishing of its substance.[73]

Whereas Böhm-Bawerk looked at individual capital goods, each of which has a period of production, Clark argued that the capital fund was far more important, having no periods but acting incessantly. Furthermore, where Jevons and Böhm-Bawerk saw the essence of capital as permitting production to be spread out over time, Clark argued the reverse: capital permits different stages of the productive process to be carried on simultaneously.

Though Clark and Böhm-Bawerk were advocating radically different views of capital they had one thing in common: both tried to measure capital by a single number, whether the period of production or the value of the capital fund. Both used highly aggregative models of production. It can be shown, as was done in the 1960s, that similar criticisms are applicable to both theories: in circumstances where the period of production fails, so too does Clark's concept of the capital stock.

## Cassel

A third approach to the theory of capital was the one adopted by Marshall, and later in *The Nature and Necessity of Interest* (1901) by Cassel, namely to define capital in such a way that it could be regarded as an original factor of production, standing alongside land and labour. The independent, or primary factor to which capital corresponded was found in "abstinence" (Marshall) or "waiting" (Cassel). For all his stress on time preference this was something Böhm-Bawerk had refused to do, seeing land and labour as the only two primary factors. Cassel's argument was that waiting had to be regarded as an independent factor: it could not be reduced to more elementary factors; and it could be substituted for other factors.[74] The interest rate was a price, determined by same factors as the price of any other good, arising because waiting was scarce, while its outcome (saving) was in demand for capital investment. To determine the rate of interest it was necessary simply to look at the demand and supply of waiting.

## Fisher

Fisher too acknowledged a debt to Böhm-Bawerk, for while he objected to the latter's assumption that longer processes were more productive than shorter ones, he accepted most of the rest of his theory. Fisher's solution to the problem of interest, taking into account Böhm-Bawerk's discussion of time and the provision for wants at different times in the future, was

that the rate of interest depends on the character of the income stream, – its size, composition, probability, and above all its distribution in time. It might be called a theory of *prospective provision of income*.[75]

This theory was expounded in *The Rate of Interest* (1907), later revised as *The Theory of Interest* (1930). His earlier work is also important, however. In *The Nature of Capital and Income* (1906) he defined capital value as the discounted present value of a future income stream. The rate of interest was the price linking the flow of income with the stock of capital value. And in *Appreciation and Interest* (1896) he investigated the distinction between real and nominal interest rates.

Fisher developed his theory in three stages. In the first he assumed that the income stream facing each individual was given. Given the rate of interest the consumer has to choose a consumption stream with the same present value as the given income stream, a point Fisher illustrated with the now-familiar diagram shown as Figure 14.2 (at this stage consider only the budget line and the indifference curves). The difference between income and consumption is the individual's demand or supply of loans, this depending on the interest rate. Market equilibrium requires that the interest rate be such as to equate demand and supply of loans in the market as a whole.

Borrowing and lending as in the example above are not the only ways of altering the income stream: the owner of "capital-wealth" has alternative uses to which he may put it. In Clark's terms, the capital fund may correspond to different physical capital goods, each of which yields a different income stream. Fisher, however, recognized that, "when an income stream is modified by a change in the use of the capital yielding it, its present value may not remain the same.".[76] For Fisher, unlike Clark, the

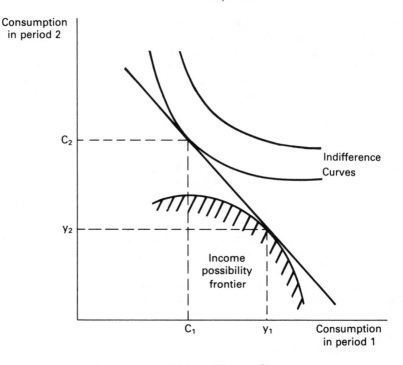

FIGURE 14.2  *Fisher's Theory of Interest*

value of the capital stock could not be regarded as a given factor of production. Given the ability to change the income stream through changing the use of the capital stock, which Fisher illustrated with the income possibility frontier shown in Figure 14.2, and the rate of interest, an individual's optimum will be that shown in Figure 14.2. As in the previous case demands and supplies of loans can be calculated for all the individuals in the economy, the equilibrium interest rate occurring where these sum to zero.

Finally there is the third stage where uncertainty is introduced. Fisher argues that the market will become segmented, different interest rates applying to different degrees of security and to different time periods. In addition, risk will increase time preference. But despite this Fisher failed to provide a detailed analysis to match his discussion of the determination of interest under certainty. He contented himself with arguing that risk introduced disturbing influences into the static scheme: for example, not all borrowers and lenders would face the same interest rate, and so their rates of time preference would differ. His conclusion, in *The Theory of Interest*, is worth quoting at length, for it indicates his view of what economic theory is capable of doing, and his view as to the limitations of economic analysis.

We must, therefore, give up as a bad job any attempt to formulate completely the influences which really determine the rate of interest. ... In short, the theory of interest in this book merely covers the simple rational part of the causes actually in operation. The other or disturbing causes are those incapable of being so simply and rationally formulated.[77]

Study of these disturbing causes had to be empirical and statistical, not rational and theoretical.

In conclusion, two further things are worth noting about Fisher's theory. In *The Theory of Interest* the analysis of production was supplemented by the important concept of the rate of return over cost, substantially identical to Keynes' marginal efficiency of capital. This is a concept founded on the notion, central to Fisher's work, of capital as the present value of an income stream. It was not a physical rate of return on capital, but a variable determined by comparing two streams of income. The second point is that, in contrast to the theories of both Clark and Böhm-Bawerk, Fisher's theory is microeconomic. Though, like Clark, he views capital as a fund of value, the similarity ends there: there is nothing of Clark's social capital in Fisher's work; nor anything paralleling Böhm-Bawerk's period of production.

*Schumpeter and Knight*

The only aspect of profits considered so far has been interest. Pure profits do not appear in static equilibrium because entrepreneurial activity reduces them to zero. The fact that entrepreneurial profits are zero in static equilibrium, however, does not mean that they are unimportant. J. B. Clark, for example, had argued that whilst entrepreneurial profits were a dynamic phenomenon, occurring only in disequilibrium, they were important because it was the prospect of such profits which provided the incentive to innovate. The economist who placed the greatest stress on this, however, was Schumpeter. Schumpeter, in his *Theory of Economic Development* (1912) argued that without innovations and technical change an economy would eventually settle down to a stationary state in which there was no uncertainty about the future. It is innovations which disturb this situation, these leading to unforeseen opportunities for profit.[78]

A similar view was later taken up by Knight in *Risk, Uncertainty and Profit* (1921), who used uncertainty, in a carefully defined sense, to explain not interest but pure profit, the surplus above the costs of all factors of production. He distinguished two types of uncertainty: a *measurable* uncertainty (such as in games of chance) which he called risk, and an *unmeasurable* uncertainty which, he argued, constituted true uncertainty. True uncertainty, when people do not know what they are doing, is the essence of profits, but as people learn, this uncertainty will be reduced, and with it profits.

*Hayek and Knight*

Debate over the theory of capital re-emerged in the 1930s, the stimulus being Hayek's *Prices and Production* (1931). In this book Hayek used the

Böhm-Bawerkian theory of capital as part of an explanation of the trade cycle. The characteristic of a cyclical upswing was seen to be a lengthening of the period of production, caused by a primarily monetary expansion. When monetary expansion ceased, according to Hayek, a crisis would emerge because long, capital-intensive production processes would become unprofitable and would be stopped. The result would be over-production of investment goods relative to consumption goods, unemployment emerging until labour could be redeployed.[79] Though it can be argued that the crucial factor here is the inflexibility of the capital stock rather than the Böhm-Bawerkian theory *per se*, this book started a debate on the capital theory used by Hayek, his most notable critic being Knight, whose first contribution appeared in 1933.[80]

Knight's criticisms of the Böhm-Bawerk/Wicksell/Hayek view were varied. He argued (i) that Böhm-Bawerk's distinction, taken from the classics, between primary and secondary factors was misconceived, the relation between capital and labour being "strictly mutual, co-ordinate and simultaneous"; and (ii) that there is no period of production with any determinate length or meaning. The justification for the former assertion is contained in the following quotation.

In the historical view the creation of the productive system itself, including labourers as well as capital instruments, which in turn include "land", has been a cumulative, uninterrupted process of the hen-and-egg sort, going back as far as we care to trace it; in this process, moreover, all productive instruments existing at any time, including labourers, have participated on a joint co-operative basis.[81]

As for the second point, he had a variety of explanations. As indicated above, he saw production as a process with its origins infinitely far back, and with implications stretching infinitely far into the future. Associated with this was the impossibility of distinguishing between maintenance and new investment. Only if such a distinction is made can new processes being started be distinguished from old ones being continued. But more important than this was the claim that there was no necessary connection between roundaboutness and the stock of capital. Roundaboutness might increase without any increase in the stock of capital. As regards the stationary state, Knight accepted Clark's view of production as a process in which "the productive equipment of society yields want-satisfying services which are consumed as soon as they are created".[82]

Some of Knight's criticisms, such as his argument that a single infinitely-lived item of capital equipment makes the average period of production infinite, were unfounded. He was right, however, in claiming that the period of production could not, except under very special circumstances, be used to measure the capital stock.[83] As for his own view of capital, this was similar to Fisher's. Capital was regarded as identical to wealth, the capital value of a consumption stream. In a stationary economy this will equal the cost of the capital goods. It does indeed take time to change the capital stock, but the rate at which this can be done depends not on the structure of investment, the Böhm-Bawerkian answer, but on the amount of saving.

## 14.6  CONCLUSIONS

Although it remained firmly based on the ideas of Jevons, Menger, Walras, Marshall and Clark, the theory of economic equilibrium was by 1939 very different from that of the pioneers of marginal analysis. (1) By 1939 it had been made abundantly clear that the maximizing model of consumer behaviour did not depend on any hedonistic psychology. (2) Market equilibrium, both competitive and non-competitive, was now understood much better. (3) The application of mathematical techniques, which in the post-war period was to be used to produce even more fundamental changes in economic theory, had become firmly established. (4) There had been significant progress, notably by the Swedish school, and by Hicks, in analysing an economy characterised by time and uncertainty. (5) Finally, underlying all these developments were important developments as regards method.[84] Most economists had turned away from Marshall's attempt to blend history and economic theory, and from Menger's search for causal laws. When we take account of the increased interest in econometrics, the method of the new establishment in value theory was probably closer to that of Jevons than to that of any of his contemporaries. Taken together, these developments implied a theory of value radically different from that prevailing half a century before.

# 15

# Welfare Economics

## 15.1 INTRODUCTION

Welfare economics can be regarded as a branch of economics dating from the late nineteenth century. This is not to imply that earlier economists were not concerned with the welfare of society as a whole – far from it, for the classical economists were very much concerned with this.[1] What happened towards the end of the nineteenth century was that welfare economics began to develop as a separate branch of economics, for several reasons. Firstly, there was a desire to stress the distinction between the positive and normative aspects of economics, which necessitated separating welfare economics from the positive branches of the subject.[2] Secondly, there was a need to examine more carefully the role of the state in economic life. Not only was the state playing a greater role in the economy, but socialism, or collectivism, was an important issue towards the end of the nineteenth century. Criteria had to be developed to evaluate proposals for state intervention, and these had to be provided by welfare economics.

Equally important, however, were two reasons connected with the new theory of value. Marginalism meant that economists were equipped, for the first time, with a technical apparatus for dealing with allocation problems, and these came to constitute an important part of welfare economics. Most important, however, is the fact that the marginal utility theory of value meant that wealth could no longer be regarded as synonymous with welfare, for the utility of a commodity need not equal its price. This difference between value (in the sense of utility) and price was something of which economists had long been aware, but it was only after the marginal utility theory of value became widely accepted that its full implications became apparent.

The development of welfare economics as a separate branch of economics came only gradually. As with the doctrine of marginal utility itself, precursors can be found, such as Dupuit's use of consumers' surplus, or Bastiat's doctrine of maximum satisfaction,[3] but it is only from the 1870s that the issues involved were confronted systematically within the main body of economic analysis. It then took several decades before welfare economics attained its present form, this occurring from the 1940s and 1950s. The intervening period, during which the foundations for modern welfare economics were laid, is the subject of this chapter. In dealing with it, it is helpful to distinguish two streams of thought: the utilitarian, associated above all with English economists such as Sidgwick, Marshall and Pigou; and the non–utilitarian, of which Pareto was the most prominent exponent.

## 15.2 UTILITARIAN WELFARE ECONOMICS

*Bentham and J. S. Mill*

We have already met utilitarian welfare economics in the work of Jevons,[4] who saw pure economics as comprising the mechanics of utility and self-interest, and who used the utilitarian criterion in his analysis of economic policy. However if we are to understand developments in welfare economics, in which differences of opinion over the nature of utility played a major role, we need to consider in more detail what economists of the time meant by the term utility. To do this it is useful to go back not simply to Jevons but to Bentham and J. S. Mill.

For Bentham, the utility which served both to explain behaviour (individuals seeking to maximize their own happiness) and as a standard of morality (the "principle of utility", or the greatest happiness of the greatest number) was a very down-to-earth, commonsensical concept.

By utility is meant that property in any object, whereby it tends to produce benefit, advantage, good or happiness, (all this in the present case comes to the same thing) or (what again comes to the same thing) to prevent the happening of mischief, pain, evil or unhappiness to the party whose interest is considered.[5]

I use the words *pain* and *pleasure* in their ordinary signification ... *Pain* and *pleasure* are what everybody feels to be such – the peasant and the prince, the unlearned as well as the philosopher.[6]

He saw no problem of principle in basing theories on individual feelings in this way, arguing that "the sensations of men are sufficiently regular to become the objects of a science and an art".[7]

Bentham recognized that the pleasure a person received from something (its utility to him) depended on both "the particular sensibility of individuals" and "the exterior circumstances in which they are placed".[8] However, he saw these as practical problems, not conceptual ones. For example, in discussing criminal law he argued that whilst these differences in character and individual circumstances could not, in general, be taken account of by legislators, "provision of them may be made by the judge, ..., to whom the several individuals that happen to be concerned may be made known".[9] Utility is made into a practical concept by the proviso that where character and circumstances cannot be ascertained or measured, either directly or indirectly, "they have no claim to be taken notice of".[10] Implicit in this is the judgement that where all ascertainable characteristics are the same for two individuals, so too are their utilities. This makes sense of Bentham's argument that every individual is to count as one.[11]

It is because pleasure and pain, and hence utility, were seen as common-sense concepts of practical application that Bentham's discussions of utility measurement seem so unsatisfactory from a modern point of view. Apart from attempts to relate the measurement of pleasure to the least and greatest perceptible pleasures, his discussions deal only with the mechanics of utility measurement, leaving the principles untouched. Inter-personal comparability was an issue never confronted, his only justification for the utilitarian criterion being the absence of any consistent alternative.

Bentham's utilitarianism raised the question as to whose judgement is to be used in applying the utilitarian criterion. Presumably the answer is that it is the judgement of whoever is making the decisions. The paternalistic bias implicit in this approach, which implies that some people (the judge in the example cited above) can evaluate the pleasures experienced by others, was made explicit by J. S. Mill. Mill argued that only those who are acquainted with both can compare two pleasures. Thus only the educated can judge the utility of education, since the uneducated are not acquainted with its benefits. In other words, inter-personal utility comparisons are based on the judgements, and hence the values, of a small, wealthy and leisured class.[12] Although solving the problem from a logical point of view, the ethical basis for this is questionable.

To sum up, utility was, for both Bentham and Mill, a practical concept, something that properly qualified people could recognize and measure. The problems in deciding on the competence of alternative judges, and the ethics involved, were simply not perceived in the way we would perceive them today.[13]

## Jevons

Like Mill Jevons separated clearly the issues of utility as an explanation of behaviour and as a standard of morality. Rejecting the notion of inter-personal utility comparisons, he used utility maximization as an explanation of behaviour. When he turned to questions involving social welfare he recognized that the utilitarian criterion was not an objective one, but a matter of individual judgement.[14] In his discussions of practical issues his use of the utilitarian criterion was thus little more than a form of words, nothing in his arguments depending on it.

However, although Jevons himself denied the possibility of inter-personal utility comparisons, this was not true of his successors. These can be divided into two groups: there is the practical utilitarianism of Sidgwick, Marshall and Pigou; and there is the more abstract utilitarianism associated with Edgeworth.

## Sidgwick

It can be argued that it was Sidgwick who was the originator of the utilitarian tradition in welfare economics which culminated in the work of Pigou. Sidgwick's contributions were threefold. Firstly, he stressed the distinction, fundamental to welfare economics, between the positive and normative aspects of economics.[15] Secondly, the classical economists were concerned with measures to increase the wealth of nations, wealth being taken to measure what we now think of as welfare. Sidgwick used Jevons' value theory to show that wealth in the sense of the sum of individuals' utilities (which we might call welfare) did not necessarily correspond to wealth in the sense of the sum of produced goods valued at their market prices. Sidgwick found three reasons for this. (1) Prices correspond to *marginal* utilities, whereas to calculate the utility resulting from the consumption of a good we need to multiply the quantity of the good not by its marginal utility, but by its *average* utility. In other words, people may benefit from *unpurchased utilities*, explained by Sidgwick in terms of consumer's surplus, a concept he learnt from Marshall's early work. (2) Similar problems arise in the case of free goods, the price of which has nothing to do with either marginal or average utility. (3) The total utility derived from a given collection of goods will depend on their distribution between individuals, for by redistributing goods from consumers with a low marginal utility (the rich) to those with a high marginal utility (the poor) total utility will be raised, even though the value of goods consumed will be unchanged.

However, despite these differences between wealth and welfare, Sidgwick argued that for practical reasons, and because it corresponded with common usage, the term wealth had to be defined in terms of market prices, except in the specific cases where "the standards of the market fail us".[16] He argued that where comparisons are being made between communities similar in time and place this will be a reasonable approximation. This therefore provides the justification for Sidgwick's aggregative, classical approach, in which he considers first the production of wealth, followed by its distribution and exchange. The fundamental problem of production was seen in classical terms, as concerning the causes influencing "the average annual produce per head of a given community".[17] Utilitarianism, seeing welfare as the sum of individual utilities, was thus used to justify the aggregative approach of the classical economists.

The theory of utility on which this analysis was based had much in common with that of Bentham. Despite the long discussions of utility in *The Methods of Ethics* (1874), utility was almost taken for granted. As with Bentham and Mill, it was an *assumption* that degrees of desirability (pleasure) were "definitely given in experience",[18] and that they were commensurable.[19] However, Sidgwick clearly rejected Mill's paternalistic approach, arguing that individuals had to be taken as the judges of their own utilities, seeing "the immediate decision of consciousness" as "the only conceivable means of estimating pleasure".[20] Sidgwick recognized that inter-personal utility comparisons involved "those vague and uncertain balancings of different quantities of happiness with which the politician has to content himself",[21] but, like Bentham, he appears to have seen the main problems as practical rather than conceptual.

Finally, Sidgwick contributed to practical welfare economics by providing a systematic account of the principles of economic policy. This problem too is approached in a classical manner, through analysing in turn production and distribution. He starts by systematically investigating the reasons why a system of *laissez faire* will not necessarily maximize production. From a modern perspective the most interesting of these are probably those involving what Sidgwick describes as involving "a conflict of private and social interests".[22]

(1) There is the "large and varied class of cases" in which individuals cannot obtain adequate remuneration for the services they provide to society, such as the provision of lighthouses.[23]

(2) Entrepreneurs may, on the other hand, be able to obtain rewards exceeding the benefits to society (e.g. a second railway line).

(3) There are cases where the co-operation of everyone is needed (e.g. in controlling diseases).

(4) Inequalities may have adverse effects on efficiency (e.g. low wages affecting health).

(5) Individuals may fail to save enough to provide for future generations.

(6) The production of maximum wealth (at market prices) may not correspond to the production of maximum utility, if prices do not reflect the utilities of the commodities concerned.

Any of these, Sidgwick argued, *might* call for state intervention, but he stressed that abstract principles could provide no more than a framework in which government intervention could be discussed. In reaching definite conclusions, practical, empirical considerations were decisive. The merits and demerits of intervention had to be weighed up against those of non-intervention in each particular case. When he did this, Sidgwick found considerable scope for government intervention.

In addition to this concern with production, Sidgwick put forward as a second major objective of government policy the objective of bringing about a just or equitable distribution of the produce.[24] His conclusion was that "fair" wages (and this extended to that part of profits which could be seen as the wages of management) could be defined as "market wages as they would be under the least possible inequality of opportunities".[25] Although equality of opportunity was desirable, and although there were many ways of moving towards it (such as the provision of free education) there were in practice many obstacles in the way of achieving complete equality. Particularly important was the effect of many redistributive schemes on incentives, and hence on the amount of wealth to be distributed. "I object to socialism not because it would divide the produce of society badly, but because it would have so much less to divide."[26] Thus, for example, although he conceded that it would be possible for society to be organized on a socialist basis, without any interest being paid on capital, he nonetheless came down against this.

## Marshall

Although Marshall's approach is utilitarian, it is easier to separate out the utilitarian elements in his economics than is the case with either Jevons or Sidgwick. Unlike Sidgwick, Marshall makes it completely clear that wealth is a sum of money values (the national dividend) and that this is an object of study in its own right. Utility is brought in as consumer's surplus. Maximizing the sum of consumers' surpluses, and maximizing wealth, are clearly distinguished.

Marshall's crucial contribution to welfare economics is his development of the idea of consumer's surplus. Not only is it a concept which has remained in economics ever since; but also Marshall was able to use it to examine the doctrine of maximum satisfaction, showing that consumers' surplus will be maximized at the competitive equilibrium of supply and demand. According to Schumpeter, this "spelled a new departure" in welfare economics, being the first time that the doctrine had been considered on a purely theoretical plane.[27] At the same time, however, Marshall pointed out the limitations of consumer's surplus much more clearly than did Sidgwick. He showed that consumer's surplus could be used to measure utility only if the marginal utility of income was constant, and that the sum of different individuals' consumer surpluses could be said to correspond to a sum of utilities only if the marginal utility of income were the same for all individuals. Marshall's response to this was to confine his use of the concept to situations where these conditions might be approximately satisfied:

On the whole, however, it happens that by far the greatest number of the events with which economics deals, affect in about equal proportions all the different classes of society; so that if the money measures of the happiness caused by two events are equal, there is not in general any very great difference between the amounts of happiness in the two cases.[28]

This approach has much in common with the intensely practical utilitarianism of Bentham and Sidgwick.

## Pigou

The practical, aggregative, utilitarian approach to welfare economics reached its culmination in the work of Pigou, who gave the subject its name. Just as much as Sidgwick and Marshall, Pigou believed that it was "the realistic, not the pure, type of science that constitutes the object of our search".[29] This desire for a practical approach led him to follow Sidgwick and Marshall in adopting the classical approach, of discussing welfare in terms of the production and distribution of wealth, or national dividend.

Although using very different terminology, Pigou, like Marshall, separated much more clearly than did Sidgwick the concepts of wealth and welfare. His definition of welfare was explicitly utilitarian: (1) "the elements of welfare are states of consciousness"; (2) "welfare can be brought under the category of greater and less".[30] This was clearly a very broad concept, so to make it practical Pigou restricted his attention to *economic welfare*: "that part of welfare that can be brought, directly or indirectly, into relation with the measuring rod of money".[31] It was economic welfare to which the national dividend was the objective counterpart, for it comprised "the balance of satisfactions from the use of the national dividend over the dissatisfactions involved in the making of it".[32] The links between economic welfare and the national dividend may, as Sidgwick showed, be indirect, and economic welfare may be an unsatisfactory concept, but the terminology nonetheless has the virtue of making very clear the distinction between wealth and welfare.[33]

Perhaps Pigou's more important contribution, *vis à vis* Marshall, was that he abandoned the latter's consumers' surplus analysis in favour of a marginal approach. He started with the question of the conditions under which *laissez faire* would not result in maximum welfare, tackling this by examining the factors which might cause private interests to diverge from the interests of society. If marginal private products differed from the corresponding marginal social products, then *laissez faire*, even if it maximized wealth, would not maximize welfare. There were three reasons for such discrepancies to occur.

(1) Separation of tenancy from ownership of a factor might lead to inadequate compensation being provided for improvements made by a tenant.

(2) Problems are created by externalities and public goods, these being defined in the following way:

> the essence of the matter is that one person A, in the course of rendering some service, for which payment is made, to a second person B, incidentally also renders services or disservices to other persons C, D and E, of such a sort that technical considerations prevent payment being exacted from the benefited parties or compensation being enforced on behalf of the injured parties.[34]

Despite the clarity of his definition, however, Pigou failed to think through all the difficulties involved, and his analysis has been subjected to severe criticism.[35]

(3) Problems were also caused by the co-existence of industries with increasing and decreasing returns to scale. This was an extension of Marshall's argument,[36] that the government ought to take measures to increase production of commodities the price of which will fall as their production increases, reducing production of commodities the price of which rises as production is increased. This argument was, however, subjected to severe criticism: in particular, Pigou failed to distinguish real externalities from effects which were merely transfers.[37] Given Pigou's concern with maximizing welfare this distinction was crucial, for transfers did not affect total welfare.

Economic policy, for Pigou, involved eliminating discrepancies between marginal private and social products. Using these concepts Pigou, after considering the practical details of various cases, constructed a detailed programme for economic policy, described by one historian as providing "virtually a blue-print for the welfare state".[38]

## Edgeworth

Edgeworth, like Sidgwick, owed much to Jevons, but his use of utilitarianism was very different. Where Sidgwick, Marshall and Pigou were very practical, Edgeworth's work was much more abstract. He remained very close to Jevons, seeing economics as concerned with examining the implications of utility maximization, but he pursued far more rigorously than did Jevons the idea that ethics involved analysing the implications of maximizing the sum total of utilities. Three aspects of Edgeworth's work was worth discussing here: his attempts to provide a means of measuring utility; his attempts to provide a rationale for utilitarianism; and his use of utilitarianism to argue the case for progressive taxation.

(1) The issue of utility measurement is discussed right at the start of *Mathematical Psychics* (1881), where Edgeworth writes,

> Utility, as Professor Jevons says, has two dimensions, *intensity* and *time*. The unit in each dimension is the just perceivable increment. The implied equation to each other of each *minimum sensibile* is a first principle, incapable of proof.[39]

The idea of measuring utility in terms of the smallest difference that people could distinguish was an idea Edgeworth took from contemporary psychology, which attempted to measure such differences experimentally. Such an approach may provide a means of measuring utility, but severe problems are raised by the last sentence quoted above. In it Edgeworth is making an ethical judgement about the relative values of different persons' utilities, without giving any defence of the implied value judgements involved.[40] Despite appearances, therefore, Edgeworth's approach does not solve the problem of inter-personal utility comparisons.

(2) Edgeworth introduced the utilitarian criterion into the theory of bargaining, as a principle of arbitration:

> competition requires to be supplemented by arbitration, and the basis of arbitration between self-interested contractors is the greatest possible sum-total of utility.[41]

He gave two reasons why the utilitarian solution might appeal to both sides. The first was that in the absence of such a principle of arbitration the bargainers might end up anywhere on the contract curve. Faced with the alternative of a random outcome somewhere on the contract curve, the utilitarian position would have much to recommend it. The second was the argument that "splitting the difference" would lead to a point nearer to the utilitarian position than to either extreme position.

(3) In *Mathematical Psychics* Edgeworth clearly recognized that utilitarianism implied that incomes should be equally distributed. However, this result applied only if all individuals had the same capacity for pleasure (i.e. the same utility functions): if some people had a greater capacity than others for pleasure, maximizing the sum of utilities generally meant that they should end up with more pleasure.[42] This, however, was already well known. Edgeworth's contribution was to apply this to the theory of taxation. Where his predecessors, such as Sidgwick, had interpreted the notion of equality of sacrifice as implying proportional taxation, Edgeworth interpreted sacrifice in terms of utility. Rejecting the criteria of equal absolute sacrifice and equal proportional sacrifice as giving inadequate guidance as to whether or not taxation should be progressive, Edgeworth argued that the total disutility imposed by taxation should be minimized. Edgeworth followed Sidgwick, howev-

er, in finding many reasons why, despite this, taxation should not be sufficiently progressive to create complete equality of incomes. These reasons ranged from differences between individuals' utility functions, to the need to guard against eroding the incentive to work.[43]

## 15.3   NON-UTILITARIAN WELFARE ECONOMICS

*Walras*

The origins of the branch of welfare economics based on the denial of the possibility of making scientific inter-personal utility comparisons go back to Walras. Though Walras used the concept of utility, he did not make inter-personal comparisons, basing his welfare economics instead on the concepts of commutative and distributive justice.[44] Though derived from the concept of commutative justice, the doctrine of maximum satisfaction he developed proved capable of a different interpretation, providing the basis for a non-utilitarian welfare economics. The economist who saw the possibility of developing Walras's ideas in this way was Pareto.

*Pareto*

In his *Cours d'Economie Politique* (1896) Pareto approached the problem of welfare economics through examining the allocation of resources that would be pursued by a socialist state seeking to achieve "the maximum well-being of its citizens".[45] He was able to show that this allocation would be the same as that occurring under free competition. What did he mean by "well-being" in this context?

(1) He argued that if a reallocation of resources would make everyone better off, society would be better off if it were undertaken.

(2) Where a proposed change made some people better off and some worse off, it was necessary to separate the questions of production and distribution. Pareto tackled this by looking for an allocation of resources such that "the sum of goods obtained, *if they were distributed in a suitable manner*, would maximize each individual's utility".[46]

In other words, Pareto assumes that society as a whole gains if the gainers from a change are able to compensate the losers and still remain better off.[47] Thus Pareto had come a long way towards what we now call "Pareto optimality", but despite his refusal to make inter-personal utility comparisons he was still seeking a single optimum.

The final step towards what we now think of as "Pareto optimality" came in the *Manual of Political Economy* (1906), where he wrote:

We will say that the members of a collectivity enjoy *maximum ophelimity* [Pareto's term for utility] in a certain position when it is impossible to find a way of moving from that position very slightly in such a manner that the ophelimity enjoyed by each of the individuals of that collectivity increases or decreases. That is to say, any small displacement in departing from that position necessarily has the effect of increasing the ophelimity which certain individuals enjoy, and decreasing that which others enjoy, of being agreeable to some and disagreeable to others.[48]

It is the last sentence of this which contains the crucial insight – that where some gain and others lose it is impossible, without making further ethical judgements, to say whether society as a whole gains or loses. By seeing this, Pareto was able to develop a concept of social welfare, albeit a very limited one, which did not depend on any ability to make inter-personal utility comparisons. It is this insight which distinguishes Pareto's contribution from that of Edgeworth who, although he had shown that on the contract curve it was impossible to increase one person's utility without reducing another's, and that the competitive equilibrium was one point on the contract curve, had not drawn these conclusions from his results.

## 15.4 LATER DEVELOPMENTS

By the end of the 1920s the Sidgwick–Marshall–Pigou approach to welfare economics had developed to such an extent that one of its critics was able to describe it as "the most impressive and most unified body of thought in economic science", no other school having developed a detailed welfare economics.[49] However, as we have seen, implicit in much of this work was the possibility of making inter-personal utility comparisons. For example, it is not, except in special cases, possible to speak of a welfare gain for society without having some means of balancing the utility gained by one person against that lost by another. No adequate justification for such inter-personal utility comparisons had been given. This assumption was strongly attacked, in particular by Myrdal (1929) and Robbins (1932). In addition, the concept of externalities was subject to severe criticism. The result was that by the mid 1930s, according to Hicks, "Pigou's foundations seemed hopelessly eroded".[50]

The argument used by Robbins was that there was no *scientific* way of comparing one individual's utility with another's. Thus whilst comparisons of satisfactions are, and must continually be, made in everyday life, such comparisons have no scientific basis, and as such should be clearly distinguished from positive economics. Robbins' critique was thus not that inter-personal utility comparisons could not be made, but that the way they had been introduced into economics was confusing the distinction between positive and normative issues. This essentially methodological critique was similar to that of Myrdal, who argued that economics, both past and present, was permeated by political values. Although his conclusion, that there was a need for an economics based on "explicit and concrete value premises",[51] was radically different from that of Robbins, the implications of Myrdal's critique for Pigovian welfare economics were seen as being much the same.

These ideas were not new. Economists had long since recognized both the difficulties involved in comparing different individuals' utilities, and the need to be careful about the distinction between positive and normative economics. The criticisms of Myrdal and Pigou, however, were nonetheless effective in destroying the foundations of welfare economics as it then stood. In the attempt to find an alternative basis for welfare economics, economists began to make use of what Hicks described as the "hint [which] was discovered in one of the more obscure chapters of Pareto's *Manuel*".[52] The work of Pareto, which had been neglected by English speaking economists, was rediscovered, and the stage was set for the emergence of the so-called "New Welfare Economics" in the late 1930s.[53]

# 16

# Money and the Trade Cycle

## 16.1  INTRODUCTION

In the years following 1870 there was no change in monetary economics comparable with the changes which took place in the theory of value and distribution, though Jevons, Menger and Walras all made important contributions.[1] Jevons' contribution was primarily statistical, developing index numbers and using them to analyse the effects of the Californian gold discoveries. Walras integrated monetary theory into his general equilibrium model in a way not matched by his contemporaries. Menger, in complete contrast, analysed money as an institution which emerged as a natural result of men's economizing behaviour. As regards monetary policy, both Jevons and Walras were concerned with schemes to stabilize prices, Jevons proposing his tabular standard of value, Walras his *billon d'argent régulateur*. There was, however, within these contributions, no new theme comparable with the new ideas which emerged in the theory of value and distribution. There was no significant dividing line between monetary economics before and after 1870.

There was, however, one problem which dominated discussions of monetary policy during the period: that of fluctuating prices. Fluctuating prices were of concern not only to Jevons and Walras, but to all the major contributors to the period's monetary economics. Wicksell, Marshall and Fisher, for example, all produced schemes designed to produce greater price stability than was afforded by the gold standard. This concern carried through into the decades leading up to 1930, when price fluctuations were used by many economists to explain the trade cycle. There was, however, no break with classical monetary economics. Indeed, it could be argued that the key to much of the period's monetary economics is Wicksell's cumulative process, itself a rediscovery of Thornton's theory of interest and prices.[2]

This continuity extends to discussions of the trade cycle. Marshall, for example, took his analysis of the trade cycle from Overstone.[3] There were, however, important statistical contributions dating from the 1860s, which made the nature of the trade cycle much clearer. Jevons, through analysing time series data, established the existence of a regular cycle of 10 to 11 years' duration.[4] Probably more important was the work of Juglar who, though he also analysed time series data on the cycle, contributed the terminology which came to be used to describe the various phases of the cycle. Unlike Jevons, Juglar saw the cycle as fundamentally independent of outside events, such as harvests and wars, seeing cycles as arising "out of the behaviour, the activities, and above all the saving habits of the population, and the way they employ the capital and credit available".[5] He saw depression as a response to the preceding prosperity, rather than as brought about by outside forces. In common with Mitchell, Juglar was more concerned to explain how cycles develop, in particular their financial aspects, rather than to provide a theoretical explanation of what caused what.[6]

## 16.2   MONETARY THEORY BEFORE 1930

*Wicksell*

Wicksell's main contributions to monetary theory came in *Interest and Prices* (1898), a book whose concern was to restate and defend the quantity theory of money, the classic statement of which Wicksell found in Ricardo.[7] In developing the quantity theory he was influenced above all by two things: (1) the capital theory of Jevons and Böhm-Bawerk, which had laid the foundations for a real theory of the rate of interest; and (2) Tooke's objections to the quantity theory, which comprised both a number of puzzles (e.g. why do interest rates rise with inflation and fall with depression?) and a number of suggestions, such as his statement that only incomes determine prices. Wicksell argued that although the quantity theory was the only theory with any claim to scientific importance, it was incomplete, in that it failed to give any explanation of *how* prices changed. His solution involved arguing, in denial of Say's Law, that prices change because supply is not equal to demand.

The first step was to define the *normal, or natural rate of interest*, the rate of interest at which the supply of savings equals the demand for loan capital.[8] This will be roughly equal to the expected yield on newly-created capital. In a simple credit economy, in which savers lend directly to borrowers, competition between borrowers would ensure that the rate of interest on loans equalled this natural rate of interest. In an organized credit economy, however, the situation is more complicated, for banks can grant loans in excess of the amount of savings deposited with them, for the money they lend will be returned to them as deposits. In a "pure credit" economy, where the only form of money is bank deposits backed by loans, there is no limit to the amount of credit that can be created in this way. It is only when banks have to hold reserves of metallic money that this process of credit creation has limits.

In such a credit economy the crucial factor is the *money rate of interest*, the rate of interest charged on loans. Consider a pure credit economy. If the money rate of interest is less than the natural rate, borrowing will exceed saving, with the result that demand for goods will exceed supply, and the price level will rise. Similarly, prices will fall if the money rate is above the natural rate. Price stability requires that the money rate of interest equal the natural rate. Thus Wicksell argued that in a pure credit economy the money supply was completely elastic, being able to sustain any equilibrium price level, changes in this price level depending on the banking system's interest rate policy. The quantity theory and Say's Law held in equilibrium, but not in disequilibrium. Similar arguments would be true of an economy in which money comprised both credit money and metallic currency, but here there were limits to the ability of the banking system to change the money supply. In an expansion, for example, a shortage of reserves might force the banking system to raise the money rate of interest, bringing the expansion to an end.

To explain cyclical variations in interest rates (Tooke's puzzle mentioned above) Wicksell assumed that the natural rate of interest fluctuated, with the banking system changing the money rate of interest only with a lag. He thus had a view of the cycle in which increased optimism, or an increase in the rate of technical progress, could raise the natural rate of interest. Because the market rate lagged behind this, borrowing would exceed saving, credit would expand, and the excess of demand over supply would raise prices. In recessions this process would be reversed.

Wicksell thus supplied a theory of a credit economy, based on the ability of the banking system to cause divergences between the natural and the money rates of interest. Though developed independently, this had much in common with Thornton's theory. This monetary theory was then combined with a real theory of the trade cycle to provide an explanation of interest rates and the price level over the cycle. These ideas, in particular the *cumulative process* whereby a divergence between the money and natural rates of interest produces, not a once-for-all rise in the price level, but continuous inflation, influenced most twentieth century monetary theory, though the degree of Wicksell's influence varied enormously. Prior to the 1930s, for example, Wicksell's influence on English speaking economics was only indirect, coming in particular through Fisher, Cassel and Mises; whereas in the 1930s, due to the work of Hayek and Keynes, Wicksellian ideas were widely discussed. In Sweden itself, a definite Wicksellian school emerged.

*Fisher*

The second major contribution on which twentieth century monetary economics rests is that of Irving Fisher. Though contributing to the subject throughout the inter-war period, his major contributions date from before 1914: *Appreciation and Interest* (1896), *The Rate of Interest* (1907) and *The Purchasing Power of Money* (1911). Of his interest theory,[9] the aspect most relevant for monetary economics is his emphasis on the distinction between real and nominal interest rates.[10] As for his theory of money itself, this was, like Wicksell's, expressed in terms of the quantity theory, Fisher being responsible for the most widely used version of the equation of exchange,

$$MV = PT,$$

where $M$ is the quantity of money, $V$ its velocity of circulation, $P$ the price level, and $T$ the volume of transactions. When bank deposits were brought in as well as currency (it was still currency that was thought of as money) the equation became,

$$MV + M'V' = PT,$$

$M'$ and $V'$ being the quantity and velocity of circulation of bank deposits. In this version of the quantity theory the emphasis was on the circulation of the means of payment, something Fisher took from Newcomb, whose *Principles of Political Economy* (1885) had contained a section on "the societary circulation", in which the equation of exchange was stated. This emphasis on the circulation of money used to finance transactions led Fisher to define $T$ so as to include all transactions: not simply income, but transactions in intermediate goods and financial assets.[11]

In using the equation of exchange Fisher distinguished carefully between the "permanent or ultimate effects" of a change in, say, the quantity of money, and "temporary effects during periods of transition".[12] Permanent effects were obtained using a simple quantity theory: changes in the quantity of money would ultimately produce equiproportionate changes in the price level; the interest rate, velocity and the volume of transactions settling down at their normal values. During transition periods, however, monetary changes would produce changes in *all* the variables in the equation of exchange. The major reason for these temporary effects was, according to Fisher, the failure of the interest rate to respond sufficiently rapidly to price changes. For example, if $M$ increased, this would increase the inflation rate, but if the money interest rate did not respond fully, the real interest rate would fall, and business would be stimulated. The volume of bank lending would increase, raising $M'$ relative to $M$, and velocities would increase, causing prices to rise still further. Prices would continue to rise so long as the interest rate lagged behind its normal rate. During this inflation output would expand excessively, for prices "have to be pushed up, so to speak, by increased purchases".[13] Eventually, however, a rise in the interest rate will bring this process to an end.

Several points need to be made about Fisher's theory. (1) Fisher used this theory of transition periods to provide a monetary theory of the cycle, claiming that when taken in conjunction with maladjustments in the rate of interest, it was monetary factors that were the main cause of crises.[14] He argued that "overconsumption" and "overinvestment", in terms of which other economists were explaining crises,[15] arose because of monetary causes: "people spend more than they can afford [because] they are relying on the dollar as a stable unit when as a matter of fact its purchasing power is rapidly falling".[16] (2) He laid much more stress than did many of his contemporaries on the level of indebtedness relative to the changes in capital values brought about by changing prices and interest rates. This emphasis is clearest in his later "Debt-deflation theory of great depressions" (1933), in which he explained the great depression as resulting from the effects of deflation on an economy in which the level of indebtedness had risen excessively. (3) Though Fisher stressed variations in the quantity of money, where Wicksell emphasized changes in the natural rate of interest, his analysis of transition periods had much in common with Wicksell's cumulative process. However, Fisher chose to stress the long run in a way Wicksell did not. For example, in *The Purchasing Power of Money* he wrote,

So far as I can discover, *except to a limited extent during transition periods, or during a passing season* (e.g. the fall) there is no truth whatsoever in the idea that the price level is an independent cause of changes in any of the magnitudes, $M$, $M'$, $V$, $V'$, or the $Q$'s.[17]

This emphasis on the long run was reinforced by his illustration, comparing the effects of a monetary change to the movement of cars in a train:

The peculiar effects during transition periods are analogous to the peculiar effects in starting or stopping a train of cars. Normally the caboose keeps exact pace with the locomotive, but when the train is starting or stopping this relationship is modified by the gradual transmission of the effects through the intervening cars.[18]

### The Cambridge school

Marshall's successors at Cambridge developed his cash balance approach to the quantity theory, according to which people desire to hold a certain fraction, $k$, of their resources, $R$, as money, $M$, with $P$ being the *value of money* (i.e. the reciprocal of the price level as we are used to thinking of it). This is of course equivalent to Fisher's formula, with resources, or income, substituted for transactions. Despite this, however, the difference in formulation mattered, for it put greater stress on psychological factors and individual decisions. Thus all the major advocates of the "Cambridge equation" were led to stress changes in expectations and confidence as an important cause of changes in the value of money.

This emphasis is perhaps clearest in Pigou, who argued that people had two uses for resources, consumption apart: to hold money for the convenience and security it gives; or to use resources for the production of commodities, in order to obtain a profit. Resources will be allocated between these two uses so as to equate the marginal utility of investing (dependent on "the expected fruitfulness of industrial activity") with the marginal utility of holding money (dependent on the pattern of income receipts, the availability of other means of settling debts, and expectations of price changes).[19] These expectations were liable to change, this being the main factor explaining changes in the value of money.

The Cambridge version of the equation of exchange was thus regarded as a framework within which to analyse various effects on the value of money, not as the expression of a rigid quantity theory. According to Pigou,

The quantity theory is often defended and opposed as though it were a definite set of propositions that must either be true or false. But in fact the formulas employed in the exposition of that theory are merely devices for enabling us to bring together in an orderly way the principal causes by which the value of money is determined.[20]

Yet the theory was regarded as more than a truism, for, in Keynes' words, it "flows from the fact that money as such has no utility except what is derived from its exchange value, that is to say from the utility of things which it can buy".[21] This was the justification for the assertion that demand for money was demand for a certain quantity of real cash balances, and for asserting that *ceteris paribus*,[22] the demand curve for money was a rectangular hyperbola.[23] However, even this was not consistently asserted. For example, Keynes argued that in the short run changes in $M$ and $P$ might cause changes in $kR$.[24]

As with Fisher's quantity theory, the Cambridge version was developed to allow for bank deposits, this being done in Pigou's equation,

$$P = (kR/M)[c + h(l - c)],$$

where $M$, this time, is the quantity of legal tender money (what we might call high-powered, or base money), $c$ is the fraction of money balances held as legal tender money and $h$ is the fraction of their deposits that banks hold as reserves of legal tender money.[25] As with the other versions of the Cambridge equation, this provided a framework within which causes of price level changes could be analysed.

The evils of fluctuating prices were stressed both by Marshall and his followers, a variety of schemes being proposed to deal with the problem. Marshall emphasized the uncertainty introduced by price fluctuations, and the element of speculation this introduced into business life. He integrated this into a theory of the trade cycle:

The consequence of this uncertainty is that, when prices are likely to rise, people rush to borrow money and buy goods, and this helps prices to rise; business is inflated ...; those working on borrowed money pay back less real value than they borrowed.

Because nominal wages are fixed,

the employer pays smaller real salaries and wages than usual, at the very time when his profits are largest in other ways, and is thus prompted to over-estimate his strength, and engage in ventures which he will not be able to pull through after the tide turns.[26]

When credit is shaken, and prices fall, the process is reversed. Employees are unwilling to let money wages fall, so falling prices raise real wages and workers become unemployed as businesses are shut down. Firms reduce production in order to improve the market for their own goods, but in doing so they reduce demand in other markets. Thus fluctuations in the standard of value, according to Marshall, are always "either flurrying up business activity to an unwholesome fervour, or else closing factories and workshops by the thousand".[27]

Marshall's remedy for this situation was twofold. Firstly, he revived the idea of a tabular standard of value, whereby contracts could be made in terms of a unit of fixed purchasing power. This would reduce the significance of fluctuations in the value of money. Secondly, he advocated

ˉbasing the currency on both gold and silver, a unit of currency corresponding to a fixed quantity of gold *plus* a fixed quantity of silver. The value of
such a currency would fluctuate with the average of the values of gold and
silver, fluctuating by less than either metal alone.

Whereas for Marshall money was thought of primarily as metal, this was
not the case for his successors. Though Keynes and Pigou both shared his
view as to the effects of price fluctuations,[28] together with his desire to
stabilize the price level, they attached greater importance to credit money,
and their remedies varied accordingly, both of them stressing the management of the money supply. This stress on the need for management was
particularly marked in the case of Keynes, whose emphasis on it, though
going back to his *Indian Currency and Finance* (1913), was most clearly stated
in his *Tract on Monetary Reform* (1923).[29]

To understand the *Tract on Monetary Reform* we need to consider the other
side of the value of money: the exchange rate, which was explained in terms
of purchasing power parity, the elements of which, although the name was
coined by Cassel,[30] can be found in Marshall, and, before him, Ricardo.
Purchasing power parity, in the Cambridge version, determined the
equilibrium value of the exchange rate. If the exchange rate were too high,
for example, equilibrium required that the price level fall sufficiently for
purchasing power parity to be restored. In such circumstances, Keynes
argued in the *Tract*, the government had to decide between devaluation and
deflation. This involved management: a *decision* as to the appropriate price
level. Given that capitalism could not be efficient, and might not even
survive, without a stable price level, Keynes had no hesitation in advocating
devaluation rather than deflation:

For these grave causes we must free ourselves from the deep distrust which exists
against allowing the regulation of the standard of value to the subject of *deliberate
decision*. We can no longer leave it in the category of ... matters which are settled by
natural causes, or are the resultant of the separate actions of many individuals acting
independently, or require a revolution to change them.[31]

## 16.3 BUSINESS CYCLE THEORY BEFORE 1910

### Before 1900[32]

In the period before 1900 there was little sustained analysis of the trade
cycle. As was the case with Marshall and Wicksell, most of the leading
economists were more concerned with the formulation and development of
equilibrium theory. Discussion of the trade cycle was, apart from brief
treatments, such as those considered above, confined to others. During the
period, however, a variety of ideas were put forward, many of these
anticipating ideas found in later writing. Nasse, for example, in 1879,
attributed booms to inventions, associating particular booms with particular industries. In the period after the crisis of 1873, Price ascribed crises and
depressions to over-consumption's destroying more wealth than was

produced, something that might happen as a result of excessive investment in fixed capital, high wages, or high government consumption. Similar was the explanation of Guyot who, in 1892, argued that over-investment in fixed capital could produce a shortage of 'circulating capital. Set against these "real" theories were ones stressing psychological factors and credit. We have already mentioned Marshall. Similarly Bagehot, referring to "a great many stupid people" having "a great deal of stupid money",[33] argued that credit gets extended during the optimism of a boom, but that this over-optimism will eventually be discovered, whereupon the structure of confidence and credit will collapse. In his account elements of multiplier and accelerator processes can even be discerned.

In addition to all these theories were those which attacked Say's Law: the under-consumptionist theories. An American, Hawley (1882) reached such a theory via the route of Mill's stagnation thesis, of the tendency of the rate of profits to a minimum.[34] He argued that there was a tendency towards over-accumulation, especially when profits were high during a boom. Another American, Crocker, in the 1880s reached similar conclusions through attacking Mill's doctrine of the impossibility of general over-production.[35] The main performance here, however, was that of Hobson. In his first book, *The Physiology of Industry* (1889)[36] he claimed that production was not equal to the maximum set by factor supply, being kept below this by excessive saving. Although Hobson was taken by Keynes as a precursor, this analysis, although containing many insights into the macroeconomics of saving and investment, was not altogether free from the Smithian perspective: saving was equated with investment, and differences between a barter and a monetary economy were not recognized.

*Tugan Baranovsky*

Despite this variety of earlier writings on the trade cycle, the modern literature stems, above all, from one work: Tugan-Baranovsky's *Industrial Crises in England* (1894). The background to this work was the debate amongst Russian Marxists in the 1890s over the question of whether Russian capitalism was in a position to create a market sufficient for its own development, an issue with important political implications.[37] Tugan-Baranovsky's position was that capitalism could expand indefinitely, demand being sustained by increased production of capital goods, accumulation being an end in itself. Contrary to Marx, but in agreement with Lenin, Tugan-Baranovsky argued that though capitalism would suffer periodic crises, these would not cause its collapse.

In this context Tugan-Baranovsky viewed cycles as an integral part of the process of capitalist development, explicitly rejecting "exogenous" explanations of the cycle, such as those of Jevons and Juglar. Cycles were connected with the persistent tendency, in a capitalist economy, towards over-production of capital goods, something which could, in a monetary economy, lead to general over-production. Whilst he denies Say's Law, recognizing the possibility of general over-production, Tugan-Baranovsky argued that it was the behaviour of investment that was crucial. He found empirical evidence for this in fluctuations in iron production, iron being used above all, Tugan-Baranovsky claimed, in the production of capital goods.

Why, however, should the accumulation of fixed capital not proceed at a steady rate? Tugan-Baranovsky's answer was that, because so much of national income goes to the capitalist class, capital is not accumulated in the right proportions. In the upswing capitalists draw on accumulated funds to accumulate capital as fast as they dare. But the result is that eventually the accumulated funds become exhausted, and the interest rate rises. Because too many capital goods have been produced investment then falls, and a depression begins. In the following depression, loanable capital accumulates, for savings continue at a fairly steady rate, but before this can be transformed into productive capital it needs to be appropriately distributed amongst the various branches of production, something that need not occur, given the anarchy of an individualistic, competitive economy. So loanable capital accumulates until the pressure of funds seeking investment outlets is sufficient to overcome industry's resistance, and it begins to be transformed into fixed capital. As expansion in one area tends to spread throughout the economy, new demand is rapidly created and the economy enters a new phase of prosperity.[38]

## Spiethoff

Spiethoff's contributions, dating from the year after the German edition of *Industrial Crises in England*, were strongly influenced by Tugan-Baranovsky's work, as well as by the German historical school.[39] Like Tugan-Baranovsky, he rejected Say's Law as inappropriate to a monetary economy, but where Tugan-Baranovsky explained fluctuations in investment in terms of alternating shortages and gluts of loanable capital, Spiethoff introduced other features. Firstly, he explained the boom in terms of innovations, or the discovery of overseas markets, either of which could raise profitability in some particular sector, thus starting the upswing. Secondly, he explained the crisis in terms of limited opportunities for investment: during the boom, output of consumption goods will lag behind investment, so consumption goods prices stay high, keeping profits high. However, when the new investment eventually starts to result in increased production of consumption goods, prices must eventually fall, even though cartels may manage to maintain prices for a while. Investment will have to be curtailed, because once the new plant is installed, there remains only the task of maintenance and replacement.

These influences, operating on investment through profitability and the incentive to invest, were seen by Spiethoff as complementary to Tugan-Baranovsky's explanations in terms of the supply of capital. In a boom the process of expansion was limited not only by limits to the demand for real capital, but also by shortages of capital. These shortages, occuring at the peak of the cycle, were very much real shortages, for it was shortages of real capital goods which underlay the tightened conditions in the capital market. The wrong type of goods had been produced. Thus monetary and credit policies would do nothing to prevent the crisis.

## 1900–1910

The work of Tugan-Baranovsky and Spiethoff stimulated much work on business cycles, and in the first decade of the twentieth century a number of important contributions were made. The first of these concerns the acceleration principle, the theory that a relatively small increase in the demand for consumption goods can produce a much larger increase in the demand for investment goods. The essence of the idea was first put forward by Carver (1903), but the credit for developing it and integrating it into a theory of the cycle is due to Aftalion (1910).[40]

The key to Aftalion's theory of the cycle was the idea that wants could become saturated, something he explained in an Austrian manner, in terms of diminishing marginal utilities. The stock of capital goods had to be adjusted to the demand for consumer goods, something that was difficult, for three reasons: (1) the acceleration principle meant that even small fluctuations in demand for consumer goods could produce large fluctuations in the demand for capital goods; (2) the long period required for the construction of capital goods; and (3) the durability of capital goods. Thus in a boom projects would be started without initially producing any goods to satisfy demand; when they started to produce, demand would become saturated, and investment would fall. Depression would follow, and this would last until a sufficient number of capital goods had worn out for there to be a shortage of capital goods relative to demand. The gestation lag in new investment projects, and the durability of capital, were thus important in determining the length of the cycle. Aftalion thus found the amplitude and the timing of the cycle to be inherent in the techniques of production.

Another important contribution was that of Schumpeter, who emphasized the role of innovations in the process of economic development. Schumpeter's argument was that innovations inevitably occur in waves: when an entrepreneur innovates, others follow, for the task of following an innovator is easier than that of first making the discovery. The appearance of an innovation moves the economy out of equilibrium, creating new opportunities for profit, which are gradually exploited. Depression then follows as the economy settles down to a new equilibrium. Boom and slump are, for Schumpeter, essential aspects of the process through which equilibrium is re-established after a wave of innovations.

As regards the monetary aspects of the cycle, an important contribution was that of Johannsen (1908) who, though not alone in arguing the under-consumptionist case, was the most original. His originality was twofold: a perceptive analysis of the relationship between saving and investment; and a statement of the "multiplying principle" linking consumption to investment. Johannsen distinguished carefully between saving, the act of refraining from consumption, and investment, the purchase of capital goods. It is only when savings are invested in new wealth (what Johannsen calls the "capitalistic form" of savings) that aggregate demand will be unaffected by the level of saving. If savings are hoarded, or are used to purchase already-existing property ("impair savings") this will reduce demand and hence profits, something akin to Keynes' theory in the *Treatise on Money*. Johannsen's version of the multiplier, too, is reminiscent of Keynes: a fall in one group's spending lowers the incomes of another group, which in turn reduces its spending, thus reducing the incomes of a third group, and so on.

## 16.4  BUSINESS CYCLE THEORY, 1910–1930

If the previous period was the one in which the main explanations of the business cycle were first put forward, virtually all the materials for a comprehensive theory being available by 1910, it was the following two decades that constituted the heyday of business cycle theory. Between 1910 and 1930 many studies of the cycle were published, the major ones being by Mitchell (1913, 1927), Cassel (1918a), Hawtrey (1913, 1919), Robertson (1915, 1926) and Pigou (1912, 1927). From the 1930s the question of the trade cycle became, in part due to Keynesian influence, to a certain extent a theme subsidiary to the theory of employment.

### *Mitchell*

Arguably the most important of these writers on the cycle was, at the time at least, Mitchell, for it was his work which popularized the notion of the business cycle, not merely amongst economists but amongst businessmen and politicians.[41] In addition, the statistical work on the business cycle undertaken both by Mitchell and his students, marks him out from other economists working on the problem of cycles.

Mitchell's emphasis was on the business cycle as an integral part of business life, its rhythmic pattern being evident not merely in one or two major aggregates, but permeating all economic activity. He saw his task as investigating the nature of these cycles – the nature of the process whereby prosperity is transformed into depression, and depression into prosperity – and to do this he accumulated and brought together an ever-increasing wealth of statistical data. This task of building up a comprehensive picture was started in Mitchell's *Business Cycles* (1913), continuing in his work with the National Bureau for Economic Research, an organization Mitchell was instrumental in founding, becoming its director from its foundation in 1920 to 1945. It was through the National Bureau that his *Business Cycles: the Problem and its Setting* (1927), and *Measuring Business Cycles* (1946) were produced.

This statistical work on business cycles, together with the other statistical work associated with it, such as estimates of national income, and studies of its distribution, constitute in their own right a chapter in the history of economics. Our main concern here is with the implications of Mitchell's work for the theory of the business cycle. Mitchell has been portrayed as an advocate of measurement without theory, but this is far from the case.[42] There is a sense in which it is truer to see Mitchell as synthesizing the various theories of the cycle. He argued that we need working hypotheses to guide the selection and analysis of data, this being provided, in his work in business cycles, by a survey of current theories.[43] In surveying these theories Mitchell found a place for virtually all the then current theories, seeing them as differing in emphasis rather than in principle.[44] It is possible to view Mitchell as being too uncritical when he claims that the problem is not that there are too few acceptable theories, but that virtually every theory appears justifiable.

Where Mitchell considered earlier writers to have gone wrong was in isolating one particular factor, seeing that as the true cause of the cycle. He argued that because the cycle was an extremely complex phenomenon, comprising numerous actions and reactions, it was more profitable to concentrate on trying to understand the nature of the process as a whole, rather than on trying to single out any one cause as fundamental. This was a task which, according to Mitchell, required statistical analysis, not deductive theory.[45]

However, just as it would be wrong to see Mitchell as a pure empiricist, so too would it be wrong to see him simply as an eclectic in his theory. There was, though it was deliberately not formulated as a formal theory, a theoretical framework underlying his approach, one very much influenced by Veblen.[46] Mitchell saw the business cycle as rooted in a particular institutional structure – that of a system of inter-related, large-scale organizations, the object of which was to make money. The interdependence of all prices was described in almost Walrasian terms. There was substitution between goods on the demand side; prices and costs were linked; competition equalized the rate of profit; and security prices were linked to profits.

> At whatever point analysis may begin, tracing the interlocking links of the price chain, to that point will it come round again if it proceeds far enough. ... Thus all prices in a business economy are continually influencing one another. To account for any one item in the system, one must invoke the whole.[47]

Despite this, however, his assumptions were not Walrasian, for he claimed that the notion of equilibrium was inappropriate for describing an economy, for any economy would always be in motion. Furthermore, he did not accept the hypothesis of perfect competition: not only might there be imperfections of competition (Mitchell was never very clear as to exactly what he assumed here), but also prices and profits were to a substantial extent determined by institutional factors. Many prices were rigid because of contracts and conventions. The institution, however, to which Mitchell attached most importance was that of money. In contrast with the Walrasian, or even the Marshallian system, which in other ways had something in common with Mitchell's, relative prices, and hence profits, depended as much on credit conditions as on real factors.

Business cycles emerged naturally from this framework. Revival emerges naturally from depression as profits rise, something which occurs as a matter of course through costs falling relative to output prices, falling interest rates and the increased availability of finance through the banking system. Profits rise and an expansion develops, until it in turn generates forces which disrupt it: costs rise relative to selling prices, and credit becomes scarce, and hence expensive, or it might be due to other factors, such as errors in businessmen's expectations. Depression begins and the cycle is completed.

For Mitchell, therefore, the business cycle was seen as inherent in an economy organized around making money. The choice of the term "business cycle" as opposed, for example, to the term "industrial fluctuations" favoured by Robertson and Pigou, was no accident: on the one hand it echoed Veblen's distinction[48] between the business, or pecuniary, aspect of economic activity, and the "industrial", or technological, aspect; and on the other hand, it stressed the rhythmic, or cyclical nature of variations in the level of activity.

However, although this framework proved fruitful for empirical research, Mitchell and the National Bureau filling out much of the statistical detail, Mitchell stopped short at explaining *how* this process worked itself out. Nowhere, for example, does he explain *why* prices move relative to costs in the way they must do if his theory is to hold. Despite Mitchell's impressive statistical work, and despite his bringing together many theories of the cycle, we have to look elsewhere to find progress in the theory of the business cycle.

### Cassel

Although written in 1914, Cassel's work on the cycle, published as Book IV of *The Theory of Social Economy*, was published in 1918. Like Mitchell, he dealt with cycles rather than crises, seeing them as the product of a specific epoch in economic history:[49] and he used statistical evidence to support his theory. Beyond this, however, he has little in common with Mitchell. Whereas Mitchell stressed the pervasiveness of the cycle, Cassel drew from his statistics the conclusion that the cycle was a phenomenon associated primarily with fixed capital formation, not with consumption, the latter fluctuating little over the cycle. Furthermore, where Mitchell was eclectic in his use of previous theories, Cassel built on Spiethoff's over-investment theory. Where he differed from Spiethoff was in seeing a greater role for monetary factors.

At the start of the upswing, according to Cassel, profits will be high relative to wages, and banks will be lending at too low a rate of interest. These two effects combine to stimulate the production of fixed capital. As the boom proceeds, the proportion of production devoted to capital formation rises, whilst the proportion devoted to savings does not. A shortage of capital develops, and interest rates rise. At the same time wages rise relative to profits, causing demand for investment goods to fall.

Important too is the accelerator, transforming a fall in the growth rate of consumption demand into a fall in the level of investment. In the down-swing which follows, these forces are reversed, savings increasing in relation to the production of capital goods, and interest rates falling. At the trough, however, the link between monetary factors and investment is much weaker than at the peak, a conclusion Cassel found to be supported by statistical evidence.

In this theory Cassel explained the role of lags in preventing the economy from being in equilibrium continuously, these including lags in the response of investment to changes interest rates; the reaction of interest rates to changes in investment; and the time taken between the start of an investment project and its completion. In addition, the economy is periodi-cally subject to disturbances which renew the cyclical activity, such as advances in technology (e.g. railways, electricity) or the opening up of new countries. His main difference with Spiethoff was in arguing that the shortage of capital at the crisis was a shortage of *monetary* savings, not a shortage of real capital goods. Banking policy was thus seen as important.

### Mises

A theory which laid even greater stress on monetary factors in the cycle was that of Mises (1913). Using a model which in other respects had much in common with Cassel's, Mises brought in Wicksell's cumulative process, whereby prices change in response to any discrepancy between the natural and money rates of interest, to analyse the monetary aspects of the cycle. According to Mises it was the failure of the banking system to keep the money rate of interest equal to the natural rate, together with an ideology, prevalent amongst businessmen and politicians, in favour of low interest rates, which was responsible for the persistent tendency of the economy to expand excessively, producing crises and hence the cycle[50] This view of the cycle is considered below, as it was later taken up by Hayek.

### Hawtrey

Whilst Cassel and Mises both emphasized the role of money in the cycle, neither gave it so prominent a place as did Hawtrey, whose most important works during this period were *Good and Bad Trade* (1913) and *Currency and Credit* (1919), the latter in particular being extremely influential in the 1920s.[51] Hawtrey was strongly influenced by Marshall, but differed from him in attaching more importance to money: he argued that although they were correct in claiming that money was not the same thing as wealth, orthodox economists had failed to recognize that money was nevertheless "a most potent factor in economic organization".[52] Whilst Cassel and Mises allowed for the influence of real as well as monetary factors in the cycle, Hawtrey stressed that it was only the latter that really mattered.

The basis of his theory was a distinctive view of the relationship between money and income (*nominal* spending), one which goes beyond the conventional quantity theory relationship. When a *new* credit is created, Hawtrey argued, through a bank granting a new loan, it will be spent, this expenditure constituting income for its recipients. This income will raise spending, which in turn will generate further income, a process which will carry on until the purchasing power in circulation is returned to the bank to pay off the original loan. It is thus crucial to Hawtrey's theory that when he refers to a given stock of money (or the margin of unspent purchasing power, as he calls it) he is envisaging a situation in which new credit is continually being created, this being counterbalanced by the repayment of older loans. This means that for Hawtrey an increase in the quantity of money occurs when the flow of new credit exceeds the flow of purchasing power being returned to the banks to cancel old loans. Changes in the money supply are thus *directly* linked to changes in the flow of income.

This link between money and income is central to Hawtrey's theory, but it needs to be supplemented by two things: an explanation of why changes in nominal spending produce changes in employment; and an account of Hawtrey's view of the role of interest rates.

Hawtrey saw a strong link between the short term interest rate and the supply of bank credit, the crucial role being played by *dealers*. It is dealers from whom producers receive their orders, and because they hold large stocks of goods, financed by a volume of credit which is large in relation to their turnover, they are very sensitive to changes in the rate of interest. Thus a rise in the short term rate of interest makes dealers wish to reduce their inventories, causing them to reduce their orders from producers. Production falls and unemployment rises. At the same time, because dealers hold lower inventories, demand for credit falls, and the money supply is reduced. Thus a rise in the short term rate of interest would have a strong effect on both money and employment.

The reason why this process leads to a fall in output and unemployment is that prices take time to adjust. In particular, wages are sticky. Thus when, in response to a fall in spending following a monetary contraction, prices and wages fall, interest rates can fall again, monetary demand and the level of employment being restored to their former levels. Money wage rigidity was, for Hawtrey, the key to the link between money and employment.

Three factors in particular are brought in to explain why cycles will emerge in this setting. The first is the inherent instability which Hawtrey sees in the system of bank credit. High profits cause lending to rise, and this in turn raises profits still further, and so on. The second is the lag which occurs between the increase in the volume of spending and the increase in the demand for money which follows it. When new credit is granted, it is used, by dealers, to purchase goods from producers, these being transactions which are settled by cheque rather than with currency. It is as the increase in purchasing power spreads to wage-earners that the demand for currency increases, this occurring only some time after the initial increase in credit. Finally, there is the lag involved in the production process. This is important because Hawtrey assumes that producers require a continual stream of new credit throughout the production process; which means that once bankers are committed to supporting a project they will be committed, morally if not legally, to continue to advance credit until the process is complete. The outcome of these three factors is that the banking system is unable to respond appropriately. For example, in an expansion, by the time rising demand for currency causes banks to lose reserves and they raise interest rates, the level of demand will already have expanded too far. In addition, despite raising interest rates, banks will be unable to cut back their lending immediately, due to their commitments to producers. Thus monetary expansion will typically be excessive, this necessitating a contraction as banks attempt to restore their reserves to an appropriate level. The downswing is, however, likely to be carried too far, and a cycle is the result.

Hawtrey worked out his theory not only for an isolated economy, but also for an open one, both with fixed and flexible exchange rates (a gold standard and an inconvertible paper currency). He incorporated into it the Wicksellian natural rate of interest and Fisher's theory of the real interest rate. Although Hawtrey did use his theory to analyse the effects of real disturbances, this was only in order to argue that the important influences on the level of activity were monetary in origin: without a change in the money supply there could not be any significant fluctuations in the flow of purchasing power, and hence the scope for fluctuations was very limited.

Hawtrey's analysis, in addition to its influence in the 1920s, is important in the development of Keynesian economics. Although the ideas are not developed so thoroughly as in Keynes' *General Theory*, the multiplier and the view that changes in demand have a direct effect on the volume of output are both present in *Good and Bad Trade*.

*Robertson*

In contrast to Hawtrey, Robertson, in *A Study of Industrial Fluctuations* (1915) analysed the cycle in terms of real factors: in addition to following Jevons in giving considerable attention to crop cycles and the influence of agriculture on trade, Robertson provided an account, independently of Schumpeter, of the stimulating effect of innovations, and he made use of Aftalion's over-investment theory. Innovations could start an upswing through their effects on costs and demand. During the upswing it would take time before investment led to increased output, and so one possible reason for the downturn, when this came, was that a surplus of particular capital goods might emerge. Shortage of saving provided an alternative reason. Robertson's achievement, in distilling these conclusions out of a welter of facts, has been described by Hicks as involving "almost miraculous insight".[53]

Very different was Roberton's later *Banking Policy and the Price Level* (1926), a book in which he cooperated closely with Keynes,[54] in which he analysed more thoroughly than anyone before him the process of saving and investment. In the key chapter in this book, entitled "The different types of saving", Robertson distinguishes between a multitude of types of saving. His use of the term "lacking", as being more neutral than the more traditional "abstinence" or "waiting", was one of the reasons why his terminology appears very strange. Whilst Robertson's terminology was far too complicated to appeal to other economists,[55] it was important in that it defined saving and investment (the supply of and demand for lacking) in such a way that they could be unequal. The reason for this was the possibility of forced saving, something which could be brought about through the banking system. Suppose the banking system expands the supply of credit through lending to investors: investors will be able to purchase a larger share of output, doing so at the expense of consumers.

In applying these concepts to the cycle, Robertson retained the idea that there could be real causes of the business cycle, describing fluctuations due to such causes as "appropriate". When real costs or real demand changed, it was quite appropriate for output to change. However, in addition to these fluctuations, there were fluctuations in output that were caused by price fluctuations and the behaviour of the banking system. It was the duty of banking policy to prevent this. However, and this is where Robertson's analysis of saving and investment was so important, the task of the banking system was not so simple as it might sound, for credit creation had two aspects. On the one hand, there was the effect of banking policy on the price level, but on the other there was its effect on forced saving. In addition to the task of assisting price stability, the banking system had the task of ensuring that an appropriate volume of savings, forced if not voluntary, was available for investment. These two tasks could conflict, Robertson arguing that under some circumstances the banking system should abandon the goal of price stability, in order to achieve an adequate supply of savings.

## Pigou

We close our discussion of the period up to 1930 with a discussion of Pigou, whose *Industrial Fluctuations* (1927) can be regarded as the best attempt at a synthesis of alternative theories. Pigou's first analysis of the cycle was provided in *Wealth and Welfare* (1912), where it arose naturally out of his aggregative approach to welfare economics. After investigating the factors determining the size and distribution of the national dividend, Pigou turned to the question of its variability, and hence the variability of employment. He argued that the causes of fluctuations were too closely bound up with the general body of economic activity to permit an isolated treatment of them. It was from the second edition of *The Economics of Welfare* (1924) that Pigou dropped this arrangement, assigning discussion of fluctuations to a separate volume.

There were two main features of the framework within which Pigou brought together much of the previous literature on the cycle. The first was his systematic use of the distinction between two problems: that of the initiating impulses disturbing the economic system; and that of the conditions under which such impulses operate to cause fluctuations in economic activity. Pigou was not the first to draw this distinction between what came to be known as the impulse and propagation problems, credit for this being due to Wicksell,[56] but Pigou was influential in bringing it into general use. The second aspect of Pigou's approach was that, like Mitchell, he stressed expectations of industrial profit as the mechanism through which various impulses affected the economy. Thus although Pigou can, in some respects, be thought of as having a "psychological" explanation of the cycle, his framework was sufficiently elastic to allow for a large variety of influences: autonomous real or monetary factors, just as much as psychological factors, could influence expected profits and hence economic activity.

Pigou's method was very much in the Marshallian tradition. Like Marshall's work, *Industrial Fluctuations* comprised a blend of theory and empirical analysis. More important, however, was the fact that Pigou's theoretical framework was Marshallian. It deals with a competitive, though not perfectly competitive, world; one in which the changing economic equilibrium can be analysed in terms of the elasticities of industry demand and supply curves.

In view of developments in the 1930s and beyond, two features of *Industrial Fluctuations* must be emphasized. The first of these is Pigou's stress on the role of fluctuations in demand as the main cause of fluctuations in employment. In analysing the propagation of demand from one sector to another, Pigou is describing what is essentially a multiplier process: what is missing as compared with later theories is not the idea so much as the *technical* device of the multiplier.[57] It was due to technical limitations that Pigou reached the conclusion that it was not possible to estimate quantitatively the effects on economic activity of an increase in demand.

The second feature of Pigou's work is his emphasis on the labour market. Although in many ways in the tradition of earlier writing on the cycle, *Industrial Fluctuations* is in other ways much closer to modern theory, in which the theory of employment is primary. The key concept here is Pigou's elasticity of supply of floating capital, for it is this which determines the extent to which an increase in profit expectations, caused by whatever initiating impulse, will affect unemployment. Through this elasticity, the reduction in unemployment resulting from an increase in expected profits will depend on the elasticity of supply of credit (and hence on the banking system), and on the extent of any changes in prices and wages (which affect the volume of real resources that a given supply of finance will command). Pigou supplied a variety of reasons why prices and wages would be sticky, failing to equate the supply of and demand for labour. It would be wrong, however, to conclude that Pigou saw wage stickiness as the fundamental problem. If demand were severely depressed, for example, wages might have to fall very low, or even become negative, for full employment to be achieved: aggregate demand, rather than wage stickiness, could well be the problem when there was unemployment.[58]

## 16.5   THE THEORY OF MONEY AND EMPLOYMENT,
### 1930–1936

The 1930s opened with two influential works, appearing almost simultaneously – Hayek's *Prices and Production* and Keynes' *Treatise on Money* –

works which dominated discussion of money and the cycle for the next few years. Though both their conclusions and the routes by which they reached these were very different, the ideas in both these books can be traced back to Wicksell, of whose theory they were logical extensions. Given this, together with the influence of Wicksell on Swedish economists working on similar problems, it could be argued that the first half of the 1930s was when Wicksell's influence was at its height.[59]

## Hayek

Although Hayek's ideas became neglected after the success of the *General Theory*, they were at the time highly regarded, and the centre of much controversy. Schumpeter refers to the "sweeping success" of *Prices and Production*, a success not equalled by that of any theoretical book at a comparably abstract level.[60] Hayek's key argument was that the trade cycle arose because the organization of the banking system made it difficult to avoid periods of excessive monetary expansion. When, as must inevitably happen, such monetary expansion is brought under control, the result will be depression, the severity of the depression being directly proportional to the length of the previous boom.

The framework Hayek used to reach this conclusion comprised two main elements: Wicksell's cumulative process, and Böhm-Bawerk's theory of capital.[61] During the period of expansion, which might owe its origins to real causes, excessive monetary expansion would lead to forced saving, lowering interest rates, and raising the prices of producers' goods relative to those of consumers' goods.[62] Production of producers' goods would thus rise, but because Hayek assumed an initial state of full employment,[63] the only way in which the capital stock could be increased was through a lengthening of the period of production. However, when monetary expansion ceased, forced saving would also cease, total savings returning to their previous level, thus raising the rate of interest. The price of consumption goods would then rise relative to that of producers' goods. This rise in the interest rate, and the associated shift in relative prices, makes the longer processes of production that were started during the boom unprofitable, and they will be shut down, thus releasing labour. Shorter production processes will be expanded, but this will take time as stocks of all the appropriate intermediate goods have to be built up, and during the time it takes to do this there will be unemployment.

Unemployment occurs because the employment of labour requires capital goods, and the capital goods released when the longer, capital intensive processes are terminated are unsuitable to be used in the shorter processes that need to be started up. Demand for labour is thus, in the short run, very inelastic, and unemployment is the inevitable result of a shortening of the period of production. Monetary expansion will not prevent it: if investment were to be increased, this would merely postpone the required adjustment, making the crisis, when it eventually came, worse; if consumption were to be increased, this too would raise the price of consumption goods relative to that of producer goods, making still shorter processes profitable, thus exacerbating the situation. The only way the situation could, according to Hayek, be restored, is through an increase in the level of voluntary saving sufficient to make the longer processes of production, introduced during the expansion, profitable.

### Keynes' treatise on money

Very different was the *Treatise on Money*, in which a Wicksellian construction was used to argue that monetary expansion could cure unemployment through raising the price level. To understand the argument Keynes was using, we have to consider what he called his *fundamental equations*. The starting point for these was Keynes' idiosyncratic system of national income accounting, in which earnings ($E$) were defined as including only the *normal* earnings of factors of production, excluding "windfall" profits or losses ($Q$). Defining the value of output as a whole as $Y$, the value of investment as $I$ and the value of consumption as $C$, we have

$$Y = C + I$$
$$Y = E + Q.[64]$$

Defining savings as *earnings* less consumption,

$$S = E - C,$$

we obtain

$$I = S + Q.$$

That is, investment is equal to savings plus windfall profits, which may be positive or negative. If we now define real output, $y$, and the price level, $P$, such that $Y = Py$, we can derive the following equation for the price level:

$$P = (E/y) + (I - S)/y.$$

This shows the price level to be determined by two terms: normal earnings per unit of output, plus the difference between investment and savings (i.e. windfall profits) per unit of output.

The fundamental equations enabled Keynes to distinguish between two types of inflation: *income inflation*, where normal earnings per unit of output were increasing, and *profit inflation*, arising because the actions of the banking system caused investment to exceed saving. The significance of this distinction was that it was only in a profit inflation that entrepreneurs would have an incentive to increase production. It led also to the so-called "widow's cruse" (sic) theory of distribution, for if entrepreneurs were to increase their spending on investment, they would find that this increased their prices and hence their profits: profits were like the widow's cruse,[65] in that however much they were spent, they would never be exhausted.

In using the fundamental equations the crucial factor was the rate of interest. The rate of interest depended on supply and demand for money, where the latter comprised two categories: *cash deposits*, deposits needed to finance transactions; and *savings deposits.* Demand for cash deposits was explained by Keynes in terms of a quantity theory, but demand for savings deposits was determined very differently, depending on the "bearishness" of the public. The behaviour of the rate of interest thus depended on the willingness of the banking system to respond to the changing demands of the public, these depending on investors' expectations.

A monetary expansion would thus act on the economy in the following way. (1) Given the level of "bearishness", it would lower the rate of interest. (2) This would raise the level of investment relative to savings. (3) The rise in investment relative to savings would raise prices relative to earnings, increasing windfall profits. (4) Finally, the rise in profits would cause entrepreneurs to expand production and increase employment. Monetary expansion could thus be used to lower unemployment, this operating through its effect on prices and profits.

### The Swedish contribution

In the early 1930s Wicksellian ideas were also being developed in Sweden. Whether or not they can justifiably be called a "Stockholm School"[66] the economists concerned, Lindahl, Myrdal, Ohlin, Hammarskjold and Lundberg, shared a Wicksellian heritage, and they built upon it to produce works often considered to anticipate the *General Theory* in important respects.[67] Myrdal, for example, claimed that Keynes' *General Theory* constituted, for Swedish economists, an important development along a familiar line of thought, not a revolutionary breakthrough[68] Despite this, however, there were important differences between their approach and that of their British contemporaries.[69]

The first of their contributions was that of Lindahl, in particular his essay "The rate of interest and the price level" (1930). In this Lindahl, after arguing that the quantity theory, though remaining a significant part of the theory of value, failed to provide a "satisfactory and generally valid" explanation of changes in the value of money. Such a theory, he argued, had to be sought through extending the general theory of price to the problem of price relations between periods.[70] To provide such an explanation, Lindahl constructed a dynamic period analysis, in which a "period" had two characteristics: during it, the factors directly influencing prices are taken as constant; and prices are in equilibrium such that supply equals demand.[71] The price level within each period is explained in terms of the relation

$$E(1 - s) = PQ,$$

where $E$ denotes money income, $s$ the proportion saved, and $P$ and $Q$ the price and quantity of consumption goods. Using this framework Lindahl could then analyse the effects, under different circumstances, of a change in the rate of interest. Starting from an initial situation of full employment, he obtained Wicksellian conclusions, but when he started from a situation of unemployment he found that the rise in incomes caused by the fall in the rate of interest would raise consumption, thus increasing employment, not only in the investment goods sector, but also in the consumption goods sector.[72] Lindahl's emphasis, however, was not on this so much as on the fact that the price level would rise by less in such a situation than in a situation of full employment.[73]

Two years later there appeared the first version of what was to be the most important Swedish contribution: Myrdal's *Monetary Equilibrium*,[74] a book which developed Lindahl's interpretation of Wicksell's cumulative process. Myrdal described his main contribution as being "to include anticipations in the monetary system".[75] He did this through introducing the distinction between the *ex ante* and *ex post* values of a variable. Though he did not provide a full dynamic analysis, the fact that he was, like Lindahl, thinking in terms of a dynamic period analysis was crucial: *ex ante* quantities were defined in terms of the action planned at the start of a period; *ex post* quantities were those measured at the end of the period.[76] This distinction was important only in a dynamic economy, for in a stationary state it would be unimportant whether a period was viewed from the beginning or the end.

This approach led Myrdal to start from the position that,

In the *ex post* calculus there is, …, by necessity an exact balance between the invested waiting and the value of gross investment. Looking forward there is no such balance except under certain conditions which remain to be ascertained. In the *ex ante* calculus it is a question not of realized results but of the anticipations, calculations and plans driving the dynamic process forward. [If investment or saving changes] there must be a tendency *ex ante* to a disparity. The real problem to be solved in monetary theory is: How does this tendency to disparity in the saving–investment equation develop into *ex post* balance?[77]

Along with his emphasis on the importance of the period implicit in monetary analysis, Myrdal considered the concepts of *ex ante* and *ex post* to have been his chief contribution.

Using these concepts Myrdal was able to proceed to his "immanent criticism" of Wicksell, reformulating the latter's concept of monetary equilibrium. After replacing Wicksell's natural rate of interest with an anticipated, *ex ante*, yield on investment, he concluded that monetary equilibrium required a profit rate sufficient to stimulate "just the amount of total investment which can be taken care of by the available capital disposal".[78] Though retaining what Myrdal described as the "fundamental part" of Wicksell's theory, he thus abandoned Wicksell's zero profit condition (equality of the natural and money rates of interest). Central to Myrdal's own equilibrium condition was that it was defined *ex ante*. He also parted company with Wicksell when considering the relationship between monetary equilibrium and price stability, for he argued that monetary equilibrium was compatible with any inflation rate.[79] However, because some prices are stickier than others, monetary policy needed, according to Myrdal, to aim at "adapting the flexible prices to the absolute level of the sticky ones".[80]

It is in considering sticky prices that Myrdal derived results which paralleled those of the *General Theory*. He considered a tightening of credit, this lowering capital values, reducing profit margins and lowering investment. This will cause incomes to fall, both in the investment goods and the consumer goods sectors, unemployment rising in both due to wage stickiness. When incomes fall in this way, Myrdal argues, consumption will fall by "significantly less" than total income, savings being reduced despite the rise in the rate of interest[81] He thus sees the possibility that this fall in saving will serve to maintain monetary equilibrium. However, Myrdal is still seeing price changes as the motive force behind the process, for he argues that if consumption goods prices do not fall, the process will come to an end.[82] After this, Myrdal goes on to assert the following, Keynesian sounding, proposition:

If the forces maintaining consumption are strong enough and if the reaction of total real investment to a shrinking profit margin is sufficiently small, then the effects of the credit policy will be neutralized.[83]

We thus have here two familiar ideas: that monetary equilibrium (savings equal to investment) is possible at a variety of levels of employment; and that monetary policy will, under certain circumstances, be ineffective. Notice, however, that Myrdal's emphasis is throughout, as befits his objective of providing an "immanent criticism" of Wicksell, on the implications of his analysis for the price level rather than for the level of employment.

Although Lindahl and Myrdal made what were probably the most important of the Swedish contributions to the monetary theory, they were far from alone. Others worth mentioning are Hammarskjold, Ohlin and Lundberg. Hammarskjold's contribution was twofold. He not only provided a formal, algebraic exposition of period analysis, but also stressed windfall profits as the link between successive periods. In this he was strongly influenced by Keynes' *Treatise on Money*. Ohlin, as was the case with his work on international trade, stressed quantity adjustments as part of the mechanism whereby equilibrium was brought about. Finally, it was Lundberg (1937) who analysed a process in which there is continual disequilibrium, in the sense that expectations are not fulfilled in each period.

## The multiplier

The view that an increase in spending in one sector of the economy might, through its effect on incomes, raise spending in other sectors, was widely held in the late 1920s. Not only was it present, albeit without being given a prominent role, in theoretical writings on the trade cycle, from Hawtrey's *Good and Bad Trade* to Pigou's *Industrial Fluctuations*, but it was also important in discussions of public works expenditure.[84] What was missing from these discussions was the technical device of the multiplier, whereby the secondary effects on employment were determined by the marginal propensity to consume.[85]

One source of the multiplier was Hawtrey who, in a paper prepared for the MacMillan Committee[86] at the beginning of 1931, produced a numerical example relating an increase in investment to an increase in output. In his example, 40% of income was saved, and Hawtrey argued that a £5m increase in investment would produce a £12.5m increase in output.[87] The other, and more well known, source of the multiplier was Kahn's article "On the relation of home investment to unemployment" (1931). In this he calculated the amount of secondary employment that would result from employing an extra man on road building. The ratio of secondary to primary employment was determined by the distribution of income, and the fractions of profits and wages spent on home-produced consumption goods.[88] Meade's contribution to the theory of the multiplier was to show that at the end of the multiplier process, the increase in savings would, ignoring changes in imports and exports, equal the initial increase in investment. In other words, an increase in investment could, under some circumstances, generate enough savings to finance itself.

Because of the way the multiplier is often presented nowadays, it is important to emphasize that Kahn's multiplier was *not* a theory of aggregate demand. It was simply a relationship between the primary and secondary employment effects of an increase in public investment. Similarly, in discussing the relationship between saving and investment, the emphasis was on (1) the reduction in unemployment benefits, and (2) the fall in the balance of trade that would result from a rise in investment. The multiplier was not derived, as in modern theory, from a saving–investment equilibrium condition.

### Keynes' General Theory

Immediately after its publication it became clear that there were serious defects in the central theoretical chapters of Keynes' *Treatise on Money*: in particular in those dealing with the "fundamental equations" and the dynamics of the price level. To a certain extent Keynes was aware of the book's inadequacies,[89] but far more important was the barrage of criticism to which the book was immediately subjected. Some criticisms could be dismissed, but there were many that could not be. In particular, it was argued that the fundamental equations were merely truisms, explaining nothing; that there were problems with the units in which Keynes measured quantities; and, above all, that he failed to deal adequately with changes in output. This point had been made by Hawtrey who, even before the book's publication, had criticized Keynes for not recognizing that a fall in demand might, even without any fall in prices, lead to a fall in output.[90] More important, however, was the sustained investigation of this issue by a group of younger Cambridge economists (the so-called "circus", of which Robinson, Meade and Kahn were the most prominent members) which met regularly to discuss the *Treatise*.[91] Kahn's article on the multiplier had been available before the *Treatise* was published, but was too late to have any influence on it. It was as a result of his trying to combine his analysis with that of the *Treatise* that Kahn reached the conclusion that the fundamental equations applied in their full simplicity only at full employment. It was Kahn who pointed out the error, in the *Treatise*, of ascribing the price levels of investment and consumption goods to completely different causes. It was out of this process of re-examining the *Treatise on Money* that a theory of output began to emerge, albeit one expressed in the same language.[92]

The gist of Keynes' ideas at this time is contained in a series of lectures he gave in Chicago in June 1931.[93] As in the *Treatise*, he spoke of booms and slumps as being determined by excesses or deficiencies of investment over saving, but though still attaching great importance to the role of profits, he emphasized changes in employment more than in the *Treatise*. He came close to the idea of an unemployment equilibrium:

> Now there is a reason for expecting an equilibrium point to be reached. A given deficiency of investment causes a given decline in profit. A given decline in profit causes a given decline in output. Unless there is a constantly increasing deficiency of investment, there is eventually reached, therefore, a sufficiently low level of output which represents a spurious kind of equilibrium.[94]

Although this is not the *General Theory* it is a significant step towards it, the final steps being taken in the next couple of years.[95]

These origins explain some of the puzzling features of the *General Theory*.[96] Because Keynes had little to add to much of the discussion of the monetary system contained in the *Treatise,* the *General Theory*'s treatment of money is fairly rudimentary. More importantly, however, the criticism to which the fundamental equations were subjected explains why Keynes, in the *General Theory*, avoided any measurement of either levels of output or price levels. Everything in the *General Theory* is measured either in terms of quantities of money, or in terms of employment. Thus, for example, the aggregate supply curve relates not price to output, but revenue to employment.

The crucial part of the *General Theory*, as is evident even from a glance at the table of contents, is the theory of aggregate demand. This theory will be familiar, but it is important to point out that there is more to this than the idea of the multiplier. Three main propositions can be distinguished: (1) that an increase in expenditure will produce "multiplier" effects; (2) that there may be equality of saving and investment at a variety of levels of income; and (3) that changes in the level of output provide a mechanism through which, independently of changes in profitability, savings and investment can be brought into equilibrium. Kahn had provided only the first. By the time of his Chicago lectures, quoted above, Keynes had reached the second proposition, though he had still not integrated this with the idea of the multiplier. For the *General Theory* all three propositions were necessary. There is a radical difference between understanding the dynamic multiplier and seeing how this can be used as the basis for a theory of aggregate demand. Keynes achieved the latter; Kahn did not.

The theory of the consumption function, however, can explain the level of demand only given the level of investment. Keynes' explanation of the latter, the inducement to invest, comprised two parts: the marginal efficiency of capital, and the theory of liquidity preference. The marginal efficiency of capital, the discount rate at which prospective returns from investment equal the cost of the investment, turned out to be the same as Fisher's rate of return over cost.[97] To understand Keynes' use of it, however, we need to consider his approach to the problem of expectations. This was to divide expectations into long and short term expectations.[98] The former are concerned with the proceeds an entrepreneur can expect to derive from the output he is producing; the latter with what he can expect to earn through future production if he purchases an item of capital equipment. Short term expectations are capable of being checked frequently in the light of experience, and so Keynes argues that it is reasonable to neglect them, looking simply at realized proceeds. Long term expectations, however, are a different matter, being based on much more precarious information in which investors have limited confidence. To a large extent, therefore, long term expectations are based on conventions, these being liable to change arbitrarily, and for no apparent reason. This means that the marginal efficiency of capital was, for Keynes, something very volatile, liable to change arbitrarily as investors changed their opinions. This contrasted with consumption decisions, which, being based on short term expectations, could be portrayed as a function of realized income.

Expectations were also important in Keynes' theory of the rate of interest, in which the rate of interest depended on liquidity preference. Demand for money depended on expectations of future interest rates as much as on current interest rates. More important, however, than the details of Keynes' treatment is the fact that it was, as was the treatment of demand for money in the *Treatise*, demand for the *stock* of money which determined the rate of interest. Demand for money was being seen as part of the theory of portfolio choice.[99]

In presenting all the material discussed so far, the main part of the *General Theory*, Keynes made the preliminary assumption that the money wage rate was constant, many variables being measured in wage units, an assumption not relaxed until chapter 19. Despite its coming so late in the *General Theory*, however, this chapter is of particular importance in view of the role of money wage rigidity in previous theories of unemployment. Keynes' argument about money wage changes is the following. (1) Given the propensity to consume, the marginal efficiency of capital and the rate of interest, a reduction in money wage rates can have no effect on employment. If entrepreneurs were to respond to a fall in money wage rates by increasing their production, they would find that demand would, unless the marginal propensity to consume were equal to unity, fail to grow by as much as supply. The additional output would remain unsold, so firms would not have an incentive to produce it. (2) Alternatively, a reduction in money wage rates might affect demand through the propensity to consume (through affecting the distribution of income), through the marginal efficiency of capital (through affecting the ratio of current costs to expected proceeds), or through the rate of interest (through raising the real value of the money supply). It is through the last of these that Keynes argues that wage reductions must operate. This means that wage reductions have effects exactly equivalent to those of an appropriate increase in the money supply. Two conclusions can be drawn from this. (a) For exactly the same reason that an increase in the money supply may fail to raise employment, a reduction in money wage rates may be ineffective. (b) Any increase in employment which could be brought about by a wage reduction could, much more easily, be brought about by an increase in the quantity of money. (3) Finally, having shown that an increase in the money supply can mimic the effects of a reduction in wage rates, Keynes then argues that money wages *ought not* to be flexible, for changes in the money wage rate cause unfair changes in the distribution of income, changes in the burden of debt, and instability in the price level. Thus, not only does Keynes not blame unemployment on wage rigidity, but he argues that it is better for money wage rates to be inflexible.

## 16.6  CONCLUSIONS

The period covered by this chapter was an extremely fertile one as regards theories of money and the cycle. Although the quantity theory remained, right up to the time of the *General Theory*, the framework within which such issues were discussed, it was the vehicle for much thought on short run problems. Wicksell's cumulative process and Fisher's transition periods, contain much worthwhile analysis of the relationship of monetary changes and changes in output and the price level. Though they have been expounded separately in this chapter, theories of money and the cycle were closely linked, even by economists for whom monetary factors were not primary. Thus although there was no separate subject of "macroeconomics", the issues we now consider under that heading were far from neglected. Despite the revolutionary claims made in the *General Theory*, therefore, it is very misleading to view Keynes as having created the subject of macroeconomics almost single-handed.

# 17

## International Trade and Colonies

### 17.1 BACKGROUND

The new theories of value developed in the 1870s did not result in any dramatic changes in the theory of international trade and the empire. Two reasons suggest themselves. The first is that because of concern with the question of the gains from trade, real cost theories of value, with their associated welfare implications, continued to be used. As a result the labour theory of value survived, albeit in a modified form, in international trade theory into the twentieth century.[1] The second is that the dominant influence was that of Mill, whose theory of reciprocal demand was completely compatible with the new theories of value, for it described a general equilibrium of supply and demand.

### 17.2 THE PURE THEORY OF TRADE, 1870–1914

*Developments within the classical tradition*

In the period after 1970 a number of economists worked to extend and to develop the Ricardo–Mill theory from within the classical tradition. The first important contributor was Cairnes (1874).[2] Cairnes accepted the main elements of Mills's theory, seeing comparative costs as explaining why countries trade, with reciprocal demand determining international values within the limits set by comparative costs.[3] He departed from Mill, however, in important respects. Firstly, he made it clear that the costs relevant to comparative advantage were the subjective sacrifices involved, these comprising both labour and abstinence, though in practice labour costs alone provided an acceptable approximation.[4] Cairnes carefully examined the relationship between comparative costs, calculated in this way, and relative prices. Secondly, because Cairnes extended Mill's theory of reciprocal demand to cover not simply trade, but exchange between non–competing groups *within* a country, he had to modify the Ricardian theory of comparative costs accordingly. The reason was that whereas for Ricardo and Mill relative prices within a country corresponded to relative costs, this would not be so if competition were imperfect. When they differed, it was relative prices, rather than relative costs, which had to be used in calculations of comparative advantage and trade flows.

It follows from this that, although a staunch defender of the classical theory of value, Cairnes greatly enlarged, albeit emphasizing imperfections of competition, the role of demand. The importance of demand came out in his discussion of the effects of increases in wages. Where effective competition prevailed, Cairnes followed the Ricardian view that a rise in wages would not affect the volume of trade: its effect would be to lower profits, leaving costs unaffected. Outside the limits of effective competition, however, whilst a uniform change in all wage rates would not affect trade, a change in wages within *one* non-competing group could affect trade. The mechanism was as follows. A fall in one industry's wages, assuming its workers do not compete directly with workers in other industries, would reduce that industry's costs and prices causing an increase in its exports. Depending on the elasticity of demand for these exports[5] the export revenue might rise, fall or stay the same, any change in export revenue producing a trade imbalance, and hence gold flows. These gold flows would alter the relative price levels of the countries concerned, as a result of which relative wage levels would be brought back into equilibrium. Whether or not the outcome of this process was a net increase in trade as a whole depended on elasticities of demand for the industry concerned and for other industries.

A later writer to develop Mill's theory along classical lines was Bastable (1897). He continued to use comparative costs, though measuring these not in terms of labour or sacrifice but in units of productive power: "a given amount of labour, working with an average amount of capital, and thus producing a definite amount of a commodity".[6] Like Cairnes he discussed non-competing groups and analysed the effects of variations in the elasticity of demand. Where he went further was in bringing in non-constant returns to scale. Variations in demand might, for Bastable, alter comparative advantage by changing relative costs.[7] A similar position was held by Taussig (1911, 1927), the dominant figure in trade theory, especially in the United States, in the early twentieth century. His position was fundamentally a classical one as modified by Cairnes and Bastable. His exposition had, however, the advantage of greater clarity.

## Mill's critics

The Ricardo–Mill system was subject to criticism from several economists.[8] McLeod (1872) and Cliffe Leslie (1879a) criticized the distinction between home and foreign trade, arguing that the same principles must apply to both, an argument effectively met by Cairnes' application of reciprocal demand to home trade between non-competing groups. Leslie went on to argue that lack of information caused numerous discrepancies between actual incomes and prices.[9] These were, however, criticisms from economists hostile to classical economics. An example of criticism by a follower of classical economics can be found in Sidgwick's *Principles of Political Economy* (1883). Sidgwick argued that the peculiarity of international trade was not factor immobility but distance.[10] He came to the conclusion that limits to international relative prices would be set not by comparative costs but by home costs with and without the double cost of transportation.[11] The exact position of prices within this range depended on how the two countries shared the costs of transportation.

Characteristic of all these criticisms was their failure to provide a fundamental challenge to the Ricardo–Mill orthodoxy. They were all criticisms which could be passed over as missing the main point of the Ricardo–Mill theory. Sidgwick was concerned with a more limited problem: the division of the costs of transport, rather than the gains from trade.[12] Of the criticisms offered by McLeod and Leslie, some were incorrect; others raised much wider issues.[13]

*Mathematical extensions of the Ricardo–Mill system*

Of more significance were attempts by economists to analyse the Ricardo–Mill system mathematically. The most important was that of Marshall (1879) who analysed Mill's reciprocal demand using offer curves. His theory, however, was not for some time published, being merely circulated, by Sidgwick, to a limited number of economists. The first actual publication of his offer curves was in Italian, in Pantaleoni's *Manual of Pure Economics* (1889).

Though Marshall described these as demand curves they were very different from the demand curves used by Marshall in his theory of domestic values, for they were not partial equilibrium constructions describing demand for a single commodity on the assumption that the prices of all other commodities remained unchanged, but were general equilibrium constructions drawn on the assumption that changes in trade were accompanied by readjustments in domestic production. This was made clear by Edgeworth who at one point described an offer curve as a "supply and demand curve".[14] Offer curves were effective in clarifying several aspects of the Ricardo–Mill theory, in particular the analysis of stability and changes in cost conditions. They could also be used to analyse the effects of tariffs and, when combined with indifference curves, as was done by Edgeworth, to draw conclusions about welfare.[15] Marshall's offer curves thus provided a useful means of expounding the Ricardo–Mill theory, but without altering its substance.

An alternative mathematical approach was to apply to international trade the Walrasian method of general equilibrium, as was done by Pareto (1896, 1908). Pareto, however, failed to get beyond the counting of equations, adding little of real interest.[16] He was, however, able to make the notion of sacrifice more precise, relating it to *ophélimité*, or utility. He criticized the classical economists for being imprecise in their definition of costs.[17]

## 17.3   THE PURE THEORY OF TRADE: THE INTER-WAR PERIOD

*Graham*

It was the inter-war period which saw the first serious challenge to Mill's theory of international values, this coming from Graham (1923, 1932). He attributed the errors of those following Mill's approach to

Mill's dictum, too slavishly accepted by his followers, that trade among any number of countries, and in any number of commodities, must take place on the same essential principles as trade between two countries and in two commodities.[18]

Results drawn from the two country–two commodity case had, according to Graham, "no application to reality."[19] He adduced a variety of reasons for this.[20] (1) When there are more than two commodities or more than two countries comparative advantage ceases to be something dependent on cost conditions alone, but depends on the actual terms of trade: if the terms of trade change a country may import and export different commodities. This was a well-known point, discussed by, for example, Edgeworth. (2) When there are more than two countries demand conditions change dramatically: the existence of alternative sources of supply makes demand for an individual country's product more elastic. (3) A large number of countries and commodities means that the limits to variations in international values set by comparative cost become narrower. (4) It becomes inappropriate to assume that two countries' demands for each others' products will be of the same order of magnitude. Consider, for example, English matches exported in return for German cloth: it is likely that within the limits set by comparative costs German demand for matches will be very small relative to English demand for German cloth, with the result that their relative price will be set by comparative costs in England, all the advantage from trade accruing to Germany.[21]

Using this approach Graham was able to re-evaluate many of the conclusions reached by Mill and his successors.[22] Fundamental to his argument was his claim that

the terms of international exchange are established not in the way posited by the neoclassical school [Mill and his successors] but through the play of indirect, or "linked", competition, on the basis of opportunity cost.[23]

Though going beyond the Ricardian theory in analysing multi-commodity, multi-country exchange, and in analysing much more thoroughly the interplay of supply and demand, Graham was thus restoring the Ricardian approach to trade theory. His objection was very much to Mill's theory of reciprocal demand, which, unlike Ricardo's comparative advantage, Graham believed, did not take account of each country's internal production conditions. It is for this reason that Haberler described Graham's approach as "ultra classical".[24] It was not until Meade's work in the 1950s that the link between internal production conditions and offer curves was made explicit.

## Heckscher and Ohlin

An alternative approach to the pure theory of trade originated, under Wicksell's influence, in the work of two Swedish economists, Heckscher (1919) and his pupil Ohlin (1933).[25] Heckscher's purpose was to analyse the effects of trade on the distribution of income between factors of production, to do which he had to explain why comparative costs differed between countries. Making the assumption, which distinguished his theory from the classical theory, that "the same efficiency" prevailed in both countries (that they both had access to the same technology)[26] Heckscher came to the conclusion that differences in comparative costs arose due to differences in the relative scarcity of factors of production. A country where labour, for example, was abundant would have a comparative advantage in relatively labour intensive products. This framework enabled Heckscher to argue that trade tended to even out the scarcity of factors of production among countries.[27] Through exporting commodities which used a country's relatively abundant factor, and importing those which required large amounts of its relatively scarce factor, demand for abundant factors would be increased and demand for scarce factors reduced. Heckscher claimed that where the same technique was used in two countries[28] trade would expand until relative factor prices were equalized. This tendency to equalization would partially be offset, however, if there were any scope for factor substitution, in which case equalization of relative factor prices would be only partial. Where different techniques were used, both absolute and relative factor prices would differ between countries, such differences explaining the migration of capital and labour.[29]

Ohlin, through whose book *Interregional and International Trade* (1933) Heckscher's ideas became known to the English speaking world, adopted substantially the same position. He found explanations of differences in comparative costs, and hence of trade, in differences in factor endowments; and he found that trade would lead to a partial equalization of factor prices. There were, however, important differences between the two treatments. (1) He made explicit the general equilibrium nature of his theory, describing inter-regional equilibrium in a system of equations analogous to Cassel's system for a single region.[30] (2) He pointed out that trade could be caused not only by differences in factor endowments, but also by differences in demands, and by gains through specialization where there were increasing returns to scale. (3) He provided a discussion of dynamic aspects of trade and factor pricing, including international factor movements and changing factor supplies.

Ohlin presented his theory as an alternative to the orthodox theory. Referring to Pareto's theory, of which his was a development, he wrote, "Pareto did not bring some minor modifications of the classical doctrine, but attacked the problem in an entirely different way."[31] Ohlin criticized Pareto for not formally rejecting the Ricardian doctrine, for he argued that by measuring comparative costs in terms of marginal utility instead of labour costs, Pareto had fundamentally altered the Ricardian theory.[32] Despite Ohlin's view, however, it can be argued that it is the opportunity cost aspect of the Ricardian theory which is fundamental, and that the labour theory of value, with which Ohlin disagreed, was a subsidiary feature. Given this, Ohlin's theory appears as a development of, not an alternative to, classical theory.

*Opportunity cost*

The third approach to the pure theory of trade to emerge in the inter-war period was that stemming from the work of Haberler (1930, 1933). Like

Ohlin, Haberler was concerned "to display the Theory of International Trade as a constituent part of the modern doctrine of economic equilibrium".[33] He started from Ricardo's comparative cost theory, but instead of rejecting it he argued that the labour theory of value, from which Ricardo had derived relative costs, could be replaced with the concept of opportunity cost.[34] To do this he introduced what he called the "substitution curve" (the production possibility frontier, or transformation curve) which described the rate at which commodities could be substituted for each other in production, without bringing in any specific theory of costs.

In a series of papers in the early 1930s this approach was developed into the geometric version of trade theory that is found in modern textbooks. Viner in 1931 combined Haberler's substitution curve with indifference curves.[35] The nature of such an equilibrium was further investigated by Lerner (1932, 1934) and Leontief (1933), the latter using the theory to derive Marshall's offer curves, and explaining, without using either real or labour costs, the effects of factor endowments and demand conditions on trade.[36]

## 17.4 THE TRANSFER MECHANISM

### Bastable and Nicholson

In the closing decades of the nineteenth century discussion of the transfer mechanism was stimulated by a number of works analysing the terms of trade between England and India, arguing that the large sums paid to England on "extra-commercial accounts" had turned the terms of trade to India's disadvantage.[37] Many of these writings relied on Mill's version of the price-specie-flow mechanism: starting from a position of internal and external equilibrium, a unilateral transfer would, through causing specie to flow into the receiving country, raise its prices relative to those in the paying country, this resulting in an excess of imports over exports. This view was challenged by Bastable and Nicholson, both of whom argued that transfers were effected through changes in incomes.

Bastable claimed that Mill had omitted to allow for the effect of the transfer on incomes. Even without any multiplier effects, and these were absent from the discussion until the 1930s, a transfer payment would cause a once-for-all increase in the receiving country's income. This would, independently of any specie flow or changes in prices, cause the creditor to demand more imports. If this effect is sufficiently large there will be no need for any change in relative prices: "The inhabitants of the [creditor country], having larger money incomes, will purchase more *at the same price*, and thus bring about the necessary excess of imports over exports".[38] Indeed, in actual circumstances, where there are many countries and many commodities, competition will fix the terms of trade between relatively narrow limits, preventing the price changes on which Mill's mechanism relies. Despite such a clear account, however, Bastable never fully integrated this with the rest of his work on trade and foreign exchange.[39]

Bastable's theory was taken up a few years later by Nicholson (1897), who improved on it in several ways. In addition to the receiving country's increase in income, Nicholson brings in the loss of income in the paying country:

The government of the paying country must levy taxes to the amount of the annual tribute, and thereby will *diminish the consuming power* of the people by so much. Assume that, in the first place, actual money is taken from the pockets of the people. We may suppose that in consequence there will be partly a lessened demand for imports and partly an excess of home commodities available for export. At the same time the receiving country – when the money is sent to it – will *have so much more to spend* and can take more imports and also consume things formerly exported. In this way an excess of exports from the paying country equivalent to the tribute can be brought about without any change in prices.[40]

Though aware of problems which might arise, Nicholson is making it clear that transfer can be effected without any change in prices. The issue is how quickly the relevant adjustments take place.

Though Bastable and Nicholson saw themselves as challenging an established orthodoxy,[41] they were in fact arriving at conclusions reached in the first half of the nineteenth century by economists, from Foster to McCulloch and Cairnes, concerned with the effects of Irish absenteeism.[42] The quotation from Nicholson might well have come from one of these earlier writers.

### Taussig

Despite the work of Bastable and Nicholson, however, the price-specie-flow approach remained dominant, its outstanding exponent being Taussig, whose article "International trade under depreciated paper. A contribution to theory" (1917) prompted widespread discussion. Though concerned with a different financial situation Taussig's theory was fundamentally the same as Mill's: a transfer would raise prices in the receiving country relative to those in the paying country, the resulting "bounties" on exports and imports producing the required trade balance.[43] Taussig did consider the case where neither specie flows nor price level changes were required, but he dismissed it as "extremely rare", occurring mostly in cases where loans were, as part of a "neo-mercantilist" policy, tied to exports from the lending country.[44]

One result of this paper was a re-statement, by Wicksell (1918) and J. H. Hollander (1918), of the classical mechanism. This is done most clearly by Wicksell who, considering two countries whose prices cannot vary, concludes:

The stimulus to these altered conditions of trade is not to be found in a difference of prices in the two countries, [ruled out by the assumptions]; the increased *demand* for commodities in one country, the diminished demand in the other would in the main be sufficient to call forth the changes alluded to.[45]

The other result of Taussig's article was a series of PhD theses by his students, each studying the balancing mechanism for a particular country at a time of large capital transfers. Examples of these are Viner's *Canada's Balance of International Indebtedness* (1924a), and J. H. Williams' *Argentine International Trade under Inconvertible Currency, 1880–1900* (1920). It was in the light of these studies that Taussig wrote:

> One thing, however, stands out from the British phenomena ... the unmistakably close connection between international payments and the movements of commodity imports and exports. And this closeness of connection is found again and again in other countries also.[46]

There was, however, a puzzle, for imports and exports moved surprisingly fast, "almost as if there were an automatic connection between these financial operations and the commodity exports and imports". The intermediate stage, predicted by the Thornton–Mill theory, involving gold flows and price changes, was hard to find, and if it was there it was certainly extremely short. Taussig did not, however, abandon the theory: "I find it impossible to see how there can be a complete skipping of the intermediate stage – anything in the nature of an automatic connection." The evidence remained, for Taussig, a puzzle.

### Keynes and Ohlin

The transfer problem was brought into prominence in the inter-war period by the question of German reparations payments, required by the treaty of Versailles: could Germany afford to pay reparations on the scale demanded. In addition to the issue of whether sufficient money could be raised, by taxes or other means, within Germany (the so-called budgetary problem) there was the transfer problem, the issue of whether any financial payments could be translated into an export surplus. Rather than consider the controversy in detail[47] we will concentrate on one episode where theoretical issues emerged very sharply: the exchange between Keynes and Ohlin in the 1929 *Economic Journal*.

Keynes argued that the budgetary problem was solved, for Germany was by 1929 already paying enough taxes to cover reparations. He was doubtful, however, as to whether it was possible to translate this into an export surplus. The reason was that although Germany was capable of increasing the supply of exports, these could be sold abroad only if their price fell sufficiently to increase demand. The problem as Keynes saw it lay with the elasticity of demand: the value of exports had to be increased by 40%. Because the Allies refused to let Germany devalue, an *enormous* reduction in domestic prices and costs was required.[48] Indeed, if the elasticity of demand were less than unity it would be *impossible* for Germany to produce an export surplus[49]

Ohlin's response to this was to argue that Keynes had neglected the direct effects of reparations on buying power, and hence on the balance of trade. Suppose country A borrows (or receives as a gift) 100m marks from country B. A fraction (say 20m marks) will be spent on imports, the remainder being spent on domestic goods. Keynes, in the tradition of

Taussig, stressed that this would produce only *a part* of the required balance of trade adjustment of 100m marks, the remainder being produced through price changes. Ohlin, in contrast, took up an argument made earlier by Viner[50] to the effect that this 80m marks spent on domestic goods would lead, through attracting resources away from export and import-competing industries, to an import surplus of 80m marks additional to the initial 20m. Though there would be price changes internally, the required surplus would thus be produced independently of any change in the terms of trade. Ohlin thus saw the transfer problem as much less of a problem than Keynes.[51]

*Conclusions*

In these disagreements over the transfer mechanism a variety of issues were involved. One cause of difficulty was that the advocates of the demand transfer mechanism separated changes in demand from changes in the quantity of money. In contrast to Wicksell and Ohlin, Taussig and Keynes argued that, under convertible currency, transfers of demand required movements of gold.[52] The most important issue, however, was whether adjustment could come about through changes in income or changes in relative price levels. The difference was not, as Taussig and Keynes argued,[53] that the demand-transfer theorists skipped the period of adjustment, dealing instead with equilibria, but was rather that a different mechanism was being proposed. Having said this, however, it is important not to exaggerate the contributions of the advocates of the demand transfer mechanism. Despite the similarity of their ideas to those later advocated by Keynes, the crucial concept of the multiplier was missing.[54] This makes pre-1930 discussions of the transfer mechanism very different from post-1936 discussions of the problem.

## 17.5　THE THEORY OF THE EXCHANGE RATE

*Cassel's theory of purchasing power parity*

The currency instability of the first world war and after, when many countries suffered from periods of severe inflation and rapidly depreciating currencies, brought into prominence the question of exchange rates, something which had not been relevant when convertibility into gold at a fixed exchange rate could be assumed. The most widely discussed theory of international exchange rates was that of Cassel, the creator of the term "purchasing power parity".[55] The earliest version of the theory was the simplest.

If we consider two countries, A and B, with independent paper currencies, the money of A can have value in B only on the ground that it represents buying power, or more generally paying power in A. The price in B of the money of A will, therefore, be broadly proportional to the buying power of the money of A and will consequently stay in inverse proportion to the general prices in A. Furthermore, the price in B will, of course, tend to be proportional to the general level of prices in B. Thus the rate of exchange between the two countries will be determined by the quotient between the general levels of prices in the two countries.[56]

In other words, people value foreign currency only for the goods it will buy in the country concerned. If foreign prices double, foreign currency will be worth half as much. Similarly, if domestic prices were to double and foreign prices were to remain unchanged, the value of domestic currency would be halved and people would pay twice as much domestic currency for a unit of foreign currency. If both domestic and foreign prices doubled the exchange rate would be unchanged.

This theory of the exchange rate was completed with a simple quantity theory of money:

Now, according to the quantitative theory of money the general level of prices varies, other things being equal, in direct proportion to the quantity of the circulating medium in a country. If this be true, the rate of exchange between two countries must vary as the quotient between the quantities of their representative circulating media.[57]

To confirm this theory Cassel looked at data for Britain and Sweden. Cassel's approach was determined by the availability of data. Using an index of British prices and measures of currency circulation in Sweden[58] he calculated the inflation which had taken place since 1910–1913.[59] From this he could calculate what should have happened to the exchange rate since 1910–1913 if the purchasing power parity theory were true. He found that, for the 12 months in 1915, the period he investigated, there was very little divergence between the actual exchange rate and its theoretical rate given by purchasing power parity.

*Criticism and development of the theory*

The theory, as first stated by Cassel, was very straightforward, but it soon became clear that it had to be modified. One of the first modifications was that restrictions on trade might cause the exchange rate to diverge from purchasing power parity, provided they affected a country's exports and imports unequally. Restrictions on imports, for example, might cause a country's currency to appreciate.[60] Exchange rates might also depart from purchasing power parity as a result of speculative capital movements, these perhaps caused by expectations of inflation or particularly severe balance of payments deficits.[61] The outcome of this type of modification to Cassel's theory was that purchasing power parity came to be seen as a theory of the, longer term, equilibrium exchange rate. This tendency is most clearly stated by the most prominent British exponent of purchasing power parity theory, Keynes (1924):

the essence of the purchasing power parity theory, considered as an explanation of the exchanges, is to be found, I think, in its regarding internal purchasing power as being in the long run a more trustworthy indicator of a currency's value than market rates of exchange, because internal purchasing power quickly reflects the monetary policy of the country, which is the final determinant.[62]

Though the theory thus became very different from Cassel's original version, a theory of month-by-month exchange rates, it retained the notion that causation ran from domestic monetary policy to changes in the exchange rate. This was criticized by several economists who argued that causation ran the other way round. In the US, for example, it was argued that from 1862 to 1879, a period when the dollar was inconvertible (the Greenbacks), commodity prices had *followed* changes in the exchange rate. It was variations in the probability of paper currency being redeemed in gold that caused, firstly, variations in the exchange rate, and secondly, changes in commodity prices.[63] Amongst American economists it was Fisher, the foremost exponent of the quantity theory, who was the most important supporter of purchasing power parity.[64]

Even if causation did run from money to the exchange rate, there were still important problems with purchasing power parity. Pigou (1922) raised several important technical problems with the theory. Particularly important is the fact that not all goods enter into international trade. For non-traded goods there is no reason why there should be any relation between two countries' prices. To show the importance of this for purchasing power parity we need to consider the distinction between absolute and relative purchasing power parity (Pigou called them "positive" and "comparative" respectively). Absolute purchasing power parity states that the exchange rate is the ratio of the price levels in two countries: if a given bundle of goods costs $6 in the US, and £2 in the UK, then purchasing power parity implies $3=£1. Against this version of purchasing power parity, the existence of non-traded goods is decisive, for it means there is no reason why purchasing power parity should hold. Relative purchasing power parity, however, states that the change in the exchange rate since some base period is given by the difference between two countries' inflation rates. This version of the theory can be defended in the presence of non-traded goods, provided that, within each country, the ratio of the prices of traded and non-traded goods has not changed.

This question of non-traded goods raises the question of what price index should be used in calculations of purchasing power parity. If relative prices of traded and non-traded goods are changing then a general index of prices cannot be used. On the other hand, if the price of traded goods alone is used, the theory becomes, as Keynes later pointed out, almost a truism: it follows from the fact that, allowing for transport costs, there can be only one price in the world market for a commodity.[65] In addition, when the price index used is the price index of only those goods entering into world trade, it becomes much harder to see causation as running from prices to exchange rates, rather than vice versa.

Still further complications arise from the fact that divergences between purchasing power parity and exchange rates can occur through shifts in demand, or through changes in productivity. Any demand shift, for example, which causes a change in the terms of trade should produce a discrepancy between purchasing power parity and the exchange rate.[66] Whilst some economists (e.g. Keynes[67]) supported an appropriately qualified version of purchasing power parity, others rejected the theory altogether. Thus Taussig (1927) argued that "there is no normal or settled rate of exchange based on purchasing power parity".[68]

Some of the problems faced by economists writing on exchange rates in the inter-war period stemmed from the paucity of the available data. Of particular interest here is an attempt by Brisman (1933) to introduce a cost parity into the discussion. He argued that

equilibrium consists in balance between the rates of exchange on the one hand and the international competitive power of the paper currency country on the other. The latter is determined by the effective costs of production in the paper currency country compared with the same costs of production in the gold standard countries
.... [69]

This was the idea that underlies indices of competitiveness, such as relative unit labour costs. However, whilst such indices of international competitiveness, often referred to as "real" exchange rates, are routinely calculated today, Brisman was forced to accept that such "effective costs of production cannot be determined statistically". His conclusion was the pessimistic one that, "we must consequently give up any idea of a numerical expression for the state of equilibrium".[70]

## 17.6  EMPIRE AND COLONIAL DEVELOPMENT

*Hobson*

Amongst non-Marxist economists there was, in the late nineteenth and early twentieth centuries, only one who developed a new approach to the empire: Hobson.[71] The theory for which Hobson is best known is his theory of "financial imperialism", expounded in *Imperialism: a Study* (1902) and a series of writings in the years up to 1914.[72] In its simplest version his theory started from the unequal distribution of income in capitalist countries, which led to chronic over-saving. Hobson took up the idea, going back to Smith and Wakefield, that imperial expansion could be used to provide an outlet for investment and for exports of commodities. Protection was an aspect of this process, for protection could raise profits, accentuating the maldistribution of income and hence the surplus of capital seeking investment outlets. Thus despite his earlier advocacy of protection and imperial expansion as a means of counteracting under-consumption at home, Hobson turned against protection as being one facet of imperialism.

In arguing the case for free trade Hobson was following the radical tradition of which Cobden had been the outstanding exponent in an earlier era.[73] His reasons for supporting free trade, however, changed substantially. In 1902 Hobson was adopting the view that prosperity depended primarily on the home market. Given radical domestic reforms, which would reduce inequality and correct the tendency to under-consumption, foreign trade would become comparatively unimportant:

[if] the industrial revolution had taken place in an England founded upon equal access by all classes to land, education and legislation, specialization in manufactures would not have gone so far ... for trade would have been less important, though more steady; the state of life for all portions of the population would have been high and the present rate of national consumption would have given full, consistent, remunerative employment to a far larger quantity of public and private capital than is now employed.[74]

Given equality in the distribution of income, demand would be sufficient to ensure full employment. In later writing, on the other hand, Hobson moved towards a more Cobdenite position, stressing the contribution of free trade, and the resulting interdependence of nations, to world peace.[75]

An important aspect of Hobson's thought is his view of the effects of imperialism on the colonial territories. Hobson's subtlest analysis of the prospects for colonial territories came in (1902)[76] where he argued that capital export was capable of transforming the world economy: countries such as China could develop to such an extent as to become a serious competitive threat to Europe and America.[77] This outcome, however, was not inevitable, or even likely, for all regions, for two reasons. Firstly, Hobson saw an enormous difference between countries such as China and India, with a long history of civilization, where the local social organization might prove sufficient to cope with development; and other areas, such as Africa, where orderly development and the avoidance of exploitation might require external supervision.[78] Secondly, and more importantly, a natural development of Asian and African countries based on local needs was contingent on reforms within western societies. In the absence of radical, egalitarian reforms in western countries, imperialism would lead both to a vast growth in the wealth and power of the western financial class at the expense of the Chinese and western working classes,[79] and to unsuitable, exploitative forms of development being imposed on Asia and Africa.[80] Hobson's fear at this time was a de-industrialization of the West, with manufacturing becoming concentrated exclusively in the East due to lower labour costs. Western prosperity would then be confined to finance and services. Later, however, he moved towards a less radical, and more orthodox, view of the prospects for the international division of labour.

*Colonial development*

In the inter-war period several specialists on colonial problems wrote about issues that would now be included under the heading of development economics, an important example of such work being Lilian Knowles' *The Economic Development of the British Overseas Empire* (1924–1936). This inter-war literature shows how differently the subject was then conceived. Firstly, the term development was usually used to denote the development of natural resources, whether by government or private enterprise, rather than in the Marxist sense of the progressive evolution of an economic system.[81] Secondly, this development of a region's resources was seen as something separate from increasing the welfare of the region's inhabitants.

This distinction was embodied in the doctrine of the "dual mandate", which had parallels in other colonial powers, whereby the British colonial government was thought to have two responsibilities: development and the welfare of colonial peoples.[82]

Though on a limited scale, and comparatively neglected until the growth of interest in development economics after 1940, some important work was done on analysing the problems facing colonial territories. Two contributions stand out, those of Boeke, writing about Dutch colonies, and Furnivall, writing about the British. Both stressed the different social structure of many colonies compared with that of European countries. Boeke[83] developed a theory of a dual society, one comprising an imported, usually capitalist, social system, together with an indigenous, often pre-capitalist, society. Different economic principles were needed to analyse the behaviour of the two sectors of the economy, western economic principles being applicable to the capitalist part, the indigenous population being slow to accept western values and to respond to economic incentives. Though he differed from Boeke in not accepting that their native populations did not respond to economic incentives, Furnivall similarly analysed colonial territories as having social structures different from those of western economies.[84]

In the words of one commentator,

there existed by the 1930s a large literature of colonial economics, in scholarly books and articles, as well as in mountains of official reports, on which the profession at large could have drawn had the subject interested them.[85]

# 18

## Alternative Approaches

### 18.1   ENGLISH HISTORICAL ECONOMICS

*Background*

The 1870s saw the rise to prominence of historical economics, both in England, where confidence in classical political economy had collapsed, and in Germany, where the deductive, Ricardian version of classical political economy had never gained a firm hold.[1] Though there were links between the two, Cliffe-Leslie and Ingram in particular being well aware of the writings of the German school, the origins and nature of the two variants of historical economics were very different.[2]

The man usually taken to be the forerunner of English historical economics is Richard Jones, whose *Essay on the Distribution of Wealth and the Sources of Taxation* (1833) contained a forthright criticism of Ricardian doctrines, blaming their inadequacies on Ricardo's method. On rent, for example, Jones argued that Malthus had proposed his theory of rent as an explanation of specific historical circumstances, but that

Mr Ricardo, however, overlooking altogether the limited extent of the field to which these principles were readily applicable, underook from them alone to deduce the laws which regulate the nature and amount of the revenue derived from land at all places, and under all circumstances; and not content with this, proceeded from the same narrow and limited data, to construct a general system of the distribution of wealth, and to explain the causes of variations which take place in the rate of profits, or amount of wages over the surface of the globe. [Ricardo had produced a hypothetical system which] a single comprehensive glance at the world as it actually exists, is sufficient to show to be utterly inconsistent with the past and present condition of mankind.[3]

The reason for these errors was that men preferred "the way of *anticipation* to that of *induction*": a structure of doctrines was erected on observations of only a small portion of the earth's surface.[4] This is not to say that Jones rejected deductive reasoning altogether, but rather that he believed that economists needed to spend more time on observation before proceeding to deduction: "they have quitted *too soon* the duty of dwelling long and humbly among things, that they might *prematurely* take up the more fascinating employment of laying down those maxims of imposing generality".[5] Thus when Jones investigated rent, his treatment comprised an analysis of numerous different types of rent.

There was also, however, another side to Jones' work. This was his contention that political economy must be concerned with "the economical structure of nations", by which he meant the relations between the different classes which are established in the first instance by the institution of property in the soil, and by the distribution of its surplus produce; afterwards modified and changed ... by the introduction of capitalists.[6]

Only a knowledge of this structure, or "economical anatomy" could explain the past fortunes of different peoples.[7]

In addition to Jones, two other influences need mentioning as important background to English historical economics. Firstly, there was Sir Henry Maine's work on jurisprudence in which, instead of trying to reconstruct law in the light of rational principles, as was the approach of Bentham, he argued that law was to be studied historically and comparatively. Cliffe Leslie pointed to Maine's having exposed the fallacies inherent in the concepts of nature and natural law, exploding the myth that there was a "code of nature" against which legislators could go at their peril.[8] Secondly, there was the influence of Comte, and his call for a unified social science. This ruled out of order the classical abstractions.

## Cliffe Leslie

The writer who opened the English debate on method in the 1870s was Cliffe Leslie,[9] with his article on "The political economy of Adam Smith" (1870). Leslie's main argument was that political economy did not comprise a body of natural laws, for its "laws" were not universal and immutable, but varied from age to age and from place to place.[10] Smith, Cliffe Leslie contended, whilst recognizing this for earlier writers, had failed to see that it applied to his own system.[11] Cliffe Leslie also stressed the importance of induction in Smith's work, arguing that his combination of induction and deduction enabled him to avoid errors into which his followers had fallen.[1] Smith's use of induction, however, had not gone far enough, for

under the bias given by the theory itself, partly because the method of interrogating nature itself was new, and the canons of induction unsettled, conceived that ... nature when interrogated, confirmed his anticipations of nature.[13]

In addition, Cliffe Leslie criticized the notion that political economy should be based on the assumption of selfish behaviour, arguing that this was not Smith's approach.[14] Cliffe Leslie thus argued that Smith's authority could not be claimed for the contentions of contemporary, abstract political economy.

This argument was developed in what Ingram (1893) later described as "the first systematic statement by an English writer or the philosophic foundation of the historical method",[15] Cliffe Leslie's article "On the philosophical method of political economy" (1876). In this, his first contention was that the heterogeneity both of wealth itself, and of the desire for wealth, was important, but that deductive economics neglected both. Because it threw no light on the nature of wealth (whether it comprised, for example, buildings, land or ornaments),[16] and because it failed to consider the variety of human motivations (treating those other than the desire for wealth as disturbing causes, or frictions), "the abstract a priori and deductive method yields no explanation of the causes which regulate either the nature of the amount of wealth".[17] As regards the distribution of wealth, this depended not only on exchange, but also on the ownership of property, to explain which historical investigations were needed.

From this Cliffe Leslie went on to argue that the evolution of society must be considered as a whole.

The truth is, that the economy of every nation, as regards the occupations and pursuits of both sexes, the nature, amount, distribution and consumption of wealth, is the result of a long evolution in which there has been both continuity and change, and of which the economical side is only a particular aspect or phase. And the laws of which it is the result must be sought in history and the general laws of society and social evolution.[18]

Moral, political and economic causes had to be considered together: "Every successive economic stage [in social progress] … has an economy which is indissolubly connected with the physical, intellectual, moral, and civil development."[19] The philosophical method of political economy had to be one which expounded this evolution, involving economic, political and social institutions.[20]

Three years later (1879) Cliffe Leslie published a further, and in some ways more penetrating criticism of orthodox political economy, one based not so much on inductive reasoning as on a theoretical argument.[21] This argument was that orthodox political economy postulated more than simply a general pursuit of wealth: it also postulated "full knowledge and foreknowledge", or full information and perfect foresight, to use modern terminology. Without this postulate, Cliffe Leslie argued, the uniformity of wage and profit rates crucial to orthodox theory would disappear: competition will work to equalize returns only if people can identify lines of business in which returns are unusually high or low.[22] If uniformity of wage and profit rates were abandoned, so too must be the cost of production theory of value. Cliffe Leslie argued that the complexity of the economy was increasing, and with this the extent of uncertainty.

Industrial liberty and the division of labour, the two pillars of Adam Smith's system, produce an economic world, the vastness, complexity, and incessant changes of which are absolutely incompatible with the main postulates of the Ricardian theory.[23]

### Bagehot

The historical relativity of economic doctrines was also accepted by Bagehot (1876), a supporter of deductive political economy. He criticized those who suggested that English political economy was applicable to all states of society with the argument that the causes with which it dealt were the main ones only in "a society of grown-up competitive commerce, such as we have in England".[24] In such societies other causes could be grouped under the heading of "friction", whereas in other "un-economic" societies these other causes were the most effective ones. Bagehot thus wanted the authority of political economy "minimized" in the sense that "its authority should be upheld, but its frontiers marked".[25] If this were done, political economy could be less abstract, for once the claim to universal applicability had been abandoned, doctrines could be illustrated with facts from the societies to which they did apply. Bagehot's aim, in examining the postulates of English classical political economy, namely the free mobility of capital and labour, was to show that "it is not a questionable theory of unlimited extent, but a most certain and useful thing of limited extent".[26]

Whilst he accepted the logic of the historical criticism, Bagehot still accepted the scientific status of orthodox economics. His reason for accepting much of classical economics, rather than rejecting it as did Cliffe Leslie, was simply his interpretation of what he observed going on around him. Where Cliffe Leslie saw factors as being immobile, what struck Bagehot was their mobility. They reached different conclusions not because they held different methodological views, but because they interpreted the empirical evidence in different ways.

## Ingram

Whereas Cliffe Leslie and Bagehot derived their ideas from English sources, Ingram's approach was influenced by Comte, whom he described as "the greatest master who has ever treated of sociological method".[27] In his address to the British Association in 1878 he presented a Comtean critique of orthodox economics, made up of four points.[28] (1) He argued, like Jones and Cliffe Leslie, that economic phenomena could not be separated from other aspects of society.[29] Even on issues where the economic aspects were the most important, such as that of free trade versus protection, an adequate treatment would require non-economic aspects to be considered. (2) He criticized orthodox economists for conceiving and presenting their concepts in a "viciously abstract" way.[30] His criticism was not abstraction per se, but that it lost contact with reality. As an example, he cited Cliffe Leslie's argument that "desire for wealth" was used to include a great variety of wants, different in their nature and effects. (3) The place of deduction had been exaggerated, according to Ingram, for deduction was possible only in simple cases: "social phenomena are in general too complex, and dependent on too manifold conditions, to be capable of such a priori determination".[31] In contrast to Senior's unjustifiable attempt to deduce all the phenomena of industrial life from four postulates, Ingram argued that the place for deduction was in verifying and controlling inductions. Furthermore, the historical dimension of economics could not be ignored, social facts of any complexity being incomprehensible apart from their history.[32] (4) Related to this was Ingram's final point, that the conclusions, both theoretical and practical, to be drawn from political economy were much less absolute than orthodox economists suggested.[33] Economic theorems were applicable only to a certain stage of development. For Ingram, the conclusions of orthodox political economy were not valueless, but were limited in their applicability.

## Sidgwick and Marshall

Of the economists who sought to preserve the Ricardian tradition the most important were Sidgwick and Marshall. Sidgwick's approach in his *Principles of Political Economy* (1883) was conciliatory, arguing that the wave of criticism to which political economy had been subject, from Cliffe Leslie as well as from Jevons, had been salutary, but that it had been carried too far. Sidgwick described his aim as being "to eliminate unnecessary controversy, by stating these results in a more guarded manner, and with due attention to the criticisms and suggestions of recent writers".[34] He argued that the opposition between inductive and deductive methods had been urged in "needlessly sharp and uncompromising terms".[35]

Sidgwick's approach to method could be described as pragmatic, for rather than advance a particular method for general use he considered separately the three branches of the subject: production, distribution and exchange.[36] For production, he found predominantly inductive methods appropriate.[37] Distribution and exchange, on the other hand, were more amenable to deductive treatment, except when it came to dynamics, for which induction from historical facts was most important.[38] Whilst Sidgwick saw an important role for the deductive, hypothetical method, however, he argued that its application always required the use of induction, the line later taken J. N. Keynes.[39]

Marshall's method[40] followed Sidgwick's, though he went further towards the historical approach. Important was his argument that

> we may not assign any universality to economic dogmas. For that part of economic doctrine, which alone can claim universality, has no dogmas. It is not a body of concrete truth, but an engine for the discovery of concrete truth, similar to, say, the theory of mechanics.[41]

Marshall thus stressed continuity with the English classical economists, whilst sidestepping the issue as to whether their doctrines were valid or not.[42] Whilst Marshall argued that it would be "difficult to overrate" the importance of the work done by the historical school in "tracing the history of economic habits and institutions",[43] he contended that "they do not in any way help us to dispense with the use of the economic organon: but rather make use of its aid at every step".[44]

## The emergence of economic history

The outcome of these controversies was twofold. Orthodox economists came, by and large, to recognize, to a greater or lesser extent, a role for historical as well as deductive analysis. But more important was the emergence of economic history as a subject separate from both economics and history. One economic historian has placed the subject's "take-off" in the period 1882–1904, its creation a a subject in its own rights, being due in particular to four pioneers: J. E. Thorold Rogers, Arnold Toynbee, W. J. Ashley and William Cunningham.[45]

Rogers remained orthodox in his economic theory, seeing historical research as providing illustrations of independently derived historical laws. This approach was exemplified in his *History of Agriculture and Prices in England* (1866–1902) and his *Six Centuries of Work and Wages* (1884), in which he brought together a wealth of statistical information on English economic history. Toynbee's importance, by contrast, was that, in Ashley's words,

at a time when the study of political economy had sunk to its lowest point in England, he did perhaps more than any other man to create a new interest in it, a new belief in its seriousness as a scientific discipline, a new hope that in it might be found some help towards the solution of pressing economic problems. ... He turned this new interest in the direction of the historical examination of social development, and of the direct examination of existing phenomena.[46]

His lectures of 1881–1882[47] first popularized the term "the industrial revolution", laying great stress on its adverse social consequences.

Perhaps the most important figure in the development of the subject, however, was Cunningham,[48] whose contribution was twofold. Firstly, he provided the subject's first textbook, *The Growth of English Industry and Commerce* (1882). He continued to advance the subject in successive editions of this, which grew enormously in size. Secondly, Cunningham emphasized the need for economic history to be treated as a separate subject from economics. In 1889 he provided the first direct attack on Marshall's "The present position of economics", arguing that as long as economists such as Mill and Marshall were

prepared to exclude a large range of phenomena from consideration, or take pains to represent the transactions of mediaeval life in such a shape as they shall appear conformable to modern practice, they must expect to be charged with a disregard of the facts.[49]

Economic history, Cunningham claimed, was not to be treated merely "as a field from which we can cull additional illustrations of universal truths", but should "enable us to understand actual life both in the past and in the present".[50] This attack on Marshall's position was followed by a further attack on economists' use of economic history. In "The perversion of economic history" (1892b), Cunningham criticized Marshall's use of economic history in his *Principles*.[51] Economic history, Cunningham contended, was paying the price of being too fashionable, ordinary economists, assuming free competition and the laws of supply and demand, professing themselves extremely interested in history, wishing to do anything they can for it. He continued, "To this polite desire it is surely not discourteous to reply, *Laissez faire, laissez aller*." This, however, was what economists would not do; they would neither leave it alone nor pursue it seriously, trying "to incorporate some of its results into that curious amalgam, the main body of economic tradition; and the result is the perversion of economic history".[52]

The first professor of economic history was not Cunningham, but Ashley, appointed to a chair at Harvard in 1892. Whilst Ashley derived his interest in economic history from English sources, he was the English historical economist most influenced by the German historical school.[53] Comte's influence was strong, Ashley seeing the generalizations towards which historical inquiry must work, not as "mere corrections or amplifications of current economic doctrines", but as "conclusions as to the character and sequence of the stages of economic development".[54] Ashley's overall tone, however, was, unlike Cunningham's, conciliatory.[55] He called, in his inaugural lecture (1893) for a truce in the controversy, suggesting that economic theorists and economic historians should try for the next twenty years to leave each other "severely alone", remaining silent where they could not reach agreement.[56]

This agreement to compartmentalize the subject was not, however, the result of Ashley's abandoning his Comteist ideas, for he remained sceptical as to the value of economic theory. It was rather that he was content for the two approaches to be judged by their results. His early hopes of creating a historical economics capable of proving a serious rival to economic theory were, however, disappointed. Thus he was unable to reconcile himself to the compartmentalization he had earlier advocated, seeking closer links with economics which might, he hoped, transform the latter.[57]

The consolidation of economic history came in the 1920s, when a number of economic historians tested, in a series of detailed studies, the generalizations made by the pioneers. Typical of the work resulting from this stage was Clapham's *Economic History of Modern Britain* (1926).[58] The subject had become separate from economics, economics becoming increasingly innocent of history, and historians increasingly innocent of theory.[59] After Clapham's "Of empty economic boxes" (1922) there were no more methodological battles between economic historians and economists.[60] Economic history of the inter-war period was a very different creature from the historical economics of the late nineteenth century.[61]

## 18.2   GERMAN HISTORICAL ECONOMICS

*Background: the "older historical school"*

German historical economics, it is usually argued, stemmed from the work of three economists, whose writings date from the late 1840s, Roscher, Hildenbrand and Knies, the first important contribution being by Roscher in 1843. Roscher was concerned not to oppose but to supplement and complete the Ricardian theory.[62] As to Ricardian methods, he considered that they could serve as a counter to any laziness in the use of "historico-statistical" and "practical-political" methods.[63] He was, however, unlike the Ricardians, concerned with the social organism as a whole, wishing to analyse the effects of various institutions on the nation's well-being, and to supply rules which could guide statesmen.[64] This approach was characterized by Schmoller as an attempt to connect the teaching of political economy with the "cameralist" tradition of training administrators. If the classical doctrines were to be of any use to administrators they had to be corrected and kept as close as possible to facts.[65]

Hildenbrand, on the other hand, set a very different objective for his work. It was

to open a way for an essentially historical standpoint in political economy and to transform the science of political economy into a body of doctrines dealing with the economic development of nations.[66]

Hildenbrand, in contrast to Roscher, was thus a critic of the classical conception of political economy which viewed the economy as a network of exchanges between men motivated by the pursuit of self-interest.[67] His more positive contribution to providing laws of development was to distinguish three stages, based on observable changes in monetary and credit institutions, these being those of natural, monetary and credit economies.

Yet another, different, view was taken by Knies (1853) who questioned not only English classical political economy, but also Hildenbrand's claim that there existed natural laws of development. He adopted a relativistic approach to political economy.

The conditions of economic life determine the form and character of economic theory. Both the process of argument employed and the results arrived at are products of historical development. The arguments are based on the facts of concrete economic life and the results bear all the marks of historical situations. The generalisations of economics are simply historical explanations and progressive manifestations of the truth. Each step is a generalisation of the truth as it is known at that particular stage of development. No single formula and no collection of such formulae can ever claim to be final.[68]

## *Schmoller and the "younger" historical school*[69]

Though Roscher, Hildenbrand and Knies did much to establish historical economics in Germany, their approaches were very different from each other, and despite the frequent use of the term, no true "school" emerged. The emergence of a distinctive historical school occurred in the 1870s with the work of Schmoller, whose influence dominated German economics until 1918. One of the reasons for the sudden waning of Schmoller's influence was his close association with the Hohenzollern empire, for he was instrumental in founding, in 1872, the *Verein für Sozialpolitik*, an organization committed to drawing the working class away from revolutionary causes by a policy of social reform.[70] Unlike the American Economic Association, which soon abandoned similar aims, the *Verein* continued to support this policy, its members, including Schmoller, becoming closely involved with Bismarck's social policies. This is not to say, however, that Schmoller subordinated political economy to political purposes, for his emphasis was very much on letting facts speak for themselves.

Like his predecessors and his English historical contemporaries, Schmoller stressed the organic nature of social phenomena. Where he differed from Hildenbrand and the Comteists was in denying that historical research should be concerned with discovering natural laws of economic development. "We cannot even say whether the economic life of humanity possesses any element of unity or shows any traces of uniform development, or whether it is making for progress at all."[71] He argued that whilst some generalizations might be made,

By cloaking propositions as "laws", one gives them an appearance of necessity which they do not possess, or one gives too high an importance to comparatively insignificant truths, thereby misleading those who apply them.[72]

Though for practical purposes it might be necessary to refer to a law of development, such a law was neither an empirical law nor similar to scientific laws.

The method adopted by Schmoller's school was the production of detailed historical monographs. Judgements were to be made on the basis of the facts of each individual case. Despite his opposition to Menger's use of abstract methods, however, Schmoller, especially in his later work, did not advocate pure empiricism, devoid of theory, and neither did he claim economics to be an exclusively historical subject. He himself worked primarily, though not exclusively, on historical material, but this was not the case with all his pupils. Spiethoff being the prime example of one who gave much attention to theory.[73]

Schmoller's main work, his *Grundriss der Volkswirtschaftslehre* (Outline of Economic Doctrines) (1900) illustrates his method. Perhaps its main characteristic is its wide scope (Ashley, for example, described it as an "olympian survey") covering issues such as the nature and origin of various institutions, neglected in most treatments of economics. Each topic was treated in four ways: historically, statistically, analytically and practically.[74] Though Schmoller's theory was weak, he showed no reluctance to theorize, taking, for example, part of his theory of value from Menger and Böhm-Bawerk.[75] The value of Schmoller's *Outline*, and of the historical school more generally, was in its bringing together an enormous variety of historical and empirical material. Its weakness was that it failed to integrate it. Schmoller's *Outline* remained, in Mitchell's words, "a treatise of beginnings".[76]

### Spiethoff, Sombart and Weber[77]

In the reaction against the ideas of Schmoller and the *Verein für Sozialpolitik* which took place in the early part of the twentieth century, a variety of directions were pursued. In some ways closest to Schmoller was Spiethoff, with his work on business cycles.[78] Whilst Spiethoff made much greater use of theory than did Schmoller, he confined himself to fairly simple theories, investigating facts in detail, and describing the patterns which emerged. In addition he claimed to be providing an explanation relevant only to specific historical circumstances. Thus, for example, his business cycle theory was applied only to the period 1822–1913. There were, however, substantial differences between his approach and Schmoller's. One was that he confined his attention to economics. More important, however, was his later recognition of a large number of "styles" of economic life, analysis of each requiring its own economic theory as well as concepts drawn from timeless pure theory.[79] A "style" was the form economic activity assumed in a given era, and it was charcterized by certain uniformities, in particular uniformities in institutional patterns.[80] Such generalizations were far from Schmoller's scepticism as to the possibilities of discovering economic regularities.

Even further from Schmoller's cautious approach was that of Sombart, exemplified in his *Modern Capitalism* (1902). Where Schmoller had been careful in building up historical evidence, Sombart appeared careless and insubstantial. What he did provide, the reason for the book's success, was a speculative framework, influenced by Marx, for understanding economic history. An economic system was characterized, for Sombart, not only by its technology and institutions, but by its "spirit", the force embodying the creative drives of a culture and inspiring the whole life of an era.[81]

More important, especially for the social sciences as a whole, however, than either Spiethoff or Sombart, was Weber, known primarily for his work on the Protestant origins of capitalism[82] and for his methodological writings.[83] His contribution to the latter was twofold. Firstly there was the neutrality, or value-free nature, of economic science.[84] Definite policy conclusions could not be drawn from positive studies, as a result of which he argued that social scientists should not attempt to use their authority to advance their own ethical or political ideas. Secondly, Weber advanced the concept of the "ideal type". These were mental constructions that emphasized certain features of reality at the expense of others in order to facilitate the formulation of hypotheses. The classic example of this is the "economic man" of economic theory.

Though Weber's plea for a value-free social science influenced economists, and though Spiethoff's contribution to the business cycle formed the starting point for much future work, the main influence of the historical school's successors was outside economics. Economics never became sufficiently wide in scope to encompass the ideas of Sombart and Weber. The issues they raised were left to sociologists and economic historians.

## 18.3 AMERICAN INSTITUTIONALISM: VEBLEN

*Introduction*

It would be very misleading to project the present-day situation backwards and to see American economics as having been dominated, throughout the twentieth century, by "neoclassical" economics. Equally important, at least until the 1920s, was Institutionalism. Institutionalism owed something to German historical economics: the aims of the American Economic Association, for example, were very similar to those of the *Verein für Sozialpolitik*.[85] The main influence on Institutionalism, however, was not German but American: the savage critique of orthodoxy provided by Thorstein Veblen.

Veblen was concerned, however, with much more than economics. His attacks on economic orthodoxy formed but a part of a sustained critique of American society and culture. His *Theory of the Leisure Class* (1899), in which he made full use of his unrivalled literary powers to satirize American society, brought him popular acclaim.

### Cultural evolution

Central to Veblen's theory is the view that economic development is about changes in the methods of doing things. Where orthodox economists laid great stress on capital accumulation, Veblen argued that it was changes in the human factor which were more important:

The physical properties of the materials accessible to man are constants: it is the human agent that changes, – his insight and his appreciation of what these things can be used for is what develops. ... The changes that take place in the mechanical contrivances are an expression of changes in the human factor.[86]

As for capital goods, these are

facts of human knowledge, skill and predilection; that is to say, they are, substantially, *prevalent habits of thought*, and it is as such that they enter into the process of industrial development.[87]

Veblen's main task, therefore, was to explain changes in the prevailing habits of thought, or institutions.

All economic change is a change in the economic community, – a change in the community's methods of turning material things to account. The change is always in the last resort a change in habits of thought. This is true even of changes in the mechanical processes of industry.[88]

Veblen's theory of how these institutions change was based on a complicated evolutionary process in which the material conditions of life interact with habits of mind. The starting point is that the prevailing conditions of life give rise to certain habits of mind, or institutions. From this starting point, several processes then operate. (1) Technology develops, the character of this development depending on the nature of the prevailing institutions. (2) Institutions develop, but, because people become conditioned to accept certain ideas, and because of the power of vested interests, institutions can be sustained after they have lost touch with the underlying material conditions of life. (3) Sometimes, however, technological development results in the creation of new habits of mind, strong enough to overthrow the dominant institutions. The process then repeats itself.

The evolution of institutions is central to this process. A crucial aspect of this evolution is the interaction of economic with non-economic institutions. This works in both directions. On the one hand, economic institutions (habits of mind formed in the process of earning a living) come to permeate other areas of life. Veblen's *Theory of the Leisure Class*, for example, is an examination of the impact of business values on taste and fashion. His *The Higher Learning in America* deals with universities, showing how business principles have displaced principles of scholarship.[89] Thus Veblen could write,

The economic history of any community is its life history in so far as it is shaped by men's interest in the material means of life. This economic interest has counted for much in shaping the cultural growth of all communities. ... An evolutionary economics must be a theory of a process of cultural growth as determined by the economic interest.[90]

On the other hand, economic interests are influenced by other interests (aesthetic, sexual, humanitarian, devotional, etc.), because

since each of these passably isolable interests is a propensity of the organic agent man, with his complex of habits of thought, the expression of each is affected by habits of life formed under the guidance of all the rest.[91]

Related to this interaction of habits developed in different activities is the tendency of any institutional system to develop an internal coherence. An institutional system comes to be

pervaded by a certain characteristic logic and perspective, a certain line of habitual conceptions having a degree of congruity among themselves, a "philosophy" as it would once have been called.[92]

Over time this institutional logic comes to be elaborated and refined, and to find expression in laws and organizational forms.[93] It is thus because of the complexity of the forces influencing the way in which a culture develops, rather than because a culture becomes completely static, that discrepancies can develop between a culture and the habits appropriate to the underlying material conditions of production.

### Business enterprise and the machine process

Veblen's theory of cultural evolution is illustrated by his analysis of American industrial society as he found it in the 1890s. His analysis ran in terms of two institutions: the machine process and business enterprise, different habits of thought being associated with each. The machine process for Veblen meant more than simply the use of mechanical devices, though this was included.[94] It denoted the whole system of production in which mechanized processes were used, a system which had several important aspects. No individual process was self-sufficient, the system containing "a more or less delicately balanced complex of sub-processes". It required quantitative precision and uniformity: "mechanical standardisation" had replaced "craftsmanlike skill" as the means whereby different processes were made to work efficiently together.[95]

The machine process is run, however, for the sake of business enterprise, the motive of which is pecuniary gain. Because pecuniary gain, rather than production or economic welfare, is the criterion according to which industry is run, production will not be organized in such a way as to maximize welfare.

The economic welfare of the community at large is best served by a facile and uninterrupted interplay of the various processes which make up the industrial system at large; but the pecuniary interests of the businessman in whose hands lies the discretion in the matter are not necessarily served by an unbroken maintenance of the industrial balance.[96]

Businessmen might gain, for example, by disturbing the system, providing opportunity for speculation.[97] In addition, prices are raised where possible, and attempts are made to increase monopoly power through acquisition of other businesses or through advertising. A feature of advertising is that it is competitive, which means that sellers have to undertake it, even though it contributes nothing to the usefulness of the goods produced: "It gives vendibility, which is useful to the seller, but has no utility to the last buyer."[98] Veblen thus sees the existence of "parasitic" lines of business:

Work that is, on the whole, useless or detrimental to the community at large may be as gainful to the business man and to the workman whom he employs as work that contributes substantially to the aggregate livelihood.[99]

The gains of these unproductive occupations come out of the aggregate product of the other occupations.[100]

These two types of activity are important, according to Veblen, because each type of activity inculcates a different spiritual attitude:

The spiritual ground of business enterprise ... is given by the institution of ownership. "Business Principles" are corollaries under the main proposition of ownership; they are the principles of property, – pecuniary principles.[101]

In contrast, the machine process enforces a standardization of conduct and a habits of explaining things in terms of cause and effect. "Its metaphysics is materialistic, and its point of view is that of causal sequence."[102]

Veblen thus saw American industry and society as dominated by the institution he called business enterprise, business habits of mind pervading all American culture. One result of this business activity and the continual search for pecuniary gain was mechanization and the extension of the machine process. The machine process, however, inculcates habit of mind inconsistent with the principles of business enterprise.

On the basis of this, Veblen argued that two classes would emerge: those employed in running business, and those running the machine process. These two classes would have different habits of thought: one class would think in terms of natural rights, the other in terms of cause and effect. Of particular importance would be the growth of matter-of-fact habits amongst the working class, for they, ceasing to think in terms of natural rights, would be unable to understand the justification for business enterprise and would turn to socialism. His conclusion was that the regime of business enterprise was unlikely to be long lasting.[103]

This conclusion was similar to that reached by Marx, but with a fundamental difference. This difference is the difference between the Hegelian and Darwinian versions of evolution: where Marx saw the historical process as leading to a definite goal, Veblen's view of the world was Darwinian.[104] Evolution, for Veblen, involved a "colorless sequence of phenomena" linked by chains of cause and effect.[105] It was only individual behaviour which was purposive, or teleological. On the other hand, it can be argued that Veblen's evolutionary scheme is a dialectical one. In the words of a recent writer,

competing institutional principles arise from the technological changes introduced as a result of the institutional structure of the old system. ... The internal logic of a system [gives] rise to contradictions that create its own transformation.[106]

### Economic theorizing and culture

This theory of cultural evolution forms the basis for Veblen's critique of economic theories. This critique is centred on the distinction between two "spiritual attitudes or points of view":[107] the evolutionary and the non-evolutionary. Characteristic of all non-evolutionary points of view is the explanation of economic phenomena in terms of some purpose. The most basic such attitude is animism: attributing purpose to aspects of nature. He described the Physiocratic system as animistic.

Nature then is the final term in the Physiocratic speculations. Nature works by impulse and in an unfolding process, under the stress of a propensity to the accomplishment of a given end. The propensity, taken as the final cause that is operative in a given situation, furnishes the basis on which to co-ordinate all our knowledge of those efficient causes through which nature works to her ends.[108]

The Physiocrats were never satisfied with an explanation, according to Veblen, until they had related an economic phenomenon to this process of nature working towards a given end.

The nature of the teleology underlying economic reasoning changed substantially between the Physiocrats and, for example, Clark or the Austrians, particularly important in the transition being the Utilitarians' stress on human pleasure and pain, rather than the design of God, as the ultimate standard for judging economic life. Behind these changes, however, the animistic method of reasoning persisted.

The ultimate laws and principles which they formulated were laws of the normal or the natural, according to a preconception regarding the ends to which, in the nature of things, all things tend. In effect, this preconception imputes to things a tendency to work out what the instructed common sense of the time accepts as the adequate or worthy end of human effort. It is a projection of the accepted ideal of conduct. This ideal of conduct is made to serve as a canon of truth, to the extent that the investigator contents himself with an appeal to its legitimation for ... the "controlling principles" that are conceived intangibly to underlie the process discussed.[109]

Thus, though the nature of the teleology changed substantially, economic phenomena were still explained by showing how they could be deduced from generally accepted postulates, such as "economic man" and perfect competition. This approach Veblen called "taxonomic". Referring to such reasoning, he perceptively argued the following.

Of course, this perfect competitive system, with its untainted "economic man", is a feat of the scientific imagination, and is not intended as a competent expression of fact. It is an expedient of abstract reasoning; and its avowed competency extends only to the abstract principles, the fundamental laws of science, which hold only in so far as the abstraction holds. But, as happens in such cases, having once been accepted and assimilated as real, though perhaps not as actual, it becomes an effective constituent in the inquirer's habits of thought, and goes to shape his knowledge of facts. It comes to serve as a norm of substantiality or legitimacy; and facts in some degree fall under its constraint, as is exemplified by many allegations regarding the 'tendency' of things.[110]

Against the attitude underlying such reasoning Veblen set the evolutionary point of view, which he regarded as the attitude of modern science. From an evolutionary point of view the sole type of explanation involved cause and effect:

The modern scientist is unwilling to depart from the test of causal relation or quantitative sequence. When he asks the question Why? he insists on an answer in terms of cause and effect .... This is his last recourse.[111]

Impersonal sequences of cause and effect are *all* that is sought.

What gave this interpretation of economic theories its power was that these points of view were not taken as a datum, but were explained as the products of certain types of economic activity. The late eighteenth and nineteenth centuries, for example, saw the growth of the machine process and the extension of business enterprise, each bringing with it its own habits of thought. At the time of Smith and the Physiocrats, for example, the machine process, though still very underdeveloped by later standards, was more highly developed in England than in France.[112] Veblen uses this to explain why the matter-of-fact attitude was stronger in British than in French thought: despite its fundamentally teleological design, for example, stronger traces of a cause-and-effect attitude can be seen in *The Wealth of Nations* than in French work of the same period. Turning to the nineteenth century, the dominance of the taxonomic approach, in both classical and neoclassical economics, can be accounted for as reflecting the ever stronger influence of business enterprise, with its judgement of everything in terms of value. The utilitarian emphasis on value as the main problem of political economy, in contrast to Smith's stress on production, is explicable in terms of this habit of mind.

Veblen produces an interesting explanation of the crises which occur in economic theory. Confidence in economic theories is shaken, not because they are disproved, but because they become out of touch with the prevailing habits of mind, as is illustrated by his account of the demise of classical political economy.

In the days of the early classical writers economics had a vital interest for the layman of the time, for it formulated the common sense metaphysics of the time in its application to a department of human life. But in the hands of the later classical writers the science lost much of its charm in this regard. It was no longer a definition and authentication of the deliverances of current common sense as to what ought to come to pass; ... and it was also out of touch with that realistic or evolutionary habit of mind which got under way in the middle of the century in the natural sciences. It was neither vitally metaphysical nor matter of fact, and it found very few outside of its own ranks.[113]

### *Veblen's critique of orthodox economics*

These ideas formed the basic for Veblen's devastating critique of orthodox economics. There were several strands to this.[114] (1) He criticized orthodox economics for being based on outmoded, "animistic" and "teleological" preconceptions, as a result of which it suffered from being "taxonomic".[115] (2) He attacked hedonism, on which, he argued, orthodox economics was based, as being inadequate as an account of human motivation. (3) He criticized both deductive and inductive methods.

A natural inference from Veblen's view of knowledge as determined by prevailing habits of thought would be that he held a purely relativistic view of knowledge. This was, however, not the case. Veblen clearly regarded "matter-of-fact", or "evolutionary", knowledge, which explained things in terms of cause and effect, as superior to the "pre-Darwinian" theories at which he directed his criticism. The habits of mind engendered by the machine process, which led people to see things in terms of cause and effect, gave genuine insights into how the world worked.

There are two aspects to Veblen's criticism of hedonism. One is his theory of instincts. He argued that people are motivated by a variety of instincts: the drive for technological improvement (workmanship); the drive towards providing for the welfare of family and society (parental bent); and the drive to produce coherent explanations of the world (idle curiosity).[116] Hedonism is inadequate as a psychology on which to base economics. There was, however, a more profound objection to hedonism. Veblen argued that the main determinant of behaviour was not instincts, but institutions. Institutional principles, once established, come to replace the instincts as the goals of action: they occupy the interest to such an extent as commonly to throw their own ulterior purpose into the background and often let it be lost sight of.[117] Because of this Veblen argued that it was wrong to take behaviour as determined by psychology. Individual preferences should be treated as endogenous, not exogenous, the most well known example being "conspicuous consumption", where the value of a good bears no relation to its real worth. The real importance of Veblen's theory of instincts was rather that the instincts provided a normative criterion against which to judge institutions: institutions are judged on the basis of their compatibility with the instincts (as an example, see his denunciation of advertising, quoted above).[118]

Veblen's criticisms of deductive theory (that it was defended irrespective of whether or not it was consistent with empirical evidence) and of induction (which did not provide a theory of anything) were designed to pave the way for the acceptance of the genetic methodology which he continually advocated.[119] Veblen never succeeded, however, in providing a workable alternative methodology. His main success (assuming that it is regarded as a success), therefore, was as a critic. According to one commentator, "It cannot be doubted that his destructive attacks caused bewilderment among his contemporaries and, in so far as they were successful, tended to undermine their faith in orthodox economic theory."[120] In Arrow's words, Veblen's attacks "undermined the never-very-secure hold of neoclassical thought on [the] teaching of American economics".[121] The task of providing a workable alternative to neoclassical economics thus fell to others.

## 18.4 AMERICAN INSTITUTIONALISM: MITCHELL

### Mitchell and Veblen

Mitchell's claim to immortality rests with the empirical work for which he and his colleagues at the National Bureau of Economic Research were responsible. Mitchell was, however, one of Veblen's two leading disciples, and it is important to see him in this light.

Three aspects of Veblen's theory were particularly important for Mitchell. (1) Mitchell, like Veblen, was very critical of theories based on the assumption that wants, or preferences, were given. (2) He accepted the importance of Veblen's distinction between business and industry, or between the pecuniary and technological phases of economic life. The business cycle, the subject of Mitchell's most important work, was seen as a phenomenon arising out of the nature of business enterprise, but one which had important repercussions on the process of making goods. (3) He took over Veblen's view of the organic, evolving nature of society. He thus objected to the use of simple theories, stressing the complexity of economic phenomena.

Beyond this, however, Mitchell's approach was *very* different from Veblen's. Despite his scepticism as to the value of much orthodox theory, he nonetheless used those parts of it which seemed appropriate. For example, although Mitchell's conception of the business cycle problem may have been taken from Veblen, it can be argued that the details of his theoretical account of the business cycle, in which the interdependence of all prices and quantities played an important role, owed as much to Walras as to Veblen.[122]

### Mitchell's method

Mitchell's clearest statement of his method is provided in his Presidential Address to the American Economic Association, "Quantitative analysis in economic theory" (1925). He started by quoting Marshall's dictum that "qualitative analysis has done the greater part of its work".[123] However, rather than finding the makings of a new *methodenstreit* in these words, he went on to argue:

We do not speak of qualitative *versus* quantitative analysis. We do not seek to prove that one type should predominate over the other. Instead of dogmatizing about method at large, we are experimenting with method in detail. In the measure of our proficiencies, we all practise both qualitative and quantitative analysis, shifting our emphasis according to the tasks we have in hand. ... Such differences of opinion as flourish among us turn chiefly on our expectations concerning the relative fruitfulness of qualitative and quantitative work.[124]

Thus when Mitchell, later in this address, criticized the deductive economics of Jevons and Marshall, the tone of his criticism was very different from that of Veblen's attacks on hedonism. Mitchell was content to argue that, because of better data and access to better techniques, quantitative workers were in a position to estimate directly phenomena such as the influence of supply and demand on price, that qualitative workers had been forced to approach only indirectly through deduction. From this he drew the conclusion that

it seems unlikely that the quantitative workers will retain a keen interest in imaginary individuals coming to imaginary markets with ready made scales of bid and offer prices. Their theories will probably be theories about the relationships among the variables that measure objective processes.[125]

The old explanations provided by economists such as Marshall and Jevons would be disregarded rather than refuted. He likened this change towards quantitative reasoning to the shift amongst psychologists towards stimulus–response sequences and the quantitative analysis of behaviour.

This attitude also underlay Mitchell's work on the cycle. Though he started his work with a survey of previous theories of the cycle, he did not see the task of quantitative work as being to test these. Though such theories might give insights into some of the processes at work, the phenomenon of the cycle was too complicated to be explained by any simple model. The features of actual cycles had to be distilled from statistical data.

More importantly, Mitchell re-interpreted the concepts he took over from Veblen. Consider Mitchell's description of the relation between business and industry:

Much of their [quantitative workers'] data will consist of two great groups of time series. One group shows variations in the output, stocks, shipment, or orders for economic goods expressed in physical units .... The second group of time series shows variations in quantities expressed in monetary units. The relations between these two groups will be an obvious problem of just the kind that quantitative workers enjoy attacking. They cannot content themselves by staying always on the money level of analysis, or always on the commodity level; and they cannot pass back and forth between the two levels without realizing what they are doing.... Out of this technical characteristic of the statistical data we may expect to come to a close scrutiny of the relations between our pecuniary institutions and our efficiency in producing and distributing goods.[126]

Though the theme is Veblen's, the methodology is very different. Similarly, for Mitchell, the organic nature of society implied that it was not possible to represent the evolution of the economy with a single time series (such as GDP). To describe the business cycle, for example, it was necessary to examine a whole variety of indicators.[127]

### Interpretation

Mitchell was not an advocate of pure empiricism, for it was only certain types of economic theory that he rejected. It was because Mitchell attached great importance to the complexity of economic phenomena that he spurned simple theories. In the light of this, a recent writer concluded that:

Mitchell was, of course, extremely foresighted in recognising so long ago the crucial distinction between simple hypotheses readily recognisable as embryonic, if relatively useless, economic theory and complicated hypotheses less recognisable but far more likely to lead to progress in solving economic problems.[128]

The most important example of this is probably Mitchell's rejecting the "neoclassical" emphasis on equilibrium (a relatively simple hypothesis) in favour of the "institutionalist emphasis on economic process" (a complicated, but allegedly more fruitful hypothesis).[129]

On the other hand, despite Mitchell's use of economic theory, his emphasis was overwhelmingly on induction: on the need to derive hypotheses directly from empirical data. Furthermore, a crucial characteristic of deductive reasoning is that assumptions have to be stated sufficiently precisely for it to be possible to work out exactly what the theory does predict. Mitchell's preference for very complicated theories, therefore, made the use of deductive reasoning very difficult. Thus although Mitchell did use economic theory, it is not very misleading to regard him, at least in his Presidential Address, as having advanced an inductivist research programme. It is possible to say of Mitchell what he said of Marx: "He may not have gotten his leading ideas out of his study of historical records, that is quite true, *but no one does.*"[130]

## 18.5  AMERICAN INSTITUTIONALISM: COMMONS

### Collective action

The starting point for Commons' economics is the fact of scarcity. He differs from neoclassical economists, however, in arguing that in the absence of any constraints on individual action, disputes between individuals concerning command over scarce resources will be settled by physical force. Such a situation is inefficient, not least because it creates insecurity, making it difficult to plan for the future. Collective action, therefore, is needed to impose constraints on individual behaviour, thereby creating opportunities for others.

If transactions are to go on peaceably without resort to violence between the parties there must always have been a fifth party to the transaction, namely a judge, priest, chieftain, ..., who would be able to settle the dispute, with the aid of the combined power of the group to which the parties belonged.[131]

Institutions, for Commons, are the mechanisms through which collective control is exercised: "we may define an institution as collective action in control, liberation and expansion of individual action".[132] Such collective control may comprise either unorganized customs or organized action through *going concerns*, such as the state, the family, the church, the corporation, the trade union, etc. Each of these institutions will have its own set of *working rules*:

Working Rules are continually changing in the history of an institution, and they differ for different institutions; but, whatever their differences, they indicate *what individuals can, must, or may, do or not do, enforced by collective sanctions*.[133]

Three aspects of such collective control of individual action need to be mentioned.

(1) The existence of rules governing behaviour creates opportunities as well as imposing constraints:

collective action is more than control of individual action – it is ... a *liberation* of individual action from coercion, duress, discrimination, or unfair competition by other individuals. ... [In addition] it is *expansion* of the will of the individual far beyond what he can do by his own puny acts. The head of a great corporation gives orders whose obedience, enforced by collective action, executes his will at the ends of the earth.[134]

Perhaps the most basic opportunity is that provided by *property*: the institution of property gives one individual control over a resource through restraining others from exercising control over it.

(2) Because of the variety of types of control, institutional economics, for Commons, comprised not only economics, but also ethics and jurisprudence:

ethics deals with the rules of conduct arising from conflict of interests, arising, in turn, from scarcity and enforced by the *moral* sanctions of collective *opinion*, but economics deals with the same rules of conduct enforced by the collective economic sanctions of *profit* or *loss* in case of obedience or disobedience, while jurisprudence deals with the same rules enforced by the organized sanctions of *violence*. Institutional economics is continually dealing with the relative methods and efficiency of these three types of sanctions.[135]

(3) It was the availability of an outside arbitrator which enabled ethical considerations to be brought in, for without the possibility of appeal to some objective authority, bargains would be determined simply by power. Against the charge that concepts such as "reasonable value" were merely matters of opinion, he argued that such concepts could be given precision by arbitrators or through the legal system, the final arbitrator being the Supreme Court of the United States. Thus for Commons, "Reasonable Value is the Court's decision of what is reasonable as between plaintiff and defendant. It is objective, measurable in money, and compulsory."[136]

*Transactions*

Commons' basic unit of analysis was the *transaction*. A transaction involves "the alienation and acquisition, between individuals, of the *rights* of property and liberty created by society".[137] Commons distinguished three types of transaction: bargaining, managerial and rationing transactions. The first two are transactions between a legal superior and a legal inferior. A rationing transaction involves the "rationing of wealth or purchasing power by a superior authority",[138] an example being the levying of taxation by the state. Managerial transactions involve the relationship of command and obedience involved in the organization of production, as between a manager and an employee.[139]

Bargaining transactions, on the other hand, involve a voluntary agreement between legal equals. A characteristic feature of a bargaining transaction is that it involves a double transfer of ownership: ownership of one resource is exchanged for ownership of something else.[140] Legal equality, however, does not imply that the two sides to a bargain have equal bargaining power, for the terms of a bargain will depend on the ability of each party to withhold something that the other party wants. This will depend on the alternative opportunities available. The use of such bargaining power may, however, be restrained by working rules: some alternatives may be ruled out, or limitations may be placed on the use of power. The law, for example, may require equal opportunities, fair competition; or it may prevent unreasonable use of bargaining power, and ensure due process of law.[141]

The relationship between scarcity and working rules is summed up by Commons when he argues that implicit in any transaction are three social relations:

the relations of conflict, dependence and order. The parties involved are involved in a conflict of interest on account of the universal principle of scarcity. Yet they depend on each other for reciprocal alienation and acquisition of what the other wants but does not own. Then the working rule is not a foreordained harmony of interests, but it actually creates, out of a conflict of interests, a workable mutuality and orderly expectation of property and liberty.[142]

Thus collective action, for Commons, is a prerequisite for bringing order out of the conflicts of interest created by scarcity.

*Institutional change*

Transactions thus depend on the working rules of the going concern within which they take place? But where do such institutions, such going concerns with their working rules, originate? Commons rejected any idea that institutions were given once-for-all, as if by some fixed social contract. The key requirement of working rules is *workability*: the requirement that they enable the going concern to function properly. Working rules, Commons argued, are necessary and their survival in history is contingent on their fitness to hold together in a continuing concern the overweening and unlimited selfishness of individuals pressed on by scarcity of resources.[143]

Institutions are problem solving mechanisms which evolve in response to new problems:

They grow out of the settlement of disputes and the combined action of the group as a mass in offense or defense with other groups. This necessarily means the selection of good habits and practices of individuals as against bad habits and practices that weaken the group as a whole.[144]

One means of changing working rules is through political power. Political and judicial institutions are subject to change as much as any other institution, for they must be workable: they must be capable of solving problems in a sufficiently equitable and efficient manner to enable the system to continue. As is any form of activity, the use of political power is itself subject to working rules.[145]

The means of changing working rules on which Commons placed most emphasis, however, was the process of common law. When a dispute arises, it may be settled by the courts. The courts decide, on the basis of what they consider reasonable, whether or not certain practices are desirable. In coming to their decisions they consider not only statute law, but also

the inducements to efficiency, the Circumstances of Scarcity at the time and place, the expectation of the Future, the good and bad practices of the two parties, as well as the good and bad Common Practices of similar persons under similar conditions.[146]

The decisions of the courts give precision to customs and rules. Through the courts, not only ethical and ideological attitudes, but also economic considerations are brought to bear on institutions.

Commons' attitude towards economic policy followed as a natural corollary of this view of institutions and the way they evolve. He saw policy as being concerned with the development of improved working rules. The task of policy makers was not to search for ideal solutions to problems, but to search for workable improvements. Though Commons also made proposals for constitutional reform, designed to make the political and judicial processes more effective in solving problems,[147] his most important work was on specific economic problems. Throughout his career Commons was involved in proposing, and advising, on legislation, both in Wisconsin and at the Federal level.[148] His influence on legislation was *enormous*, covering civil service reform, factory legislation, workmen's compensation, unemployment insurance, interest rate control, rural credit and taxation measures, inheritance taxation, property assessment laws, immigration laws, monetary policy and industrial relations. In addition, he had an enormous influence on policy through his students: "through his students Commons was the intellectual origin of the New Deal, of labor legislation, of social security, of the whole movement in this country [the US] towards a welfare state".[149]

*Commons, Veblen and economic theory*

Commons' ideas had much in common with those of Veblen: they both stressed the purposive nature of economic activity; and they both emphasized the evolving nature of economic institutions. Commons' ideas differed from Veblen's, however, in several important respects, the result being that his system is *substantially* different from Veblen's.

Most important is Commons' view of institutions as constraining behaviour. For him, individuals' desires and instincts still operate, but are controlled and guided by institutions. This led Commons to reject Veblen's dichotomy between business and industry. Veblen had seen a sharp distinction between pecuniary and technological criteria as criteria for social choice.[150] This dichotomy, according to Commons, arose because Veblen had failed to consider the constraints which have been evolved, through the courts, to control business activity:

The historical explanation of Veblen's cynical antithesis of business and industry is in the failure to trace out the evolution of business customs under the decisions of the courts, as he had traced the technological customs. Such an investigation reveals the evolution of his "intangible property", which has consisted in making the distinction, not allowed by Veblen, between goodwill and privilege, goodwill being the reasonable exercise of the power to withhold, and privilege being the unreasonable exercise of that power.[151]

Through the courts property had been linked to "reasonable" value:[152] anything reasonable, whether reasonable value, reasonable wages, reasonable safety or reasonable conduct, would be sustained by the courts.[153] This explains his remark, in the preface to his *Legal Foundations of Capitalism* (1924), that in trying, with his students, to reconcile the decisions of the courts with the writings of the economists, "what we were really working on was not merely a theory of Reasonable Value, but the Legal Foundations of Capitalism itself".[154]

Because of his starting point, namely the conflicts arising from the scarcity of resources, Commons' economics is easy to relate to orthodox, "neoclassical" economics. Commons minimized the novelty of his own teaching:

The problem now is not to create a different kind of economics – "institutional" economics – divorced from previous schools, but how to give to collective action, in all its varieties, its due place throughout economic theory.[155]

His *Institutional Economics* (1934) was subtitled "Its Place in Political Economy".

Commons' concerns, however, were much wider than those of orthodox economics. Orthodox economics dealt only with bargaining transactions, whereas Commons saw these as merely one type of transaction. In addition, Commons was concerned to investigate the constraints on behaviour, seeing these as endogenous. Commons' main interest was in what he called *strategic* transactions: transactions which altered the constraints within which what he called *routine* transactions took place.[156] Thus he was, for example, more interested in the transactions which established property rights and the limits on competition, than in how product prices were determined subject to these constraints. This explains his emphasis on legal processes. His approach was thus in a sense complementary to that of orthodox economics.

Despite the profundity of his contributions, Commons' economic *theory* has largely been neglected. To many economists his writings were incomprehensible.[157] His writings have been described as "a tangled jungle of profound insights".[158] Though he had influential students, their influence was on legislation, not on basic theory. He has also suffered from being grouped together with Veblen as an "Institutionalist", for this has helped obscure his place as an independent economic thinker.

## 18.6 MARXIST ECONOMICS

### *The golden age of Marxism*

The decades leading up to 1914 can legitimately be described as the golden age of Marxism. In the words of one authority,

> The period of the Second International (1889–1914) may be called without exaggeration the golden age of Marxism. Marxist doctrine had been clearly enough defined to constitute a recognizable school of thought, but it was not so rigidly codified or subjected to dogmatic orthodoxy as to rule out discussion or the advocacy of rival solutions to theoretical and tactical problems.[159]

In continental Europe in particular, there was extensive discussion of many aspects of Marxist theory, both amongst people describing themselves as Marxists, and with opponents of Marxism who nonetheless took Marxism seriously.

Despite this interest in Marxism, and despite the roots of Marxist economic theory in English classical economics, Marxist and mainstream economics, with notable exceptions, went their separate ways. In England few prominent economists took Marxism seriously, an exception being Wicksteed's (1894) attempt to use Jevonian marginal utility analysis to criticize the Marxian theory of value.[160] Edgeworth, for example, reviewing a book published in 1920, wrote "We have much sympathy with those who hold that the theories of Marx are beneath the notice of a scientific writer".[161] In the United States, with its greater tolerance for divergent approaches, there was a tendency to treat Marxian economics as yet another system to be considered alongside others. Thus although prominent economists, such as Mitchell,[162] commented favourably on Marx, his ideas had little impact on economic thinking. It was in Europe that both developments in Marxist economics, and the interaction of Marxian and orthodox ideas were greatest. Within Marxist economics the most important development was perhaps the theory of imperialism, associated with the names of Hilferding, Bukharin and Lenin, according to which imperial expansion overseas could be explained in terms of surplus capital seeking profitable investment opportunities. Imperialism was thus important as a means of explaining why it was that capitalism was managing to survive, and even prosper, despite Marx's predictions to the contrary.[163] It was out of debates on the viability of capitalism, an issue connected in Marx's theory with the recurrence of economic crises, that Tugan-Baranovsky's work on cycles emerged.[164] But although Tugan-Baranovsky's work on the cycle fed into the emerging orthodox literature on the business cycle, the most important instance of the interaction of Marxist and orthodox economics during the period was the interchange between Böhm-Bawerk and Hilferding, Böhm-Bawerk being widely regarded as the period's most important critic of the Marxian system.[165] This interchange is revealing, for it explains the difference between the orthodox and Marxist approaches to the subject, and hence why their interaction was so unproductive.

### Böhm-Bawerk and Hilferding

The occasion for Böhm-Bawerk's attack on the Marxian system in his *Karl Marx and the Close of his System* (1896) was the publication, in 1894, of the third and final volume of *Capital*.[166] This was particularly important because in the first volume Marx had promised that he would later provide a reconciliation of the contradiction involved in assuming both a labour theory of value based on a uniform rate of exploitation, and the fact that competition will produce a uniform rate of profit. Böhm-Bawerk had earlier (1884) predicted that no satisfactory explanation would be forthcoming, since the assumptions of a uniform rate of exploitation and a uniform rate of profit were, except in certain very simple cases, irreconcilable.

When Marx's volume III was published, Böhm-Bawerk found that Marx's solution had been simply to abandon the labour theory of value, in the sense that he accepted that prices would not be proportional to labour values.[167] In Böhm-Bawerk's view this undermined the whole Marxian system, for it could no longer provide an explanation of the ratios in which goods were exchanged.[168] The explanation that the labour theory of value "ultimately" determined prices – the line of causation running from aggregate surplus value to prices via aggregate profits and the average rate of profit – was considered, by Böhm-Bawerk, unacceptable. All this argument achieved was to show that labour value was one of the factors determining price. Furthermore, Marx's system could cope neither with explaining the prices of goods not produced by labour, nor with the problems caused by differences in the quality of labour.[169]

To show the importance of this for Marx's system as a whole Böhm-Bawerk argued that Marx had simply taken the labour theory of value on the authority of Smith and Ricardo, because it fitted in with his socialist preconceptions, building up a system based on this. As he realized that it was insufficient simply to postulate a labour theory of value, for this could not be taken as a self-evident proposition, he constructed a variety of artificial and fallacious arguments to support it. Marx, in his attempt to justify a system based on an out-dated and refuted theory of value, simply ignored the evidence that exchange values were not determined by labour values.

Herein lies, I believe, the alpha and omega of all that is fallacious, contradictory, and vague in the treatment of his subject by Marx. His system is not in close touch with the facts. Marx has not deduced from facts the fundamental prices of his system, either by means of a sound empiricism or on a solid economico-psychological analysis.[170]

Hilferding's response was to argue that Böhm-Bawerk's criticism was the result of a much too narrow view of economics, according to which the main purpose of the subject was to explain relative prices. Bourgeois economics, according to Hilferding, considers merely the relationship between man and nature, between commodities and individual wants.[171] In contrast, Marxian economics was concerned with exchange value as a social phenomenon, not as a means of determining prices.[172] Böhm-Bawerk, according to Hilferding, confused value and exchange value and price.[173] Thus Hilferding did not attempt to refute Böhm-Bawerk's arguments on their own ground, for he saw something more to the labour theory of value than merely a means of explaining prices. "It is therefore because labor is the social bond uniting an atomized society, and *not because labor is the matter most technically relevant*, that labor is the principle of value".[174] Labour value had, for Hilferding, a deeper meaning connected with the role of exploitation in Marx's view of history.[175] Marx, according to Hilferding, was concerned not to explain relative prices, but to explain the evolution of capitalism.

Connected with this last point is Hilferding's other main criticism of Böhm-Bawerk: that the subjectivist approach, explaining prices in terms of the relationship between needs and wants, was ahistorical, for "The natural conditions under which labor is performed are unalterably given to society, and from these conditions therefore changes in social relationships *cannot* be derived."[176]

Because value was a social relationship, it could not depend on the factors posited by the Austrians. It would be more correct to argue, however, not that the Austrian theory of value denied the social nature of value, but that it interpreted it in a different way. Instead of making almost animistic generalizations about the way society worked, the Austrian approach was to look for the underlying factors that explained why social relationships took the particular forms they did.[177]

In conclusion, it can be argued that the main difference between Böhm-Bawerk and Hilferding was that they had different views of the purpose of economic theory. As one historian of Marxism has said of Marx's theory,

Its purpose is not to describe the quantitative relations between phenomena so that we can more easily influence events, but to unmask the anti-human character of a society in which production is entirely geared to the multiplying of exchange value; to lay bare the "alienation" of social life. ... A theory of this kind is not so much an explanation as an ideological appeal, and must be understood as such."

Referring to the exchange between Böhm-Bawerk and Hilferding, he goes on to argue, "The controversy between Marxists and critics of the theory of value is thus insoluble, as the latter expect from a general economic theory something that Marx's doctrine is unable to provide".[178] Böhm-Bawerk's desire was for a scientific economics based on facts, which meant that, once the labour theory of value had been abandoned as an explanation of relative prices, it was almost inevitable that he, and similarly-minded contemporaries, would dismiss the partly normative and metaphysical labour theory of value as of no significance.

### The transformation problem

In 1907 an important contribution was made to the Marxian theory of value with von Bortkiewicz's solution to the transformation problem. Von Bortkiewicz pointed out that in his solution to the transformation problem Marx had illegitimately mixed together prices and values. To obtain prices Marx had added profits to the *value* of the constant and variable capital used up on production.[179] Von Bortkiewicz argued, correctly, that the appropriate procedure was rather to add profits to the *price* of the capital used up in production. This meant that it was necessary to formulate two separate systems, one dealing with values, the other with prices.

In the *value system*, using the notation of chapter 12,

$$c_I + (1 + e)v_I = o_I$$
$$c_{II} + (1 + e)v_{II} = o_{II}.[180]$$

The value produced by each sector comprises constant capital used up in production, vairable capital and surplus value, surplus value being a fraction $e$ of variable capital. In the *price system*, on the other hand,

$$(1 + r)(p_I c_I + p_{II} v_I) = p_I o_I$$
$$(1 + r)(p_I c_{II} + p_{II} v_{II}) = p_I o_{II}$$

where $r$ is the profit rate, and $p_I$ and $p_{II}$ are the ratios of price to value in each of the two sectors.[181] The significant features of these equations are: (1) that the rate of profit is applied to the total capital stock, not merely to variable capital;[182] and (2) that constant capital is valued using the price of capital goods, with variable capital being valued using the price of wage goods.

Making the further assumption that "simple reproduction"[183] was taking place, and that total profits equalled total surplus value, von Bortkiewicz went on to show that these equations could be used to determine a set of prices.[184]

### 18.7  CONCLUSIONS

Throughout the period, and above all from the 1870s to the mid 1920s, orthodox economics was subject to a sustained attack from the advocates of rival approaches. Common to all these attacks was the charge that contemporary deductive theory was unhistorical, but despite this common strand, there was much greater diversity amongst critics of orthodoxy than amongst its supporters. Whilst there were substantial differences between, for example, Marshall's "neoclassical" approach and Austrian "subjectivism", their theories shared a common structure, differences concerning primarily the interpretation of this structure. With the critics of orthodoxy, on the other hand, the differeces were more fundamental. The approach of the German historical school was close to those of Mitchell and Ashley, for example, but the differences between English, German and American variants remained, nonetheless, substantial. Given the nature of the historical approach, it was perhaps inevitable that differences in national circumstances would cause economists to have different outlooks. Historical economics travelled less well than more mathematical economics.[185] American concern with big business, for example, had no real parallel in England, for the structure of the industrial system was very different. When we take account of Veblen and Marx, who also wished to emphasize the historical evolution of economic systems, the picture becomes even more complicated.

This welter of historical criticism had remarkably little impact on the main body of economic thought, though particular branches of the subject owed much to it. A variety of reasons for this have been suggested. The Marxian explanation, for example, runs in terms of the class interests of the bourgeoisie. Whilst this explanation is hard to refute, there are strong grounds for scepticism. Many mainstream economists, for example, were keenly interested in the interests of the working class, and in projects of social reform. Similar objections can be raised to Veblen's explanation that hedonistic economics, of which marginal utility theories form a part, reflect pecuniary habits of mind.

An important reason for the survival of mainstream economics was that some of the criticisms were answered very effectively. Particularly important here is Allyn Young's criticism of the view, put forward by Veblen, and taken up by Mitchell, that mainstream economics was flawed because it was based on a defective view of human nature, namely hedonism. The part of this critique that Young attacked was the view that "Economic theory rests and always has rested, upon the concept of human nature posited by the economist".[186] Taking as his example Ricardo's system, Young argued,

It is impossible to deduce Ricardo's system from psychological postulates, unless the postulates are made so numerous that there is a one-to-one correspondence with every separate *element* in his system. In short, Ricardo's postulates are found only *in* his system; in fact, I believe it is substantially accurate to say that they *are* his system. Professor Mitchell has charged economists with having rationalized economic behaviour. He himself ... has rationalized economic science. For exposition's sake, or because they thought logical consistency required it, or for some much more subtle and obscure reason, economic theorists have often presented their doctrines as though they flowed from some first principle. But the first principle is generally purely ornamental, like the meaningless "desire for wealth". The real soundness of a system of thought depends on its internal consistency and upon the accuracy with which it summarizes the pertinent parts of experience. These considerations hold true not only for so-called deductive economics (the "deduction" is only a matter of expositional form) but also for 'institutional' or any other variety of economics.[187]

Whatever its merits as a view of the capitalist system, institutionalism did not score highly on this criterion. Young reached the conclusion that "Veblen is a man of genius, but the term scientist does not fit him. He is something that may be as good or better: an artist, an impressionist, painting the picture of the world as he sees it".[188]

The fundamental reason for the survival and prosperity of the orthodox approach, however, would appear to be the inadequacy of the alternatives offered, none of which provided a satisfactory means of analysing the questions to which most economists sought answers. There was widespread agreement, for example, that historical analysis could play an important role in analysing the evolution of national economies over long periods of time, though even here few generalizations could be sustained, but most economists were interested in far more than this. Historical generalizations could not, for example, say anything about the effects of new forms of taxation or new forms of labour organization, both of which were important issues around the turn of the century. In addition, German historical economics was not equipped to analyse the inflation of 1923, and in the 1930s Institutionalism had little to contribute to an analysis of the world slump.

A further factor was that the advocates of a more inductive method failed to provide an alternative to "deductive" theory. When it came to constructive work, for example, both Schmoller and Mitchell made use of marginalist theories, Schmoller making use of Böhm-Bawerk's work, Mitchell of Walras'. The method of the neoclassical programme, on the other hand, was one which proved capable of being employed to answer an ever-increasing range of issues. This is not to say that the insights of the historical economists or the institutionalists were not capable of being used to provide the foundation for an alternative to marginalist theory, though perhaps this is the case. It is rather that no one managed to show how this could be done.

Marxian theory did provide a real alternative to the marginalist conceptual framework, but here too there were serious inherent weaknesses. As Böhm-Bawerk pointed out, Marxian value theory was essentially Ricardian, and could be rejected on the same grounds: the objections concerning the pricing of non-produced goods, the problems raised by differing capital–labour ratios and those caused by the non–homogeneity of labour were all well known from classical criticisms of Ricardian theory. Thus in raising them Böhm-Bawerk was not introducing new arguments, but citing well established results. Though Marxists may have been able to justify the use of labour values as a normative concept, this was not the "scientific" concept that most academic economists were looking for.

# 19

## Economics and Policy in Britain

### 19.1 INTRODUCTION

*Background*

Though economic policy and attitudes towards it changed only very gradually, it is possible to point to a number of events in the years around 1870, all significant in producing a change of attitude towards state intervention in the economy.[1] 1873 is often taken as marking transition from the "great Victorian boom" to the "Great Depression" of the 1870s and the 1880s.[2] From 1873 prices fell steadily, and some sectors of the economy, in particular parts of agriculture, suffered. This was the period when Britain's economic position in the world was being challenged by the growth of the German and American economies, and when forebodings concerning Britain's economic decline were first raised, as in Jevons' *The Coal Question*.[3] From 1879, with Germany's move to protection, the system of free trade established in the 1860s began to crumble. Domestically, important developments were the Reform Acts of 1867 and 1884, which greatly widened the franchise, creating an electoral base for policies of social reform. In addition, legislation in 1871 and 1875 enormously increased the scope for trade union activity. The spread of socialist ideas provided further pressure for social reform. Thus by the 1880s the setting for discussions of economic policy was very different from that twenty years earlier.

Of the changes which took place in economic theory, by far the most important concerned the distribution of income. With the final demise of the wage fund doctrine, one of the obstacles to attempting to raise wages had been removed. But even more important was the removal of what Cairnes called "the great Malthusian difficulty": the threat of population growth no longer inhibited proposals to raise the standard of living. Though utilitarian arguments could be used to support proposals for income redistribution, developments in the theory of income distribution were more important than the changes which occurred in the theory of value.

*Economists and state intervention*

The last three decades of the nineteenth century saw a change, albeit a very gradual one, in economists' attitudes towards the role of the state in the economy. There was a movement towards seeing a much greater role for the state than was the case in the middle of the century[4] Though there may have been some bias towards *laissez faire* and individualism,[5] it is less misleading to stress the enormous increase in the number of cases economists discovered which required state intervention. Representative of this transition from the mid-nineteenth century classical view, to the more modern view is Jevons. In 1869 he described "freedom for *all* commercial transactions" as "the spirit of improved legislation", whereas by 1883 he saw "hardly any limits to the interference of the legislator".[6] In addition to cases where his arguments for intervention were paternalistic, he found cases of public goods. This argument for state intervention was taken up and stated more forcefully by Sidgwick, the culmination of this line of argument coming in Pigou's *Economics of Welfare*, a systematic exposition of the case for state intervention.[7]

In parallel to this discovery of more and more cases requiring state intervention to tackle problems the market could not cope with, was an increased concern for greater equality in the distribution of income. It is true that neoclassical economics abandoned the simplicities of classical macroeconomic distribution theories, and it is true that distribution did not occupy the same place in the new theory of value as in classical theory, but the distribution of income was not neglected. Indeed, the new approach made it possible to examine, in a way not possible for the classical economists, the distribution of income between persons, something of more importance than the factor distribution central to classical theory. Sidgwick was important here, positing a right distribution of income as an object of government policy together with ensuring that production was as high as possible.[8] This emphasis on distribution as an objective of government policy followed from marginal utility analysis, for Sidgwick found that total utility depended not only on the level of income, but also on its distribution.[9] In the following decades marginal utility analysis may not have been taken to what some economists have seen as its logical conclusion, namely the advocacy of complete equality,[10] but the assumption of diminishing marginal utility was used to argue the case for some degree of progression in taxation.

Perhaps the main contribution was that of Edgeworth.[11] Where his predecessors, such as Sidgwick, had interpreted equality of sacrifice to imply proportional taxation, Edgeworth interpreted sacrifice in terms of utility. Rejecting equal absolute and equal proportional sacrifice as giving inadequate guidance as to whether or not taxation ought to be progressive, Edgeworth argued that the total disutility imposed by taxation should be minimized. Edgeworth followed Sidgwick, however, in finding many reasons why this did not imply that there should be complete equality in the distribution of income. These ranged from differences in individuals' utility functions to the need to guard against eroding the incentive to work.

The change of attitude this represented was concisely summed up by Cannan (1893):

The economist of today is far less hostile to socialism in general than his predecessors of the classical school... . The doctrine of marginal utility stamps as economical many things which could formerly be recommended only on "sentimental" grounds... . Assuming needs to be equal, modern economics certainly teaches that a given amount of produce or income will "go further" the more equally it is divided. The inequality of the present distribution has no pretension to be in propotion to needs.[12]

## 19.2   TARIFF REFORM BEFORE 1914

*The campaign for tariff reform*

Discussions of tariff reform did not begin with Joseph Chamberlain, the issue of "fair trade" having been raised in the 1880s, a period when Britain was suffering severely from the effects of foreign competition on interest and profits; but it was with Chamberlain's arguments for tariff reform, dating from the 1890s, and reaching their climax in 1903, that tariff reform was at its height as a political issue. Chamberlain, as Colonial Secretary, promoted in 1896 the idea of an "Imperial *Zollverein*", an imperial customs union with free trade internally and a common protective tariff.[13] Such a system would not, however, suit colonies that wished to protect their industries from the effects of British competition. Thus Chamberlain moved towards a system whereby Britain would discriminate in favour of colonial foodstuffs and raw materials, the colonies in turn discriminating in favour of British industrial goods. Some moves in this direction were taken, but the critical problem arose in 1903 when Chamberlain failed to get the cabinet to agree to a permanent duty on grain imports,[14] for without such a duty it was impossible to discriminate in favour of colonial produce. Starting in May 1903 Chamberlain embarked on a campaign to convert his party and the electorate to a programme of tariff reform. Though the debate was most intense during 1903, tariff reform remained a major political issue right up to 1914.

In the tariff reform controversy there were not merely two, but an enormous variety of standpoints. There were extremists on both sides: some tariff reformers claimed this to be a remedy for virtually every economic problem; whilst on the other side there were those for whom to question free trade came close to blasphemy.[15] But even within less extreme opinion there was a wide range of attitudes. In part this was because political arguments were, right from the start, inseparable from economic ones. For Chamberlain, for example, tariff reform was merely part of a political programme in which imperial unity and social reform were the over-riding issues. Relations with the empire apart, tariff reform raised the question of British relations with Germany and the US. Some supporters of tariff reform failed to share Chamberlain's views on imperial unity; others feared extensive social reform.

Protection could, furthermore, be advocated on quite different grounds, as was done by Balfour, Prime Minister in 1903, in his attempt to find a way in between Chamberlain's tariff reform and free trade as advocated by other members of his party. Balfour's "Insular Free Trade" was based on the premise that, though universal free trade was desirable, free trade might not be desirable in a world in which other countries were protectionist. It would be wrong to give up the bargaining position offered by a tariff: "we should openly and avowedly announce that this country no longer considers itself debarred by economic theories from making the best commercial bargain it can with other countries".[16]

Against both these positions were ranged free traders, who included not only politicians but a substantial number of academic economists. The most significant expression of academic opinion came in what was described as the manifesto of the 14 professors, contained in a letter to *The Times* on August 12th 1903, the signatories to which included Edgeworth, Pigou, and, most important of all, Marshall.[17]

This was an attempt to use the authority of scientific, academic economics in opposition to the protectionist cause.[18] Its outcome, however, was to emphasize the lack of unanimity amongst economists. Though there were exceptions, Clapham, for example, supporting free trade, and Price opposing it, free trade was generally supported by economists sympathetic towards economic theory, and protection by those favouring a more historical approach to the subject, Hewins and Ashley being perhaps the most prominent.

## The economic issues

Perhaps the most important economic aspect of the controversy concerned the effect of a tariff on food prices: would the so-called "stomach taxes" raise the price of food? This was a problem ideally suited to the Marshallian apparatus of supply and demand. Even within this framework, however, the effects of a tariff were complicated, for they depended on the relative magnitudes of various elasticities: domestic, colonial and foreign elasticities of supply and demand.[19] Whilst such reasoning should have been able to counter some of the more simplistic arguments as to why the tax should have been paid by foreigners, it carried no weight against arguments that would not fit in to the Marshallian framework. These included not only political arguments, but also important dynamic arguments about the effects of a tariff in stimulating industry and employment in Britain, and in encouraging the development of new sources of food supply in the colonies. The importance of factors that could not be fitted into the framework, together with the absence of reliable statistical evidence on the relevant elasticities, made the Marshallian "organon" of little direct relevance.

There were also considerable differences of opinion on what use could be made of empirical data on trade flows, and on the performance of countries that had adopted protection. Against the protectionists' claim that tariffs had been an important cause of German and American industrial success, it was possible to point, for example, to the size of their domestic markets, or to the extent of their natural resources. It was hard to use trade statistics even to establish the weakness of British industry without protection:[20] not only were the statistics subject to enormous margins of error, but even growing exports could be interpreted as indicative of either weakness or strength.[21]

These issues were complicated enough, but there were still further economic issues. Tariff reform became linked with unemployment. An example here illustrates the danger academic economists faced of their carefully worded comments being misused. In early 1903 Ashley made the following remark, citing Bagehot's work[22]: "the older writers minimised unduly the difficulty with which labour transfers itself from one industry to another, even a closely allied one".[23] In Chamberlain's hands this argument was re-phrased as an attack on

This doctrine, this favourite doctrine, of the "transfer of labour" is a doctrine of pedants who know nothing of business, nothing of labour. It is not true.... . You cannot teach men who have attained to skill and efficiency in one trade, you cannot teach them on a moment's notice, skill and efficiency in another.[24]

Another economic issue was the revenues to be obtained from protection, this being one reason for the increase in support for tariff reform gained within the Unionist Party in the years leading up to 1914. Revenue from a tariff was a means whereby military expenditures and social welfare measures could be financed without the increases in direct taxes that Churchill and Lloyd George, in the Liberal Party, were demanding.[25] Yet another issue was the link between the gold standard and trade policy, some free traders arguing that the system of international economic relations, of which the gold standard was a part, was founded on free trade.[26]

### The outcome

Free trade, together with the desire to avoid the "dear loaf" was one of the main issues on which the Liberal victory in the 1906 election was based.[27] Within the Unionist Party, protectionism became strongly established; this did not, however, mean that Chamberlain's original campaign had succeeded. Support for protection was, especially in times of depression and high unemployment, such as 1908–1909, stronger than support for imperial preference. Furthermore, the revenue arguments for protection as an alternative to what were seen as the Liberals' attacks on property through income taxation, appealed to very different interests from those at which Chamberlain had wished to appeal with his strategy of vigorous social reform and imperial regeneration. Though tariff reform became accepted by the Unionist Party, its purpose, the ideas on which it was based, and the interests to which it appealed, had changed to such an extent as to raise the question of whether it should really be described as the same policy.

The implications of the tariff reform campaign for the economics profession are also interesting. The manifesto of the professors backfired in the sense that, far from asserting the authority of academic opinion, it demonstrated the lack of agreement amongst economists, providing occasion for ridicule of abstract theorizing. In addition, the controversy helped re-open the division within the profession that had been patched over since the methodological controversies of the 1880s and the early 1890s.[28] Though this has been questioned, it has been argued that Pigou's support for free trade was a significant factor in his election as Marshall's successor in 1908, in preference to Foxwell and Ashley, two supporters of tariff reform.[29] Whilst it seems hard to believe that the election of Foxwell or Ashley rather than Pigou would have made any significant difference to the way economic doctrines developed over the following decades, the institutional structure of the profession in England might well have been different.


## 19.3    UNEMPLOYMENT POLICY BEFORE 1914

*The emergence of employment as an object of economic policy*

Although protection came to be proposed as a remedy for unemployment, it was not originally seen in these terms, an important reason for this being that it was not until the very end of the nineteenth century that unemployment came to be seen as an economic problem. The term "unemployment" itself came into common use only in the mid 1890s.[30] For most of the nineteenth century unemployment, or "irregularity of employment" as it was more commonly called, was seen primarily as a social problem caused by the normal working of the economic system. The New Poor Law of 1834 was based on the assumption that unemployment was, at least for the able bodied, an inevitable occurrence which men should predict and provide for out of their earnings whilst employed.

Though it was recognized by the middle of the century that unemployment could be wasteful, unemployment being seen by Senior, for example, as eroding workers' skills and habits of regularity, it was in the 1880s that perspectives began to change. Unemployment came to be seen as one of the most harmful consequences of trade depressions, and as a chronic social problem amongst certain groups of the population. One of the earliest contributions by an economist was Foxwell's *Irregularity of Employment and Fluctuations of Prices* (1886), in which it was argued that it was the irregularity and insecurity of employment, rather than the average level of earnings, which lay at the root of many social problems. Rather than encourage the dependence of wages on market forces, Foxwell argued, the government should aim, as a major object of policy, to increase the regularity of employment, "giving to the artisan and the labourer as much social security as is enjoyed by the salaried and professional classes".[31] Another economist who clearly saw unemployment as an economic problem was Hobson.[32] It was Hobson who provided a formal definition of unemployment, defining it to cover "all forms of involuntary leisure suffered by the working classes". Though he defended this as corresponding to the general usage of the word, he went on to argue that "The more scientific definition would, however, identify unemployment with the total quantity of human labour power not unemployed in the production of social wealth, which would rank ... as superfluity or waste."[33] This was wider than official definitions, which excluded, for example, seasonal unemployment, on the grounds that taking the year as a whole workers unemployed in one season were nonetheless essential to production. In addition, he provided an economic theory treating unemployment as an aspect of trade depression, with under-consumption being its "direct economic cause".[34] As a remedy he proposed income redistribution aimed at increasing the level of consumption.

The most important work, however, on unemployment was done not by economists, but by what one historian has described as "a group of intellectual hybrids, who were concerned partly with general economic hypotheses, partly with sociological investigation, and partly with administrative reform",[35] the most important being Hubert Llewellyn Smith, Charles Booth, William Beveridge, and Sidney and Beatrice Webb. Llewellyn Smith, author of the Board of Trade's index of unemployment, helped to clarify and define the nature of the problem by providing, in 1893, what became for many years the standard classification of types of unemployment.[36] Booth and the Webbs, in the late 1880s and the early 1890s, conducted detailed investigations into the nature of unemployment, its connection with poverty and the nature of the labour market. The focus of attention was above all on casual labour, the case receiving most attention being London dock labour. In these studies, unemployment was seen as a problem associated with the organization of the labour market, their aim being to find administrative methods of improving this, and hence alleviating the problem of unemployment. Booth, for example, proposed the decasualization of dock labour. Unemployment was not seen primarily in macroeconomic terms.

## Beveridge

In 1909 two works were published which between them contained most of the remedies for unemployment discussed in the next two decades. One of these was Beveridge's *Unemployment, a Problem of Industry* (1909). Beveridge's starting point was the same as that of Booth and earlier investigators, but he went beyond their work in looking at employment in a wider range of industries, those unionized as well as ones dominated by casual labour, and in considering the organization of the labour market in general. Beveridge saw unemployment as an inevitable aspect of growth in a competitive economy.

Unemployment arises because, while the supply of labour grows steadily, the demand for labour, in growing, varies incessantly in volume, distribution and character. ... [S]o long as the industrial world is split up into separate groups of producers ... there must be insecurity of employment. ... Unemployment, in other words, is to some extent at least part of the price of industrial competition – part of the waste without which there could be no competition at all.[37]

He argued, however, that the problem of unemployment could be reduced to "relative insignificance" with two types of policy. The first was a system of labour exchanges, designed to increase the "fluidity" of labour between different employments. Beveridge saw this as

a policy of making reality correspond with the assumptions of economic theory. Assuming the demand for labour to be single and the supply to be perfectly fluid, it is not hard to show that unemployment must always be in the process of disappearance – that demand and supply are constantly tending to an equilibrium. The ideal for practical reform, therefore, must be to concentrate the demand and to give the right fluidity to the supply.[38]

Labour exchanges would, of course, alleviate the problem of casual labour through helping workers to find alternative employment, and they would assist the movement of workers out of declining industries. But their significance went beyond this. For example, young people could be better guided as to choice of careers and into industrial training.[39]

Labour exchanges were also important for Beveridge's other main proposal: the extension of unemployment insurance. Whilst he saw this as coming about in a variety of ways, he argued that it should be supported by the state, either through assisting trade unions in their provision of unemployment insurance, or through the provision of unemployment insurance directly. It was only if an efficient system of unemployment registration were instituted that an insurance scheme could be protected from abuse, which meant that a system of labour exchanges was a pre-requisite for adequate unemployment insurance.[40]

Beveridge did not reject other means of alleviating unemployment, such as altering the timing of public works schemes, and wage flexibility, but he described such schemes as "minor measures". It was the reorganization of the labour market to which he attached most significance.

## The Royal Commission on the Poor Laws

The other important contribution made in 1909 to the discussion of unemployment was the report of the Royal Commission on the Poor Laws. The background to this was that, especially since the 1880s, local authorities had been empowered to provide unskilled relief work to alleviate the worst instances of unemployment, a policy which eventually found expression in the Unemployed Workmen's Act of 1905. These schemes had many faults, and from 1905 to 1909 were investigated by a Royal Commission. Whilst the majority report of this Royal Commission favoured continuing the existing policy of relief works, a more ambitious proposal was put forward in the minority report, the main authors of which were the Webbs, together with A. L. Bowley, who worked out the statistical details. The minority's main proposal was that a substantial part of the normal public works expenditure of the national government and local authorities should be earmarked as to be undertaken in years when unemployment was particularly high. In other words, the pattern of government spending was to be altered so as to smooth out the demand for labour, thus removing cyclical unemployment. Other types of unemployment could be alleviated by improving the operation of the labour market.

It was in the same year, 1909, that an act was passed establishing labour exchanges all over the country. Two years later, the National Insurance Act provided a system of insurance against unemployment.

*The Ricardian view of public works*

The Ricardian view of public works expenditure was that, in providing work for the unemployed the government merely "takes work from people employed by private individuals, and gives it to people selected by the state".[41] Though this view came into prominence in the late 1920s as the "Treasury View", it was being put forward in discussions of public works before 1914.

Its leading academic exponent, Hawtrey, wrote in 1913,

> The writers of the Minority Report appear to have overlooked the fact that the Government by the very fact of borrowing for this expenditure is withdrawing from the investment market savings which would otherwise be applied to the creation of capital.[42]

Hawtrey, however, was virtually alone amongst academic economists in supporting this view. Another writer on the cycle, Robertson, criticized this argument two years later. The earliest modern critique of this argument, however, was that of Pigou in his inaugural lecture (1908). Citing the use in Parliament of an argument similar to that later used by Hawtrey, Pigou argued that though raising loans or taxes to finance relief works might reduce private employment to some extent, only a part of the money would be taken from funds destined for the employment of labour. There would thus be a net increase in employment.[43]

## 19.4   THE GOLD STANDARD AND EMPLOYMENT POLICY, 1918–1939

*Background*

In the inter-war period unemployment dominated discussion of economic policy as never before. Thus although, for example, protection was still an important issue, especially within the Conservative Party,[44] the context of the discussion was very different. Furthermore, the nature of the employment problem had changed significantly since before 1914. After the collapse of the immediate post-war boom, unemployment remained substantially higher than before 1914, averaging approximately 10% throughout the 1920s. Furthermore, due to the publication of monthly unemployment statistics, people were much more aware of the extent of unemployment than was the case before 1914. It was not only the level of unemployment, however, that distinguished the post- and pre-war situations, for its character was very different too. Unemployment could no longer be seen as a problem associated primarily with casual labour, for it was clearly associated with the decline of certain traditional staple industries, in particular coal mining, textiles and shipbuilding. The situation was also very different from the pre-war in that unemployment insurance, its coverage having been substantially increased by the Unemployment Insurance Act of 1920, now covered most of the working population. Furthermore, the contributory nature of the scheme was immediately under-mined, for the scheme was based on the assumption that the normal level of unemployment was 4–5%, whereas unemployment rose to 17% in 1921, before any reserves had been built up in the National Insurance Fund. Though attempts were made to "disguise" this as loans to the National Insurance Fund, a large part of unemployment compensation was met out of taxation. Thus not only did the cost of unemployment benefits provide a further reason for concern about the level of unemployment, but the issues of unemployment and budgetary policy became linked much more closely than before the war.

The situation changed yet again in the 1930s, after the slump of 1929. In the 1920s unemployment was primarily a British problem, for though some other countries, such as Germany, had high unemployment, this could be explained in terms of specific factors. For the United States in particular, the 1920s were a period of expansion and prosperity. But not only was the unemployment problem of the early 1930s more severe than that of the 1920s, it was also very clearly a world problem, not explicable in terms unique to Britain. Indeed, Britain suffered less from the slump after 1929 than did the United States and many other countries.

The monetary situation was also very different after 1918. Prior to 1914 the gold standard was, with the exception of the controversies over bimetallism, virtually unquestioned. During the war Britain left the gold standard. This meant that after 1919 monetary policy was a topic for discussion, if only because a decision about the standard had to be taken: even if it was taken for granted that the pre-war gold standard had to be restored, there were the issues of how and when to do so.

The questions of money and unemployment came to be linked in a way not true of pre-1914 policy discussions. An important reason for this was the changed nature of the employment problem, for unemployment was now substantially a problem of the export industries, whose performance depended on their competitiveness. The exchange rate, costs and wage rates were thus brought into the discussion of unemployment in a new way.

### The gold standard

Following the recommendations of the Cunliffe Committee in 1918 and 1919, the decision was taken to return to the gold standard at the pre-war parity of £1 = $4.86.[45] The return could not take place immediately, however, for British prices were too high relative to American prices for this exchange rate to be feasible.[46] From 1920 to 1925 there was a 40% fall in the price level, with British prices falling relative to American, which made it possible to contemplate returning to the pre-war parity in 1925. The problem was that, despite the price fall, sterling was still overvalued at $4.86, the exact amount being the subject of dispute, and the following years saw attempts to reduce wages in order to reduce exporters' costs. It was this downwards pressure on wages that was responsible for the General Strike in 1926. The gold standard was maintained for six years, until 1931, when as a result of a financial crisis it had to be abandoned and sterling was devalued. There were thus three distinct phases of exchange rate policy: the period from 1920 to 1925 when preparations were being made to return to gold; the period of the restored gold standard, from 1925 to 1931; and the period off gold after 1931. In each of these the constraints on, and the background to, the use of monetary and fiscal policy were very different.

The arguments used by the proponents of the return to gold were centred on the uncertainty to which investors were subject under a managed currency. Without the constraint on currency expansion of its having to be convertible into gold there was the persistent danger of credit expansion and inflation. Given the examples of wartime inflation and, a few years later, of inflation in the Weimar republic, such a view made much more sense then than it would today. There was also the moral argument that sterling debts had been incurred under the understanding that sterling could be exchanged for gold at a certain price, and that to devalue was to renege on a contract.[47] Such behaviour was inconsistent with the maintenance of a stable international financial order on which trade and prosperity were dependent.

The decision as to just when to return to gold was taken in the light of the report by the Bradbury Committee in February 1925. The Bradbury Committee did not consider the question of a lower parity for sterling – indeed it hardly had to, for the Anglo-American price gap was, wrongly as it turned out, estimated to be as little as 4.5%. Allowing for the margin between gold points (the maximum and minimum values between which sterling could fluctuate on the gold standard) this would necessitate a deflation of only about 1.5%. In addition the committee viewed the prospects of deflation with equanimity, the 40% fall in prices since 1920 being taken as evidence for this. It was felt important to return to gold while the prospects were favourable, for delay might reduce confidence in sterling, lowering the exchange rate and making a return to the pre-war parity more difficult.

The most prominent opponent of the decision to return to gold was Keynes. In his *Tract on Monetary Reform* (1923) he acknowledged the injustices resulting from inflation, but he saw the consequences of deflation as worse.[48] He argued that it was time to abandon prejudices about entrusting the management of the price level to the government. When the return to gold did come, Keynes responded with his *The Economic Consequences of Mr Churchill* (1925), directed against the then Chancellor of the Exchequer. He argued that the price gap was much greater than the Bradbury Committee thought, nearer 10%, and that because of the difficulty in reducing wages the resulting overvaluation of sterling would have severe consequences, especially on the export industries.

To a great extent, therefore, the difference of opinion between Keynes and the advocates of the return to gold concerned the interpretation of empirical evidence rather than differences in economic theory. They had different beliefs as to the extent of the deflation required by the return to gold, Keynes' estimate of the price gap being much higher than that of the Bradbury committee. In addition, Keynes argued that the deflation seen since 1920 had been possible only because wages had never properly adjusted to the rise in prices up to 1920; he argued that *because of* the deflation which had occurred, any further deflation would be very difficult. In contrast, his opponents saw past deflation as evidence that future deflation would also be possible.

### Public works policy in the 1920s

After 1918 the view of most British economists was that public works expenditure could be used to reduce the level of unemployment, this view being held not only by socialists such as the Webbs, but also by more orthodox economists. Several years before, both Pigou (1908 and 1912) and Robertson (1915) had rejected the Ricardian view that public expenditure would merely divert expenditure from private investment, a view which they continued to advocate after the war. The only prominent British economist to argue against public works in the 1920s was Hawtrey.[49] Though Hawtrey was joined in the 1930s by economists such as Hayek and Robbins, influenced by Austrian theories of the cycle,[50] it remained true that the majority of economists supported the use of public works policies to tackle unemployment. It would involve only a slight exaggeration to endorse Keynes' remark, made in 1929, that "I know of no British economist of reputation who supports the proposition that schemes of National Development are incapable of curing unemployment."[51]

It was in the Treasury and the City, not amongst economists, that opposition to public works was to be found. Even here, however, there were important changes of emphasis through the period.[52] In the early 1920s there was some official support for relief works and contra-cyclical public works, of the type proposed in the Minority Report of the Royal Commission on the Poor Laws in 1909.[53] Experience of previous slumps meant that unemployment was expected to be temporary, and public works organized by local authorities were a fairly cheap form of unemployment relief, not involving the Exchequer. It was only after 1925, when high unemployment was no longer seen as temporary, that attitudes hardened and moves were taken to restrict relief work. There was a shift from seeing unemployment as a cyclical problem towards seeing it as a structural one, for which the appropriate remedies were industrial reorganization, labour mobility and cost reductions. In the words of one historian, "Within the space of a few years, therefore, both relief and contracyclical public works had been discredited, and the Treasury was enunciating the view for which it became infamous."[54] Moreover, not only did the Treasury start disputing the value of public works schemes, but it also started using new theoretical arguments to defend its view. Thus a Treasury statement made in 1927 could argue that

The decision taken by the Government at the end of 1925 to restrict grants for relief schemes was based mainly on the view that, the supply of capital in this country being limited, it was undesirable to divert any appreciable proportion of this supply from normal trade channels.[55]

By 1929 Churchill, addressing the House of Commons, claimed that

It is *orthodox treasury dogma, steadfastly held,* that whatever might be the political or social advantages, very little additional employment can, in fact, and as a general rule, be created by State borrowing and expenditure.[56]

According to this orthodoxy, Britain's economic problems were not due to insufficient demand, but were explicable in terms of four factors: the burden of unproductive debt and overlavish spending by central government and local authorities, these resulting in budgetary problems; excessive costs in certain industries; and the attempt by all classes to maintain an unduly high standard of living.[57]

*Real wages and unemployment*

In view of the tendency in post-war writings on "Keynes and the Classics" to see wage cuts as the "classical" remedy for unemployment, it is worth pointing out that support for wage cuts was, amongst economists, very limited. Though there were of course prominent economists, most notably perhaps Cannan, who supported a policy of wage reductions, the economist most commonly associated with "classical" economics, Pigou, did *not* advocate such a policy.[58] On the issue of wage cuts versus policies to expand demand there was little difference between his view and that of Keynes. Although Pigou's position was stated in his *Industrial Fluctuations* (1927) an even clearer statement is to be found in the evidence he later gave to the MacMillan committee.[59] In this he conceded that *given the level of demand,* reductions in real wages would increase employment, but he argued that an expansion of demand would be preferable. It was because he took the existence of unemployment as indicating that supply of labour exceeded demand that he believed that an increase in demand could raise employment without any fall in real wages.[60]

*Keynes and public works, 1924–1929*

Although, as has already been argued, it would be completely misleading to represent Keynes as standing alone, he was one of the most vigorous advocates of public expenditure as a remedy for unemployment. When Keynes first began supporting public investment programmes in the mid 1920s this was not seen as a remedy for cyclical fluctuations, such as the pre-war public works proposals, but as a remedy for the persistent slump in certain industries, a slump destined to continue because of the return to gold.[61] In 1929 he wrote,

I began to advocate schemes of National Development as a cure for unemployment four years or more ago – indeed as soon as I realised that, the effect of the return to gold having been to put our money rates of wages too high relatively to our foreign competitors we could not, *for a considerable time,* hope to employ as much labour as formerly in the export industries.[62]

Thus Keynes, in an article posing the rhetorical question, "Does unemployment need a drastic remedy?" (1924) supported Lloyd George's proposals for a large programme of public investment. Keynes argued that lack of confidence was inhibiting the recovery of private investment, and that to undertake a programme of public investment would both provide employment directly and restore the confidence of the private sector. Keynes' association with Lloyd George and the Liberal Party continued throughout the 1920s, Liberal Party work culminating in its 1929 election manifesto, *We Can Conquer Unemployment*. This contained the argument that public investment, in schemes ranging from road building to investment in electricity generation and the telephone system, would not only generate employment directly, but also generate further employment in the private sector. The manifesto contained an explicit criticism of the argument that the supply of savings was limited, the claim being made that a large quantity of saving was not finding its way into productive investment, but was being hoarded as bank deposits.[63] This manifesto was publicly endorsed by Keynes.[64]

*Depression and recovery, 1929–1939*

To understand the nature of the discussions which took place in these years it is necessary to provide a brief outline of the events which took place.[65] The Wall Street crash occurred in September 1929[66] and there followed a worldwide slump. Unemployment in Britain, though it rose less than in the US, rose from 10% in 1929, to 16% in 1930 and to 22% in 1931. This created the prospect of an enormous budget deficit. Taxes were raised in the 1930 budget, and in February 1931 a committee, the May Committee, was set up to find ways of reducing public expenditure. Up to this point the consequences for sterling of the slump had been favourable, for with the collapse of the US stock market boom money became less tight, British interest rates falling substantially from the Autumn of 1929 to the Spring of 1930. In May, however, the failure of an Austrian bank resulted in a financial crisis which spread, first to Germany and then, by July, to Britain.[67] The government's response was to attribute the crisis in large measure to a lack of confidence, this being caused by the large budget deficit.[68] The remedy was seen as involving public expenditure cuts such as those the May Committee recommended in its report, published early in July. The Labour Government split over the issue of a 10% reduction in unemployment benefits, and was replaced on August 24th by a National Government under MacDonald, until then Prime Minister in the Labour Government. Cuts were agreed and an emergency budget passed on September 10th. This failed, however, to alleviate the situation, and on September 21st the Bank of England was relieved of its responsibility to pay gold on demand. The gold standard was thus maintained until the government was forced to abandon it.

Despite the almost universal desire, whilst it was in operation, to stay on the gold standard, there was little support for the idea of returning to it once it had been abandoned.[69] Discussion was rather over the rate at which sterling should be allowed to settle. Though the departure from gold was accompanied by a temporary rise in interest rates, it was soon followed by a period of cheap money, and a relatively low exchange rate, these being intended to aid recovery. The Exchange Equalization Account was set up in 1932 to make it possible to continue this policy in the face of the inflow of capital which occurred as confidence in sterling was restored.[70] Budgetary policy, however, changed little in the early 1930s. The expenditure cuts introduced in 1931 were restored by 1935, but the budget was still balanced. The government objected to, for example, Keynes' proposals for expenditures to be met by future increases in taxation, on the grounds that this was merely a way of attempting to disguise an unbalanced budget. It was only from 1936, and above all from 1937, when it became caught up in rearmament, that budgetary policy changed.[71]

### The MacMillan report

Whilst the May Committee took a very short term view, ignoring the wider effects of their proposed expenditure cuts on the economy, a broader perspective was taken by the Committee on Finance and Industry, the MacMillan Committee, which reported later in July. The report of this committee, of which Keynes was a prominent member, is important, for it illustrates the case for expansion as it appeared whilst Britain was still on the gold standard.

In its opening section the report put forward a view of the need for economic management similar to that expressed by Keynes in *The End of Laissez Faire*:

we may well have reached the stage where an era of concerted and deliberate management must succeed the era of undirected natural evolution. ... We stand in need as never before of a definite national policy in our financial disposition.[72]

Though the committee argued a case for expansion, however, it did not dispute the advantages of remaining on gold.

This brings us to the question whether adherence to an international standard may involve the payment of too heavy a price in the shape of domestic instability... . If we leave aside the position today, experience does not show that a creditor country with diversified trade is liable to suffer undue strain merely as the result of adherence to an international standard. We are of the opinion, therefore, that we should not be influenced merely by the exigencies of the moment, if there is reason to believe that there may be important countervailing advantages on a longer view. If we need emergency measures to relieve the immediate strain, we should seek them in some other direction.[73]

As for these long term advantages the committee mentioned the earnings from banking and financial services, but more important was the need for a world monetary standard: "there is, perhaps, no more important object within the field of human technique than that the world as a whole should achieve a sound and scientific monetary system".[74] By abandoning gold, Britain would be reducing the possibility of progress towards a rational world monetary system, for the committee saw no possibility of early progress towards such a system "except as the result of a process of evolution starting from the historic gold standard".[75] Though Ernest Bevin, who had consistently advocated devaluation, together with one other member of the committee, dissented,[76] devaluation was emphatically rejected.[77]

This cosmopolitan outlook was reflected in the main policy prescription, that

our object should be, so far as it lies within the power of this country to influence the international price level, first of all to raise prices a long way above the present level, and then to maintain them at the level thus reached with as much stability as can be managed.[78]

As for divergences between national interests and the interests of the world as a whole, it was thought that "such apparent divergences of interest would generally prove to be illusory or avoidable if fully understood".[79] Price stability was to be achieved by central bank credit policy, aimed at stabilizing the rate of investment, both long and short term.[80] By undertaking not to allow "unwanted and unnecessary" accumulations of gold, central banks would avoid transmitting deflation from one country to another. It was only after considering how to make the international monetary system operate better that the committee turned to other issues.[81]

A substantial minority of the committee, including Keynes and Bevin, went further, arguing that wider issues had to be considered. "For if the situation remains unchanged in other respects, we doubt whether it lies within the power of the banking system to restore unemployment to a satisfactory level".[82] The reason given for this was that the main problem was not lack of bank credit, but "the reluctance of acceptable borrowers to come forward".[83] To change this, either the long term rate of interest had to be considerably reduced, or some form of state action had to be taken. Either would put strain on the balance of payments. It was in this context that a system of tariffs and bounties was suggested as an alternative "immeasurably preferable to devaluation".[84]

The policies proposed by the MacMillan Committee are consistent with the framework of the *Treatise on Money* which Keynes had published the previous year. The emphasis was on the need for inflation, for a rise in the price level on a worldwide scale, to raise profits and the incentive to invest.[85] Public spending and expansionary credit policies were a part of this process. The crucial aspect of the committee's recommendations, however, is that neither were these proposals seen as an alternative to the gold standard, nor did the committee reject the long term arguments put forward in favour of the gold standard. Indeed, as the quotation above shows, they could hardly have attached more importance to the maintenance of a stable international monetary system.[86] Thus proposals for protection were not seen as a means of cutting Britain off from the rest of the world, but as a means of enabling Britain to stay on the gold standard, the only feasible starting point for progress towards an improved international monetary system.

*The development of Keynes' views*

In assessing the development of Keynes' views it is crucial to bear in mind the changing circumstances in which he was writing, for he was continually attempting to apply his ideas to the current situation, bearing in mind the constraints on what was feasible. There was a consistent theme in his writings, however; namely the undesirability of deflation.[87] In the early 1920s he criticized the return to gold on the grounds that the authorities underestimated both the extent and the significance of the deflationary effects of their policy. From 1925 to 1931 he sought ways of inflating the economy, both national and international, whilst retaining the benefits of the gold standard. His motives for supporting the gold standard were a natural extension of his earlier views, for he saw it as a step towards introducing some sort of rational decision making as to the course of the world economy.[88] He continued to argue for expansionary policies after 1931, though with the collapse of the gold standard he switched his hopes for the international monetary system to some sort of sterling area.

This emphasis on inflation contrasted with the orthodox position, which was one dominated by fear of inflation. A major reason why the gold standard was thought to inspire confidence was that managed currencies were associated with inflation. In the early 1930s fiscal policy was motivated by fear of the inflationary consequences associated with an unbalanced budget.

Keynes' advocacy of inflation was, however, contingent on circumstances, as is illustrated by the views he expressed in a series of articles and letters he wrote in 1937.[89] By that time the economy was, Keynes believed, passing beyond the point where there was general excess capacity, as a result of which it was important to pay as much attention to the composition of demand as to its volume. Because of the possibility that a slump might soon develop, and given that suitable investment projects take time to create, he argued that certain items of spending should deliberately be held back so that they could be used, when the time came, to counteract the slump. Thus Keynes was urging restraint, even though unemployment was still over 10%.

Keynes' policy prescriptions, whether on domestic monetary policy, public works or the international monetary system, were all based on the same attitude towards the role of government in the economy. This attitude was spelt out in detail in *The End of Laissez Faire* (1926). The bulk of this comprised a long disquisition on social philosophy, in which he criticized *laissez-faire* orthodoxy, describing it as a "lethargic monster", which had "ruled over us by hereditary right rather than by personal merit".[90] Seeing state socialism as equally anachronistic,[91] he argued, borrowing Bentham's phrase, that it was necessary "to distinguish afresh the *Agenda* of government from the *Non-Agenda*".[92] As regards the former, he argued

The most important *Agenda* of the State relate not to those activities which private individuals are already fulfilling, but to those functions which fall outside the sphere of the individual, to those decisions which are made by *no one* if the State does not make them. The important thing for government is not to do things which individuals are doing already, and to do them a little better or a little worse; but to do those things which at present are not done at all.[93]

Seeing the main evils of his time as "the fruits of risk, uncertainty and ignorance" he cited three areas where state action was needed: deliberate control of currency and credit; "some coordinated act of intelligent judgement" as to the desirable level of savings and the directions into which they are channelled; and attention to the size and quality of the population.[94] Keynes thus argued for the deliberate management of the currency, first at a national level and later, when the circumstances required it, at an international level, and measures to ensure a rational level of investment. Underlying all his writings on policy was a philosophy according to which the world was amenable to rational decision-making, and that such decisions should be taken by someone.[95]

## 19.5   CONCLUSIONS

*The complexity of economic policy*

In this chapter no attempt has been made to tackle two of the questions most often asked about economics and economic policy, namely what were the main reasons why particular economic policies were pursued, and which policies were the appropriate ones to pursue? There are two reasons for this. The first is that to tackle either of these questions properly would take us further into British economic history than it is appropriate to go here.[96] But the second, and more fundamental reason is that, although these are important questions, they are not necessarily the most important ones from the point of view of understanding the way in which economic ideas have evolved. For this, it is often more important to see how the ideas are related to the circumstances in which they were put forward than to know how the ideas stand up in the light of a modern interpretation of the economic history of the period. To examine ideas about economic policy in this way is not to justify them:[97] they may of course be completely explicable yet erroneous.

During the period covered by this chapter, economic theories were important in discussions of economic policy, academic economists having ample opportunity to make their views known, both before and after the war. The relationship of this advice to the policies pursued was, however, complicated, not simply because policy makers chose to take account of other issues, had vested interests, and failed to understand the ideas of academic economists, but for more fundamental reasons connected with the nature of economic theories. The first reason is that whilst the development of economic theory is to a substantial extent autonomous, in the sense that its evolution is influenced primarily by theoretical considerations, the way economic theories develop is also influenced by the problems economists choose to tackle, and the way they choose to tackle them. These depend on how economists conceive the economy, and on the nature of the economic problems with which policy makers are confronted. The best example of this is perhaps the evolution of attitudes towards unemployment. As long as economists' conceptions of unemployment were dominated by the problems of casual labour in the London docks, they were most unlikely to analyse the problem of unemployment even in the way it was analysed in the inter-war period, let alone in the way economists usually tackle the problem today.

A second reason why the relationship between theory and policy is so complicated is that not only are theories developing, but also there is rarely a one-to-one correspondence between theories and policy prescriptions. A good example of this is provided by the attitudes of Keynes and Pigou towards unemployment policy in the late 1920s. Their positions on unemployment policy were very close indeed, both arguing against wage reductions, and in favour of public investment policies. These policy prescriptions were, however, based on different theories. The theoretical approach of Pigou's *Industrial Fluctuations* is different from that of Keynes' *Treatise on Money*.[98] As an example of the opposite instance, of differing policy prescriptions being derived from the same theory, it is possible to cite the different views on policy derived by economists using the purchasing power parity theory in the early 1920s.

An aspect of this problem, sufficiently important to be worth singling out, is the fact that an economic theory focuses only on certain aspects of a problem. Whilst such "blinkers" may for some purposes, and the logical analysis of economic relationships is one of these, be invaluable, the aspects which are ignored can rarely be left out of discussions of economic policy. A good example here is the use of the Marshallian theory in the Tariff Reform campaign. Problems of economic development are virtually impossible to analyse in a Marshallian supply and demand model,[99] but they were issues which could not be neglected because of the importance many tariff reformers attached to them.

In assessing debates on economic policy it is important to note that certain aspects of economic problems are amenable to quantitative treatment, in the sense that they concern functional relationships between economic variables. Since 1939, especially with the increase in the use of mathematics in economics, the emphasis on these aspects of economic problems has increased. The result of this is the tendency to attach too little importance to factors which cannot be quantified. Consider the orthodox case on the gold standard and public works policy. The Keynesian counter-argument can easily be expressed formally and the weaknesses of the Treasury View stand out clearly. The arguments put forward on the other side, in contrast, *whatever their intrinsic merits*, cannot, at least at present, be analysed in this way. Factors such as confidence, and the reaction of other countries to an "immoral" action, cannot usefully be expressed in terms of simple functional relationships. This would seem one of the reasons, and it is worth emphasizing that it is only one reason, why the orthodox position has been taken less seriously than the Keynesian. It is for this reason that the MacMillan Committee report is so interesting, for it shows Keynes and other advocates of expansionary policies arguing an aspect of the "orthodox" case, namely the importance of the gold standard.

## British and American policy discussions

This chapter has been very parochial in its outlook, for unlike economic theory, discussions of economic policy in the period were, to perhaps a greater extent than today, very much affected by the particular circumstances and background against which the economists were writing. This can best be illustrated by considering some of the ways in which the context for American discussions of policy was very different from that of British discussions.

As in Britain, the context in which American discussions of economic policy took place changed substantially in the last third of the nineteenth century, but the reasons for this were very different.[100] The event dividing the century, both politically and economically, was the Civil War of 1862–1865, the decades following 1865 seeing not only a different political balance but an enormous expansion of the economy in terms of both production and geographical area. It was between 1865 and 1914 that the frontier was extended from the Mississippi to the Pacific. During the Civil War a policy had been established favouring the rapid expansion of industry, with minimal controls on business activity. Especially with the enormous concentration of economic power which emerged in the 1890s, due in part to the importance of railroads in the US economy, an enormous concentration of economic power took place, especially in the 1890s. As a result of this the need for controls on business was an issue of immensely greater importance than in Britain.

Monetary problems, too, were the subject of more intense discussion in American than in Britain, the Civil War again having set the scene with enormous increases in the national debt, and with the issue of inconvertible currency (the greenbacks). Further factors underlying the importance of monetary issues in the US were the need of a rapidly expanding economy for circulating medium, and the political importance of farmers. In the depressions of the 1870s and the 1890s, and above all in the Presidential election of 1896, the silver question achieved a prominence unrivalled elsewhere, the free coinage of silver being advocated as a means of expanding the supply of currency.[101] Thus although the theories American economists produced were of the same genus as contemporary theories in other countries, discussions of economic policy were radically different.

As in Britain, labour unions and their behaviour were an important issue, but again the context was different. American labour unions faced much greater problems than their British counterparts, their membership remained low, right up to 1914, and they were relatively weak. Although explicitly socialist ideas did not gain much support, radical ideas were strong in the US. In addition, the tolerance of American economists towards rival viewpoints meant that the association of unemployment with the business cycle, and of the business cycle with under-consumption, was stronger in the US than in Britain. Thus Hobson, for example, received more attention in the US than in Britain. Discussions of unemployment policy had a very different background.

# 20

# Scope and Method in Neoclassical Economics

## 20.1 INTRODUCTION

Despite the enormous differences in the way they approached their economic inquiries, Jevons, Menger and Walras were seen by many of their contemporaries to stand alongside the English classical political economy of Ricardo, Senior and Mill as placing abstract, deductive theory at the centre of economics. It was the historical school which challenged English classical political economy on methodological grounds, the work of Jevons, Menger and Walras being seen, in words written not long after, as "a reversion to the abstract method ... just at the moment when Historical study seemed to be triumphantly forging ahead".[1]

This chapter is concerned with the views on method put forward by the successors of Jevons, Menger and Walras. This is not to say that other economists had nothing to say on method – far from it, for most neoclassical methodological writings were in response to arguments of critics who cast doubts on the propriety of their approach. However, because the attacks on neoclassical methodology were frequently the major part of the case against orthodox economics, it makes sense to consider these methodological criticisms in chapter 18 rather than here.

## 20.2  J. N. KEYNES[2]

The most important British work on methodology in the late nineteenth century was John Neville Keynes' *Scope and Method of Political Economy* (1891), in which he tried to resolve the differences between the abstract, "English" school and its historical, "German" critics.[3] Keynes presented his views in a spirit of compromise: "The besetting fallacy of writers on economic method has been well said to be one of exclusiveness."[4] Different methods, according to Keynes, were appropriate for different problems, and he claimed that economists of both schools used the same methods when they were discussing the same problems. Their differences really concerned the relative importance of different problems.[5] Furthermore, it was only the extreme exponents of each school who disagreed; most economists were agreed over method.

Although Keynes presented his argument as one of compromise he clearly sided with the abstract, "English" school. Most importantly, he argued for a clear separation of positive and normative economics, rejecting the claim that economics was an ethical science: "The attempt to fuse together the enquiries into what is, and what ought to be, is likely to stand in the way of our giving a clear and unbiased answer to either question."[6] Keynes also denied the historical school's claims that the economic aspects of behaviour could not be isolated from other social phenomena.

The best starting point for discussing Keynes' methodological views is his definition of a science as "a connected and systematized body of truths possessing generality of form".[7] Keynes saw scientific activity as a search for *truths*, the basis for this being observation, or induction. Though, for reasons considered below, deduction was vital, deduction would be of no significance unless the premises on which it worked were founded on observation: "all deduction is barren, so long as it does not start from observation".[8] Two remarks need to be made about this role for observation and induction. The first is that observation, for Keynes, was an elastic term, including not only experiments (for example to test diminishing returns, or the effects of the division of labour on productivity),[9] but also common sense[10] and the results of introspection.[11] Though Keynes realized that observation was theory-dependent, this was not seen as a barrier to the inductive testing of theories: it was rather that understanding of the correct theory could help remove "personal bias": "The more complete our knowledge of the laws by which economic phenomena are regulated, the more accurate will our description and classification of them become."[12] The second remark is that the task of inductive reasoning was confined to the observation of "elementary economic forces", not "complex economic facts".[13] Keynes' rejection of the historical method was not based on any objection to induction *per se*, but was rather because he believed the subject matter of economics to be too complicated to be amenable to an inductive treatment. Thus, writing on the method of differencs (which involves, for example, finding two countries that are identical in all respects save the one in which we are interested) he argued that whilst

a connection of cause and effect can be established by this method with a more or less high degree of probability[,] the cases of which this can be said are, however, exceptional; and even in the most favourable instances, confirmation by some independent line of reasoning is indispensable.[14]

The greater the number of causes in operation, and the more complicated the mode of their interaction, the less possible it becomes to fulfil the conditions required for valid inductive reasoning.[15]

Deduction was also important, not only because of the inability of inductive reasoning to establish complex economic laws, but also because scientific activity was seen by Keynes as going beyond mere description to the establishment of links between economic facts. For this deductive reasoning was vital. It was this which led Keynes to quote with approval Jevons' claim that,

It is, in fact, in proportion as a science becomes deductive, and enables us to grasp more and more apparently unconnected facts under the same law, that it becomes perfect. He who knows why a thing happens, will also know exactly in what cases it will happen, and what differences in the circumstances will prevent the thing from happening.[16]

It is important to stress, however, that Keynes was concerned not merely with prediction, but with finding the true causes (*verae causae*) of economic phenomena.[17]

The truths of which political economy consisted were to be *general* truths, as is made clear both in Keynes' definition of science, and in the passage from Jevons just quoted. There are two aspects to this generality of economic laws. The first is that the desire for general laws supported Keynes' emphasis on deductive reasoning. Keynes claimed that abstract, deductive theory could be made "demonstrative and necessary", with little grounds for dispute as to its conclusions. In contrast, inductive laws were seen as "contingent and indeterminate", limited in their application and less certain.[18]

The other aspect of the search for generality is that economic laws had to be laws of tendency, asserting what would happen in the absence of disturbing or countervailing causes. A *ceteribus paribus* qualification usually applies.[19] Whilst Keynes stressed the importance of comparing predictions with observations, the purpose of this was not so much to test the theory as to establish whether the conditions necessary for the theory to be applicable were met. Thus although Keynes quoted Mill to the effect that confidence in deductive reasoning is derived from the accordance of the results of such reasoning with those of observation, he does so only in order to qualify the statement.

We may have independent grounds for believing that our premises correspond with the facts, and that the process of deduction is correct; and we may accordingly have confidence in our conclusions, although their complete verification is almost impossible.[20]

Discrepancies between theories and the facts might arise through aspects of the theories being unobservable; in other words, even if all the *ceteris paribus* assumptions were specified, it might be impossible to tell whether or not they were satisfied.

Though conciliatory in tone, contributing to the decline of methodological controversy in England,[21] Keynes' book constituted a vigorous defence of abstract economics, Keynes attaching less importance to historical studies than did Marshall.[22] Despite Marshall's eminence, it could be argued that it was Keynes' conciliatory defence of abstract theory, rather than Marshall's attempt to combine theory and history, which prevailed. Keynes' methodology was used to justify the use of Marshall's theoretical tools. Research in English economics was concerned above all with theory,[23] the ideas of Marshall's *Industry and Trade* not being followed up. Clapham's "empty boxes"[24], the Marshallian categories of constant, increasing and decreasing returns industries, remained unfilled: the research needed to say which industries came into which category was never done. The dominant trend in English economics was that leading up to Robinson's *Economics of Imperfect Competition*, developing Marshall's theoretical tools and neglecting history. It can also be argued that the positive–normative distinction, to which both Keynes and Marshall attached so much importance, became diluted over the decades which followed. The main development here was Pigou's decision to place "economic welfare"[25], an essentially normative concept, at the centre of economics.[26] Robinson later claimed that as an undergraduate at Cambridge in the 1920s, she had never been taught the importance of upholding the positive–normative distinction.[27]

## 20.3  AUSTRIAN APPROACHES[28]

### *Böhm-Bawerk and Schumpeter*

Though Böhm-Bawerk wrote no really important work on methodology, it is important to mention his views to show that the views of Wieser and Mises do not represent the only Austrian response to Menger's work. Böhm-Bawerk was, of course, just as committed as Menger to the development of deductive economic theory. There was, however, a softening in his attitude towards deductive economic theory, analogous to the shift in emphasis between Cairnes and Keynes, in that Böhm-Bawerk used the terms "isolating" or "abstract-deductive" rather than "exact" to describe deductive theory. Where Menger treated "exact" laws as irrefutable,[29] Böhm-Bawerk saw economic laws as founded on observation:

The abstract-deductive method ... has no fancy *a priori* axioms as a basis for its inferences, nor does it confine itself to inferences and deductions. On the contrary, it starts exactly as the historical school would have it start, with observation of actual conditions and endeavours from this empirical material to build general laws.[30]

Even the doctrine of marginal utility, for which Menger claimed so much, was, for Böhm-Bawerk, based on observation.

Böhm-Bawerk emphasized the methodological parallels between economics and the natural sciences, his empiricist methodology becoming clear in his criticism of Marx, whose system he saw as being out of touch with the facts.[31] This emphasis on the parallels between economics and the natural sciences was characteristic also of Schumpeter's writing (1908). In this book Schumpeter expounded and defended the Walrasian general equilibrium system on the grounds that, although abstract and unrealistic in character, it enabled the economist to understand, better than he otherwise would, an important set of experiences. It was solely for the purposes of gaining insight into empirical observations that the assumptions of abstract economic theory were chosen.[32]

### *Wieser*

The claims of Böhm-Bawerk and Schumpeter that economics was an empirical science analogous to the natural sciences was completely rejected by Wieser. His main argument was that economics was in a privileged position *vis à vis* the natural sciences, in that it had available to it insights obtained from "inner observation".

We can observe natural phenomena only from outside but ourselves from within.... . This psychological method chooses the most advantageous position for observation. It finds that certain acts take place in our consciousness with a feeling of necessity. What a huge advantage for the natural scientist if the organic and inorganic world clearly informed him of its laws, and why should we neglect such assistance.[33]

The situation facing natural scientists was that they

must be content to describe a series of happenings, abandoning the hope of showing how the effect springs from the cause... . For all actions unaccompanied by a consciousness of necessity, economic theory need never strive to estimate a law in a long series of inductions. In these cases we, each of us, hear the law pronounced by an unmistakable inner voice.[34]

Thus where Böhm-Bawerk tried to take economics in a direction similar to that advocated by Keynes, Wieser attempted to move it the other way, much closer to the position of Senior and Cairnes, claiming that significant conclusions could be deduced from a few fundamental, self-evident and indisputable assumptions.[35]

## Mises

Wieser's arguments were carried a stage further by Mises, whose ideas, brought together in *Epistemological Problems of Economics* (1933) were very influential in the 1930s. He summarized the aim of his book as being to establish the logical legitimacy of the science that has for its object the universally valid laws of human action.[36]

These laws covered not merely economic activity, but "extended to all human action and all social phenomena".[37] His concern was thus much wider than simply economics. Economics was special because it was the discipline in which, due primarily to the work of the English classical school, the science of human action had been most fully worked out.[38] The wide nature of Mises' concern led him to discuss not only the historical school, the combat of whose ideas was his main task, but also the views of sociologists. Thus the writings of men such as Dilthey, Weber and Bergson receive from Mises attention they receive in the writings of few other economists.

For Mises not only was observation incapable of furnishing laws of human action, but it could not even provide a basis for deriving such laws. Despite asserting that both theory and history were indispensable,[39] he went far beyond Keynes in completely rejecting induction as a means of providing a basis for theoretical argument.[40] He argued that observations were dependent on theory.

It is only with the aid of a theory that we can determine what the facts are... . To apply language, with its words and its concepts, to anything is at the same time to approach it with a theory.[41]

The study of history always presupposes a measure of universally valid knowledge.[42]

This theory comprised a priori theorems, neither based on experience nor verifiable.

But no kind of experience can ever force us to discard or modify a priori theorems. They are not derived from experience; they are logically prior to it and cannot be either proved by corroborative experience or disproved by experience to the contrary.[43]

If theories could not be based on observation, on what could they be based? Mises found the answer to this in the logic of human action.

The science of human action that strives for universally valid knowledge is the theoretical system whose hitherto best elaborated branch is economics. In all of its branches this science is a priori, not empirical. Like logic and mathematics, it is not derived from experience; it is prior to experience. It is, as it were, the logic of action and deed.[44]

Knowledge of action, or rational action, came, for Mises as for Wieser, from introspection. Unlike Keynes, however, Mises regarded this not as empirical knowledge, but as knowledge prior to experience.

What we know about the fundamental categories of action – action, economizing, preferring, the relation of means and ends ... – is not derived from experience. We conceive all this from within, just as we conceive logical and mathematical truths, a priori, without reference to any experience. Nor could experience ever lead anyone to the knowledge of these things if he did not comprehend them from within himself.[45]

The knowledge derived in this way was universally valid.[64] The only role for experience in this "praxeology" as he called it,[47] was that of distinguishing interesting from uninteresting problems.

For Mises, therefore, economics comprised the working out of the implications of economizing behaviour, of behaviour in accordance with given preferences. The assumption of rational behaviour, the striving after goals, or the attainment of ends, was not an empirical hypothesis, but an axiom: to speak of irrational behaviour was for Mises meaningless.[48]

Like Keynes, Mises pointed out the importance of distinguishing scientific explanation from political value judgements.[49] It can be argued, however, that Mises' methodology provided no means for preventing the impermissible obliteration of this boundary. Despite claiming economic science to be neutral as regards value judgements,[50] Mises argued that economic laws showed the existence of a limit to political power, beyond which it could not successfully go, this leading to policies of liberalism and the transformation of the world under capitalism.[51] Liberalism was nothing to do with value judgements, but was an implication of properly understood economic science. Collective organization of production was impracticable, for it would make impossible any form of economic calculation.[52] Collectivism, therefore, could be no more than a "partisan dogma" involving both "commitment to a definite ideal" and "condemnation of all others".[53] "For that reason all collectivist doctrines are harbingers of irreconcilable hatred and war to the death."[54] It is hard to argue that the positive–normative distinction is being upheld here.

## 20.4 ROBBINS[55]

The outstanding contribution to the revival of the Senior–Mill–Cairnes approach to methodology was Robbins' *An Essay on the Nature and Significance of Economic Science* (1932), probably the most widely quoted book on economic methodology in the twentieth century. Robbins claimed not to be putting forward any new approach to economics, but to be making precise the nature of the already firmly established generalizations of which economics consisted.[56] He argued that progress towards unifying the subject had been sufficiently great for this to be not only feasible, but a vital task.[57] His approach to this task was strongly influenced by the Austrians, in particular Mises.

Crucial to the whole book is his oft-quoted definition of economics: "Economics is the science which studies human behaviour as a relationship between ends and scarce means which have alternative uses."[58] It dealt with an aspect of behaviour, not with certain kinds of behaviour.[59] It was crucial to this definition that nothing was said as to the nature of the ends which governed behaviour: these were taken as given, economics being entirely neutral between ends. Despite this, however, Robbins did make some assumptions about the nature of these ends, for he assumed that "individuals can arrange their preferences in order, and in fact do so".[60] He described this assumption as "one of the conditions which must be present if there is to be economic activity at all. It is an essential constituent of our conception of conduct with an economic aspect."[61] But though Robbins took rational behaviour for granted, he did not share Mises' view that this was an a priori truth: it was merely a generalization from common experience.[62]

No one will really question the universal applicability of such assumption[s] as to the existence of scales of relative valuation, or of different factors of production, or of different degrees of uncertainty regarding the future, *even though there may be room for dispute as the best mode of describing their logical status.*[63]

Knowledge based on such premises was, nonetheless, more securely based than knowledge based on empirical evidence, even evidence from controlled experiments.[64]

In Economics ... the ultimate constituents of our fundamental generalizations are known to us by immediate acquaintance. In the natural sciences they are known only inferentially. There is much less reason to doubt the counterpart in reality of individual preferences than that of the assumption of the electron.[65]

The role of realistic studies was seen by Robbins as testing the *applicability* of a theory, not the theory itself,[66] for in addition to the universally applicable assumptions discussed above, it was necessary to introduce subsidiary postulates. Because these subsidiary postulates were "historicorelative", valid only under specific historical circumstances, theories would rarely be universally applicable. In addition to ascertaining the applicability of theories, empirical research could suggest appropriate subsidiary postulates, and suggest new problems to be tackled.

Whilst economics was, according to Robbins, privileged as regards the sources of its knowledge, it was limited to making qualitative, not quantitative, predictions. Robbins dismissed the argument that economics ought to be seeking to estimate quantitative laws of supply and demand, for example, with the argument that this is a field "where there is no reason to suppose that uniformities are to be discovered".[67] Supply and demand will depend on individual valuations and technical facts, both of which lie "outside the sphere of economic uniformity".[68] Thus he was critical of Mitchell's attempts to use statistical methods to find common features of business cycles.[69] Going even further, he claimed that not a single "law" worthy of the name had emerged from the enormous empirical efforts of the historical and institutionalist schools.[70]

## 20.5  HUTCHISON

*Logical positivism*

Although it is Robbins' *Essay* which is so often quoted, and despite the fact that it is Robbins' definition of economics which gets quoted in most modern introductory texts, the modern period in discussions of economic methodology should be dated not from this, but from the appearance of a book published six years later: Hutchison's *On the Significance and Basic Postulates of Economic Theory* (1938). The reason for this is Hutchison's introduction into economics of the ideas associated with the so-called "Vienna Circle" of the 1920s and 1930s, namely "logical positivism", or "logical empiricism".[71] The central theme of logical positivism was that only meaningful statements were to be accorded any scientific status, and these comprised only two types of statement. There were analytic statements (either tautologies or self-contradictions), which could be evaluated using the rules of logic. And there were synthetic statements, factual statements, verifiable or falsifiable by empirical evidence.[72] Other, metaphysical, statements were meaningless, neither true nor false, being incapable of evaluation, either by logical analysis or by confrontation with empirical evidence. During the 1930s and 1940s these ideas were extensively discussed, as a result of which they were substantially modified. For example, the testability criterion for distinguishing synthetic statements from meaningless ones was modified; attempts were made to provide a justification for the role of theoretical entities not capable of direct observation; and the analytic–synthetic distinction was investigated. As a result it became clear, as early as the mid 1930s, that the initial hopes of ridding philosophy and positive science of metaphysical ideas had been overoptimistic, a more moderate "logical empiricism" emerging by the mid 1950s.[73]

Despite these developments, however, the initial concern to apply logical analysis to scientific statements, and the concern to ensure that such statements were clear and unambiguous, remained the dominant theme.

### The Significance and Basic Postulates of Economic Theory

The purpose of Hutchison's book was clearly stated in its opening paragraph.

The purpose of this essay is to help in elucidating the significance of that body of "pure theory" the possession of which distinguishes Economics from the other social sciences. It is concerned, therefore to mark off clearly propositions which belong to "pure theory" from those that do not, to investigate the source of the validity of these propositions, to clarify their relation to the assumptions or postulates on which they rest, including the "ceteris paribus" assumption, and finally to clarify these assumptions themselves by analysing the main concepts ... which they contain.[74]

The technique Hutchison used to analyse the nature of economic theories was to distinguish between three types of proposition: the analytic propositions of pure theory; the synthetic propositions of applied theory, in which predictions were deduced from empirically established premises; and inductive inferences (also synthetic propositions). The propositions of pure theory were indeed, as Robbins had claimed, more certain than empirical propositions, but they were also empty, in the sense that they were merely tautological: they had no empirical content. In contrast, the characteristic feature of synthetic propositions was that they "must conceivably be capable of empirical testing, *or be reducible to such propositions* by logical or mathematical deduction".[75] Hutchison argued that it was the acceptance of empirical testing which marked out "scientific" from "philosophical" activity, and which permitted science to progress.

It is this acceptance of the testing of propositions according to definite criteria which is the source of that steady secular piecemeal agreement and advance of "science", and its cumulative, international, impersonal, and "coral-reef-like" growth.[76]

Thus whenever any economist advances as possessing empirical content any proposition which is neither capable of being confirmed or falsified, nor deducible from any such proposition, he is "transgressing the frontiers of his subject".[77] Introspection might be vital psychologically, but it could *never* be a substitute for empirical testing.[78]

Though he argued it was tautological, Hutchison did not dismiss pure theory as worthless, but he argued that its only scientific justification lay in its being a step towards the formulation and confirmation of testable, empirical laws. Thus he criticized the way in which the ceteris paribus condition was used, arguing that its effect was frequently to remove any potential factual content from a theory, for it was only if the *cetera* were precisely specified that a theory would be testable. This was rarely done.[79] Furthermore, when he came to analyse the basic postulates of economic theory he became sceptical as to whether it could ever be used to produce testable propositions. Scarcity alone was insufficient as a basic postulate: rational conduct, the fundamental postulate of pure theory, had to be postulated as well. The definitions of rational conduct, however, offered by the leading economists, made sense only if perfect foresight were also assumed.[80] In other words, the assumption of rational behaviour was clearly specified only for a world in which most economic problems were absent. Further problems were created by the existence of monopoly, for "monopolistic" behaviour based on perfect expectations was a logical impossibility.[81] "Under oligopoly conditions there is no one clear and unambiguous answer to the question 'How would a sensible man act in such a situation?'"[82] The only way to find out how oligopolists behave is thus to look and see; it cannot be deduced from pure theory.

Finally, Hutchison argued that it was justifiable to consider conditions of equilibrium only if the tendency towards equilibrium were postulated as a testable, empirical truth.[83] Most formulations of the tendency to equilibrium simply rendered the theory untestable, thus depriving the theory of any empirical content.

*Knight's attack*

Hutchison's introduction of the testability requirement for economic propositions elicited a fierce attack from Knight (1940). Knight's main argument was that economic truth is unlike truth in natural sciences, for economic activity is goal-directed.

Propositions about economic behaviour relate to purposiveness in human behaviour, and depend for their meaning upon knowledge of its purposive character... . And it is obvious that we do not know the purpose or motives of human behaviour by inference from the observation of behaviour itself in the same sense in which we infer positive empirical laws or propositions of behaving material.[84]

Knight claimed that it was impossible to verify any proposition about economics by any empirical procedure. This was summed up in his rejoinder to Hutchison's reply to his article.

In short: my point was and is that the categorical contrast drawn by Mr Hutchison, and by so many others, between propositions which can be tested and the 'vague conceptions of common sense' and the insistence that only propositions of the former character are admissible in economic theory is a false pretence and must be abandoned. *The testable facts are not really economic*, for positive process is not of the economizing character. This inability to test may or may not be regarded as 'too bad'; anyhow, it is the truth.[85]

The opposition to Hutchison's stress on testability could hardly be more clearly stated.

# IV

## THE MODERN PERIOD, 1939–1980

# 21

# The 1930s as a Turning Point

*Economic theory*

Although the work of economists such as Pareto, Böhm-Bawerk, Wicksell, Fisher and Clark, the "second generation" of neoclassical economists, had established deductive, marginalist theory as the main method of economic inquiry, the streams of dissent were still extremely strong. There was American Institutionalism, Veblen's attacks on neoclassical economics having been very effective.[1] Equally important was Marshall's refusal to place too much weight on simple, abstract economic models, and his insistence on blending theory and history.[2]

The place of deductive theorizing at the centre of economic analysis was considerably strengthened in the 1930s. It was in the 1930s that the influence of Institutionalism waned,[3] and that the movement away from Marshall's value theory was completed. Robinson's *Economics of Imperfect Competition* (1933) was based on a more abstract method, much closer to modern economics than was the method of Marshall's *Principles*.[4] In addition, Marshall's consumer theory came to be superseded by that of Hicks and Allen (1934) and Samuelson (1938), whilst the attacks of Myrdal (1929) and Robbins (1932) undermined the utilitarian approach to welfare economics. With Hicks' *Value and Capital* (1939) and Samuelson's *Foundations of Economic Analysis* (published in 1947, but dating from the late 1930s) the establishment of an alternative to the Marshallian theory of value was complete. The new approach to economics was represented in Samuelson's *Economics* (1948).

The 1930s also saw the appearance of Keynes' *General Theory* (1936), on the basis of which macroeconomics was to emerge as a distinct branch of economics. In macroeconomics, as in microeconomics, there was a shift towards a more formal, abstract method, many of those involved in developing Keynesian ideas also being associated with what Shackle[5] has called "the new establishment in value theory": Robinson (1937), Samuelson (1938a, 1948a), and, above all, Hicks (1937, 1939a).

*Econometrics*

One of the main features distinguishing post-war economics from that of previous periods is the development of econometrics. The link between macroeconomics and econometrics is clear: many post-war developments were concerned with reconciling Keynes' behavioural functions, in particular the consumption function, with empirical data. More generally, however, it is hard to imagine "positive economics" becoming as popular as it did without the availability of econometric techniques, for even if economists have rarely rejected theories on the basis of econometric evidence, it seems reasonable to conjecture that the availability of econometric techniques provided a justification (excuse?) for developing formal mathematical models[6]: the availability of formal econometric techniques enabled economists to separate the analysis of economic theories from the analysis of empirical data more easily than might otherwise have been the case.

It was in the 1930s that the term econometrics came into use, the Econometric Society being established in 1930. There were two aspects to this. One was the use of mathematical methods to analyse economic models. Of particular importance was the use of mathematics to analyse economic dynamics, Frisch's work (1933) being particularly influential. The other aspect of econometrics was the use of statistical techniques to test and to estimate the parameters of economic models. Though there were important contributions much earlier in the century, Moore's work being particularly widely noticed,[7] it was only by the 1930s that the conceptual problems underlying such techniques were beginning to be sorted out. With problems such as the identification problem, the nature of the disturbance term, the theory of least squares estimators and the theory of confidence intervals, for example, it was work in the late 1920s and 1930s which provided the foundations on which post-war work could build.[8] Particularly important were Tinbergen's pioneering attempts to construct economy-wide, simultaneous-equation models, first of the Dutch economy (1935) and then of the US economy (1939).

A prerequisite to the use of econometric methods was the availability of statistical data, and here again the 1930s mark a turning point. Data collection on a large scale, as has characterized post-war economics, requires government involvement. In the US the NBER had been collecting and analysing statistical data since its foundation in 1920, but it was not until 1932, when the US Senate requested estimates of national income for 1929–1931, that the US government became involved. The resulting estimates, produced under Kuznets' direction, were published in 1934. In the UK, though Colin Clark worked on national income accounts throughout the thirties, the first officially produced national income estimates did not appear until 1941 (produced by Meade and Stone). It was only after the *General Theory* that the now familiar organization of national accounts was established.[9]

*Conclusion*

Although they form part of a continuous line of development going back to the 1870s and beyond, these developments, taken together, can be seen as marking a turning point in economic analysis. There was no sharp break with the past, but these developments in economic theory and in econometrics imparted to the economics of the post-war period a character very different from that of the period up to the 1920s.

# 22

# Scope and Method

## 22.1 FALSIFICATIONISM

*Samuelson's operationalism*

In his influential *Foundations of Economic Analysis* (1947)[1] Samuelson advanced a methodology of operationalism. Operationalism arose from the work of Bridgman (1927), a physicist, having much in common with logical positivism, and dating from the same period.[2] The main thesis in Samuelson's version of operationalism was that the task of economists was to discover "operationally meaningful theorems", by which he meant "hypotheses about empirical data which could conceivably be refuted, if only under ideal conditions".[3]

Though Samuelson's emphasis is very different from that of Hutchison, Hutchison placing a much greater emphasis on the information that can be obtained through testing assumptions, this is nothing other than falsificationism, albeit under a different label. Samuelson dismissed the view that economic laws deduced from a priori assumptions had any claim to rigour or validity independently of any empirical behaviour, criticizing the large number of economists who had failed to derive meaningful theorems from their theories. Though in no way original, Samuelson's operationalism was the basis for his economic theory: the search for comparative statics predictions dominated his *Foundations* to an extent without parallel in earlier treatises on economic theory.[4] His methodological views were influential due to the influence of his economic theory.

*Friedman's methodology of positive economics*

The second, and most important, post-war attempt to state a falsificationist methodology was that proposed in Friedman's influential article, "The methodology of positive economics" (1953). After starting with an endorsement of Keynes' views on the importance of the positive–normative distinction Friedman went on to argue that

The ultimate goal of a positive science is the development of a "theory" or "hypothesis" that yields valid and meaningful (i.e., not truistic) predictions about phenomena not yet observed.[5]

Four criteria for judging the theories of positive economics were then invoked:[6] (1) they must be logically consistent, containing categories with meaningful empirical counterparts; (2) they must advance testable hypotheses; (3) the only relevant test of the validity of a theory is the comparison of its predictions with experience; and (4) since an infinite number of theories are consistent with the data, other criteria (such as simplicity and fruitfulness) must be introduced in order to choose amongst competing theories.

The most distinctive feature of this approach is that, unlike Hutchison, Friedman rejected as fundamentally wrong the idea that the testing of assumptions could provide a test of the value of a hypothesis "different from" or "additional to" the test by implications.[7] Going still further, Friedman made the claim that

> In so far as a theory can be said to have "assumptions" at all, and in so far as their "realism" can be judged independently of the validity of predictions, the relation between the significance of a theory and the "realism" of its "assumptions" is almost the opposite of that suggested by the view under criticism. Truly important and significant hypotheses will be found to have "assumptions" that are wildly inaccurate descriptive representations of reality, and, in general, the more significant a theory, the more unrealistic the assumptions (in this sense).[8]

The reason for his claim was that a good theory is one which predicts successfully on the basis of a few important elements. "To be important, therefore, a theory must be descriptively false in its assumptions." Friedman thus argued that the relevant issue was not the "realism" of assumptions, but whether the assumptions were good enough approximations for the purpose in hand. The test of this was the theory's predictions. In other words, testing predictions and assumptions amounted to the same thing: testing assumptions does not provide a test additional to testing the conclusions.

### Discussion of Friedman's thesis

Friedman's article produced an enormous response and stimulated extensive discussion, in particular concerning his thesis that the realism of a theory's assumptions was irrelevant to its validity.[9] Several important weaknesses in the argument were pointed out, in particular his failure to make clear the sense in which the term "realistic" was used, and his failure to distinguish between the different ways in which assumptions are used in economic models. Consider first the term "realism". There are four ways in which an assumption might be unrealistic.[10] (1) It might be incomplete as a description of some object. (2) It might be false, or at least inconsistent with the available evidence. (3) It might be used to define an "ideal type", not descriptive of any actual object. (4) It may mean that the assumption postulates individual behaviour which we find incomprehensible. Even if Friedman were justified in arguing against the need for realistic assumptions, the case would have to be argued separately with respect to each type of realism.

Similar arguments have been made concerning Friedman's failure to distinguish between different uses of assumptions. Assumptions are used in different ways in economics,[11] and the relevance of their realism needs to be argued separately for each usage.

Problems are also raised for Friedman's argument by the fact that hypotheses are never tested singly. A theory usually contains a variety of hypotheses, which means that when a theory's predictions are being tested it is rarely clear which hypotheses are being tested.

Possibly the most well-known response to Friedman was that of Samuelson, who named Friedman's argument the "F-twist".[12] In trying to prove the relevance of the realism of assumptions, Samuelson argued that theories were equivalent restatements of conclusions and assumptions: it made no difference whether the assumptions or the conclusions of a theory were tested, for the theory could be reformulated so that the assumptions were conclusions, and the conclusions assumptions. The main reason, however, why Samuelson's response to Friedman is interesting is not this argument (which can be shown to be unjustifiable) but that, in his response to Friedman, Samuelson advanced the argument that theories could provide no more than *descriptions* of economic phenomena:

A description ... that works to describe well a wide range of observable reality is all the "explanation" we can ever get (or need desire) here on earth ... *An explanation, as used legitimately in science, is a better kind of description, and not something that ultimately goes beyond description.*[13]

## 22.2  DEFENCES OF ABSTRACT THEORIZING

### Machlup

In the discussions which, in the 1950s and 1960s, stemmed from the methodological writings of Hutchison,[14] Samuelson and Friedman, an important contributor, not yet mentioned, was Machlup. Machlup is important because his views reflect what had, by the 1950s, become the dominant view amongst philosophers of science.[15] This was the view which had emerged out of the discussion of logical positivism, its most important characteristic, for our purposes, being that it recognized a role in scientific theory for unobservable, theoretical terms. Theoretical terms form part of a hypothetico-deductive system. Though some theoretical terms may be unobservable, and hence statements about them may be untestable, the system as a whole may produce testable, empirical statements. Theoretical terms gain meaning (they are "indirectly tested") through being part of a system which is tested.[16]

The role in scientific explanation of a theoretical system was important to Machlup's criticisms of both Hutchison and Samuelson.[17] He characterized Hutchison as an "ultra-empiricist": as one who required that every assumption of a theory be directly testable. In contrast, Machlup argued that indirect testability was enough to justify the use of a theoretical term. Indirect testability also enabled Machlup to reject Hutchison's argument that because the fundamental postulates of economics were part of a deductive system and were protected by a *ceteris paribus* clause, they were unfalsifiable and hence devoid of any empirical content.

Hutchison replied by dismissing the charge of ultra-empiricism, for he had claimed only that meaningful propositions had to be either testable, or *reducible* to testable propositions.[18] He still argued, nonetheless, that the behaviour postulates should reflect the observed behaviour of economic agents, something Machlup did not require. It can be argued[19] that Machlup's position was perfectly consistent with the view then prevailing amongst philosophers of science, and that there is no objection to the assumption of maximizing behaviour as a meaningful, though not falsifiable, heuristic postulate. Against this, however, it can be argued that Hutchison was right in claiming that Machlup was adopting a position far too defensive of conventional economic theories. Not only was Machlup arguing that certain assumptions might not be testable, a legitimate argument, but he was also challenging the desirability of testing them, arguing that it may not matter if assumptions are shown to be false, as opposed to being untestable: "... the assumption of consistently profit-maximizing conduct is contrary to fact ... we are defending an assumption of which we are certain that it does not always conform to the facts". After arguing that we can never know whether the extent of the discrepancies between assumed behaviour and the facts is significant he goes on to conclude,

What then should be done? Just what is being done: to accept maximizing conduct as a heuristic postulate and to bear in mind that the deduced consequences may sometimes be considerably out of line with observed data ... the "indirect verification" or justification of the postulate lies in the fact that it gives fairly good results in many applications of the theory.[20]

This approach to theories also provided the basis of Machlup's criticism of Samuelson's methodology. Firstly, Machlup could oppose Samuelson's operationalism on grounds similar to those on which he objected to Hutchison's falsificationism. Furthermore, Machlup was able to point to Samuelson's own practice. Taking as an example Samuelson's work on factor price equalization, Machlup argued that Samuelson produced his best work not when he followed his methodology of operationalism, but "when he deduces from unrealistic assumptions general theoretical propositions which help us interpret some of the empirical observations of the complex situations with which economic life confronts us".[21] Secondly, Machlup's views of theory explain why he objected to Samuelson's claim that explanation was no more than description.

A theory, by definition, is much wider than any of the consequences deduced. If the consequences were to imply the "theory" just as the theory implies the consequences, that theory would be nothing but another form of the empirical evidence (named "consequence") and could never "explain" the observed empirical facts.[22]

Following the contemporary philosophy of science, therefore, Machlup asserted that explanation was something more than mere description.

*Koopmans*

A related, though different, view of economic theories was provided by Koopmans in the second of his *Three Essays on the State of Economic Science* (1957). Koopmans sided with Hutchison in his desire to test the propositions of economic theory,[23] but he nonetheless provided a justification for abstract and unrealistic theory. He proposed regarding economic theory

as a sequence of conceptional *models* that seek to express in simplified form different aspects of an always more complicated reality.... . The study of the simpler models is protected from the reproach of unreality by the consideration that these models may be prototypes of more realistic, but also more complicated, subsequent models.[24]

In this process, aspects of reality have to be perceived before they can be incorporated into a model: realism is therefore always ahead of rigour. Models are always unrealistic.

Koopmans also presented the argument that the relative importance of theoretical and empirical work will depend on the nature of the problem in hand.[25] Considering the postulates of production possibilities, for example, he argued that mathematical difficulties presented the main obstacle to progress, economic theory having failed to digest "the simplest facts establishable by the most casual observation".[26] With the postulates concerning behaviour, on the other hand, theoretical and empirical work needed to be co-ordinated.

Without concurrent theoretical effort, however, the fact finding or statistical testing runs a risk of proliferation or maldistribution ... the study of hypothetical models is needed for us to see which hypotheses about individual behaviour have first claim to verification or testing, because of their relevance to questions ... to which we seek answer.[27]

## 22.3 THEORIES OF THE GROWTH OF KNOWLEDGE

*Background*

From the late 1960s the nature of the discussion of economic methodology changed fundamentally, this change reflecting equally dramatic changes which took place in the philosophy of science. During the 1960s the "received view" of scientific theories, dominant for over thirty years, was successfully challenged, most philosophers of science repudiating it by the end of the decade.[28] A variety of alternatives was offered to replace it,[29] ranging from explanations (such as those of Feyerabend[30] and Kuhn[31]) which laid great stress on sociological factors, to views (such as those of Toulmin[32] and Lakatos[33]) based on historical examination of scientific reasoning, based on the assumption that scientific activity does yield knowledge of how the world really is.[34] Out of this welter of ideas, however, relatively few filtered through to discussions of economic methodology.[35] Of those which did, overwhelmingly the most influential were those of Kuhn, and then Lakatos.

The major new element introduced into the discussion was the idea that the focus of attention could profitably be shifted from the question of how an isolated scientific theory could be justified, to the question of how scientific knowledge grows. Though it was Kuhn who first made economists think in this way, the idea goes back much further, in particular to Popper's *Logic of Scientific Discovery* (1934). An important aspect of Popper's argument, neglected in earlier discussions of falsificationism in economics, was his emphasis on falsificationism not as a means of ensuring that scientific knowledge is true, but as a means of ensuring its growth. Popper is as much a growth of knowledge theorist as Kuhn. It was out of discussions of Popper's and Kuhn's contrasting views that Lakatos's "methodology of scientific research programmes" emerged.[36]

*Economic methodology*

As a result of these developments, and following the example set by many philosophers of science, methodological inquiries in economics became more closely linked to the history of economic thought. Economists began, around 1970,[37] to ask whether Kuhn's paradigms could be used to interpret what Schumpeter had called "classical situations" in the history of economics, such as classical, neoclassical and Keynesian economics. An example of such an inquiry was Coats' (1969) "Is there a 'Structure of Scientific Revolutions' in Economics?" Coats came to the conclusion that whilst there were (due to the vagueness of economic paradigms and to their being less liable to falsification) no phases of paradigm change in economics quite like those in the natural sciences, the process of paradigm change could nonetheless "serve as an ideal type, which can be used to clarify the interrelationships between the terminological, conceptual, personal and professional elements involved in the development of economic ideas".[38] These applications of Kuhn's ideas were supplemented, from the mid-1970s, by similar attempts using Lakatos's "methodology of scientific research programmes", particularly influential being the volume *Method and Appraisal in Economics* (ed. Latsis, 1976).

The significance of this work for methodology, as opposed to its significance for the history of economic thought, is that although dealing with the history of the subject, it does have methodological implications for the theory itself. Theories can be evaluated in the light of the way they are developing. For example, the use of Lakatos's distinction between progressive and degenerating research programmes[39] can provide a way out of the Machlup–Hutchison disagreement. We may agree with Machlup that because of the complexity of the economy relative to what our theories can handle, and because of the inadequacy of the empirical data, important assumptions will have to remain untested, and at the same time agree with Hutchison that this opens the way to defending any theory we like. If so, we can follow Lakatos in arguing that protectiveness towards an untested theory is permissible only if the research programme is progressive, successfully predicting new facts.[40]

The result of the introduction of these new ideas appears to have been a move towards methodological pluralism, something perhaps inevitable with the undermining of empiricism.[41] Such a change is present even in the work of economists who would still strongly defend falsificationism.[42]

# 23

## Microeconomic Theory

### 23.1 BACKGROUND

*Improvements in technique*

The most obvious difference between the economic theory of the post-war period and that of the previous period is the enormous increase in the use of mathematics, combined with the use of more advanced mathematical techniques. Given that the system of static, competitive equilibrium analysis was established in its essentials by 1939, it is tempting to argue that what has happened since then amounts to little more than the application of superior techniques at the expense of attempting to derive new economic insights. Whilst there may be some truth in this, however, it would be wrong to dismiss modern economic theory on these grounds without attempting to see what has been achieved and how.[1]

Advances in technique are relevant for the history of economic analysis only in so far as they affect the content of economics. Since 1939 there have been several areas where improvements in technique have been very important in affecting the way in which economic inquiry has been undertaken. Two types of development need to be distinguished. Firstly there are mathematical developments which enable results to be derived more elegantly and at a greater degree of generality, and which permit a more unified treatment of the theory than would otherwise be possible. Examples of such techniques include the theory of convex sets and certain aspects of duality theory. Such developments, however, despite their producing enormous changes in the way economic models are handled, and despite their improving economists' understanding of these models, have had little effect on the way the economy has been viewed. Secondly, there are those developments which have had a fundamental effect on the way the economic system is conceived. These include linear models, game theory and the theory of choice under uncertainty.[2]

*Linear models*

In *Linear Programming and Economic Analysis* (1958) Dorfman, Samuelson and Solow commented that economists had been doing linear economics for 40 years without being conscious of it. They argued that economists had for a long time passed over the linear aspects of their problems as "obvious, trivial and uninteresting".[3] This had changed in the two decades prior to the book's publication, when a variety of new methods had been developed, all dependent on the linear structure of certain economic problems[4] – in particular input–output analysis, linear programming and game theory.

Input–output analysis, outlined by Leontief in 1936, and more fully expounded in *The Structure of the American Economy, 1919–29* (1941) was, in Leontief's words, "an attempt to apply the economic theory of general equilibrium – or better, general interdependence – to an empirical study of interrelations among different parts of a national economy."[5] Of Leontief's three sets of equations, two were inherently linear: the conditions that an industry's net output must, in static equilibrium, equal the consumption of that industry's output by all other industries plus final demand; and that the price of an industry's output equal the value of the inputs used in producing it. What turned the problem into a completely linear one was the assumption that the technical coefficients relating outputs to inputs were fixed.[6] The implications of this approach were not simply that it made possible statistical estimation of relations between industries, important though this was, but that it stressed the complementarity rather than the substitution between factors, and that it pushed intermediate goods to the forefront. The importance of complementarity relative to substitution was an empirical issue.[7] The emphasis on intermediate goods became clearer when, during the war, Leontief analysed an "open" system: one in which final demand was taken to be exogenous. In such a model it was possible to use an input–output model to examine the effects of, for example, a change in military expenditure, not simply through analysing its direct effects, but also through working out its implications for the use of intermediate goods, such as chemicals and steel. It was possible to examine the effects of changes in the composition of demand on production in various industries, and on demand for labour.

Only a little later came the first work on linear programming, again inspired by practical problems, the "transportation problem" (given a certain number of factories and a number of consumers who must be satisfied, all in different locations, how can production be organized so as to minimize transportation costs?)[8] and the "diet problem" (what combination of different foods will give essential nutrients at minimum cost?). Though both problems were solved in 1941, the important developments came with the work of Koopmans (1947a) and Dantzig (1951) who, rediscovering the transportation problem in their work for the US Navy and Air Force, posed and solved the more general linear programming problem. Two developments were of particular importance. One was the simplex method, which provided a means of solving more than a very simple problem (Dantzig, 1951); and, most important of all, the theory of duality (Gale, Kuhn and Tucker, 1951). The theory of duality was important because of its economic interpretation. Suppose the original problem is to maximize profit subject to given factor supplies. The solution to the dual problem yields the value of each of the factors. Hicks interprets this as showing that the price system is inherent in the economic problem, not something brought in from outside.[9]

*Game theory*

Though it initially arose as one aspect of linear theory, game theory has been sufficiently important in the development of post-war economics to merit separate attention.[10] The theory of games was first outlined by von Neumann in 1929, but the work which brought it to the attention of economists at large was *The Theory of Games and Economic Behaviour* (1944) written with Morgenstern. After discussing the use of mathematical methods, von Neumann and Morgenstern open their book with a discussion of rational behaviour.[11] Following the lead given by Menger and Böhm-Bawerk in placing emphasis on exchange between a limited number of individuals, they argue that rational behaviour must be analysed in a situation where "strategy" is important: where one individual's action can influence the actions of others, and where there is the possibility of coalitions being formed. This is a situation that von Neumann's theory of games was designed to analyse.

In simple games the minimax criterion was adopted as the criterion for individual rationality: each player chooses the strategy which keeps the maximum loss (the actual loss depending on the other player) as low as possible. The device of choosing mixed strategies (for example tossing a coin to decide which strategy to play) was introduced to ensure that an equilibrium could always be found. Probably of more significance for economic theory, however, was their analysis of bargaining, the strength of their approach being that they analysed the conditions under which coalitions would be formed. To do this they introduced the concept of "dominance":

> $x$ dominates $y$ [$x$ and $y$ are two allocations of individual gains] when there exists a group of participants each one of whom prefers his individual situation in $x$ to that in $y$, and who are convinced that they are able as a group – i.e. as an alliance – to enforce their preferences.[12]

The significance of the concept of dominance is that if one outcome (call it $y$) is dominated by another ($x$) then $y$ will never occur, for there will be a group which will not accept $y$, for it prefers $x$, and believes it can achieve $x$. What von Neumann and Morgenstern described as the "solution" to the game was not a unique outcome, but the set of all the outcomes not dominated by outcomes which were themselves feasible.

Since the appearance of *The Theory of Games and Economic Behaviour* much work has been done by economists and others on both co-operative and non-co-operative games. Particularly important have been Nash's (1950) solution for a non-co-operative game, a generalization of the "Cournot duopoly equilibrium"; the concept of the "core", first defined by Gillies (1959);[13] and various solution concepts offered for co-operative games (e.g. Nash (1953).[14] The core, the set of allocations not blocked by any possible coalition,[15] was applied to market equilibrium by Shubik (1959) and proved useful in understanding the nature of competitive equilibrium, for it could be shown rigorously that, as Edgeworth had argued some 80 years earlier, the core (Edgeworth's contract curve) contained any competitive equilibria;

and that as the number of traders increased the core shrank until in the limit only competitive equilibria remained. Competitive equilibria were thus the only feasible equilibria in an economy where all traders were too small to have any bargaining power.[16]

### Choice under uncertainty

One of the most important characteristics of post-war microeconomics is the widespread use of various techniques for dealing with choice under uncertainty. Though such techniques can be found in earlier work[17] they were not widely used. Three, related, approaches to the problem of choice under uncertainty have been particularly important. The first is that due to von Neumann and Morgenstern (1944), who developed a theory of expected utility maximization, basing this on a series of axioms about human behaviour.[18] In the early 1950s there was controversy over these axioms, for they implied that a cardinal utility index could be constructed. It was from the appearance of Savage's *The Foundations of Statistics* (1954), which contained a more complete statement of the axioms on which the theory was based that the theory began to be much more widely accepted.

The second approach is Arrow's (1953) "state preference" theory. This distinguishes goods according to the "state of nature" in which they are available. An example of such a "contingent commodity" would be "an umbrella if it is raining". Individuals are assumed to have preferences between such goods. Though state preference theory is quite compatible with von Neumann–Morgenstern expected utility maximization, it provides a more useful way of tackling certain problems.

Finally there is the "mean–variance" approach, used in particular by Tobin (1958) and Markovitz (1959) to analyse the demand for securities. Here it is assumed that an individual's utility depends on the mean and the standard deviation (or variance) of the return on a portfolio of assets. This is equivalent to the von Neumann–Morgenstern approach only if the individual's utility function has certain special properties. Though many economists consider these special properties unacceptable, the mean–variance approach nonetheless continues to be used because of its simplicity.

### Aggregation

For a variety of reasons economists in the post-war period have been much more aware of aggregation problems than were their predecessors: improved mathematical techniques made it possible to analyse such problems much more thoroughly, but above all aggregation was unavoidable in statistical work. Two theorems on aggregation were widely known: those of Leontief and Hicks. In *Value and Capital* Hicks proved that where the relative prices of a group of commodities were constant, this group of commodities could be treated as a single commodity. Slightly more general was Leontief's theorem (1947) that a group of commodities could be aggregated if the marginal rate of substitution between any two commodities in the group was independent of the quantity of any commodity outside the group. These were not conditions which could generally be assumed to be satisfied. Though similar results were produced in other contexts (e.g. Gorman's (1953) conditions for aggregating individual demands and Fisher's (1969) conditions for aggregating production functions), the conditions under which aggregation was possible were so strict as to emphasize that it was not in general possible.[19] For example, the aggregation of consumers' demands to obtain a market demand curve with similar properties is, apart from special cases, possible only where all the individuals are identical, or have homothetic preferences (loosely, this means that each indifference curve is an enlarged or reduced version of any other indifference curve).

## 23.2 GENERAL COMPETITIVE EQUILIBRIUM

*Samuelson's* Foundations

The work which in a sense laid the foundations for contemporary economic theory was Samuelson's *Foundations of Economic Analysis* (1947). Though published eight years after Hicks' *Value and Capital* it was independent of it, parts having been written as early as 1937. From the start, Samuelson made full use of mathematics, arguing that "the laborious working over of essentially simple mathematical concepts" should be regarded as unrewarding mental gymnastics of a particularly depraved type.[20] He aggressively and explicitly reversed Marshall's view on the role of mathematics in economics.[21] This stress on mathematics, however, constitutes only the background to Samuelson's contribution, of which three aspects are particularly important.

(1) He defended the use of the concept of equilibrium, arguing that many problems could be viewed as maximization or minimization problems. The theory of consumer behaviour and the theory of the firm were, for Samuelson, simply applications of the theory of constrained maximization. Not only did this framework reveal a unified structure underlying apparently diverse problems, but it was a source of predictions. For example, the fact that demand functions described the solution to a constrained maximization problem might in itself be enough to make it possible to say something about their properties.

(2) The task of economic theory was argued to be the derivation of "operationally meaningful" theorems: hypotheses about empirical data which might conceivably be refuted.[22] Whatever the merits of this from a methodological point of view,[23] its significance was that it led him to stress the importance of comparative statics: it was not enough to enumerate the factors influencing the price of a commodity, for example, if nothing could be said about how changes in these factors would cause the price to change. As regards such predictions, Samuelson found two sources of information. Some theorems about comparative statics could be derived from the

assumption of maximizing behaviour on the part of individuals, in particular from the second order conditions for an optimum, but more important were those derived from stability conditions. For example, in Marshallian theory where, for a given output, the market sets the price, an equilibrium will be stable if the supply curve cuts the demand curve from below.[24] Given this information we can immediately deduce that a rise in demand will lead to an increase in output. This relationship between stability conditions and comparative statics results was named by Samuelson the "correspondence principle".[25] The correspondence principle, however, turned out to be much less useful than Samuelson had claimed. The main reason for this is that where consumers are maximizing their utility, and producers are maximizing their profits, the conditions for stability turn out to be equivalent to the conditions for the existence of an equilibrium. Stability conditions are thus superfluous.

(3) Finally, there is Samuelson's stress on the need to analyse stability in terms of an *explicit* dynamic process. It was not enough, according to Samuelson, simply to ask whether, for example, a fall in the price of a commodity raised excess demand for the commodity. It was necessary to specify a process linking price changes to excess demands, and to examine the conditions for this process to converge to an equilibrium. Although Samuelson's treatment of dynamics was not new (he acknowledged a debt to Frisch (1935–1936)[26] it was his approach which became the standard one.

## The Arrow–Debreu model

A problem not dealt with by Samuelson or Hicks was that of the existence of a competitive equilibrium, the main contributions here being made in the 1950s. The main paper here was by Arrow and Debreu (1954), who produced a much more general existence result than those produced by Wald and his contemporaries in the 1930s.[27] In particular Arrow and Debreu started from assumptions about consumers' preferences, rather than marginal utility functions, and they used more general assumptions about technology than the fixed coefficients assumed by Wald and von Neumann. During the 1950s various attempts were made, working within the same basic framework, to generalize these results, the economists involved including McKenzie, Gale, Nikaido and Uzawa.[28] The canonical statement of what has become known as the Arrow–Debreu model was provided in Debreu's *Theory of Value* (1959).

Because of its importance to contemporary economics it is important to be clear about what this model involves, about the conclusions drawn from it, and about what the model does not do. Of particular importance is the way goods are defined. A good is defined in terms of *four* attributes: physical characteristics; location; date of delivery; and the state of nature in which it is available.[29] Thus, for example, "black umbrellas delivered in London on St. Swithun's day 1995 if it is raining" would be a different good from similar umbrellas delivered at the same time and place in the event that it is not raining. The term used to denote goods defined in this way is "dated, contingent commodities", for their availability is contingent on certain events (as is, for example, a payment under an insurance contract). The assumption is then made that *all* goods defined in this way have markets. This amounts to assuming that there is a *complete set of futures and insurance markets*, which in turn means that agents (firms and households) can determine their entire production and consumption plans, for they know the prices of all goods in all future periods, and they can insure themselves against all eventualities.

Arrow and Debreu were able to prove that, provided firms' production sets and consumers' preferences exhibited certain properties, an equilibrium would exist for such an economy.[30] Later work in the 1950s was concerned with proving the existence of an equilibrium under weaker (less restrictive) assumptions about production sets and household preferences. The basic framework was left unchanged.

To see the significance of this result we have to see it in conjunction with the so called fundamental theorems of welfare economics derived a few years earlier about the relationship between Pareto efficiency and competitive equilibrium.[31] In 1951 Arrow and Debreu had shown (1) that any competitive equilibrium must be Pareto efficient, and (2) that any Pareto efficient allocation could, by an appropriate redistribution of endowments (the initial stocks of goods, including factors of production, owned by households) be achieved as a competitive equilibrium. It could thus be claimed that the Arrow–Debreu existence result provided a rigorous demonstration of the conditions under which the "invisible hand" would work and that they had shown that it is *possible* to describe an economy in which resources are allocated in an orderly fashion. It is important to note, however, that no claim has been made that these results describe *any* actual economy. Indeed, it can convincingly be argued that they could not possibly describe any actual economy.

Compared with earlier work the novelty in this approach rested in the introduction of dated, contingent commodities to deal with the problems of time and uncertainty. This treatment of these problems is, however, unrealistic, not least because it provides no role whatsoever for money, and there is no reason for a market in firms' shares to exist. This is because when the economy "opens", transactions can be undertaken governing sales and purchases at all future dates. There is no reason for markets to continue to operate after the opening period – this is the result of postulating a complete set of futures markets.

If the Arrow–Debreu model is so patently unrealistic, why is it used? One reason is simply that it renders the problem of proving the existence of an equilibrium tractable. By dealing with time and uncertainty in this way, the problem is reduced to one of static equilibrium, for all market activity takes place at the beginning of the economy's life. The complete set of insurance markets removes problems of uncertainty and expectations. The second reason, however, is more fundamental, namely that the Arrow–Debreu model helps redefine the real issues facing economists as why the sufficient conditions for equilibrium do not hold. Because of this the Arrow–Debreu model provides a benchmark with which other equilibrium concepts can be compared. For example, though it can be argued that it has little in common with Smith's use of the term, it has been claimed (e.g. Hahn, 1982c) that the Arrow–Debreu model shows what we need to ensure that the "invisible hand" works. In particular, it shows the need for a full set of markets. This provides a framework for seeing why the "invisible hand" breaks down in other models: the absence of Pareto optimality in more "realistic" models can, for example, often be explained in terms of missing markets.

*Stability*

In the 1950s much work was done not only on the existence, but also on the stability, of competitive equilibrium. Here the starting point was Samuelson's work – the approach adopted was to specify a specific dynamic process and to examine the conditions under which this process would converge on an equilibrium. One of the first tasks was to reconcile Samuelson's stability conditions with Hicks' which, though not derived from an explicitly dynamic model, had an economic interpretation. It was shown by Smithies (1942) and Metzler (1945) that under some circumstances the two were equivalent.

In analysing stability it was necessary, as Samuelson had shown, to make assumptions about the specific dynamic process involved. Here the benchmark was the *tâtonnement*: the imaginary process, taken from Walras, whereby an auctioneer raises or lowers prices according to whether excess demands are positive or negative. A crucial aspect of the process is that no transactions take place until markets are in equilibrium. The reason for these assumptions was not the realism of the process they describe, but theoretical problems. If agents' plans are inconsistent (as must be the case if supply and demand are not equal) it is very difficult indeed to say how much will be bought and sold. In addition, given that all agents are price-takers (there is perfect competition), who, if there is no auctioneer, sets prices?

In the 1950s a series of papers appeared on the stability of *tâtonnement* processes. However, although the results were more rigorously proved, and more general, there was, as regards economically interesting stability conditions, little advance beyond Hicks' condition that all goods must be gross substitutes. That nothing more general was likely to be available was made clear by Scarf (1960), who produced a range of interesting cases which were unstable. Further work in the early 1970s confirmed that stability was something that could be proved for only very special cases.[32] The search for more and more general stability conditions was a waste of time.

Despite the problems involved, attempts were made to analyse non-*tâtonnement* processes. For example, Hahn and Negishi (1962) analysed a process where exchange took place out of equilibrium, this being governed by the condition that where a good was in excess demand (supply) overall, no agent was constrained in the amount he or she could sell (buy). Another example is Uzawa (1962), who investigated a process, analogous to that described by Edgeworth, where exchange takes place whenever two agents can do so to their mutual advantage. Although, however, it was possible to deduce conditions under which such processes converged upon a competitive equilibrium, this approach, despite its potentially greater realism, did not get very far. The main reason for this was the lack of any firm criterion as to what should happen out of equilibrium.

### Alternatives to the Arrow–Debreu model

One of the most obvious alternatives to the Arrow–Debreu model is to consider an economy with an incomplete set of markets, in particular one with an incomplete set of futures and insurance markets. This is of fundamental importance, for it provides a role for money. The reason for this is that, if some of these markets are missing, decisions cannot all be taken at once. Trading will need to take place all the time, not merely in the beginning. Economies like this, where trading takes place at every date, were named, by Radner (1968), *sequence economies*. Such an economy was considered by Hicks in *Value and Capital*. Hicks' work was important because he pointed out the importance of the way in which expectations are formed, distinguishing between two types of equilibrium: a *temporary equilibrium*, in which expectations of the future are taken as exogenous; and a *perfect foresight equilibrium*, in which expectations are correct.[33] One virtue of this approach, apart from its being clearly less unrealistic than the Arrow–Debreu model, is that it is a prerequisite for constructing a model of a monetary economy. Money (an asset of no intrinsic value, held only because of what it can buy) only makes sense if markets are open at a sequence of dates, though other conditions are needed as well, such as the existence of transactions costs. Research along these lines was widespread in the 1970s. The main issue investigated was that of the conditions under which an economy would have an equilibrium in which the price of money was positive.[34]

The temporary equilibrium models discussed so far may allow for the possibility of money, but they are still inadequate to explain how Keynesian problems might arise, for the assumption that markets are in equilibrium rules out the possibility of unemployment in the sense of supply labour exceeding the demand. One way of introducing the possibility of unemployment is to assume that prices are, at least temporarily, fixed. If prices cannot adjust to equate supply and demand, either buyers or sellers will be unable to trade as much as they wish at the prevailing prices. In the former case, for example, some goods will be rationed. If agents are rationed in one market (for example, suppose that households cannot sell as much labour as they wish) they will have to adjust their demands or supplies in other markets (for example, reduce their demand for consumption goods). Although these ideas were developed in the concept of macroeconomics,[35] they lead to an equilibrium concept which can be applied in more general models.

Although the first microeconomic analysis of an equilibrium with rationing was that of Glustoff (1968) the most widely used notions of equilibrium with rationing are those of Dreze (1975) and Benassy (1975).[36] In formulating such models there are three problems to be solved: (1) to decide what information agents have about the quantities they can buy or sell when markets are not in equilibrium (note that in a market clearing model this problem does not arise, for prices contain all the relevant information); (2) to decide how the constraints that agents perceive affect their supplies and demands;[37] and(3) to specify a scheme whereby agents are rationed (for example, do all workers work short hours, or do some work as much as they wish, with others totally unemployed). It is differences in the answers suggested to these problems that account for the differences between Dreze and Benassy equilibria, though the problem they are tackling is fundamentally the same.

Attractive as these models may seem in providing a rigorous framework for discussing Keynesian phenomena, they suffer from very serious drawbacks, in particular from two, possibly related, problems. The first is that they fail to explain why prices do not adjust to clear markets. The second is that if agents face constraints on the amounts that they can buy and sell, then competition cannot be perfect. If, for example, there is a maximum to the amount a firm can sell, then its demand curve cannot be completely horizontal. This observation leads naturally into the suggestion that monopolistic competition rather than fix-price equilibrium may be a better framework. With the exception of an early paper by Negishi (1960) research along these lines dates from the 1970s, examples being Benassy (1976), Grandmont and Laroque (1976) and Hahn (1978).[38]

## 23.3 FURTHER DEVELOPMENTS

*The theory of choice*

The theory of general competitive equilibrium, whether in its Walrasian or Arrow–Debreu form, is based on the assumptions that consumers and firms know the situation confronting them, and that they have no influence on the market. Even theories of growth[39] make sense only in such a context. The treatment of such firms and consumers has remained, in its essentials, unaltered since Hicks' *Value and Capital* and Samuelson's *Foundations*. The axioms on which consumer theory is based have been worked out more thoroughly, and more efficient techniques are available for deriving results from it. Though the result of this is that the theory is now much better understood, it can be argued that the effort put into work such as Hicks' *Revision of Demand Theory* (1956) has not been very well rewarded.[40]

Although the fundamental assumptions involved have changed little, the range of problems to which consumer theory has been applied has increased to such an extent as to make the theory significantly different from what it was 40 years ago. This will be illustrated with three examples.[41] The first of these concerns the supply of labour and the choice between consumption and leisure. An interesting aspect of this example is that it is one where the typical budget constraint will be non-linear: if the household has any non-labour income, for example, non-linearity arises immediately from the constraint on the number of hours in the day. Possibly more important, however, is the fact that most of the interesting applications of consumer theory involve non-linear budget constraints (for example, the implications of different wage structures, or the impact of the tax and benefit systems). The resulting emphasis on the form of the budget constraint, rather than on the nature of preferences, as the critical factor influencing consumer behaviour, applies not simply to labour economics, but to many applications.[42] Also important is the use of consumer theory to analyse the question of labour supply over time, raising the issue of investment in education, usually analysed in terms of "human capital". Although modern discussions of human capital started a few years before this,[43] the main stimulus to work in this area came from Becker's *Human Capital* (1964).

The emphasis on constraints rather than preferences is also a feature of the second example, theories of the household "production function". Becker (1965) proposed a theory in which the goods on which utility depends (such as eating a meal) require both purchased goods (food) and time (for preparation and eating). Households thus face both time and budget constraints, which means that the opportunity cost of an activity depends on the inputs it requires, the cost of any goods required and on the value of time. Related to this is Lancaster's (1966a and b) theory,[44] where utility is assumed to depend not on goods consumed, but on "characteristics". Goods (e.g. baked beans) comprise bundles of characteristics (flavour, nourishment). Consumers choose their preferred bundle of characteristics, achieving this by an appropriate choice of goods.

The final example is the theory of rationing, to which wartime controls provided the stimulus.[45] The main interest here has been in "spillover effects" – with how a change in consumption of a rationed good affects demand for unrationed goods. Although it was in the early 1970s that interest in this subject was at its height, the foundations for subsequent work were provided by Tobin and Houthaker (1951). They had shown that if one commodity were rationed, the elasticity of demand for other commodities would be reduced. Whether a change in one ration increased or reduced demands for other commodities depended on whether they were substitutes for, or complements to, the rationed good. During the 1950s interest in rationing theory waned, for obvious reasons, but it revived in the 1970s in response to work on equilibria with rationing.[46] As with the other two examples, the basic consumer theory here is identical to that of Hicks and Samuelson: the novelty lies in its application to new situations.

### Choice under uncertainty

As this problem was most often handled using expected utility maximization together with a von Neumann–Morgenstern utility function, attention was confined to what Knight[47] called risk – measurable uncertainty. With very few exceptions[48] the problem of choice under circumstances where the individual has no information on which to base a calculation of probabilities was neglected. Given this, existing theory could be reworked, replacing utility or profits with expected utility or profits, and with random parameters introduced into some of the constraints. For example, it is a simple exercise to assume that the firm faces a randomly shifting demand function, with a given probability distribution, and to work out conditions under which expected profit is maximized.[49] To interpret such results, however, we need a way of measuring risk and attitudes towards it, so that we can investigate why the introduction of risk affects the results. Various measures of both risk and risk aversion were developed, such as the Arrow–Pratt measure of risk aversion, and the Rothschild–Stiglitz measure of risk.[50]

Given such a framework a number of issues can be tackled. One of them is risk – both how it affects decisions, and how it is shared between individuals and firms. The obvious example here is insurance, but it is important to point out that insurance is not the only mechanism for transferring risk from one individual to another. Consider the wage contract between workers and a firm, when the demand for the firm's product is uncertain. If a fixed wage is specified, the firm bears the entire risk, whereas if wage rates vary with the price of the product the risk is shared with the workers. Such considerations have been applied to situations as diverse as labour contracts, in an attempt to explain the stickiness of wage rates,[51] to the issue of labour managed firms,[52] and tenancy agreements in underdeveloped countries.[53]

### The economics of information

In recent years much attention has been devoted to the question of how markets work when information is limited. This is a complicated question, for not only is there the problem of how information is acquired, but it is frequently necessary to allow for imperfect competition. Consider the case, for example, where consumers have limited information about the prices charged by different firms, a case first analysed by Stigler (1961). In such models the optimal strategy for consumers to follow is often to set a "reservation price", buying from the first firm they encounter which offers a price below this. The higher are the costs of searching, the lower the reservation price will be. If consumers are different, and have different reservation prices, then any individual firm will face a downward–sloping demand curve. In any period a number of consumers will come to this firm, and the higher its price, the greater the number of customers who will choose not to buy, but to continue searching for a cheaper price. Competition is thus necessarily imperfect. The outcome of such processes depends on the precise assumptions made about how much firms and consumers learn: it might, for example, be either the monopolistic or the competitive price.[54]

*Asymmetric information*

Once uncertainty is introduced there arises the possibility that not only will information be listed, but that different agents will have access to different information. This situation is known as one of asymmetric information. In many situations it could be argued that asymmetric information is the rule, because for an individual uncertainty comprises not only uncertainty about the "state of nature", but also uncertainty as to the preferences, and hence the behaviour of the other agents in the economy. This raises, as was established in the 1970s, fundamental issues concerning the way in which markets operate. Two particular problems need mentioning: moral hazard, and adverse selection.

The problem of moral hazard can be illustrated by an insurance contract. If an individual is completely insured, he or she will have no incentive to avoid accidents, and may thus be less careful than if he or she were uninsured. Insurance may thus affect the probability of an accident. This problem, however, is *much* more general: it is related to the issue of whether individuals can be provided with an incentive to tell the truth, or not to cheat.[55]

Adverse selection can also be illustrated with reference to insurance markets, though this problem too is much more general. Suppose an insurance company offers medical insurance at a premium appropriate to the health of the average member of the population. Those whose health is very good will decide that the policy is too expensive to be worth buying.[56] The result is that the average health of those buying the insurance will be *worse* than that of the population as a whole. This problem, known as adverse selection, can arise whenever the quality of a commodity traded is uncertain, and where there is asymmetric information. For example if the seller of a used car knows how good it is, but potential buyers have no means of assessing the car's quality until after they have bought it, the average quality of used cars offered for sale should be worse than the average quality of cars of the same age and type.

A seminal paper here was Akerlof's (1970) model of the market for "lemons" (poor quality used cars). His conclusion was that, given certain, not unreasonable, assumptions, trade would be impossible. The only feasible equilibrium price was zero. The argument is quite simple. Suppose the market price for cars of a certain age and type were positive. Because sellers know the quality of the cars they are selling, cars worth more than this will not be offered for sale. The average value of cars offered for sale will therefore be less than the market price. Given that buyers have no idea of the quality of the particular car they are buying, buyers will be prepared to pay only this average price. They will not be prepared to pay the market price. A positive price cannot, therefore, be an equilibrium price.

A still more fundamental result is that of Rothschild and Stiglitz (1976), who investigated the possibility of equilibrium in an insurance market. They assumed that the insurance company had no means of telling whether potential purchasers of insurance fell into a high or low risk category. Rothschild and Stiglitz were able to show that if insurance companies were to offer only a single type of contract, no equilibrium would exist, not even one with a zero price. An equilibrium, might, however, exist if two types of policy were offered, designed so that high risk customers would purchase one type of policy, and low risk customers the other. For example, one type of policy might have a lower premium, but with the customer being responsible for a certain fraction of any claim. High risk individuals might find such a policy unattractive (remember, individuals are assumed to know their own health). Under some circumstances, however, even such a *separating equilibrium*, as it is called, may not exist. Rothschild and Stiglitz were also able to show that if such an equilibrium were to exist, some individuals would be rationed: low-risk individuals would find that they were unable to purchase as much insurance as they wanted to buy. These results, that an equilibrium may not exist, that even if it does there may be more than one price in equilibrium, and that agents may face quantity constraints, have been obtained in a variety of models of asymmetric information.[57]

Offering two types of policy, designed to attract different types of customer, is an example of *screening*: of agents finding ways of distinguishing high quality from low quality goods or customers. An alternative would be for sellers to find ways of *signalling* the quality of their product (guarantees, or brand names, for example). Such issues have been extensively discussed in recent years.[58]

A characteristic of the markets discussed above is that prices convey information. A natural question to ask, therefore, is how much information can prices convey? As an example, consider a model put forward by Grossman and Stiglitz (1980). Grossman and Stiglitz assume that there is some uncertainty about which firms can, if they are prepared to pay the cost, become fully informed. If firms choose to acquire this information, it will affect their behaviour, and hence the market price. Suppose that every firm were to become informed. For any individual firm the incentive to become informed would disappear, for it could deduce all the information it needed from observing the prices produced by the behaviour of its fully-informed competitors. Thus there cannot be an equilibrium in which firms are fully informed: firms would have an incentive to stop acquiring the information. Now suppose that firms all chose not to buy the information. In this case any firm would find it profitable to buy the information: because other firms are uninformed, prices cannot carry any information. Thus a situation where no firms buy the information cannot be an equilibrium either. No equilibrium exists, neither one in which firms choose to become informed, or one in which they do not. Now suppose that there is some additional uncertainty, which no firm can predict. This "noise" may, if it is sufficiently large, serve to prevent uninformed firms from deducing the information they wish to know from prices. They will thus choose to become informed (or to remain uninformed if the costs of the information are too high), and an equilibrium may exist. Equilibrium is thus possible only where prices fail to convey all the relevant information. This shows that, if information is costly to acquire, there will be a limit to the amount of information that can be carried by price signals, and that a market equilibrium may fail to exist.

*Transactions costs*

An area which has received considerable attention in the post-war period is that of transactions costs. A seminal article here was Coase's "The nature of the firm" (1937) in which he argued that transactions costs provided a way of understanding the firm. Coase argued that the characteristic feature of the firm was that, within it, decisions about the allocation of resources could be made administratively, rather than through the market.[59] This raises the questions of why such "islands" of conscious planning should exist, and why their scope varies so much between industries.

Coase found the answer to these questions in *transactions costs*. Organizing production through the market is not costless: relevant prices have to be discovered, and contracts have to be negotiated. In addition there are costs arising from uncertainty and from taxation (which may apply to market transactions, but not to non-market ones). Against this have to be set the costs of organizing production within the firm. Profit maximization implies that,

a firm will tend to expand until the costs of organising an extra transaction within the firm becomes equal to the costs of carrying out the transaction by means of an exchange in the open market or the costs of organising in another firm.[60]

The transactions cost approach which has developed from this follows Commons[61] in taking the individual transaction as the unit of analysis. The economic problem is thus seen as how to organize transactions so as to promote efficiency. It is a hallmark of the approach that the emphasis is on comparing *alternative* modes of making transactions, rather than on comparisons with a frictionless ideal. Government action, for example, is merely one among many ways of organizing transactions. As such it cannot be assumed that government action can necessarily out-perform the market. To decide for or against government intervention it is necessary to compare the costs of having the government organize transactions with those of bringing transactions about through the market.

The fact that all transactions are costly implies that the allocation of property rights between individuals is far more important than if transactions were costless. In the absence of transactions costs the allocation of property rights, except in so far as it affected the distribution of wealth, would be irrelevant, for an appropriate set of contracts could enable resources to be allocated in an optimal manner. When transactions are costly this is not the case. For example, someone might retain the use of a resource that could much more profitably be used by someone else, simply because the costs of transferring the resource (finding a suitable buyer, negotiating and enforcing an appropriate contract) are prohibitive.[62]

*Oligopoly*

Advance in the theory of equilibrium with small numbers of buyers and sellers, each of whom has a significant influence on the market and on the behaviour of others, was limited, until the 1970s when game theory began to be used on a large scale to tackle the problem. This is not to say that there were not advances before then. There were, but they were limited in scope. Bain (1947) proposed the idea of limit pricing, a firm choosing the highest price consistent with making it unprofitable for any competitor to enter the market. This idea was later extended by Bain (1956) and Sylos-Labini (1962) who related entry prevention to technology: increasing returns to scale could provide a barrier to entry, for new producers have either to incur high costs by producing a small output, or else flood the market, producing at lower cost, but depressing the price.

Though the theory of games has been applied to the problem of non-collusive oligopoly, the main development has been the use of bargaining theory to handle situations where agents negotiate with each other. Much recent interest has been in the theory of contracts, especially in the labour market. This is considered below.

*Firms' behaviour*

In most of microeconomics, firms are assumed, making due allowance for possible risk aversion, to be profit-maximizers. This assumption has, however, been questioned. One alternative is to retain the notion that firms maximize something, but to alter the maximand. This is the approach underlying much of the literature, stemming from Penrose (1959), Baumol (1959) and Marris (1964) on the growth of the firm. In this literature firms are treated as more than producers of a single product, for it is assumed that if a firm faces limits to its expansion in one market, it can diversify into other markets. Along with this went an emphasis on the separation of ownership from control in large corporations.[63] Firms were controlled not by their shareholders, but by managers, whose interests might diverge from those of the shareholders. For example, managers' salaries, their status and their power, might depend more on the size of the firm than on its profitability. Managers would, however, be constrained in their activities, for if these diverged too far from what shareholders wanted, the price of a firm's shares might fall, raising the possibility that the firm would be taken over by another firm, its managers losing their power altogether. Thus Marris, for example, assumed firms to be managed so as to maximize *growth*, subject to the constraint that the value of the firms' shares remained above some minimum level required to prevent takeover.

These models, though abandoning the assumption of profit maximization, still assume maximization of some sort. An alternative approach is to abandon the assumption of maximizing altogether. Particularly important here is the work of Herbert Simon (1956, 1957) who has denied that maximizing behaviour is, as many economists assume, synonymous with rationality.[64] Simon has distinguished between two types of rationality. (1) *Substantive rationality* defines, "behaviour which is appropriate to the achievement of given goals within the limits imposed by given conditions and constraints".[65] This is the rationality of traditional maximizing models: finding the behaviour appropriate to maximizing profits, utility, or some other objective. (2) *Procedural rationality*, on the other hand, defines behaviour "which is the outcome of appropriate deliberation".[66] With procedural rationality the emphasis is on the *process* whereby decisions are made.

Given that searching for alternative, more profitable, strategies is costly, it may make sense to stop searching as soon as a satisfactory strategy has been discovered. This process of discovering a satisfactory (as opposed to optimal) set of decisions is what Simon calls *satisficing*. It is not that decision makers do not wish to have higher profits (or any other objective), but rather that given the costs of acquiring information, and the uncertainty as to the benefits that will result from it (perhaps there is no better strategy) maximization may not make sense.

One development from this is behavioural theories, such as those of Cyert and March (1963). Empirical evidence is collected on the decision rules used by organizations, and the implications of these decisions are investigated. A model of the firm, the behaviour of which is determined by the decision rules of its component parts, can be used to generate predictions, which can be tested.[67] An alternative approach, followed by Simon himself, is to analyse the principles underlying the search process. Simon has investigated, for example, the principles on which an efficient search for a satisficing solution could be based.

### The theory of employment

An issue which has attracted much attention since the early 1970s is that of unemployment. The persistence of high unemployment has caused economists to seek an explanation, for in a competitive market the wage rate should adjust to equate supply and demand. In the attempt to explain the persistence of unemployment, economists have used many of the concepts and ideas discussed above.[68] No attempt will be made to survey this literature, but it is important to indicate some of the ways it has been tackled.

Lack of information has underlain most attempts to explain unemployment. The earliest theories were search models (e.g. Phelps, 1970) in which unemployment arises because workers take time to find suitable employment. Such models, however, explain only "voluntary" unemployment. Further progress can be made by assuming not only that information is incomplete, but also that there is asymmetric information. Firms, for example, may not know the quality of potential workers until after they have hired them. When wage offers may act as screening devices, it is possible to find further reasons why the wage rate may fail to equate supply and demand for labour. Much of the literature on signalling is concerned with the labour market.

A more recent development has been the use of bargaining models to explain why the wage rate may remain above the market clearing rate, much attention being paid to so called *implicit contracts*: contracts which are not written down. For example, if workers are risk averse but firms, being better able to spread risks, are risk neutral, it may be in the interests of both parties to negotiate a contract in which wages fluctuate by less than the marginal product of labour. Workers could gain from being exposed to less risk, and firms might thus be able to negotiate a lower wage rate. Asymmetric information provides another reason why fixed wage contracts may be preferred. Suppose, for example, that there is uncertainty as to the demand for a firm's product. The firm may have more information about what is happening in the market than does the union with which it is negotiating. If the firm were allowed, for example, to reduce wages when the marginal product of labour fell, it might have an incentive to pretend that productivity had fallen, in order to reduce wages. A contract in which wages are fixed, but where the firm chooses how much labour to employ, may thus be preferable for the union.

## 23.4 CONCLUSIONS

Although the underlying theoretical framework has remained the same as that used by Hicks and Samuelson, microeconomic theory has changed substantially in the post-war period. The availability on a wide scale of new techniques has enabled economists to extend the scope of microeconomic theory to encompass issues that were previously thought incapable of formal analysis. The extension of microeconomic theory to deal with uncertainty and lack of information promises to be particularly important, not least because it calls into question some common assumptions about the way competitive markets work, such as the notion that in equilibrium agents will be able to buy and sell as much as they wish at the prevailing prices. Such work is in its infancy, but it is possible that, it may, even though it is based on the "neoclassical" assumptions of maximizing behaviour and competitive markets, change the way in which economists think about market equilibrium. Though empirical evidence may be vital, both in raising questions which need answering and in choosing between alternative theories, such a change could never be brought about without theoretical work at a fairly abstract level.

# 24

## Welfare Economics[1]

### 24.1 THE NEW WELFARE ECONOMICS, BERGSON AND SAMUELSON

*The New Welfare Economics*

By the late 1930s many economists had come to accept the arguments of Myrdal and Robbins, that interpersonal utility comparisons could not be used as the basis for a scientific welfare economics. In response to this there arose a series of attempts to construct a welfare economics free from interpersonal utility comparisons, this becoming known as the "New Welfare Economics", as opposed to the old welfare economics of Marshall and Pigou. These attempts were made possible by developments in consumer theory, where a theory of the consumer based on utility was being replaced with one based on the concepts of preference and indifference.

The starting point for the New Welfare Economics was the idea that a change increased potential welfare if the gainers from the change could compensate any losers and still remain better off. This criterion was first used by Pareto (1896) and was taken up by Barone (1908), but after that it was neglected until its revival by Kaldor (1939).[2] Kaldor attached great importance to this compensation test, for it provided a means of separating welfare economics into two parts: one dealing with production; the other with distribution. This separation was something Pigou had been able to do because of his utilitarianism: Pigou was able to consider separately factors affecting the sum total of utility, and factors affecting its distribution. The merit of the compensation test was that this separation could, it was claimed, be achieved without any interpersonal utility comparisons. Kaldor was thus able to argue that a scientific welfare economics was possible, this being one which analysed situations with a view to establishing whether or not it was *possible* to make everyone better off. This left the issue of distribution to be settled outside economics, for, he argued, it was "quite impossible to decide on economic grounds what particular pattern of income distribution maximizes social welfare".[3]

Hicks took up Kaldor's idea of separating the issues of production and distribution, defining an *optimum* as a situation in which "every individual is as well off as he can be made, subject to the condition that no reorganization permitted shall make any individual worse off".[4] It was only later that such an optimum was called a "Pareto optimum" (Little, 1950). Hicks was able to use this definition to show: (1) that there was an infinite number of such optima; and (2) that an optimum required certain conditions to be satisfied, in particular that the marginal rate of substitution between any two commodities be the same for all consumers consuming the two commodities, and for all producers producing both of them. These results provided a framework in which Hicks, without referring to utilitarianism, was able to discuss discrepancies between social and private costs, and the welfare implications of monopoly and imperfect competition.

Where did the compensation principle come into all this? The answer is that it could be used to enlarge the set of welfare improvements beyond the set of Pareto improvements, which Hicks considered virtually empty. There were, however, problems with this approach, the most notable being pointed out by Scitovsky (1941). Scitovsky derived the paradoxical result that it was possible for a change from A to B to pass the Kaldor–Hicks compensation test, and for the change from B to A to pass it as well. In other words, the Kaldor–Hicks compensation test could give contradictory results.

The nature of the problem here, and the reason for the Scitovsky paradox, can be seen most clearly by using the concept of the utility possibility frontier, developed by Samuelson (1950). Suppose we have an economy in which there are two individuals, one of which produces commodities, the other consuming them. Assume that the utilities of these individuals are initially those indicated by the point X in Figure 24.1. By redistributing income from the producer to the consumer we can increase the consumer's utility at the expense of the producer's utility, and in so doing we trace out the utility possibility frontier associated with the point X.[5] Now suppose that we consider a change, such as the introduction of protection, which moves the economy to point Y, and that, by the same method of redistributing income, we construct the utility possibility frontier corresponding to Y. If the situation is as shown in Figure 24.1, we have the Scitovsky paradox: if we are at X we could reach point Y' by introducing protection and redistributing income so as to compensate the consumer; similarly, if we were at Y we could move to X' by bringing in free trade and compensating the producer. Both the introduction of protection and its removal pass the Kaldor–Hicks compensation test.

Scitovsky's response to this was to require that the Kaldor–Hicks criterion be satisfied in one direction, and to be violated in the other direction: the so called Scitovsky double criterion. It turns out, however, that even this is not enough, for the only case where it can be said that one situation is *unambiguously* better than another is, as Samuelson pointed out, where one utility possibility frontier is completely outside the other.

The problem with both the Kaldor–Hicks and the Scitovsky criteria is that they do not require that compensation is actually paid. In our example this means that the introduction of protection alters the distribution of income, something which matters because the choice between protection and free trade depends on the distribution of income: if the consumer is very well off compared with the producer (we are in top left part of Figure 24.1) then protection is preferable; whilst if the producer is well off (we are in the bottom right part of the diagram) then free trade is better.

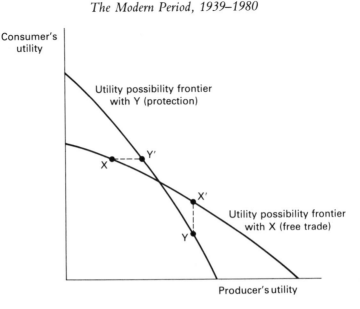

FIGURE 24.1   *Compensation Tests*

The reason why this issue is so important is that the arguments involved undermine the idea that the issues of production and distribution can be separated. Without knowing the distribution of income it is impossible to say whether or not a change is desirable, except in the very special case where everyone is made better off, or everyone worse off. This had implications not only for abstract welfare economics, but also for the significance of the statistics on national income, which were being compiled on a large scale for the first time in the 1940s. At the time when statisticians were beginning to calculate figures for national income, its justification as a measure of welfare, provided by Pigou, was being undermined. In this context the significance of the Kaldor–Hicks criterion was that it provided a reason, so its proponents believed, for claiming that an increase in national income corresponded to an increase in potential welfare: if national income rose, it would be possible to make everyone better off. Thus some of the main contributions to the New Welfare Economics were made in articles dealing with the measurement of national income (e.g. Hicks, 1940; Samuelson, 1950).

The issue of compensation tests was not, however, the only issue in welfare economics relevant to the problem of measuring national income, for the following questions also had to be answered:
(1) How should commodities entering into national income be valued?
(2) How should the public sector be treated?
(3) What was the *economic* significance of the various types of index number which might be used?

Economists were returning to the problems discussed by Pigou at the start of his *Economics of Welfare*, but they were considering them differently, in the context of the new theory of value. In the same way that Sidgwick, Marshall and Pigou had had to reconsider the significance of national income in the light of the marginal utility theory of value, so too did the economists of the 1930s and 1940s have to reconsider the issue in the light of the new consumer theory.[6]

### Hicks' rehabilitation of consumers' surplus

Even if utility were measurable, there were problems with Marshall's concept of consumer's surplus, but with the criticisms of utility theory made by Myrdal and Robbins it became completely untenable. The main architect of the revival of consumers' surplus as a usable concept was Hicks, first in *Value and Capital* (1939) and then in a series of articles in the 1940s. Marshall had argued that consumer's surplus required the assumption that the marginal utility of income was constant. Hicks' contribution was to show that the definition of consumer's surplus was a separate issue from the issue of whether or not it could be measured by the area under a demand curve – it was only the latter that depended on the marginal utility of income being constant. He then argued that consumer's surplus could be measured by what he called the *compensating variation* in income, "whose loss would just offset the fall in price and leave the consumer no worse off than before".[7] This is a perfectly well-defined, measurable concept. Similarly, *consumers'* surplus was interpreted in this way as "the amount of money consumers as a body would have to lose in order to make each of them as badly off as he would be if the commodity disappeared".[8] Although *it can no longer be interpreted as a utility sum*, this has a perfectly clear meaning. It is at this stage of the argument that issues are raised similar to those involved in the measurement of real income, for it is because Hicks goes on to define an optimum as a situation where "no reorganisation is possible which will leave any individuals so much better off that they will be able to compensate the losers and still be left with a net gain",[9] that he can use changes in consumers' surplus as a measure of changes in welfare. Hicks' rehabilitation of consumers' surplus was thus only partial.

### Bergson and Samuelson

The outcome of the New Welfare Economics was that an optimum came to be defined as a situation in which it was not possible to make anyone better off without making someone else worse off. In the absence of utilitarianism, however, it was not at first clear exactly what it was that was optimal in such an optimum. An answer to this question was first provided by Bergson (1938), who defined what Samuelson later described as an individualistic social welfare function. Bergson started from the general statement that social welfare must be a function of the quantities of all the commodities consumed, and all inputs including labour. As it stands, such a social welfare function says no more than that social welfare depends, in an unspecified way, on the resources available to society. The merit of the approach was that it enabled Bergson to do two things. (1) He was able to work out the value judgements implicit in various statements of the conditions for a welfare optimum (in particular the judgement that welfare depends only on individual utilities; and that social welfare increases when all individuals become better off).[10] The utilitarian social welfare function is clearly a special case of a more general function embodying these judgements. (2) He showed that many of the optimum conditions, such as equal marginal rates of substitution, applied whatever the exact form of the social welfare function: in other words, whatever additional value judgements we choose to make.

This concept of a social welfare function was further developed by Samuelson (1947 and 1950), who related it to the utility possibility frontier, using these concepts to put into perspective many of the ideas discussed earlier in this section. Samuelson was able to show that the Pareto-optimum conditions give necessary conditions[11] for being on the utility possibility frontier, but that they do not establish any particular point on the frontier. To single out a particular point on the frontier, further ethical judgements are required. According to Samuelson, potential welfare can be said unambiguously to increase only if the *entire* utility possibility frontier shifts outwards, something that a single index number could never show. In the words of one contemporary survey, "Samuelson has shown that we cannot even be *sure* that group A is better off than group B even if A has collectively more of everything."[12]

### The theory of the second best

The first order conditions for a Pareto optimum yield results such as marginal cost pricing, the inefficiency of tariffs, and so on. Arguments such as these, however, are based on the assumption that everything else in the economy is optimally adjusted: that price equals marginal costs in all other industries; that there are no other tariffs; and so on. In the early 1950s economists began to question whether these results were justified should the Pareto optimality conditions not be satisfied in other parts of the economy. For example, if there are monopolies in the private sector, should marginal cost pricing be adopted in the public sector? The conclusion was reached that such conclusions were generally not justified.[13] These results were brought together and integrated under the name of the general theory of the second best by Lipsey and Lancaster (1956). They showed that, in general, where more than one of the Pareto optimality conditions was violated, it would not necessarily be an improvement to satisfy one of them if the others remained violated.

## 24.2 ARROW AND SOCIAL CHOICE THEORY

*Arrow's general possibility theorem*

A completely different approach to the problem of social welfare was taken by Arrow in his influential book, *Social Choice and Individual Values* (1951a). Starting from the proposition that if social choices are to be made on the basis of individual preferences, value judgements have to be made, Arrow investigated the problem of whether various generally accepted value judgements were compatible with each other. To do this he defined a social welfare function in a different way from Bergson and Samuelson. He assumed that each individual could rank *all the possibilities open to society* in order of preference. The social welfare function is then a mechanism for deriving a social ranking (order of preference) for the various alternatives from the set of individual rankings. Examples of such mechanisms include majority voting, or the dictatorship of one individual. So Arrow's problem can be restated: does there exist a social welfare function (a mechanism for getting from the set of individual preferences to a social preference) which satisfies reasonable ethical criteria?

The criteria Arrow thought ought to be satisfied are: (1) unrestricted domain (it should work whatever are the individual preferences); (2) the Pareto criterion;[14] (3) independence of irrelevant alternatives (choice between two alternatives should depend neither on whether or not a third, irrelevant, alternative is available, nor on individuals' preferences between alternatives not being considered); (4) non-dictatorship (which should be self-explanatory). Arrow then showed that there existed no social welfare function satisfying all these conditions. In other words,

If we exclude the possibility of interpersonal comparisons of utility, then the only methods of passing from individual tastes to social preferences which will be satisfactory and which will be defined for a wide range of sets of individual orderings are either imposed or dictatorial.[15]

This was his general possibility theorem.

Arrow's theorem, frequently referred to as his *impossibility* theorem, had a widespread influence on economists, contributing to the general pessimism as to the scope of welfare economics in the early 1950s. The New Welfare Economics had failed to provide a value-free basis for welfare economics; the theory of second best suggested that even the limited guidance provided by Pareto optimality conditions might be unreliable; and Arrow had shown that it was impossible to derive an ethically acceptable social welfare function.[16] In this situation economists were faced with three possible responses. (1) To lose interest in welfare economics altogether. (2) Simply to assume that there did exist some set of ethical principles on which social choices could be based, these being represented by, say, a Bergson–Samuelson social welfare function. If they went ahead and used these, they would eventually discover which of Arrow's postulates was violated.[17] (3) To investigate Arrow's result further, replacing his conditions with alternative ones, and seeking ways round his possibility theorem. This route led to the development of social choice theory as a distinct branch of welfare economics.[18] When economists came to investigate Arrow's result in this way they found it to be remarkably robust, similar theorems emerging when the problem was formulated in a variety of ways.

### The implementability of social choice rules

Arrow's theorem is concerned with the problem of using individual preferences to obtain a social ranking of the various alternatives open to society. Such social choice rules are, however, useless unless there is a way of finding out what the individuals' preferences are. This raises the issue of whether individuals would, if a given social choice rule were implemented, reveal their preferences correctly. Suppose a given social choice rule were being used to determine public policy. If individuals knew this rule they might be able to obtain a better outcome for themselves by misrevealing their preferences (i.e. by lying). A social choice rule is said to be *strategy-proof* if it is impossible for any individual to obtain a more preferred outcome by misrevealing his or her preferences: if individuals have no incentive to lie.

A theorem which some economists would consider as equal in importance to Arrow's theorem is the Gibbard–Satterthwaite theorem.[19] This states that, assuming there are at least three alternatives to be chosen from, any strategy-proof social choice function is dictatorial: one individual gets his or her way irrespective of what other individuals prefer. In other words, there is no solution to the problem of providing each individual with an incentive to reveal his or her preferences correctly. As with Arrow's theorem, economists have sought ways round this very undesirable result.[20]

### Utility measurement

Since Arrow, economists have turned again to the issue of utility measurement and interpersonal utility comparisons. In a sense this represents a revival of the utilitarian approach discussed in chapter 14, but to see it in this way would be misleading. Utility, as used by Bentham, Sidgwick and Pigou, was essentially a practical, commonsensical concept, one for which little justification was given, utilitarianism emerging naturally from it. In contrast, utility in its modern incarnation is very different, not being vulnerable in the same way to criticisms such as those of Myrdal and Robbins.

There are two main ways in which testable, interpersonal utility comparisons can be made, neither of which is vulnerable to the Myrdal–Robbins critique. One is to correlate utility with observable individual characteristics (for example, if A smiles more than B then he must be happier, and hence have a higher utility). Such judgements may be controversial, but they can nonetheless be stated sufficiently precisely for interpersonal utility comparisons to be meaningful in the sense of being testable. The other way is to assume that individuals can make judgements of the form, "I would prefer to be her in her situation than to be me in mine." Such a statement is a subjective opinion, but it expresses a preference, just as much as if an individual expresses a preference for one bundle of goods rather than another. As such it can be argued that such subjective statements can form the basis for a scientific welfare economics, in the same way that preferences between bundles of goods form the basis for a scientific consumer theory.

Consider, for example, the case where there are two individuals, A and B, both of whom would prefer to be A (i.e. have all A's personal characteristics, tastes and so on) in A's position (i.e. consuming the bundle of goods that A consumes) than to be B in B's position. There is a strong case here for saying that A's utility is higher than B's. This instance, of unanimity in making interpersonal utility comparisons, may be of only limited relevance, but it is sufficient to establish the *possibility* of making interpersonal utility comparisons, if only under a limited range of circumstances.

Economists adopting this approach have thus been able to clarify the issues involved in making interpersonal utility comparisons in a variety of ways.

(1) Interpersonal utility comparisons *do* involve subjective judgements, but these can be stated explicitly, and they can be the subject of rational discussion.

(2) Utilities may be *partially* comparable, the choice not being solely between total comparability and the complete absence of any comparability, as was assumed in the literature on the New Welfare Economics.[21] This partial comparability is something that can be stated formally, in order to derive the implications of different degrees of comparability.

(3) Economists have also looked more closely at the types of interpersonal utility comparability required for the use of various welfare criteria. For example, to use the utilitarian criterion it is enough to be able to compare the units in which utilities are measured (i.e. *differences* in utility): there is no need to compare utility *levels*.

These points may seem unduly technical, but they have important implications for the way welfare economics is viewed. Modern utilitarianism, for example, is very different from earlier utilitarianism, for although both may refer to maximizing the sum of individual utilities, the reasoning behind them is different: modern utilitarianism is based on precisely formulated premises, premises which can be, and have been, compared with alternatives.

## *Justice*

There are two ways in which considerations of justice can be brought into social choice theory. One is to use arguments about justice in order to say something about the appropriate form for the social welfare function. The other is to bring concepts of justice into social choice theory as alternatives to the traditional welfare criteria. Both approaches have been used.

The use of concepts of justice related to the idea of fairness in order to justify certain forms of social welfare function stems above all from Harsanyi (1955) and Rawls (1958, 1971). Their ideas have in common the notion that a fair allocation of resources is one that people would be able to agree upon if they did not know which position in society they were themselves to occupy. Such a social contract theory, however, can still lead to very different social welfare functions. Harsanyi used it to justify utilitarianism: if individuals each believe that they have an equal chance of any position in society, then they will maximize their expected utility by agreeing to a utilitarian allocation of resources. Rawls, on the other hand, assumed that people were completely ignorant as to the positions they would occupy in society, and he inferred from this[22] that a fair allocation of resources was one that took most care of the worst-off person in society.[23] Rawls' work, in particular, has had a substantial influence on welfare economics, though it could be argued that this is not so much because of his discussion of justice, as because he provided economists with a new, easily-applied welfare criterion.

Ideas of justice have also, however, been used to raise doubts about social welfare functions, whether of the Bergson–Samuelson or the Arrow type, and even to raise doubts about the Pareto criterion itself. An issue which has attracted a lot of attention is one raised by Sen (1970b), namely whether or not liberalism is compatible with the Pareto criterion. His argument is that there are certain personal choices (e.g. whether to sleep on one's back or on one's belly; or one's choice of reading matter) which are no-one else's business. In other words, people have certain rights which should be respected by any social welfare function. Though the idea is not inconsistent with the most general formulations of Bergson–Samuelson and Arrow social welfare functions, the properties that these social welfare functions are usually assumed to exhibit (e.g. the Pareto criterion) are inconsistent with it. Sen's liberalism implies that social welfare depends on more than simply individual preferences: in order to evaluate social welfare, for example, we need to know whether my utility is derived from eating bananas or from torturing you. If this argument is accepted, it undermines the Pareto criterion, for in the case where a change makes everyone better off, the Pareto criterion *rules out* the use of non-utility information. If we accept that people have certain rights, Sen argues, then non-utility information cannot be ruled out in this way.

### Social choice theory after Arrow

Although he was not the first to introduce the problem of group decision making into economics,[24] it was Arrow's work which inspired much of modern social choice theory. The general possibility theorem was a challenging, paradoxical result, thought by many to be catastrophic in its implications for welfare economics. At the same time, it provided great scope for the application of advanced mathematical techniques. Recent work has made Arrow's theorem much more comprehensible: if economists are confined to using only utility information, and if the available utility information is very poor (i.e. no interpersonal comparability whatsoever) then it is hardly surprising that acceptable social welfare functions are hard to find. These restrictions are, however, inappropriate if recent arguments on interpersonal utility comparisons, and on the use of non-utility information, are accepted. Thus though modern social choice theory owes much of its inspiration to Arrow's possibility theorem, it has developed beyond it.

## 24.3   WELFARE ECONOMICS AND PUBLIC POLICY

*Pareto-efficiency and social welfare functions*

The two fundamental theorems of welfare economics – that competitive equilibria are Pareto-efficient, and that, under certain conditions, any Pareto optimum can be achieved as a competitive equilibrium – were established in their modern form by Arrow (1951c) and Debreu (1951). These theorems constitute the modern equivalent of the doctrine of maximum satisfaction. To understand them it is necessary to note that they are more than the old doctrines dressed up in more sophisticated mathematical techniques, for they show, in a way that the older doctrines were unable to do, the stringency of the conditions required to ensure an efficient equilibrium, even when efficiency is defined in the weak sense of Pareto-optimality.[25] These conditions require not only perfect competition in all markets, but also complete information, and a complete set of both futures and insurance markets.

Probably of more significance than this, however, is the fact that in the period under consideration the use of the criterion of Pareto-efficiency has become completely routine. When constructing a model of economic equilibrium, whether a static model, an intertemporal model, a model with rationing, a bargaining model, or any other, economists examine the solution in terms of Pareto-efficiency as a matter of course.[26] This may seem an obvious thing to do, but that is only because we are now so used to the idea. In part this arises, no doubt, from the increased use of mathematics (establishing Pareto-optimality, or its absence, means one more theorem), but its main motivation stems from the developments in welfare economics discussed above. The outcome of the New Welfare Economics was that the Pareto criterion (that at least one person be made better off, with no-one being made worse off) was apparently the only generally acceptable criterion for an increase in welfare.[27] Where Pigou would have asked whether the national dividend was being maximized, post-war economists have asked whether an equilibrium is Pareto-optimal.

Economists have not, however, defined their attention to Pareto-efficiency, being increasingly willing to use explicit social welfare functions of the Bergson–Samuelson type. It might be thought that this involved a reversion to pre-Paretian welfare economics, the only real different lying in the greater degree of abstraction permitted by the use of more complicated mathematical techniques This, however, is not the case, for social welfare functions are frequently used to make explicit the implications of alternative value judgements, rather than to argue for a particular policy objective. The example of the literature on optimal taxation is considered below. Another example worth mentioning is Atkinson's index of inequality – a measure which can be used, for example, to show whether income is more equally distributed in one country than in another. This measure is defined as "the proportion of the present total income that would be required to achieve the same level of social welfare as at present if incomes were equally distributed".[28] This measure of inequality clearly depends on the form of the social welfare function, but the reason for using it is to show that the measurement of inequality depends on attitudes towards inequality. These value judgements are introduced in the form of a parameter, the value of which reflects the degree of aversion to inequality. The point of introducing a social welfare function is not to bring in implicit value judgements, but to make explicit the implications of alternative value judgements.

One of the characteristics of economic theory in recent decades has been the attention given to public policy. In the same way that it is now routine for economists to investigate the welfare implications of their models, it is also routine for economists to examine the implications of their models for government policy. An important branch of welfare economics is thus concerned with criteria for government policy. To give some idea of the way in which economists have approached the question of government policy in recent years, three particularly important examples will be discussed: the theory of optimal taxation, Samuelson's theory of public goods, and Coase's theorem on externalities. Though these are very important examples, it is important to stress that these are only examples, chosen from a literature that covers an enormous variety of issues not mentioned here.

### *The theory of optimal taxation*[29]

The aim of this section is not to present technical details but to give an idea of the type of argument that is used in the theory of optimal taxation, and of the type of conclusion that can be obtained. As representative of much recent work on the subject, consider the treatment of optimal taxation contained in Atkinson and Stiglitz's *Lectures on Public Economics* (1980). Their starting point is Pareto-optimality and the two fundamental theorems of welfare economics. They introduce these, however, not to argue that competition is thereby justified, but to point out why free markets may *fail* to produce an efficient allocation of resources. Competition may be imperfect, markets may be missing, and information may be incomplete.[30] In addition, they point out that "Pareto efficiency does not ensure that the distribution of income that emerges from the competitive process is in accord with the prevailing concepts of equity (whatever these may be)."[31]

Recognizing that the Pareto criterion provides inadequate guidance on most matters of policy, Atkinson and Stiglitz make extensive use of social welfare functions. Their defence of the use of social welfare functions is worth quoting at length:

> a complete incidence analysis [i.e. of how the burden of taxation is distributed amongst different people] would specify the effect of any tax policy on every individual in the economy, but such an approach, even were it practicable, would not be of much use for public policy purposes, and the information, once obtained, would undoubtedly be reduced to some form of summary statistics. The social welfare functions we employ ... can be seen as forms of summary statistics, embedding both judgements about the distribution of income and trade-offs beween 'mean income' and inequality.[32]

These value judgements are made as explicit as possible, the implications of a variety of social welfare functions being considered.[33]

A further important aspect of their treatment is that they see the design of public policy is seen as inherently a second best problem. The reason for this is that not only are the only non-distortionary taxes lump sum taxes, but "the information on which to base lump sum taxes is not observable, or it is observable only at great cost, and individuals have an incentive not to reveal it".[34] This means that only a restricted range of lump sum taxes is available. For example, to reach a social optimum (to find this we need to make the necessary value judgements) it might be necessary to tax people according to their earning *capacity* (the maximum that they could earn) so that the tax does not induce them to work less hard. Earning capacity, however, is not directly observable. Because a lump sum tax based on earning capacity (the "first-best" solution) is not available, it is necessary to find a "second-best" solution. It is necessary to develop ways of relating tax to observable characteristics (such as actual income) in such a way as to achieve the desired relation of taxation to the unobservable characteristics (such as earning capacity) in which we are interested.[35]

The first problem Atkinson and Stiglitz tackle is the structure of indirect taxation: how to raise a given amount of revenue, using indirect taxes (taxes on different types of expenditure) in such a way as to minimize the loss of utility.[36] Because all individuals are assumed to be identical, the criterion of maximizing one individual's utility is equivalent to adopting a utilitarian social welfare function. It can be argued that if all individuals are identical a utilitarian social welfare function is acceptable, for the question of equity in the distribution of income does not arise. In addition to investigating the optimal structure of indirect taxation, Atkinson and Stiglitz go on to analyse the second-best problem: what can be said about the possibilities for increasing welfare by changing taxation. After that the model is extended to cover differences between individuals, at which stage considerations of equity are brought in.

There follows a similar analysis of optimal income taxation. Their starting point is the utilitarian approach of Sidgwick and Edgeworth, with its implication that the structure of taxation should be such as to render the marginal utility of income the same for all individuals.[37] Like Sidgwick and Edgeworth they recognize the need to modify this to take account of the effect of taxes on incentives. There are three ways in which they are able to take their analysis well beyond that of earlier economists.[38] Firstly, their use of social welfare functions enables them to discuss alternatives to the utilitarian criterion. Rawlsian and non-Paretian functions are discussed, the concept of social welfare functions providing a framework within which to discuss the value judgements involved. Secondly, they tackle the second-best problem of what should be done when the choices available to the government are restricted. Finally, the improved mathematical techniques available make it possible to investigate aspects of the problem that could not otherwise be tackled. Does it, for example, make much difference whether the government is constrained to have a constant marginal tax rate?

Given that even the most complicated of the models used are nonetheless highly simplified compared with any real economy, what does such analysis achieve? Atkinson and Stiglitz do not prescribe definite policies on the basis of their theories. Speaking of indirect taxation, for example, they conclude that "There are not typically simple rules of wide applicability."[39] They provide three main arguments for the value of such research.

(1) It casts doubt on conventional rules, such that a uniform sales tax is more efficient than a rate which varies from commodity to commodity.[40] Once we start considering second-best problems, Atkinson and Stiglitz argue, intuition becomes an unreliable guide.[41] Consider, for example, the notion that equity implies that luxuries should be taxed more heavily than necessaries. If high taxes on necessaries were to raise enough revenue to enable a regressive poll tax to be reduced, it might be more equitable to retain the taxes on necessaries than to abolish them.[42]

(2) The results obtained in the literature on optimal taxation depend critically on parameters about which we have little empirical knowledge (e.g. the elasticity of supply of labour, elasticities of demand for commodities).[43] The theory of optimal taxation provides an indication of where empirical research might produce the greatest improvements in the design of taxation.

(3) Analysis of particular problems such as that of optimal taxation helps us understand the implications of alternative objectives which might be pursued:

The exploration of the implications for tax policy of the Rawlsian difference principle, for example, has helped to clarify the nature of that principle, and has influenced the degree to which it has been accepted as a basis for redistributive policy.[44]

### Public goods

The theory of public goods and externalities could be considered under the heading of either positive or normative economics, but is considered here for convenience. Modern theories of public goods stem from two articles by Samuelson (1954a, 1955).[45] He examines what he called "a strong polar case" where each individual's consumption of a collective consumption good (public good) led to no subtraction from the quantity consumed by any other individual. The total supply of the public good enters every individual's utility function. Samuelson went on to derive Pareto-optimality conditions for an economy comprising both public and private goods, thus deriving conditions for the optimal supply of public goods.

Samuelson reached the conclusion that "no decentralized pricing system can serve to determine optimally these levels of collective consumption".[46] No individual will supply the socially optimal amount of a public good, for he or she will be prepared to provide it only up to the point where its marginal cost equals the marginal benefit to him or her personally: the social benefits, comprising the sum of individuals' benefits, must exceed the benefits to any individual.[47] Public goods raise even more fundamental problems, however. Suppose the state were to decide to supply the optimal quantity of a public good, charging individuals according to the benefits they derive from it. To do this it would have to ascertain the benefits to individuals of the public good. Any individual, however, will have an incentive to understate the value of the public good to him or her: if others value the good it will be provided anyway, even if one individual contributes nothing. This is the so called "free rider" problem.[48]

From the starting point provided by Samuelson, economists have developed the theory in a variety of directions. For example, a problem with Samuelson's theory is that pure public goods are very difficult to find. The analysis, therefore, has to be extended to cover "impure" public goods, such as ones where people can choose not to consume the good (e.g. broadcasting) or cases where people can, possibly at a cost, be excluded from consuming the good. Alternative methods of financing various types of public good can be investigated with respect to various welfare criteria. Schemes for inducing potential consumers to reveal their preferences can be devised and evaluated.

## Externalities

Like public goods, externalities raise the possibility of market failure. Following Pigou,[49] economists have often argued that externalities call for government action, such as taxes or subsidies, in order to bring marginal private costs into line with marginal social costs. The problem of inducing people to reveal their preferences correctly, however, causes problems with this argument: because many externalities (e.g. pollution) have the character of public goods, people will often have an incentive to misreveal their preferences. It cannot be assumed that the government will necessarily be able to perform better than the market, though of course it may be able to do so.

The aspect of the literature on externalities that will be considered here is Coase's "The problem of social cost" (1960). Apart from being one of the most frequently cited economics articles,[50] this article is important for changing economists' perspective on the problem of externalities. Coase argued that where one business's actions caused damage to another business (e.g. a grazier's cattle may damage a farmer's crops if there are no fences) it was wrong to assume that such damage should necessarily be prevented. The crucial issue, Coase argued, was whether total production was higher with or without the damage taking place.

Coase started by considering the case where markets work freely: where "the operation of the pricing system is without cost".[51] He then compared two cases: where the damaging business does, and does not, have to pay for any damage caused. Coase argued that total production would be the same in either case. Consider the case of the grazier whose cattle destroy crops. if the grazier is liable for the damage his cattle cause, then he will allow damage to occur only where the benefits to him exceed the damages he has to pay. He will take account of crop damage in deciding, for example, how many cattle to rear, and whether or not it is worth putting up fences. This was well understood. Where Coase went further was in pointing out that similar conclusions would hold if the grazier was *not* liable to pay damages. The mechanism in this case was that, if the prevention of crop damage would result in higher overall production, it would be in the farmer's interest to pay the grazier not to damage his crops. The allocation of resources would be optimal whether or not damages had to be paid.

The implication of this argument was that, provided property rights were properly defined (i.e. businesses know whether they are liable for damages or not), and provided that all necessary transactions could occur costlessly, the distribution of property rights affected only the distribution of income, not the level of output. When market transactions are costly, however, the situation is very different.

Firstly, the distribution of property rights may affect the outcome. With certain externalities, even if liability to damage is well defined, transactions costs may make the payment of damages prohibitively expensive. Transactions costs are likely to be particularly high, for example, where damage is inflicted not on a single business, but on a large number, for it may be expensive even to find out who is affected, let alone enter into a contract with each of them.

Secondly, where the costs of undertaking market transactions are high, businesses will have an incentive to find alternative forms of economic organization. If production is organized within a firm, for example, certain transactions can be organized administratively, within the firm, rather than through the market. The optimal way of organizing production, therefore, will depend on the relative costs of making different types of transaction.[52] The government can, from this perspective, be regarded as a "super-firm", able to influence the use of factors by administrative decision.[53] Coase thus reached the conclusion that "All solutions have costs, and there is no reason to suppose that government regulation is called for simply because the problem is not well handled by the market or the firm."[54]

## 24.4  CONCLUSIONS

Welfare economics provides an excellent example of how developments in economic theory can result in a new perspective on the history of economic thought. By the 1960s it had become generally accepted that there was no scientific basis for making inter-personal utility comparisons, and as a result of this utilitarian welfare economics appeared completely discredited. Although subsequent developments have not re-instated the utilitarian welfare economics of Sidgwick and Pigou, they have shown that the movement towards Paretian welfare economics went too far: although the scope for scientific inter-personal utility comparisons may be very limited, it is an exaggeration to say that such comparisons cannot be made at all. From the perspective of the 1980s, therefore, the shift from utilitarian to Paretian welfare economics is seen to have involved Kuhnian losses as well as gains.

# 25

## Growth and Capital

### 25.1 THE THEORY OF GROWTH

*Harrod and Domar*

Modern growth theory stems from the work of Harrod (1939) and Domar (1946). Though the equation central to both their models has come to be called the Harrod–Domar model,[1] they approached the problem of growth very differently.

Harrod's theory centred on the concept of the *warranted rate of growth*:

that rate of growth which, if it occurs, will leave all parties satisfied that they have produced neither more nor less than the right amount ... it will put them into a frame of mind which will cause them to give such orders as will maintain the same rate of growth.[2]

The relationship of supply and demand was analysed, in a Keynesian manner, in terms of savings and investment. Saving was assumed to be a fraction, $s$, of output. Investment was determined by the acceleration principle, and depended on the growth of output. Defining $v$ as "the value of capital goods required for the production of a unit increment of output",[3] equality of planned savings and investment requires that

$$sY = vY,$$

which implies that the growth rate, $Y/Y$, equals $s/v$. This growth rate was Harrod's warranted rate of growth.

Harrod went on to draw pessimistic conclusions about the possibility of steady growth. The main problem was that divergences of the actual growth rate from the warranted rate would be cumulative. If, for example, the actual growth rate were less than the warranted rate, the result would be that producers would find themselves with too much capital (either unwanted inventories, or too much equipment) and they would reduce their investment. The result of this would be that the growth rate would, because of the multiplier effect on income, fall even further below the warranted rate. This problem of the instability of the warranted rate was reinforced by the existence of a limit imposed on the actual rate of growth by what Harrod called the *natural rate of growth*. This was

the maximum rate of growth allowed by the increase of population, accumulation of capital, technological improvement and the work/leisure preference schedule, supposing that there is always full employment in some sense.[4]

If the natural rate were less than the warranted rate (and there was no reason why this should not be the case) then depression would result, for the economy could not possibly expand at the warranted rate for very long.

Although $s$ and $v$ are treated as constants in Harrod's algebra, he does not assume them to be fixed. Harrod refers to investment depending on the rate of interest, and on long term plans as well as on the increase in output.[5] The level of savings will depend not only on the level of output, but also on the level of unemployment. Thus the warranted rate of growth ($s/v$) might be "dragged down by depression", or be "twisted upwards by an inflation of prices and profit".[6]

Domar's starting point, on the other hand, was the dual role of investment.[7] On the one hand it produces demand, via the multiplier, and on the other it increases productive capacity. Domar was thus concerned to find the conditions under which demand would grow at the same rate as productive capacity. He argued that it was important to see unemployment as dependent not on the level of national income, but on the ratio of income to productive capacity.[8] He distinguished between unemployment caused by deficient demand, and that due to the productivity of investment being less than its maximum value. The latter might arise, for example, if investment were inefficiently allocated between different uses. Domar came to the conclusion that the economy would converge towards a degree of capacity utilization given by the ratio of the growth rate of investment to the required growth rate, the latter being given by the same formula as Harrod's warranted growth rate.[9] A low rate of growth would thus lead to permanent stagnation.

It is important to note that although Harrod and Domar both derived the equation that has become associated with their names, they used it in very different ways. Firstly, their interpretations of $v$ were different. Domar postulated a direct link between $v$ and increases in productive capacity, something which Harrod did not do: for Harrod the accelerator was a theory of the demand for investment.[10] Secondly, they had completely different accounts of what went on when the economy was not growing at the warranted, or required, growth rate.

*Neoclassical growth theory*

Although Harrod and Domar recognized that $s$ and $v$ would in practice vary, their formal models treated them as constants. In the 1950s economists tried to construct formal models which allowed for changes in $s$ and $v$. The predominant approach was the "neoclassical" one, this originating in papers by Solow (1956) and Swan (1956). Solow, for example, criticized Harrod and Domar for studying the problem of the long run with short run tools. Harrod and Domar had, according to Solow, assumed fixed coefficients whereas, argued Solow, "One usually thinks of the long run as the domain of the neoclassical analysis, the land of the margin."[11] Solow proposed to accept all the Harrod–Domar assumptions, except that of the constant capital–output ratio.[12] There is, however, much more to Solow's model than this, for he assumes perfect competition, an assumption not made by either Harrod or Domar. In Solow's model the economy is a miniature general equilibrium model, with competitive equilibrium prevailing in the markets for labour, capital and output. At any moment there are given stocks of capital and labour, with competition ensuring full employment, and the equality of factor prices to marginal products. Output is linked to inputs of capital and labour by a production function exhibiting with marginal products. Growth comes about because a fraction of output is saved and invested, this increasing the capital stock. The labour force is assumed to be growing at an exogenously given rate. If capital accumulates at a rate different from the rate at which the labour force is growing, the capital–labour ratio will change, this in turn causing factor prices to change. Solow was able to show that, starting from any arbitrary capital stock, the economy would converge on an equilibrium where capital and labour were growing at the same rate, and where factor prices were constant.

When Solow's model, which was essentially the same as Swan's, is compared with the earlier models of Harrod and Domar, stress is often laid on the production function which allowed capital to be substituted for labour, but this is not the main difference. The significant point about Solow's model is that it tackled the problem of growth from the point of view of general equilibrium theory: as mentioned above, it is a miniature competitive equilibrium model, with competition ensuring that supply and demand are equal in all markets, all the time. It is a dynamic version of the model analysed by Hicks in *The Theory of Wages* (1932), a model in which competition ensures that Keynesian problems do not arise. This is in marked contrast to the models of both Harrod and Domar which, for all their differences, both claimed to say something about the course of unemployment over time.

Much of the vast literature appearing on growth theory in the 1960s was concerned with relaxing the heroic abstractions made in Solow's one-sector model. The most obvious was to disaggregate, the first step being to construct models with two sectors, one producing consumption goods, the other investment goods (Meade, 1961; Uzawa, 1961). This model worked in much the same way as Solow's model, though making the general equilibrium aspects of the model more explicit: supply and demand determine the relative prices of the two goods as well as factor prices.[13] Attempts were made to consider alternative technologies, and to allow for technical progress in a more realistic way – for example, so called "vintage models", in which the productivity of capital goods is assumed to depend on when they were made, newer ones being more productive than old ones. However, whilst there was no problem in extending the model to cover a wide variety of consumption goods, problems emerged when a variety of capital goods was introduced.

One of the most significant problems is what has become known as the "Hahn problem" (Hahn, 1966). The essence of this problem is that the value of a capital good depends on its yield, this including any capital gains from holding the capital good. A rise in the price of any capital good will result in a capital gain, this raising the yield and hence raising the demand still further, giving a further capital gain. The instability this causes was found to apply to a wide class of models.

An alternative approach was to move closer to macroeconomics, introducing money explicitly into growth models. The most common approach here, though there were exceptions, was to postulate a government which financed its debts by issuing debt which the private sector purchased. Instead of holding only capital, the private sector now held two assets, capital and government debt, demands for these two assets depending on their relative yields. Though its only function was to be held as an asset, this government debt was called "money". Some of the economists who analysed this type of model retained the competitive equilibrium assumptions (e.g. Tobin, 1965; Sidrauski, 1969), whereas others departed from the competitive equilibrium framework by allowing markets to be out of equilibrium, admitting the possibility of unemployment. (e.g. Rose, 1973; Uzawa, 1973; Stein, 1971). Within this framework an extra variable, the growth rate of the money supply, was introduced, and it was possible to analyse the effects of this on the equilibrium growth path.

In virtually all this literature, the long run equilibrium growth rate was taken as exogenous, determined by the rate of population growth and the rate of growth of productivity. What then did growth models show? (1) They showed how an economy might, starting from an arbitrary starting point, move towards an equilibrium growth path on which the growth rate would be that set by population growth and technical progress. (2) Although the equilibrium *growth rate* was exogenous, other characteristics of the long run equilibrium, such as consumption per head, did depend on parameters such as the propensity to save, or, in "monetary" models, the growth rate of the money supply. These relationships could be investigated.

### Von Neumann, Ramsey and optimal growth

An alternative approach to the problem of production, which avoids the problem of measuring capital, is to deal with capital as a list of specific physical capital goods. The seminal paper dealing with growth within this framework was that of von Neumann (1938). This paper used a linear model of production. There was a set of productive processes, each using a specified list of inputs to produce a specified list of outputs. No capital aggregate was needed. The problem of fixed capital was dealt with by including old capital goods in the list of outputs. This means that, for example, a process might comprise:

1 unit labour + 1 new machine → 1 unit food + 1 old machine.

To obtain a growth model von Neumann assumed that the supply of labour was perfectly elastic at a fixed, subsistence wage rate, and that all profits were invested. His model, apart from the absence from it of any scarce resources, thus had a very classical flavour.

Von Neumann went on to prove that there existed a balanced growth path along which the economy could expand, and to find the growth path with the highest growth rate. He was able to show that on this growth path with the maximal growth rate: (1) there would be a set of prices and a rate of interest such that, if they prevailed, a competitive economy would grow at this growth rate; and (2) this interest rate would equal the growth rate.[14]

A natural development from this model was that economists tried to generalize it, and to analyse similar models, such as Leontief's, one based on a simpler technology than von Neumann's model. For example, if the assumption of a subsistence wage rate were dropped, it was possible to show that as the real wage rose, the von Neumann growth rate fell. Thus if the growth rate of the labour force were fixed, it was possible to find the real wage rate at which the economy (and hence demand for labour) would grow at the same rate as the supply of labour. If the assumption that all profits were saved was relaxed, it followed that the rate of growth was equal to the rate of interest multiplied by the fraction of profits saved.

The von Neumann model raised the question of optimal growth, which is where we need to bring in another pre-war contribution, that of Ramsey (1927). Like von Neumann, Ramsey was concerned with optimal growth, but where von Neumann was concerned to find the highest growth rate consistent with the technology, Ramsey tackled the problem from the consumers' point of view. Ramsey's problem involved finding the path of capital accumulation, not necessarily with a constant growth rate, which maximized the present value of consumers' utility. Much work was done in the 1950s and 1960s on the problem of optimal growth, both capital orientated (von Neumann's problem of maximizing the rate of capital accumulation) and consumption orientated (Ramsey's problem), such problems being seen as relevant to the problem of planning. Several contributions to this literature are worth picking out. An influential early paper was Malinvaud (1953), which looked at the relationship of Pareto efficiency and competitive equilibrium in a model with an infinite time horizon.[15] Another important contribution was that of Dorfman, Samuelson and Solow (1958), which brought the notion of the "turnpike" to the notice of less mathematical economists.[16] Though proofs of turnpike theorems usually involve complicated mathematics, the basic idea is very simple. Suppose that there are two goods, $x$ and $y$, and that an economy starts with initial stocks of $x_0$ and $y_0$ in Figure 25.1. Assume the objective is to accumulate as much capital as possible by time $T$, but to retain the initial ratio of $x$ to $y$. In other words the objective is to move as far as possible along the line OR. The problem is what path to follow. Now assume the von Neumann path is ON. This is the balanced growth path along which the growth rate is maximized. The turnpike theorem says that the optimal path will be one which goes towards the von Neumann path (the "turnpike", of "motorway"), moves along it for a while, and then returns towards the target shortly before time $T$. In the same way that it pays a driver to use a turnpike even if it is not the most direct route, if her journey is sufficiently long, so it is optimal for the economy to grow along the von Neumann growth path if the time horizon is sufficiently long. It could thus

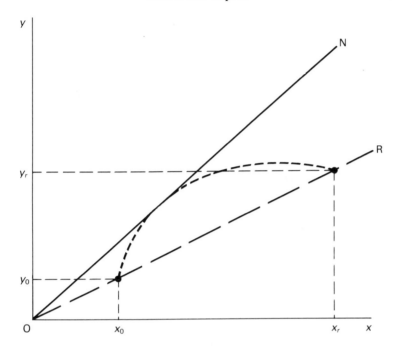

FIGURE 25.1 *The Turnpike*

be argued that the turnpike theorem gives relevance to the von Neumann growth path, for there is, in general, no reason to assume either that planners will desire balanced growth for its own sake, or that the economy will have exactly the right initial stocks to follow the von Neumann path immediately.

When approaching the problem of optimal growth from the consumption side, contact was made with aggregative growth models. The main result here was that derived simultaneously by Robinson (1962b), who called it the "neoclassical theorem", and Phelps (1961), whose name "the golden rule of accumulation" became the accepted one. The golden rule deals with the problem of maximizing steady state consumption per head, stating that it will be maximized if the rate of interest, equal to the marginal product of capital, equals the growth rate.[17] Planners may not wish to maximize steady state consumption per head, but it was shown that the golden rule growth path was related to Ramsey's more general problem in much the same way that the von Neumann growth path was to the capital orientated planning problem discussed above.

### "Keynesian" growth models

Most of the growth models discussed so far fall under the heading "neoclassical".[18] Throughout the period, however, a small but widely noticed group of economists argued against this approach, with its assumptions of smooth factor substitution and competitive markets, putting forward alternative theories of growth and distribution. The main members of this group were Robinson, Kaldor and Pasinetti. The main thrust of their critique of neoclassical models concerned the theory of capital, considered below. In addition, however, the neoclassical method of studying equilibrium was vehemently criticized. The main critic was perhaps Robinson, who argued that neoclassical models neglected what she called "historical time". Her own models, however, were not much better in that she concentrated her attention on *golden age growth*, a concept identical to the neoclassical steady state, where an economy is in equilibrium with a constant growth rate. Her approach did, however, have the merit of stressing the unrealistic nature of the concept.[19]

Common to the theories of Robinson, Kaldor and Pasinetti was the so called "Keynesian" theory of income distribution. There were two sources from which this theory sprang. One was the "widow's cruse" theory of profits contained in Keynes' *Treatise on Money*, taken up again in his *How to Pay for the War*.[20] The other source was Kalecki's theory of the trade cycle. Kalecki was a Polish economist who, as early as 1933, had derived a theory which had much in common with Keynes' *General Theory*.[21] An important aspect of Kalecki's work was that, as a result of his Marxist background, he concentrated on income distribution, something neglected in the *General Theory*. Kalecki argued that profits were proportional to the sum of capitalists' consumption and investment.[22]

The most widely known version of the Keynesian theory of distribution is, however, that of Kaldor (1956).[23] In deriving this theory Kaldor's starting point was that, in equilibrium, national income, which is identically equal to the sum of profits and wages, must equal consumption plus investment. Using self-explanatory notation,

$$P + W = C + I.$$

The simplest case is obtained by assuming that all wages are consumed, and that a fraction, $s$, of profits is saved, so that

$$C = (1 - s)P + W.$$

From these two equations it follows that

$$P/K = (1/s)\ I/K$$

where $P/K$ is the rate of profit on capital and $I/K$ the growth rate.[24] The rate of profit is determined by the growth rate and the propensity to save out of profits. The Keynesian theory asserts that it is investment that is exogenous, and that this determines the rate of profit.

Though this theory was used by its authors to provide an alternative to the marginal productivity theory of profits, the two are in no way contradictory. Savings behaviour and whether or not firms maximize profits,[25] the basis for marginal productivity theory, are separate issues.

Although attempts were made to destroy the theory, either by ridicule, or by criticizing its formulation,[26] it was a theory for which a defence could be provided. It might depend on assumptions which, from a neoclassical point of view, look peculiar, but that is a different matter.

## 25.2   THE THEORY OF CAPITAL

*Robinson's complaints*[27]

The post-war controversies over the theory of capital, to which Joan Robinson was the main contributor, are sometimes seen as a reaction against aggregative growth models. But though such growth models clearly fuelled the controversy, they were not its starting point, for Robinson's original article, "The production function and the theory of capital", which started the controversy, was published in 1953, the first neoclassical growth models appearing only in 1956. Robinson's target was rather marginal productivity theories of distribution of the Hicksian type.

Robinson opened her article with a direct attack on the neoclassical concept of the production function. Firstly, she argued that by emphasizing the role of factor substitution, it diverted attention from the more important issues of factor supply and technical change. More important, however, was her argument that the proponents of an aggregate production function had evaded the issue of how capital was to be measured.

Moreover the production function has been a powerful instrument of miseducation. The student of economic theory is taught to write $O=f(L,C)$ where $L$ is a quantity of labour, $C$ is a quantity of capital and $O$ a rate of output of commodities. He is instructed to assume all workers alike, and to measure $L$ in man-hours of labour; he is told something about the index number problem involved in choosing a unit of output; and he is then hurried on to the next question, in the hope that he will forget to ask in what units $C$ is measured. Before he ever does ask, he has become a professor, and so sloppy habits of thought are handed on from one generation to the next.[28]

In this article and in her subsequent writings[29] the neoclassical theory is attacked on three grounds.[30] It is important to keep these separate as they are completely separate arguments. (1) There is the Keynesian objection that demand may be insufficient to ensure full employment.[31] (2) Next there are Robinson's strictures against the use of the concept of equilibrium. She argued that equilibrium was not something an economy could ever get into: either an economy was, and always had been, in equilibrium, or else it would never be in equilibrium.[32] Her arguments here raised a variety of issues, concerning expectations, the age structure of the capital stock and the extent to which technical coefficients were fixed when capital goods were installed. (3) The most important argument, however, was that the production function could not be used *even to compare two equilibrium paths*, let alone to say anything about an economy out of equilibrium.

To understand this last point we have to consider the role of capital in the neoclassical account of capital accumulation.[33] The essence of the neoclassical story is that capital is accumulated by saving, the amount of consumption sacrificed being equal to the amount of capital created. This capital earns the marginal product of capital, which is the yield (interest) available to the saver. "Capital" here represents *two* things: the amount of saving undertaken, and the resulting change in the stock of goods (on which the marginal product of capital depends). Robinson's argument was that it was in general *impossible* to find a single measure of capital which could represent these two things. The reason why the value of the capital stock on which interest was calculated (the stock of savings) could not be the same as the physical capital stock was found in the so called price–Wicksell effect. This was the effect whereby any difference in the capital stock would result in a different rate of interest and hence a different relative price between consumption goods and capital.[34] At different interest rates the same sacrifice of consumption goods would produce different changes in the real capital stock.

In the 1950s and 1960s a typical response to this argument was to admit that Robinson was right in principle, but to treat the one-sector model, in which these problems are assumed away (there is a single commodity, usable either for consumption or as capital) served as a rough approximation to more realistic models. Consider Swan's defence of the one-sector model:

From the idea of capital as a single stock there is in principle no sudden transition to the enormous who's who of all the goods in existence. Between the two extremes lies an ascending scale of nth-order dynamic systems, in which capital like everything else is more and more finely subdivided and dated, with ascending degrees of (potential) realism and (actual) complexity.[35]

A similar view was taken by Solow (1957) who, in defending econometric work using an aggregate production function, argued: "One can at least hope that the aggregate analysis gives some notion of the way a detailed analysis would lead."[36] He makes it clear, however, that he cannot provide a rigorous justification for this hope:

let me make explicit that I would not try to justify what follows [the use of an aggregate production function] by calling on fancy theorems on aggregation and index numbers. Either this kind of aggregate analysis appeals or it doesn't. Personally I belong to both schools. If it does, I think one can draw some crude but useful conclusions from the results.[37]

## Sraffa

Before considering some of the arguments which arose as a result of Robinson's claims, we have to consider another contribution which had a profound influence on the way the debate proceeded, namely Sraffa's *Production of Commodities by Means of Commodities* (1960). This was subtitled "Prelude to a Critique of Economic Theory", and was intended to revive the Ricardian and Marxian approach to the problem of value and distribution. In contrast to the neoclassical tradition where commodity prices and the distribution of income are determined simultaneously, distribution is, in the Ricardian tradition as interpreted by Sraffa, determined *prior to* commodity prices: distribution is determined at the macroeconomic level, after which prices can be calculated from costs of production. The book's influence was threefold.

(1) Sraffa influenced the way in which the problem of capital was approached. His method, followed in the "reswitching" controversy which followed, was to consider a linear technology of the Leontief type. A technique of production was made up of a series of processes such as:

4 tons corn + 3 tons iron + 2 units labour → 5 tons iron
2 tons corn + 2 tons iron + 1 unit labour → 3 tons wheat.

For such a technique it was possible to write down equations relating commodity prices, the wage rate and the rate of profit:

$$(4P^C + 3P^I + 2W) (1 + r) = 5P^I$$
$$(2P^C + 2P^I + 1W) (1 + r) = 3P^C.$$

Bearing in mind that we are free to take one of these prices as *numéraire*, these equations can be solved to give a relation between the rate of profit and the real wage rate (in terms of the *numéraire*). It can be shown that there will be a negative relationship between the rate of profits and the real wage rate, the exact form of the relationship depending on the capital–labour ratios in the two sectors.

Although Sraffa was not the first to use this type of technology, his work led to the technological possibilities open to the economy being represented by a set of techniques of production, each technique having its own set of input–output coefficients. At any real wage rate, the technique actually used would be the one which yielded the highest rate of profit. From such a set of techniques it is possible to derive relationships between the wage rate, the rate of profit, output and capital per head.

(2) Sraffa's book revived interest, as Sraffa had intended, in the Ricardian/ Marxian theory of value, relating the problem of capital measurement to the problems Ricardo and Marx had encountered with the theory of value.[38] One of the reasons for this was that Sraffa solved the technical problems underlying Ricardo's search for an invariable measure of value. He showed that prices could be measured in terms of the "standard commodity", an artificial commodity constructed so as to be produced with the economy's average capital–labour ratio. This invariable measure, however, could not do what Ricardo had wanted it to do, for whenever the technique of production changed, so too would the standard commodity itself.[39]

(3) Sraffa provided an alternative view of economics, one free from some of the alleged ideological implications of neoclassical theory.[40] The argument was that equations such as those above are insufficient to determine both the real wage rate and the rate of profit. Sraffa interpreted this to mean

that the distribution of income must be determined *outside* the system of pricing. One way is the Ricardian one of assuming the real wage rate to be fixed at subsistence; alternatively we might add a rate of exploitation (the ratio of profits to wages) in a Marxian manner. For Sraffa the details were not so important as the fact that it made it possible for him to argue that distribution and price determination were not simultaneous: distribution was logically prior to pricing, for once distribution is determined, the equations described above can be used to determine commodity prices. Sraffa saw this approach as radically different from the neoclassical.[41]

### Reswitching

The issue which dominated discussions of capital theory in the 1960s was "reswitching". To understand this we must consider a conventional neoclassical production function with diminishing marginal products. Such a production function implies that as the rate of interest falls,[42] more capital-intensive techniques of production are introduced, and output per head rises. When the technology is analysed in terms of a set of Sraffian techniques, however, the possibility arises that as the rate of interest falls, the economy may, instead of moving towards a more capital-intensive technique, return to a less capital-intensive technique previously adopted at a lower rate of interest. In other words, as the rate of interest is reduced, the capital–output ratio, and possibly output per head as well, may first rise and then fall. This is the phenomenon known as "reswitching". Its importance was that it made it clear that the technology could be represented by a neoclassical production function only under very special circumstances.[43]

By the mid 1960s it became accepted that these arguments undermined the one-sector neoclassical model, the classic statement of this being that of Samuelson (1966b):

> The phenomenon of switching back at a very low interest rate to a set of techniques that had seemed viable only at a very high interest rate involves more than esoteric technicalities. It shows that the simple tale told by Jevons, Böhm-Bawerk, Wicksell and other neoclassical writers – alleging that, as the interest rate falls in consequence of abstention from present consumption in favour of future, technology must become in some sense more "roundabout", more "mechanized" and more "productive" – cannot be universally valid. ... There often turns out to be no unambiguous way of characterizing processes as "more capital intensive", more "mechanized" more "roundabout", except in the *ex post* tautological sense of being adopted at a lower interest rate and involving a higher real wage.[44]

### Capital and general equilibrium

Controversy continued throughout the 1960s, however, for a variety of reasons, the main one being that the implications of reswitching for disaggregated neoclassical models were still not clear. Critics claimed that the whole of general equilibrium theory, based on supply and demand, was undermined, whilst others argued that only aggregative models were affected.[45]

From a methodological point of view, two responses to this situation are particularly interesting. One was to argue that the possibility of reswitching was an empirical issue.[46] Samuelson (1966b) doubted whether reswitching was very important,[47] whilst others investigated conditions necessary to rule out reswitching.[48] Most extreme of all was Ferguson's declaration that the whole issue was an empirical one, and that "Until the econometricians have the answers for us, placing reliance on neoclassical economic theory is a matter of faith."[49]

The other interesting response was that of Solow (1963), for he tried to re-instate the neoclassical vision through adopting a different approach, one which dispensed, so he claimed, with the need to measure capital. His approach was to ask what we needed to know about the technology in order to construct an optimal plan. Thus he argued that the crucial concept was not capital but the rate of return on investment: if a unit of consumption is sacrificed in one period, what return will it provide in terms of additional consumption in the following period. This was Fisher's rate of return.[50] Solow's argument was criticized by Pasinetti (1969), who argued that implicit in the Fisher approach was an "unobtrusive postulate", which amounted to *assuming* that capital intensity varied inversely with the rate of interest. The details of his argument are not so important as the reason why it attracted so much interest: it claimed to show that not only was the one-sector parable untenable, but so too were more general models. Solow's approach of diverting attention to the rate of return on investment did not lessen the controversy.

## Intertemporal general equilibrium

The reason why the critics of neoclassical economics were so persistent is obvious: they believed that neoclassical theories of growth and distribution were fundamentally flawed. Why, however, did the proponents of neoclassical economics not simply ignore these criticisms? Why was reswitching seen as more than a minor puzzle? The answer would appear to be that it concerns a fundamental assumption made throughout the theory of competitive equilibrium: the assumption of diminishing marginal rates of substitution.[51] Without diminishing marginal rates of substitution there is no assurance that the familiar tangency conditions will yield a maximum rather than a minimum of profits. To emphasize the importance of the idea, note that a similar assumption has to be made about utility functions, otherwise the tangency of an indifference curve with a budget line would imply minimization, not maximization, of utility. The assumption of diminishing marginal rates of substitution is as fundamental to the theory of competitive equilibrium as is the assumption of rational behaviour (maximization of profits or utility).

An implication of diminishing marginal rates of substitution is that the price system is "connected": that if an allocation of resources is optimal at two sets of prices, it will be optimal at all intermediate sets of prices. To see this, consider an isoquant of the type often found in linear programming:

one with a series of corners. The corner points are optimal at a range of factor price ratios: for example, in Figure 25.2, B will be an optimum provided that the iso-cost lines are steeper than BC and flatter than AB. The point is that if a point, B, is optimal at two factor price ratios, then it is also optimal at any intermediate factor price ratios.[52] Reswitching, however, implies that an allocation of resources may be optimal at two sets of prices, but not at intermediate sets of prices. In other words, that the price system is not connected. Thus reswitching raised doubts about a fundamental assumption: about part of the "hard core" of neoclassical economics.

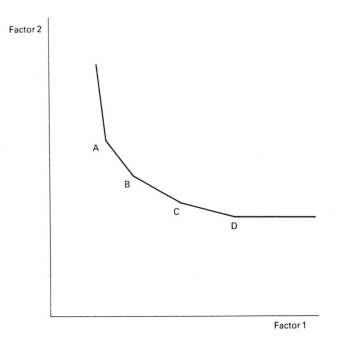

FIGURE 25.2   *An Isoquant*

A resolution of this paradox was provided in Bliss's *Capital Theory and the Distribution of Income* (1975).[53] The key to this book is that capital theory is discussed in the context of an explicit model of intertemporal general equilibrium. This distinguishes goods not only in terms of their physical characteristics, but also in terms of their date of delivery. Thus if we have $n$ types of good, and $T$ time periods, we have $nT$ dated "commodities". If there is a market for each dated commodity, we have $nT$ prices. Denote the price of the $i$th commodity in period $t$ as $p_{i,t}$. Implicit in these prices is a set of interest rates. For example, the interest rate on good $i$ at time $t$, $r_{i,t}$, is given by $(p_{1i,t} - p_{i,t-1})/p_{i,t-1}$. This is the yield to be obtained from holding good $i$ for one period at time $t$.

Reswitching is paradoxical because it implies that the set of prices at which a particular technique is chosen is not connected: that a technique is optimal at two sets of prices, but not at sets of prices in between. Bliss, using this intertemporal general equilibrium framework, was able to show that this was an illusion.

Bliss used this intertemporal general equilibrium framework to argue that the paradox of reswitching arose because economists were in the habit of assuming only a limited set of prices: economists werein the habit of considering only those sets of prices in which the rate of interest was constant. If we broaden the set of prices we consider, so that we allow for price paths on which the rate of interest is changing, then the paradox disappears. This rather abstract idea is best understood with the aid of a simple example. Assume that there is a single commodity, and three time periods. Suppose that there is reswitching in the sense that a given technique is optimal at rates of interest of 10% and 20%, but that some other technique is chosen if the interest rate is 15%. The question is whether this implies that the price system is not connected?

Take the price of the commodity in period 1 as numeraire. If the rate of interest is 10%, the price must be 1.1 in period 2, and 1.21 in period 3. If the rate of interest is 20%, the corresponding prices are 1.2 and 1.44. These prices are shown in Table 25.1. If the price system is connected, the

Table 25.1

|   | A $r = 10\%$ | B $r = 20\%$ | C |
|---|---|---|---|
| 1 | 1 | 1 | 1 |
| 2 | 1.1 | 1.2 | 1.15 |
| 3 | 1.21 | 1.44 | 1.325 |

technique we are considering must be optimal at an average of these two sets of prices. Such an average is shown in column 3 of the table. For example, the price in period 2 is $(1.1 + 1.2)/2 = 1.15$. The important thing to note about column 3 is that the rate of interest is *not* 15%: it is 15% from periods 1 to 2, but only 14% from periods 2 to 3.

By showing that a technique may be optimal at 10% and at 20%, but not at 15%, reswitching suggests that the price system is not connected. This is, however, an "optical illusion", for if we allow for price paths with a variable rate of interest, the price system appears completely connected.[54] The paradox disappears.

## 25.3  CONCLUSIONS

For all the intellectual effort that went into growth and capital theory in the 1950s and 1960s, it can be argued that little light was shed on the factors causing some countries to grow faster than others. The origins of modern growth theory lay with Harrod and Domar, who were concerned about the possibility of secular stagnation. From the mid-1950s growth theory came to be incorporated within general equilibrium theory, and it attracted attention as the theory of dynamic equilibrium. From the early 1970s interest in growth theory lessened. Why?

(1) Growth theory ceased to be topical: the problems of inflation, unemployment and exhaustible resources came to be seen as more important than the problem of explaining the conditions under which steady growth might occur. In addition, the concept of rational expectations opened up new areas of theoretical research outside growth theory.

(2) More importantly, however, the main results obtainable within the framework of neoclassical growth theory had, by the early 1970s, been worked out. Growth theory was understood, and ceased to be a separate subject. Models of dynamic equilibrium could be used routinely by economists whose main concerns lay in other fields, such as public finance or monetary economics.

(3) Though many economists continued to defend the general neoclassical model, the Cambridge critique of the neoclassical production function did serve to emphasize that the one-sector neoclassical model could be no more than a parable. It also undermined the attempt to provide an empirical basis for growth theory through estimating aggregate production functions. Thus though the Cambridge critique was not the main reason for the loss of interest in growth theory, it was a contributory factor.

With the theory of capital, controversy was stimulated by economists who believed that the neoclassical research programme, based on maximization and marginal productivity, was fundamentally flawed, and in need of replacement. To explain the persistence of the controversy, however, we need to explain why neoclassical economists could not simply ignore the criticisms, as they ignore so many others. The reason would seem to be that reswitching the "paradox" of reswitching cast doubt on the assumption of convexity, fundamental to so much of mainstream economic theory. It was because it cast doubt on such a fundamental postulate that dismissing reswitching as "unlikely" was beside the point.

It is because of this that Bliss's defence of the neoclassical theory, showing that reswitching does not imply any non-convexity at all, is so important. It is important, however, that this defence of neoclassical theory was achieved only at the cost of making it even clearer that the economy under discussion could not possibly describe any actual economy. With an aggregative neoclassical growth model it is possible to imagine that it could be extended to cope with the presence of uncertainty. With Bliss's intertemporal general equilibrium model it is clear that the introduction of time and uncertainty would involve radical changes in the theory.

# 26

# Money, Employment and Inflation

## 26.1 THE DEVELOPMENT OF THE KEYNESIAN SYSTEM

*The reception of the* General Theory

Keynes' *General Theory*[1] was the outcome of two decades in which an enormous amount of work was put into macroeconomic theorizing. For all Keynes' claims to novelty, much of the *General Theory*'s contents can be found elsewhere in the literature of the 1920s and 1930s, in particular in the writings of Pigou, Hawtrey and the Swedish school. Despite this continuity, however, discussions of modern macroeconomics have to start with the *General Theory*, the reason being that certain interpretations of it came to dominate post-war macroeconomics. Earlier contributions, irrespective of their merits, were almost completely eclipsed.

The *General Theory* was immediately successful, the extent and speed of its impact being unparalleled: the following year's *Economic Journal* was, perhaps not surprisingly, filled with reactions to the book; a symposium on it filled an issue of the 1937 *Quarterly Journal of Economics*; and within a couple of years the framework provided by the *General Theory* was being used not simply by Keynes' colleagues, but by complete outsiders and even by economists initially critical of it. One historian has made the claim that "During the ten or twelve years after its appearance the *General Theory* received more attention than Alfred Marshall's *Principles of Economics* had received in over 50 years."[2] A survey of contemporary economics published at the end of the 1940s indicates the extent of his influence: he was cited 98 times, compared with 56 citations for Hicks, his nearest rival. In addition, ideas stemming from the *General Theory* formed the subject matter of at least part of 15 out of the 23 chapters in the survey.[3]

To a certain extent the reception of Keynesian economics can be seen in terms of the emergence of a new generation of economists, the disciples of Keynes (e.g. Samuelson, Robinson, Harrod, Meade, Lerner) belonging to the younger generation, the critics (e.g. Leontief, Schumpeter, Knight, Viner) to the older generation.[4] This still leaves open, however, the question of why Keynesian ideas were found so attractive. One reason was undoubtedly that Keynes was addressing an important contemporary problem: though recovery from the depression was by 1937 well under way, the depression of 1929 to 1933 had had a profound impact. Samuelson has argued that although it still survived, events since 1929 had caused belief in the existing orthodoxy to atrophy, and that the *General Theory* provided an alternative.[5] Also important was the theoretical challenge provided by the *General Theory*, for not only did it contain a wealth of ideas capable of development, but it also contained many puzzles requiring solution. Some economists have gone so far as to claim that its complexity was an essential ingredient of its success.[6]

With hindsight, however, it is perhaps the arguments used in criticism of the *General Theory* which are most interesting, for it is easy to see its attractions. Consider the arguments used by Schumpeter and Leontief, both of whom criticized Keynes on methodological grounds. Leontief concentrated on Keynes' method, shared with other members of the "Cambridge school", which Leontief described as "implicit theorizing".[7] By implicit theorizing Leontief meant the practice of defining terms in such a way as to imply a definite theoretical relationship between these terms and the basic postulates of the theory, but without ever specifying this relationship.[8] Such a procedure, according to Leontief, made rational discussion of a theory very difficult, for it was never clear to a critic exactly what the theory involved. An example was Keynes' use of aggregate demand and supply curves without specifying the factors on which they depended sufficiently carefully for it to be possible to say whether or not it was correct to treat them as independent of each other. He agreed with Schumpeter's accusation that Keynes shared what Schumpeter described as the Ricardian vice: "the habit of piling a heavy load of practical conclusions upon a tenuous framework, which was unequal to it yet seemed in its simplicity not only attractive but also convincing". Schumpeter saw this as having dramatic implications, for not only did Keynes influence the best minds of the economics profession, but he also "brought back the happy times of Mrs. Marcet, when every schoolgirl, by learning the use of a few simple concepts, acquired competence to judge all the ins and outs of the infinitely complex organism of capitalist society".[9] The simplifications to which Schumpeter objected included the theory's static and short run nature; its neglect of the effects of investment on capacity; and the assumption that people respond to real values everywhere except when it comes to bargaining over money wages. It was only with all the givens implied by these assumptions that "the three great simplifiers", as Schumpeter called the consumption function, the marginal efficiency of capital and liquidity preference, could determine national income and implement Keynes' vision of the economic system.[10]

It was in the course of the debates over the *General Theory* that the contributions of the Swedish economists were brought to a wide audience. This was done by Ohlin (1937), who coined the phrase "the Stockholm school" to describe the work of Lindahl, Myrdal and himself; work which he saw as anticipating the essential ideas of the *General Theory*.[11]

*Extensions of the* General Theory

Much of the literature appearing in the decade after 1936 was concerned with clarifying and debating detailed points made in the *General Theory*: liquidity preference versus loanable funds theories of the interest rate; the value of aggregative economics; the nature of the multiplier; the role of hoarding in the theory of liquidity preference. These controversies were, in the words of one historian, "long and tedious",[12] for though there were many points at which Keynes' arguments needed correcting, and though some important modifications were introduced (such as the *ex ante/ex post* distinction), they did not result in any fundamental changes to the Keynesian theory.

Of more interest are the investigations into the individual functions used in the *General Theory*. The notable success here concerned the consumption function, where Keynesian theory was examined in the light of empirical data, especially in the US. Studies of family budgets proved consistent with Keynes' consumption function, but against this evidence were cyclical variations in the propensity to consume, and evidence that in the long run the consumption function was, for the US at least, shifting upwards. This proved an ideal area for development, the most well-known theories being those of Duisenberry (1948), Friedman (1957) and Modigliani and Brumberg (1954). Of these the one that took firmest root was the permanent income/life cycle theory (it can be argued that the two are substantially the same). The reason usually given for the success of this theory[13] is that the Keynesian hypothesis was refuted by the evidence, the permanent income/life cycle theory replacing it because of its ability to explain this evidence. This is, however, only part of the story, for it could be argued that the success of the permanent income/life cycle theory arose because it explained the consumption function in terms of individual maximizing behaviour: until it had been explained in these terms there was a sense in which it was not understood.

This interpretation of the theory of the consumption function is supported by developments in other areas, such as money and wages. Shortly after the *General Theory* evidence was produced to show that wages did not vary over the cycle in the way predicted by the *General Theory*.[14] Though this added to the controversy surrounding the *General Theory* this did not stimulate new theoretical developments until the 1970s. Two reasons suggest themselves. The first is that the Keynesian system emphasized demand rather than supply, so the behaviour of money and real wages could be regarded as an anomaly, peripheral to the main theory. This changed in the 1970s. The other reason is that until "disequilibrium" models appeared, economists did not have a theoretical framework in which to analyse the problem: there was no microeconomic theory available to explain why firms should not employ labour to the point where the real wage equalled the marginal product of labour. The availability of suitable techniques was also important in attempts to improve on the Keynesian theory of the demand for money, where the main achievements were the theories of Baumol (1952) and Tobin (1958). The contribution of both these theories was to make sense of the demand for money, through providing an explanation in terms of individual maximizing behaviour. Thus it can be argued that, in these areas, a crucial factor was the desire to make sense of Keynesian ideas in terms of individual maximizing behaviour.

The *General Theory* was also extended by being applied to new areas: the business cycle (e.g. Harrod, 1936), growth (e.g. Harrod, 1939), the balance of payments (e.g. Robinson, 1937), and inflation (e.g. Keynes, 1940). These areas are discussed elsewhere in this chapter.

### Keynes and the classics

In discussing the debates over the *General Theory* we have so far avoided the central issue – that of the nature of the *General Theory* itself. The tone of the debate was set by Keynes himself when he presented his theory as an alternative to a "classical" theory, his own theory being the more general. Controversy was aroused, not only because of Keynes' claim to have provided a more general theory, but also because Keynes' version of the classical theory was based on Pigou's *Theory of Employment* (1933), a modern work which to many economists was as hard to understand as the *General Theory*. There were thus two aspects to the controversy: working out what the classical theory really was,[15] and working out how it related to Keynes' theory, for it was by solving these problems that economists hoped to sort out what were the essential features of the *General Theory*. Here the outstanding contribution was that of Hicks (1937, 1939a) whose interpretation of the *General Theory* became accepted to such an extent that it became, for many economists, not only synonymous with Keynesian economics, but the only framework within which macroeconomics could be conducted.

As mentioned above,[16] Hicks came to the *General Theory* familiar with both Walrasian general equilibrium theory, and the writings of the Swedish economists. Furthermore he has already produced both a diagram with which to analyse three-way exchange, and an aggregative model involving labour, loans and output.[17] Though in no way an anticipation of the *General Theory*, this led naturally into an interpretation of the *General Theory* as a temporary general equilibrium model, analysed in terms of IS and LM curves. The Swedish influence was most prominent in *Value and Capital* where expectations were treated more thoroughly than in his 1937 article, and where Myrdal's *ex post/ex ante* distinction was used to sort out the relationship between saving and investment, Keynes' exposition of this having caused great confusion.[18] His 1937 article showed what could be done with the diagram, in particular using the liquidity trap and the horizontal LM curve to portray the *General Theory* as being concerned with the "economics of depression", applying when the prospective attractiveness of investment is so low that the IS curve cuts the flat portion of the LM curve. A higher incentive to invest would cause the IS curve to cut the steep portion of the LM curve, producing "classical" results.[19]

The IS–LM apparatus permitted Hicks to relax certain of Keynes' assumptions, inserting income in the investment function and the interest rate in the savings function. This was significant in that it enabled him to find a similarity between Keynes and Wicksell, relating Keynesian ideas to Wicksell's distinction between the natural and money rates of interest.[20]

Differences between Keynes and the classics were argued to depend on the slopes of the IS and LM curves, and hence on the elasticities of savings, investment and demand for money with respect to income and the interest rate.

This approach, of using a simple four-market general equilibrium model, dominated discussion of Keynesian economics until the 1960s, controversy settling on the specific assumptions necessary to produce Keynesian results: was unemployment caused by wage stickiness (in which case some of Keynes' critics would consider themselves vindicated) or could it be caused by a liquidity trap or insufficient and interest-inelastic investment demand? It was in this discussion that the "real balance effect" came to be seen as crucial, for it was this which undermined the claim that insufficient investment demand or a liquidity trap was sufficient to create the possibility of an unemployment equilibrium, independently of wage rigidity. If wages were not rigid, unemployment would cause deflation which, through raising the real value of people's money balances, would raise consumption and increase employment.[21]

The climax of this debate came with Patinkin's *Money, Interest and Prices*, published in 1956 with an extensively revised edition in 1965. This book did two things. It provided a microeconomic theory on which monetary theory could be based, "redoing" Hicks' *Value and Capital* with money treated properly as a "very special good".[22] In addition it provided a definitive account, within the Hicksian framework, of the difference between Keynes and the classics. His conclusion was that a full employment equilibrium would exist and that it would be stable. Keynesian economics was the economics of disequilibrium, arising when the equilibrating forces were too weak to restore full employment "within a socially acceptable period of time".[23] Thus Keynes was seen not as having made a fundamental theoretical contribution so much as having drawn attention to the case relevant to policy-making, namely disequilibrium.

### The economics of disequilibrium

The interpretation of Keynesian economics described above became the established orthodoxy, enshrined in macroeconomics textbooks.[24] This changed, however, in the late 1960s when it was challenged first by Clower (1965), and later by Leijonhufvud in a widely read book *On Keynesian Economics and the Economics of Keynes* (1968). As its title implies, the book's claim was that what was generally taken to be "Keynesian economics" (namely the Hicksian interpretation) was in fact nothing like the economics of Keynes himself. Clower's point, which was taken up by Leijonhufvud, was present in *Money, Interest and Prices*, but was not fully developed there. It was that the Walrasian model, used by Hicks and Patinkin, did not deal with supply and demand in a manner appropriate to a discussion of Keynesian economics. The basis for this claim was that when markets fail to clear, transactors face not only budget and technological constraints, but also constraints on how much they can buy and sell. These constraints will affect demands and supplies in other markets. For example, if a household finds that it cannot sell as much labour as it wishes, it will have to demand a smaller quantity of consumption goods than it would otherwise demand. This explains why "Walras's Law", which states that the sum of realized excess demands must be zero, may fail: it is possible to have, for example, an excess supply of labour without there being any corresponding excess demand. It was on the basis of this argument that Clower and Leijonhufvud were able to claim that Keynes had made a fundamental contribution to the theory of value: he had analysed the behaviour of an economy in which markets do not necessarily clear.

Leijonhufvud buttressed this argument with many detailed arguments concerning aggregation, wage rigidity and expectations in order to show that the orthodox interpretation of Keynes was wrong. His central theme was that Keynesian economics was about what happened when there was no Walrasian auctioneer, and when quantities adjusted faster than prices in response to an imbalance between supply and demand. It is the absence of the auctioneer which means that transactions take place at disequilibrium prices, resulting in quantity constraints being imposed on buyers and sellers. Keynesian economics is thus about coordination failures which are inherent in the market mechanism, not about what happens when certain prices are held constant. It is thus Keynesian economics which is the more general case.

Clower and Leijonhufvud challenged the orthodox interpretation of Keynes, but neither of them provided an alternative, usable framework for doing short run macroeconomics. Indeed Leijonhufvud has, in the 1970s, reacted strongly against formal modelling of Keynesian economics, seeing the crucial aspects of the *General Theory* as lying at the "presuppositional level", it being possible to appraise Keynesian economics only in terms of "an informal and improvised meta-language", not in terms of a formal model.[25] A more formal analysis of Keynesian problems, embodying Clower's insight, was produced by Barro and Grossman (1971), who provided what they called a "general disequilibrium model".[26] Taking a model simplified so that only two markets (for labour and goods) need be considered, they showed the possibility of an equilibrium where output is low because demand for goods is low; and demand for goods is low because output, and hence income, is low. The significance of such an equilibrium is that it can arise even if the real wage rate is at its equilibrium level. In such a framework multiplier effects arise naturally. Though these "disequilibrium" models started off as attempts to provide theoretical explanations of Keynesian problems they did not stop there, for it proved possible to analyse other cases, in particular classical unemployment (caused by an excessive real wage rate) and repressed inflation (where there is general excess demand, both for goods and for labour). In addition such models could be used to explain the behaviour of wages over the cycle, to analyse the balance of payments (Dixit, 1978) and to analyse capital accumulation (Malinvaud, 1980). The basic ideas were also used at a microeconomic level.[27]

These models were still, however, not completely satisfactory, for they all took prices as given, failing to answer the question of why prices did not adjust to ensure full employment equilibrium. This was something to which answers could not be found at a macro level.

## 26.2   MONEY AND INFLATION

*The theory of inflation before 1958*

In the wake of the *General Theory* inflation began to be explained in terms of the flow of spending relative to the flow of output, rather than in terms of the quantity (stock) of money. The application of Keynesian ideas to inflation was made by Keynes himself in *How to Pay for the War* (1940): inflation was there viewed as produced by the combination of high purchasing power (and hence high expenditure) caused by war production and the reduced availability of goods caused by the diversion of goods into the war effort. The crucial assumption was that, because the economy was operating at full employment, any rise in demand would be met by a rise in prices rather than by a rise in output. In advancing this theory Keynes revived the "widow's cruse" theory of the *Treatise on Money*,[28] for he assumed that rising prices would cause a rise in profits, the shift in the distribution of income towards profits being the means through which output and expenditure were brought into balance. Such theories of inflation subsequently became known as "inflation gap" theories, inflation being caused by the "gap" between expenditure and the quantity of goods available to meet that expenditure, the most widely read account of such a model being that enshrined in Samuelson's (1948a) textbook. These inflation gap models differed from Keynes' in that there was less emphasis on changes in the distribution of income as the means whereby savings and investment would be brought into equilibrium: rising prices might reduce demand through money illusion, rising marginal tax rates, the real balance effect as well as or instead of through a change in income distribution.

A particularly interesting version of the inflation gap theory was Hansen's (1951) "two gap" model. The interesting feature of this model was that it dealt with both goods and labour markets: excess demand for goods would cause changes in the price of output; whilst excess demand for labour would cause changes in the money wage rate. Equilibrium required that prices and wages rise at the same rate, and hence that the goods gap and the labour, or factor, gap be equal. If the goods gap were larger than the factor gap, for example, the real wage would fall and so output and employment would be increased, thus reducing the goods gap and increasing the factor gap, bringing them into equality. The significance of the model is that it gives a particular equilibrium inflation rate; and that it represents inflation as the outcome of processes affecting the economy as a whole: inflation results not from what happens in a single market, but from the interaction of all the markets in the economy.

The 1950s was the era when it was common to distinguish between "demand", or "demand pull" and "cost", or "cost push" inflation.[29] Demand inflation covered the inflation gap theories just discussed, and also theories such as that of "demand shift" inflation, according to which inflation arose because prices were inflexible downwards: if demand shifts from good A to good B the price of A will rise, whereas that of B will not fall, so the overall price level rises.[30] Cost inflation, on the other hand, resulted from market power being used to push up wages or profit margins, with monetary and fiscal policy accommodating to the resulting rises in prices. Much attention was concentrated on unions and wage bargaining as a source of inflation. Issues raised included the degree of competition, oligopoly being seen as conducive to inflation; union rivalry; attempts to maintain or create wage differentials; and the pricing policies of firms.

*The Phillips curve*

Of more importance for subsequent developments in the theory of inflation was the emergence of the Phillips curve as the standard tool with which to analyse the problem of inflation.[31] The curve derived by Phillips (1958) was an *empirically determined* relationship between the rate of change of money wage rates and the rate of unemployment; Phillips claimed that a curve which he had derived from data for the period 1861 to 1913 would also explain data for both the inter-war and post-war periods. What gave this model its significance was that it could be explained theoretically in terms of a standard model of the labour market. Lipsey (1960a) provided such an explanation, taking the standard theory, according to which wage changes were proportional to excess demand for labour, and modifying it to allow for frictional unemployment and vacancies. This explained the position and the shape of Phillips' curve. The Phillips curve was discussed in relation to the US by Samuelson and Solow (1960), who also examined its implications for anti-inflation policy. In the late 1950s and the early 1960s an enormous number of empirical studies appeared which confirmed the negative relationship between inflation and unemployment that Phillips had discovered.[32]

The Phillips curve, in a sense, marked the demise of the distinction between demand and cost inflation. Though it could be used alongside the demand–cost distinction[33] this was unnecessary. Arguments could instead be conducted by incorporating more variables into the Phillips curve. One such attempt was that of Hines (1964), who inserted a measure of unionization to measure union power. This provoked much research, in the late 1960s and early 1970s, on appropriate measures of union power which could be inserted in a Phillips curve, either to prove or to disprove Hines' contention that union power had a significant impact on the inflation rate.[34] Far more significant, however, was the introduction of inflationary expectations into the Phillips curve. The main contributions here were two papers appearing in 1967–1968. Friedman's presidential address to the American Economic Association (1968) and Phelps (1967). The introduction of inflationary expectations was not new (for example, Samuelson and Solow had in 1960 raised the possibility that if the economy were run at high levels of unemployment inflationary expectations might fall, shifting the Phillips curve down)[35] but its implications had not been fully worked out before. Phelps and Friedman both argued that in the short run a downward-sloping Phillips curve would emerge, but that in the long run any trade-off between unemployment and inflation would disappear.

Friedman's argument was that the Phillips curve was, from the point of view of economic theory, mis-specified in that because supply and demand for labour both depended on real wages it was the rate of growth of real wages, not money wages, which should depend on unemployment. It was for this reason that expected inflation should appear on the right hand side of the Phillips curve: because everyone was concerned with real wages, a 1% rise in the expected inflation rate should lead to a 1% rise in the actual rate. Crucial to Friedman's argument was the concept of the "natural rate of unemployment", the unemployment rate consistent with a constant rate of inflation. He described this as the unemployment rate

that would be ground out by the Walrasian system of general equilibrium equations, provided that there is embedded in them the actual structural characteristics of the labour and commodity markets, including market imperfections, stochastic variability in demands and supplies, the cost of gathering information about job vacancies and labor availabilities, the costs of mobility, and so on.[36]

Unemployment would differ from this natural rate only if people made mistakes in their inflationary expectations: low unemployment would be the result of inflation being underestimated, high unemployment the result of its being overestimated.

The emphasis of Phelps' argument was rather different, but its conclusions were remarkably similar. Phelps was concerned, in a way that Friedman was not, with the microeconomics of the labour market: with the question of how labour markets operate when information is incomplete and costly. His argument was that information about wages would travel only slowly, the result of this being that in the short term a rise in demand would induce workers to supply more labour – when they received higher wage offers they would at first interpret this as meaning that they had been offered an unusually good wage rate; only later would they discover that wages generally had risen and that there was nothing special about the wage they had been offered. This approach was explored by Phelps and others in *Microeconomic Foundations of Employment and Inflation Theory* (1970), where all but one of the contributors used a version of the natural rate hypothesis.

These theoretical developments were reflected in empirical work, where, making the assumption that expectations could be modelled as a lagged function of past inflation rates (so-called "adaptive expectations") emphasis was on estimating the size of the coefficient attached to expected inflation: did a 1% increase in inflationary expectations cause inflation to rise by a full 1%, or would inflation rise by only a fraction of 1%?[37] This was important because if it was the latter then there would still be a trade-off between inflation and unemployment in the long run, albeit with a much steeper

Phillips curve than in the short run. If, on the other hand, the coefficient were unity then the natural rate hypothesis was vindicated. Initially empirical work suggested a coefficient significantly less than unity, with the result that the natural rate hypothesis was not accepted.[38] This attitude changed during the 1970s, however, when it became generally accepted that the long run Phillips curve must be vertical. One reason for this was empirical work: wage equations, perhaps due to the acceleration of inflation in the early 1970s, began to produce higher values for the coefficient on inflationary expectations. In addition, the relationship between unemployment and vacancies involved in the traditional approach appeared to break down. But more important were theoretical developments, in particular the arguments surrounding rational expectations. As long as the Phillips curve was thought of as something "tacked on" to a basically Keynesian model, there was no incongruity in having a non-vertical long run Phillips curve. As the Phillips curve became a more integral part of the model, a model supposedly grounded in the assumption of rational behaviour, it became natural to assume that the long run Phillips curve must be vertical. A symptom of this change was the replacement, in macroeconomics textbooks, of the IS–LM model with the aggregate supply and demand model as the main explanation of output and the price level.[39]

*Friedman and the quantity theory of money*

In the wake of Keynesian economics the quantity theory of money was neglected as an explanation of inflation and output in preference to the income expenditure approach. The quantity theory was far from neglected in economic theory, however, where the literature contained extensive discussion of two issues: the "classical dichotomy",[40] attacked by Keynes, according to which the real factors underlying supply and demand determined relative prices, with the quantity of money determining only the absolute price level; and the neutrality of money (whether an increase in the money supply will do anything other than raise all prices in the same proportion). Discussion was, however, at a purely theoretical level.[41] The main contribution towards reviving interest in the quantity theory as a useful macroeconomic tool was Friedman's article, "The quantity theory of money: a restatement" (1956). The central argument of this article is contained in the following quotation.

The quantity theory is in the first instance a theory of the *demand* for money. It is not a theory of output, or of money income, or of the price level. Any statement about these variables requires combining the quantity theory of money with some specifications about the conditions of supply of money and perhaps about other variables as well.[42]

In formulating a theory of the demand for money Friedman stressed that it was one asset, one way of holding wealth, and that demand for it could be analysed using the standard theory of consumer choice. This led him to write the demand for money function as

$$M = f(r_b, r_e, (1/P) \, (dP/dt), w, Y/P, u)$$

where demand for money depends on the expected yields on holding bonds and equities, the expected inflation rate, the ratio of human to non-human wealth, real income $(Y/P)$ and variables affecting tastes and preferences (summarized by $u$). Though the stress on price expectations and the inclusion of the ratio of human to non-human wealth (which caused demand for money to fluctuate over the cycle) differentiated Friedman's theory from that of Keynes, there is considerable justification for describing Friedman's theory as a more elegant statement of Keynes' theory of liquidity preference. The velocity of circulation is simply $1/f$.

The quantity theory, according to Friedman, comprised two assertions:

(i) the empirical hypothesis that the demand for money is stable – more stable than functions such as the consumption function that are offered as alternative key relations.
(ii) there are important factors affecting the supply of money that do not affect the demand for money.[43]

Friedman presents his ideas as a restatement of an oral tradition existing at Chicago, where a version of the quantity theory was kept alive by Simons, Mints, Knight and Viner,[44] a tradition more flexible than the Hayekian version dominant at LSE.[45] Because of this tradition, Friedman argued, Chicago economists were less vulnerable to the lure of Keynesian ideas. There is considerable evidence, however, that Friedman's restatement should rather be regarded as a new interpretation of the quantity theory, albeit one following on closely from the Chicago tradition. In addition, there is evidence that later versions of this Chicago tradition owed something to the Keynesian theory of liquidity preference.[46]

Whether a restatement of an earlier tradition, or an original interpretation of the quantity theory, Friedman's article set the pattern for the development of the quantity theory for the next decade. Friedman himself undertook empirical investigations into the two assertions listed above, research culminating in *A Monetary History of the United States, 1861–1960* (1963, with Schwarz).[47] In these studies he reached the conclusion that the supply of money had been to a substantial extent independent of demand, and that money had a strong influence on the economy. A particularly important conclusion was that there was a long and variable lag between monetary changes and their effects on the economy. This link, however, was strongest for large changes (deep depression cycles and substantial inflations): if changes in the money supply were only moderate then other factors were also important.[48] Though Friedman found a strong link operating from money to prices and income, he was able to defend the policy he had long since advocated (in *A Program for Monetary Stability*, 1946): that the object of monetary policy should be to expand the money supply at a steady rate.[49] Limitations of knowledge concerning the other factors affecting the economy, factors which were important in mild cycles, imposed definite limits to the possibilities for fine tuning the economy through monetary policy. The most that could be achieved was to prevent money from being a major source of disturbance.

Of particular interest is an episode which arose out of an attempt by Friedman and Meiselman (1963) to find a way of testing the quantity theory against the Keynesian theory. The test they proposed was to compare the "money multiplier" (relating income to the quantity of money) with the Keynesian investment multiplier. If the former was more stable, as Friedman and Meiselman contended, this was evidence for the quantity theory. This challenge was taken up, in particular by Ando and Modigliani (1965). Despite a whole issue of the *American Economic Review* being devoted to the question, the debate was inconclusive: it became agreed that simple models of this type were incapable of discriminating between the two theories.[50]

Throughout these discussions of the quantity theory Friedman had never provided an alternative to the Keynesian theory of how money was supposed to affect the economy – a theory of the monetarist "transmission mechanism". The overwhelming emphasis in his work was on empirical investigations based on a loosely specified theory. This situation changed in 1970–1971 when Friedman published two papers, later combined under the title "A theoretical framework for monetary analysis".[51] Here Friedman proposed a common framework in which Keynesianism and monetarism could be compared. This common framework was the Hicksian IS–LM model. As there were three variables to be determined, but only two equations (the IS and LM relations) there was a "missing equation". The simple quantity theory took output as given; the simple Keynesian theory added a fixed price level. Friedman added a theory of how changes in nominal income were broken down into changes in output and the price level.[52]

This discussion of Friedman's theoretical framework, however, was in many ways a hangover from the 1960s, for in the 1970s attention shifted, mainly because of the expectations augmented Phillips curve and the natural rate hypothesis. Attention shifted towards the dynamics of inflation and unemployment, and to the question of how expectations were formed. The arguments for monetarism came to centre on the dangers of accelerating inflation if the authorities tried to control unemployment. This argument and Friedman's earlier arguments could be combined to produce a case for aiming at a steady growth rate of the money supply: the government should try to control only what it is capable of controlling (the money supply, not unemployment), and because the lags involved made monetary policy hard to use in a discretionary manner, a fixed monetary rule should be pursued.

### Tobin's portfolio balance approach

An alternative approach to the theory of monetary policy was adopted by Tobin. Like Keynes and Friedman, Tobin viewed money as an asset, but rather than distinguish a unique asset, or set of assets, to be called money, Tobin considered a variety of assets ranging from currency at one end to physical capital at the other.[53] He constructed a series of models of the financial sector in which a market was assumed to exist for each asset – currency and various types of bank deposit being considered separately. In these models the crucial variable was the valuation ratio, Tobin's "*q*", which is the ratio of the market valuation of the capital stock to its value at replacement cost. It is this variable which measures the incentive to invest. The valuation of the capital stock, and hence "*q*", depends on supply and demand, with demand depending on the yield on capital relative to the yields available on other assets.

The significance of this approach is twofold. It stresses the existence of a range of assets, showing that the basic IS–LM model can still be used, even to represent an economy with a complicated financial sector. In Tobin's models the LM curve, instead of describing equilibrium simply in the money market, results from the equilibrium of the whole financial sector.[54] The approach recognizes the problems involved in defining money.[55] It may be possible to group together a collection of assets and to call them money, but there is no need to do this. Monetary economics can be done satisfactorily in terms of a continuous range of assets.

## 26.3  RATIONAL EXPECTATIONS AND THE NEW CLASSICAL MACROECONOMICS

*Rational expectations*

In the mid 1970s macroeconomics was transformed by the introduction and systematic use of the concept of "rational expectations", the chief architects of this being Lucas, Sargent, Wallace and Barro.[56] Though the concept of rational expectations was not new, having been developed in a different context by Muth in the early 1960s,[57] it was only in the 1970s that economists saw the implications of the concept for macroeconomics and developed them.

The basic idea underlying rational expectations is that people learn, and that they will form their expectations on the basis of all the information they have available. Their behaviour in acquiring and using information will be governed by utility maximization: if it is profitable to acquire new information, or to use the information they have in a more efficient way then people will do so. To analyse such a process of learning is, however, immensely complicated, an alternative to which is to analyse an equilibrium in the process of learning: to analyse a situation where the process of learning has come to an end in the sense that people have no incentive to change the method by which they form their expectations. The simplest such situation to analyse is the situation where people have learnt everything there is to be learnt: in other words, a situation where everything that is predictable is predicted correctly. If there is no uncertainty this amounts to assuming that expectations are correct. If there is uncertainty it implies that the errors people make are completely random and unpredictable.

Why did rational expectations catch on so fast in the 1970s? Two reasons immediately suggest themselves. The first is that work on expectations-augmented Phillips curves showed that the formation of inflationary expectations was crucial in determining how an economy worked, in particular how it responded to monetary and fiscal policy. There was, however, no satisfactory theory of expectations. Expectations were explained by economists in terms of various ad hoc rules, such as "adaptive expectations",[58] all of which implied that people were failing to use the information available to them. There was a clear need for a better theory of expectations. The second reason is that the concept represents the application of individual maximizing behaviour, an assumption that was being progressively applied to other areas of economic theory, to the formation of expectations.

*The new classical macroeconomics*

The new classical macroeconomics combines the hypothesis of rational expectations with the natural rate hypothesis. The implications of this were dramatic, as was shown in a series of papers in the mid 1970s.[59] By the mid 1970s the Phelps-Friedman expectations-augmented Phillips curve was becoming generally accepted, but there was still controversy as to whether the long run Phillips curve was completely vertical, this hinging on whether expectations responded fully to changes in the inflation rate. The introduction of rational expectations swept all this away. If expectations are rational, they must in the long run be correct on average: anything different would imply that people were ignoring easily available information. The new classical argument, however, went much further than this. The Phelps–Friedman argument had admitted that stabilization policy was not in principle impossible. It was the practical objections which were decisive. The new classical argument, on the other hand, was that it was impossible, unless the government had more information about the economy than did the private sector, for government policy, however efficiently conducted, to have any systematic effect on output. Policy could affect unemployment only by causing errors in expectations, and by the assumption of rational expectations these errors must be random and unpredictable. There was no usable trade-off, even in the short run.

Of fundamental importance to the new classical view of economic policy is what is known as the "Lucas critique" of stabilization policy,[60] for this was a critique of the whole approach to macroeconomic policy prevalent since 1945. The traditional approach to economic policy is to estimate a model of the economy comprising a series of equations describing how the private sector responds to changes in exogenous variables. This model can then be used to explore the implications of various policy proposals with a view to choosing the best of these, according to whatever criterion the policymakers consider appropriate. Lucas' argument is that this approach is misconceived, for the behaviour of the private sector (and hence the initial macroeconomic model) depends on what the public believe policymakers to be doing. If policy changes, so will the model. Macroeconomic policy must be viewed as a process where the behaviour of the private sector depends on the policy being pursued by the government.

One of the attractions of the new classical macroeconomics is its ability to encompass a wide range of issues within a coherent framework. The central and overriding theme is individual rationality, the hypothesis of utility maximization being taken to its extreme. All else is subordinate to this axiom: rational expectations result from its application to the formation of expectations; continuous market clearing from its application to market behaviour (if markets do not clear people are ignoring potentially profitable opportunities for trade). It is taken as a methodological datum that explanation must be in terms of maximizing behaviour, not arbitrarily specified functions.[61]

*Responses to the new classical macroeconomics*

The ideas discussed in the previous two sections are very recent and it is much too early to assess their long term fate. Several points can, however be made. (1) Rational expectations (as distinct from the new classical macroeconomics) has established itself as an invaluable theoretical tool. It has become widely accepted, even amongst opponents of the new classical macroeconomics, that, in the absence of evidence on why expectations should differ from rational expectations, it is important at least to examine the solutions of models under rational expectations. (2) The new classical macroeconomics has unleashed a wealth of theoretical and empirical work, especially in the US. Furthermore it is still developing, as evidenced by the recent revival of the real bills doctrine.[62] (3) Questions of supply have been given a more prominent place, this being explicable in terms not only of theoretical developments, but also in terms of circumstances. (4) The Keynesian–Monetarist distinction has become an irrelevance in analysing attitudes to macroeconomics. The views now held by many economists commonly regarded as Keynesian (e.g. Tobin, Modigliani, Solow) are, though they remain critical of both Friedman and the new classical economics, very different from the views held by Keynesians twenty years ago.[63] (5) Economists have started to analyse models incorporating rational expectations, but in which the new classical conclusions do not follow.[64] Though such work is in its infancy it is clear that the new classical economics has stimulated economists to ask new questions, and to approach old questions in new ways.

## 26.4   THE BUSINESS CYCLE

*Multiplier–accelerator models*

The *General Theory* had an enormous impact on business cycle theory. As early as 1936 Harrod's *The Trade Cycle* used a multiplier–accelerator model, though it was Samuelson's (1939b) version which became the standard exposition. The attraction of this approach compared with earlier ones was that a cycle emerged naturally from the interaction of two simple relations. The accelerator explained why, for example, a fall in the *growth rate* of consumption would produce a fall in the level of investment. This in turn would, via the multiplier, lower consumption, producing a turning point in output. This approach, together with variations such as Metzler's inventory cycle (1941), dominated business cycle theory in the 1940s and early 1950s.

The Keynesian origins of this approach to the business cycle are clear, but it is important not to neglect other influences. (i) There was the accelerator itself, due in particular to Aftalion and Clark.[65] (ii) Furthermore, if the interaction of the multiplier and the accelerator were to produce cycles, lags were needed, these not being provided by Keynes, who used a static model even when this was inappropriate, but by others. Robertson (1933, 1936) postulated a lag between demand and income; Lundberg (1937) one between output and income. These changes brought the theory closer in some respects to earlier theories, such as the Swedish attempts at period analysis. (iii) Having set up a model with lags it had to be analysed, and here the application, following Frisch (1933), of mathematical methods was crucial. A critical property of the multiplier–accelerator model was, as Samuelson showed, that it would generally produce either cycles which faded away, or cycles of ever-increasing amplitude. The "realistic" case of fairly regular cycles would occur only by chance. (iv) Finally, because the multiplier–accelerator model could not pretend to be a complete model of the cycle, other factors had to be brought in. For example, Hicks' *Contribution to the Theory of the Trade Cycle* (1950), described by one authority as "the most elegant and most carefully elaborated specimen of a great variety of similar systems",[66] used a model where an unstable multiplier–accelerator process operated between a ceiling imposed by full capacity, and a floor imposed by a minimum below which investment could not fall.

Before going on to consider alternative approaches to the cycle, we need to say something about the thesis, closely tied up with views of the cycle, of "secular stagnation". Although this idea was present in the *General Theory*,[67] Keynes viewing the prospect favourably, it is a view associated, above all, with Hansen.[68] Hansen, the foremost American apostle of Keynesian ideas in the 1940s, arrived at this conclusion through combining the Keynesian theory with arguments taken from earlier business cycle theories, a mixture described by one critic as "a strange amalgam of Keynes, Schumpeter and Spiethoff".[69] The basic argument was that as the US economy matured, and the growth rate of population and resources fell, opportunities for investment would be exhausted. Autonomous investment would fall. At the same time there was a tendency for savings to rise with prosperity, reducing the multiplier. Thus government intervention, such as deficit spending, would be necessary to sustain growth and to prevent stagnation.

*Econometric models*

The Hicksian approach to the cycle was to assume a potentially explosive multiplier–accelerator process, constrained by a floor and a ceiling. The alternative approach was to use a stable multiplier–accelerator process, one in which cycles would, if left undisturbed, die away, and to postulate that it was kept going by a series of random shocks. Econometric models were important here for two reasons. The first was that evidence from such models was that they seemed to be inherently stable: in the absence of shocks, fluctuations would die away. This cast doubt on the Hicksian approach. The second, and more fundamental reason, was that this type of model requires different techniques from those required by the Hicksian approach, methods more akin to those required in econometrics. Particularly fruitful are simulation methods, an important such study being Adelman and Adelman (1959). This study took the Klein–Goldberger (1955) model of the US economy and solved it under various assumptions. They found that the model itself did not generate cycles: it settled down rapidly after a disturbance. But when a suitable series of random shocks was introduced, the model produced cyclical fluctuations considered "remarkably similar" to those described by the National Bureau.[70]

These results are interesting because they illustrate two things. (i) Progress in economic theory is dependent on the availability of appropriate techniques: in this instance the development of simulation methods, this in turn being dependent on the availability of computers. (ii) The availability of techniques may influence the way in which the economy is perceived. Thus the use of a simple second-order difference equation to represent cyclical fluctuations suggested a clear-cut difference between the Hicksian use of the multiplier–accelerator model, according to which cycles result from the structure of the economy, and the Frisch–Adelman view, according to which they result from the way in which the economic system responds to exogenous shocks.

*Money and the business cycle*

Though not alone in arguing that monetary factors had, under Keynesian influence, been unduly neglected,[71] responsibility for arousing interest in the monetary aspects of business cycles rests above all with Friedman. In the tradition of Mitchell and the National Bureau, under the aegis of which much of his research was undertaken, Friedman's approach was primarily empirical, being concerned with the behaviour of money, income and the velocity of circulation over the cycle.[72] Typical is "Money and business cycles" (1963b), where extensive discussion of empirical evidence is followed by what Friedman and Schwarz describe as "a tentative sketch" of mechanisms linking monetary changes to the cycle. Aside from his contributions to the quantity theory more generally, Friedman's main contribution was the use of permanent income to explain cyclical variations in the velocity of circulation.[73]

Despite Friedman's advocacy, however, monetary theories of the cycle failed to catch on. In part this was due to Friedman's approach, with its attempt to demonstrate the importance of money through examining evidence on the timing of cycles in money income and velocity. As Tobin (1970) pointed out with some carefully worked out counter-examples, empirical evidence on timing may be able to refute the theory that monetary factors are responsible for cycles, but it cannot possibly establish it. Furthermore, attempts to develop a monetary theory to pose against the Keynesian theories could hardly proceed until a suitable theory of the relationship between money, output and prices had been developed. Such a theory was not available.

After a period of comparative neglect in the 1960s, when interest in dynamics was focused instead on growth, interest in the business cycle, and with it interest in monetary theories of the cycle, was revived by the work of Lucas in the mid 1970s.[74] In the same way, however, that the new classical macroeconomics constituted a radical departure from the more traditional monetarism associated with Friedman, so the new classical theory of the business cycle was radically different from that of Friedman and Schwarz. The object was to provide an "equilibrium" theory of the cycle: one in which all markets were assumed to be in equilibrium continuously, and in which expectations were rational. The source of fluctuations was found in errors in inflationary expectations, these in turn resulting from unanticipated changes in the growth rate of the money supply. The interpretation of the resulting cycles is, however, very different from that of fluctuations in Keynesian theory. Unemployment arises in equilibrium theories of the cycle because workers choose to work less because of mistakes they make in evaluating current and future real wage rates. Thinking that the current real wage rate is unduly low, for example, workers choose to take leisure now rather than in the future.

The fundamental axioms of the new classical macroeconomics, however, are insufficient in themselves to generate a cycle. As expounded so far, the theory can only explain random fluctuations in output, whereas business cycles are not random – the essence of the business *cycle* is that fluctuations in output follow a pattern. To explain this pattern lags have to be introduced into the model. Whilst there is nothing inherently wrong with this, it is important to notice that it is not the equilibrium elements of the theory that produces cycles: it is just as much the factors introduced from outside – the lags, about which macroeconomic theory has little to say. The theory looks very close to the econometric theories discussed above: the cycle results from the interaction of the economic system with a system of exogenous shocks.

## 26.5   CONCLUSIONS

It would be natural to think of the conflict between Keynesianism and monetarism as the main feature of post-war macroeconomics, and to a great extent this is correct. It is arguable, however, that the dominant theme, from Hicks's work on Keynes and the "classics" to Lucas's work on rational expectations, has been the attempt to establish a macroeconomic theory based on secure microeconomic foundations. This has been a crucial factor, even in areas (such as the theory of the consumption function, or the theory of inflation and unemployment) where econometric work has been undertaken on a large scale. It is, on the whole, developments in theory, not the results of empirical work, which change the way economists conceive the economy. Thus, though interest in a new line of inquiry has sometimes been prompted by the discovery of a new empirical regularity (e.g. the Phillips curve), it has been more common for a new departure in macroeconomics to be the result of a new theoretical idea. Important examples are Hicks's interpretation of Keynes in terms of a general equilibrium model, the "general disequilibrium" theory based on the work of Clower and Leijonhufvud, and the new classical macroeconomics.

# 27

# International Trade and Development

## 27.1 THE PURE THEORY OF TRADE

*General equilibrium and geometry*

During the previous period international trade had increasingly been viewed in terms of general equilibrium theory, a tendency which became even more complete with Samuelson's work, dating from the late 1930s. This was achieved to a great extent through confining attention to simple cases in which definite results could be obtained. Following the lead of Haberler, Lerner and Leontief, diagrammatic analysis of the 2×2 (two country, two commodity) case became common, enormous emphasis being placed on geometric analysis.[1] The classic work here was Meade's *Geometry of International Trade* (1952), which consolidated earlier contributions using its "trade indifference curve",[2] a device which enabled Meade to represent in a single diagram a free trade equilibrium involving two countries, each with its own production possibility frontier and consumption-indifference curves.[3]

The derivation of Meade's trade-indifference curves is shown in Figure 27.1a. There are two commodities, $X$ and $Y$, and two countries, $a$ and $b$. Country $a$'s consumption is shown in quadrant II, its preferences being described by a set of consumption-indifference curves, of which two, $I'_{ca}$ and $I''_{ca}$ are shown. Country $a$ has the production-possibility curve PP', and in the absence of trade would be in equilibrium at A.

Corresponding to each consumption-indifference curve it is possible to derive a trade-indifference curve. For example, to derive the trade-indifference curve corresponding to consumption-indifference curve $I'_{ca}$, we slide the quadrilateral OPAP' round $I'_{ca}$. The trade-indifference curve corresponding to $I'_{ca}$, $I'_{ta}$ is the path traced out by the origin of the production possibility diagram as it slides round $I'_{ca}$. It is an indifference curve, for country $a$, relating quantities of exports and imports. For example, if country $a$ were to import OC units of $Y$ and export CD units of $X$, it could consume at point B (in Figure 27.1a) and be exactly as well off as if there were no trade and it was consuming at point A.

If we derive a whole set of trade-indifference curves, one for each consumption-indifference curve, we can use them to derive an offer curve for country $a$. The process can then be repeated for a second country, $b$, country $b$'s consumption being measured in quadrant IV. Putting the two

(a)

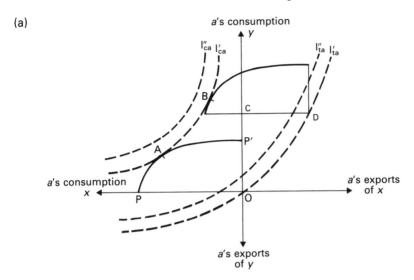

(b)

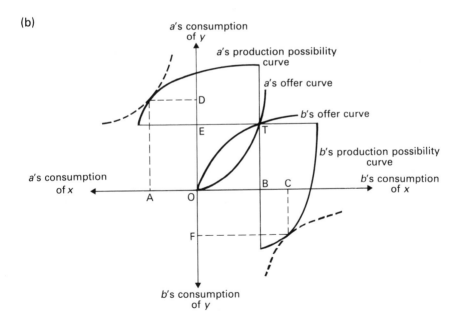

FIGURE 27.1   *Meade's International Trade Geometry*

offer curves together we can find the equilibrium level of trade. If we draw not only the two offer curves, but also the two countries' production possibility curves and consumption-indifference curves, we can work out how much of each commodity each country is producing and consuming. This is done in Figure 27.1b, where the quantities produced, consumed and traded are as follows:

| | Country *a* | | | | Country *b* | | | |
|---|---|---|---|---|---|---|---|---|
| | Imp | Exp | Cons | Prod | Imp | Exp | Cons | Prod |
| X | – | OB | OA | AB | OB | – | OC | BC |
| Y | OE | – | OD | ED | – | OE | OF | EF |

It is easy to check that worldwide consumption of each good equals production, and that for each country production of each good equals consumption plus exports minus imports. Meade was thus able to show the link between internal production conditions (represented by a production possibility curve) and a country's offer curve, a link which Graham had, in the 1920s, argued was missing. Throughout the 1950s and 1960s geometry dominated trade theory to an extent not equalled in other branches of economics.[4]

A good example of a problem transformed by being considered in the context of a simple formal model is the transfer problem, and the effects of a transfer on the terms of trade. Due in part to Keynesian economics,[5] and in part to the Hicks–Allen analysis of income effects, the income mechanism was now understood, sweeping away the most controversial aspect of earlier discussions.[6] It could be shown that in the 2×2 case the change in the terms of trade would depend on the marginal propensities to spend on the two goods.[7] The change in the terms of trade was an empirical issue. Though there was still dispute as to whether any presumption could be established as to how the terms of trade would in practice move,[8] the nature of the discussion was very different. Whether a general equilibrium model or a simpler Keynesian model was used, discussion could take place within an explicit, widely accepted and understood framework. This made it possible to relate areas of disagreement much more clearly to particular properties of the model (utility functions, propensities to consume, assumptions about transport costs, the existence of non-traded goods, and so on).[9]

### The Heckscher–Ohlin–Samuelson model

The dominant approach to the pure theory of trade, certainly from the late 1940s, was that of Heckscher and Ohlin, in which trade flows were explained in terms of differences in factor endowments across countries possessing identical production functions. This approach was embodied in a specific, simple model by Samuelson in a series of papers, discussed below, dating from the 1940s. Fundamental to this approach is the result that a country will export those commodities which use its abundant factor most intensively, and import those which use its scarce factors more intensively.

Discussion of this proposition in the 1950s and 1960s was dominated by Leontief's (1953) finding, obtained using his input–output model, that the US imported relatively capital-intensive goods, exporting relatively labour-intensive ones. As the US was, and is, by any standards a capital-rich country, this appeared to contradict the Heckscher–Ohlin theory.

Several responses to this result of Leontief's can be distinguished.[10] (1) One response[11] was to argue that there was no reason to accept Leontief's conclusions, because there was no reason to assume that the conditions needed for the Heckscher–Ohlin results to hold would be satisfied in the real world. Ambiguities in the concept of factor abundance and differences in demand conditions in different countries, for example, would be enough to upset the Heckscher–Ohlin conclusions. Of particular note here is Minhas's (1962) attempt to apply constant elasticity of substitution production functions to the problem, showing the possibility of a situation where a commodity was relatively capital-intensive at one set of factor prices, but relatively labour-intensive at other prices. Such factor intensity reversals, as they are called, are inconsistent with the Heckscher–Ohlin theory. (2) Leontief's results could be investigated more closely, for example by expanding the number of factors to include natural resources and human skills.[12] (3) Finally there is the possibility of ignoring Leontief's results as a puzzle, not properly understood, but not affecting the validity of the theory. Research could continue into working out the implications of the Heckscher–Ohlin approach for various problems.

One of the main problems to be investigated was that of factor price equalization. Where Ohlin had argued that trade would result in a partial equalization of factor prices Samuelson (1948b, 1949) and Lerner (1952)[13] showed that under certain conditions, in particular the absence of transport costs, *complete* equalization of factor prices would occur,[14] the same result as would occur if factors were perfectly mobile. In other words, trade in commodities is a substitute for the movement of factors.[15] Though originally derived for a model with two countries, two goods and two factors, the result proved capable of generalization. Samuelson (1953) extended it to the case of many commodities and many factors, subsequent research during the 1950s filling in many of the gaps.[16]

The same framework also proved capable of being used to investigate the effects of trade on the distribution of income, the essential contribution here being Stolper and Samuelson (1941). Their conclusion was that trade would lower the price of the "scarce" factor of production, or in other words that protection would raise the real wage of the scarce factor. The argument is that protection raises the relative price of the importable good, increasing the real wage of the factor that this uses more intensively; as a country imports goods which are intensive in their use of its scarce factor this means that the real wage of the scarce factor will be raised by protection.[17] As with factor price equalization the Stolper–Samuelson theorem stimulated research into the exact assumptions needed for it to be valid. It turned out that the result depended on special properties of the 2×2 model that Samuelson and Lerner used. In particular, problems arise when there are more than two factors.[18]

*Alternatives to the Heckscher–Ohlin–Samuelson model*

In contrast to the extensive and well-integrated research undertaken into the Heckscher–Ohlin–Samuelson model, research into alternative explanations of trade has been more sporadic. One was that of Kravis (1956), who argued that trade was determined by the availability of goods: goods will be imported only if they are unavailable at home, either in the sense that they simply cannot be produced (perhaps due to the absence of a crucial raw material), or in the sense that they can be produced domestically only at a much greater cost than the cost at which they can be imported. Tariffs, transport costs and cartelization mean that small differences in costs do not provide a sufficient reason for trade.

A more comprehensively worked out alternative to the Heckscher–Ohlin–Samuelson theory was provided by Linder (1961) who, whilst he accepted that relative resource endowments could explain trade in primary products, denied that it could explain trade in manufactured products. For manufactured goods, however, Linder failed to provide a precise explanation of the *composition* of trade, providing instead an explanation of the *volume* of trade. His argument is that trade will be greatest between countries with similar demand patterns, and hence between countries with similar levels of income per capita. Central to the argument is increasing returns to scale, for an industry has to become sufficiently large before it can become competitive in world markets, something for which it requires a substantial home market. The strongest foreign market will be found in countries with a similar composition of demand.

Although Linder stressed increasing returns to scale, it was not until much later (Krugman, 1979) that a more formal treatment of trade under increasing returns to scale was provided. One of the problems with incorporating increasing returns to scale into a theory of trade is the need to deal with imperfect competition, a necessary implication of an equilibrium with increasing returns to scale. Krugman uses a model of monopolistic competition to show that trade can be viewed as a means of exploiting economies of scale in the presence of a less than completely elastic home market.[20]

A different approach is to concentrate on the dynamic aspects of technology, seeing exports as the result of successful innovation. A successful innovation will increase the world's demand for a country's products, the effects of this lasting until the new product is imitated abroad, at which stage demand will decline. This approach underlies the product life cycle theory put forward by Vernon (1966),[21] who explained the persistence of international differences in costs in terms of the changes in production techniques and costs which take place as a product is developed. Though a more dynamic theory, this explanation of trade has much in common with increasing returns to scale.

*Trade and welfare*

Due to the longstanding concern of economists with the gains from trade, and with the benefits or losses arising from interference with trade, developments in trade theory have always been closely linked with developments in welfare economics. Two strands of thought can be distinguished: the utilitarian and the non-utilitarian. In the modern period the main exponent of the non-utilitarian approach has been Samuelson, whose two papers (1938b and 1939a) contained the main results obtained. Samuelson's criterion for a welfare improvement is that the new situation be superior to the old one at all distributions of income: that the new utility possibility frontier lie completely outside the old.[22] Samuelson was able to show (1) that free trade was better than no trade at all, in the sense that "more of every commodity can be secured with less of every productive service".[23] Whether or not a welfare improvement resulted depended on the distribution of income and the trade pattern. Only in the case where all individuals had the same tastes was it possible to infer that trade must be beneficial, for only in that case could it be shown that all individuals would be better off with trade than without. (2) Samuelson also showed that if other countries behave competitively, it will pay a country not to trade freely, in order to exploit any monopoly power it may have. This is an argument, familiar to the classical economists, about using a tariff to produce more favourable terms of trade.[24]

Many economists adopted Samuelson's approach, his results being more precisely stated, and more general ones being derived, such as Kemp's (1962) argument that restricted trade is superior to no trade. Similar results were derived from the point of view of the world as a whole, rather from the point of view of a single country[25]

The alternative, utilitarian, approach was taken up by Fleming (1951). His concern was with choosing between alternative systems for regulating trade in order to produce a balance of payments equilibrium, on the assumption that variations in the level of employment, the exchange rate and exports subsidies and capital imports were not available.[26] To tackle this problem he adopted a utilitarian criterion, accepting the Marshallian assumption that the marginal utility of income was the same for all relevant individuals. These ideas reached their widest audience, however, through Meade's *Trade and Welfare* (1955), a book parts of which were heavily influenced by Fleming. Meade's main contributions were the introduction of "welfare weights", measuring the assumed importance to society of increases in income accruing to different individuals; and the use of Marshall's consumer surplus to measure welfare changes. The justification for this procedure was purely pragmatic, for Meade wished to deal with a wider class of problems than could be analysed using Samuelson's approach.[27] As for the welfare weights, Meade argued that whilst there might be no scientific basis for calculating them, they represented value judgements of the sort that politicians continually have to make.[28]

A further defence of Meade's procedure is that the Samuelson approach is more restrictive than it might appear. At first sight the criterion that a change represents a potential improvement if more of all commodities is available is an attractive one. Such changes, however, represent a potential welfare improvement only if income can costlessly be redistributed from one individual to another. Given that all taxes other than lump sum taxes have costs attached to them, and that appropriate lump sum taxes are rarely feasible, there will typically be costs attached to transferring income from one individual to another, which means that even if a change satisfies Samuelson's criterion it may be impossible to produce an increase in welfare.

### Customs unions and the second best

Whilst Meade's utilitarian approach to the welfare aspects of trade was important, even more important was his introduction of the term "second best" to describe the type of situation analysed by Fleming, where the ideal, or utopian, solution could not be obtained due to some constraint.[29] After developing the theory of second best Meade applied the techniques to a variety of problems in international economic policy. Meade's work, along with Ozga's (1955) analysis of tariffs, and various works on the theory of public finance, provided the starting point for Lipsey and Lancaster's general theory of the second best.[30]

Of the applications of second best theory in international trade, by far the most important was the theory of customs unions. Though customs unions, where the members of the customs union have free trade amongst themselves, imposing a common tariff barrier against outside countries, had been the subject of discussion for centuries (sixteen customs unions, for example, being formed between 1818 and 1924),[31] modern discussions of customs unions date from Viner's *The Customs Union Issue* (1950). Viner's main argument as regards the economics of the subject, the book as a whole being concerned with much more than the economics of customs unions, centred on the distinction between *trade creation* and *trade diversion*. A customs union has two aspects: internal free trade and an external tariff. The removal of barriers to trade between members of the customs union will increase trade, countries importing from other members of the customs union goods which previously either were not produced at all, or were produced elsewhere at higher cost. But in addition the external tariff may cause trade diversion: a country may switch from purchasing a good outside the customs union, to buying it from a more expensive supplier within the customs union.

Although it was in *The Customs Union Issue* that Viner applied them to the question of customs unions, the concepts of trade diversion and trade creation were not new. In the 1920s and the 1930s Viner had used these concepts to investigate the implications of preferential (discriminatory) tariffs, and before him the concepts had been used by Viner's teacher, Taussig.[32] The origin of these ideas was, however, classical; something which should not be surprising in view of the classical nature of Viner's model. Viner's model has no demand curves, and industries produce under conditions of constant cost. Though they did not neglect customs unions, the German *Zollverein* of 1834 being a subject of their discussions, the main concern of the classical economists had been with commercial treaties which discriminated in favour of a particular country's goods. The Methuen

Treaty of 1703, which diverted British trade from France to Portugal, was a longstanding and widely discussed example.

Viner's classical approach to customs union theory is not the only possible one. It is possible to argue that important aspects of customs unions are suppressed by neglecting demand and by assuming constant costs. For example, even if production is unchanged, a tariff change will enable consumers to substitute goods which have become cheaper for those which have become relatively more expensive. This will affect welfare. Though the analysis of such modifications to Viner's theory is frequently associated with Meade (1956b), Gehrels (1956), Lipsey (1957, 1960b) and Johnson (1964), it is possible to find earlier examples: De Beers (1941) and Byé (1950). Another response to Viner's work is to argue that it fails to provide any justification for a preferring a customs union to free trade: without an external tariff, the benefits of trade creation can be obtained without the costs of trade diversion. A justification for protection has been provided by Cooper and Massell (1965a and b) and Johnson (1965a), using the argument that welfare depends not only on consumption of private goods, but also on public goods, these including nationalism and industrialization, both of which can be increased by protection. As with Viner's arguments, these arguments can be traced back to the nineteenth century. Friedrich List (1841), for example, defended the *Zollverein* in terms of assisting Germany to emerge from the primary producer stage of economic development.

Of more recent contributions, one worth singling out, because of its links with recent developments in microeconomics, is that of Kemp and Wan (1976). They view the formation of customs unions as examples of the formations of coalitions in the context of game theory, reaching the conclusion that for any number of countries it is possible to form a customs union such that everyone, whether inside or outside it, is no worse off than before it was formed. The implication of this result is that there should always be an incentive to form bigger and bigger customs unions until world free trade prevails. They attribute the fact that this process has not in practice occurred to the costs and difficulties of forming coalitions. It is important to note, however, that this result assumes that lump sum (costless) transfers can be made, these being used to compensate losers from the formation of a customs union, this compensation transforming a potential improvement into an actual one. Without the availability of costless transfers their result would be much weaker.

## 27.2 THE EXCHANGE RATE AND THE BALANCE OF PAYMENTS

*The application of Keynesian theory*

The theory of balance of payments adjustment was transformed by the application to it of the Keynesian theory of aggregate demand, a process which started within months of the publication of the *General Theory* with Paish (1936),[33] shortly followed by the more thorough exposition contained in Robinson's *Theory of Employment* (1937).[34] It became accepted that the effect of changes in exports on the balance of trade would depend on the marginal propensity to import, a term coined by Paish;[35] and that the balance of trade would have an effect on income analogous to that of investment.[36] In 1940s various multipliers, both static and dynamic, linking trade and the incomes of trading countries, were derived.[37] Though this income-adjustment mechanism went well beyond the classical demand-transfer mechanism, it shared with it an emphasis on quantity as opposed to price adjustments.

*Meade's* Balance of Payments[38]

In *The Balance of Payments* (1951) Meade integrated the income approach, discussed above, with the more traditional approach stressing the role of price adjustments. In addition he related this to the issue of balance of payments policy, arguing that if the object of policy is to achieve both internal and external balance (i.e. given levels of domestic employment and the balance of payments),[39] both price and income adjustments will be needed. If only one mechanism is available the two objectives may conflict.[40] Meade argued that the solution to the policy problem was to use one policy instrument (say the exchange rate) to achieve external balance, and another (say fiscal policy) to achieve internal balance.[41]

Meade's analysis provided scope for generalization and for further analysis. His approach was a special case of the more general theory of targets and instruments developed simultaneously by Tinbergen (1952). Even within the context of internal and external balance Meade's approach could be generalized, as in Johnson (1958), to deal with expenditure switching policies (such as devaluation) and expenditure increasing or reducing policies (such as fiscal policy). A further generalization was Alexander's (1952) absorption approach, which by stressing the income effects of changes in trade remedied Meade's assumption that policy would be used to maintain internal balance all the time.[42] For example, it follows from the national income identity that the trade deficit or surplus must equal the difference between total domestic absorption (consumption and investment) and domestic production, that a devaluation cannot improve the trade balance unless either domestic absorption is reduced, or domestic production increased. Thus if there is already full employment, and domestic production cannot be increased, devaluation will fail to improve the trade balance unless accompanied by policies to reduce domestic absorption.

Another influential development along the lines set out by Meade was that of Mundell (1962). Mundell introduced the effects of policy on the capital account, arguing that internal and external balance might be maintained by combining monetary and fiscal policy. The rate of interest was introduced alongside fiscal policy as a second policy instrument.

Although neither the interest rate nor fiscal policy was an expenditure switching policy, these policies would have different effects on the capital and current accounts, enabling a trade deficit to be covered by a capital account surplus.

*Portfolio approaches to the balance of payments*

In the early 1970s a number of economists, of whom Johnson was the most prominent, began to stress a different approach to the balance of payments, the so-called monetary approach.[43] The characteristic of this approach was that it focused not on flows of goods and services but on *stocks* of assets. Of particular importance was the link between the balance of payments and the change in the money supply. A balance of payments surplus, for example, implied an increase in the money supply,[44] which, given the assumption of equilibrium in the money market, implied an increase in the demand for money. The balance of payments could thus be analysed in terms of changes in the demand for money, expenditure flows being seen as responses to such changes in stocks.

Though the early models used in the monetary approach were very simple, concentrating very much on the quantity theory of money, the approach was capable of generalization. One such generalization was to consider a much wider range of assets, not simply money and a single type of bond. The other has been to distinguish much more carefully between short and long run effects. In the short run, for example, the exchange rate can be argued to depend primarily on asset markets: speculative capital flows, dependent on expectations, dominate. In the long run, on the other hand, equilibrium in goods markets, and purchasing power parity, is much more important. Perhaps the most influential model of this type has been that of Dornbusch (1976), who used such a model to explain some of the violent exchange rate fluctuations occurring in the period after 1972. In Dornbusch's model purchasing power parity is a long run equilibrium condition. In the short run, however, exchange rate movements are explained in terms of efficient foreign exchange markets in which investors have rational expectations, and respond very quickly to information about likely trends in prices.

## 27.3   DEVELOPMENT ECONOMICS PRIOR TO THE MID 1960s

*The emergence of development economics*

Development economics in its modern form did not exist before the 1940s. The concern of development economics, as the term is now understood, is with countries or regions which are seen to be *under* or *less* developed relative to others, and which, it is commonly believed, *should*, if they are not to become ever poorer relative to the developed countries, be developed in some way. Prior to the 1940s, economists, with few exceptions, did not share this perspective, being concerned with material progress rather than the more complicated issue of development.[45] An important change in attitudes came about in the 1940s, for a variety of reasons, some political and ideological, others connected with economics itself.[46] Economic development, an issue with which colonial governments had increasingly been concerned, was brought into prominence as an official objective when "freedom from want" was included, in a speech by Roosevelt in 1941, as one of America's four peace objectives.[47] Concern for development was further stimulated with the establishment, in the mid 1940s, of several international organizations, in particular the Food and Agriculture Organisation (1943) and the International Bank for Reconstruction and Development (1944). By the time the United Nations was set up in 1945, the development of underdeveloped countries had become a generally accepted objective. The establishment of the UN confirmed this, providing a forum through which poorer countries could make their views known.[48]

An important aspect of the emergence of development economics was the increase in the role economists saw for the state and for central planning. During the war all allied governments were involved in planning to some extent, with the UK achieving a particularly high degree of planning.[49] Though there was considerable debate over the nature of the planning required, planning came to be regarded as a necessary part of the readjustment to peacetime conditions, the price mechanism alone being insufficient for the task. This belief in the need for planning carried over into development economics, a large proportion of economists concerned with the problem of development being in the UK at the time.[50] Later in the 1940s there was the example of the Marshall plan, and the successful reconstruction of the European economies.

On the economic side two factors were particularly important. The first was the availability for the first time in Clark's *Conditions of Economic Progress* (1938) of national income statistics showing the extent of the gap between rich and poor countries. From the early 1950s these figures came to be superseded, in particular by statistics, produced by national and colonial governments, emerging through the UN. The second factor was the rise of Keynesian macroeconomics, important for several reasons. It raised the possibility that a variety of types of economics might be needed: in the same way that a special type of economics were needed for advanced countries in recession, so too might a special type of economics be needed to deal with underdeveloped countries.[51] The Harrod–Domar model, an application of Keynesian ideas to the problem of growth, provided a new framework within which problems of development could be tackled. In addition, the rise of Keynesian macroeconomics increased the popularity of aggregative economics, contributing towards the view that development could be equated with increasing per capita income.[52] The stress on macroeconomic management, together with the acceptance of previously "unorthodox" fiscal measures, fitted in with the stress on planning, and the belief that aid from rich to poor countries could play an important role in the latter's development.

As development economics emerged, the problem of underdevelopment became associated with two particular problems: underemployment of labour, especially in agriculture; and late industrialization. Particularly influential was Rosenstein-Rodan's (1943) discussion of the problems of south-eastern Europe. He started from the assumption that "about 25 per cent of the population is either totally or partially ('disguised unemployment') unemployed."[53] The remedy for this lay in industrialization: "It is *the* way of achieving a more equal distribution of income between different areas of the world by raising incomes in depressed areas at a higher rate than in the rich areas."[54] This viewpoint dominated development economics for the next two decades,[55] the problem of development economics being seen as how to get industrialization started, of escaping from one or more "vicious circles": "There is ... the dominant vicious circle of low production – no surpluses for economic development – no tools and equipment – low standard of production. An underdeveloped country is poor because it is poor."[56] The vicious circle idea proved popular in the 1950s and 1960s,[57] for it tied in with the notion that development required planning, and it lent support to the notion that development required the provision of foreign aid by the developed countries. Left to themselves, the situation of poor countries would fail to improve.

*Development and growth*

One of the earliest explanations of why it was difficult to get growth started ran in terms of externalities. Rosenstein-Rodan (1943) conjectured that "External economies may [in underdeveloped countries] be of the same order of magnitude as profits which appear on the profit and loss account of the enterprise."[58] The training of workers was a particularly important example.[59] In addition, there was the complementarity which arose from the fact that expansion in one industry would create incomes which would in turn generate demand for other industries. The income generated by a shoe factory, one of Rosenstein-Rodan's examples, will not increase demand for shoes sufficient to cover more than a small proportion of the factory's output. In contrast, if the expansion covers a wide range of industries, the demand generated may be sufficient to cover a substantial fraction of the additional output. Such externalities, together with the further complementarity arising from one industry requiring as an input the output of another, this being introduced by Scitovsky (1954), came to be seen as implying that industrialization could be started only by a "big push":

Proceeding "bit by bit" will not add up in its effects to the sum total of the single bits. · A minimum quantity of investment is a necessary, though not sufficient, condition of success. This, in a nutshell, is the contention of the theory of the big push.[60]

Such a big push would have to be planned, in order to produce a balance between industries which took account of externalities, for these would be neglected by private investors.

A similar point was made in a different way by Nurkse (1952), who emphasized the creation of demand. He argued in terms of Say's Law: the output of a single industry can never create its own demand, for people involved in the industry will wish to spend only a part of their income on their own produce. If, on the other hand, a whole range of industries is expanded, this may create sufficient demand to sustain the expansion.

The notion of balance is inherent in Say's Law. Take Mill's formulation of it: "Every increase of production, if distributed without miscalculation among all kinds of produce in the proportions which private interest would dictate, creates, or rather constitutes, its own demand." Here, in a nutshell, is the case for balanced growth. An increase in the production of shoes alone does not create its own demand. An increase in production over a wide range of consumables, so balanced as to correspond with the pattern of consumers' preferences, does create its own demand.[61]

The idea that a large increase in investment was required to start growth was reinforced by conclusions reached using what was overwhelmingly the most popular growth model to be applied to the problem of development: the Harrod–Domar model.[62] According to this model the rate of growth of national income was given by the ratio of the average propensity to save to the incremental capital–output ratio (ICOR). This can be shown using the following simple algebra, where $Y$ is defined as national income and $K$ as the capital stock.

$$\mathrm{d}Y/Y = (\mathrm{d}K/Y)\,(\mathrm{d}Y/\mathrm{d}K) = (S/Y)\,(\mathrm{d}Y/\mathrm{d}K) = s/v$$

where $s$ is the average propensity to save, and $v$ is the ICOR. To increase the growth rate an increase in saving is required, the ICOR being assumed given by the technology. The implications of this were pessimistic for underdeveloped countries. Suppose the ICOR is 4:[63] this means that for each 1% increase in the growth rate, 4% of national income must be saved (invested). Thus if the population is growing at 3% per annum, 12% of national income must be invested simply to keep per capita income from falling. Given that in the early 1950s savings ratios in underdeveloped countries were mostly nearer 5%, this was a pessimistic result.[64]

A further important contribution to this view of development as requiring a sudden increase in investment was Rostow's theory of the "take-off", his most widely read exposition of this being *The Stages of Economic Growth: a non-Communist Manifesto* (1960). Rostow saw economies as progressing through five stages: traditional society; the preconditions for take-off; the take-off into self-sustained growth; the drive to maturity; and the age of high mass consumption. Of particular importance was the third stage, the take-off, this having three characteristics: a rise in productive investment from about 5% of national income to about 10%; the emergence of one or more sectors as the "leading sector"; and the modification of the political and social framework so as to exploit impulses coming from the industrial sector, enabling growth to be sustained. Rostow applied this theory to a wide range of countries, some of which had been through the take-off, some of which had not, the latter including countries identified as being in each of the first two stages. His interpretation of history was subject to severe criticism, in particular by Gerschenkron (1962), who denied that a single framework could be applied even to all the European countries which had experienced industrialization. Despite this, however, Rostow's concepts of take-off and self-sustained growth established themselves firmly in the literature to such an extent that one commentator described the 1960s as "the Rostow period" in the history of development studies.[65]

*Dualistic development*

An important aspect of the discussions of underdeveloped countries in the 1950s and 1960s was the attempt to explain the coexistence, in many underdeveloped countries, of a modern (often industrial) sector with a backward (usually agricultural) sector. The most influential of such "dual economy" models was Lewis's "Economic development with unlimited supplies of labour" (1954). Its key feature was surplus labour and disguised unemployment in the agricultural sector.[66] Thus to attract workers out of agriculture, firms in the industrial sector need offer a wage only slightly above the low average product of labour in agriculture. Growth occurs through expansion in the modern sector, capitalists reinvesting their profits, the modern sector gradually absorbing labour from the agricultural sector, a process which continues until the labour surplus is eliminated. Though the mechanism through which growth occurs is different from that of conventional growth models, the stress on capital accumulation and the need for high savings was the same: high profits result in high savings, and hence in capital accumulation and growth.[67]

An alternative approach to dualistic development was that developed by Eckhaus (1955) and Higgins (1956) who found the source of dualism in technological differences between the two sectors. The modern sector is assumed to be very capital-intensive, with only limited scope for the substitution of labour for capital. In the agricultural sector, on the other hand, capital and labour can easily be substituted for each other. Given these assumptions, employment in the modern sector is determined by the capital stock, the rest of the labour force going to the agricultural sector. The over-supply of labour to agriculture lowers the wage rate, resulting in the adoption there of very labour-intensive techniques, and low output per head. The result is a dual economy, there being an enormous difference in output per head between the two sectors. As with Lewis's model, capital accumulation is the key to the expansion of the modern sector, and to the raising of overall output per capita.

*Trade and development*

Development can also be viewed in the context of international trade.[68] Two aspects of the orthodox theory of trade are particularly important. First, the doctrine of comparative advantage, according to which countries ought to specialize in the production of commodities in which they have a comparative advantage. For many of the underdeveloped countries this would suggest that they ought to specialize in the production of primary commodities, using the proceeds to purchase manufactured goods from the developed countries. Second, the theory of factor price equalization, according to which international trade should, if competition is allowed to work, bring factor incomes in underdeveloped countries towards equality with equivalent factor incomes in developed countries. Orthodox theory suggests that underdeveloped countries, as well as developed countries, benefit from their participation in world trade. This view was challenged in the late 1940s, in particular by Singer (1950) and Prebisch (1949), who claimed tht protection could be used to stimulate development.[69]

Singer's argument had two strands to it. The first was that, although it led to specialization along the lines of comparative advantage, much investment in the export sectors of underdeveloped countries was, despite its high productivity, less beneficial to the countries concerned than other forms of investment. The reasons for this were twofold: because many export industries were more integrated with the economies of the developed countries than with the economies of the underdeveloped countries in which they were situated, many of the benefits accrued to the former: resources were diverted into industries offering less scope for technical progress and internal and external economies.[70] The second criticism of such specialization was that, because of different elasticities of demand for the products of developed and underdeveloped countries, the terms of trade were continually moving in favour of the developed countries, contributing to the continued poverty of the underdeveloped countries.

Similar ideas were put forward by Prebisch, these being developed by him and the UN Economic Commission for Latin America (ECLA) during the 1950s into an alternative view of development.[71] Prebisch and ECLA believed that the terms of trade facing underdeveloped countries were deteriorating. They linked this to the bargaining power of workers in industrial countries. Because of their workers' bargaining power, increased productivity in the industrial countries led not to falling output prices, which would have benefited underdeveloped countries, but to rising wage rates. Increased productivity in underdeveloped countries, on the other hand, led to falling output prices. In addition, because technical progress was higher in industry than in agriculture, and because the ability to save was linked to the rate of technical progress, capital accumulation was lower in the underdeveloped than in the developed countries.[72] There was thus a growing imbalance between the "centre", comprising the industrial countries, which dominated world trade, reaping most of the gains, and the "periphery". For countries in the periphery the remedy was industrialization, with the emphasis on import-substitution, not on production for export, even if this meant producing goods at a higher cost than the cost at which they could be imported. Only in this way could the imbalance between the centre and the periphery be rectified. A policy of protection and import-substituting industrialization was advocated.[73] This approach to development was also important in the movement towards integration of the Latin American countries: not only was such integration seen as a means of avoiding some of the problems which emerged with the import substitution strategy, but also it was a means of increasing the bargaining power of Latin America relative to that of the developed countries.

### Theories of uneven development

Another approach to economic development, stressing the essential unevenness of development, though in a different way from Prebisch and ECLA, was stimulated by Hirschman (1958) and Myrdal (1957).[74] Hirschman was concerned to attack the notion that development had to come through balanced growth, arguing instead that it arose through a "chain of disequilibria": expansion in one industry creates opportunities for other industries; when investment in these industries responds to the new opportunities, this creates opportunities for yet more industries and so on. In such a process two types of effect were important: "backward linkages", where expansion of an industry increased the demand for another industry's output; and "forward linkages", where an industry increased the supply, or reduced the cost of, goods to other parts of the economy. This approach was important for planning, for it suggested that planners, instead of spreading resources over a wide range of industries, should concentrate on a few industries where the linkages with other industries were particularly strong.[75] Theoretically, the approach is interesting, because of its emphasis on disequilibrium and the process through which price and profit incentives lead to changes in the economy.

Similar ideas were applied, in a less precise, but nonetheless influential, manner, by Myrdal (1957) to the issue of income distribution. He distinguished between two effects: "spread effects", making for greater equality between regions; and "backwash effects", making for inequality. Migration of capital and labour from one region to another, for example, is a "backwash" effect. Localities where the economy is expanding fastest attract migrants and capital investment, exacerbating regional inequalities. Similarly, trade provides greater opportunities for established centres of expansion. As for "spread" effects, these include the effect that increased production in prosperous regions will have on demand for the less prosperous regions' products.[76] Expansion strengthens the spread effects, recession the backwash effects, with the result that poor countries suffer more than rich countries during recessions. The problem of development was seen in terms of the relative weakness of spread effects relative to backwash effects.[77]

## 27.4 DEVELOPMENT ECONOMICS SINCE THE MID 1960s

### Changing attitudes towards development

The 1950s and 1960s saw enormous apparent progress in development economics. Though there were economists standing outside the mainstream,[78] the dominant approach emphasized economic growth through industrialization, this being promoted by policies to increase the rate of capital accumulation and detailed planning. Development plans were adopted by many countries, often in order to obtain finance from international agencies which made such plans a precondition for loans. During the 1960s, however, the emphasis began to change, this approach to economic development being criticized from a variety of points of view, the result being that by the 1970s the emphasis of the subject had changed significantly.

Perhaps the main reason for these changes was that the growth performance of the underdeveloped countries as a whole was not unsuccessful, with many countries and regions growing rapidly, and with no widening gap between rich and poor nations.[79] The problem of poverty, however, showed no signs of disappearing, growth sometimes being associated with increasing inequalities. In addition it became clear that, whatever the details of the relationship, growth could sometimes have unwelcome political implications.[80] It became increasingly clear in the 1960s, and even more so after the oil price rises of the 1970s, that it was inappropriate to lump together all underdeveloped countries, the differences between both countries and regions being enormous.[81] In 1964 Singer, contrasting the perspective of the 1960s with the pessimism of the 1950s, wrote, "In the sixties, the complexity of the real world makes a mockery of any preconceived universal optimism or pessimism."[82] This view was reinforced by studies of past experiences of industrialization which revealed the variety of ways in which this had occurred.[83]

One result of this has been a changed attitude towards capital accumulation and planning. Development was seen less in terms of capital accumulation, and mobilizing existing resources for investment, and more in terms of the creation of new resources, particularly human resources. The idea that underdeveloped countries were characterized by substantial disguised unemployment in agriculture was questioned.[84] At the same time there was a change in attitudes towards planning, many economists in the 1960s discerning a crisis in planning.[85] Planning was seen to have failed.

Another important theme in development economics of the last 20 years has been an increased stress on income distribution, and on the provision of food and other "basic needs". This concentration on the problem of poverty itself has been due to a recognition that, irrespective of whether or not traditional development policies were successful in promoting growth, growth does not necessarily produce the desired results.[86] An official exponent of this approach has been the International Labour Organisation which, in the 1970s, promoted the basic needs approach, which involved identifying the basic needs of various groups of people and the extent to which these were satisfied.[87]

### Neoclassical theorizing

An important characteristic of development economics in the 1960s and 1970s has been a resurgence of neoclassical theorizing,[88] by which is meant theorizing based on the assumption that there is a fair degree of flexibility in the economy: people adapt to changing opportunities and to changing prices, albeit sometimes slowly; firms maximize risk- and time-discounted profits, except where the institutional arrangements result in a different objective; the choice of production methods changes in response to price changes; and markets work reasonably well.[89] This neoclassical resurgence has taken a variety of forms.

In planning there has been a growing emphasis on the role of prices, with new techniques for computing "shadow prices" being developed.[90] These shadow prices cover all resources, foreign exchange being particularly important for many developing countries. They are defined so as to cover opportunity costs in terms of welfare, not simply in terms of marketed goods and services. Associated with this increased emphasis on prices have been new methods of evaluating the effects of domestic policies on trade and resource allocation. Concepts such as the "effective rate of protection" and "domestic resource costs"[91] have been used to cast doubt on some of the industrialization strategies being pursued. For example, some instances of import-substituting industrialization have been shown to amount to absurdly expensive methods of economizing on foreign exchange. Associated with this has been renewed optimism as to the possibilities for underdeveloped countries to expand their exports: the export pessimism of the 1950s is no longer dominant.[92] Where there are domestic distortions that the government wishes to correct, theoretical work has suggested that it would be better to deal with these at sources perhaps with a subsidy, rather than introducing protection.[93] Thus the emphasis has shifted away from protection and import-substitution towards greater participation in trade.

The view of underdeveloped countries as characterized by subsistence agriculture with surplus labour, and with peasant who fail to respond to market opportunities, has disappeared.[94] Particularly important was Schultz (1964), who argued that peasants maximized risk-discounted profits. Other research was produced to confirm that agricultural output would respond positively to price incentives.[95] Though not unchallenged, this work changed attitudes towards agriculture.

A substantial part of this progress can be attributed to the increased use of formal, mathematical techniques for dealing with choice under uncertainty, a development which grew out of the use of such techniques in other branches of economics. Thus formal analysis of problems ranging from the effects of different forms of land tenure on risk-bearing,[96] to the benefits of price stabilization schemes,[97] was possible.

## Dependency theories

A very different line of development has been the emergence of what are frequently known as "dependency theories".[98] The dependency involved has been defined by one of its proponents, Dos Santos (1970) in the following way:

By dependence we mean a situation in which the economy of certain countries is conditioned by the development and expansion of another country to which the former is subjected. ... [S]ome countries (the dominant ones) can expand and be self-sustaining, while other countries (the dependent ones) can do this only as a reflection of their expansion.[99]

Dependency theory is about the laws of the internal development of countries that are the object of Imperialist expansion. Dos Santos goes on to contrast this with the situation of capitalist developed economies.

This theoretical step transcends the theory of development which seeks to explain the situation of the underdeveloped countries as a product of their slowness or failure to adopt the patterns of efficiency characteristic of the developed countries (or to "modernize" or "develop" themselves). Though capitalist development theory admits the existence of an "external" dependence, it is unable to perceive underdevelopment in the way our present theory perceives it, as a consequence and part of the process of the world expansion of capitalism – a part that is necessary to and integrally linked with it.[100]

Dependency theory appears to have originated in ECLA, but it needs to be distinguished from the Prebisch/ECLA doctrine centred on the centre–periphery dichotomy.[101] Unlike dependency theories,

ECLA economic theories and critiques were not based on an analysis of social process, and did not call attention to imperialist relationships among countries, and did not take into account the asymmetric relation between classes.[102]

The new theories are more sociological and political.[103] From this new perspective the policies sought by Prebisch and ECLA, such as the liberalization of the developed countries' trade and financial policies, are of no real value to dependent economies. They would only serve to make the "centre–periphery" system more viable, whereas what is needed, according to the new perspective, is to overcome it.

Dependency theory thus stands in the Marxist tradition, though it has more in common with Lenin's view of capitalism, this owing much to Hobson, than with that of Marx himself.[104] It stands apart from most of the development economics considered in this chapter. One reason for this is that the central concept, that of "dependence", is hard to define satisfactorily. Even worse, in the words of Little (1982), a relatively orthodox (neoclassical) development economist, dependency theorists "define a concept with a value-laden connotation in a manner that often bears little relation to ordinary usage – the so called persuasive definition".[105] Marx, for example, defined "exploitation" in such a way that it occurred whenever any enterprise made a profit: in doing this he implies that the very existence of profit is unjust. A value judgement is thus concealed within a definition. In the modern literature on dependency an example is "unequal exchange", *defined* as occurring whenever wages in underdeveloped countries are lower than those in developed countries. The existence of "unequal exchange" can be defended on the grounds that such wage differentials do exist. The all important implication that such wage differentials operate to the disadvantage of underdeveloped countries is a contention that never gets proved: it is smuggled in via the definition of "unequal exchange". Little's conclusion, which would be shared by many orthodox development economists, is that "One result of this linguistic manipulation is that the possibility of serious analysis is greatly reduced."[106] When the value-content of such terms has been neutralized, what remains of the challenge to conventional development economics? The answer would appear to be very little. The *crucial* aspect of dependency theory is that contact with developed countries *worsens* the position of less developed countries, and that this is an *inevitable* aspect of the developed countries' prosperity. Both contentions are hard to prove. In response to the evidence that the standard of living in some less developed countries has improved, for example, resort has to be made to the unprovable, and unfalsifiable, counterfactual claim that in the absence of imperialist intervention living standards would have risen even more. As for reliance of developed countries on "dependent" countries, the situation is even worse for dependency theory. Trade with less developed countries is often of marginal importance for the developed countries: indeed, this is one of the reasons why less developed countries can do so little to improve their situation. If dependence is defined as lack of territorial autonomy, or in terms of trading with certain countries, then dependency becomes tautological: certain countries are simply *defined* as being dependent.[107]

# 28

## Alternative Approaches

### 28.1 INTRODUCTION

In the post-war period a number of economists have argued that the mainstream approach to economics is fundamentally flawed, and needs replacing with an alternative. From these perspectives the controversy between Monetarists and Keynesians appears as a doctrinal dispute within a shared framework, not as a dispute about fundamental assumptions. Kuhn's notion of a change of paradigm, or a scientific revolution, has been used to emphasize the magnitude of the change required, and to lend respectability to the idea that much of what now constitutes accepted theory must be abandoned. In addition, this dissent has, especially since the 1960s, become institutionalized, scholarly societies and academic journals being established to provide a forum for economists working in alternative paradigms. Thus, to name but a few, we have the *Journal of Economic Issues* centred on an institutional approach, the *Journal of Post Keynesian Economics* and the *Cambridge Journal of Economics* representing post-Keynesian economics, and the *Review of Radical Political Economy*.

There are two reasons why it is important to consider these alternative approaches here. The first is that they raise questions concerning the basic assumptions, or "hard core" of mainstream economics. The second is that it is useful to examine the extent of the differences between these alternative approaches and mainstream economics. Are the proponents of these alternative approaches, for example, merely changing a few assumptions, or are they following a completely different methodology? Are these approaches analogous to Kuhnian paradigms?

There is not space here to discuss these alternative approaches in detail, so this chapter will concentrate on examining a few alternative approaches, the emphasis being on how they impinge on mainstream economics, and on the response of mainstream economists to the challenges posed. The first five approaches to be considered are ones which are seen by their proponents as providing comprehensive, fundamentally different, approaches to that of the mainstream, namely Institutionalism, "Austrian" economics, post-Keynesian economics, Marxian and Radical economics. Also considered is the Chicago School, which, though not an alternative to mainstream economics in the same sense as the others, is sufficiently distinctive, and sufficiently important, to merit separate treatment. Some of the issues raised in discussing Chicago economics are relevant to an understanding of other approaches to economics.

## 28.2 INSTITUTIONALISM

*Ayres*

An important link between the institutionalism of Veblen and that of post-war economics is the work of Clarence Ayres. Though Ayres' first major work specifically on economics was his *Theory of Economic Progress* (1944), it is important to note that he started his graduate training at Chicago as early as *1916*, and that many of his ideas and his criticisms of orthodox economics date from the 1920s and 1930s.[1] In particular, some of the most important themes in Ayres' work can be found in two articles published in 1935.[2]

Ayres criticized orthodox, neoclassical economics on three main grounds. (1) He criticized the notion of equilibrium, claiming that they asserted more than merely cause and effect:

The laws of economics [i.e. of neoclassical economics] are "natural laws" of a distinctly theological persuasion, such as physical scientists have been struggling for a century and more to escape. In so far as they are efficacious at all, these laws take effect in a "natural" harmony or equilibrium of forces, a "balance", for instance, of supply and demand.[3]

He went on to argue that a "moderate acquaintance with modern science reveals it [this natural order] to be wholly without factual support. The affinity we feel for it is cultural".[4] He persisted in criticizing orthodox theory on these grounds, despite Knight's response that the concept of equilibrium involved no more than mechanical analogies.[5]

(2) Ayres criticized orthodox economic theory for attaching excessive importance to capital.[6] Classical economics, he argued, had erred in attributing a creative potency to capital, conceived as funds at interest:

Obviously funds, whether as interest or even as capital, create nothing. Investment brings nothing into existence. The "surplus" of which capitalists obtain (or retain) control by the institutional device of interest must have an objective existence. The real surplus is an excess of physical materials.[7]

Claiming that institutionalists had been wholly negative in their criticism of the orthodox theory of capital, Ayres argued that the explanation of the technical efficiency of western culture had to be sought in "the material culture itself".[8] The institutions of capitalism were permissive rather than creative. Ayres thus saw the evolution of technology as the dynamic force in social evolution. He saw a discrepancy between technology and institutions, for "technology grows of its own inherent character, whereas institutions do not".[9] This theme, of the dominance of technology, has remained throughout Ayres' work, in which he distinguished sharply between technological and ceremonial behaviour, seeing the former as fundamental.

(3) Technology was also important for Ayres in that it provided an absolute standard of value. He argued that individuals' attitudes could not

provide a basis on which the value of economic activities could be judged, for these were influenced by the customs of the society in which the individuals live. The only escape from the relativity of judgements based on individual preferences, and hence on customs, was to seek

some other basis of judgement altogether distinct from mores and therefore from the whole institutional aspect of civilization. That other basis is technology. I am therefore, in this sense, a complete materialist. It seems to me that technological process does indeed afford a basis of judgement which is absolute in the sense that it is in no wise dependent on any sort of moral inwardness nor upon any moral tradition whatever.[10]

Ayres thus argued the case for an instrumental theory of value: whatever contributes to the activity of a community in making a living is valuable, and whatever hinders this is economically deleterious: "The criterion of every economic judgement is 'keeping the machines running'."[11]

In addition, Ayres denied that "means" and "ends" were separate phenomena: every end is a means towards something else.[12] He thus rejected the orthodox approach of using an individualistic social welfare function: not only did he refuse to take wants as given, but also he did not see consumption as the end of economic activity.

Ayres berated classical economic theory for finding the meaning of the economy in price, arguing that "economics must be a science of value. If the economy is meaningless, no science of economics is possible. If it has meaning, the problem of economics is to elicit that meaning."[13] He argued that price theory was misleading, for not only did it create the illusion that value could be measured precisely, but also "price as we say 'sets a value' on goods and services which by other and less quantitative standards of value we do not hesitate to designate as 'anti-social' ".[14] Other ways of thinking about value were possible, provided that orthodox price theory, in which value resulted from the opposition of means and ends, were abandoned:

All that economic thinking has hitherto been obliged to exclude and reject – all that is excluded when it is assumed that "wants" and "primary" and that "scarcity" is defined by "nature" – all that we know today of social change, including the factors which actually shaped the industrial revolution: all this stands ready for assimilation into modern economics. It is only the barrier of price theory which prevents.[15]

### Galbraith

The most well-known of post-war Institutionalists is undoubtedly J. K. Galbraith, whose most important works are probably *American Capitalism* (1952), and *The New Industrial State* (1967). Galbraith views the economy as dominated not by competition, but by monopoly. He argues, however, that even monopolists are subject to constraints, these being imposed by what he calls "countervailing power".[16] Galbraith sees countervailing power as much more of a dynamic process than the bilateral monopoly of orthodox theory, for countervailing power is something which emerges in response to the growth of monopoly. For example, unionization emerges to act as a check on the power of large employers, or retailing chains are developed in response to monopoly in manufacturing.[17]

The constraints imposed by technology are crucial to Galbraith's view of how the economy works. He has argued that with the development of technology, the scale of investment becomes larger and larger, which means that firms can no longer afford to accept the risks involved in relying on the uncertainties of the market. The risks are, because of the size of the investment required, too large. Thus corporations are, according to Galbraith, forced into planning and into attempting to control the environment in which they operate. The importance of government contracts, negotiated outside the market, increases. Firms become involved in political activity. In addition, the manipulation of consumer taste, in order to ensure the success of new products, becomes a necessity. Advertising and the manipulation of consumers in the interests of large corporations is thus, for Galbraith, more than a merely accidental feature of capitalism.

Though this manipulation of consumers and the economy by large corporations has a beneficial role in the sense that it enables otherwise excessively risky investments to be undertaken, it is something of which Galbraith is as critical as was Veblen. The pattern of economic activities is distorted in undesirable directions. Particularly important is the encouragement of private consumption at the expense of public spending ("private affluence, public squalor"). In his criticism of big business, and in his appeal to wide audiences, Galbraith is the only contemporary economist to be the equal of Veblen, his *The Affluent Society* (1958) being comparable in its influence to Veblen's *Economic Theory of the Leisure Class*.

## Myrdal

A very different type of institutional economics from the institutional economics of either Ayres or Galbraith is that of Myrdal.[16] Myrdal's early work[19] was far from Institutionalism: on his first exposure to Commons' ideas, in 1930, he was not converted, seeing the rise of Institutionalist economics as a danger. His sympathies were closer to those of Fisher, Frisch and the founders of the econometric society.[20] The change in his attitudes took place with the studies of American race relations which formed the basis for *The American Dilemma* (1944). He found himself taken away from conventional economics by the need to adopt a much broader approach. This stress on factors other than purely economic ones, and on the need to consider societies as a whole, continued into his work, in the post-war period, on the problems of developing countries.[21]

The nature of Myrdal's Institutionalism is clearly shown by a quotation from the Prologue to his *Asian Drama* (1968), a study of South-east Asia.

Conditions in the rich Western countries today are such that, broadly speaking, the social matrix is permissive of economic development or, when not, becomes readily readjusted so as not to place much in the way of obstacles in its path. This is why an analysis in "economic" terms, abstracting from that social matrix, can produce valid and useful results. But that judgement cannot accurately be applied to South Asian conditions. Not only is the social and institutional structure different from the one that has evolved in Western countries, but, more important, the problem of development in South Asia is one calling for induced changes in that social and institutional structure, as it hinders economic development and as it does not change spontaneously, or, to any very large extent, in response to policies restricted to the "economic" sphere.[22]

He views people as being conditioned, even in their economic choices, "by their total mental make up" and "by the community in which they live", and as being "motivated in a variety of ways".[23] Because of this he rejects not only "economic man", but also "scientific man", arguing that "all knowledge and all ignorance tends to be opportunistic".[24] Whilst it is important to reduce such biases as far as possible through continually checking theories against empirical facts, complete objectivity is, Myrdal argues, impossible: "Valuations enter into the choice of approach, the selection of problems, the definition of concepts, and the gathering of data."[25]

If objectivity cannot be achieved through scientists being disinterested, how then can it be achieved? Myrdal's answer was the same as in his *The Political Element in the Development of Economic Theory* (1929), published nearly 40 years earlier: economics should be based on "explicit and concrete value premises"[26]:

The only way in which we can strive for objectivity in theoretical analysis is to lift up the valuations into the full light, make them conscious and explicit, and permit them to determine the viewpoints, the approaches and the concepts used.[27]

Thus in *Asian Drama*, Myrdal's first concern, after setting out the scope of the study, is to discuss *in detail* the value premises chosen, which he labels "the modernization ideals".[28]

Though Myrdal's approach is *very* different from the approaches of the other institutionalists discussed in this chapter and in chapter 18, there are nonetheless important common features. (1) Myrdal attaches great importance to the fact that social factors affect the way economists think about the problems which confront them. (2) He denies the possibility of removing value judgements from economic analysis. (3) He sees economic inquiry as concerned, in South-east Asia at least, with much more than conventional economics.

*Institutionalism*

In the late 1920s and early 1930s the influence of American Institutionalism was at its height, it being the advocates of quantitative, theoretical economics who were on the defensive,[29] but from the 1930s this influence rapidly waned.[30] In his *Theory of Economic Progress* (1944) Ayres described the victory of the orthodox over the Institutional approach as being, amongst professional economists, complete. Institutionalists, he argued, were credited merely with having called attention to the importance of matters which no economist should completely overlook although they do lie outside the field of economic analysis since they are not measured by price.[31]

Writing in 1976, Samuelson claimed that 40 years earlier, "Institutionalism withered away as an effective counterforce in economics."[32]

Institutionalism, however, did survive. The Association for Evolutionary Economics, with its *Journal of Economic Issues*, provides evidence for this. In it two viewpoints can be ascertained. One is that of Veblen and Ayres, stressing the fundamental importance of technology, and the distinction between technological and ceremonial institutions. The other viewpoint owes more to Commons', attaching much less importance, if any, to the Veblen–Ayres distinction between technology and institutions.[33] There is thus considerable variety within contemporary Institutionalism.

*The new institutional economics*

Very different from the Institutionalism discussed above is the so called "new institutional economics". Unlike the Institutionalism stemming from Veblen, the new institutional economics does not reject marginalism. Its emphasis is on extending the scope of orthodox microeconomics by taking account of previously neglected features of the economic system.[34] Greater institutional detail is introduced into theoretical models, making them less abstract. Organizational structures are perceived to affect incentives and behaviour, and are treated as a subject for economic analysis. In such analysis, transactions costs play an important role, for they provide reasons why transactions take place in one way rather than another. Coase's (1937) theory of the firm is the pioneering example of this type of theory. More recently, however, the approach has been applied much more widely. North (1981, 1984), for example, has attempted to interpret economic history in terms of the costs of political and economic organization.

Like Veblen's theory, the new institutional economics deals with institutional change, but its conception of the forces underlying this is closer to that of the "Austrians" than to Veblen's. Institutional change is seen to be generated largely by market forces, the direction of change being accounted for by the nature of transactions costs. Individuals are assumed to be pursuing their self-interest, and competition ensures that the most efficient institutions survive. The affinity with Commons' work, however, is greater. Like Commons, the proponents of the new institutional economics focus attention on transactions,[35] whilst institutions are conceived as rules and regulations which constrain behaviour.[36]

## 28.3  AUSTRIAN ECONOMICS

*Modern "Austrian" economics*

The Austrian school of economics stems from the work of Menger and his disciples. To a great extent Menger's ideas were assimilated into the mainstream of economic theory. In this process, however, Menger's ideas were combined with those of Walras and Jevons, as was done by Wicksell and Schumpeter. The result was that Austrian theory was thought to be about substantially the same basic theory as the Walrasian, the differences being those of emphasis and perspective. In Mises' words,

after some years all the essential ideas of the Austrian School were by and large accepted as an integral part of economic theory. About the time of Menger's demise (1921), one no longer distinguished between an Austrian School and other economics. The appellation "Austrian School" became the name given to an important chapter in the history of economic thought.[37]

Over the years, however, the mainstream of economic theory developed in a way very different from that intended by Menger. Subsequent generations of Austrian economists, notably Mises and Hayek, followed by certain of their students, in particular Rothbard, Kirzner and Lachman, claimed that when Austrian and Walrasian economics were combined, for example as in the work of Wicksell or Schumpeter, some of Menger's important insights were lost. What is now known as "Austrian" economics is thus not simply the economics stemming from Menger: it is the tradition that runs from Menger via Mises and Hayek, as opposed to that running via Böhm-Bawerk or Schumpeter.[38]

The first characteristic of "Austrian" economics (one shared with mainstream economics) is that it is individualistic, viewing economic activities as the outcome of the purposive activities of individuals. These individuals are assumed to operate in a changing environment in which the future is unknown, and information is limited. This has important implications for the way we view the individual. In Walrasian theory, the only relevant aspect of an individual is his or her tastes. Pareto, for example, wrote that "The individual can disappear, providing he leaves us this photograph [i.e. an indifference map] of his tastes."[39] In contrast, "Austrian" theory is based upon a richer view of the individual personality. Individuals' knowlege of their own tastes, their interpretations of current events, their expectations of future events, and their alertness to new opportunities are all considered important.[40]

It is necessary, however, to look beyond the individual, for human actions have consequences never intended by the individuals concerned. Thus "Austrians" are concerned with the evolution of social institutions, these being seen as evolving in response to the actions of individuals pursuing their own ends.[41] Money and markets are perhaps the most important such institutions.

Throughout "Austrian" economics there is a concern with time. Time is important not only because institutions develop over time, but also because the incompleteness of knowledge about the future, and the costs of obtaining information, mean that the economy will never actually be in equilibrium, but will continually be moving towards equilibrium. This leads to a much greater stress on entrepreneurship, on the process whereby new opportunities for profit are discovered, than is characteristic of general equilibrium theory.[42] "Austrian" economics is thus about explaining change. As a result of this competition is a dynamic process whereby the sources of high profits are eliminated over time. It is not the perfect competition of orthodox theory, in which no agent can influence the prices it faces, and in which profits are zero.

There is, within "Austrian" economics, a tendency to stress the gap between the methods appropriate to economic inquiry, and those used in the natural sciences. Kirzner has written of "Austrians" as being "deeply suspicious of attempts to apply measurement procedures to economics", and "sceptical of empirical 'proofs' of economic theorems".[43] There are two strands underlying this attitude. One is that of Mises' "praxeology",[44] whereby conclusions are derived from the logic of human action. Rothbard, for example, writes, "Apart from the fact that these conclusions cannot be 'tested' by empirical or statistical means, there is no *need* to test them since their truth has already been established."[45] Not altogether compatible with this is the second strand in "Austrian" methodology, according to which uncertainty and limitations of knowledge create fundamental problems for prediction in economics. On the one hand there are reasons why it is impossible to test economic theories conclusively: there are numerous unobservable variables, and aspects of economic theories, which cannot be tested. In addition, it has been argued that the act of choice is a spontaneous, creative, act, and as such is substantially unpredictable. According to Kirzner, "there is an indeterminacy and unpredictability inherent in human preferences, human expectations, and human knowledge".[46]

*Hayek*

This emphasis on uncertainty, and on the importance of knowledge, owes much to Hayek's "Economics and Knowledge" (1937).[47] He opened this article with the contention

that the tautologies, of which formal equilibrium analysis in economics essentially consists, can be turned into propositions which tell us anything about causation in the real world only in so far as we are able to fill those formal propositions with definite statements about how knowledge is acquired and communicated. In short, I shall contend that *the empirical element in economic theory* – the only part which is concerned not merely with implications but with causes and effects and which leads therefore to conclusions which, at any rate in principle, are capable of verification – *consists of propositions about the acquisition of knowledge.*[48]

In its simplest terms Hayek's argument here is that equilibrium denotes a situation in which, by definition, all agents' plans are synchronized with each other, and in which expectations are correct:

the concept of equilibrium merely means that the foresight of the different members of the society is in a special sense correct. It is correct in the sense that every person's plan is based on the expectation of just those actions of other people which those other people intend to perform[,] and that all these plans are based on the same set of external facts, so that under certain conditions nobody will have any reason to change his plans.[49]

Equilibrium relationships, according to Hayek, cannot be deduced from objective facts, for people's behaviour depends on what they know.[50] If equilibrium is then not an empirically based concept, how then can its use be defended? The only justification for its use, Hayek argues, "is the supposed tendency towards equilibrium. It is only by this assertion that such a tendency exists that economics ceases to be an exercise in pure logic and becomes an empirical science".[51] It might be thought that this was a question answered by conventional economics, for example by Walras's *tâtonnement*.[52] Hayek, however, argues that because such theories are based on the assumption of perfect markets, such theories assume what they purport to prove: they say nothing about the process whereby individuals' knowledge is changed in such a way as to make their behaviour consistent with equilibrium.[53] It is the usually "disguised and incomplete" assumptions "that people do learn from experience, and about how they acquire knowledge", which constitute the empirical content of propositions about the real world.[54]

Many of the ideas contained in Hayek's later work, and that of other "Austrians" can be traced back to this article. The centrality of individual behaviour in an uncertain world is paramount, with economic activity being seen in a dynamic context in which new information is continually being acquired and used. It is important to notice, however, that although he shares Mises' attitude towards equilibrium as indicating the direction of change, Hayek bases this on a methodology very different from Mises' praxeology. He is concerned throughout with empirical content in the sense of falsifiable propositions, a concern which has grown stronger in some of his post-war writings.[55] It is his concern with empirical content which leads him to stress the acquisition of knowledge, using the argument outlined above. Though we may, in constructing an economic theory, choose assumptions such that our theories of "perfect markets", or the logic of choice, are "a priori true", such a procedure would not provide us with what Hayek describes as "the justification which consists in the assumption that the situation in the real world is similar to what we assume it to be".[56]

### Shackle

Another economist who has laid great stress on the importance of uncertainty, and on the spontaneity of individual decision-making, is G. L. S. Shackle.[56] Shackle shares with both Keynes and Hayek a stress on the uncertainty and the ignorance involved in human affairs.

Fundamental to all Shackle's work is his stress on the prevalence of true uncertainty. It is inappropriate, Shackle argues, to analyse uncertainty in terms of probabilities, for the distinguishing feature of uncertainty, as opposed to risk, is that we have no information on which to base a calculation of probabilities.[57] Probabilities, and hence decision rules such as the maximization of expected utility, are appropriate only where the same "experiment" is repeated, to provide relative frequencies on which probabilities can be based. Where genuinely new events are involved, that is events which have never occurred before, there can be no basis on which to calculate expected probabilities, even subjective ones.

Shackle postulates an alternative treatment of uncertainty, based on two new concepts: possibility and potential surprise. Even though we may not be able to attach a probability to an event, because nothing like it has ever happened before, we may be able to say whether we think its occurrence to be possible, and how surprised we would be if it were to occur.[58]

Having suggested this alternative to the orthodox theory of probability, however, Shackle does not simply go on to replace maximization of expected utility with a maximizing model based on a different treatment of uncertainty. This is because he stresses, in a way no other economist has done, the creativity and spontaneity of human actions.[59] Conventional economic theory is based on the assumption of rational behaviour, but, according to Shackle,

> Reason is not sufficient for the guidance of conduct. … Economic choice does not consist in comparing the items in a list, known to be complete, of fully specified rival and certainly attainable results. It consists in first creating, by conjecture and reasoned imagination on the basis of mere suggestions offered by visible or recorded circumstance, the things on which hope can be fixed. These things, at the time when they are available for choice, are thoughts and even figments … if we wish to claim that reason by itself is a sufficient guide for conduct, we need to claim, not that reason can find novelty, but that it can find *all* novelty and thus *exhaust* novelty.[60]

Shackle is thus critical of what he calls the "rational ideal", the explanation of economic phenomena in terms of rational behaviour, for he sees the scope for rational action as being of necessity severely limited.

Shackle, like Hayek and modern "Austrians", sees time as central to economics, arguing that orthodox theory has failed to recognize important aspects of time. Time is irreversible, and future events are uncertain, not least because human actions are creative, and hence not completely explicable in terms of past events. Economic phenomena, therefore, must be explained in terms of a dynamic process in which the past is irrevocable, and the future inherently unpredictable. Using the analogy of a kaleidoscope, Shackle has christened such a process "kaleidics". Consider Shackle's discussion of the expectations which underlie decisions to invest:

> Expectations are *kaleidic*. Like the symmetric pattern of colours in the kaleidoscope, they can be changed comprehensively and radically by a slight shock or twist given to the instrument, or to the evidence in the mind of the expectation former. "Stretch of time" is a figment, it is memory or else imagination engendered by the evidence existing in the *actual present*. But the value to be assigned to a so-called "durable" tool or plant can be based only on the supposed content of this fundamental stretch of future time. Expectational value is a structure of thought resting at only one point on the ground of visibly recorded evidence. A small irregularity as the wheel rolls forward can lift it bodily or even deform and destroy it. The consequences of the kaleidicity of investment-values can be formidable and far-reaching.[61]

Shackle has argued that it was with such a process that Keynes was concerned.[62]


## 28.4   POST-KEYNESIAN ECONOMICS

*Interpreting the* General Theory

After the *General Theory* Keynes' ideas were interpreted and developed by Hicks, Hansen, Samuelson and others in terms of the framework provided by general equilibrium theory.[63] There also emerged, however, a tradition critical of this development.[64] Proponents of this alternative interpretation of Keynes could turn for support to several passages in Keynes' work. Firstly, there were the passages in the *General Theory* in which Keynes explicitly attacked the propositions of "classical economics".[65] More important than this, however, were passages where Keynes stressed the fundamental importance of uncertainty as to the future course of events.

In chapter 12 of the *General Theory*, for example, Keynes, in discussing the determinants of the marginal efficiency of capital, drew attention to "the extreme precariousness of the basis of knowledge on which our estimates of prospective yields have to be made".[66] Keynes, therefore, did not regard the marginal efficiency of investment schedule as stable. More importantly, however, the presence of uncertainty was fundamental to Keynes' theory of money. Differences of opinion as to the future course of interest rates, for which uncertainty was a prerequisite, underlay Keynes' speculative motive for holding money. It was the speculative demand for money which led Keynes to reject the notion of "the demand for money as a whole being proportional, or having some determinate relation, to income".[67] It was only a *portion* of the public's cash holdings that was related to income. In arguing this, Keynes was thus doing much more than merely introducing the rate of interest into the demand for money function: (1) his speculative demand meant that his demand for money function was not homogeneous (a change in income would not change demand for money in the same proportion);[68] and (2) demand for money changed with expectations, monetary policy, which would affect expectations as well as the quantity of money, affecting the interest rate via both supply and demand for money.[69] In addition, the presence of uncertainty was important to Keynes' argument that money was an asset with very special properties, not merely one asset amongst many.[70]

Thus when Keynes, in response to his critics, expounded the main themes of the *General Theory* in an article in the *Quarterly Journal of Economics* (1937), he stressed uncertainty as the factor distinguishing his theory from that of the classical economists.[71] He argued that classical economics allowed only for the possibility of risk, not for genuine uncertainty. In reality, Keynes argued, probabilities are not calculable, for "we have only the vaguest idea of any but the most direct consequences of our actions".[72] He drew the conclusion, "I accuse the classical economic theory of being itself one of those pretty, polite techniques which tries to deal with the present by abstracting from the fact that we know very little about the future."[73]

It is these two themes, the inappropriateness of supply and demand theories based on maximizing behaviour, and the importance of uncertainty about the future, which are taken by its proponents to justify the designation of their work as "Post-Keynesian". Post-Keynesian economics is claimed to be post-Keynesian, not merely chronologically, or in the sense of accepting certain aspects of the Keynesian system, but in the more profound sense of recognizing, in a way not true of mainstream economics, the fundamental criticisms of classical theories made by Keynes. Post-Keynesians, for example, seek to take seriously Keynes' claim that the importance of money lies in its being a link between the present and an uncertain future. It follows from this, for example, that it is an important characteristic of a monetary economy, for example, that wage bargains are in terms of money: that the wage bargain determines the nominal wage rate, not the real wage rate.[74] Such an assertion would not make sense in many general equilibrium models.

Although taking the lead from Keynes' *General Theory*, Post-Keynesian economics has also leaned heavily both on more recent developments in the theory of capital, and on certain other parts of Keynes' work. The criticisms of the neoclassical aggregate production function stemming from Robinson's work[75] have been used to reinforce the argument that neoclassical price theory is fundamentally, and irreparably, flawed. Not only is there, for reasons exposed in the *General Theory*, no tendency to a full employment equilibrium, but even if there were, the assumption of diminishing marginal productivity, on which neoclassical factor demand curves are based, is unjustifiable.[76] Thus the neoclassical theory cannot explain the distribution of income between factors, even should these be fully employed, and an alternative has to be found.

In seeking an alternative to the marginal productivity theory of income distribution, Post-Keynesian economists turned to the ideas put forward by Keynes in his *Treatise on Money* (1930) and by Kalecki (1933), later developed by Robinson, Kaldor and Pasinetti.[77] Though this theory of distribution, sometimes called the "Cambridge" theory, is quite compatible with factor prices being equal to marginal productivities obtained from a neoclassical aggregate production function,[78] it is used by Post-Keynesians as an alternative to this theory.

These criticisms of neoclassical economics are brought together by Robinson, one of its most persistent Post-Keynesian critics, in her discussion of "historical time". She distinguishes between two types of argument:

One kind of argument proceeds by specifying a sufficient number of equations to determine the unknowns, and so finding values for them which are compatible with each other... . The other type of argument specifies a particular set of values obtaining at a point of time, which are not, in general, in equilibrium with each other, and shows how their interactions may be expected to play themselves out.[79]

She argues that there is a fundamental difference between the two types of model, for

> in a model depicting equilibrium positions there is no causation. It consists of a closed circle of simultaneous equations. The value of each element is entailed by the values of the rest. [In contrast,] in an historical model, causal relations have to be specified.[80]

In an historical model the past is irrevocable, and the future uncertain. It is inappropriate, therefore, either to treat capital as malleable, or to neglect the importance of money.

### Neo-Ricardian economics

An important aspect of post-Keynesian economics has been the revival of interest in the Ricardian–Marxian theory of value.[81] The main contribution to this revival was Sraffa's *Production of Commodities by Means of Commodities* (1960), subtitled "Prelude to a critique of economic theory." Central to Sraffa's system is a set of equations each linking the price of a commodity to its cost of production. Production costs include the costs of produced commodities used up in production, and also the cost of labour, a non-produced input. Anything left over after paying these necessary costs of production is a surplus. Making the assumption that competition will result in a uniform rate of profit and a uniform wage rate, Sraffa thus has $n$ equations, where $n$ is the number of produced commodities:

$$(1 + r)\{p_1a_{11} + p_2a_{12} \ldots + p_na_{1n} + wl_1 \} = p_1$$
$$(1 + r)\{p_1a_{21} + p_2a_{22} \ldots + p_na_{2n} + wl_2\} = p_2$$
$$\vdots$$
$$(1 + r)\{p_1a_{n1} + p_2a_{n2} \ldots + p_na_{nn} + wl_n\} = p_n$$

In these equations $p_1$ is the price of the $i$th commodity, $w$ the wage rate, $r$ the rate of profit, $a_{ij}$ the amount of commodity $j$ used in producing a unit of commodity $i$, and $l_i$ is the labour used in producing commodity $i$.[82]

In these equations there are $n+2$ prices: $n$ commodity prices, the wage rate and the rate of profit. We can take one of these as *numéraire*, which means that there are $n+1$ prices to be determined. As there are only $n$ equations this means that something else has to be brought in before prices are fully determined. The obvious possibility is to introduce an explanation of the distribution of income, such as a subsistence wage rate, Marx's rate of exploitation, or a Keynesian theory of the rate of profit. Any of these would supply the necessary extra equation.

It is this need to bring in an extra equation which forms the basis for Dobb's claim that there is a dichotomy, "in which prices are derived from (or in part dependent on) conditions of distribution rather than distribution being derived from the structure of prices treated as being in turn a resultant of demand".[83]

Distribuion is thus, for Dobb, not a part of the general process of price-determination: "there was a crucial sense in which distribution was *prior* to exchange: namely, that price-relations or exchange values could only be arrived at *after* the principle affecting distribution of the total product had been postulated."[84]

*A neoclassical interpretation of neo-Ricardian theory*

Before considering the case in favour of Sraffa's approach it is useful to see how Sraffa's system looks from the point of view provided by general equilibrium theory. Sraffa's equations are in themselves quite compatible with neoclassical general equilibrium theory, for competitive equilibrium requires that pure profits are zero (that normal profits are earned in all industries). Indeed, it is *because* Sraffa's equations can be used to describe one aspect of a general equilibrium model that they could be used to criticize the neoclassical production function. Sraffa's system thus appears related to the linear models of Cassel, Leontief or von Neumann. Thus Hahn has written that "there is no correct neo-Ricardian proposition which is not contained in the set of propositions which can be generated by orthodoxy".[85]

From this perspective, the neo-Ricardian approach seems to depend on certain important simplifications. One of the clearest statements of such a view is that of Bliss (1975), who has argued that in what he calls the "Cambridge model",

the irritations arising from the interdependent network of influences are circumvented by some special assumptions that have the effect of allowing the state of the economy to be solved out and discussed in three distinct stages:

(1) The rate of interest (here equal to the rate of profit) is determined by a relation ... between the need for investment funds implied by the growth of the economy and the supply of these funds which is related to the level of profits. From this step is derived the rate of interest [profit[86]].

(2) Given the rate of interest it is possible to determine, independently of demand conditions and the growth rate, the costs of production of all goods ... and the techniques of production that the economy will use. From this step come relative prices.

(3) Finally, demand conditions may be brought in to determine the rates of output, given the techniques of production. ...

Here is an undeniably attractive scheme and it is not surprising that economists have found it absorbing. As a decomposable structure it has the advantage of simplicity; given a change in specification one ascertains which steps in the solution procedure are affected and it is then not difficult to work out the consequences ... and to obtain definite conclusions.[87]

He goes on to argue, however, that "the assumptions necessary to support this edifice are so restrictive that it is difficult to attach a great deal of weight to it".[85] These assumptions include: (1) saving is a constant proportion of profits, there being no other sources of saving; (2) there is only *one* non-produced input (labour); (3) there are constant returns to scale.[89] Bliss is thus very critical of this approach:

We have here an example of a general analytical method which proceeds by embedding the variable whose magnitude is desired in an equation in which all other terms are deemed by assumption to be constants. The method has been called "Ricardian" by Schumpeter [90] and "implicit theorizing" by Leontief [91]. The trouble with this method of treating problems is not merely that things are assumed to be constant which are certainly not constant, though that is indeed a tendency; but also that *factors which ought to be analysed and made the subject of economic theories remain unanalysed, or are analysed only crudely.*[92]

*A defence of Neo-Ricardian theory*

If Sraffa's equations can be seen as describing merely certain aspects of a simplified general equilibrium system, how can it provide the basis for an *alternative* to the neoclassical theory of value? To answer this question it is useful to note that Sraffa started work on what became *Production of Commodities by Means of Commodities* in the late *1920s*. Thus although it was not published until 1960, the book arose *not* out of the 1950s' controversy over capital theory, but out of the discussions of Marshall's theory of the firm which took place in the 1920s.[93] Sraffa's main contribution to this discussion had been to argue that Marshallian partial equilibrium analysis was compatible only with constant returns to scale. Because he saw increasing returns to scale as being incompatible with the assumption of perfect competition, Sraffa advocated, in his *Economic Journal* article of 1926, moving towards a theory of monopoly.

In *Production of Commodities*, however, Sraffa moved even further from Marshallian theory, dropping *all* assumptions about returns to scale. He was concerned to develop only those propositions which did not depend on assumptions about returns to scale. To do this he abandoned the concepts of supply and demand curves, together with the idea that prices and quantities were determined simultaneously. Sraffa used his system of equations not to determine equilibrium prices, but to determine the prices of production which corresponded to a *given* level of output. This meant that if the level of production were to change, so too would the input–output coefficients, and hence the prices of production. It was because he interpreted his equations in this way that he did not have to make any assumption about returns to scale.

This method has been explained by Roncaglia (1977) in the following way:

Analytically, the situation of a certain economic system is considered as it might appear from a "photograph" taken at a given moment. All economic magnitudes which are not the object of analysis may be considered as data. ... In the case of *Production of Commodities by Means of Commodities* Sraffa has chosen the relationship between production prices and distributive variables (rate of profits and wage rate) as the objects of the analysis. All other variables (technology, levels of output, firm structure of all industries, etc) are taken as the data of the problem.

It must be stressed, however, that this choice does not imply an *a priori* refusal of the possibility of analyzing the problems of technological development, levels of output, strategy of firms, etc. This choice stems from the necessity of analyzing the different problems one by one, and each in isolation. The necessary assumptions and methods of analysis are not necessarily identical for all problems; for each of them only what is relevant should be included, leaving aside those elements which, as Ricardo said, simply "modify" the analysis but do not change it substantially.[94]

A similar defence of the Ricardian method has been provided by Bharadwaj (1978):

social output and methods of production were provisionally taken as data for the value problem in classical political economy *in recognition of the fact that the determinants of these were diverse and not explained on the basis of relative prices alone or within the scheme of abstraction adopted to work out the value question.*[95]

The crucial aspect of this is Bharadwaj's claim that different levels of abstraction are required for dealing with different problems. She argues that the classical framework is less restrictive than the supply and demand framework, for

it does not commit itself through its theoretical structure to any form and direction of change; in other words, the classical theory is not constrained to permit only some specific changes of the many possible ones as alone consistent with theory. Thus it does not have to presume more than is necessary for the limited objective of determining relative values at one "observed" position of the economic system.[96]

The value of the classical theory of value is seen to be twofold: (1) it emphasizes the primacy of costs of production in determining values; and (2) it does not lead us astray when we study in greater detail the conditions under which exchange takes place in particular cases, for it does not conceal from us the fact that to analyse exchange in particular circumstances it is necessary to go beyond the theory's assumptions.[97]

Roncaglia and Bharadwaj thus see an important methodological difference between neoclassical and neo-Ricardian economics. The neo-Ricardian argument, as represented by Roncaglia and Bharadwaj, is that it is pointless to seek a completely general theory. Roncaglia argues, for example, that marginalist theory is based on the premise that there is "a method which can be used to analyse *all* the relevant aspects of reality".[98] He supports this with a quotation from Samuelson's *Foundations*:

The existence of analogies between central features of various theories implies the existence of a general theory which underlies the particular theories and unifies them with respect to these central features.... It is the purpose of the pages that follow to work out [the] implications for theoretical and applied economics [of this fundamental principle of generalization by abstraction].[99]

In marginalist analysis, Roncaglia argues, the givens are consumers' tastes, technology and resource endowments. These, he argues, are "the result of complex social phenomena, which cannot be considered to be independent of the economic phenomena that the marginalists consider to be the object of the analysis".[100] He thus concludes that marginalist theory is not nearly as general as it might appear to be.

Similarly, Bharadwaj criticizes the nature of the interdependence allowed for in supply and demand theories:

the *classical* value problem was worked out in a framework of economic interdependence between production, consumption, distribution and exchanges altogether different from the equilibrium framework where these are interlinked through the market forces of supply and demand.[101]

The issue, Bharadwaj argues, is thus not one of partial versus general equilibrium analysis, but is rather one of whether the interdependence between various aspects of the economic problem can be analysed in terms of a single model. Bharadwaj chooses, for example, to follow Marx's analysis of the relation of production and consumption, seeing "historically evolved production relations" as determinng the social norms of consumption.[102] This is interdependence, but not of the type allowed for in marginalist theory.

## 28.5  MARXIAN AND RADICAL ECONOMICS

*Marxian economics*

During the period covered by this chapter a number of attempts were made to interpret Marxian economics in the light of modern non-Marxist economics, and it is these on which this section will concentrate. Most of the Marxist literature of the period will be neglected, for it is of little relevance to an understanding of developments within the mainstream of economics. Since 1939, however, non-Marxist economists have paid a significant amount of attention to Marx, many of them reaching the conclusion that Marx raised interesting technical issues, and that his attempts at solving these problems, though not always satisfactory, are worth taking seriously. The attention paid to Marx's work was probably at its height in the early 1970s, following the ferment of radical ideas associated with opposition to the Vietnam war. Marxian economics came to be re-evaluated, not merely by young economists who embraced Marxian ideas, but also by economists who remained firmly within the non-Marxian mainstream of economic thought. Symbolic of the change which took place was the change in Samuelson's attitude. In 1962 he described Marx as, "from the viewpoint of pure economic theory, a minor post-Ricardian ... a not uninteresting precursor of Leontief's input–output".[103] In contrast, the view he expressed in 1974 was that, on the basis of his schemes of reproduction, "one can claim immortal fame for Marx".[104] Since the mid 1970s, however, interest in Marxist economics has lessened.[105]

The starting point in modern attempts to evaluate Marx in the light of modern economic theory is Lange's "Marx and modern economic theory" (1935). In this article Lange claimed that Marxian and bourgeois economics were each fitted to answer a different type of question:

let us imagine two persons: one who has learned his economics from the Austrian School, Pareto and Marshall, without ever having seen or even heard a sentence of Marx or his disciples; the other one who, on the contrary, knows his economics exclusively from Marx and the Marxists and does not even suspect that there may have been economists outside the Marxist school. Which of the two will be able to account better for the fundamental tendencies of the evolution of Capitalism? To put the question is to answer it.

But this superiority of Marxian economics is only a partial one. There are some problems before which Marxian economics is quite powerless, while "bourgeois" economics solves them easily. What can Marxian economics say about monopoly prices? What has it to say on the fundamental problems of monetary and credit theory? What apparatus has it to offer for analysing the incidence of a tax, or the effect of a certain technical innovation on wages? And (irony of Fate!) what can Marxian economics contribute to the problem of the optimum distribution of productive resources in a socialist economy?

Clearly the relative merits of Marxian economics and of modern "bourgeois" economic theory belong to different "ranges".[106]

Lange went on to conclude that any superiority of Marxian economics was not due to the economic concepts Marx used, but to "the exact specification of the institutional datum distinguishing Capitalism from the concept of an exchange economy in general".[107] Marxian economics could thus explain and predict the evolution of capitalism. This was true even though the labour theory of value was inadequate for Marx's purposes, being unable to explain prices when the economy was out of equilibrium.[108]

A defence of the classical and Marxian approach to value theory was provided two years later by Dobb (1937), who argued that the choice between a cost theory of value (of which the labour theory is an example) and a subjective theory, was related to the issue of whether or not it was meaningful to talk of a surplus in the economy. According to Dobb, the concept of the surplus was crucial to classical and Marxian political economy, for it provided the basis on which to distinguish between one type of income and another. In classical and Marxian economics it is possible to say that some incomes correspond to a necessary cost of production, and that others correspond to a surplus over this cost. However, in contrast,

in the modern theory of subjective value the very concept of surplus, contrasted with cost, loses any essential meaning, and a criterion for any fundamental distinction between different classes is lacking.[109]

Dobb interpreted the transition from classical to subjective value theory in Marxian terms. According to Marx's theory of ideology,

the abstract ideas which were fashioned from a given society tended to assume a phantom or fetishistic character, in the sense that, being taken as representatives of reality, they came to depict actual society in an inverted or a distorted form. Thereby they served not merely to hide the real nature of society from men's eyes, but to misrepresent it.[110]

Following Marx in dating the significant change from 1830, an interpretation of the historical evidence for which he has, justifiably, been very strongly criticized,[111] Dobb viewed the movement to a subjective value theory in these terms. Through rendering meaningless the concept of the surplus, subjective value theory served, according to Dobb, to disguise the true nature of capitalism.[112]

In 1942 two book-length appraisals of Marxian economics were published: Robinson's *Essay on Marxian Economics* and Sweezy's *The Theory of Capitalist Development*.[113] Sweezy's book was important because it revived interest in the transformation problem, drawing attention to von Bortkeiwicz's solution. Both books viewed Marxian economics sympathetically but critically, appraising it, as had Lange, in the light of modern economic theory. Both Sweezy and Robinson, for example, were critical of Marx's doctrine of the falling rate of profit. In addition, both of them brought Keynesian ideas about under-consumption into their discussions of Marx.

Subsequent attempts to reinterpret Marxian economics have been on rather different lines, a major reason for this being developments in non-Marxian economic theory. The first of these is the development of linear production models of the type used by Leontief. The other was post-war growth theory. It was only after the developments in these two fields that non-Marxian economists possessed a framework within which Marxian economics could be evaluated. Linear models were needed to make sense of Marx's numerical examples relating both to value and to growth. Growth theory was needed in order to understand what Marx was doing in his schemes of reproduction. It was only in the light of modern theories that it became evident that the problems Marx was tackling were worth considering.[114]

It was seen, for example, that Marx's schemes of reproduction had much in common with the approach to growth found in von Neumann's work.[115] This approach to Marx is perhaps most clearly presented in Morishima's *Marx's Economics* (1973), where Morishima argues that Marx started with a multi-commodity model which he wished to aggregate in order to obtain a macroeconomic growth model with only two sectors, namely the model used in volume II of *Capital*. This is an interpretation of Marxian economics that would have been hard to conceive in the absence of post-war discussions of growth and of aggregation in macroeconomic models. To illustrate the way in which such a new interpretation can open up possibilities previously unimaginable, it is worth noting Morishima's conclusion. This is that the labour theory of value has to be abandoned, not for any ideological reason, but because, for various technical reasons, it is unsuitable for the purpose for which it is used. Morishima argued that Marx's model could be repaired by using prices taken from von Neumann instead of labour values. This specific conclusion is far less important than the fact that interpreting Marx, or anyone else for that matter, in a new framework, can make possible radically different attitudes.

Another widely discussed aspect of Marxian economics was the transformation problem, together with the related issues of the labour theory of value, exploitation and profits. Underlying all these discussions was von Bortkiewicz's solution of the transformation problem, to which Sweezy had drawn attention. Von Bortkeiwicz's solution, however, worked only where there were three sectors. For economists familiar with Leontief and von Neumann models it was a simple step to analysing Marx's problem. Thus in 1957 Seton generalized von Bortkiewicz's solution to cover the general, *n* sector, case.

A separate influence on the discussion was that of Sraffa, for not only did Sraffa use a Leontief-type technology, but he was also, despite his un-Marxian stress on commodities as being produced by commodities rather than by labour, concerned with issues similar to those with which Marx was concerned. Sraffa was concerned with the relationship between distribution and prices in a way in which Leontief was not. The reason for this was simple: Marx and Sraffa were, in an important sense, Ricardians. Thus where Marx, in his discussions of the labour theory of value, was led to use the concept of an industry in which the organic composition of capital equalled the economy-wide average, Sraffa could use his "standard commodity".[116]

Like those who started from von Neumann, economists whose starting point was Sraffa were also led to reappraise the Marxian system. Steedman (1977), for example, reached the conclusion that

the proximate determinants of the rate of profit, the rate of accumulation, the prices of production, the social allocation of labour etc. are the physical conditions of production, the real wage and the capitalist desire to accumulate.[117]

He went on to argue that, in order to provide a materialist account of capitalist societies it was necessary to investigate the social, economic, political and technical determinants of these proximate determinants. This programme, despite its being thoroughly Marxian rather than neoclassical in its approach, would "involve no reference to Marx's value magnitudes".[118] Steedman claimed that the relationship between exploitation and profits could be understood without recourse to the labour theory of value.

Despite important differences in their attitudes to Marx, both Morishima and Steedman were attempting to keep what they considered the important aspects of Marxian theory by abandoning aspects of his theory, however important they had previously been considered, that would not stand up to criticism.

### Radical economics

The issues discussed above all relate to technical aspects of the Marxian system, its Ricardian component. This should not, however, be taken as implying that the other strand in Marx's thought, the denunciations of the injustices of the capitalist system, stemming from his early writings,[119] have been neglected in recent decades. Important here is what is often known, both by critics and supporters, as "Radical economics".[120] Though Radical

Economics is not the same as Marxian economics, Radical economists comprising some Marxists, some Post-Keynesians, plus others who fit into neither category, its concerns have strong affinities with those of Marxism, especially those of the early Marx.[121] Radical economics is the product of the 1960s, and in particular of the protest movements which centred on opposition to the American role in the Vietnam war.[122] It is to some extent the fact that many Radical economists are held together by a similar political position that accounts for the diversity of views on the technical aspects of economic theory. Though Radical economics extends far beyond this, it is represented by the Union of Radical Political Economy, founded in 1968.

Radical economics has been more than a narrowly academic movement, stressing the importance of political activism, decrying excessive technical specialization, and seeking to widen participation in economic discussion.[123] Its importance here, however, lies in the fact that Radical economists have produced a series of criticisms of conventional economic theory. Lindbeck (1971), an outsider investigating American Radical economics, listed five main criticisms of orthodox economic theory. (1) It avoids discussing the distribution of incomes, wealth and economic power. (2) Taking tastes and resources as given, it is much too restricted in its outlook. (3) It analyses small, marginal changes, rather than large changes which might fundamentally alter the nature of the economic system. (4) It pays too little attention to the "quality" of life. (5) It neglects the interaction of economic with social and political factors.[124] The role of markets and optimizing behaviour is thus played down in favour of a greater stress on the development and role of institutions. Static theorizing in terms of equilibrium models is disparaged.

There is, within Radical economics, an emphasis on inequalities and other undesirable features of the capitalist system, this determining the direction of research. Racial and sexual inequality, and the role of developing countries in exploiting the third world, are thus examples of topics Radical economists consider important. However, whilst Radical economists have made important points concerning the research agenda of mainstream economics, and whilst they have raised important questions concerning some of the assumptions often made in economic theorizing, it is far less clear that they have undermined the mainstream approach. In many areas it is the orthodox approach, of analysing the implications of maximizing behaviour under alternative assumptions, that throws light on the problems raised by Radical economists. Thus the mechanisms linking the incompleteness of labour contracts to unemployment and inflation have been analysed by economists very much within the mainstream; segmented labour markets have been the basis for much Institutionalist labour economics; discrimination has been analysed by Chicago economists, and so on.[125] A strong case can be made out to the effect that some of the most fruitful research has arisen when orthodox, neoclassical methods have been applied to the issues raised by Radical economists, not when orthodox methods have been abandoned.

## 28.6  THE CHICAGO SCHOOL

Even more than any of the "alternative approaches" considered above, the Chicago School is in many ways placed firmly within the mainstream of economic thought. It is however, appropriate to consider it here, for two reasons. The first is to emphasize the differences between Chicago economics and other branches of mainstream economics. The second reason is to point out the difference between Chicago economics and that of the "Austrians", something which is necessary because the two approaches are easily grouped together on the basis of their strongly libertarian positions, and their advocacy of free markets.

The Chicago School is the name usually given to the school, based at Chicago, though not encompassing all economists there, dominated above all by Friedman and Stigler, and before them by Knight, Viner and Simons. A succinct statement of the Chicago view has been provided by Friedman:

In discussions of economic policy "Chicago" stands for belief in the efficiency of the free market as a means of organizing resources, for scepticism about government affairs, and for emphasis on the quantity of money as a key factor in producing inflation.

In discussions of economic science, "Chicago" stands for an approach that takes seriously the use of economic theory as a tool for analyzing a startlingly wide range of concrete problems, rather than as an abstract mathematical structure of great beauty but little power; for an approach that insists on the empirical testing of theoretical generalizations and that rejects alike facts without theory and theory without facts.[126]

To understand the differences between the Chicago view and the alternatives we need to look more closely at the nature of the theory involved. Reder (1982) has argued that Chicago economics is based on what he describes as

the hypothesis that decision makers so allocate resources under their control that there is no alternative allocation such that any one decision maker could have his expected utility increased without a reduction occurring in the expected utility of at least one other decision maker.[127]

In other words, the Chicago view is characterized by the strong presumption that the allocation of resources is Pareto-efficient. To obtain testable empirical hypotheses from this starting point, four supplementary hypotheses are required: (1) most, though not all, agents take prices as being independent of the quantities they wish to buy or sell; (2) the prices at which agents agree to trade are market clearing prices; (3) information is bought and sold in the quantity that makes its price equal its marginal cost; (4) neither government intervention nor monopoly alters prices sufficiently to prevent the prices and marginal products of identical resources from being equalized.[128]

These are viewed as sufficiently good approximations to reality that the predictions of an exact model (i.e. a model containing no random variables) based on these assumptions can be taken as adequate to explain the behaviour of expected prices and quantities in the real world.[129] Chicago economists have analysed phenomena such as imperfect competition and market failure, but where the existence of such phenomena is established, they are not seen as requiring a shift of emphasis away from the basic competitive model.[130] This approach has proved extraordinarily versatile, proving capable of being applied to an enormous range of issues. Friedman has used it to analyse inflation and unemployment.[131] Stigler has applied it to models of search (such as workers searching for jobs) where information is imperfect.[132] Becker has used it to investigate the allocation of time,[133] and to investigate phenomena seemingly far from economics such as marriage and divorce.[134] Lucas has applied it to the formation of expectations.[135]

Chicago economics has been described, by a critic of both, as being "the extreme vanguard of neoclassicism".[136] There are, however, very substantial differences between Chicago methodology and that of many mainstream economists. One difference is that much of recent theoretical work on general equilibrium theory has no place within the Chicago framework. Abstract theoretical issues, such as those faced by Arrow, Debreu and their successors, concerning the existence, uniqueness and stability of equilibrium, conflicts with the Chicago criterion of empirical relevance. It is probably such theorizing that Friedman dismisses when he refers to abstract mathematical structures "of great beauty but little power".[137]

More important, however, is the extreme reluctance of Chicago economists to alter their theory to accommodate observed behaviour which appears inconsistent with the assumption that individuals are optimizing subject to constraints. If the empirical data appear sound, and if the theory cannot be extended to accommodate observed behaviour within an optimizing framework, then the problem is likely to be placed on the research agenda as a researchable anomaly.[138] Thus Chicago economists

are far less willing than others to accept reports of irrational or inefficient behaviour at face value ... and typically seek to discredit or reinterpret such reports so as to protect the basic theory.[139]

In contrast, many non-Chicago economists would not reject an argument simply because it implies a failure to optimize: for them, markets may or may not clear, individuals may or may not be completely rational, and so on.[140]

Because of their shared emphasis on competitive markets, and a common scepticism as to the possibility of using state intervention to improve on the market's allocation of resources, Chicago policy recommendations can sound very similar to "Austrian" ones. The two approaches are, however, very different. Most important, "Austrians" emphasize that the economy will never actually be in equilibrium, merely moving towards it. "Austrians" would thus not share the concern to model behaviour in terms of continuous equilibrium. Attitudes towards the empirical testing of theories are also sharply different, Chicago economists sharing none of the "Austrian" scepticism as to the value of empirical testing.[141] Even Hayek, though accepting a Popperian methodology, remains sceptical as to the extent to which the propositions of economic theory can, in practice, be tested. This contrasts with the Chicago belief that, though there is a strong presumption against accepting empirical evidence which appears to conflict with the"hard core" outlined above, the predictions of economic theory must continually be confronted with empirical evidence. With Mises' methodology there is an even sharper disagreement. A further point is that Chicago shares none of the "Austrian" reluctance to use aggregates. Friedman's stress on the virtues of simple models, for example, leads naturally into a highly aggregated approach such as is characteristic of his investigations into monetary economics.

# 29

# Economics and Policy in Britain
# 1939–1980

## 29.1 INTRODUCTION

In this chapter a number of issues arising in post-war discussions of economic policy will be considered. The first two concern general changes in attitudes to macroeconomic policy: the "Keynesian revolution" of the 1940s, and the demise of Keynesianisms in the 1970s. In addition, the issues of exchange rate policy, the European Community and policies to raise the growth rate are very briefly considered. It is important to stress that neither is this selection of topics exhaustive, nor does it necessarily include the most important topics. The topics chosen are, however, enough to support some general observations on the relationship of economic theory and policy.

## 29.2 THE ADOPTION OF KEYNESIAN POLICIES

Perhaps the most important aspect of the adoption of Keynesian ideas on managing the economy is that this was a slow and gradual process, involving pressure of circumstances and political pressures as well as simply the influence of new ideas. Keynes' *General Theory* produced no instant conversion of official opinion. The process whereby Keynesian ideas came to be adopted falls into four phases: from the *General Theory* to the outbreak of war; the problems of war finance; wartime discussions of employment policy; and the policy of the first post-war government.

### The Treasury and recovery

There was, in the late 1930s, a clear difference in approach between Keynes and the economists in the Treasury advising ministers. Particularly important was Sir Richard Hopkins, responsible for providing the government with advice on financial policy and government expenditure from 1927 to 1945. One historian has written of him, "if he thought an idea all right the official world would accept it".[1] There was considerable continuity between his ideas in the late 1930s, and the ideas he held in 1929 when Lloyd George's schemes were being discussed.[2] Two aspects of these merit attention. Firstly, he sought "good" schemes: schemes which would yield a return covering their costs. Without such a criterion, politicians would, he believed, be unable to resist the pressure to increase spending.[3] Such "good" schemes were hard to find. Secondly, he saw the fundamental policy problem as that of raising industrial efficiency, especially in the export industries, where unemployment was concentrated. Keynesian expansionary policies would raise prices, thus making the situation worse for the export industries.[4] It is important to note that, even if these arguments are thought inadequate to justify a rejection of Keynesian policies, they are not entirely without merit. To a certain extent, the differences between Keynes and Hopkins stemmed from different weights attached to political and administrative issues, as well as from different views on how the economy worked. Having said this, however, there was an important theoretical difference, in that Keynes argued that when there was substantial unemployment it was investment that determined the level of savings, whereas the Treasury persisted in believing the opposite. There was thus a difference over what Meade considered the kernel of the Keynesian revolution.[5]

Despite these differences with Keynes, the Treasury nonetheless put forward proposals for counter-cyclical public works. In particular, government officials, and later the cabinet, accepted, in 1937, the idea of postponing certain items of capital expenditure.[6] This was designed (a) to reduce the extent of the boom then developing; and (b) to ensure that when unemployment started to rise, suitable investment projects were at hand.[7] Despite the adoption of such a policy, however, it would be wrong to conclude that the Treasury was converted to Keynesian ideas.[8] Firstly, the scheme was not expounded within a Keynesian framework of national income, aggregate demand, savings and investment.[9] Secondly, it could be seen as standing in the tradition stemming from the Minority Report of the Royal Commission on the Poor Laws (1909).[10] Thus even if there was a movement towards "Keynesian" policies, it would be wrong to see this as a conversion to the Keynesian way of thinking about the economy.

*War finance*

It is the wartime discussions of policy which are most important in understanding the nature of the "Keynesian revolution" in economic policy. During the war Keynesian ideas were pertinent first of all to the question of how wartime expenditure was to be financed. Keynes' views on this were first published in two articles in *The Times* in 1939, later expanded as *How to Pay for the War* (1940). In this book Keynes applied the techniques of the *General Theory* to the problem of excessive demand. Instead of seeing inflation in terms of monetary expansion, Keynes saw it in terms of the inflationary gap: the difference between desired savings and investment. Given a situation of full employment, inflation would occur if the government wished to borrow more than the public would be willing to save *in the absence of any price rises*. The policy problem was thus seen as how to raise savings to a level sufficient to finance wartime expenditure without inflation. Rather than tax wage-earners to reduce demand, Keynes advocated a scheme of "deferred pay", a system of compulsory saving. Shortly afterwards, Keynes supplemented these arguments with his privately circulated "Budget of National Resources", which contained estimates of the inflationary gap.[11]

At the same time, Keynes was trying to make administrators see the budget not simply as a statement of public finance, but as an instrument for controlling inflationary pressures.[12] In this he was successful, the 1941 budget being "Keynesian, in principle if not in detail".[13] This budget did not, however, mark a fundamental change of outlook, so much as being an attempt to use Keynesian ideas to solve a new, temporary problem. Traditional budgetary criteria were thus not thought discredited, so much as inappropriate for the exceptional circumstances of wartime.

*Wartime discussions of employment policy*

The limited acceptance of Keynesian ideas is shown by Treasury attitudes towards employment policy when prospects for peacetime were discussed. Wartime discussions began with Meade's proposing, in 1941,[14] a series of measures: (a) policies ranging from open market operations and public works to extensions of the social services in order to maintain and control the level of demand; (b) the removal of restrictive practices in industry, in order to make industry more flexible; (c) attempts to co-ordinate monetary, budgetary and investment policies in different countries; and (d) a wage policy to prevent inflation from accelerating as unemployment was reduced.[15] These proposals contrasted with those of Hopkins. Critical of public works and tax reductions as a means of stimulating demand, and sceptical as to the political feasibility of balancing the budget over the cycle, he proposed variations in the annual rate at which debt was redeemed as a way of smoothing the cycle. Lower taxation and low interest rates could thus be used to alleviate depression, but without unbalancing the budget.[16] There was thus a clear contrast between Keynesian and Treasury attitudes.

A separate impetus was provided by Beveridge's work. Beveridge was appointed, in 1941, to investigate the system of social security. His *Report on Social Insurance and Allied Services* (1942) advocated the setting up of a comprehensive scheme of social insurance, in which various benefits, in particular a health service, child allowances and unemployment benefits, were to be provided in return for flat rate contributions. The report was an immediate success with the public, attracting enormous publicity and widespread support.[17]

In itself Beveridge's report was not concerned with unemployment policy. Employment policy was, however, crucial to it, for the scheme would be financially viable only if unemployment were kept sufficiently low. His calculations about the costs of the insurance scheme were based on the assumption of an average rate of unemployment of 8.5%, an assumption which appeared unrealistic to Treasury officials who based their expectations on pre-war experience.

After his Report on social security Beveridge himself turned to employment policy, the result being *Full Employment in a Free Society* (1944).[18] In this book Beveridge proposed a target of 3% as "a conservative, rather than an unduly hopeful, aim to set for the average rate of the future under conditions of full employment".[19] The main mechanism through which this was to be achieved was the Keynesian one of budgetary policy. The "new type" of budget Beveridge proposed was new in two respects: (a) it would be concerned with the income and expenditure of the community as a whole; and (b) taking the labour force as a datum, it would plan national expenditure in the light of this datum, rather than in view of financial considerations.[20] Beveridge was thus embracing the Keynesian approach to demand management as a tool of employment policy, an approach he saw as complementary to his earlier approach of encouraging the mobility of labour.[21]

The scope of Beveridge's 1942 report stimulated the Keynesians in the Economic Section into thinking more clearly about the post-war world.[22] Meade, for example, proposed a plan to vary National Insurance contributions as a contra-cyclical measure. The Treasury, in contrast, was concerned about the cost of Beveridge's scheme, believing, on the basis of pre-war experience, that his assumption of 8.5% unemployment was unrealistic.[23] It was out of these discussions, during 1943, in which the views of Meade, supported by Keynes, were largely opposed by Treasury officials, that the White Paper on Employment Policy emerged in 1944.[24]

Though seen as indicating the government's commitment to full employment as an objective of economic policy, the White Paper was in certain respects a compromise.[25] On the one hand it accepted the maintenance of a high and stable level of employment as one of the government's primary aims, arguing that the control of aggregate demand, through variations in investment and public works spending together with variations in the level of National Insurance contributions, could be used to achieve this. On the other hand, an important place was given to the problem of the distribution of industry, and structural unemployment. Furthermore, the principle that the budget be balanced over a long period was re-asserted.

What this survey of wartime discussions shows is that there was no sudden conversion of the government to Keynesian policies. Keynesian policies were adopted piecemeal, in response to specific events and political pressures. What Hopkins, as the chief Treasury official, attempted to do was to integrate Keynesian ideas with the ideas of traditional public finance. "Political and practical considerations of public administration, rather than economic theory, were uppermost in his mind."[26] Additionally, even though he came to accept Keynesian ideas on demand management, industrial efficiency and exports were still seen by Hopkins as the key to prosperity. The picture of anything like a simple conversion from pre-Keynesian to Keynesian ideas is misleading.

## The final phase

The progress of Keynesian ideas slowed down with the advent of the Labour government in 1945, for although the Labour Party was committed to planning the whole economy, the planning they advocated was very different from that envisaged by Keynes.[27] There was an emphasis on microeconomic planning, finance having no place in the planning machinery. Symbolic of this separation was the fact that the Economic Plan, and national income and expenditure statistics, were calculated on a calendar year basis; whilst the budget was on a financial year basis.[28] Furthermore, Dalton, Chancellor of the Exchequer from 1945, adopted a very orthodox approach to budgetary policy, regarding inflation not as a symptom of excess demand, but as an inevitable consequence of full employment, to be moderated by controls on prices and by increased production.[29] Given these attitudes, together with the need to stimulate production, especially in export industries, even at the expense of inflation, Keynesian techniques were neglected.

For a variety of reasons the final stage in the transition to the acceptance of Keynesian policies came in 1947. The main reason[30] was the emergence of a severe inflation and balance of payments crisis. One of the major problems was the rising cost of food subsidies, caused by an attempt to keep down domestic food prices in the face of rising world prices. Meade advocated letting food prices rise, in order to reduce demand and lessen inflationary pressure, a policy which was, in essentials, followed. In the words of one historian,

by 1947 the message of the *General Theory* had finally been absorbed by Whitehall. The change had scarcely been revolutionary; the whole process had taken more than ten years, and the final victory merely regained ground which had apparently been won in 1940–1.[31]

He goes on to make the point, important in view of later claims that Keynesians were not concerned about inflation, that "these changes in the role of the peacetime budget had been secured by *Keynesians worried about inflation*", the need to curb inflation being central to their advice to the Chancellor of the Exchequer.[32]

## 29.3 THE DEMISE OF KEYNESIAN POLICIES

The 1950s and early 1960s were the years when confidence in demand management was at its height. Whereas even Keynesians had, immediately after the war, thought Beveridge's 3% target for unemployment overambitious,[33] unemployment averaged less than 2% from 1950 to 1969. Whether or not they were successful, budgets were designed and justified in terms of their effects on aggregate demand.[34] From the 1960s, and to a much greater extent during the 1970s, however, confidence in this approach to macroeconomic policy weakened, and eventually collapsed.

In the 1960s there were attempts to introduce a greater degree of planning into the economy. This was in part the result of the Labour Party's winning the 1964 general election, but not entirely so, for the Conservative government had established the National Economic Development Council in 1961. These developments represented a move towards microeconomic planning, rather than simply demand management of the Keynesian type. More important, however, was the response of the government to the perceived weakness of the balance of payments in the late 1960s. Though the commitment to full employment was not abandoned, the balance of payments and associated with this, competitiveness and the inflation rate, received more attention. The emphasis had shifted slightly.

Of particular importance was the recession which came with the collapse of the 1972–1973 boom (often called the Barber boom, after the then Chancellor of the Exchequer) and the oil crisis of 1973–1974. By the end of 1974 inflation was approaching 20% p.a. (with wage inflation already over 25%), the current account deficit amounted to 4% of GDP, and the public sector borrowing requirement was at 8% of GDP. Thus although real output was *falling* and unemployment was starting to rise, Keynesian policies were ruled out. Despite worsening unemployment the government had to do something about inflation and the balance of payments.[35]

It was under these circumstances that the transition from "Keynesian" to "monetarist" policies, sometimes associated with the Conservative victory in the 1979 general election, took place. The crucial change occurred not in 1979 but several years earlier under the Labour government:

All the essentials of what became known in March 1980 as the Medium-Term Financial Strategy were contained in the Letter of Intent sent by Denis Healey to the International Monetary Fund in December 1976. There were pledges gradually to reduce the share of resources taken by the public sector and to curb public-sector borrowing in order to restrain monetary growth.[36]

In the same year, 1976, the Prime Minister argued, in opposition to the Keynesian orthodoxy of the previous 25 years, that Britain could not spend its way out of recession; and the Home Secretary questioned whether public expenditure had not grown too far.[37]

Monetarism was not the only alternative to the Keynesian orthodoxy. Also influential in 1974 was the "New Cambridge" approach. To understand the essential feature of this approach, in its early form at least, it is important to note that it is necessarily true (i.e. true by definition) that the public sector deficit must equal the sum of the private sector surplus and the balance of payments deficit.[38] It was claimed, on the basis of limited and partial empirical evidence, that the private sector surplus was roughly constant. It thus followed immediately that the public sector deficit was directly linked to the balance of payments deficit. If the public sector deficit could be reduced, this would lead to a corresponding reduction in the balance of payments deficit.[39] In other words, fiscal policy should be used to achieve a balance of payments target, not a target level of aggregate demand, as in the Keynesian theory. The counterpart to this was that changes in the exchange rate should be used to control the level of aggregate demand, the mechanism being that a fall in the exchange rate, for example, would raise exports, reduce imports, and hence stimulate demand.

Part of the attraction of the New Cambridge doctrine, an attraction it shared with monetarism, was that it dispensed with the need to rely on detailed forecasts.[40] Once the level of public spending had been decided, and a target set for the balance of payments, the level of taxation needed to produce the required public sector deficit could immediately be calculated. To work out the required level of taxation using a Keynesian theory, on the other hand, required relatively complicated calculations of multipliers, together with predictions of the other components of "autonomous" expenditure. In the 1970s, when unprecedented shocks were making forecasting very difficult, such arguments as the New Cambridge doctrine were very attractive. Although the New Cambridge approach did provide an influential alternative to monetarism for a while, however, this influence was short-lived. From 1974 onwards the New Cambridge equation broke down, for the private sector surplus changed dramatically, inflation having caused a large change in the propensity to save. As the New Cambridge doctrine was discredited, so monetarism was left as the only serious challenger to the Keynesian orthodoxy.

With the Conservative Party's victory in the 1979 general election monetary targets and the PSBR (public sector borrowing requirement) were placed at the very centre of economic policy. Keynesian economic policy, and the belief that expanding demand could raise employment, were rejected. This was made very clear in the 1981 budget when, against Keynesian principles, taxes were raised at the depth of the worst recession since the war. It is probably safe to say that in addition to this change in government policy there was a change in the general public's attitude towards unemployment: towards a greater pessimism as to the possibilities of using expansionary measures to stimulate employment.

In interpreting these events it is important to bear in mind certain aspects of the background against which economic policy-making took place. Firstly, although the 1950s and early 1960s were a period of demand management, and although fluctuations in output and employment were smaller, with average unemployment rates lower than ever before, it was never universally accepted that demand management was the cause of this stability. One of the most well-known assessments was that of Dow (1965) who, referring to fluctuations in exports and in inventories, concluded "so far from countering such basic causes of instability, the influence of policy seems rather to have exaggerated their effects".[41] Thus whilst there may have been a lot of truth in the claim that "Britain and other Western countries have had full employment since the war because governments have been committed to full employment, and knew how to secure it",[42] the truth of such claims was never established beyond question.

Secondly, there is the enormous growth in the numbers of economists, both inside and outside government. The growth of the Government Economic Service was especially marked during the 1960s: from 1964 to 1979 its size grew from about 20 to nearly 400.[43] Given the enormous increase in the availability of statistical information (the Central Statistical Office was founded in 1941), and the increased use of quantitative techniques by economists, this meant that both the extent and the nature of economic advice changes substantially. The links between statistics and economics are, of course, not in one direction alone. For example, it is because economists have, for the past decade or more, been much more interested in the money supply, that statistics on the money supply have proliferated. On the other hand, without some monetary statistics, and note that the CSO's monetary statistics go back only to 1963, thinking about recent economic policy would have to have been very different.

Finally, we need to mention the international setting. The prosperity of the 1950s was accompanied by an enormous increase in trade, especially between developed countries, and associated with this was a growth in international economic co-operation. Particularly important have been the International Monetary Fund, the General Agreement on Tariffs and Trade and the European Community.[44] In addition, there has been greater interdependence, shown by the enormous growth in the fraction of GDP accounted for by exports, not only for the UK but for many other industrial countries.

It is important not to forget that similar changes took place in most other Western economies: at around this time monetary targets were introduced throughout the OECD. Part of the reason for this was the change to floating exchange rates. With fixed exchange rates the monetary authorities had been much more constrained in their monetary policies, independent targets making more sense in the context of floating exchange rates. In addition to this, however, all countries were confronted with the same unfamiliar set of circumstances, requiring a new type of remedy.

Also relevant is the fact that, although the 1974 crisis was sudden, the situation had been changing for some time. As mentioned above, since 1964 greater weight had been attached to controlling inflation, in attempts to improve the balance of payments. Although inflation worsened dramatically in 1974, it had been gradually increasing since the mid 1960s. As the inflation rate rose, so too did the weight attached to it in economic policy-making.

Having said this, however, a shift in economic policy did take place in 1979. In the words of one commentator,

Denis Healey's monetarism was ... improvised and never had deep roots within the Labour movement. It was the response of a clever and flexible man to the breakdown of the post-war consensus on economic management and to external pressures. In contrast, the Conservative approach has been based on belief. Whereas under Mr Healey monetary policy had been juggled alongside incomes policy and measures to hold down unemployment in an uncertain mix, the early Conservative approach was more straightforward. There was a version of how the economy did (or should) work, and it was applied.[45]

This change, however, must be set against a changing background of attitudes towards the economy, both popular and academic opinion having changed substantially since the mid 1960s. Without wishing to describe the bulk of academic opinion as monetarist, the changes in economic theory, and the experience of the 1970s, have made it impossible to return to the theoretical positions of the 1960s. Whilst the shift in popular opinion towards the greater pessimism as to the ability of government to do anything about unemployment may be due in part to economic arguments, together with the simplicity of monetary explanations of inflation, it is hard to believe that it is not also due, in large measure, to the experiences of the past decade.

## 29.4 DEVALUATION, THE EUROPEAN COMMUNITY AND GROWTH

In view of the enormous growth in the use of quantitative techniques, and the vast increase in the availability of data, one question which arises is the extent to which these changes have reduced the extent of disagreement amongst economists. Two episodes in post-war policy-making suggest that progress has been less than might have been hoped. The first is the issue of devaluation, in particular between 1964 and 1967. The Labour Party came into power in 1964 faced with what appeared at the time to be an enormous balance of payments problem.[46] As the main problem seemed to be with the current account, devaluation suggested itself as a remedy. Economists, however, divided on the issue.[47]

At first sight this might seem an issue which econometricians ought to be able to settle: were the elasticities of demand supply, for imports and exports, such that devaluation would improve the balance of payments? In practice, however, more complicated issues were involved. The elasticity of supply of exports, to take one example, would depend on the extent to which spare capacity existed in the economy, on what was happening to domestic demand, and on the behaviour of costs, in particular wage costs. In addition there is the problem that because trade flows are large relative to GDP, changes in exports or imports imply changes in income. Calculating the effects of devaluation on the balance of payments is thus not simply a matter of estimating the elasticities of Marshallian, short run partial equilibrium supply and demand curves. The issues involved are much more complicated. In addition, other issues, reminiscent of those discussed in inter-war discussions of the gold standard,[48] were involved. Some people questioned the morality of devaluation; others the effects of devaluation on British earnings in the field of international banking and finance. Devaluation would, it was argued, upset the UK's role in the world financial system.

The European Community was another issue on which the application of quantitative techniques failed to have a major impact in reducing disagreement amongst economists. Econometric studies were, of course, made, but they could not settle the issue. In part this was because, as in the Tariff Reform controversy seventy years earlier, different types of factor had to be balanced against each other. There was the question of food prices and the standard of living: would entry into the European Community, with its different agricultural support system, be beneficial or harmful in both the short and the long run? Of greater importance, however, was the question of how the closer linking of British and European markets would affect industry: would increased markets provide opportunities that British industrialists would take up, or would increased European competition in the British domestic market make things worse? Customs union theory[49] could do little more than provide a framework, a terminology, within which to discuss some of these issues. It was of little direct help, not least because it had little to say on the longer term issues of the determinants of productivity growth.

This problem, of a low rate of growth of productivity, underlay all discussions of macroeconomic policy, certainly from the 1950s onwards. Prior to that post-war reconstruction had provided a different perspective. The problem of Britain's relative decline, though long-standing, was emphasized by the growth of France and Germany during the 1950s and 1960s, for this was the period when their incomes overtook Britain's. During the period a variety of remedies were tried. In the 1960s planning was tried, first by the Conservatives, but later by the Labour government with its National Plan. Planning, however, failed to do anything about raising productivity growth, for it was not known how to raise this. The Labour government also introduced the "Selective Employment Tax", a tax on employment designed to shift labour into manufacturing. The idea was that as the growth rate of productivity was higher in manufacturing than in services this would raise the growth rate, and also that as the possibilities for increasing returns to scale were greater in manufacturing, a rise in employment in manufacturing would raise productivity faster there.

The "Barber boom" of 1972–1973 was an attempt to raise productivity by creating a climate of expansion, freed from the balance of payments constraints which had brought previous expansions to a halt, through the declared willingness of the government to let the exchange rate float downwards. The idea was that by creating a climate of expansion firms would be induced to increase their investment, and the growth rate of productivity would rise, thus enabling the expansion to continue.[50] This attempt to raise the growth rate, which relied for its success on expansion being uninterrupted, came to grief, however, with the commodity price rises of 1973 and the 1973–1974 oil crisis. In the late 1970s emphasis was increasingly put on the size of the public sector as a cause of low productivity. The thesis of Bacon and Eltis (1976), that productivity growth was impaired by having an excessively high proportion of the labour force employed in producing "unmarketed" output, received much attention. Since 1979 members of the Conservative government have stressed the importance of keeping down the size of the public sector, and of the need to maintain incentives.

There has thus been no shortage of ideas on the causes and remedies of low productivity growth. It has, however, been an area in which economic theory has provided little assistance, not least because it raises so many issues that are difficult to quantify: attitudes of entrepreneurs and workers, the effects of restrictive practices, the nature of the education system and so on. Most of the literature on growth theory, showing how an economy can converge towards a balanced growth path with an exogenously given rate of technical progress, has been of no assistance whatsoever. Perhaps more than in most areas of economics, theories about productivity growth have been based on empirical generalizations which turn out to be little more than transitory trends.


## 29.5  CONCLUSIONS

The episodes discussed in this chapter suggest that there is a great deal of continuity in economic policy-making. This continuity has two aspects. One is that the attitudes underlying economic policy-making take time to change, and that, at least in the episodes considered here, it requires more than simply the appearance of a new economic theory to cause such changes. This is illustrated by both the slow progress of Keynesian ideas in the 1940s, and the gradual loss of confidence in such ideas in the 1970s.[51] In both cases force of circumstances, as governments tried to tackle new and unfamiliar problems, was an important factor, if not the major one, behind the change in attitudes. Changes in economic theories were, of course, important in both episodes, but it seems equally fair to say that it was changes in circumstances which were the direct cause of the adoption of new policies.

The other aspect of this continuity is the recurrence of certain ideas at different times. Exchange rate discussions in the post-war period raised issues discussed in the context of the inter-war gold standard. Discussions of trade and growth in the context of whether to join, or to stay in the European Community in the 1970s raised issues previously discussed during the Tariff Reform campaign in the 1900s. In part, at least, this was because, for all the changing circumstances, the underlying problem of the British economy remained the same: low productivity growth.

Whilst it would require a much more thorough investigation to be able to say anything more definite, it is far from clear that the enormous improvements in the techniques available to, and used by, economists have done much to lessen disagreement amongst economists on policy issues. There would seem to be three reasons why this has been so. (1) Prediction in economics is, because of the nature of its subject matter, extremely hazardous. Economics has produced few, if any, empirical laws comparable with those available in natural sciences, on which predictions can be based.[52] (2) Economic theory is least adequate when dealing with some of the most vital issues, in particular the question of how to stimulate productivity growth. (3) Given the great difficulty in testing economic theories, economists have frequently been excessively confident in the claims they have made on the basis of their economic theories.[53]

It is for reasons such as these that Hutchison, after surveying the extravagant claims made by economists, argues that it is particularly important to be aware of the *limitations* of economic knowledge. He claims that whereas "The naively utopian, scientistic expectations of the early twentieth century regarding the blessings which would flow from the progress of the natural sciences have long since faded away ...", such naive expectations still exist regarding the benefits to be obtained from progress in economic knowledge.[54] Even if there were to be a great leap forward in economic knowledge (and he sees no reason to expect this) such naive expectations might, he argues, prove illusory. For this reason he concludes that

to promote clarification of the extent and limitations of economic knowledge and ignorance may well do much more to reduce dissatisfaction with current economic policies and their results, than so many or most of the contributions to confused and undisciplined wrangles and debates on particular policy problems.[55]

One reason for studying methodology and the history of economic thought is to become aware of some of the limitations of economic analysis. In the words of Viner,

Men who have been trained to think only within the limits of one subject, or only from the point of view of one subject, will never make good teachers at the college level even in that subject. They may know exceedingly well the possibilities of that subject, but they will never be conscious of its limitations, or if conscious of them will never have an adequate motive or a good basis for judging as to their consequences or extent.[56]

# 30

## Contemporary Economics

### 30.1 ECONOMICS AND ITS PAST

One of the main features to emerge from this account is the enormous degree of continuity involved in the development of economic analysis. The most substantial break is probably between the classical and Jevonian theories of value, yet even here there are important elements of continuity. In other branches of the subject (the theory of international trade, monetary economics, the theory of the cycle) it is hard to detect any discontinuity. The same is true of the break referred to as the Keynesian revolution: even in the field of macroeconomics there were important elements of continuity.

Despite this underlying continuity, however, change was sufficiently rapid, and sufficiently far reaching, around both the 1870s and the 1930s to justify the use of the word "revolutionary". It is important to note, however, that these revolutions involved much more than simply the emergence of a new theory, or theoretical framework. Referring to the Smithian, Jevonian and Keynesian revolutions, Hutchison has distinguished four, very different, types of change.

(1) New policy objectives are urged or given much greater priority than previously.
(2) There may be changes in interests, or research priorities.
(3) A new terminology, or conceptual framework, may be introduced.
(4) There may be changes in testable, refutable empirical content.[1]

These are, of course, interrelated. In addition to these types of change we could add changes in intellectual standards: the "marginalist" revolution occurred at roughly the same time that economics was becoming established as an academic subject, something which may have been a factor behind the increasing preference for more formal, if somewhat narrower, analysis.[2] Similarly, the Keynesian revolution is hard to separate from the quantitative revolution which took place at around the same time. There was, therefore, much more to the changes which occurred in both the 1870s and the 1930s than can be encompassed within either the Kuhnian or the Lakatosian framework.

Although they are clearly incapable of explaining all the developments which took place in the 1870s and the 1930s, the theories of Kuhn and Lakatos are nonetheless useful. Many aspects of these revolutions can be explained in terms of Kuhnian or Lakatosian terms. The Jevonian and Keynesian revolutions, and the rise of monetarism in the 1970s, for example, exhibit many features of Kuhnian revolutions: empirical anomalies which become too important to be neglected; increased interest, in times of perceived crisis, in methodological issues; losses as well as gains when economists move from one "paradigm" to another; and so on. In addition, it is easy to identify phases of "normal science", in which research is directed towards solving Kuhnian "puzzles". Similarly, the changes which took place in the 1870s and the 1930s exhibit many of the features of Lakatosian research programmes. Both the spread of marginalist economics in the 1870s, and the spread of Keynesian economics in the 1930s and 1940s, can be seen in terms of economists switching from a research programme thought to be degenerating into a progressive one.

## 30.2 THE STATE OF CONTEMPORARY ECONOMICS

*Criticisms of contemporary economics*

Economic theory has, especially since the 1970s, come in for a barrage of criticism, to such an extent that several commentators have written of a "crisis" in economic theory.[3] Economics, by which is usually meant mainstream, "neoclassical" economics, has been criticized for having no empirical content, for being too abstract, and for amounting to little more than intellectual game-playing.[4] In responding to such criticisms, however, it is important to separate two, distinct, issues. (1) Is the mainstream approach misguided, and in need of replacement with some other approach? (2) Is the emphasis (i.e. the allocation of intellectual resources within the research programme) wrong and in need of improvement? These questions are very different, and need considering separately.

*Criteria for appraisal*

To answer these questions we need a standard of judgement. It will therefore be assumed that the task facing economists is to produce empirical propositions: propositions which could be falsified, but which have survived attempts to falsify them. There may be severe limitations as to the extent to which this is possible, but it should nonetheless remain the underlying objective.

There is, however, as was pointed out in chapter 1, more to the question of methodology than this. Of particular importance is the fact that theoretical propositions are not isolated, but form part of a larger theoretical structure. The unit of appraisal has therefore to be something analogous to a Lakatosian scientific research programme: the set of assumptions and procedural rules which is used to generate empirical propositions. Given that the aim of economic analysis is to generate empirical propositions, a research programme should be judged in terms of whether it is progressive or degenerating.[5]

This Lakatosian extension to the falsificationist methodology is particularly important in economics, for a number of reasons. Falsification, although in principle problematic in *any* discipline, is particularly difficult in economics. Firstly, because controlled experiments are rarely possible, it is rarely possible to test the various components of a theory independently of each other. Thus in practice many hypotheses have to be tested "indirectly": as economists use certain concepts they find that they can neither understand economic phenomena, nor explain empirical data, without them.[6] Such "indirect" testing may be considered inadequate, but frequently nothing better is possible.

Secondly, the subject matter of economics is itself changing: we cannot even assume that people always respond in the same way to economic stimuli. For example, it is quite plausible that people today respond to inflation differently than they did even 20 years ago. This has two implications. (1) It imposes limitations on the ability of economists to build up data with which to test their theories in the way that, for example, astronomical data has been built up over centuries. Pre-war data, for example, may be useless for testing hypotheses about how people behave today. (2) More important than this, changes in the economy mean that economic theories are continually being applied under new circumstances, under which they have never been tested. This means that economists will, or perhaps should, never have confidence in any empirical generalization, unless it has been generated by a theory in which they have confidence. Economic theory has therefore to be more than merely a means of generating predictions.[7] For these reasons it is worth evaluating contemporary economics as a Lakatosian research programme.

### The "neoclassical" research programme[8]

Using the Lakatosian criterion, a strong case can be made in defence of the neoclassical research programme. In any research programme it is inevitable that there will be a hard core of assumptions which are provisionally accepted as irrefutable. In economics this hard core will inevitably be more important than in many disciplines. The difficulties involved in testing assumptions have already been mentioned. In addition, the complexity of the societies with which economists are concerned means that economic theories must, of necessity, neglect certain phenomena. The question to be asked of many of the assumptions made in economics is, therefore, not whether they are true, but whether they provide a useful way of isolating the phenomena which are important for the problem in hand.[9] The existence of unfalsifiable, or even descriptively false, assumptions,[8] therefore, does not *necessarily* render a research programme unsatisfactory, provided that the research programme is progressive.[10]

In considering whether or not the neoclassical research programme is progressive, we will assume that it has succeeded in explaining much of what has happened to the economy (it should soon become clear that by assuming this we are not conceding very much). Two questions can be raised concerning the manner in which economic phenomena have been explained.

The first question is whether or not economic events have been predicted *in advance*, or merely explained after the event? Whilst the former is obviously desirable, it is not *quite* so important as it might at first sight appear to be. Consider the example of including inflationary expectations in the Phillips curve. When Phillips curves were first estimated, from around 1960, they appeared to work, even though they did not contain any allowance for inflationary expectations. More important, however, if economists had tried, in their econometric work, to allow for inflationary expectations they might well have turned out to be empirically unimportant, either because the public was not then aware of inflation in the same way as it is today, or simply because there were then far more important factors affecting inflation.

The second, and more important, question is whether new facts have been explained in a way which preserves the integrity of the research programme, or whether they have been explained simply by *ad hoc* modifications to the theory. Here the record of mainstream economics would seem very favourable, for anomalies have frequently been solved not through introducing *ad hoc* modifications, but through applying the underlying maximizing model of behaviour to more and more problems. *Ad hoc* assumptions have been *removed* rather than introduced. Consider some examples. (1) Kuznets' data on long run consumption patterns were incompatible with the Keynesian consumption function.[11] This anomaly was accommodated by replacing an *ad hoc* generalization about the propensity to consume with a theory in which consumers maximized utility: the permanent income and life-cycle theories.[12] In the 1970s further problems arose in that the savings ratio rose dramatically. Again this was explained, not by any *ad hoc* expedient, but through applying the theory more carefully and defining income correctly so as to allow for the effects of inflation on asset-values.[13] (2) When he introduced inflationary expectations into the Phillips curve, Friedman (1968) was not making an *ad hoc* modification, but was making the theory *more* consistent with basic price theory. Associated with this, the recent literature on the microeconomics of unemployment has been concerned with applying the theory of maximizing behaviour to new situations in order to explain the new fact of persistent unemployment.[14]

Though these examples are taken from macroeconomics, similar examples can be found in virtually any field of economics. It is thus possible to conclude that mainstream economics has been reasonably progressive.[15] This, however, is only one side of the coin, for if one research programme is to be abandoned, it is necessary to find a better one to replace it. For many economists, none of the alternatives seems any better. As an example, consider Weintraub's explanation of what would be required to cause him to support the post-Keynesian research programme:

I could be convinced by two distinct but related lines of argument.

The first would involve a demonstration that the neo-Walrasian program was degenerating, and the second would involve a demonstration that the (post) Keynesian program was progressing.

Demonstrating the former would require, at best, arguments showing repeated ad hoc adjustments of the neo-Walrasian hard core in order to assimilate anomalies. It would further require a relative absence of new empirical facts which were explicable with theories derived from the hard core.

Neither am I aware of reduced scope for the program. Rather than drawing in its extension over time, it has helped to explain, in recent years, new facts from female labor force participation rates to migration flows, from the relationship between race and earnings to the decline in US fertility.

Demonstrating the progressivity of the (post) Keynesian program would require, at a minimum, an articulation of the hard core, and heuristics, of the (post) Keynesian program. Repeated announcements of what post Keynesians do not believe does not constitute an investigative logic. Further, what are the successes of the program? What extension has there been in its domain? What previously inexplicable, or unrecognised, features of economic life has it illuminated?[16]

Similarly, Blaug argues that, for all its failings, "it is only orthodox, timeless equilibrium theory – in short, the neoclassical SRP – that has shown itself willing to be judged in terms of its predictions".[17]

### The direction of research

If the above arguments are accepted, then much of contemporary economics can be justified as constituting part of a progressive research programme. Despite this, however, it would be wrong to use this as a reason for dismissing all the criticisms which have been levelled against contemporary economics. Even if there are reasons for continuing with the same approach, it is possible to question whether research is being directed towards answering the most important questions.

One argument that has been used is that the structure of rewards in the economics profession is such as to lead to an inappropriate valuation of the different activities to which economics devote their attention. It has been argued that: (1) there is an incentive to go for research which yields novel results rather than genuine insights;[18] (2) there is an excessive emphasis on economic theory, and on formal econometrics, rather than on more mundane empirical work, such as gathering new data;[19] (3) that there is a tendency to seek confirmations of theory, not falsifications.[20]

Broadly, the argument is that academic career prospects depend on publications. It is thus all-important for academics to produce work which stands a high chance of being published. This, it is argued, has adverse consequences. The need to satisfy editors and referees, many of whom judge papers in terms of their compatibility with neoclassical economics, makes it unsafe to produce work that conflicts with this approach. In addition, it is safer to produce a paper which offers some small, but definitely novel, development of a well-established, or fashionable theory, than to work on genuinely new problems. With the latter, not only is there a greater risk of failure, but even if the work is successful it may not be appreciated.

The counter-argument is of course that such procedures do serve to maintain academic, or scientific, standards. However, even if rewards were to accrue in proportion to the value of an academic's research, risk-aversion would stop individuals from choosing the research strategy which maximized the expected value of their output. They would choose to forgo a fraction of their expected earnings in exchange for a reduction in the uncertainty they faced. Having said this, however, it has to be conceded that theoretical work is probably too highly regarded relative to empirical work. Whether this is of much importance, however, is a much more complicated question to answer.

Similar arguments have been put forward to explain why there is so little emphasis on falsifying theories, and so much emphasis on confirmations of theories. It is argued that journals require significant regression results, and that as a result negative results do not get published. Again, though there may be some truth in this, it is worth pointing out that it is important to get results consistent with a theory, for the task of economics is not only to test theories, but to discover empirical regularities.

Whilst it may be true that excessive resources are being devoted to abstract theoretical work, it is important to emphasize that even the most abstract theory is not necessarily valueless. Consider, for example, the work in the 1950s on proving the existence of a competitive equilibrium.[21] Such proofs are *of necessity* highly abstract, but if the competitive equilibrium model is to be used at all, such proofs are important. Their function, in the words of one contributor to this literature, "is to assure the theorist that his model is not vacuous. And *he has no business taking this for granted*".[22] It is thus inappropriate to criticize work on existence proofs on the grounds of excessive abstraction. They may be criticized on the grounds that the competitive equilibrium model is not worth taking seriously, but that is a very different type of argument.

It can, however, be argued that economic theories have been too abstract in the sense that economists have pursued excessive generality. Though this may be true, it is important to note that it is sometimes only *after* considerable research has been undertaken that it becomes clear whether or not general results are going to be available. In addition, if models are oversimplified, there is the danger that factors which ought to be analysed and made the subject of economic theory, will be left unanalysed, and that definite theoretical relationships may be implied where none exist.[23] Until more general models are investigated it may not be clear which simplifications matter and which do not.

## 30.3 CONCLUSIONS

Progress in economic analysis seems most likely to arise as the result of economists investigating specific problems, using whatever techniques seem most likely to result in the production of testable, and tested, hypotheses, rather than through attempts to replace mainstream economics with something radically different. There are two reasons for saying this. Firstly, even though it may have many failings, mainstream economics does not appear to be fundamentally flawed and in need of replacement: it would appear to be at least as progressive as any of the alternatives offered.

Secondly, though progress has been far from uniform, economic analysis would appear to have progressed as much through the gradual accretion of knowledge as through revolutionary transformations in the subject. This is not to say that a new "paradigm" may not emerge, but that if it does, this is at least as likely to arise out of attempts to solve specific empirical problems, as to arise out of methodological criticisms of contemporary economics.

Acceptance of these arguments, however, does not imply a complete rejection of the arguments put forward by the proponents of alternatives to mainstream economics. One reason for this is that, of all the successes of neoclassical economic analysis, there are nonetheless vital issues where its powers are severely limited, perhaps the most important example of this being its failure to explain why some countries have grown so much faster than others. Where issues can be related to simple functional relationships between variables, neoclassical theorizing has shown itself extremely powerful, but where this is not possible, it is very weak. Another reason is that economists critical of mainstream economics have raised a number of important issues which should not be neglected. The Austrian and Post-Keynesian arguments about the implications of uncertainty, the Institutionalist arguments about the welfare criteria used in mainstream economics, and Simon's arguments about satisficing would seem particularly important. It is quite possible to recognize the importance of these issues without accepting the claim that mainstream economics is fundamentally flawed. For all its limitations, and these are many, neoclassical economics has, over the past century, been successfully applied to an ever-wider range of problems, including ones which had previously been considered beyond the scope of formal economic analysis.

# Notes

1 Schumpeter (1954), p. 3.
2 Ibid., p. 5.
3 For a slightly broader perspective on the philosophy of science in economics, see ch. 22.
4 Lakatos (1970), p. 91.
5 Popper (1972), p. 30.
6 Ibid.
7 Kuhn (1962), p. 10.
8 Ibid., pp. 47–8.
9 Ibid., p. 44.
10 Ibid., pp. 37–9.
11 Ibid., p. 19.
12 Ibid., pp. 46–7.
13 Ibid., p. 80.
14 Ibid., ch. VI.
15 Ibid., pp. 67–8.
16 Ibid., p. 68.
17 Ibid., p. 83.
18 Ibid., p. 83.
19 Ibid., pp. 87–8.
20 Ibid., p. 85.
21 Ibid., pp. 96–7.
22 Ibid., p. 111.
23 Ibid., pp. 94, 135.
24 Ibid., p. 107.
25 Ibid., p. 122.
26 Ibid., p. 162.
27 See Lakatos (1970 and 1974b).
28 Lakatos (1974a), p. 4; (1974b), p. 149.
29 Lakatos (1974a).
30 Lakatos (1970), p. 71.
31 Lakatos (1974a), pp. 5–6.
32 See Lakatos (1970), pp. 49–52.
33 Ibid., p. 50.
34 Ibid., p. 65.
35 Merton (1963), p. 371.
36 Merton (1961), p. 356.
37 Merton (1963), p. 376.
38 Ibid., p. 375.
39 Ibid., p. 380.
40 Schumpeter (1954), p. 6.
41 Blaug (1978), p. 1.
42 Note that Blaug adds important qualifications to the sentence quoted here.
43 On relativism and absolutism, see Blaug (1978), pp. 2 f.
44 See chs 13 and 21.

CHAPTER 2

1   O'Brien (1976b), p. 133.
2   E.g. Sidgwick, Nicholson. See O'Brien (1976b).
3   Hutchison (1978), p. 24.
4   Cf. Gide and Rist (1909), p. 50.
5   Schumpeter (1954), p. 185.
6   This was a project which remained unfinished.
7   O'Brien (1976b).
8   Smith (1759) quoted in Skinner (1979), p. 105.
9   Bowley (1973) makes an interesting comparison with Cantillon in this respect.
10  E.g. Roll (1973).
11  Blaug (1978), pp. 39–40.
12  Hollander (1973), ch. 3; Mathias (1983).
13  Smith (1776), p. 1; cf. p. 4 n. 2.
14  Ibid.
15  Ibid., p. 352.
16  Transport and retailing, for example, counted as productive.
17  Ibid., p. 291.
18  Ibid., pp. 296–8. Note that money fits in here as a technical device.
19  Ibid., pp. 1–2.
20  Ibid., p. 7.
21  Ibid., p. 21.
22  Define the following variables:
    $X^t$   — output in period $t$
    $L^t$   — labour employed in period $t$
    $P$   — productivity of productive labour
    $w$   — wage rate
    $k$   — fraction of output devoted to employing productive labour

    The two basic relationships are:
    $$X^t = pL^t$$
    and
    $$L^t = kX^{t-1}/w,$$

    from which can be derived the equation
    $$X^t = k(p/w) X^{t-1}$$

    The growth rate then follows as $k(p/w) - 1$.
23  Ibid., p. 359.
24  Ibid., pp. 32–3.
25  Ibid., p. 34.
26  Ibid., pp. 54–6.
27  Ibid., pp. 53–4; cf. pp. 72–3.
28  There is *one sentence* which can be construed as supporting a labour theory of value, on p. 40. But compare with pp. 37–8.
29  Ibid., p. 62.
30  Ibid., p. 61. See diagram in O'Brien (1975), pp. 80–1.
31  Ibid., p. 77.
32  Ibid., pp. 92–3.
33  Ibid., pp. 88–9.
34  Ibid., p. 95.

35 Ibid., p. 98.
36 Ibid., p. 375.
37 Ibid., ch. 10.
38 Ibid., p. 111.
39 Ibid., p. 161.
40 Ibid., p. 162. Smith has been criticized for neglecting competition between landlords. The monopolistic interpretation is more justifiable if it is assumed that the landlord always has the option of cultivating the land himself.
41 Ibid., p. 180.
42 Ibid., p. 182.
43 Ibid., pp. 103–4. Samuelson instances Smith's analysis of the situation in colonies to argue that he envisaged diminishing returns. However, this is not the case in the part of the WN where Smith deals with rent. One defence of Smith's apparent inconsistency would be to argue that once lands were fully developed constant returns prevailed, but that until then returns would be higher, and diminishing.
44 Ibid., p. 208.
45 Ibid., Bk. II, ch. V.
46 Similar arguments can be advanced on the basis of Smith's trade theory.

## CHAPTER 3

1 This is the abbreviated title by which the essay is commonly known.
2 See O'Brien (1975), p. 126, n. 49.
3 Because labour and capital are used in fixed proportions, either capital or labour could be used on the horizontal axis. When one increases, so too does the other.
4 Ricardo (1817), p. 21.
5 A bundle of agricultural products would work, provided that the items in the bundle were always produced and consumed in fixed proportions.
6 Ricardo (1817), p. 55.
7 Ibid., p. 130.
8 For further discussion of this, see Sraffa (1960).
9 Ricardo (1817).
10 Similar problems also occur if the capital used in different industries differs as to its durability, or if the ratio of circulating capital to fixed capital varies across industries.
11 This argument appears only in the third edition of Ricardo's *Principles*. He had earlier argued that mechanization could not harm workers.
12 Schumpeter (1954), p. 473.
13 Compare this with the criticisms levelled against Keynes: p. 334.
14 Blaug (1978), p. 140.
15 O'Brien (1975), p. 45. It is important to note that Ricardo's influence extended to much more than the theory of value and distribution.
16 There has been a revival of interest in Ricardo since Sraffa (1960), but the nature of this interest is rather different. See pp. 384–5.

## CHAPTER 4

1 Gide and Rist (1909), p. 106.
2 See p. 51.

3  The fact that the capitalist and the entrepreneur were usually the same in early nineteenth century England has been suggested as a reason why the concept of the entrepreneur never became prominent in English economics. See Blaug (1958).
4  Bowley (1973), p. 144.
5  Ibid., pp. 144–6.
6  Ibid., p. 146.
7  Cournot (1838), p. 20.
8  Ibid., p. 57.
9  See pp. 140 ff.
10  See Ekelund and Hebert (1983).
11  The first edition was in 1816, prior to Ricardo's *Principles*.
12  See Hutchison (1978), ch. 2, on the relation between Mill and Ricardo.
13  Torrens (1821), p. xiii, quoted in Blaug (1958), p. 52.
14  Bailey (1825), pp. vii–viii.
15  Ibid., p. 1.
16  Ibid., p. 2, 4.
17  Ibid., p. 185.
18  Ricardo (1817), p. 56.
19  Bailey (1825), p. 229.
20  See Blaug (1958), pp. 55–8.
21  Senior (1836), p. 12, quoted in O'Brien (1975), p. 101.
22  Longfield (1834), p. 110.
23  Ibid., p. 28.
24  Bowley (1973), p. 150.
25  Longfield (1834), pp. 111f.; Senior's statement of diminishing marginal utility was probably not available to Longfield when he wrote this – see Bowley (1973), p. 153.
26  Longfield (1834), p. 115.
27  Bowley (1973), p. 153.
28  Senior (1836), p. 178.
29  Ibid., pp. 166–7.
30  Ibid., p. 153.
31  Ibid., pp. 153, 187.
32  Longfield (1834), p. 191.
33  Ibid., p. 192.
34  Ibid., p. 193.
35  Ibid., p. 210.
36  Ibid., p. 209.
37  Ibid., pp. 210–11.
38  Schumpeter (1954), p. 466.
39  Ibid., p. 603; cf. Blaug (1978), ch. 9, especially p. 167.
40  See Mill's summary of his theory of value, (1848), Bk. III, ch. VI.
41  See p. 76.
42  O'Brien (1983), pp. 89–90.
43  See Hutchison (1953), ch. 1.
44  See pp. 64 ff.
45  See pp. 212 ff.

## CHAPTER 5

1  For example, Locke (1691), Law (1705), Cantillon (1730).
2  Hicks (1967), p. 177.
3  See pp. 172–3.
4  Thornton (1802), pp. 118–19.
5  See Thornton's analysis of the 1797 crisis where he defends the decision to suspend cash payments.
6  Ricardo (1810), sect. 22. This telescoping of the short and long runs was characteristic of his work, not just of his monetary economics.
7  Ibid. Note that this was written before his *Essay on Profits* (see p. 26).
8  See p. 53.
9  Overstone, quoted in Tooke (1844), p. 8.
10  Tooke (1844), p. 70.
11  Ibid., p. 82.
12  Ibid., p. 84.
13  Say (1803), pp. 113–14.
14  Compare the statements on ibid., pp. 116, 117.
15  Mill (1808), p. 135.
16  Ibid., emphasis added.
17  Ibid., p. 137
18  Ibid., p. 138. Note that here Mill was arguing against Smith's "vent for surplus" theory.
19  Keynes (1936), pp. 362–3.
20  Ricardo (1817), p. 296; cf. ch. 3.
21  Mill (1844), p. 69.
22  Ibid., p. 70.
23  Ibid., p. 73.
24  Overstone (1837a), p. 44; (1857), p. 31.
25  Overstone (1857), p. 167.
26  Overstone (1857), pp. 264 ff.
27  Overstone (1857), p. 167.
28  Overstone (1837b), p. 36.
29  Tooke and Newmarch (1838), vol. II, p. 214.
30  See ch. 16 on more recent theories. See Schumpeter (1954), pp. 738–47 for details of other classical theories.
31  Cf. Schumpeter's assessment (1954), p. 747. He argues that Marshall did no more than elaborate on Mill's suggestions. Hansen (1964) also links Mill with later work.
32  Mill (1848), p. 654.
33  Ibid., p. 655.
34  Ibid., p. 320.
35  Ibid., p. 323.
36  Ibid.
37  Ibid., p. 401.

## CHAPTER 6

1  See O'Brien (1975).
2  See p. 18.
3  O'Brien (1975), pp. 174–5.

4   Ricardo (1817), pp. 152–3.
5   Ricardo (1817), p. 152.
6   Ricardo (1817), pp. 153–4.
7   Ricardo (1817), p. 158; cf. p. 155.
8   These essays were written as early as 1829–30.
9   Edgeworth (1894), p. 7.
10  Mill (1848), p. 250, quoted in Black (1971).
11  Ibid., p. 251.
12  Ibid., p. 255.
13  Ibid., p. 261.
14  Ibid., p. 261.
15  Ibid., pp. 263 f.
16  It is worth mentioning that the last sections of the chapter, added in later
    editions, were neglected for many years because economists could make no
    sense of them. Edgeworth (1894) and Viner (1937) are perhaps the most
    eminent examples. In these sections Mill confronts the issue of the possible
    indeterminacy of the terms of trade, dealing with it by considering the special
    case where demands have unit elasticity (Mill (1848), p. 268). See Chipman
    (1966).
17  See pp. 47 f.
18  Wheatley (1807); see Viner (1937), pp. 296–7.
19  See Mason (1955), pp. 529 ff.
20  Quoted in Mason (1955), p. 530.
21  Ibid.
22  For references see Mason (1855), p. 531; O'Brien (1970), pp. 208 ff.; Viner
    (1937), pp. 297 ff.; Fetter (1968), and O'Brien (1975).
23  The following argument is taken from Mason (1957).
24  This section relies very heavily on Winch (1965).
25  Smith (1776), p. 424 as quoted in Winch (1965).
26  Winch (1965), p. 12.
27  See p. 21.
28  Ibid., p. 25.
29  See pp. 50 ff.
30  Winch (1965), p. 32.
31  Ibid., p. 30.
32  Ibid., p. 26.
33  Hutchison (1956); Winch (1965), p. 33.
34  See pp. 27 and 56.
35  Winch (1965), p. 41.
36  Ibid., p. 48.
37  Ibid., pp. 51 ff.; Ghosh (1964).
38  Wakefield (1833), note I, especially p. 328. Note that Wakefield preferred the
    term "combination of labour" to Smith's "division of labour". The terms mean
    the same thing.
39  Cf. Smith (1776), Bk. III, ch. I.
40  Wakefield (1833;, p. 375.
41  Ibid., p. 376.
42  Winch (1965), p. 99.
43  Wakefield (1833), p. 522 for examples of the inefficiencies which occurred ·on
    colonies where land was very cheap.
44  Ibid., pp. 467–8.
45  O'Brien (1970), pp. 342–3.

46  Ibid., pp. 336 ff.
47  See p. 22.
48  O'Brien (1975), p. 275.
49  O'Brien (1975).

## CHAPTER 7

1   See pp. 123–5.
2   Keynes (1933).
3   Black (1973).
4   See pp. 212 ff.
5   Jevons (1879), p. viii.
6   Ibid., p. ix.
7   Jevons (1871), p. 90.
8   Ibid., p. 91.
9   Ibid., p. 110.
10  Ibid., p. 148.
11  Ibid., p. 194.
12  Ibid., p. 202.
13  Ibid., p. 205.
14  Ibid., p. 226.
15  Ibid., p. 236.
16  Ibid., p. 241.
17  Jevons (1865), p. 241.
18  Ibid., p. 149.
19  Ibid., p. 151.
20  Ibid., p. 155.
21  Ibid., p. 222.
22  Jevons (1863), p. 20.
23  See Black (1960), p. 219.
24  Cairnes (1874).
25  Jevons (1875, 1878).
26  Jevons (1882), p. 12.
27  Jevons (1882), p. 171.
28  Jevons (1872–81), vol. II, p. 287.
29  Jevons (1883), pp. 191–2.
30  Jevons (1882), p. 14.
31  Ibid., pp. 33–4.
32  Jevons (1871), p. 72.
33  See pp. 36 ff.
34  de Marchi (1973); Black (1960).
35  See pp. 241 f.

## CHAPTER 8

1   Walras (1874), p. 40.
2   Ibid., p. 84.
3   Ibid., p. 86; note that although monopoly was defined as an aspect of applied economics, the *Elements* contain a section on monopoly.
4   Jaffe (1978), p. 574.
5   Jaffe (1975), p. 820.

6   See pp. 34 ff.
7   He distinguished between "extensive", "intensive", "effective" and "rectangu-
    lar" utility, making the subject seem unnecessarily complicated.
8   See p. 35.
9   Cournot (1838), p. 127.
10  Walras (1874), p. 44.
11  Let $p$ be the rental and $P$ the price of the asset. Assume the depreciation charge is
    $mP$, and the insurance premium $vP$. The net income derived from the asset is
    therefore $p-mP-vP$, which gives a percentage yield of $(p-mP-vP)/P$.
12  Using the notation from note 11, this implies that the return from buying a
    capital good, $p-mP-vP$, equals the return, $iP$, where $i$ is the rate of interest,
    that could be obtained from lending the purchase price, $P$, at the going market
    rate of interest.
13  See chs. 9 and 14.
14  This is the familiar formula for the yield on a long-term bond.
15  Walras (1874), pp. 143, 255, 305.
16  See pp. 164–5.
17  Cf. Jaffe (1977), p. 379. Although Walras derives conditions equivalent to those
    for a Pareto optimum, the value judgements involved were very different:
    uniform competitive price was itself the ethical ideal, Walras's value judgement
    being that exchange should not alter the *numéraire* value of an individual's
    endowment of goods. This is very different from the value judgements usually
    used to support Pareto optimality.
18  Wicksell (1906), vol. I, pp. 72 ff.; cf. Hutchison (1953), pp. 206–7.
19  Walras (1874), p. 601 and references there.
20  See pp. 175 ff.
21  See ch. 16.
22  Schumpeter (1910), p. 79.
23  This order for the material occurs only from the 4th edition.
24  Walras appreciated the significance of variable production coefficients only after
    this was pointed out to him by Barone in 1894. Walras (1965), vol. II, pp. 619
    ff. For the history of marginal productivity theory, see pp. 146 ff.
25  Marginal productivity itself occurs only from the 4th edition, despite the
    appearance of variable coefficients in earlier editions. Walras (1874), pp. 549–53.
26  This follows from the assumption of diminishing marginal utility.
27  Harrod (1956), p. 316.
28  Walras (1874), pp. 390–1.
29. Walras's phrase was "mettre en ruines". Walras (1965), vol. I, p. 646; and
    Jevons (1872–81), vol. V, p. 95.
30  Walras criticized the Marxian labour theory of value on similar grounds. Walras
    (1896), pp. 226 ff.
31  Jaffe (1975), p. 882.
32  Walras (1898), p. 76.
33  Ibid., p. 198.
34  See p. 171.
35  This was also the view of Auguste Walras; Jaffe (1975), p. 813.
36  Jaffe (1975), p. 815.
37  This argument is developed in Jaffe (1975).
38  See note 7 above.
39  Blaug (1978), p. 587. He also provides a good discussion of some of the
    technical aspects of the problems Walras was analysing.
40  Morishima (1980), p. 552; cf. (1977), p. 4.

## CHAPTER 9

1 Note that before 1914 Austria was not a small, neutral state, but the centre of a large empire.
2 See p. 13.
3 The nationalistic emphasis of the Historical School might be an explanation of why it was less important in Austria than in Germany; this emphasis could have been divisive in a country containing many nationalities.
4 The original wording, though the English is obscure, is important in view of Menger's attitude to causation. See p. 90.
5 Menger (1871), p. 52.
6 This division of goods into orders is clearly intended as a simplification, made to clarify the exposition.
7 Menger (1871), p. 115.
8 Menger's objections to the use of the term utility are little more than a quibble over the exact use of words, and is not evidence against this. Ibid., pp. 118–19.
9 Ibid., p. 132.
10 Menger does not suggest that these measurements can have more than ordinal significance.
11 Ibid., p. 150.
12 Ibid., p. 149.
13 Ibid., p. 164; cf. p. 165.
14 Ibid., p. 63.
15 Ibid., p. 165. Menger does not seem to be aware of the existence of an adding-up problem.
16 Ibid., p. 157; cf. p. 153.
17 Ibid., p. 161.
18 Ibid., p. 191.
19 See Hutchison (1981), especially ch. 6.
20 Menger (1871), p. 217
21 Ibid., p. 97.
22 Ibid., pp. 260–1.
23 This view of the development of wants has something in common with that of Marshall. See p. 99.
24 Ibid., pp. 152–5.
25 See ch. 18.
26 See Hutchison (1981), ch. 6, and Alter (1982).
27 Menger (1883).
28 Menger (1871), p. 51.
29 See p. 85.
30 Alter (1982).
31 Antonelli (1953).
32 Menger (1883), p. 218.
33 Wieser (1893), p. 60.
34 Ibid., p. 61.
35 Ibid., p. 62.
36 See p. 166.
37 Wieser (1893), p. 66.
38 Ibid.
39 See Hayek (1935).
40 Schumpeter (1954), p. 847.

41 Ibid., p. 234. See Hutchison (1981). There seems some similarity here with Walras's use of the competitive model.
42 See pp. 151 ff.
43 See pp. 265 ff.
44 See pp. 266–8 and 379.
45 See Hayek (1935).
46 See p. 379.
47 See pp. 189 f.
48 See p. 157.

## CHAPTER 10

1 This has been disputed. See below.
2 Because of Marshall's emphasis on continuity with the English classical economists, the term "neoclassical" is in a sense more applicable to Marshall than to the Jevons, Walras or Menger.
3 Whitaker (1975).
4 Cf. Marshall's review of Jevons (1871), reprinted in Marshall (1925).
5 See Marshall's paper on mechanical and biological analogies in economics, reprinted in Marshall (1925).
6 Marshall (1925), p. 417.
7 Marshall (1890).
8 Cf. the diagrams in Whitaker (1975) and Marshall (1879).
9 Marshall (1890), p. 502; emphasis added.
10 Ibid., p. 317.
11 Ibid., p. 501.
12 Ibid., p. 665.
13 Ibid., p. 545.
14 Marshall (1879).
15 See pp. 175 ff.
16 Marshall (1890), p. 1.
17 Parsons (1931 and 1932).
18 Marshall (1890), p. 689.
19 Ibid., p. 470.
20 See pp. 167 and 242.
21 Whitaker (1977), p. 163.
22 Marshall (1907).
23 Marshall (1890). It is worth noting that many of Marshall's pupils were involved in surveys which were gradually revealing the extent of poverty in Britain.
24 Hutchison (1953), p. 70.
25 See pp. 212 ff.
26 Marshall (1925), p. 159.
27 Ibid., p. 437.
28 See n. 5 above.
29 Marshall (1961), vol. II, p. 72.
30 Marshall (1897).
31 Guillebaud (1952), p. 114.
32 Marshall (1890), pp. 9–10.

33  Quoted in Whitaker (1975), p. 110 and in Coats (1967a).
34  Samuelson (1967), pp. 109, 111.
35  Cf. pp. 142–3.
36  Cf. Hayek's argument, p. 379.
37  Hutchison (1981), p. 53.
38  Marshall (1925), p. 165. cf. p. 244.
39  Taussig (1924), p. 1.

## CHAPTER 11

1  John Bates Clark should not be confused with his son, also an eminent economist, John Maurice Clark.
2  Dorfman (1946–59), vol. III, p. 192.
3  Ibid.
4  See p. 147. See also Dorfman (1946–59), vol. III.
5  These publication dates are slightly misleading, for much of the contents was contained in earlier articles.
6  Clark (1886), p. iii.
7  Ibid., p. iv.
8  Ibid., p. 15.
9  Ibid., p. 74.
10  Ibid., pp. 107–8.
11  Wieser probably comes closest to this. See p. 91 f.
12  Ibid., p. 120.
13  Ibid., p. 151.
14  Ibid., prefaces.
15  He still considered that it was his stress on social value which distinguished his views from those of his European contemporaries. Clark (1899), p. 376.
16  Ibid., p. vi.
17  Ibid., pp. 29–30.
18  Ibid., pp. 67–70.
19  Ibid., ch. VI.
20  ibid., pp. 106–7.
21  See ch. 14 for discussion of Böhm-Bawerk and Clark's disagreement with him.
22  Clark (1899), pp. 334–40.
23  Ibid., pp. 401–2.
24  Ibid., p. 404.
25  Ibid., p. 405.
26  Ibid., p. 410. Note the similarity to Schumpeter's theory of profits. See p. 157.
27  Ibid., p. 418.
28  Ibid., p. 434.
29  Ibid., p. 436.
30  Ibid., p. 9.
31  See pp. 227 f.
32  Clark (1896), pp. 12–14.
33  Cf. Hutchison (1953); Jalladeau (1975); Henry (1982).

## CHAPTER 12

1  Texts on Marx abound, and this chapter attempts to do no more than provide a brief introduction to some of the themes most relevant to developments in mainstream economics.

2 Kolakowski (1978), vol. I, p. 401.
3 Much of this paragraph is taken from Pribram (1983), pp. 246 ff.
4 Morishima and Catephores (1978), p. 10; much of this section is taken from ch. 1 of this book.
5 Ibid., pp. 3, 12–13.
6 Schumpeter (1954).
7 See Morishima (1973), p. 11; Marx (1867–94), pp. 46–7. Marx needed to assume something like this to avoid the absurdity of implying that the value of a commodity could be increased simply by expending more labour on it. Subsequent references to *Capital* simply give the volume number.
8 To simplify the exposition the distinction between stocks and flows is ignored. Marx brings in assumptions about rates of turnover of capital to link together the stock of capital (the base on which to calculate the rate of profit) and the flow of capital used up in production (which enters into the value of commodities).
9 Vol. III, ch. 9.
10 A further problem is that if we accept that total surplus value is defined as equal to total profits, it no longer follows that total output will be the same in value terms as in price terms. This problem does not arise in the simple example used here because in it values and prices are not separated as they should be. See p. 238; also, Seton (1957).
11 Vol. III, ch. 9, p. 155; note that the only reason why, in this example, all prices turn out to be the same is that the capital in each sector is the same. In other words, it is assumed that the depreciation rate on fixed capital is 100%. Nothing of importance hangs on this. In Marx's example where the turnover rates of the various types of capital are different, prices differ.
12 Vol. II, ch. 19, pp. 363 ff.
13 See Eltis (1975).
14 In Quesnay's *tableau* gross output is 2500, this being because he includes an interest charge of 500 (assumed equal to 10% of a capital invested of 5000). This interest charge is used to cover depreciation, being spent entirely within the productive sector. It does not affect the balance between the sectors and it is simpler to leave it out.
15 See Eltis (1975), p. 195.
16 If we adopted the assumptions about depreciation mentioned in note 14 there would be an entry of 500 here.
17 Vol. II, ch. 20, pp. 396 ff.
18 Vol. II, p. 397.
19 This condition was derived from the condition that demand and supply for investment goods are equal; exactly the same can be derived from the condition that output of consumer goods equals demand (total variable capital plus total surplus value).
20 It can be shown that for simple reproduction, $v_I/v_{II}=k_{II}/(1+e)$. If $e$ rises, department I must become smaller relative to department II.
21 Vol. II, ch. 21; Morishima (1973), pp. 117 ff.
22 It was important for Marx not so much because of its greater realism as because of its importance in Marx's Hegelian scheme.
23 Morishima (1973), p. 118f.; for other objections see Blaug (1978), p. 263.
24 See ch. 25.
25 Vol. III, ch. 14.
26 There are, of course important senses in which Marx was not one of the classical economists. For example, the classical economists can be regarded as a

reasonably well defined sociological group, of which Marx was clearly not a member.
27  Blaug (1980), ch. 2.
28  See p. 237.


## CHAPTER 13

1   This is taken from the title of Bowley (1972).
2   Hutchison (1955), p. 3.
3   See pp. 43–4 and 212 ff. The classic reference on the state of the subject in 1870 is Hutchison (1953), ch. 1. See also Coats (1964), pp. 95 f; Hutchison (1955), pp. 3 f.; Hutchison (1978), ch. 3.
4   Hutchison (1978), p. 75.
5   Ibid., p. 81.
6   Ibid., p. 86.
7   Hutchison (1955), p. 7.
8   Ibid., p. 9.
9   Ibid. See also Coats (1964, 1967a).
10  Hutchison (1953), pp. 63–4.
11  Coats (1967a), p. 714 f.; Kadish (1982).
12  See Coats (1967b).
13  Coats (1967a), p. 710.
14  Coats (1980), p. 601. Most of this section is taken from this article.
15  It is significant that the American Economic Association was founded before the Royal Economic Society.
16  Coats (1980), p. 594.
17  Ibid., p. 602.
18  Ibid., p. 605. To get an impression of the variety within American economics, see Mitchell (1969).


## CHAPTER 14

1   In this chapter we are concerned solely with the meaning of utility as applied to a single individual. Questions of interpersonal utility comparisons are discussed in ch. 15.
2   Jevons (1871), pp. 112–14.
3   Edgeworth (1881), p. 7.
4   Bonar (1888), esp. pp. 24–5; Mitchell (1969), p. 253.
5   See Mitchell (1969), p. 257.
6   Fisher (1892), p. 11.
7   Ibid., p. 23.
8   Ibid., p. 89.
9   Pareto (1893).
10  Johnson (1913), p. 103.
11  Schumpeter has suggested that Johnson's failure to acknowledge Pareto earned Slutsky's resentment amongst Italian economists. The circumstances of 1915 go partly to explain the neglect of Slutsky amongst English-speaking economists.

The mathematics in both articles was also very difficult for most contemporary economists.

12  An additively separable utility function is one that can be written in the form $U = u_1(x1) + u_2(x2) + \ldots + u_n(xn)$ where $x1, \ldots xn$ are the quantities of the $n$ goods consumed.

13  Fisher (1892), pp. 64–75.

14  This was also done by Barone. See Shackle (1967), p. 81, but note Shackle's complete neglect of Fisher.

15  Hicks recalls coming to the new consumer theory via the elasticity of substitution as applied to the production function. Hicks (1981), pp. 3–4.

16  See p. 95.

17  Cassel (1918), p. 82.

18  There were of course exceptions, such as Mill's theory of reciprocal demand; but it is with Cairnes' extension of this aspect of Mill's theory that is associated the demise of classical economics.

19  Schumpeter (1954, pp. 963 ff) distinguishes between a static state and a stationary one.

20  Pareto (1906), p. 106.

21  Marshall (1890), p. 810; quoted by Hutchison (1953), p. 81.

22  Schumpeter (1954), p. 978.

23  Chamberlin (1933), p. 8.

24  Ibid., p. 68.

25  Ibid., p. 3.

26  Ibid., pp. 82, 110; Chamberlin (1937), p. 195.

27  Chamberlin (1937), p. 195.

28  Blaug (1978), p. 417.

29  Robinson (1933a), p. 1. Her quotation is from Pigou.

30  Ibid., p. 11.

31  Ibid.

32  She has later (1973) argued that this was her main purpose. For an argument that this reflects her later concerns see Harcourt (1984), p. 641.

33  Robbins (1928), p. 393.

34  See O'Brien (1983a).

35  The marginal revenue curve was discovered independently by Harrod, Chamberlin and Yntema. See the contrasting comments of Shackle (1967) and Samuelson (1967a) on this.

36  Harrod (1930), p. 91.

37  Robinson (1932), pp. 549–52.

38  Robinson (1933a), p. 15.

39  Ibid., p. 6, emphasis added.

40  Shove (1933), p. 121.

41  Robinson (1933b), p. 124.

42  E.g. Loasby (1976); O'Brien (1983a).

43  Loasby (1976), p. 202.

44  See p. 103.

45  See p. 35.

46  This is hinted at in Bowley (1924) and used by Frisch (1933) and Hicks (1935b).

47  Robinson (1933a), pp. 38, 81.

48  Sweezy (1939), Hall and Hitch (1939).

49  Stigler (1947), p. 410.

50  Arrow and Hahn (1971); much of the following is taken from here.

51  Moss (1984), p. 307.

52 Hicks (1939a), pp. 83–5.
53 See pp. 191 ff.
54 This and the following three paragraphs owe much to Gordon (1973).
55 See Marshall (1890), Appendix J.
56 See article on Wood in Stigler (1965).
57 Note that Walras held similar views on taxing land.
58 See Coase and Stigler (1969).
59 Berry (1891), p. 315.
60 Wicksteed (1894), p. 7.
61 Ibid.
62 Linear homogeneity means that if $Y=F(K,L)$ then $aY=F(aK,aL)$ where $a$ is any positive constant.
63 Note that the first of these assumptions implies constant returns.
64 Wicksell had himself (1893) put forward a similar theory, but he was unaware of this.
65 Edgeworth (1925), vol. I, p. 31.
66 Such a function had previously been used by Wicksell.
67 Schumpeter (1954), p. 909.
68 See below.
69 Böhm-Bawerk (1889), p. 347.
70 Ibid., p. 358.
71 Ibid., p. 365.
72 See ch. 25.
73 Clark (1893), p. 308.
74 Cassel (1901), p. 89.
75 Fisher (1907), p. 74.
76 Ibid., p. 139.
77 Fisher (1930), p. 321.
78 See pp. 108 f.
79 See pp. 189 f.
80 For a list of the numerous contributions to this debate see Kaldor (1938).
81 Knight (1933), p. 328.
82 Ibid., p. 329.
83 See pp. 325 f.
84 See ch. 20.

## CHAPTER 15

1 See Myint (1948).
2 See Hutchison (1981), ch. 3.
3 See p. 36.
4 See pp. 70 ff.
5 Bentham (1789), p. 2.
6 Bentham (1818;, p. 3.
7 Ibid., p. 102.
8 Ibid., p. 103.
9 Bentham (1789), p. 66.
10 Ibid.
11 In modern theory this assumption would be expressed as saying that all

individuals have a common utility function, in which all ascertainable individual characteristics enter as arguments.

12  Cf. Sidgwick's attitude, discussed below.
13  This is not to imply that Bentham and Mill held exactly the same theory of utility. There were differences, but they are not relevant to the present argument.
14  See p. 75.
15  See Hutchison (1981), ch. 3.
16  Sidgwick (1887), p. 71.
17  Ibid., p. 90.
18  Sidgwick (1874), p. 129.
19  Ibid., p. 123.
20  Ibid., pp. 144, 398.
21  Sidgwick (1874), p. 397.
22  Ibid., p. 409.
23  Ibid., p. 406.
24  See Hutchison (1978), p. 104.
25  Sidgwick (1874), p. 506.
26  Ibid., p. 517.
27  Schumpeter (1954), p. 1070.
28  Marshall (1890), p. 108.
29  Pigou (1920), p. 6.
30  Ibid., p. 10.
31  Ibid., p. 11.
32  Ibid., p. 86.
33  See Hicks (1975), pp. 219–20.
34  Pigou (1920), p. 185; quoted in Hutchison (1953), p. 291; see Collard (1981), p. 114.
35  See pp. 315 f.
36  See p. 100.
37  See the symposium in the *Ecnomic Journal*, 1928.
38  Blaug (1978).
39  Edgeworth (1881), p. 7.
40  Suppose individual A can distinguish between "good" and "awful". whereas B can distinguish between "good", "fairly good", "acceptable". "poor" and "awful". Edgeworth is assuming that if A moves from "awful" to "good", this has the same value to society as if B moves from "awful" to "poor". This clearly involves an ethical judgement. See Sen (1970a), pp. 93–4.
41  Edgeworth (1881), p. 56.
42  Ibid., p. 64.
43  Edgeworth (1894). See Creedy (1981), pp. 89–91.
44  See p. 77.
45  Pareto (1896), para. 721. p. 92.
46  Ibid., para. 721, n. 2., pp. 92–4.
47  This idea is developed in Chipman (1976), p. 92.
48  Pareto (1908), p. 201.
49  Myrdal (1929), p. 128.
50  Hicks (1975), p. 220.
51  Myrdal (1929), p. 199.
52  Hicks (1975), p. 220.
53  See pp. 302 f.

## CHAPTER 16

1 Marshall's contributions to monetary economics came later and considered below.
2 See pp. 46 f.
3 See p. 53.
4 See p. 74.
5 2nd edn, p. xix; quoted in Hutchison (1853), p. 372.
6 See pp. 181 ff.
7 These ideas were developed in Wicksell (1906), vol. II.
8 The problem of defining the natural rate is more complicated than suggested here, for the rate at which inflation is zero may not be the same as the rate equating saving and investment. This formed the basis for Myrdal's later development of Wicksell's theory. See below pp. 192 f.
9 See p. 155.
10 Fisher was not the first to draw this distinction, but it was he who was responsible for popularizing the idea.
11 This contrasts with the Cambridge approach. See below.
12 Fisher (1911), p. 55.
13 Ibid., p. 62.
14 Ibid.
15 See section 16.3.
16 Fisher (1911), p. 66.
17 Ibid., p. 169.
18 Ibid., p. 161.
19 Pigou (1917).
20 Pigou, quoted in Keynes (1923), p. 61.
21 Keynes (1923), p. 61.
22 Note that the ceteris paribus conditions included the expected rate of inflation.
23 Linking the quantity of money to the value of *money*.
24 Keynes (1923), p. 65.
25 Pigou (1917), p. 179. Note that if we divide both sides by $c+h(1-c)$ we obtain something much more familiar: the condition that the demand for money must equal the quantity of high-powered money multiplied by the money multiplier.
26 Marshall (1887), p. 181.
27 Ibid., p. 192. Note that he refers to general over-production as a "monstrous fallacy".
28 Particularly notable is ch. 1 of Keynes (1923).
29 See also p. 251.
30 See pp. 206 ff.
31 Keynes (1923), p. 36.
32 Much of the following is taken from Hutchison (1953), ch. 22.
33 Ibid., p. 367.
34 Cf. Parrini and Sklar (1983). Note that Marx also criticized Say's Law, and stressed the falling rate of profit.
35 See ch. 5.4.
36 Written jointly with A. F. Mummery.
37 See Kolakowski (1978), vol. I, p. 327, who describes the question of markets as "one of those most discussed in Marxist circles".
38 Hansen (19164), p. 286.
39 See pp. 218 ff.

40  Schumpeter (1910). These ideas were developed in Schumpeter (1912) and (1939).
41  Hansen (1964), p. 397; Dorfman (1946–59), p. 360.
42  Cf. Koopmans (1947b).
43  Mitchell (1927), p. 3.
44  Ibid., p. 11.
45  Ibid., pp. 54–5.
46  See pp. 223 f.
47  Mitchell (1927), pp. 113–15.
48  See p. 223.
49  Cassel (1918a), vol. II, p. 545.
50  Haberler (1936), p. 64.
51  Hicks (1977), p. 118; Schumpeter (1954), p. 1121; Davies (1981), pp. 204, 211.
52  Hawtrey (1913), p. 5.
53  Hicks (1982), p. 129.
54  Preface to Robertson (1926).
55  To get the flavour of this note that lacking might be: short, long or unproductive; spontaneous, induced or automatic; imposed; applied or abortive; and that there were similar classifications for hoarding, stinting and splashing!
56  Frisch (1933), p. 178.
57  The exposition was similar to that of a two-country multiplier model, though he analysed a supply shock, and allowed for the elasticity of supply. Pigou (1927), pp. 51–64.
58  Ibid., p. 284.
59  It was at this time that English translations of Wicksell's major works were first published.
60  Schumpeter (1954), p. 1120. This followed Hayek (1929).
61  See pp. 151 ff. and 172–3.
62  For a discussion of how this situation might come about see Hicks (1967).
63  For Hayek this starting point was a methodological assumption.
64  This is not Keynes' notation. Note that Keynes had separate equations for the prices of consumption and investment goods.
65  The reference is to the Old Testament, 1 Kings, ch. 17.
66  Ohlin (1937) is the source of this description.
67  See the symposium in *History of Political Economy*, 1978, Patinkin (1982), Hansson (1982).
68  Myrdal (1973), pp. 4–5.
69  Steiger (1978); Patinkin (1982), pp. 45–6.
70  Lindahl (1939), p. 141.
71  Ibid., p. 159.
72  Ibid., pp. 166, 178.
73  Ibid., pp. 184–5.
74  Published in Swedish in 1931, in German in 1933, and in English in 1939. The last is not simply a translation, though the main ideas are to be found in the Swedish edition.
75  Myrdal (1939), p. 32.
76  Ibid., p. 47.
77  Ibid., p. 46.
78  Ibid., p. 83.
79  Ibid., pp. 131–3.

80  Ibid., p. 135.
81  Ibid., pp. 164–5.
82  Ibid., pp. 167–8.
83  Ibid., p. 168.
84  See p. 249.
85  Cf. Pigou (1927), p. 64.
86  The MacMillan Committee is discussed on pp. 255–6.
87  See Davies (1981), pp. 216–17.
88  Like Myrdal, Kahn explained the MPC in terms of the increase in income
    which occurred when a man moved from the dole to receiving a wage, not in
    terms of a fundamental psychological law.
89  See the preface.
90  Keynes (1971–1983), vol. XIII, pp. 54, 152.
91  Ibid., pp. 337–43.
92  See Robinson (1933c), written in the summer of 1931.
93  The Harris Lectures, Keynes (1971–83), vol. XIII, pp. 343 ff.
94  Ibid., pp. 355–6.
95  Patinkins's answer to this is in 1933; Patinkin (1982), p. 30.
96  In discussing the *General Theory* it is assumed that the reader is familiar with the
    standard macro textbook expositions of Keynesian economics. Ackley (1961),
    Branson (1979), Blaug (1978).
97  Fisher (1930).
98  Cf. Kregel (1973).
99  Hicks (1935a) and Hicks (1982), p. 8.


CHAPTER 17

1   See Viner (1937).
2   Cairnes' views on the transfer mechanism, written rather earlier, are considered
    in ch. 6.
3   Cairnes (1874), pp. 372, 418, 423. This was described as the difference between
    the theory of international trade (why countries trade) and international value
    (the terms on which they trade).
4   Ibid., pp. 373, 416.
5   Cairnes did not use the term, but the concept is clear.
6   Bastable (1897), p. 24.
7   Ibid., pp. 29–31.
8   Cf. pp. 43–4 and 212 ff.
9   Cliffe Leslie (1879).
10  Sidgwick (1883), pp. 205–9.
11  Ibid., p. 212.
12  Bastable (1897), p. 176.
13  See pp. 213 f.
14  Edgeworth (1894), p. 32. Note that both Marshall and Edgeworth applied
    reciprocal demand to representative "bales" of commodities; Edgeworth
    (1894), p. 157; Marshall (1879), p. 2. An economist who did use partial
    equilibrium supply and demand curves to analyse trade was Barone, in 1908.
    See Viner (1937), pp. 589–91.

15 Edgeworth (1894), p. 39.
16 Pareto (1908), pp. 269–71.
17 See Angell (1926).
18 Graham (1932), p. 584.
19 Graham (1923), p. 328.
20 Graham (1932), pp. 584–6.
21 This objection is not applicable to the Marshall–Edgeworth approach of aggregating all exports and all imports into "bales". As Graham points out, however, this approach is invalid when the relationships between different items within the bales change. Graham describes the Marshall–Edgeworth approach as building "imaginary bricks with imaginary clay" (Graham, 1932) p. 583.
22 Graham (1923), pp. 326–30.
23 Graham (1932), p. 581.
24 Haberler (1955), p. 11.
25 This was presented as a dissertation in Swedish in 1924.
26 Heckscher (1919), p. 277.
27 Ibid., p. 285.
28 I.e. exactly the same combinations of inputs were used to produce each commodity.
29 Ibid., p. 291.
30 Ohlin (1933), Appendix 1, pp. 553–62; also pp. 305–6 See p. 144 for discussion of Cassel's system.
31 Ibid., p. 564.
32 A similar criticism was also directed at Marshall: ibid., pp. 567–8.
33 Haberler (1933), p. 175.
34 Ibid., pp. 175 ff.
35 Viner (1937), p. 521. The diagram was presented at LSE in 1931.
36 This derivation of the offer curve was contained in earlier discussions of consumer theory. See p. 135; Cf. Chipman (1965), p. 687.
37 Bastable (1889), pp. 12–13.
38 Ibid., p. 16.
39 Cf. Angell (1926), pp. 100–2.
40 Nicholson (1897) quoted by Iversen (1935), p. 244.
41 Bastable (1889, p. 114) saw himself as attacking an unchallenged orthodoxy. Iversen refers to the income approach as being consigned to oblivion for 20 years (Iversen, 1935) p. 244).
42 See pp. 59 f.
43 Taussig (1917), p. 389.
44 Ibid., p. 393.
45 Wicksell (1918), p. 405.
46 Taussig (1927), p. 260.
47 Iversen (1935), pp. 259 ff.
48 Keynes pointed out that even if the elasticity of demand were as high as 2, a 10% fall in costs would raise the value of exports by only 8% (Keynes, 1929a, p. 166).
49 Ibid., p. 162.
50 Viner (1924a), pp. 204–6; cf. Viner (1937), p. 305 ff.
51 This is by no means the whole of the discussion; many other issues such as German borrowing abroad in the 1920s, and the relation between international

investment and trade flows, were discussed. See Iversen (1935), pp. 278 ff; Haberler (1933), pp. 6 ff; Viner (1937), pp. 307 ff.

52  Keynes (1929b), p. 479.
53  Keynes (1930), ch. 21. See Haberler (1933), p. 74.
54  Cf. p. 193. Ohlin does not have the multiplier. For Ohlin here the increases in imports are not due to successive rounds of expenditure and income, but are due to supply responses.
55  The term was introduced in 1918, but the concept was used earlier.
56  Cassel (1916), p. 62.
57  Ibid.
58  Given the quantity theory it makes no difference whether the growth of the money supply or of the price level is used.
59  The average of these years was used.
60  Cassel (1918b), p. 413.
61  Cassel (1919), pp. 494–5. The example which drew attention to this factor was post-war Germany (Cassel (1922), pp. 147 ff.).
62  Keynes (1923), p. 79; cf. Angell (1926), p. 191.
63  Anderson (1920).
64  Fisher (1920).
65  Keynes (1930), pp. 72–4.
66  Bresciani-Turroni (1934), p. 80.
67  Keynes (1924), p. 80.
68  Taussig (1927), p. 357; see Bresciani-Turroni (1934), p. 434.
69  Brisman (1933), p. 73; cf. Officer (1976), which contains an outline of developments since the 1930s.
70  Ibid., p. 74.
71  For the views of more orthodox economists see Wood (1983).
72  He held a different view in his earlier writings. See Cain (1978, 1979a), from which most of this section is taken.
73  See p. 65.
74  Hobson (1902), 2nd edn, quoted in Cain (1978), p. 572.
75  This can be explained in terms of changes in the political climate: see Cain (1978), Clarke (1981), Cain (1981).
76  Later (1911) Hobson adopted a more orthodox view of increasing international division of labour.
77  Cain (1975), p. 512.
78  Cain (1979a), p. 419.
79  Ibid., p. 413.
80  Ibid., p. 418.
81  Arndt (1981), p. 460.
82  This was reflected in the replacement, in 1939, of the Colonial Development Act by the Colonial Development and Welfare Act.
83  Boeke (1953), a brief excerpt from which is in Meier (1970).
84  For a brief excerpt from Furnivall's work see Meier (1970).
85  Arndt (1972), p. 21.

## CHAPTER 18

1  For some exceptions, see pp. 40–1.
2  Spiegel (1983) refers to these as the Baconian and Hegelian variants of historical economics.

3  Jones (1833), p. vii.
4  Ibid., pp. xxii–xxiii.
5  Ibid.
6  Jones (1859), p. 560.
7  Spiegel (1983), p. 398.
8  Cliffe Leslie (1870), p. 152; see Koot (1975), pp. 326–7.
9  Koot (1975), p. 313. Cliffe Leslie was concerned to find solutions to the problems of agrarian Ireland, for which the methods of classical economics were no use.
10  Cliffe Leslie (1870), p. 148.
11  Ibid., p. 149.
12  Ibid., p. 160.
13  Ibid., p. 162.
14  Ibid., p. 150.
15  Ingram (1893), p. 228.
16  Cliffe Leslie (1876), p. 217.
17  Ibid., p. 227.
18  Ibid.
19  Ibid.
20  Ibid., p. 242.
21  The economist who has paid most attention to this argument of Cliffe Leslie's is perhaps Hutchison, from 1937 to 1981.
22  Cliffe Leslie (1879), p. 939.
23  Ibid., p. 941.
24  Bagehot (1876), p. 26, cf. p. 9.
25  Ibid., p. 27.
26  Ibid., p. 33.
27  Ingram (1878), p. 47.
28  These ideas were developed in Ingram (1893).
29  Ingram (1878), pp. 48 ff.
30  Ibid., p. 55.
31  Ibid., p. 59.
32  Ibid., p. 60.
33  Ibid., p. 66.
34  Sidgwick (1883), p. 7.
35  Ibid.
36  Ibid., pp. 28–9.
37  Ibid., pp. 30–2.
38  Ibid., pp. 33–4.
39  See pp. 262 ff.
40  See also pp. 101 ff.
41  Marshall (1885), p. 159.
42  Cf. Kadish (1982), pp. 131 f, 135.
43  Marshall (1885), p. 165.
44  Ibid., pp. 165–6.
45  Harte (1971), pp. xii, xix. Much of the following account as taken from this source. For details of the Rostovian metaphor see p. 364.
46  Ashley (1889), p. 429.
47  These were published posthumously in (1908).
48  Harte (1971), p. xi.
49  Cunningham (1889), pp. 109–10.
50  Ibid., p. 110. Note that Marshall was in fact careful *not* to make exaggerated claims concerning the universal validity of economic doctrines. See p. 102.

51 See Kadish (1982), pp. 150–1. Cunningham's inaugural lecture (1892a) is also worth mentioning.
52 Cunningham (1892b), p. 491.
53 Koot (1980), pp. 188–9.
54 Ashley (1893), p. 7.
55 Kadish (1982), pp. 217–18 explains the difference in terms of their academic positions, Cunningham having little to lose by attacking Marshall, Ashley having little to gain
56 Ashley (1893), p. 8.
57 Koot (1980), p. 192.
58 Harte (1971), p. xxvii.
59 In the 1960s links between economics and economic history were revived with the *New Economic History*, but the influence here was solely from economics to economic history. Influence in the reverse direction was confined to the literature on economic development, and to certain aspects of work on growth.
60 Hartwell (1973), p. 33.
61 Hartwell (1973) provides a comparison of the economic history of the two periods.
62 Gide and Rist (1909), p. 582.
63 Pribram (1983), p. 215.
64 Ibid., p. 214; see also Gide and Rist (1909), p. 382.
65 Ibid., p. 382–3.
66 Hildebrand (1848), p. v, translated in Gide and Rist (1909), p. 383.
67 Pribram (1983), p. 215.
68 Knies (1853), pp. 24–5, translated in Gide and Rist (1909), pp. 390–91.
69 See Hutchison (1953), Spiegel (1983) and Mitchell (1969).
70 Hutchison (1953), p. 185.
71 Schmoller (1900) translated in Gide and Rist (1909), p. 385.
72 Schmoller (1900) p. 356 quoted in Hutchison (1953), p. 182.
73 Hutchison (1953), p. 183; see p. 179.
74 Ibid., p. 184; cf. Mitchell (1969), pp. 556 ff.
75 Hutchison (1953), p. 184; cf. Schumpeter (1954), p. 813.
76 Mitchell (1969), p. 574.
77 Hutchison (1953), pp. 185–6; Schumpeter (1954), pp. 816–17.
78 See Spiegel (1983), pp. 428 ff and p. 179.
79 Spiethoff (1932); cf. Schumpeter (1954), p. 816; Seligman (1962), pp. 34 ff.
80 Seligman (1962), p. 36.
81 Ibid., p. 15; cf. Spiegel (1983), p. 428.
82 Weber (1904).
83 Selections in Brodbeck (1982).
84 This is the meaning of the term "wertfreiheit".
85 Two of the easiest introductions to Veblen, containing details of his back-ground, are Dorfman (1949), ch. XIX, and Mitchell (1965), ch. XX. See also Spiegel (1983); Ekelund and Hebert (1983); Hutchison (1953).
86 Veblen (1898), p. 71.
87 Ibid., emphasis added.
88 Ibid., p. 75.
89 Rutherford (1984), p. 335.
90 Veblen (1898), pp. 76–7.
91 Ibid., p. 77.
92 Veblen (1915), p. 267; see Rutherford (1984), p. 334.
93 Rutherford (1984), p. 334.

94 Veblen (1904), ch. II.
95 Ibid., p. 9.
96 Ibid., p. 27.
97 Ibid., p. 28.
98 Ibid., p. 59.
99 Ibid., p. 63.
100 Ibid., p. 64.
101 Ibid., p. 66.
102 Ibid., p. 67.
103 Veblen (1904), pp. 374 ff., (1921).
104 Coats (1954a).
105 Veblen (1898), pp. 60–1.
106 Rutherford (1984), p. 341.
107 Ibid., p. 60.
108 Veblen (1899–1900), p. 92.
109 Veblen (1898), p. 65. He refers to this criterion as that of "ceremonial adequacy".
110 Veblen (1899–1900), pp. 142–3.
111 Veblen (1898), p. 60.
112 Veblen (1899–1900), p. 145.
113 Veblen (1898), p. 69.
114 See p. 239.
115 Veblen (1898), p. 79.
116 Rutherford (1984), p. 332.
117 Veblen (1914), pp. 7–8; quoted in Rutherford (1984), pp. 333–4.
118 Rutherford (1984), p. 333.
119 Coats (1954a), p. 531.
120 Ibid.
121 Arrow (1975), p. 5.
122 See p. 182.
123 Marshall (1907), quoted in Mitchell (1925), p. 20.
124 Mitchell (1925), pp. 20–1.
125 Ibid., p. 26.
126 Ibid., pp. 29–30.
127 Klein (1983), pp. 876 ff.
128 Ibid., p. 875.
129 Ibid.
130 Mitchell (1965), p. 586; emphasis added.
131 Commons (1924), p. 67.
132 Commons (1931), p. 649.
133 Ibid., p. 650; emphasis added.
134 Ibid., p. 651.
135 Ibid., p. 650.
136 Commons (1936), p. 244; cf. Chamberlain (1963), p. 85.
137 Commons (1931), p. 652.
138 Commons (1934a), pp. 67–8.
139 See Rutherford (1983), p. 725.
140 Commons (1950), p. 48; note that this was published posthumously.
141 Rutherford (1983), p. 725.
142 Commons (1931), p. 655.
143 Commons (1924), p. 138.
144 Ibid.

145 Cf. Rutherford (1983), pp. 726–9.
146 Commons (1925), p. 380; quoted in Rutherford (1983), p. 728.
147 Rutherford (1983), p. 729.
148 Dorfman (1946–59), vol. IV, pp. 379 ff.; Chamberlain (1963).
149 Boulding (1957), p. 7.
150 Rutherford (1983), p. 731.
151 Commons (1934a), p. 673; cf. Rutherford (1983), p. 731.
152 Chamberlain (1963), pp. 83–7; cf. Mitchell (1965), p. 729 ff.
153 Commons (1924), p. vii.
154 Ibid., pp. vii–viii.
155 Commons (1934a), p. 5; cf. Mitchell (1935), pp. 339–40.
156 Commons (1950).
157 Boulding (1957), p. 7.
158 Boulding (1957), p. 8.
159 Kolakowski (1978), vol. II, p. 1; the following pages contain a discussion of Marxism in the context of Socialism in Europe at the end of the nineteenth century. See also Pribram (1983), pp. 267 ff.
160 In reading Wicksteed's article it is important to remember that it was written before the third volume of *Capital*, containing Marx's discussion of the transformation problem, had appeared.
161 Edgeworth (1925), vol. III, p. 273.
162 Mitchell (1969).
163 See Brewer (1981).
164 See pp. 178 f.
165 Sweezy (1949), pp. ix–x.
166 A correct translation of the title would be *On the Completion of the Marxian System.*
167 See pp. 114–15.
168 When thinking about the technical aspects of Böhm-Bawerk's criticism, not discussed here, it is important to note that it was published before Bortkiewicz had published his solution to the transformation problem. Thus when Böhm-Bawerk argues that Marx mixes values and prices, he is not using the statement of the transformation problem expounded in p. 000.
169 Cf. Jevons' similar criticism of the English classical theory of value. See p. 76.
170 Böhm-Bawerk (1896), p. 101.
171 Hilferding (1904), p. 196.
172 Ibid., pp. 130, 139.
173 Ibid., pp. 156–9.
174 Ibid., p. 134.
175 Cf. Veblen (1906–7), where the metaphysical nature of the Marxian theory is argued.
176 Hilferding (1904), p. 134; emphasis added.
177 Cf. pp. 000–000 on Menger and institutions.
178 Kolakowski (1978), vol. II, pp. 296–7.
179 See p. 114.
180 Bortkiewicz (1907), p. 200. He used a three-department model, the third sector producing luxury goods for the capitalists.
181 Ibid., p. 202.
182 Note that we are here assuming that fixed capital turns over once a year, and that the capital stock is the same as depreciation.
183 See p. 117.

184 For a straightforward explanation see Blaug (1978), p. 243.
185 Hutchison (1955).
186 Mitchell (1919) quoted in Young (1925), p. 176.
187 Young (1925), pp. 179–80.
188 Ibid., p. 183.

CHAPTER 19

1 Hutchison (1978), pp. 94 ff.; Crouzet (1982), pp. 105–12.
2 For a critical discussion of these terms see Crouzet (1982), pp. 56–63.
3 See p. 73.
4 Much of this section is taken from Hutchison (1978), ch. 4; see ibid., pp. 256 ff. for a discussion of some views very different from those presented here.
5 Cf. Deane (1978), p. 101.
6 Hutchison (1978), p. 97; see p. 75.
7 See pp. 165 ff.
8 Sidgwick (1883), p. 403; see Hutchison (1978), p. 104.
9 See p. 163.
10 This conclusion would also require the assumption that all utility functions were identical, and that utilities were inter-personally comparable.
11 Hutchison (1978), p. 104; Creedy (1981), pp. 89–91.
12 Hutchison (1978), p. 117, quoting the 3rd edition of Cannan (1893).
13 Cain (1979), p. 40 f.
14 Because temporary import duties had been introduced during the Boer War, discussion centred on whether these temporary duties should be removed, not on whether new duties should be introduced.
15 Ibid., p. 41.
16 Balfour, quoted in Coats (1968), p. 194.
17 Bastable *et al.* (1903).
18 Coats (1964), pp. 99–103.
19 See the quotation from Pigou, quoted in Coats (1968), p. 216.
20 Cain (1979), pp. 45 ff. contains an appraisal of whether tariffs would in fact have worked.
21 Coats (1968), p. 207.
22 See pp. 214 f.
23 Quoted in Coats (1968), pp. 214–15.
24 Ibid., p. 215.
25 Cain (1979a), p. 55.
26 Tomlinson (1981), p. 55.
27 Cain (1979a), pp. 54 ff.
28 Coats (1968), p. 224; see pp. 212 ff. and 262 ff.
29 Ibid., pp. 225 ff.; cf. Coase (1972).
30 Hutchison (1978), p. 409; Harris (1972), p. 4 attributes first use of the term to Marshall in 1888. Much of this section is from Harris (1972), pp. 1 ff.
31 Foxwell (1886), quoted in Hutchison (1953), p. 412.
32 For a discussion of Hobson see Alett (1981).
33 Hobson (1896), pp. 9–10.
34 Hobson (1896), p. viii; cf. pp. 56 ff.

35  Harris (1972), p. 11.
36  Harris (ibid.) suggests that it was the search for such measures which led to the theoretical explanations used.
37  Beveridge (1909), p. 235.
38  Ibid., p. 237.
39  For other effects see ibid pp. 210 ff.
40  Ibid., pp. 228 ff.
41  Hutchison (1953), pp. 416–17.
42  Hawtrey (1913), p. 260, quoted in Hutchison (1953), p. 417; see pp. 184 ff.
43  Blaug (1978), pp. 684–5 provides an interpretation of Pigou's argument in terms of the balanced budget multiplier.
44  The election of 1923 was fought, and lost, by Baldwin on the issue of protection.
45  Pigou later argued to the MacMillan committee that the issue was seen as how, not whether, to return to gold.
46  See section 17.5 for discussion of the purchasing power parity theory which underlay this discussion.
47  Cf. Moggridge (1972), p. 228: "The 'Norman Conquest of $4.86' was ultimately an act of faith in an incompletely understood adjustment mechanism undertaken for largely moral reasons."
48  See p. 177.
49  See pp. 184 ff. and 249.
50  See pp. 189–90.
51  Keynes (1971–1983), vol. XIX, p. 813.
52  Winch (1969), pp. 104–7.
53  See p. 248.
54  Winch (1969), p. 106.
55  Ibid.
56  Quoted in ibid., p. 109.
57  This summary is taken from Bradbury's note of dissent to the report in MacMillan Committee (1931), p. 263.
58  For an extensive discussion of attitudes to wage cuts see Hutchison (1978), ch. 6; Pigou's views are in Collard (1981).
59  Hutchison (1978), pp. 182–3.
60  See below.
61  Keynes' advocacy of public works predates the actual return to gold.
62  Keynes (1971–1983), vol. XIX, pp. 812–13; emphasis added.
63  Liberal Party (1929), pp. 54–5.
64  See Harrod (1951), p. 465.
65  For an account of the period see Alford (1972).
66  Galbraith (1955) provides a good account of this.
67  Winch (1969), pp. 120–35; Howson (1975), p. 75.
68  Confidence was impaired also by the exaggerated estimates the May Committee provided of the likely deficit, and by the MacMillan Committee's estimates of the extent of British short-term indebtedness.
69  Howson (1975), pp. 80 ff.
70  This is not the same as saying either that government policy was the cause of cheap money, or that this was the cause of the recovery. See Nevin (1955); Howson (1975), pp. 86 ff.
71  Howson (1975), pp. 90 ff; Sabine (1970).
72  MacMillan Committee (1931), p. 5.

73 Ibid., p. 108.
74 Ibid., p. 109.
75 Ibid.
76 Ibid., pp. 239 ff.
77 Ibid., p. 110.
78 Ibid., p. 117.
79 Ibid., p. 126.
80 Ibid., pp. 131–3.
81 Other major recommendations concerned the need for greater statistical information, and the so-called "MacMillan gap" – the inability of firms of a certain size to obtain finance.
82 Ibid., p. 190.
83 Ibid., p. 191.
84 Ibid., p. 200.
85 See p. 191.
86 Given the collapse of world trade following the monetary collapse of the 1930s this fear was perhaps less unjustifiable than it might now seem.
87 Cf. pp. 177 and 251.
88 Winch (1969), p. 138.
89 Hutchison (1981), pp. 114 ff.
90 Keynes (1926), p. 287.
91 Ibid., pp. 290–1.
92 Ibid., p. 288.
93 Ibid., p. 291.
94 Ibid., p. 292.
95 See Skidelsky (1983) for a broader discussion of Keynes' philosophical outlook.
96 For discussion of these issues see Aldcroft (1984); Alford (1972); Cain (1979a); Floud and McCloskey (1981); Moggridge (1972); Pollard (1970); Tomlinson (1981).
97 Cf. the position taken by Rogin (1956).
98 See pp. 187 and 190.
99 Problems of long-term development were of course important to Marshall, but these were grafted on to, rather than being analysed within, the supply and demand framework.
100 Dorfman (1946–1959) is the most important reference. See also texts such as Scheiber *et al.* (1976).
101 E.g. Scheiber *et al.* (1976), pp. 304 ff.

## CHAPTER 20

1 Gide and Rist (1909).
2 Cf. Blaug (1980), pp. 81–6.
3 The terms English and German were used to describe the two though there were of course exceptions. See ch. 18.
4 Keynes (1891), p. 8. Note that John Neville Keynes was the father of John Maynard Keynes.
5 Ibid., pp. 10, 29.
6 Ibid., p. 47.

7  Ibid., p. 143.
8  Ibid., p. 165, cf. p. 211.
9  Ibid., p. 172.
10  Ibid., p. 144.
11  Ibid., p. 165.
12  Ibid., p. 168.
13  Ibid., p. 166.
14  Ibid., p. 183.
15  Ibid., p. 193.
16  Ibid., p. 196.
17  Ibid., p. 211.
18  Ibid., p. 140.
19  Ibid., p. 206.
20  Ibid., p. 220.
21  See Robertson's illuminating comment on the English attitude being that methodological controversy was a subject more suitable for Germans than for Englishmen. He doubted whether many of his contemporaries actually read Keynes' book; Robertson (1951), p. 14, quoted in Hutchison (1981), pp. 63–4.
22  See pp. 101 ff.
23  See pp. 140–1.
24  Clapham (1922).
25  See p. 165.
26  Hutchison (1981), pp 64 f.
27  Robinson (1962), p. 72; see Hutchison (1981), p. 57.
28  Much of this section is taken from Hutchison (1981), ch. 7.
29  See p. 90.
30  Böhm-Bawerk, quoted by Hutchison (1981), pp. 203–4.
31  Böhm-Bawerk (1896), pp. 101, 117; quoted by Hutchison (1981), p. 204.
32  See Mitchell (1969), pp. 376 ff.
33  Wieser (1929), p. 17; quoted by Hutchison (1981), p. 206.
34  Wieser (1913), p. 8; quoted by Hutchison (1981), p. 206.
35  Hutchison (1981), p. 205.
36  Mises (1933), pp. xiii–xiv.
37  Ibid., p. 2.
38  Ibid., p. 12.
39  Ibid., p. xv.
40  Ibid., p. 9.
41  Ibid., p. 28; cf. p. 9.
42  Ibid., p. 2.
43  Ibid., p. 27.
44  Ibid., pp. 12–13.
45  Ibid., pp. 13–14.
46  Ibid., p. 2.
47  Ibid., p. 14.
48  Ibid., pp. 33–5.
49  Ibid., p. 37.
50  Ibid., pp. 38, 40.
51  Ibid., pp. 3–4.
52  See Hayek (1935).
53  Mises (1933), p. 42.
54  Ibid., p. 42.

55 See also p. 169.
56 Robbins (1932), pp. xiv, 1.
57 Ibid., p. 3.
58 Ibid., p. 16.
59 Cf. Marshall's definition in terms of economic welfare; ibid., p. 4.
60 Ibid., pp. 78–9; cf. p. 75.
61 Ibid., p. 76.
62 Caldwell (1982), pp. 103–6.
63 Robbins (1932), p. 81.
64 Ibid., pp. 74, 79.
65 Ibid., p. 105.
66 Ibid., pp. 116–18.
67 Ibid., p. 107
68 Ibid., p. 106.
69 Ibid., p. 113.
70 Ibid., p. 114.
71 Caldwell (1982), chs. 2–4, from which much of this section is taken. Note that this statement does not label Hutchison as a positivist; for other influences on Hutchison see Coats (1983).
72 Caldwell (1982), pp. 13 f.
73 Ibid., pp. 30–31; see ch. 24.
74 Hutchison (1938), p. 3.
75 Ibid., p. 9.
76 Ibid., p. 7.
77 Ibid., p. 10.
78 Ibid., pp. 140–1.
79 Ibid., pp. 40 f.
80 Ibid., pp. 84 f.
81 Ibid., p. 98.
82 Ibid., p. 100.
83 Ibid., p. 107.
84 Knight (1941), p. 752.
85 Ibid., p. 753.

## CHAPTER 21

1 Cf. p. 228.
2 See p. 101; also Perlman (1977), who places Marshall alongside the American Institutionalists.
3 See pp. 239, 376–7.
4 See pp. 142–3
5 Shackle (1967).
6 Note (a) that these remarks do not apply to all economic theorizing, and (b) that they do not apply to Friedman, the principal exponent of "positive economics". See p. 277.
7 See Stigler (1954).
8 See Darnell (1984).
9 See Patinkin (1976a).

## CHAPTER 22

1   See p. 288.
2   Caldwell (1982), p. 15.
3   Samuelson (1947), p. 4. Hypothesis has been changed to the plural. Samuelson's version of operationalism differs from Bridgman's – see Blaug (1980), pp. 99–100; Caldwell (1982), p. 189.
4   Whether Samuelson's methodology as illustrated by his subsequent work is best characterized as falsificationism is another matter. See Machlup's comment below.
5   Friedman (1953), p. 26. Note that Friedman uses "meaningful" in a slightly different sense from Hutchison.
6   Ibid., pp. 26–8; cf. Caldwell (1982), p. 174.
7   Friedman (1953), p. 30.
8   Ibid. Note that Friedman explicitly denies that unrealistic assumptions guarantee a good theory.
9   For lists of the contributions to this controversy see Blaug (1980), p. 110; Boland (1979).
10   Nagel (1963).
11   E.g. Archibald (1959) distinguished five types; Blaug (1980), p. 107.
12   Samuelson (1963).
13   Samuelson, quoted in Blaug (1980), p. 113.
14   See p. 270.
15   For an account of this view see Nagel (1961) or Suppe (1977).
16   Caldwell (1982), p. 23.
17   Machlup (1955, 1956, 1964).
18   See p. 270.
19   Caldwell (1982), pp. 144–5.
20   Machlup (1956).
21   Machlup (1964), p. 735.
22   Ibid., p. 753.
23   Koopmans (1957), p. 132. He argues that observations should be collected with a view to testing the least well-established postulates of economic theory (p. 142).
24   Ibid., pp. 142–3.
25   Ibid., p. 150.
26   Ibid., p. 154.
27   Ibid., p. 164.
28   Suppe (1977), pp. 617–18; this is the view which underlies Machlup's methodology, described above.
29   Ibid., Afterword; Blaug (1980), ch. 2.
30   Feyerabend (1975).
31   Kuhn (1962).
32   Toulmin (1972).
33   Lakatos (1970).
34   Suppe (1977), pp. 652–3.
35   Blaug (1980) cites an unusually wide variety of philosophical views.
36   See ch. 1.
37   E.g. Gordon (1965), Bronfenbrenner (1971), Kunin and Weaver (1971).
38   Coats (1969), p. 295.
39   See ch. 1.

40  E.g. Blaug (1980).
41  E.g. Boland (1982), Caldwell (1982)
42  Blaug (1980), Hutchison (1981); cf. Coats (1983), pp. 27–8.


## CHAPTER 23

1   Cf. Hicks (1960), pp. 76–7.
2   We neglect here developments relevant primarily to other chapters.
3   Dorfman *et al.* (1958), p. 1.
4   The simplest inherently linear structure is the simple budget constraint.
5   Leontief (1941), p. 3.
6   This assumption found some justification in non-substitution theorems.
7   Leontief (1941), p. 40.
8   Dorfman *et al.* (1958), p. 107.
9   Hicks (1960), p. 111.
10  When non-zero sum games are considered the problem is no longer linear.
11  von Neumann and Morgenstern (1944), pp. 8–15.
12  Ibid., p. 38.
13  Though tackling a more specific problem it could be argued that the true originator of the concept was Edgeworth.
14  It is important to distinguish the two concepts associated with Nash: what is often called the Cournot–Nash equilibrium, a solution to a non-cooperative game, and the Nash bargain, a solution to a cooperative game.
15  The core is similar to von Neumann and Morgenstern's "solution", though not exactly the same. See Shubik (1981).
16  Scarf (1962), Aumann (1964).
17  E.g. See Nicholl (1941); cf. the quotation from Fisher on p. 157.
18  They developed this to deal with the theory of games.
19  Green (1964) contains a thorough treatment of the problem. See also Bliss (1975) and Green (1976).
20  Samuelson (1947), p. 6.
21  See p. 102.
22  Samuelson (1947), pp. 3–4.
23  See p. 280; see also Hahn (1983), pp. 31–6.
24  See p. 96.
25  Samuelson (1947), pp. 5, 257–8.
26  Ibid., p. 314.
27  See p. 144.
28  For references see Debreu (1982).
29  See section 23.1
30  Debreu (1959), pp. 83–4.
31  See p. 311.
32  Hahn (1982d), p. 745.
33  It is worth noting that this is an equilibrium concept, not simply an assumption about expectations.
34  Hahn (1971), p. 3; Kurz (1974); Starratt (1973).
35  See pp. 337 f.
36  Grossman (1969).
37  See pp. 337–8.

38　Arrow and Hahn (1971), p. 167.
39　See section 25.1.
40　See Lancaster (1957).
41　See Deaton and Muellbauer (1980) for more details.
42　Ibid., p. 3.
43　*JPE* 1962, issue on "Investment in human beings"; the idea of human capital goes back to Smith.
44　Although it is Lancaster's theory of goods characteristics which is most widely cited, the theory can be found in earlier work: Gorman (1980), written in 1956; and Ironmonger (1972).
45　Tobin (1952) surveys this literature.
46　See pp. 292 and 338.
47　See p. 157.
48　Arrow and Hurwicz (1972), Milner (1954), Shackle (1949, 1961).
49　For a survey see McCall (1971); Hey (1979).
50　See Hey (1979).
51　See Azariadis and Stiglitz (1983).
52　Hey (1981b).
53　Stiglitz (1974).
54　Hey (1979), pp. 178 ff.; Hey (1981a), pp. 171 ff.
55　See p. 308.
56　If consumers are risk neutral, then anyone with above-average health will refuse to buy the policy; if consumers are risk-averse then the cut-off point will be higher.
57　See symposium introduced by Stiglitz (1977).
58　Hey (1981a), pp. 172 ff.; Spence (1974); symposium introduced by Spence (1976).
59　Coase (1937), p. 389.
60　Ibid., p. 395.
61　See p. 232.
62　This subject is briefly treated in Williamson (1977), pp. 190 ff.; see also p. 377.
63　The issue of separation of ownership from control dates from Berle and Means (1932).
64　See also Simon (1978). Simon's theory has implications for all behaviour, not merely that of firms.
65　Simon (1976), p. 130.
66　Ibid., p. 131.
67　Baumol (1984), p. 477.
68　Solow (1980), Okun (1981).

## CHAPTER 24

1　Parts of this chapter are based on the assumption that the reader will have read a standard treatment of welfare economics, such as Bator (1957), or the relevant chapters of texts such as Hirschleifer (1976).
2　For a list of earlier contributors, who between them developed the conditions for a Pareto optimum, see Boulding (1952).
3　Kaldor (1939), p. 389.
4　Hicks (1939b).

5   This assumes that income is efficiently redistributed, by lump sum transfers. Note that although the exposition is in terms of utility, it does not require any interpersonal utility comparisons.

6   For example, Smith's distinction between productive and unproductive labour could be related to the issue of whether to include in national income the cost of producing government services. A survey of the theory of index numbers, as applied to individuals, is found in Frisch (1936).

7   Hicks (1939a), p. 41.

8   Hicks (1941), p. 104.

9   Ibid., p. 106.

10  This gives a social welfare function of the form
$$W = W\{U_1(x_1),\ U_2(x_2),\ \ldots\}$$
where $W$ is social welfare, and $U_i$ is the $i$th individual's utility function.

11  This assumes that there is an interior solution.

12  Boulding (1952), p. 31.

13  See Mishan (1965).

14  This condition was introduced in the second edition, replacing two conditions (positive association of individual and social values, and citizens' sovereignty) which were used in the first edition.

15  Arrow (1951a), p. 59.

16  See Graaf (1957); Baumol (1965), ch. 14.

17  E.g. Little, Samuelson.

18  See Sen (1970a and 1985).

19  Gibbard (1973), Satterthwaite (1975).

20  Sonnenschein (1983).

21  Sen cites the example of the welfare implications of Nero's fiddling while Rome burned. We can say that the utility gained by Nero was less than the utility lost by all other Romans put together without committing ourselves that we could always compare the utilities of any two Romans.

22  This link is very hard to establish formally.

23  Note that although economists have usually described as Rawlsian a social welfare function where social welfare depends on the welfare of the worst-off person in society, Rawls himself defined his criterion differently, in terms of the quantity of socially necessary goods consumed by the worst-off person.

24  E.g. Duncan Black (1948).

25  The use of the term Pareto optimal comes from Little (1950).

26  The terms Pareto-efficient and Pareto-optimal are used interchangeably.

27  The *Pareto condition* is that a change be a *Pareto improvement*. A *Pareto optimum* is a situation such that no Pareto improvements are feasible.

28  Atkinson (1975), p. 48.

29  See also Sandmo (1976); Musgrave (1959); Pigou (1928a).

30  Atkinson and Stiglitz (1980), pp. 347–50.

31  Ibid., p. 6.

32  Ibid., p. 352.

33  Ibid., pp. 336–42.

34  Ibid., p. 357

35  Ibid., p. 359.

36  This goes back to Ramsey (1927).

37  See p. 242. The modern treatment stems from Mirrlees (1971).

38  Atkinson and Stiglitz (1980), pp. 394–7.

39  Ibid., p. 393.

40  Ibid.

41 Ibid., pp. 355–6.
42 Ibid., p. 433.
43 Ibid., p. 456.
44 Ibid., p. 335.
45 For discussion of earlier treatments see Musgrave (1939), pp. 213–17.
46 Samuelson (1955), p. 182.
47 See Samuelson's diagram (1955), p. 196.
48 See p. 297.
49 See ch. 15.
50 Elsinga (1984).
51 Coase (1960), p. 424.
52 Ibid., p. 435.
53 Ibid., p. 436.
54 Ibid., p. 437.

## CHAPTER 25

1 See p. 364.
2 Harrod (1939), p. 45.
3 Ibid., p. 46.
4 Ibid., p. 61.
5 Ibid., p. 47.
6 Ibid., p. 62.
7 Domar (1946), p. 68.
8 Ibid., p. 67.
9 Ibid., pp. 72–3.
10 Harrod included the effects of capital accumulation on capacity in his natural rate of growth, not his warranted rate.
11 Solow (1956), p. 162.
12 Ibid.
13 See Solow (1961) for a simple exposition of the two-sector model as a miniature general equilibrium model.
14 See Hicks (1965) for a simple exposition.
15 Special problems arise when infinite time is considered. See Shell (1971).
16 Cf. Hicks (1965), p. 208.
17 If there is steady growth, capital and labour must grow at the same rate. Investment, therefore, must equal $nK$, where $n$ is the growth rate of the labour force, and $K$ is the capital stock. Investment per head, $i$, is thus equal to $nK/L = nk$ where $k$ is capital per head. Assuming output per head is related to capital per head by $y = f(k)$, consumption per head, $c = y - i = f(k) - nk$. For $c$ to be a maximum, $dc/dk = f'(k) - n = 0$, from which the golden rule follows.
18 Harrod and Domar are exceptions.
19 See Harcourt (1984).
20 See pp. 190 and 397.
21 Translated in Kalecki (1969).
22 Kalecki (1969), p. 3. For an explanation, see the discussion of Kaldor's model.
23 See also Robinson (1956).
24 $P + W = C + I = (1-s)P + W + I = (P + W) + (I - sP)$, therefore $I = sP$.
25 Kaldor (1957); Kaldor and Mirrlees (1962).

26  E.g. Tobin (1960).
27  Cf. Harcourt (1972), p. 15.
28  Robinson (1953), p. 47.
29  Robinson (1956) and numerous articles: see Harcourt (1972).
30  She also raised the issue of whether technical coefficients could in reality be varied.
31  Harcourt (1972), pp. 99 ff.
32  Robinson (1953), pp. 54–9.
33  Cf. Samuelson (1948a), 7th edn, pp. 573–6; Burmeister (1980), pp. 112–15.
34  See Harcourt (1972), pp. 39 ff.
35  Swan (1956), p. 103.
36  Solow (1957), pp. 401–2.
37  Ibid.
38  See pp. 29 and 114.
39  See Harcourt (1982).
40  See pp. 384 ff.
41  See, for example, Dobb (1973); cf. Bliss (1975), ch. 6.
42  Although reference is made to "changes" this is solely to simplify the exposition: the changes involve comparisons across steady states, not changes over time.
43  See Harcourt (1972), recent editions of Samuelson (1948a), or Blaug (1975). Note that Price–Wicksell effects are more important than reswitching. Price–Wicksell effects, necessary if reswitching is to occur, are on their own sufficient to rule out an aggregate production function.
44  Samuelson (1966b), pp. 233, 250.
45  Garegnani and Nell are examples of critics; Laing provides a defence.
46  Cf. Blaug (1975), pp. 39–40.
47  Samuelson (1966), p. 249.
48  E.g. Bruno, Burmeister and Sheshinski (1966).
49  Ferguson (1969), p. 266; cf. Robinson (1973a), chs 16, 16a; Blaug (1975).
50  See p. 157.
51  It would be more correct to say "non-increasing", as there is no reason why the MRS should not be constant over a certain range, as in Figure 25.2.
52  The terminology sometimes used is that a set of prices "supports" a given allocation of resources.
53  Cf. Dixit (1977) for a helpful review, which stressed the importance of Bliss's book.
54  Bliss (1975), p. 63.


CHAPTER 26

1  See pp. 194 ff.
2  Pribram (1983), p. 496; cf. introduction to Harris (1947).
3  Moggridge (1975), p. 73.
4  Schumpeter (1954), p. 1180; Samuelson (1946), p. 187.
5  Samuelson (1946), p. 189.
6  Schumpeter (1954); Johnson (1971).
7  Leontief (1937).

8 Guillebaud's description of Marshall's habit of "leaving the context to explain the meaning"; see p. 102 above.
9 Schumpeter (1954), p. 1171.
10 Ibid., p. 1176.
11 See pp. 191 ff.
12 Pribram (1983), p. 504.
13 E.g. Branson (1979), pp. 183–7.
14 Dunlop (1938), Tarshis (1939).
15 See Samuelson (1968) on how the classical theory was never rigorously stated.
16 See p. 145.
17 Hicks (1982), pp. 69, 319.
18 Hicks' (1939a), p. 178.
19 Hicks (1937), pp. 135–8.
20 See p. 172; Hicks (1984), pp. 198–9.
21 Cf. Schumpeter's view discussed on p. 334.
22 Weintraub (1979), p. 63.
23 Patinkin (1965), p. 343. This was limited in that Patinkin did nothing to solve the aggregation problem; cf. section 23.1.
24 Ackley (1961), Dernberg and McDougall (1960).
25 Leijonhufvud (1976), p. 82.
26 Solow and Stiglitz (1968) contains a model containing many of Barro and Grossman's ideas, but they are to a great extent left implicit in the mathematics of the model.
27 See p. 292.
28 See p. 190.
29 Bronfenbrenner and Holzman (1963), Samuelson and Solow (1960).
30 See Bronfenbrenner and Holzman (1963), p. 63.
31 Gordon (1976), pp. 259–62; Bronfenbrenner and Holzman (1963), p. 64 f.
32 Lipsey and Parkin (1975), p. 149; Bronfenbrenner and Holzman (1963); there is more to the Phillips relation than merely a negative slope – see Lipsey and Parkin (1975), p. 150.
33 Samuelson and Solow (1960).
34 Lipsey and Parkin (1975), pp. 156–9. There were serious problems with this model, not least the fact that unionization might well depend on the state of demand.
35 Samuelson and Solow (1960), p. 384.
36 Friedman (1968), p. 102.
37 Lipsey and Parkin (1975), p. 154.
38 Gordon (1976), p. 264.
39 Villard (1948), pp. 319–20.
40 Patinkin (1949).
41 Johnson (1956b), pp. 2–6; Patinkin (1965).
42 Friedman (1956), p. 52.
43 Ibid., pp. 62–3.
44 Ibid., pp. 51–2.
45 Ch. 18; Friedman (1974), pp. 162–3.
46 Patinkin (1969), pp. 100–1 on influence of Keynes.
47 Much of this is contained in Friedman (1969).
48 Friedman (1969), p. 181.
49 Ibid., p. 259.
50 See Blaug (1980a).

51  In Gordon (1974).
52  For reactions see Gordon (1974).
53  Tobin (1963, 1969).
54  A slight modification is needed in that the yield on capital, not the yield on bonds, should appear on the vertical axis of the ISLM diagram.
55  There is a large literature on this, not discussed here.
56  Lucas (1972), Sargent and Wallace (1975); see Begg (1982), Sheffrin (1983).
57  Muth (1961).
58  See e.g. Begg (1982).
59  Lucas (1972), Sargent and Wallace (1975).
60  One of the simplest expositions is Sargent and Wallace (1976).
61  Lucas (1980).
62  Hall (1982), Sargent and Wallace (1982).
63  House of Commons (1981), ch. 4. This contains a survey of recent attitudes to policy, and the fourfold classification it employs can usefully be compared with the Monetarist–Keynesian classification found in many textbooks.
64  E.g. Hahn (1982a).
65  See p. 180.
66  Haberler (1956), p. 137.
67  Keynes (1936).
68  E.g. Hansen (1941).
69  Simons (1942).
70  Adelman and Adelman (1959), p. 301.
71  E.g. Haberler (1956).
72  E.g. Friedman (1969), chs 6 and 9.
73  Ibid., pp. 116–21.
74  Lucas (1975, 1977, 1978); see Sheffrin (1983), pp. 31–40 for a simple account.

## CHAPTER 27

1   On pre-1940 contributions see section 17.3. Note that the geometry of international trade theory is general equilibrium geometry, using Edgeworth boxes and similar constructions.
2   Meade (1952), p. 12.
3   Ibid., pp. 19–26.
4   Cf. Corden (1965), p. 29. It is worth noting that in addition to the developments mentioned in the text there was Mosack (1945), which discussed the theory of trade in the context of Hicks' *Value and Capital*.
5   See p. 336.
6   See p. 206.
7   Samuelson (1952); see also Samuelson (1954b), Bhagwati (1964), pp. 190–2.
8   E.g. Jones (1970).
9   Jones (1983).
10  Cf. de Marchi (1976), p. 114.
11  E.g. Jones (1956).
12  Bhagwati (1964), pp. 175 f.; de Marchi (1976), p. 119.
13  This was written in the early 1930s; de Marchi (1976), p. 115.
14  This is partly a reversion to Heckscher's original result. It is important to note,

however, that the way in which it was derived differed from the way Heckscher derived his, for he was averse to the use of general equilibrium theory. See Ohlin (1933), appendix to 2nd edn, p. 306. See also Chipman (1966) and Samuelson (1971). There Samuelson points out that, if there is one immobile factor, Ohlin's claim that there would be only partial factor price equalization was right.

15 Mundell (1957).
16 E.g. Kuhn (1959).
17 Bhagwati (1959), p. 271.
18 See Pearce (1970), ch. 16.
19 Corden (1965), pp. 31–4; Bhagwati (1964), pp. 181–4.
20 See Dixit and Stiglitz (1977).
21 See Caves and Jones (1977), pp. 137–41.
22 See p. 306.
23 Samuelson (1939a), p. 204.
24 Samuelson (1938b), p. 265.
25 Bhagwati (1964), pp. 214–17.
26 These assumptions described the problem facing many countries in the immediate post-war period.
27 Meade (1955a).
28 Ibid.
29 E.g. in Fleming (1951) the constraints preventing the utopian solution were the inability to devalue, the inability to impose export subsidies, and so on.
30 See p. 306.
31 O'Brien (1976a), p. 540; see also Machlup (1977).
32 Viner (1924b, 1931); Taussig (1892). See O'Brien (1976a), pp. 556–8. Much of the following is taken from this.
33 The balance of payments did of course feature in the early versions of the multiplier. See p. 194.
34 Corden (1965) claims that Robinson's book served as the principal text on the balance of payments until Meade (1951).
35 Paish (1936), p. 46. The concept itself was not new.
36 E.g. Robinson (1937), p. 214.
37 Metzler (1942); Machlup (1943). For a more detailed discussion see Pribram (1983), pp. 537–8; Haberler (1955), pp. 44–8.
38 See Corden (1965), pp. 10–15; Allen and Kenen (1978), pp. 13 f.
39 Meade (1951), pp. 104–5.
40 Ibid., pp. 114 f.
41 Ibid., pp. 157–62.
42 Corden (1965), pp. 15–21.
43 Frenkel and Johnson (1976); Johnson (1977); Whitman (1975).
44 It was argued that in the long run it is impossible to sterilize a balance of payments imbalance.
45 See p. 210 for earlier views.
46 In addition to the factors discussed below, there is also the obvious one of the number of underdeveloped countries which became independent, especially in the 1950s and 1960s.
47 Arndt (1972), p. 24.
48 The Economic Commission for Asia and the Far East, and the Economic Commission for Latin America, both established in the late 1940s.
49 Little (1982), pp. 35 ff.

50  Little (1982), 35n for a list.
51  Hirschman (1981), pp. 3, 6.
52  Arndt (1981), p. 465.
53  Rosenstein-Rodan (1943), p. 245.
54  Ibid. It is also worth mentioning another influential contribution: Mandelbaum (1945).
55  Cf. Brookfield (1975), p. 71, n. 13.
56  Singer (1949), p. 5.
57  Myrdal (1968).
58  Rosenstein-Rodan (1943), p. 250.
59  Ibid., p. 248.
60  Rosenstein-Rodan (1961), quoted in Meier (1970), p. 396.
61  Nurkse (1952), pp. 257–8, quoting Mill, *Essays on Some Unsettled Questions of Political Economy* (1844).
62  This is discussed in a different context in section 25.3.
63  Clark (1953).
64  Cf. Singer (1952), especially pp. 396–9.
65  Brookfield (1975).
66  Lewis (1954), pp. 402–3. Surplus labour is defined as involving a zero marginal product of labour.
67  There is of course an enormous difference in the distribution of the benefits of growth: workers do not benefit at all. See ibid., pp. 448–9.
68  See section 28.1.
69  Little (1982), pp. 70 ff.
70  Singer (1950), p. 165.
71  See Cardoso (1977); Brookfield (1975), pp. 139–42.
72  Cardoso (1977), pp. 12–13.
73  Ibid., p. 26. For discussion of the reactions of orthodox economists to this see ibid., pp. 16–24, or Little (1982), pp. 70 ff.
74  Hirschman's argument owed a lot to Scitovsky (1954), especially pp. 300 ff.
75  Hirschman (1958), ch. 6.
76  Hirschman used the terms "trickling down effect" and "polarization effect" to describe these phenomena.
77  The ideas of Hirschman and Myrdal have important implications for geographical aspects of development. For discussion of such issues amongst geographers see Brookfield (1975), ch. 4.
78  E.g. Friedman (1958), Bauer (1984).
79  For details of the growth performance see Sen (1983), Brookfield (1975), Little (1982).
80  Hirschman (1981), p. 20.
81  Livingstone (1981a), pp. 8–9. He adds a further explanation, that increasing numbers of development economists came from the underdeveloped countries themselves.
82  Singer (1964a), p. 17.
83  Gerschenkron (1962). See Hirschman (1981), p. 11.
84  Little (1982), p. 149.
85  Ibid., pp. 125 f.
86  Sen (1983) argues forcefully that traditional development economics does work, but that it does not produce the desired results in terms of reducing hunger.
87  Rimmer (1981) points out that this is a reversion to earlier ideas.

88 Little (1982), p. 123 refers to the resurgence of neoclassical economics. The word theorizing is used here to indicate an approach, not a particular theory.
89 The definition is taken from ibid., p. 25, where this is contrasted with the "structuralist" view of the world as inflexible (p. 20).
90 Ibid., pp. 128–9.
91 Ibid., pp 128, 136 f.
92 Ibid., pp. 138–9.
93 Ibid., p. 40.
94 Ibid., p. 149.
95 Ibid., pp. 160–1.
96 Stiglitz (1974).
97 Newbery and Stiglitz (1981).
98 E.g. Baran (1957), Frank (1968), Emmanuel (1974), Amin (1976).
99 Dos Santos (1970), p. 143.
100 Ibid.
101 See p. 366.
102 Cardoso and Faletto (1979), quoted in Little (1982), p. 409, n. 1.
103 Cardoso (1977), p. 35.
104 For discussion of Marx's and Lenin's theories of Imperialism see Brewer (1981). Some of the economists listed in note 99 are discussed there.
105 Little (1982), p. 220.
106 Ibid., p. 221.
107 Rimmer (1984), pp. 228–9; Little (1982), pp. 218 ff.

## CHAPTER 28

1 See Breit and Culbertson (1976a); Dorfman (1946–59), vol. IV, pp. 126–9.
2 Ayres (1935a and b) which should be read together with Knight (1935).
3 Ayres (1935a), p. 175.
4 Ibid., p. 176.
5 Ayres (1935b), pp. 356–7.
6 Ayres (1935a), p. 181.
7 Ibid., p. 186.
8 Ibid., p. 189.
9 Asyres (1935b), p. 358.
10 Ibid.
11 Ayres (1944), p. 223.
12 Ibid., p. 224.
13 Ibid., p. 85.
14 Ibid., p. 226.
15 Ibid., p. 85.
16 The subtitle of *American Capitalism* was "A theory of countervailing power."
17 It is in some ways closer to the Austrian concept of competition.
18 Myrdal (1978).
19 See p. 192.
20 Myrdal (1978), p. 772.
21 See p. 367.
22 Myrdal (1968), p. 26.
23 Ibid., p. 7.

24  Ibid., p. 25; see his discussion of the sources of bias, pp. 8–24.
25  Ibid., p. 32.
26  Myrdal (1929), p. 128; cf. p. 169.
27  Myrdal (1968), p. 33.
28  Ibid., pp. 49–125.
29  See pp. 238 ff.; cf. Myrdal (1978), p. 772.
30  Myrdal, ibid., attributes the decline of Institutionalism to the depression, a problem on which Institutionalists had no effective advice to offer.
31  Ayres (1944), p. 12.
32  Samuelson (1976) 10th edn, quoted in Klein (1978), pp. 252–3.
33  See Samuels (1977, 1978).
34  Much of this paragraph comes from Furobtn and Richter (1984).
35  See Williamson (1977), p. 191.
36  See North (1984), p. 8.
37  Mises (1969), p. 10, where he excepted his own work from this generalization; quoted in Littlechild (1978), p. 14. Much of the following argument is from this source.
38  This is not to imply that Hayek and Mises held identical views, as is shown below. Hutchison (1981), pp. 210 ff., argues that fundamental change in Hayek's views took place with his 1937 article, his early views being close to those of Mises.
39  Quoted in Littlechild (1978), p. 20.
40  This list is taken from Littlechild (1978), p. 20.
41  See p. 89.
42  This is not completely absent from theories involving Walrasian elements; see pp. 108 and 157.
43  Kirzner (1976), p. 40.
44  See p. 266.
45  Rothbard (1976), p. 21; see p. 267.
46  Kirzner (1976), p. 42.
47  Much of the following argument is owed to Hutchison (1981), pp. 214 ff., where it is argued that this article constitutes a significant break with his earlier views.
48  Hayek (1937), p. 33. In a footnote to this passage Hayek interprets verification in terms of falsificationism, citing Popper (1934).
49  Ibid., p. 42; cf. discussions of conjectural variation (p. 143) and rational expectations (p. 345).
50  Ibid., p. 44.
51  Ibid.
52  See pp. 79 and 291.
53  Ibid., p. 45.
54  Ibid., p. 46.
55  The argument is developed further in Hutchison (1981), pp. 216 ff.
56  Hayek (1937), p. 48.
57  Cf. Knight's view: see p. 157.
58  See Ford (1983).
59  Shackle (1972).
60  Ibid., p. 96.
61  Ibid., p. 183; cf. p. 428.
62  Ibid., pp. 429 ff.; Shackle (1967).
63  See pp. 336 f.

64 S. Weintraub was one of the first economists to question the Hicks–Hansen interpretation of Keynes.
65 Keynes (1936), pp. v, 4 ff.
66 Ibid., p. 149.
67 Ibid., p. 194.
68 Keynes wrote the demand for money as $M^d = L_1(Y) + L_2(r)$.
69 Ibid., ch. 15.
70 Ibid., ch. 17.
71 Note that Keynes defined the term "classical" to include neoclassical economics as well as what is usually thought of as classical economics.
72 Keynes (1937), p. 216.
73 Ibid., p. 218.
74 See Kregel (1973).
75 See pp. 325 ff.
76 E.g. Garegnani (1970); Harcourt (1972).
77 See p. 324.
78 See Hahn and Matthews (1964).
79 Robinson (1962b), p. 23.
80 Ibid., p. 26.
81 Sraffa is also discussed on pp. 326 ff.
82 A simpler version of these equations is on p. 327.
83 Dobb (1973), p. 261.
84 Ibid., p. 169.
85 Hahn (1982b), p. 353.
86 This is the Kaldorian theory of distribution. Given the growth rate, the rate of profit (interest) is $r = g/s_p$.
87 Bliss (1975), p. 121.
88 Ibid.
89 Ibid., pp. 122–3, 276.
90 See p. 32.
91 See p. 334.
92 Bliss (1975), p. 125, emphasis added.
93 See p. 140.
94 Roncaglia (1977), p. 172.
95 Bharadwaj (1978), p. 41; emphasis added.
96 Ibid., p. 67.
97 Ibid., p. 66.
98 Roncaglia (1978), p. 120.
99 Samuelson (1947), quoted by Roncaglia (1978), p. 120.
100 Ibid. The sentence quoted refers to technology, but similar remarks are made concerning preferences.
101 Bharadwaj (1978), p. 60.
102 Ibid., pp. 60–2.
103 Samuelson (1962), quoted in Samuelson (1974), p. 270.
104 Samuelson (1974), p. 270.
105 See Klamer (1984), p. 7, and the quotation from Solow on p. 130.
106 Lange (1935), p. 191.
107 Ibid., p. 201.
108 Ibid., p. 196.
109 Dobb (1937), p. 22.
110 Ibid., p. 135.

111   Ibid., p. 136; see Hutchison (1981) for a severe criticism of Dobb on this point.
112   He has continued to express similar views: e.g. (1973).
113   Schumpeter (1942) also contained an extensive discussion of Marx.
114   Many economists would prefer to say that Marx is as worthwhile as much modern growth theory, being sceptical as to the value of both.
115   See pp. 321 f.
116   Meek (1967), p. 176; see p. 327.
117   Steedman (1977), p. 207.
118   Ibid., italics in orginal.
119   See p. 112.
120   Bronfenbrenner (1970), Lindbeck (1971).
121   Blaug (1983), p. 750.
122   Bronfenbrenner (1970), p. 748 gives a list of reasons.
123   Ibid., p. 753.
124   Lindbeck (1971), pp. 9 ff.
125   See Blaug (1983).
126   Friedman (11974), quoted in Samuels (1976).
127   Reder (1982), p. 11; much of the following argument is taken from here.
128   Ibid.
129   Such an assertion requires strong assumptions about the nature of the disturbances involved.
130   Ibid., p. 16.
131   See p. 341.
132   Stigler (1961, 1962).
133   Becker (1965); see p. 294.
134   Becker 1976). It is important to note that an assumption Becker maintains throughout is that preferences do not change.
135   See pp. 345 f.
136   Samuels (1976), p. 4.
137   See quotation above.
138   Reder (1982), p. 13.
139   Ibid., p. 15.
140   Ibid., p. 17.
141   Littlechild (1978), pp. 23–4.

## CHAPTER 29

1    Peden (1983), p. 282.
2    See p. 254.
3    Ibid., p. 283; Middleton (1982).
4    Peden (1983), p. 284.
5    Meade (1975).
6    Howson (1975), pp. 127–8.
7    By the time the policy was agreed, however, the recession had begun and it was too late to implement it.
8    Peden (1980).
9    Peden (1983), p. 285.
10   See p. 248.
11   Harrod (1951), pp. 579 ff.

12 Booth (1983), pp. 106–7.
13 Ibid., p. 107.
14 Meade was one of a group of economists in the Economic Section of the War Cabinet secretariat.
15 Booth (1983), pp. 107–8.
16 Ibid., pp. 108–9.
17 Beveridge (1953).
18 In contrast with his earlier report, this was not produced in any official capacity. See Beveridge (1953), ch. 15.
19 Beveridge (1944), p. 128.
20 Ibid., pp. 30–1.
21 Ibid., p. 106; see pp. 247 f.
22 Booth (1983), p. 109.
23 Ibid., p. 110.
24 Ibid., p. 114.
25 Note that Keynes was not involved in the production of this White Paper.
26 Peden (1983), p. 295.
27 Booth (1983), pp. 119 ff.
28 Ibid., pp. 119–20.
29 Ibid. Dalton's orthodoxy did not extend to monetary policy, where he tried to get the interest rate as low as possible.
30 For other reasons see ibid., p. 120.
31 Ibid., p. 122.
32 Ibid.
33 Peden (1983), p. 295; see Harrod (1968).
34 Dow (1965), pp. 178 ff.; cf. Matthews (1968).
35 For further details on what was happening to the British economy see Backhouse (1983), chs 1 and 12.
36 Riddell (1983), p. 59.
37 Ibid., pp. 28, 59.
38 This follows from there being only three sectors in the economy (i.e. public, private and overseas) for one sector's deficit must be matched by a surplus in one or both of the other two sectors.
39 Cf. discussion of the Ricardian vice, pp. 32 and 386.
40 Stewart (1977).
41 Dow (1965), pp. 391–2.
42 Stewart (1972), p. 188.
43 Coats (1981), p. 33. Discussion of the reasons for the growth in numbers is discussed here.
44 Before this there was the European Free Trade Area, a group of countries not in the EEC.
45 Riddell (1983), pp. 59–60.
46 Reference is to the *apparent* deficit, because subsequent revisions of the statistics resulted in a substantially lower deficit for these years. Backhouse (1983), p. 242.
47 Hutchison (1977), ch. 5.
48 See pp. 250 ff.
49 See pp. 358 f.
50 OECD (1971), pp. 24–31.
51 No suggestion is being made as to the permanence of this change of attitude, other than to suggest that things can never be quite the same again.

52    Hutchison (1977), ch. 2.
53    Ibid., p. 6; see Appendix, "Knowledge and ignorance in action", for some examples.
54    Ibid., p. 4.
55    Ibid., p. 5; this sentence is emphasized in the original.
56    Viner (1958), quoted in Hutchison (1977), p. 7.


# CHAPTER 30

1    Hutchison (1978), pp. 291 ff.
2    See pp. 125 ff.
3    See Coats (1977), Eichner (1983) and Heller (1975).
4    Leontief (1971), Hutchison (1977).
5    See section 1.2.
6    See pp. 279 f.
7    See p. 280.
8    Cf. Blaug (1980a).
9    See p. 278.
10    See p. 6.
11    See, e.g., Branson (1979).
12    See p. 335.
13    Income has, at least since Fisher (1906) been defined as the amount someone can consume without reducing his or her wealth. If inflation reduces the real value of financial assets, it is necessary to save a certain amount simply in order to prevent real wealth from falling. Given the level of measured income, therefore, a higher level of inflation implies a lower level of income.
14    See pp. 300 f.
15    It is perhaps worth noting that Lakatos distinguished between research prog-rammes which were empirically progressive and those which were only theoretically progressive (see chapter 1, and the references cited there).
16    Weintraub (1982), pp. 302–3.
17    Blaug (1980a).
18    See Katouzian (1980).
19    Leontief (1971).
20    Canterbery and Burkhardt (1983), Blaug (1980), p. 261.
21    See pp. 289 ff.
22    Hahn (1984), p. 961.
23    See p. 386.

# Bibliographical Note

Most of the important bibliographical references are contained in the text, or in the notes. In addition, excellent, very comprehensive, bibliographies are contained in Blaug (1978), Spiegel (1983) and, for classical economics, O'Brien (1975). It is often worth checking what has been published in *History of Political Economy*, the main journal devoted to the history of economic thought. An index to Volumes 1–15 (1969–1983) is contained in the Winter 1983 issue. The purpose of this note is therefore confined to: (1) suggesting starting points for further reading; and (2) providing references to some material used in writing this book, but not mentioned elsewhere; and (3) pointing out some topics omitted, for reasons of space, in the text. Because the work of economists discussed in the text can easily be found in the alphabetical list of references, the emphasis here is on secondary material.

## CHAPTER 1

Most texts on the history of economic thought contain discussions of how the subject ought to be approached. Particularly important are the introductions to Blaug (1978) and Schumpeter (1954). See also the appendix to Pribram (1983). Very different points of view are to be found in Rogin (1956) and Stark (1944). Stigler (1960) and Hutchison (1978, ch. 9) are essential reading.

On methodology Blaug (1980a) and Caldwell (1982) adopt a historical approach. Stewart (1977) focuses directly on the logic underlying economic arguments, and although the result may be less exciting to read than either of the other two books, it is nonetheless well worth reading. Also useful are Boland (1982) and Coats (1982). See also the references for chapters 20 and 22.

On the philosophy of science as seen by non-economists, the papers contained in Lakatos and Musgrave (1970) are all worth reading. Lakatos (1971) explains Lakatos' own view of how his methodology of scientific research programmes can be used to appraise the history of science: his method of "rational reconstructions". A brilliant example of his technique is Lakatos (1976), well worth reading even though it deals with the history of mathematics, not economics.

## I: POLITICAL ECONOMY BEFORE 1870

With all the chapters in part I the best starting point is O'Brien (1975), together with the relevant chapters of Blaug (1978), Schumpeter (1954) and

Pribram (1983). Also well worth reading are Blaug (1958) (Blaug's later book is not a substitute for this), Winch (1973) and Eltis (1984). On specific economists, see O'Brien (1970), Bowley (1937), Robbins (1958) and Schwarz (1972). More recently there has been Hollander's work on Smith (1973) and Ricardo (Hollander, 1979). On Ricardo, it is worth reading O'Brien (1981b) and Hollander (1982). Finally, Cannan (1893) is also, despite its age, worth reading.

Samuelson (1978) provides a concise account of the classical theory of value and distribution, though this should be read in conjunction with Hollander (1980), where it is argued that Smith's theory differs from Samuelson's "canonical" model. New editions of all Smith's works have recently been brought out by the University of Glasgow, together with two volumes of essays on Smith, edited by Skinner and Wilson, editors of the Glasgow edition of the *Wealth of Nations*. Several of Skinner's papers on Smith are contained in (1976).

Ricardo's works can be found in Sraffa's *Works and Correspondence of David Ricardo*. Sraffa's Introduction to Ricardo's *Principles* (Volume I) is essential reading for any student of Ricardian economics. Although it probably goes too far in dismissing Ricardo, Hutchison (1952) is a useful antidote to texts which attach too much importance to Ricardo. See also Hutchison (1978) ch. 2.

On the material covered by chapters 4–6, books which must be mentioned are Viner (1937) (useful on money as well as trade), Fetter (1965), Winch (1965), Grampp (1960, 1965), Gordon (1979), and Robbins (1952). On the question of Ireland, discussed only tangentially in chapter 6, see Black (1960). Useful collections of articles on classical attitudes to policy and the colonies are found in Coats (1971) and Shaw (1970). Taylor (1972) provides a useful review of the literature on *laissez-faire* in nineteenth century England. For further references on all these subjects see O'Brien (1975), Blaug (1978) and Gordon (1979).

## II: THE NEW SYSTEMS

Hutchison (1953) contains chapters on Jevons, Walras, Menger, Marshall and Clark, all of which are still worth reading. Jaffe (1976) provides a concise discussion of the differences between the first three of these. See also Howey (1960).

Keynes' article in 1933 still provides a useful introduction to the work of Jevons. The most important articles on Jevons are probably those of Black (R.D.C.) (1962, 1972, 1973, 1981), the editor of Jevons' correspondence. See also Bowley (1972), Robertson (R.M.) (1951) and Checkland (1951). On Walras, Jaffe's articles are essential reading, as are the relevant parts of Schumpeter (1954). See also Pirou (1938), Ricci (1933), Collard (1973) and Menard (1980). Useful discussions of Menger's work can be found in Hutchison (1981, ch. 6), Kauder (1957) and Alter (1982). See also the symposium in *Atlantic Economic Journal 6* (3), Sept. 1978.

The classic piece on Marshall is Keynes (1925), reprinted in Marshall (1925). This volume contains Marshall's most important articles on economics. In addition, many of Marshall's most important ideas were put forward, not in published works, but in papers prepared for the government. For these see Marshall (1926). To understand the evolution of Marshall's thought see Whitaker (1975). Whitaker (1974) contains an interesting account of Marshall's (unpublished) attempts to construct a mathematical model of growth. Of recent work on Marshall, particularly useful is O'Brien (1981a). Though old, Parsons (1931, 1932) are still worth reading. See also Perlman (1977), Shove (1942), Guillebaud (1952) and Viner (1941), Whitaker (1977), Coats (1968) and Coase (1975).

On J. B. Clark, see Dorfman (1946–1959, vol. III), Mitchell (1969), Jalladeau (1975) and Henry (1982).

One of the best introductions to Marx's economics is in Blaug (1978). Blaug criticizes Marx from a methodological point of view (1980b). For a short and helpful guide to what is in *Capital*, see Brewer (1984). Morishima's (1973) attempt to provide a mathematical interpretation of Marx's economics is well worth reading. See also Morishima and Catephores (1978), Schumpeter (1942) and Robinson (1942).

On the material covered in chapter 13, see Black *et al* (1973), Blaug (1978), Hutchison (1955 and 1978, chs. 3, 4), Coats (1967a and 1980), Spengler (1968), Perlman (1977).

## III: THE NEOCLASSICAL PERIOD

One of the most useful books on this is still Hutchison (1953). The chapters in Part I of his book provide a good starting point for investigating the work of individual economists. Economists treated by Hutchison, but who have perhaps not received the attention they deserve in Part II above, are Wicksell, Pareto, Wicksteed and Hobson. For further treatment of individuals see Homan (1952), O'Brien and Presley (1981) and Mitchell (1969). The last of these is based on students' notes on lectures given many years earlier, and fascinating, not only because it reveals the rich variety in the early twentieth century's economics, but also because of what it reveals about Mitchell's attitude to economics. On Pareto, Pirou (1938) and Ricci (1933) are well worth reading. A very brief overview is provided in Rima (1977).

Blaug (1978), Schumpeter (1954) and Pribram (1983) provide a thematic treatment and are highly recommended. With Schumpeter it is well worth making full use of both the table of contents and the index to find what he has to say on a particular economist or topic. Because Blaug uses modern theory to explain earlier theories it is sometimes necessary to be careful to distinguish the two, but his treatment of the subject is particularly valuable because he discussed in detail some of the technical issues glossed over in Part II.

On consumer theory see Stigler (1950), Schumpeter (1954) and Shackle (1967), though note that Shackle completely ignores Fisher. Shackle (1967) is also useful on the theory of imperfect competition, as are Hicks (1935), O'Brien (1983a and 1984a), and Moss (1984). On early discussions of the existence of competitive equilibrium, see Arrow and Hahn (1971). Stigler (1941) is the classic reference to the marginal productivity theory of distribution. See also the important article by Gordon (1973).

Welfare economics is discussed in Hutchison (1953), Blaug (1978), and Schumpeter (1954). See also the chapter on Pigou in Spiegel (1952), Collard (1981), and Myint (1948). For a useful discussion of a problem not discussed in chapter 15, see Ruggles (1949 and 1950).

Haberler (1936) is seen by many as the classic survey of pre-Keynesian business cycle theories. For the period up to 1929 the two chapters of Hutchison (1953), are invaluable. Hansen (1964) is also extremely useful, being easier to consult on specific economists than is Haberler. Earlier work is usefully surveyed in Mitchell (1913 and 1927). For an account of developments in the early thirties (Keynes' *Treatise* and Hayek) see Hansen and Tout (1933). As usual, Schumpeter (1954) is well worth consulting, as is Pribram (1983). For a discussion of some early American contributions not discussed in chapter 16, see Parrini and Sklar (1983). Two economists who were widely cited, though usually very critically, were Foster and Catchings (1923, 1925, 1927 and 1928). Foster and Catchings (1926) contains a short and simple introduction to their work. For references to contemporary critics of their under-consumptionist doctrines see Haberler (1936), ch. 5. Their views have recently been examined in Gleason (1959) and Carlson (1962). On monetary theory, see Marget (1930) and O'Brien (1984b).

The literature on Keynes is vast. A selection of early reactions to Keynes is in Harris (1947). Of more recent discussions Patinkin (1976a and 1982), Winch (1969), and Keynes (1975) are particularly worth reading. The June 1983 issues of *The Economist* contain appraisals of Keynes by Samuelson, Hicks, Hayek and Tobin. Keynes' writing, ranging from his books to his correspondence, some of which is very useful in explaining the evolution of his ideas, is in *Collected Writings of John Maynard Keynes* (1971–83). See also the references in chapter 26.

The standard treatment of the theory of international trade is once again Viner (1937). To this should be added Chipman's survey articles, (1965 and 1966), and Haberler (1933 and 1955), Metzler's contribution to Ellis (1948), Iversen (1935), and Angell (1926). In using the last two items it is necessary to be careful when reading about classical theories of the transfer mechanism. On this see the articles by Mason, cited above. On development economics before 1945 see Arndt (1972 and 1981), and Rimmer (1981).

English historical economics is covered by Coats (1954b), Koot (1975 and 1980), Kadish (1982), Hartwell (1973) and Harte (1971). See also Coats (1982a) and Koot (1982). The last of these is the introduction to a volume containing inaugural lectures by the majority of British professors of economic history, many of which contain reflections on the state of their

subject. Texts containing useful discussions, in English, of German historical economics include Mitchell (1969), Hutchison (1953), Ekelund and
Hebert (1983) and Pribram (1983).

The institutionalism of Veblen, Commons and Mitchell is discussed in
the articles contained in Dorfman *et al.* (1963) and in Dorfman (1946–1959,
vols 3–4). Dowd (1958) contains a bibliography of Veblen's works,
together with a wide range of articles on Veblen. On Veblen, see also
Mitchell (1969), Coats (1954a), Arrow (1975), and Rutherford (1984).
Commons' thought is helpfully discussed in Gruchy (1940), Parsons (1950),
Gonce (1971 and 1976), Dugger (1980) and Rutherford (1983). See also
Parsons' introduction to the 1970 edition of Commons (1950). Of the
American institutionalists not mentioned in chapter 18, the most important
is undoubtedly J. M. Clark: see, for example, Clark (1923, 1926, 1957 and
1961).

Marxism was far from the only variety of socialism discussed during this
period. Particularly important was Henry George. On US discussions see
Dorfman (1946–1959). On British socialism see the discussions of Fabian-
ism in Stigler (1965), McBriar (1962) and Ricci (1969). On Hobson's
socialism see Alett (1981). On discussions in the 1920s and 1930s on the
organization of a socialist economy see Hayek (1935) and the article by
Bergson in Ellis (1948).

Economics and policy in Britain is discussed in Hutchison (1953), Harris
(1972), Winch (1969) and the articles contained in Pollard (1970). The tariff
reform campaign is discussed in Coats (1964 and 1968), and in Cain (1979b).
The subject is surveyed in Tomlinson (1981).

Caldwell (1982) and Blaug (1980) between them cover most of the
methodological debates discussed in chapters 20 and 22. In addition, the
most important references, or at least excerpts from them, are reprinted in
Hausman (1984) and Caldwell (1984). Hausman's selection has more on
older discussions, Caldwell's on more recent debates, and although there is
some overlap the two volumes complement each other. Both are strongly
recommended.

## IV: THE MODERN PERIOD

Useful collections of articles have been produced by the AEA, only some of
which are in the list of references. In addition, the many books of readings
published by Penguin, most of which are now out of print, generally
contain much important material. Also useful are the survey articles in
AEA/RES (1965), and in the *Journal of Economic Literature.* The papers of
several contemporary economists have been collected, the most important
being those of Hicks and Samuelson. Hicks' collected papers are particularly
helpful as they contain his later reflections on his earlier work. For
discussion of particular economists, see Spiegel and Samuels (1984).

On the material covered by chapters 23 and 26, I have little to add to the
footnotes, beyond stressing the usefulness of Weintraub (1979), Blaug

(1980a, part III) and Pribram (1983). Lucas (1980) contains some helpful comments on the way macroeconomics has developed. Though much of their content is of a very technical nature, Arrow and Intriligator (1981 and 1982) are useful for chapter 23. Drazen (1980) surveys the literature on disequilibrium models. On welfare economics, Sen (1970a) is much more accessible than it might at first appear to be. The non-mathematical sections can on the whole be read without reading the mathematical parts. Many of the articles collected in Sen (1982) are also quite accessible.

It is probably because many, if not most, economists found it difficult to see why so much fuss was made about capital theory, that surveys abound. For surveys from very different points of view see Harcourt (1972) and Bliss (1975). Sen (1974) contains an amusing account of the controversy, but which nonetheless makes some important points. On the outcome of the controversy, see the very different assessments of Harcourt (1976) and Dixit (1977). Most of the important references are in Sen (1970c) and Harcourt and Laing (1971). A text on growth theory which contains comprehensive bibliographies is Wan (1971).

Two of the best introductions to development economics are Little (1982) and Brookfield (1975). See also Seers (1979), Livingstone (1981a), Killick (1978, ch. 2), Lal (1983) and Rimmer (1984, ch. 6). Hirschman (1981) should not be missed. On international trade, Haberler (1955) and Corden (1965), together with Pribram (1983) provide an excellent starting point.

On Ayres and institutionalism see Breit and Culbertson (1976a), together with the review symposium in *Journal of Economic Issues* 11 (1977), pp. 635–65. Different views of institutionalism, as presented in the *JEI*, are provided by Klein (1978) and Samuels (1977 and 1978). An attempt to formulate an institutionalist methodology is Wilber and Harrison (1978) – see Coats (1982b). Hutchison (1984) provides an overall perspective on institutionalism. On the New Institutional Economics, see the symposium introduced by Furobtn and Richter (1984). Dugger (1983) argues that these two varieties of institutionalism have little in common with each other.

Introductions to "Austrian" economics are provided by Littlechild (1978 and 1982), Dolan (1976) and Shand (1984). Hutchison (1981, ch. 7) provides a critical account of modern "Austrian" methodology. Coats (1983c) contains an attempt to explain the recent revival of interest in subjectivism. Introductions to post-Keynesian economics include Kregel (1973 and 1983), and Eichner and Kregel (1975). See also Roncaglia (1977 and 1978) and Bharadwaj (1978). In my view the best account of Radical economics is Blaug (1983). On Chicago, see not only Reder (1982), but also Bronfenbrenner (1962), Coats (1963) and Rima (1967, ch. 19).

The reception of Keynesian economics is discussed in Peden (1980 and 1983), Booth (1983), Middleton (1982), as well as in Winch (1969) and Keynes (1975). On economics and policy in subsequent years see Hutchison (1968).

A spate of articles and books critical of the current state of economics has appeared recently. Heller (1975) and Coats (1977) both repay reading, and between them provide a long list of references. More recent books include

Bell and Kristol (1981) – this contains several useful pieces, not all critical of mainstream theory, Eichner (1983), Katouzian (1980), Thurow (1983), Kamarck (1983), Ward (1972), Wilber and Jameson (1983). To keep the situation in perspective it is worth reading Schumpeter (1982) and Hutchison (1983). Hahn (1984) contains a brief statement of some of the merits of contemporary economic theorizing.

# Abbreviations used in the Bibliography

| | |
|---|---|
| AAA | Annals of the American Academy of Political and Social Science |
| AEA | American Economic Association |
| AE | American Economist |
| AER | Atlantic Economic Review |
| AEJ | Atlantic Economic Journal |
| BA | British Association for the Advancement of Science, section F |
| CJE | Cambridge Journal of Economics |
| CJEPS | Canadian Journal of Economic and Political Science |
| EA | Economie Appliquée |
| Eca | Economica |
| Ecta | Econometrica |
| EDCC | Economic Development and Cultural Change |
| EHR | Economic History Review |
| EJ | Economic Journal |
| FR | Fortnightly Review |
| GdE | Giorgnale degli Economisti |
| HOPE | History of Political Economy |
| IER | International Economic Review |
| IMFSP | International Monetary Fund Staff Papers |
| JEH | Journal of Economic History |
| JEL | Journal of Economic Literature |
| JES | Journal of Economic Studies |
| JET | Journal of Economic Theory |
| JIE | Journal of International Economics |
| JLE | Journal of Law and Economics |
| JPKE | Journal of Post Keynesian Economics |
| Kyk | Kyklos |
| LBR | Lloyds Bank Review |
| MS | Manchester School |
| REP | Revue d'Economie Politique |
| RES | Review of Economic Studies |
| REStats | Review of Economics and Statistics |
| SEJ | Southern Economic Journal |
| SJE | Swedish/Scandinavian Journal of Economics |
| SJPE | Scottish Journal of Political Economy |
| WA | Weltwirtschaftliches Archiv |
| YLJ | Yale Law Journal |
| YR | Yale Review |
| ZgS | Zeitschrift für die Gesamte Staatswissenschaft |
| ZN | Zeitschrift für Nationalokonomie |

# Bibliography

*Note*

As these dates are used not only to identify items in the bibliography, but also to indicate when works were written, the date which appears after an author's name is normally that of the first edition. Where details of a later edition (or of a reprint in the case of journal article) are given, any page references normally refer to this.

Ackley, G. (1961) *Macroeconomic Theory*. New York.

Adelman, I. and Adelman, F. L. (1959) The dynamic properties of the Klein–Goldberger model, *Ecta*, **27**. In AEA (1965).

AEA (1949) *Readings in the Theory of International Trade*. Philadelphia.

AEA (1953) *Readings in Price Theory*, ed. G. J. Stigler and K. E. Boulding. London.

AEA (1965) *Readings in Business Cycles*, ed. R. A. Gordon and L. R. Klein. Homewood, Ill.

AEA (1969) *Readings in Welfare Economics*, ed. K. J. Arrow and T. Scitovsky.

AEA/RES (1965) *Surveys of Economic Theory*. London: Macmillan.

Aftalion, A. (1909) La réalité des surproductions générales, *REP*.

Agarwala, A. N. and Singh, S. P. (ed) (1958) *The Economics of Underdevelopment*. Oxford: Oxford University Press.

Akerlof, G. A. (1970) The market for "lemons": quality uncertainty and the market mechanism, *QJE* **84**, 488–500.

Aldcroft, D. H. (1984) *Full Employment: the Elusive Goal*. Brighton: Harvester Press.

Alett, J. (1981) *The New Liberalism: the Political Economy of J. A. Hobson*. Toronto: University of Toronto Press.

Alexander, S. S. (1952) Effects of a devaluation on a trade balance, *IMFSP* **1**, 379–96.

Alford, B. W. E. (1972) *Depression and Recovery?* London: Macmillan.

Allen, P. R. and Kenen, P. B. (1978) *The Balance of Payments, Exchange Rates and Economic Policy*, Princeton University reprints in International Finance, **19**, 1979.

Alter, M. (1982) Carl Menger and homo oeconomicus: some thoughts on Austrian theory and method, *JEI* **16**, 149–60.

Amin, S. (1976) *Unequal Development*. Brighton: Harvester Press.

Anderson, B. M. (1920) Some observations on Professor Cassel's paper, *AAA* **89**, 268–73.

Anderson, J. (1777) *An Enquiry into the Nature of the Corn Laws*.

Ando, A. and Modigliani, F. (1965) The relative stability of monetary velocity and the investment multiplier, *AER* **55**, 693–728.

Angell, J. W. (1926) *The Theory of International Prices*. Cambridge, Mass.

Antonelli, E. (1953) Leon Walras et Carl Menger à travers leur correspondance, *EA* **6**, 269ff.

Appleyard, D. R. and Ingram, J. C. (1979) "A reconsideration of the additions to Mill's 'great chapter'". *HOPE* **11**, 459–76.

Archibald, G. C. (1959) The State of Economic Science, *BJPS* **10**, 58–69.

Arndt, H. W. (1972) Development economics before 1945. In J. Bhagwati and R. S. Eckhaus (eds), *Development and Planning, Essays in Honour of Paul Rosenstein-Rodan*. London: Allen and Unwin.

Arndt, H. W. (1981) Economic development: a semantic history, *EDCC* **29**, 456–66.

Arrow, K. J. (1951a) *Social Choice and Individual Values*, 2nd edn, 1963. New York: Wiley.

Arrow, K. J. (1951b) Alternative approaches to the theory of choice in risk-taking situations, *Ecta* **19**, 404–37.

Arrow, K. J. (1951c) An extension of the basic theorem of Classical welfare economics. In J. Neyman (ed.), *Proceedings of the Second Berkeley Symposium on Mathematical Statistics and Probability*.

Arrow, K. J. (1953) The role of securities in the optimal allocation of risk-bearing. Translated in *RES* **31**, 91–6.

Arrow, K. J. (1975) Thorstein Veblen as an economic theorist, *AE* **19**, 5–9.

Arrow, K. J. and Debreu, G. (1954) Existence of an equilibrium for a competitive economy, *Ecta* **22**, 265–90.

Arrow, K. J. and Hahn, F. H. (1971) *General Competitive Analysis*. Edinburgh: Oliver and Boyd.

Arrow, K. J. and Hurwicz, L. (1972) An optimality criterion for decision-making under ignorance. In C. F. Carter and J. L. Ford (eds), *Uncertainty and Expectation in Economics*. Oxford: Basil Blackwell.

Arrow, K. J. and Intriligator, M. D. (1981) *Handbook of Mathematical Economics*, vol. I. Amsterdam: North Holland.

Arrow, K. J. and Intriligator, M. D. (1982) *Handbook of Mathematical Economics*, vol. II. Amsterdam: North Holland.

Ashley, W. J. (1889) Arnold Toynbee, in Ashley (1900).

Ashley, W. J. (1893) On the study of economic history. In Ashley (1900) and in Harte (1971).

Ashley, W. J. (1900) *Surveys Historic and Economic*. London: Longmans Green.

Ashley, W. J. (1888) *An Introduction to English Economic History and Theory*, 3rd edn, 1894. London.

Atkinson, A. B. (1975) *The Economics of Inequality*. Oxford: Oxford University Press.

Atkinson, A. B. and Stiglitz, J. E. (1980) *Lectures on Public Economics*. London: McGraw-Hill.

Aumann, R. J. (1964) Markets with a continuum of traders, *Ecta* **32**, 39–50.

Auspitz, R. and Lieben, R. (1889) *Untersuchungen über die Theorie des Preises*.

Ayres, C. E. (1935a) Moral confusion in economics, *IJE* **45**, 170–99.

Ayres, C. E. (1935b) Confusion thrice confounded, *IJE* **45**, 356–8.

Ayres, C. E. (1944) *Theory of Economic Progress*. Chapel Hill.

Azariadis, C. and Stiglitz, J. E. (1983) Implicit contracts and fixed price equilibrium, *QJE* **98**, suppl., 1–22.

Backhouse, R. E. (1983) *Macroeconomics and the British Economy*. Oxford: Martin Robertson.

Bacon, R. W. and Eltis, W. A. (1976) *Britain's Economic Problem: Too Few Producers*. London: Macmillan.

Bagehot, W. (1976) The problems of English classical political economy, *FR*. Reprinted as book of same title, 1885.

Bailey, S. (1925) *A Critical Dissertation on the Nature, Measure and Causes of Value*, LSE series of reprints, 7. London: LSE.

Bain, J. S. (1947) A note on pricing in monopoly and oligopoly, *AER* **39**, 448–64.

Bain, J. S. (1956) *Barriers to New Competition*. Cambridge, Mass.

Baran, P. (1957) *The Political Economy of Growth*, New York.

Barone, E. (1908) The ministry of production in the collectivist state. Translated in Hayek (1935).

Barro, R. J. and Grossman, H. I. (1971) A general disequilibrium model of income and employment, *AER* **61**, 82–93.

Bastable, C. F. (1889) Some applications of the theory of international trade, *QJE* **4**, 1ff.

Bastable, C. F. (1897) *The Theory of International Trade*, 3rd edn, 1900. London.

Bastable, C. F. *et al.* (1903) Letter to *The Times*, 12 August. Reprinted in *EJ* **13**, 446–9.

Bator, F. M. (1957) The simple analytics of welfare maximization, *AER* **47**, 22–59.

Bauer, P. T. (1984) *Reality and Rhetoric*. London: Weidenfeld.

Baumol, W. J. (1965) *Welfare Economics and the Theory of the State*, 2nd edn. London: LSE.

Baumol, W. J. (1952) The transactions demand for cash: an inventory theoretic approach, *QJE* **66**, 545ff.

Baumol, W. J. (1959) *Business Behaviour, Value and Growth*, 2nd edn, 1967. New York.

Baumol, W. J. (1984) Baumol on Simon. In Spiegel and Samuels (1984).

Baumol, W. J. and Goldfield, S. M. (1968) *Precursors in Mathematical Economics: an Anthology*, LSE Series of Reprints, 19. London: LSE.

Becker, G. A. (1964) *Human Capital*. New York.

Becker, G. A. (1965) A theory of the allocation of time, *EJ* **75**, 493–517.

Becker, G. A. (1976) *The Economic Approach to Human Behaviour*. Chicago: Chicago University Press.

Beers, J. S. de (1941) Tariff aspects of a federal union, *QJE* **56**, 49–92.

Begg, D. C. K. (1982) *The Rational Expectations Revolution in Macroeconomics*. Oxford: Philip Allan.

Bell, D. and Kristol, I. (eds) (1981) *The Crisis in Economic Theory*. New York: Basic Books.

Benassy, J. P. (1975) Neokeynesian disequilibrium in a monetary economy, *RES* **42**, 502–23.

Benassy, J. P. (1976) The disequilibrium approach to monopolistic price setting and general monopolistic equilibrium, *RES* **43**, 69–81.

Bentham, J. (1789) *An Introduction to the Principles of Morals and Legislation*, ed. J. H. Burns and H. L. Hart, 1982. London: Methuen.

Bentham, J. (1818) *Theory of Legislation*. Translated by R. Hildreth, 1874. London.

Bergson, A. (1938) A reformulation of certain aspects of welfare economics, *QJE* **52**, 310–34.

Berle, A. A. and Means, G. C. (1932) *The Modern Corporation and Private Property*. New York.

Berry, A. (1891) The pure theory of distribution, BA. Reprinted in Baumol and Goldfield (1968).

Beveridge, W. (1909) *Unemployment, a Problem of Industry*. London.

Beveridge, W. (1942) *Report on Social Services and Allied Services*, CMND 6404.

Beveridge, W. (1944) *Full Employment in a Free Society*. London.

Beveridge, W. (1953) *Power and Influence: an Autobiography*. London.

Bhagwati, J. (1959) Protection, real wages and real incomes, *EJ* **69**, 733–44. Reprinted in Bhagwati (1969).

Bhagwati, J. (1964) The pure theory of international trade: a survey, *EJ* **74**. In *AEA/RES* (1965), vol. II.

Bhagwati, J. (ed.) (1969) *International Trade: Selected Readings*. Harmondsworth: Penguin.

Bhagwati, J. (ed.) (1981) *International Trade: Selected Readings*. Cambridge, Mass.: MIT Press.

Bharadwaj, K. (1978) *Classical Political Economy and the Rise to Dominance of Supply and Demand Theories*, RC Dutt Lectures. Calcutta: Orient Longman.

Black, D. (1948) On the rationale of group decision-making, *JPE*, 23–34.

Black, J. (1962) The technical progress function and the production function, *Eca* **29**, 166ff.

Black, R. D. C. (ed.) (1971) *Readings in the Development of Economic Analysis, 1776–1848*. Newton Abbot: David and Charles.

Black, R. D. C. (1960) Jevons and Cairnes, *Eca* **27**, 214–32.

Black, R. D. C. (1960) *Economic Thought and the Irish Question*. Cambridge.

Black, R. D. C. (1962) W. S. Jevons and the economists of his time, *MS*, 203–21.

Black, R. D. C. (1970) Introduction to 1970 edition of Jevons (1871).

Black, R. D. C. (1972) Jevons, marginalism and Manchester, *MS* **40**, 2–8.

Black, R. D. C. (1973) W. S. Jevons and the foundation of modern economics. In Black et al. (1973).

Black, R. D. C. (1981) W. S. Jevons, 1835–1882. In O'Brien and Presley (1981).

Black, R. D. C., Coats, A. W. and Goodwin, C. (1973) *The Marginal Revolution in Economics*, Durham NC: Duke University Press.

Blaug, M. (1958) *Ricardian Economics*. New Haven.

Blaug, M. (1975) *The Cambridge Revolution: Success or Failure?* London: Institute of Economic Affairs.

Blaug, M. (1978) *Economic Theory in Retrospect*, 3rd edn. Cambridge: Cambridge University Press.

Blaug, M. (1980) *The Methodology of Economics*. Cambridge: Cambridge University Press.

Blaug, M. (1980b) *A Methodological Appraisal of Marxian Economics*. Amsterdam: North Holland.

Blaug, M. (1983) A methodological appraisal of Radical economics. In Coats (1983a).

Bliss, C. J. (1975) *Capital Theory and the Distribution of Income*. Amsterdam: North Holland.

Boeke, J. H. (1953) *Economics and Economic Policy in Dual Societies*, excerpt in Meier (1970).

Böhm-Bawerk, E. v (1884) *History and Critique of Interest Theories*, translated by G. D. Huncke and H. F. Sennholz, 1959. South Holland, Ill.: Libertarian Press.

Böhm-Bawerk, E. v (1889) *The Positive Theory of Capital*, translated by G. D. Huncke and H. F. Sennholz, 1959. South Holland, Ill.: Libertarian Press.

Böhm-Bawerk, E. v (1896) *Karl Marx and the Close of His System*, translated by P. Sweezy 1949. New York.

Boland, L. (1979) A critique of Friedman's critics, *JEL* **17**, 503–22.

Boland, L. (1982) *The Foundations of Economic Method*. London: George Allen and Unwin.

Bonar, J. (1888) The Austrian economists and their views on value, *QJE* **3**, 1ff.

Booth, A. (1983) The "Keynesian Revolution" in economic policy-making, *EHR* **34**, 103–23.

Bortkiewicz, L. v (1907) On the correction of Marx's fundamental theoretical

construction in the third volume of Capital. Translated in Böhm-Bawerk (1896).
Boulding, K. E. (1952) Welfare economics. In Haley (1952).
Boulding, K. E. (1957) A new look at institutionalism, *AER* **47**, suppl., 1–12.
Bowley, A. L. (1924) *The Mathematical Groundwork of Economics*. Oxford.
Bowley, M. (1937) *Nassau Senior and Classical Economics*. London.
Bowley, M. (1972) The predecessors of Jevons – the revolution that wasn't, *MS* **40**, 9–29.
Bowley, M. (1973) *Studies in the Theory of Value before 1870*. London: Macmillan.
Branson, W. H. (1979) *Macroeconomic Theory and Policy*, 2nd edn. New York: Harper and Row.
Breit, W. and Culbertson, W. P. (1976b) Clarence Edwin Ayres: an intellectual's portrait. In Breit and Culbertson (1976a).
Breit, W. and Culbertson, W. P. (ed.) (1976a) *Science and Ceremony*. Texas University Press.
Breit, W. and Hochman, H. M. (1968) *Readings in Microeconomics*. London: Holt, Rinehart and Winston.
Bresciani-Turroni, C. (1934) The "Purchasing Power Parity" doctrine, *L'Egypte Contemporaine* **25**, 433–64.
Brewer, A. A. (1981) *Marxist Theories of Imperialism*. London: Routledge and Kegan Paul.
Brewer, A. A. (1984) *A Guide to Marx's Capital*. Cambridge: Cambridge University Press.
Bridgman, P. (1927) *The Logic of Modern Physics*. New York.
Brisman, S. (1933) Some reflections on the theory of foreign exchange. In Cassel (1933).
Brodbeck, M. (1982) *Readings in the Philosophy of the Social Sciences*. London: Macmillan.
Bronfenbrenner, M. (1962) Observations on the "Chicago school(s)", *JPE* **70**, 72–5.
Bronfenbrenner, M. (1970) Radical economics in America: a 1970 survey, *JEL* **8**, 747–66.
Bronfenbrenner, M. (1971) The "structure of scientific revolutions" in economic thought, *HOPE* **3**, 136–51.
Bronfenbrenner, M. and Holzman, F. D. (1963) Survey of inflation theory, *AER* **43**, 593–661, reprinted in AEA/*RES* (1965), vol. I.
Brookfield, H. (1975) *Interdependent Development*. London: Methuen.
Bruno, M., Burmeister, E. and Sheshinski, E. (1966) Nature and implications of the reswitching of techniques, *QJE* **80**, 526–53.
Burmeister, E. (1980) *Capital Theory and Dynamics*. Cambridge: Cambridge University Press.
Byé, M. (1950) Customs unions and national interests, *EA*. Translated in *IEP*, 1953, 208–34.
Cain, P. J. (1978) J. A. Hobson, Cobdenism and the radical theory of economic imperialism, 1898–1914, *EHR* **31**, 565–84.
Cain, P. J. (1979a) International trade and economic development in the work of J. A. Hobson before 1914, *HOPE* **11**, 406ff.
Cain, P. J. (1979b) Political economy in Edwardian England: the tariff reform campaign. In A. O'Day, (ed.) *The Edwardian Age: Conflict and Stability*, 1900–1914. London: Macmillan.
Cain, P. J. (1981) Hobson's developing theory of imperialism, *EHR* **34**, 313–16.
Cairnes, J. E. (1874) *Some Leading Principles of Political Economy*. London.
Caldwell, B. (1982) *Beyond Positivism*. London: George Allen and Unwin.

Caldwell, B. (1984) *Appraisal and Criticism in Economics*. London: George Allen and Unwin.

Cannan, E. (1893) *A History of Theories of Production and Distribution in English Political Economy from 1776 to 1848*, 3rd edn, 1917. London.

Canterbery, E. R. and Burkhardt, R. J. (1983) What do we mean by asking whether economics is a science? In Eichner (1983).

Cantillon, R. (1730) *Essay on the Nature of Commerce in General*.

Cardoso, F. H. (1977) The originality of a copy: CEPAL and the idea of development, *CEPAL Review*, **2**, 7–40.

Cardoso, F. H. and Faletto, L. (1979) *Dependency and Development in Latin America*. Berkeley: University of California Press.

Carlson, J. A. (1962) Foster and Catchings: a mathematical appraisal, *JPE* **70**, 400ff.

Carver, T. N. (1903) A suggestion for a theory of industrial depressions, *QJE* **17**, 497ff.

Cassel, G. (1899) Grundriss einer elementaren Preislehre, *ZgS* **55**.

Cassel, G. (1901) *The Nature and Necessity of Interest*. London.

Cassel, G. (1916) The present position of the foreign exchanges, *EJ* **26**, 62ff. and 319ff.

Cassel, G. (1918a) *Theory of Social Economy*. Translated by J. McCabe, 1923. London.

Cassel, G. (1918b) Abnormal deviations in international exchanges, *EJ* **28**, 413ff.

Cassel, G. (1919) The depreciation of the German Mark, *EJ* **29**, 492–6.

Cassel, G. (1920) Some leading propositions for an international discussion of the world's monetary problems, *AAA* **29**, 259–67.

Cassel, G. (1922) *Money and Foreign Exchange after 1914*. London.

Cassel, G. (1933) *Economic Essays in Honour of Gustav Cassel*. London: George Allen and Unwin.

Casson, M. (1983) *Economics of Unemployment*. Oxford: Martin Robertson.

Caves, R. E. and Jones, R. W. (1977) *World Trade and Payments*, 2nd edn. Boston: Little Brown.

Chamberlain, N. R. (1963) The institutional economics of John R. Commons. In Dorfman *et al.* (1963).

Chamberlin, E. H. (1933) *Theory of Monopolistic Competition*. Cambridge, Mass.: Harvard University Press.

Chamberlin, E. H. (1937) The difference between monopolistic and "imperfect" competition, *QJE*. Reprinted in 6th edn, 1948, of Chamberlin (1933).

Checkland, S. G. (1951) Economic opinion in England as Jevons found it, *MS* **19**, 143–69.

Chipman, J. (1979) Mill's "superstructure": how well does it stand up? *HOPE* **11**, 477–500.

Chipman, J. S. (1965) A survey of the theory of international trade, part 1: the classical theory, *Ecta* **33**, 477–519.

Chipman, J. S. (1965) A survey of the theory of international trade: part 2: the neoclassical theory, *Ecta* **33**, 685–760.

Chipman, J. S. (1966) A survey of the theory of international trade: part 3, the modern theory, *Ecta* **34**, 18–76.

Chipman, J. S. (1976) The paretian heritage, *Cahiers Vilfredo Pareto, Revue Européene des Sciences Sociales*, **14**, 65–171.

Clapham, J. H. (1922) Of empty economic boxes, *EJ* **32**, 305–14. Reprinted in AEA (1953).

Clark, C. (1938) *Conditions of Economic Progress*. London.

Clark, C. (1953) Population growth and living standards, *International Labour Review*. Reprinted in Agarwala and Singh (1958).

Clark, J. B. (1886) *The Philosophy of Wealth*, 2nd edn, 1887. New York: A. M. Kelley.

Clark, J. B. (1891) Distribution as determined by a law of rent, *QJE* **5**, 289–318.

Clark, J. B. (1893) The genesis of capital, *YR* **2**, 302–15.

Clark, J. B. (1896) The theory of economic progress, *AEA Economic Studies* **1**, 5–22.

Clark, J. B. (1899) *The Distribution of Wealth*, 2nd edn, 1902. New York.

Clark, J. M. (1923) *Studies in the Economics of Overhead Costs*. Chicago.

Clark, J. M. (1926) *Social Control of Business*. Chicago.

Clark, J. M. (1957) *Economic Institutions and Human Welfare*. New York: Borzoi Books.

Clark, J. M. (1961) *Competition as a Dynamic Process*. Washington: Brookings.

Clarke, P. F. (1981) Hobson, free trade and imperialism, *EHR* **34**, 308–12.

Cliffe Leslie, T. E. (1870) The political economy of Adam Smith, *FR*. In Cliffe Leslie (1879a).

Cliffe Leslie, T. E. (1876) On the philosophical method of political economy, *Hermathena* **4**. In Cliffe Leslie (1879a).

Cliffe Leslie, T. E. (1879) The known and the unknown in the economic world. In Cliffe Leslie (1879a).

Cliffe Leslie, T. E. (1879a) *Essays in Political and Moral Philosophy*. Dublin.

Clower, R. W. (1965) The Keynesian counter-revolution: a theoretical appraisal, in F. H. Hahn and F. Brechling, (eds), *The Theory of Interest Rates*. Reprinted in Clower (1969).

Clower, R. W. (ed.) (1969) *Monetary Theory*. Harmondsworth: Penguin.

Coase, R. H. (1937) The nature of the firm, *Eca* **4**, 386–405.

Coase, R. H. (1960) The problem of social cost, *JLE*, 1–44. In Breit and Hochman (1968).

Coase, R. H. (1972) The appointment of Pigou as Marshall's successor, *JLE* **15**, 473–85.

Coase, R. H. (1975) Marshall on method, *JLE* **18**, 25ff.

Coase, R. H. and Stigler, G. J. (1969) Alfred Marshall's lectures on progress and poverty, *JLE* **12**, 181–226.

Coats, A. W. (1954) The influence of Veblen's methodology, *JPE* **62**, 529–537.

Coats, A. W. (1954b) The historicist reaction in English political economy, 1870–1890, *Eca* 143–53.

Coats, A. W. (1963) The origins of the "Chicago schools(s)" ? *JPE* **71**, 487–93.

Coats, A. W. (1964) The role of authority in the development of British economics, *JLE* **7**, 85–106.

Coats, A. W. (1967a) Sociological aspects of British economic thought (ca 1880–1930), *JPE* **75**, 706–29.

Coats, A. W. (1967b) Alfred Marshall and the early development of the London School of Economics: some unpublished letters, *Eca* **34**, 408–17.

Coats, A. W. (1968) Political economy and the tariff reform campaign of 1903, *JLE* **11**, 181–229.

Coats, A. W. (1969) Is there a "structure of scientific revolutions" in economics? *Kyk* **22**, 289–96.

Coats, A. W. (1977) The current "crisis" in economics in historical perspective, *Nebraska Journal of Economics and Business* **16**, 3–16.

Coats, A. W. (1980) The culture and the economists: some reflections on Anglo-American differences, *HOPE* **12**, 588–609.

Coats, A. W. (1981) Britain: the rise of the specialists, *HOPE* **13**, 365–404. In *Economists in Government*. Durham, N.C.: Duke University Press.

Coats, A. W. (1982a) The distinctive L.S.E. ethos in the inter-war years, *AEJ* **10**, 18–34.

Coats, A. W. (1982b) The methodology of economics: some recent contributions, *Kyk* **35**, 310–21.

Coats, A. W. (1983b) Half a century of methodological controversy in economics: as reflected in the writings of T. W. Hutchison. In Coats (1983a).

Coats, A. W. (1983c) The revival of subjectivism in economics. In Wiseman (1983).

Coats, A. W. (ed.) (1971) *The Classical Economists and Economic Policy*. London.

Coats, A. W. (ed.)(1983a) *Methodological Controversies in Economics: Historical Essays in Honor of T. W. Hutchison*. Greenwich, Conn.: JAI Press.

Collard, D. A. (1973) Leon Walras and the Cambridge caricature, *EJ* **83**, 465–76.

Collard, D. A. (1981) A. C. Pigou, 1877–1959. In O'Brien and Presley (1981).

Commons, J. R. (1924) *The Legal Foundations of Capitalism*. New York.

Commons, J. R. (1925) Law and economics, *YLJ* **34**, 371–82.

Commons, J. R. (1931) Institutional economics, *AER* **21**, 648–57.

Commons, J. R. (1934a) *Institutional Economics*. University of Wisconsin Press.

Commons, J. R. (1934b) *Myself*. University of Wisconsin Press.

Commons, J. R. (1936) Institutional economics, *AER* **26**, 237–54.

Commons, J. R. (1950) *The Economics of Collective Action*, University of Wisconsin Press.

Cooper, C. A. and Massell, B. F. (1965a) A new look at customs union theory, *EJ* **75**, 742–47.

Cooper, C. A. and Massell, B. F. (1965b) Towards a general theory of customs unions for developing countries, *JPE* **73**, 461–76.

Cooper, R. N. (ed.) (1969) *International Finance: Selected Readings*. Harmondsworth: Penguin.

Corden, W. M. (1965) *Recent developments in the theory of international trade*, Princeton Special Papers in International Economics, 7.

Cournot, A. A. (1838) *Researches into the Mathematical Principles of the Theory of Wealth*. Translated by I. Fisher, 1927. New York.

Creedy, J. (1981) F. Y. Edgeworth, 1845–1926. In O'Brien and Presley (1981).

Creedy, J. and O'Brien, D. P. (ed.) (1984) *Economic Analysis in Historical Perspective*. London: Butterworths.

Crouzet, F. (1982) *The Victorian Economy*. London: Methuen.

Cunningham, W. (1882) *The Growth of English Industry and Commerce*. Cambridge.

Cunningham, W. (1889) The Comteist criticism of economic science, BA. In Smyth (1962).

Cunningham, W. (1892a) The relativity of economic doctrine, *EJ* **2**, 1–16.

Cunningham, W. (1892b) The perversion of economic history, *EJ* **2**, 491–506.

Cyert, R. M. and March, J. G. (1963) *A Behavioural Theory of the Firm*. New York: Prentice Hall.

Dantzig, G. B. (1951) Maximization of a linear function of variables subject to linear inequalities. In Koopmans (1951).

Darnell, A. C. (1984) Economic statistics and econometrics. In Creedy and O'Brien (1984).

Davies, E. G. (1981) R. G. Hawtrey, 1879–1975. In O'Brien and Presley (1981).

Deane, P. (1978) *The Evolution of Economic Ideas*. Cambridge: Cambridge University Press.

Deaton, A. S. and Muellbauer, J. (1980) *Economics and Consumer Behaviour*. Cambridge: Cambridge University Press.

Debreu, G. (1951) The coefficient of resource allocation, *Ecta* **19**, 273–92.

Debreu, G. (1959) *The Theory of Value.* New York: Wiley.

Debreu, G. (1982) Existence of competitive equilibrium. In Arrow and Intriligator (1982).

Dernberg, T. F. and McDougall, D. M. (1960) *Macroeconomics*, 4th edn, 1972. London: McGraw-Hill.

Dixit, A. K. (1977) The accumulation of capital theory, *OEP* **29**, 3–29.

Dixit, A. K. (1978) The balance of trade in a model of temporary equilibrium with rationing, *RES* **45**, 393–404.

Dixit, A. K. and Stiglitz, J. E. (1977) Monopolistic competition and optimum product diversity, *AER* **67**, 297–308.

Dobb, M. (1937) *Political Economy and Capitalism.* London.

Dobb, M. (1973) *Theories of Value and Distribution since Adam Smith.* Cambridge: Cambridge University Press.

Dolan, E. G. (ed.) (1976) *The Foundations of Modern Austrian Economics.* Mission, Kan.: Sheed and Ward.

Domar, E. (1946) Capital expansion, rate of growth and employment, *Ecta* **14**, 137–47. In Sen (1970c).

Dorfman, J. (1946–59) *The Economic Mind in American Civilization*, 5 vols. New York: Viking.

Dorfman, J. *et al.* (1963) *Institutional Economics: Veblen, Commons and Mitchell Reconsidered.* Berkeley: University of California Press.

Dorfman, R., Samuelson, P. A. and Solow, R. M. (1958) *Linear Programming and Economic Analysis.* New York.

Dornbusch, R. (1976) Expectations and exchange rate dynamics, *JPE* **84**, 1161ff.

Douglas, P. H. (1934) *Theory of Wages.* New York.

Dow, J. C. R. (1965) *The Management of the British Economy 1945–60.* Cambridge: Cambridge University Press.

Dowd, D. F. (ed.) (1958) *Thorstein Veblen: a Critical Reappraisal.* Ithaca, N.Y.

Drazen, A. (1980) Recent developments in macroeconomic disequilibrium theory, *Ecta* **48**, 283–306.

Dreze, J. (1975) Existence of an equilibrium under price rigidity and quantity rationing, *IER* **16**, 301–20.

Dugger, W. M. (1980) Property rights, law and John R. Commons, *Review of Economics and Sociology* **38**, 41–53.

Dugger, W. M. (1983) The transaction cost analysis of Oliver E. Williamson: a new synthesis, *JEI* **17**, 95–114.

Duisenberry, J. S. (1948) Income–consumption relations and their implications. In L.A. Metzler (ed.) *Income Employment and Public Policy: Essays in Honor of A. H. Hansen.* New York.

Dunlop, J. T. (1938) The movement of real and money wage rates, *EJ* **48**, 413ff.

Eckhaus, R. S. (1955) The factor proportions problem in underdeveloped countries, *AER* **45**. In Agarwala and Singh (1958).

Edgeworth, F. Y. (1881) *Mathematical Psychics.* London.

Edgeworth, F. Y. (1889) On the application of mathematics to political economy, BA. In Edgeworth (1925), vol. II.

Edgeworth, F. Y. (1894) The pure theory of international values, *EJ* **4**. In Edgeworth (1925), vol. II.

Edgeworth, F. Y. (1925) *Papers Relating to Political Economy*, 3 vols. London.

Eichner, A. S. (ed.) (1983) *Why Economics is not Yet a Science.* London: Macmillan.

Eichner, A. S. and Kregel, J. A. (1975) An essay on post-Keynesian economic theory: a new paradigm in economics, *JEL* **13**, 1293–1314.

Ekelund, R. B. and Hebert, R. F. (1983) *A History of Economic Theory and Method*, 2nd edn, London: McGraw-Hill.

Elliott, J. E. (1978) Institutionalism as an approach to political economy, *JEI* **12**, 91ff.

Ellis, H. S. (1948) *A Survey of Contemporary Economics*. Homewood, Ill.: R. D. Irwin.

Elsinga, K. E. (1984) Elsinga on Coase. In Spiegel and Samuels (1984).

Eltis, W. A. (1975) François Quesnay: a reinterpretation. 1 The Tableau Economique. 2 The Theory of Growth, *OEP* **27**, 167–200, 327–51.

Eltis, W. A. (1984) *The Classical Theory of Economic Growth*. London: Macmillan.

Emmanuel, A. (1974) *Unequal Exchange, a Study of the Imperialism of Trade*. London: New Left Books.

Ferguson, C. E. (1969) *The Neo-Classical Theory of Production and Distribution*. Cambridge: Cambridge University Press.

Fetter, F. W. (1965) *The Development of British Monetary Orthodoxy, 1797–1875*. Cambridge, Mass.

Fetter, F. W. (1968) The transfer problem: formal elegance or historical realism. In C. R. Whittlesey and J. S. G. Wilson (eds), *Essays in Money and Banking in Honor of R. S. Sayers*. Oxford.

Feyerabend, P. (1975) *Against Method*. London: New Left Books.

Fisher, F. M. (1969) The existence of aggregate production functions, *Ecta* **37**, 553–77.

Fisher, I. (1892) *Mathematical Investigations into the Theory of Prices*. From *Transactions of the Connecticut Academy*, **9**.

Fisher, I. (1896) *Appreciation and Interest*.

Fisher, I. (1906) *The Nature of Capital and Income*. New York.

Fisher, I. (1907) *The Rate of Interest*. New York.

Fisher, I. (1911) *The Purchasing Power of Money*. New York.

Fisher, I. (1920) A discussion of Professor Cassel's article, *AAA* **89**, 276–79.

Fisher, I. (1930) *The Theory of Interest*. New York.

Fisher, I. (1933) Debt-deflation theory of great depressions, *Ecta* **1**, 337ff.

Fleming, J. M. (1951) On making the best of balance of payments restrictions on imports, *EJ* **61**, 48–71.

Floud, R. and McCloskey, D. (1981) *The Economic History of Britain since 1700*. Cambridge: Cambridge University Press.

Flux, A. W. (1894) Review of Wicksteed (1894), *EJ* **4**, 305–13.

Ford, J. L. (1983) *Choice, Expectation and Uncertainty*. Oxford: Basil Blackwell.

Foster, J. L. (1804) *An Essay on the Principle of Commercial Exchanges and More Particularly of Exchange between Great Britain and Ireland*.

Foster, W. T. and Catchings, W. (1923) *Money*. Cambridge, Mass.

Foster, W. T. and Catchings, W. (1925) *Profits*. Boston and New York.

Foster, W. T. and Catchings, W. (1926) Old King Cole in trouble, *Atlantic Monthly*, July 1926. Reprinted as pamphlet of same name.

Foster, W. T. and Catchings, W. (1927) *Business without a Buyer*. Boston.

Foster, W. T. and Catchings, W. (1928) *The Road to Plenty*. Boston.

Foxwell, H. S. (1886) *Irregularity of Employment and Fluctuations of Prices*.

Foxwell, H. S. (1887) The economic movement in England, *QJE* **2**, 84ff.

Frank, A. G. (1968) *Development and Underdevelopment in Latin America*. New York: Monthly Review Press.

Frenkel, J. A. and Johnson, H. G. (ed.) (1976) *The Monetary Approach to the Balance of Payments*. London: Allen and Unwin.

Friedman, M. (1953) The methodology of positive economics. In *Essays in Positive*

*Economics*. Reprinted in Breit and Hochman (1968).

Friedman, M. (1956) The quantity theory of money – a restatement. In Friedman (ed.) *Studies in the Quantity Theory of Money*. Reprinted in Friedman (1969).

Friedman, M. (1957) *The Theory of the Consumption Function*. Princeton.

Friedman, M. (1958) Foreign aid: means and objectives, *YR* **47**, 24–38.

Friedman, M. (1968) The role of monetary policy, *AER* **58**. In Friedman (1969).

Friedman, M. (1969) *The Optimum Quantity of Money and Other Essays*. London: Macmillan.

Friedman, M. (1970) A theoretical framework for monetary analysis, *JPE* **78**, 193–238. In Gordon (1974).

Friedman, M. (1974) Comments on the critics. In Gordon (1974).

Friedman, M. and Meiselman, D. (1963) The relative stability of monetary velocity and the investment multiplier in the United States, 1897–1958. In *Stabilization Policies*, Prentice Hall for Commission on Money and Credit.

Friedman, M. and Schwarz, A. J. (1963a) *A Monetary History of the US, 1861–1960*. Princeton: Princeton University Press.

Friedman, M. and Schwarz, A. J. (1963b) Money and business cycles, *REStats* **45**. In Friedman (1969).

Frisch, R. (1933) Propagation problems and impulse problems in dynamic economics. In Cassel (1933) and in AEA (1965).

Frisch, R. (1936) Annual survey of general economic theory: the problem of index numbers, *Ecta* **4**, 1–38.

Furobtn, E. G. and Richter, R. (1984) The new institutional economics, *ZgS* **140**, 1–6.

Galbraith, J. K. (1952) *American Capitalism*. Harmondsworth: Penguin, 1963.

Galbraith, J. K. (1955) *The Great Crash, 1929*. Harmondsworth: Penguin, 1961.

Galbraith, J. K. (1958) *The Affluent Society*. Harmondsworth: Penguin.

Galbraith, J. K. (1967) *The New Industrial State*. Harmondsworth: Penguin, 1969.

Gale, D., Kuhn, H. W. and Tucker, A. W. (1951) Linear programming and the theory of games. In Koopmans (1951).

Garegnani, P. (1970) Heterogeneous capital, the production function and the theory of distribution, *RES* **37**, 407–36. In Hunt and Schwarz (1972).

Gehrels, F. (1956) Customs unions from a single country viewepoint, *RES* **24**, 61ff.

George, H. (1879) *Progress and Poverty*. New York.

Gerschenkron, A. (1962) *Economic Backwardness in Historical Perspective*. Cambridge, Mass.: Harvard University Press.

Ghosh, R. N. (1964) The colonization controversy: R. J. Wilmot-Horton and the classical economists, *Eca* **31**, 385–400. In Coats (1970).

Gibbard, A. (1973) Manipulation of voting schemes: a general result, *Ecta* **41**, 587–601.

Gide, C. and Rist, C. (1909) *A History of Economic Doctrines*. Translated by R. Richards, 1917. London: Harrap.

Girvan, N. (1973) The development of dependency economics in the Caribbean and Latin America: review and comparison, *Social & Economic Studies* **22**, 1ff.

Gleason, A. H. (1959) Foster and Catchings: a reappraisal, *JPE* **67**, 156ff.

Glustoff, E. (1968) On the existence of Keynesian equilibrium, *RES* **35**, 327–34.

Gonce, R. A. (1971) John R. Commons's legal economic theory, *JEI* **5**, 80–95.

Gonce, R. A. (1976) The new property rights approach and Commons's Legal Foundations of Capitalism, *JEI* **10**, 765–97.

Gordon, B. (1979) *Economic Doctrines and Tory Liberalism, 1824–1830*. London: Macmillan.

Gordon, D. F. (1965) The role of the history of economic thought in the understanding of modern economic theory, *AER* **55**, suppl., 119–27.

Gordon, R. J. (1976) Recent developments in the theory of inflation and unemployment, *JME* **2**, 185–219. In Korliras and Thorn (1979).

Gordon, R. J. (ed) (1974) *Milton Friedman's Monetary Framework*. Chicago: Chicago University Press.

Gordon, S. (1973) The wage fund controversy: the second round, *HOPE* **5**, 14–35.

Gorman, W. M. (1953) Community preference fields, *Ecta* **21**, 63–80.

Gorman, W. M. (1980) A possible procedure for analysing quality differentials in the egg market, *RES* **47**, 843–56.

Gossen, H. H. (1854) *Entwicklung der Gesetze des menschlichen Verkehrs und der daraus fließenden Regeln für menschliches Handeln.*

Graaf, J. de V. (1957) *Theoretical Welfare Economics*. Cambridge.

Graham, F. D. (1923) The theory of international values re-examined, *QJE* **37**. In AEA (1949).

Graham, F. D. (1932) The theory of international values, *QJE* **46**, 581ff.

Grampp, W. D. (1960) *The Manchester School of Economics*. London: Oxford University Press.

Grampp, W. D. (1965) *Economic Liberalism*, 2 vols. New York: Random House.

Grandmont, J. M. and Laroque, G. (1976) On Keynesian temporary equilibrium, *RES* **43**, 53–67.

Green, H. A. J. (1964) *Aggregation in Economic Analysis*. Princeton.

Green, H. A. J. (1976) *Consumer Theory*, 2nd edn. London: Macmillan.

Grossman, H. (1969) Theories of markets without recontracting, *JET* **4**, 476–9.

Grossman, S. and Stiglitz, J. E. (1980) The impossibility of informationally efficient markets, *AER* **70**, 393–408.

Gruchy, A. G. (1940) John R. Commons's concept of twentieth century economics, *JPE* **48**, 823–49.

Guillebaud, C. W. (1952) Marshall's Principles of Economics in the light of contemporary economic thought, *Eca* **19**, 111–30.

Guyot, Y. (1892) *Principles of Social Economy.*

Haberler, G. (1930) Die Theorie der komparativen Kosten, *WA* **32**, 356–60.

Haberler, G. (1933) *The Theory of International Trade*. Translated by A. Stonier and F. Benham, 1936. London.

Haberler, G. (1936) *Prosperity and Depression*, 3rd edn, 1943. Geneva: League of Nations.

Haberler, G. (1955) *A survey of international trade theory*, Princeton Special Papers in International Economics, 1.

Haberler, G. (1956) Monetary and real factors affecting economic stability: a critique of certain tendencies in economic theory, *BNLQR*. In AEA (1956).

Hahn, F. H. (1962) A theorem on non-tâtonnement stability, *Ecta* **30**, 463–69.

Hahn, F. H. (1966) Equilibrium dynamics with heterogeneous capital goods, *QJE* **80**, 133–46.

Hahn, F. H. (1971) Equilibrium with transactions costs, *Ecta* **39**, 417–39.

Hahn, F. H. (1978) On non-Walrasian equilibria, *RES* **45**, 1–17.

Hahn, F. H. (1982a) *Money and Inflation*. Oxford: Basil Blackwell.

Hahn, F. H. (1982b) The neo-Ricardians, *CJE* **6**, 353–74.

Hahn, F. H. (1982c) Reflections on the invisible hand, *LBR*, April, pp. 1–21.

Hahn, F. H. (1982d) Stability. In Arrow and Intriligator (1982).

Hahn, F. H. (1983) On general equilibrium and stability, in *Paul A. Samuelson and Modern Economic Theory*, ed. E. C. Brown and R. M. Solow. New York: McGraw-Hill.

Hahn, F. H. (1984) Review of Hicks (1983), *EJ* **94**, 960–2.

Hahn, F. H. and Matthews, R. C. O. (1964) The theory of economic growth: a survey, *EJ* **74**. In AEA/*RES* (1965), vol. II.

Haley, B. F. (ed.) (1952) *A Survey of Contemporary Economics*, vol. 2. Homewood, Ill.: R. D. Irwin.

Hall, R. E. (1982) Monetary Trends in the United States and the United Kingdom: a review from the perspective of new developments in monetary economics, *JEL* **20**, 1552–6.

Hall, R. L. and Hitch, C. J. (1939) Price theory and business behaviour, *OEP* **2**, 12–45.

Hansen, A. H. (1941) *Fiscal Policy and Business Cycles*. London.

Hansen, A. H. (1964) *Business Cycles and National Income*, 2nd edn. London.

Hansen, A. H. and Clemence, R. V. (1953) *Readings in Business Cycles and National Income*. London: George Allen and Unwin.

Hansen, A. H. and Tout, H. (1933) Annual survey of business cycle theory: investment and saving in business cycle theory, *Ecta* **1**, 119–47.

Hansen, B. (1951) *A Study in the Theory of Inflation*. London: Macmillan.

Hansson, B. (1982) *The Stockholm School and the Development of the Dynamic Method*. London: Croom Helm.

Harcourt, G. C. (1972) *Some Cambridge Controversies in the Theory of Capital*. Cambridge: Cambridge University Press.

Harcourt, G. C. (1976) The Cambridge controversies: old ways and new horizons – or dead end, *OEP* **28**, 25–65.

Harcourt, G. C. (1982) The Sraffian contribution: an evaluation. In I. Bradley and M. Howard (eds), *Classical and Marxian Political Economy: Essays in Honour of Ronald L. Meek*. London: Macmillan.

Harcourt, G. C. (1984) Harcourt on Robinson. In Spiegel and Samuels (1984).

Harcourt, G. C. and Laing, N. F. (eds) (1971) *Capital and Growth*. Harmondsworth: Penguin.

Harris, J. (1972) *Unemployment and Politics, 1886–1914*. Oxford: Oxford University Press.

Harris, S. E. (ed.) (1947) *The New Economics*. New York.

Harrod, R. F. (1930) Notes on supply, *EJ* **40**, 232ff.

Harrod, R. F. (1936) *The Trade Cycle*. Oxford.

Harrod, R. F. (1939) An essay in dynamic theory, *EJ* **49**, 14–33. In Sen (1970c).

Harrod, R. F. (1951) *The Life of John Maynard Keynes*. Harmondsworth: Penguin, 1972.

Harrod, R. F. (1956) Walras: a re-appraisal review article, *EJ* **66**, 307ff.

Harsanyi, J. C. (1955) Cardinal utility, individualistic ethics and interpersonal comparisons of utility, *JPE* **63**, 309ff.

Harte, N. B. (1971) The making of economic history. In Harte (ed.), *The Study of Economic History*. London: Frank Cass.

Hartwell, R. M. (1973) Good old economic history, *JEH* **33**, 28–40.

Hausman, D. (ed.) (1984) *The Philosophy of Economics*. Cambridge: Cambridge University Press.

Hawley, F. B. (1882) *Capital and Population*.

Hawtrey, R. G. (1913) *Good and Bad Trade*. London.

Hawtrey, R. G. (1919) *Currency and Credit*. London.

Hayek, F. A. (1929) *Monetary Theory and the Trade Cycle*. Translated by N. Kaldor and R. M. Croome, 1933. London.

Hayek, F. A. (1931) *Prices and Production*. London.

Hayek, F. A. (ed.) (1935) *Collectivist Economic Planning*. London: Routledge.

Hayek, F. A. (1937) Economics and knowledge, *Eca* **4**, 33–54. In Hayek (1949).

Hayek, F. A. (1949) *Individualism and Economic Order*. London.

Heckscher, E. (1919) The effect of foreign trade on the distribution of income, *Ekonomisk Tidskrift*. Translated in AEA (1949).

Heller, W. (1975) What's right with economics, *AER* **65**, 1–26.

Henry, J. F. (1982) The transformation of John Bates Clark: an essay in interpretation, *HOPE* **14**, 166–77.

Hey, J. D. (1979) *Uncertainty in Microeconomics*. Oxford: Martin Robertson.

Hey, J. D. (1981a) *Economics in Disequilibrium*. Oxford: Martin Robertson.

Hey, J. D. (1981b) A unified theory of the behaviour of the profit-maximizing, labour-managed and joint-stock firms operating under uncertainty, *EJ* **91**, 364ff.

Hicks, J. R. (1932) *The Theory of Wages*. London: Macmillan.

Hicks, J. R. (1935a) A suggestion for simplifying the theory of money, *Eca* **2**. In Hicks (1967).

Hicks, J. R. (1935b) The theory of monopoly, *Ecta* **3**. In Hicks (1983).

Hicks, J. R. (1936) Mr Keynes's theory of employment, *EJ* **46**, 238ff. In Hicks (1982).

Hicks, J. R. (1937) Mr Keynes and the classics: a suggested interpretation, *Ecta* **5**, 147–59. In Hicks (1967).

Hicks, J. R. (1939a) *Value and Capital*. Oxford: Oxford University Press.

Hicks, J. R. (1939b) Foundations of welfare economics, *EJ* **49**, 696–712.

Hicks, J. R. (1940) Valuation of social income, *Eca* **7**. In Hicks (1981).

Hicks, J. R. (1941) Rehabilitation of consumer's surplus, *RES* **8**. In Hicks (1981).

Hicks, J. R. (1950) *A Contribution to the Theory of the Trade Cycle*. Oxford: Oxford University Press.

Hicks, J. R. (1956) *A Revision of Demand Theory*. Oxford: Oxford University Press.

Hicks, J. R. (1960) Linear Theory, *EJ* **70**. In AER/RES (1965), vol. III.

Hicks, J. R. (1965) *Capital and Growth*. Oxford: Oxford University Press.

Hicks, J. R. (1967) *A Revision of Demand Theory*. Oxford: Oxford University Press.

Hicks, J. R. (1967) *Critical Essays on Monetary Theory*. Oxford: Oxford University Press.

Hicks, J. R. (1975) The scope and status of welfare economics, *OEP* **27**. In Hicks (1981).

Hicks, J. R. (1977) *Economic Perspectives*. Oxford: Oxford University Press.

Hicks, J. R. (1981) *Wealth and Welfare*. Oxford: Basil Blackwell.

Hicks, J. R. (1982) *Money, Interest and Wages*. Oxford: Basil Blackwell.

Hicks, J. R. (1983) *Classics and Moderns*. Oxford: Basil Blackwell.

Hicks, J. R. (1984) *The Economics of John Hicks*. Oxford: Basil Blackwell.

Hicks, J. R. and Allen, R. G. D. (1934) A reconsideration of the theory of value, *Eca* **1**. In Hicks (1981).

Higgins, B. (1956) The dualistic theory of underdeveloped areas, *EDCC* 99ff. In Meier (1970).

Hildebrand, B. (1848) *Die Nationalokonomie der Gegenwart und Zukunft*.

Hilferding, F. (1904) Böhm-Bawerk's criticism of Marx. Translated in Böhm-Bawerk (1896).

Hines, A. G. (1964) Trade unions and wage inflation in the UK, 1893–1961, *RES* **31**, 221–52.

Hirschman, A. O (1958) *The Strategy of Economic Development*. New Haven.

Hirschman, A. O. (1981) The rise and decline of development economics. In *Essays in Trespassing*. Cambridge: Cambridge University Press.

Hirshleifer, J. (1976) *Price Theory and Its Applications*. London: Prentice Hall.

Hobson, J. A. (1891) The law of the three rents, *QJE* **5**, 263ff.

Hobson, J. A. (1896) *The Problem of the Unemployed*. London.

Hobson, J. A. (1902) *Imperialism: A Study*. London.

Hobson, J. A. (1911) *An Economic Interpretation of Investment*.

Hobson, J. A. and Mummery, A. F. (1889) *The Physiology of Industry*. London.

Hollander, J. H. (1918) International trade under depreciated paper: a criticism, *QJE* **32**, 674ff.

Hollander, S. (1973) *The Economics of Adam Smith*. London: Heinemann.

Hollander, S. (1979) *The Economics of David Ricardo*. London: Heinemann.

Hollander, S. (1980) On Professor Samuelson's canonical classical model of political economy, *JEL* **18**, 559–74.

Hollander, S. (1982) The Economics of David Ricardo: a response to Professor O'Brien, *OEP* **34**, 224–52.

Homan, P. T. (1928) *Contemporary Economic Thought*. New York.

House of Commons (1981) *Treasury and Civil Service Committee, Monetary Policy, vol. I: Report*, 1980–81 HC163-I.

Howey, R. S. (1960) *The Rise of the Marginal Utility School*. Kansas.

Howson, S. (1975) *Domestic Monetary Management in Britain 1919–1938*. Cambridge: Cambridge University Press.

Hume, D. (1752) Essays "Of money", "Of interest" and "Of the balance of trade" in *Hume's Writings on Economics*, ed. E. Rotwein, 1955. Edinburgh.

Hunt, E. K. and Schwarz, J. G. (eds) (1972) *A Critique of Economic Theory*. Harmondsworth: Penguin.

Hutchison, T. W. (1937) Expectation and rational conduct, *ZN* **8**.

Hutchison, T. W. (1938) *On the Significance and Basic Postulates of Economic Theory*. London.

Hutchison, T. W. (1941) The significance and basic postulates of economic theory: a reply to Professor Knight, *JPE* **49**, 732–49.

Hutchison, T. W. (1952) Some questions about Ricardo, *Eca* **19**, 415ff.

Hutchison, T. W. (1953) *A Review of Economic Doctrines 1870–1929*. Greenwood Press.

Hutchison, T. W. (1955) Insularity and cosmopolitanism in economic ideas, 1870–1914, *AER* **45**, suppl., 1–16.

Hutchison, T. W. (1956a) Professor Machlup on verification in economics, *SEJ* **22**, 476–83.

Hutchison, T. W. (1968) *Economics and Economic Policy in Britain, 1946–1966*. London.

Hutchison, T. W. (1977) *Knowledge and Ignorance in Economics*. Oxford: Basil Blackwell.

Hutchison, T. W. (1978) *On Revolutions and Progress in Economic Knowledge*. Cambridge: Cambridge University Press.

Hutchison, T. W. (1981) *The Politics and Philosophy of Economics*. Oxford: Basil Blackwell.

Hutchison, T. W. (1983) From "dismal science" to "positive economics" – a century-and-a-half of progress? In Wiseman (1983).

Hutchison, T. W. (1984) Institutionalist economics old and new, *ZgS* **140**, 20–9.

Ingram, J. K. (1878) The present position and prospects of political economy, *BA*. In Smyth (1962).

Ingram, J. K. (1893) *A History of Political Economy*. Edinburgh.

Ironmonger, D. S. (1972) *New Commodities and Consumer Behaviour*. Cambridge:

Cambridge University Press.

Iversen, C. (1935) *Aspects of the Theory of International Capital Movements*, 2nd edn, 1936, Copenhagen.

Jaffe, W. (1975) Leon Walras, an economic adviser manqué, *EJ* **85**, 810–23.

Jaffe, W. (1976) Menger, Jevons and Walras de-homogenized, *Economic Inquiry* **14**, 511–24.

Jaffe, W. (1977) The normative bias of the Walrasian model: Walras versus Gossen, *QJE* **91**, 371–87.

Jaffe, W. (1978) Review of Morishima (1977), *EJ* **88**, 574–6.

Jaffe, W. (1980) Walras's economics as others see it, *JEL* **18**, 528–49.

Jalladeau, J. (1975) The methodological conversion of John Bates Clarke. *HOPE* **7**, 209–26.

Jevons, W. S. (1862) Brief account of a general mathematical theory of political economy, BA. In 4th edn of Jevons (1871).

Jevons, W. S. (1863) A serious fall in the value of gold ascertained, and its social effects set forth. In Jevons (1884).

Jevons, W. S. (1865) *The Coal Question*. London.

Jevons, W. S. (1871) *The Theory of Political Economy*, 2nd edn. 1879. Harmondsworth: Penguin, 1970.

Jevons, W. S. (1875) The solar period and the price of corn. In Jevons (1884).

Jevons, W. S. (1878) The periodicity of commercial crises and its physical explanation. In Jevons (1884).

Jevons, W. S. (1879) *The Principles of Science*. London.

Jevons, W. S. (1882) *The State in Relation to Labour*, 3rd edn, 1894. London.

Jevons, W. S. (1883) *Methods of Social Reform*. London.

Jevons, W. S. (1884) *Investigations in Currency and Finance*. London.

Jevons, W. S. (1972–81) *Papers and Correspondence*, ed. R. D. C. Black. London: Macmillan.

Johannsen, N. (1908) *A Neglected Point in Connection with Crises*.

Johnson, H. G. (1958) Towards a general theory of the balance of payments, in *International Trade and Economic Growth*. Reprinted in Cooper (1969).

Johnson, H. G. (1964) *Money, Trade and Economic Growth*, 2nd edn. London.

Johnson, H. G. (1965a) An economic theory of protectionism, tariff bargaining and the formation of customs unions, *JPE* **73**, 256–82.

Johnson, H. G. (1965b) Monetary theory and policy. In AEA/RES (1965).

Johnson, H. G. (1971)) The Keynesian revolution and the monetarist counter-revolution, *AER* **61**, 1–14.

Johnson, H. G. (1977) The monetary approach to the balance of payments: a non-technical guide, *JIE* **7**, 251ff.

Johnson, W. E. (1913) The pure theory of utility curves, *EJ* **23**, 483–513.

Jones, R. (1833) *An Essay on the Distribution of Wealth*. New York: Kelley and Millman, 1956.

Jones, R. (1859) *Literary Remains*, ed. W. Whewell. London.

Jones, R. W. (1956) Factor proportions and the Heckscher–Ohlin theorem, *RES* **24**, 1–10. In Bhagwati (1969) and Jones (1979).

Jones, R. W. (1970) The transfer problem revisited, *ECA* **37**, 178–84. In Jones (1979).

Jones, R. W. (1979) *International Trade: Essays in Theory*. Amsterdam: North Holland.

Jones, R. W. (1983) International trade, in Brown, E. C. and Solow, R. M. (eds), *Paul Samuelson and Modern Economic Theory*. New York: McGraw-Hill.

Jones, T. W. (1978) The appointment of Pigou as Marshall's successor: the other side of the coin, *JLE* **21**, 235ff.

Kadish, A. (1982) *The Oxford Economists in the Late Nineteenth Century.* Oxford: Oxford University Press.

Kahn, R. F. (1931) On the relation of home investment to unemployment, *EJ* **41**, 173ff.

Kaldor, N. (1937) Annual survey of economic theory: the recent controversy on the theory of capital, *Ecta* **5**, 201–33.

Kaldor, N. (1938) Rejoinder to Professor Knight, *Ecta* **6**, 63–82. In *Essays in Value and Distribution.* London: Duckworth.

Kaldor, N. (1939) Welfare propositions of economics and interpersonal comparisons of utility, *EJ* **49**, 549–52. In AEA (1969).

Kaldor, N. (1956) Alternative theories of distribution, *RES* **23**. In Sen (1970c).

Kaldor, N. (1957) A model of economic growth, *EJ* **67**, 591–624.

Kaldor, N. and Mirrlees, J. A. (1962) A new model of economic growth, *RES* **29**, 174–90. In Sen (1970c).

Kalecki, M. (1933) An essay on the theory of the business cycle. Translated in *Studies in the Theory of Business Cycles, 1933–1939.* Oxford: Basil Blackwell, 1969.

Kamarck, A. M. (1983) *Economics and the Real World.* Oxford: Basil Blackwell.

Katouzian, H. (1980) *Ideology and Method in Economics.* London: Macmillan.

Kauder, E. (1957) Intellectual and political roots of the older Austrian school, *ZN* **17**, 411–25.

Kemp, M. C. (1962) The gain from international trade, *EJ* **72**, 803ff.

Kemp, M. C. and Wan, H. Y. (1976) An elementary proposition concerning the formation of customs unions, *JIE* **6**, 95–7.

Keynes, J. M. (1913) *Indian Currency and Finance.* London.

Keynes, J. M. (1923) *A Tract on Monetary Reform.* London. References are to reprint in Keynes (1971–83).

Keynes, J. M. (1925) *The Economic Consequences of Mr Churchill.* London.

Keynes, J. M. (1925) Alfred Marshall, 1842–1924, *EJ* **35**. In Marshall (1925) and in Keynes (1933).

Keynes, J. M. (1926) *The End of Laissez Faire.* London. References are to reprint in Keynes (1971–83).

Keynes, J. M. (1929a) The German transfer problem, *EJ* **39**, 1–7. In AEA (1949).

Keynes, J. M. (1929b) The reparation problem: a rejoinder, *EJ* **39**, 179–82. References are to reprint in Keynes (1971–83).

Keynes, J. M. (1930) *A Treatise on Money.* London. References are to reprint in Keynes (1971–83).

Keynes, J. M. (1933) *Essays in Biography.* London.

Keynes, J. M. (1936) *The General Theory of Employment, Interest and Money.* London: Macmillan.

Keynes, J. M. (1937) The General Theory: fundamental concepts and ideas, *QJE* **51**, 209–23. In Clower (1969).

Keynes, J. M. (1940) *How to Pay for the War.* London.

Keynes, J. M. (1971–83) *The Collected Writings of John Maynard Keynes.* London: Macmillan.

Keynes, J. N. (1891) *The Scope and Method of Political Economy.* London.

Keynes, M. (ed) (1975) *Essays on John Maynard Keynes.* London: Macmillan.

Killick, T. (1978) *Development Economics in Action.* London: Heinemann.

Kirzner, I. M. (1976) On the method of Austrian economics. In Dolan (1965).

Kittrell, E. R. (1965) The development of the theory of colonization in English classical political economy, *SEJ* **31**. In Shaw (1970).

Klamer, A. (1984) *The New Classical Macroeconomics*. Brighton: Harvester Press.

Klein, L. R. and Goldberger, A. (1955) *An Econometric Model of the US, 1929–52*. Oxford.

Klein, P. A. (1978) American institutionalism: premature death, permanent resurrection, *JEI* **12**, 251–76.

Klein, P. A. (1983) The neglected institutionalism of Wesley Clair Mitchell: the theoretical basis for business cycle indicators, *JEI* **17**, 867–99.

Knies, K. (1853) *Die Politische Oekonomie vom Standpunkt der geschichten Methode*, 2nd edn, 1883.

Knight, F. H. (1921) *Risk, Uncertainty and Profit*, LSE Reprints of scarce tracts. London: LSE.

Knight, F. H. (1933) Capitalistic production, time and the rate of return. In Cassel (1933).

Knight, F. H. (1935) Confusion on morals and economics, *IJE* **45**, 200–20.

Knight, F. H. (1940) "What is truth" in economics? *JPE* **48**, 1–32.

Knight, F. H. (1941) The significance and basic postulates of economic theory: a rejoinder, *JPE* **49**, 750–3.

Knowles, L. (1924–36) *The Economic Development of the British Overseas Empire*. 3 vols. London.

Kolakowski, L. (1978) *Main Currents in Marxism*, 3 vols. Oxford: Oxford University Press.

Koopmans, T. C. (1947a) Optimum utilization of the transportation system, *Proceedings of the International Statistical Conferences*, **5**. Reprinted in *Ecta* **17** (suppl.), 1949, 136ff.

Koopmans, T. C. (1947b) Measurement without theory, *REStats*. In AEA (1965).

Koopmans, T. C. (1957) *Three Essays on the State of Economic Science*. New York.

Koopmans, T. C. (ed.) (1951) *Activity Analysis of Allocation and Production*. New York.

Koot, G. (1975) T. E. Cliffe Leslie, Irish social reform and the origins of the English historical school of economics, *HOPE* **7**, 312–36.

Koot, G. (1980) English historical economics and the emergence of economic history in England, *HOPE* **12**, 174–205.

Koot, G. M. (1982) An alternative to Marshall: history and applied economics at the early LSE, *AEJ* **10**, 3–17.

Korliras, P. G. and Thorn, R. S. (eds) (1979) *Modern Macroeconomics*. London: Harper and Row.

Krauss, M. B. (1972) Recent developments in customs union theory: an interpretive survey, *JEL* **10**, 413–36.

Kravis, I. B. (1956) "Availability" and other influences on the commodity composition of trade, *JPE* **64**, 143–55.

Kregel, J. A. (1973) *The Reconstruction of Political Economy: an Introduction to Post-Keynesian Economics*. Macmillan.

Kregel, J. A. (1983) Post-Keynesian theory: an overview, *The Journal of Economic Education*, Fall, pp. 32–43.

Krugman, P. R. (1979) Increasing returns, monopolistic competition and international trade, *JIE* **9**, 469–79. In Bhagwati (1981).

Kuhn, H. W. (1959) Factor endowments and factor prices: mathematical appendix, *Eca* **26**, 142–4.

Kuhn, T. S. (1962) *The Structure of Scientific Revolutions*, 2nd edn, 1970. Chicago: Chicago University Press.

Kunin, L. and Weaver, F. S. (1971) On the structure of scientific revolutions in economics, *HOPE* **3**, 391–7.

Kurz, M. (1974) Equilibrium in a finite sequence of markets with transactions costs, *Ecta* **42**, 1–20.

Laidler, D. (1974) *Introduction to Microeconomics.* Oxford: Philip Allan.

Laing, N. F. (1971) Introduction, part II. In Harcourt and Laing (1971).

Lakatos, I. (1970) Falsification and the methodology of scientific research programmes. In Lakatos and Musgrave (1970), and in Lakatos (1978).

Lakatos, I. (1971) History of science and its rational reconstructions, *Boston Studies in the Philosophy of Science* **8**, 91–135. In Lakatos (1978).

Lakatos, I. (1974a) Science and pseudoscience. In Lakatos (1978).

Lakatos, I. (1974b) Popper on demarcation and induction. In Lakatos (1978).

Lakatos, I. (1976) *Proofs and Refutations.* Cambridge: Cambridge University Press.

Lakatos, I. (1978) *The Methodology of Scientific Research Programmes: Philosophical Papers,* vol. 1. Cambridge: Cambridge University Press.

Lakatos, I. and Musgrave, A. (eds) (1970) *Criticism and the Growth of Knowledge,* Cambridge: Cambridge University Press.

Lal, D. (1983) *The Poverty of "Development Economics",* Hobart Paperback 16. London: Institute of Economic Affairs.

Lancaster, K. (1957) Review of Hicks (1956), *Eca* **24**, 351ff.

Lancaster, K. (1966a) Change and innovation in the technology of consumption, *AER* **56**, 14–23.

Lancaster, K. (1966b) A new approach to consumer theory, *JPE* **74**, 132–57.

Lange, O. (1935) Marx and modern economic theory, *RES* **2**, 189–201.

Latsis, S. J. (1976) *Method and Appraisal in Economics.* Cambridge: Cambridge University Press.

Law, J. (1705) *Money and Trade Considered, with a Proposal for Supplying the Nation with Money.*

Leijonhufvud, A. (1968) *On Keynesian Economics and the Economics of Keynes.* Oxford: Oxford University Press.

Leijonhufvud, A. (1976) Schools, "revolutions" and research programmes in economic theory. In Latsis (1976).

Leontief, W. A. (1933) The use of indifference curves in the analysis of foreign trade, *QJE* **47**. In AEA (1949).

Leontief, W. A. (1936) Composite commodities and the problem of index numbers, *Ecta* **4**. In Leontief (1966).

Leontief, W. A. (1937) Implicit theorizing: a methodological criticism of the neo-Cambridge school, *QJE* **51**. In Leontief (1966).

Leontief, W. A. (1941) *The Structure of the American Economy, 1929–41.*

Leontief, W. A. (1947) Introduction to a theory of the internal structure of functional relationships, *Ecta* **15**. In Leontief (1966).

Leontief, W. A. (1953) Domestic production and foreign trade: the American capital position re-examined. *Proceedings of the American Philosophical Society* **97**. In Bhagwati (1969).

Leontief, W. A (1966) *Essays in Economics.* Oxford: Basil Blackwell.

Leontief, W. A. (1971) Theoretical assumptions and nonobserved facts, *AER* **61**. In Leontief (1976).

Leontief, W. A. (1976) *Essays in Economics,* vol. 2. Oxford: Basil Blackwell.

Lerner, A. P. (1932) Diagramatical representation of cost conditions in international trade, *Eca* **12** (old series). In Lerner (1953).

Lerner, A. P. (1934) Diagramatical representation of demand conditions in international trade, *Eca* **1**. In Lerner (1953).

Lerner, A. P. (1952) Factor prices and international trade, *Eca* **19**. In Lerner (1953).

Lerner, A. P. (1953) *Essays in Economic Analysis*. London.

Lewis, W. A. (1954) Economic development with unlimited supplies of labour, *MS* **22**. In Agarwala and Singh (1958).

Liberal Party (1929) *We Can Conquer Unemployment*.

Lindahl, E. (1930) The rate of interest and the price level. In *Studies in the Theory of Money and Capital*, 1939.

Lindbeck, A. (1971) *The Political Economy of the New Left*. New York: Harper and Row.

Linder, S. B. (1961) *An Essay on Trade and Transformation*. New York.

Lipsey, R. G. (1957) The theory of customs unions: trade diversion and welfare, *Eca* **24**.

Lipsey, R. G. (1960a) The relationship between unemployment and the rate of change of money wage rates in the UK 1862–1957: a further analysis, *Eca* **27**, 1–31. In AEA (1965).

Lipsey, R. G. (1960b) The theory of customs unions: a general survey, *EJ* **70**, 496–513.

Lipsey, R. G. and Lancaster, K. (1956) The general theory of second best, *RES* **24**, 11–32.

Lipsey, R. G. and Parkin, M. (1975) Inflation: a survey, *EJ* **85**, 741–809. In Korliras and Thorn (1979).

List, F. (1841) *The National System of Political Economy*. Translated by S. S. Lloyd, 1904. New York: Longmans Green.

Little, I. M. D. (1950) *A Critique of Welfare Economics*. Oxford.

Little, I. M. D. (1982) *Economic Development*. Basic Books.

Littlechild, S. (1978) *The Fallacy of the Mixed Economy*, Hobart Paper 80. London: Institute of Economic Affairs.

Littlechild, S. C. (1982) Equilibrium and the market process. In I. M. Kirzner (ed.), *Method, Process and Austrian Economics: Essays in Honor of Ludwig von Mises*. Lexington Books.

Livingstone, I. (1981) The development of development economics, *ODI Review*, 1–19.

Livingstone, I. (ed.) (1981b) *Development Economics in Action*. London: George Allen and Unwin.

Loasby, B. J. (1976) *Choice, Complexity and Ignorance*. Cambridge: Cambridge University Press.

Locke, J. (1961) *Some Considerations of the Consequences of the Lowering of Interest and Raising the Value of Money*.

Longfield, M. (1834) *Lectures on Political Economy*, LSE Reprints of scarce tracts. London: LSE.

Lucas, R. E. (1972) Expectations and the neutrality of money, *JET* **4**, 103–24.

Lucas, R. E. (1975) An equilibrium model of the business cycle, *JPE* **83**, 1113–44.

Lucas, R. E. (1976) Econometric policy evaluation: a critique, in *The Phillips Curve and Labour Markets*, Carnegie-Rochester Conference Series on Public Policy, vol. 1. Amsterdam: North Holland.

Lucas, R. E. (1977) Understanding business cycles, in K. Brunner and A. H. Meltzer (eds) *Stabilization of the Domestic and International Economy*. Amsterdam: North Holland.

Lucas, R. E. (1978) Unemployment policy, *AER* **68**, 353–7.

Lucas, R. E. (1980) Methods and problems in business cycle theory, *JMCB* **12**, 696–715.

Lundberg, E. (1937) *Studies in the Theory of Economic Expansion*. Stockholm.

Machlup, F. (1943) *International Trade and the National Income Multiplier*. Philadelphia.

Machlup, F. (1955) The problem of verification in economics, *SEJ* **22**, 1–21.

Machlup, F. (1956) Terence Hutchison's reluctant ultra-empiricism, *SEJ* **22**, 483–93.

Machlup, F. (1964) Paul Samuelson on theory and realism, *AER* **54**, 733–6.

Machlup, F. (1977) *A History of Thought on Economic Integration*. Columbia University Press.

Macmillan Committee (1931) Report of Committee on Finance and Industry, CMND 3897.

Malinvaud, E. (1953) Capital accumulation and efficient allocation of resources, *Ecta* **21**, 233–68.

Malinvaud, E. (1980) *Profitability and Unemployment*. Cambridge: Cambridge University Press.

Malthus, T. R. (1798) *An Essay on the Principle of Population as it Affects the Future Improvement of Society*, 2nd edn, 1803.

Malthus, T. R. (1815) *An Inquiry into the Nature and Progress of Rent*.

Mandelbaum, K. (1945) *The Industrialization of Backward Areas*.

Mangoldt, H. v (1863) *Grundriss der Volkswirtschaftslehre*.

Marcet, J. (1816) *Conversations on Political Economy*, 2nd edn, 1817, 3rd edn, 1839.

Marchi, N. de (1973) Mill, Cairnes and the emergence of Marginalism in England. In Black *et al.* (1973).

Marchi, N. de (1976) Anomaly and the development of economics: the case of the Leontief paradox. In Latsis (1976).

Marget, A. W. (1930) *The Theory of Prices*, 2 vols. London.

Markowitz, H. M. (1959) *Portfolio Selection*. New York.

Marris, R. (1964) *The Economic Theory of Managerial Capitalism*. London: Macmillan.

Marshall, A. (1879) *Pure Theory of Foreign Trade and Domestic Values*, LSE reprint series. London: LSE.

Marshall, A. (1885) The present position of economics. In Marshall (1925).

Marshall, A. (1887) Remedies for fluctuations of general prices, *Contemporary Review*. In Marshall (1925).

Marshall, A. (1890) Principles of Economics, 8th edn, 1920; variorum edition, ed C. W. Guillebaud, 1961. London: Macmillan.

Marshall, A. (1892) The perversion of economic history: a reply, *EJ* **2**, 507–19.

Marshall, A. (1897) The old generation of economists and the new, *QJE* **11**. In Marshall (1925).

Marshall, A. (1907) Social possibilities of economic chivalry, *EJ* **17**. In Marshall (1925).

Marshall, A. (1919) *Industry and Trade*. London.

Marshall, A. (1923) *Money, Credit and Commerce*. London.

Marshall, A. (1925) *Memorials of Alfred Marshall*, ed. A. C. Pigou. London.

Marshall, A. (1926) *Official Papers by Alfred Marshall*, ed. J. M. Keynes. London.

Marshall, A. and Marshall, M. P. (1879) *Economics of Industry*.

Marx, K. (1867–1894) *Capital*, 3 vols. Translated by S. Moore and E. Aveling. London: Lawrence and Wishart.

Mason, W. E. (1955) Some neglected contributions to the theory of international transfers, *JPE* **63**, 529–35.

Mason, W. E. (1957) Ricardo's transfer-mechanism theory, *QJE* **71**, 107–15.

Mathias, P. (1983) *The First Industrial Nation*, 2nd edn. London: Methuen.

Matthews, R. C. O. (1968) Why has Britain had full employment since the war? *EJ* **78**, 555ff.

McBriar, A. M. (1962) *Fabian Socialism and English Politics, 1884–1918*. Cambridge.

McCall, J. J. (1971) Probabilistic microeconomics, *Bell Journal of Economics and Management Science* **2**, 403–33.

McLeod, H. D. (1872) *The Principles of Economical Philosophy*. London.

Meade, J. E. (1951) *The Balance of Payments, The Theory of International Economic Policy*, vol. 1. London.

Meade, J. E. (1952) *The Geometry of International Trade*. London.

Meade, J. E. (1955a) *Trade and Welfare, The Theory of International Economic Policy*, vol. 2. London.

Meade, J. E. (1955b) *The Theory of Customs Unions*. Amsterdam.

Meade, J. E. (1961) *A Neoclassical Theory of Economic Growth*. London: George Allen and Unwin.

Meade, J. E. (1975) The Keynesian revolution. In Keynes (1975).

Meek, R. L. (1967) *Economics and Ideology and Other Essays*. London: Chapman and Hall.

Meier, G. M. (ed.) (1970) *Leading Issues in Economic Development*. Oxford: Oxford University Press.

Menard, C. (1980) Three forms of resistance to statistics: Say, Cournot, Walras, *HOPE* **12**, 524–41.

Menger, C. (1871) *Principles of Economics*. Translated by J. Dingwall and B. F. Hoselitz, 1950. Glencoe, Ill.

Menger, C. (1883) *Problems of Economics and Sociology*. Translated by F. J. Nock, 1963. Urbana.

Merton, R. K. (1961) Singletons and multiples in scientific discovery: a chapter in the sociology of science, *Proceedings of the American Philosophical Society* **105**, 471–86. In Merton (1973).

Merton, R. K. (1963) Resistance to the systematic study of multiple discoveries in science, *Archiv Europ. Sociol.* 237–82. In Merton (1973).

Merton, R. K. (1973) *The Sociology of Science*. Chicago: University of Chicago Press.

Metzler, L. A. (1941) The nature and stability of inventory cycles, *REStats* **23**, 113ff.

Metzler, L. A. (1942) Underemployment equilibrium in international trade, *Ecta* **10**, 97ff.

Metzler, L. A. (1945) The stability of multiple markets: the Hicks condition, *Ecta* **13**, 277–92.

Middleton, R. (1982) The treasury in the 1930s: political and administrative constraints to acceptance of the 'new' economics, *OEP* **34**, 48–78.

Mill, J. (1808) Commerce Defended, in *James Mill: Selected Economic Writings*, ed. D. Winch, 1966. Edinburgh.

Mill, J. (1821) *Elements of Political Economy*. London.

Mill, J. S. (1844) *Essays on Some Unsettled Questions of Political Economy*.

Mill, J. S. (1848) *Principles of Political Economy*. References are to 1873 edn.

Mill, J. S. (1869) Review of W. Thornton, On Labour..., *FR*. Reprinted in Mill (1848), ed. W. J. Ashley, 1909.

Milner, J. (1954) Games against nature, in *Decision Processes*, and in M. Shubik (ed.) *Game Theory and Related Approaches to Social Behaviour*, 1964. New York.

Minhas, B. S. (1962) The homohyphallagic production function, factor intensity reversals and the Heckscher–Ohlin theorem, *JPE* **70**, 138–56.

Mirrlees, J. A. (1971) An exploration in the theory of optimum income taxation, *RES* **38**, 175–208.

Mirrlees, J. A. and Stern, N. H. (1973) *Models of Economic Growth*. International Economic Association.

Mises, L. v (1912) *The Theory of Money and Credit*. Translated by H. E. Batson, 1934. London: Jonathan Cape.

Mises, L. v (1933) *Epistemological Problems of Economics*. Translated by G. Reisman, 1960. Princeton.

Mises, L. v (1969) *The Historical Setting of the Austrian School of Economics*.

Mishan, E. J. (1965) A survey of welfare economics, 1939–1959. In AEA/*RES* (1965).

Mitchell, W. C. (1910) The rationality of economic activity, *JPE* **18**.

Mitchell, W. C. (1913) *Business Cycles*. New York: Burt Franklin.

Mitchell, W. C. (1925) Quantitative analysis in economic theory, *AER* **15**, 1–12. Reprinted in Mitchell (1937).

Mitchell, W. C. (1927) *Business Cycles: the Problem and its Setting*. New York.

Mitchell, W. C. (1935) Commons on Institutional Economics, *AER* **25**, 635–52. In Mitchell (1937).

Mitchell, W. C. (1937) *The Backward Art of Spending Money and Other Essays*. New York.

Mitchell, W. C. (1969) *Types of Economic Theory*. New York: Kelley.

Mitchell, W. C. and Burns, A. F. (1946) *Measuring Business Cycles*. New York.

Modigliani, F. and Brumberg, R. E. (1954) Utility analysis and the consumption function: an interpretation of cross-section data, in K. K. Kurihara (ed.) *Post-Keynesian Economics*. London: George Allen and Unwin.

Moggridge, D. (1972) *British Monetary Policy 1924–1931: the Norman Conquest of $4.86*. Cambridge: Cambridge University Press.

Moggridge, D. (1975) The influence of Keynes on the economics of his time. In Keynes (1975).

Moore, H. L. (1914) *Economic Cycles: Their Law and Cause*.

Morishima, M. (1973) *Marx's Economics*. Cambridge: Cambridge University Press.

Morishima, M. (1977) *Walras's Economics*. Cambridge: Cambridge University Press.

Morishima, M. (1980) W. Jaffe on Leon Walras: a Comment, *JEL* **18**, 550–8.

Morishima, M. and Catephores, G. (1978) *Value Exploitation and Growth*. London: McGraw-Hill.

Mosak, J. L. (1945) *General Equilibrium Theory in International Trade*. Bloomington.

Moss, S. (1984) The history of the theory of the firm from Marshall to Robinson and Chamberlin: the source of positivism in economics, *Eca* **51**, 3ff.

Mueller, M. G. (1971) *Readings in Macroeconomics*, 2nd edn. London: Holt, Rinehart and Winston.

Mundell, R. A. (1957) International trade and factor mobility, *AER* **47**, 321–37.

Mundell, R. A. (1962) The appropriate use of monetary and fiscal policy for internal and external stability, *IMFSP* **9**, 70–9.

Musgrave, R. A. (1939) The voluntary exchange theory of public economy, *QJE* **53**, 213ff.

Musgrave, R. A.(1959) *The Theory of Public Finance*. London: McGraw-Hill.

Muth, J. F. (1961) Rational expectations and the theory of price movements, *Ecta* **29**, 315ff.

Myint, H. (1948) *Theories of Welfare Economics*. London.

Myrdal, G. (1929) *The Political Element in the Development of Economic Theory*. London.

Myrdal, G. (1939) *Monetary Equilibrium*, Swedish edn. 1931. London.

Myrdal, G., Sterner, R. and Rose, A. (1944) *The American Dilemma*. New York.

Myrdal, G. (1957) *Economic Theory and Underdeveloped Regions*. London.

Myrdal, G. (1968) *Asian Drama*. Harmondsworth: Penguin.

Myrdal, G. (1973) *Against the Stream*. Translated 1974. London: Macmillan.

Myrdal, G. (1978) Institutional economics, *JEI* **12**, 771–83.

Nagel, E. (1961) *The Structure of Science*. London: Routledge and Kegan Paul.

Nagel, E. (1963) Assumptions in economic theory, *AER* **53**, 211–19. In Breit and Hochman (1969).

Nash, J. F. (1950) Equilibrium points in n-person games, *Proceedings of the National Academy of Science USA*, 48–9.

Nash, J. F. (1953) Two-person co-operative games, *Ecta* **21**, 128–140.

Negishi, T. (1960) Monopolistic competition and general equilibrium, *RES* **28**, 196–201.

Neisser, (1932) Lohnhöhe und Beschäftigungsgrad im Marktgleichgewicht, *WA* **36**, 413–55.

Nell, E. J. (1967) Theories of growth and theories of value, *EDCC* **16**, 15–26. In Harcourt and Laing (1971).

Neumann, J. v (1938) A model of general economic equilibrium. Translated in *RES* **13**, 1–9.

Neumann, J. v and Morgenstern, O. (1944) *The Theory of Games and Economic Behaviour*. New York.

Nevin, E. T. (1955) *The Mechanism of Cheap Money*. Cardiff.

Newbery, D. M. G. and Stiglitz, J. E. (1981) *The Theory of Commodity Price Stabilization*. Oxford: Oxford University Press.

Newcomb, S. (1885) *Principles of Political Economy*.

Nicholl, A. J. (1941) Probability analysis in the theory of demand, net revenue and price, *JPE* **49**, 637–61.

Nicholson, J. S.(1893) *Principles of Political Economy*, 3rd edn, 1901. London.

North, D. C. (1981) *Structure and Change in Economic History*. New York: Norton.

North, D. C. (1984) Transactions costs, institutions and economic history, *ZgS* **140**, 7–17.

Nurkse, R. (1952) Some international aspects of the problem of economic development, *AER* **42**. In Agarwala and Singh (1958).

O'Brien, D. P. (1970) *J. R. McCulloch: a Study in Classical Economics*. London.

O'Brien, D. P. (1975) *The Classical Economists*. Oxford: Oxford University Press.

O'Brien, D. P. (1976a) Customs union: trade creation and trade diversion in historical perspective, *HOPE* **8**, 540–63.

O'Brien, D. P. (1976b) The longevity of Adam Smith's vision: paradigms, research programmes and falsifiability in the history of economic thought, *SJPE* **23**, 133ff.

O'Brien, D. P. (1981a) A. Marshall, 1842–1924. In O'Brien and Presley (1981).

O'Brien, D. P. (1981b) Ricardian economics and the economics of David Ricardo, *OEP* **33**, 352–86.

O'Brien, D. P. (1983a) Research programmes in competitive structure, *JES* **10**, 29–51.

O'Brien, D. P. (1983b) Theories of the history of science: a test case. In Coats (1983a).

O'Brien, D. P. (1984a) The evolution of the theory of the firm. In F. H. Stephen (ed.), *Firms, Organizations and Labour: Approaches to the Economics of Work Organization.* London: Macmillan.

O'Brien, D. P. (1984b) Monetary economics. In Creedy and O'Brien (1984).

O'Brien, D. P. and Presley, J. R. (ed.) (1981) *Pioneers of Modern Economics in Britain.* London: Macmillan.

Officer, L. H. (1976) The purchasing-power-parity theory of exchange rates: a review article, *IMFSP* **23**, 1–60.

Ohlin, B. (1929) Transfer difficulties, real and imagined, *EJ* **39**, 172–8.

Ohlin, B. (1933) On the formulation of monetary theory, trans in *HOPE* **10**, 353–88.

Ohlin, B. (1933) *Interregional and International Trade*, 2nd edn, 1967. Cambridge, Mass.

Ohlin, B. (1937) Some notes on the Stockholm theory of savings and investment, *EJ* **47**, 53ff and 221ff.

Okun, A. M. (1981) *Prices and Quantities.* Oxford: Basil Blackwell.

Organisation for Economic Co-operation and Development (1971) *Economic Surveys: United Kingdom.* OECD.

Overstone, Lord (1837a) *Reflections Suggested by a Perusal of Mr J Horsley Palmer's Pamphlet on the Causes and Consequences of the Pressure on the Money Market.* In Overstone (1857). London.

Overstone, Lord (1837b) *Further Reflections on the State of the Currency and the Action of the Bank of England*, in Overstone (1857). London.

Overstone, Lord (1857) *Tracts on Metallic and Paper Currency.* London.

Ozga, S. A. (1955) An essay on the theory of tariffs, *JPE* **63**, 489ff.

Paish, F. W. (1936) Banking policy and the international balance of payments, *Eca* **3**, 404–22. In AEA (1949).

Pantaleoni, M. (1889) *Pure Economics.* Translated by T. B.Bruce, 1957. New York.

Pareto, V. (1894) Il massimo di utilita dato dalla libera concorrenza, *GdE* **9**, 48–66.

Pareto, V. (1896) *Cours d'Economie Politique.* Geneva.

Pareto, V. (1908) *Manual of Political Economy.*

Parrini, C. P. and Sklar, M. J. (1983) New thinking about the market, 1896–1904: some American economists and the theory of surplus capital, *JEH* **43**, 559–78.

Parsons, K. (1950) Introduction to Commons (1950).

Parsons, T. (1931) Wants and activities in Marshall, *QJE* **46**, 101ff.

Parsons, T. (1932) Economics and sociology: Marshall in relation to the thought of his time, *QJE* **46**, 316ff.

Pasinetti, L. (1969) Switches of technique and the 'rate of return' in capital theory, *EJ* **79**, 508–31. In Harcourt and Laing (1971).

Patinkin, D. (1949) The indeterminacy of absolute prices in classical economic theory, *Ecta* **17**, 1–27.

Patinkin, D. (1965) *Money, Interest and Prices*, 2nd edn. London: Harper and Row.

Patinkin, D. (1969) The Chicago tradition, the quantity theory and Friedman, *JMCB* **1**, 46–70. In D. Patinkin *Studies in Monetary Economics*, 1972. London: Harper and Row.

Patinkin, D. (1976) Keynes and econometrics: on the interaction between the macroeconomic revolutions of the interwar period, *Ecta* **44**, 1091–1123.

Patinkin, D. (1976b) Keynes' monetary thought: a study of its development, *HOPE* **8**, 1–150.

Patinkin, D. (1982) *Anticipations of the General Theory?* Oxford: Basil Blackwell.

Peace, I. (1970) *International Trade.* London: Macmillan.

Peden, G. C. (1980) Keynes, the Treasury and unemployment in the later nineteen-thirties, *OEP* **32**, 1–18.

Peden, G. C. (1983) Sir Richard Hopkins and the "Keynesian revolution" in employment policy, 1929–1945, *EHR* **34**, 281–96.

Penrose, E. (1959) *The Theory of the Firm*. Oxford: Basil Blackwell.

Perlman, M. (1977) Orthodoxy and heterodoxy in economics: a retrospective view of experiences in Britain and the USA, *ZN* **37**, 153–64.

Phelps, E. (1961) The golden rule of accumulation: a fable for growthmen, *AER* **51**, 638–43. In Sen (1970c).

Phelps, E. S. (1967) Phillips curves, expectations of inflation and optimal unemployment over time, *Eca* **34**, 254–81.

Phelps, E. S. (ed.) (1970) *Microeconomic Foundations of Employment and Inflation Theory*. London: Macmillan.

Phillips, A. W. (1958) The relation between unemployment and the rate of change of money wage rates in the United Kingdom 1861–1857, *Eca* **25**, 283–99. In Mueller (1971).

Pigou, A. C. (1908) *Economic Science in Relation to Practice*. Inaugural lecture, University of Cambridge.

Pigou, A. C. (1912) *Wealth and Welfare*.

Pigou, A. C.(1917) The exchange value of legal tender money, *QJE* **32**. In Pigou (1923).

Pigou, A. C. (1920) *The Economics of Welfare*, 4th edn, 1932. London.

Pigou, A. C. (1922) The foreign exchanges, *QJE*. In Pigou (1922).

Pigou, A. C. (1923) *Essays in Applied Economics*. London.

Pigou, A. C. (1927) *Industrial Fluctuations*. London.

Pigou, A. C. (1928a) *A Study in Public Finance*, 3rd edn, 1947. London.

Pigou, A. C. (1928b) An analysis of supply, *EJ* **38**, 238–57.

Pigou, A. C. (1933) *The Theory of Employment*. London.

Pirou, G. (1938) *Theories de l'Equilibre Economique: Walras et Pareto*. Paris.

Pollard, S. (ed.) (1970) *The Gold Standard and Employment Policies between the Wars*, Introduction by the editor. London.

Popper, K. R. (1934) *The Logic of Scientific Discovery*. Translated 1959. London.

Popper, K. R. (1972) *Objective Knowledge*. Oxford: Oxford University Press.

Prebisch, R. (1949) The economic development of Latin America and its principal problems. Translated in UN Dept of Economic Affairs, vol. of same title, 1950, and in *Economic Review of Latin America* **7**, 1962, part I.

Pribram, K. (1983) *A History of Economic Reasoning*. Baltimore: Johns Hopkins University Press.

Radner, R. (1968) Competitive equilibrium under uncertainty, *Ecta* **36**, 31–58.

Ramsey, F. P. (1927) A contribution to the theory of taxation, *EJ* **37**, 47–61.

Ramsey, F. P. (1928) A mathematical model of saving, *EJ* **38**, 543–59.

Rau, K. H. (1826–37) *Lehrbuch der Politischen Ökonomie*.

Rawls, J. (1958) Justice as fairness, *Philosophical Review* **67**, 164ff.

Rawls, J. (1971) *A Theory of Justice*. Cambridge, Mass.: Harvard University Press.

Reder, M. W. (1982) Chicago economics: permanence and change, *JEL* **20**, 1–38.

Ricardo, D. (1810) *The High Price of Bullion a Proof of the Depreciation of Bank Notes*.

Ricardo, D. (1815) *An Essay on the Influence of a Low Price of Corn on the Profits of Stock*.

Ricardo, D. (1817) *Principles of Political Economy and Taxation*. Harmondsworth: Penguin 1971.

Ricci, D. M. (1969) Fabian socialism: a theory of rent as exploitation, *Journal of British Studies* **9**(1), 105–21.

Ricci, U. (1933) Pareto and pure economics, *RES* **1**, 3ff.

Riddell, P. (1983) *The Thatcher Experiment*. Oxford: Martin Robertson.

Rima, I. (1967) *Development of Economic Analysis*. Homewood, Ill.: R. D. Irwin.

Rima, I. (1977) Neoclassicism and dissent, 1870–1925. In Weintraub (1977).

Rimmer, D. (1981) 'Basic needs' and the origins of the development ethos, *Journal of Developing Areas* **15**, 215–38.

Rimmer, D. (1984) *The Economics of West Africa*. London: Weidenfeld.

Robbins, L. (1928) The representative firm, *EJ* **38**, 387–404.

Robbins, L. (1932) *An Essay on the Nature and Significance of Economic Science*, 2nd edn, 1935. London.

Robbins, L. (1952) *Theory of Economic Policy in English Classical Political Economy*.

Robbins, L. (1958) *Robert Torrens and the Evolution of Classical Economics*. London.

Robertson, D. H. (1915) *A Study of Industrial Fluctuations*. London.

Robertson, D. H. (1926) *Banking Policy and the Price Level*. London.

Robertson, D. H. (1933) Saving and hoarding, *EJ* **43**, 399–413.

Robertson, D. H. (1936) Some notes on Mr Keynes' General Theory of Employment, *QJE* **51**, 168–91.

Robertson, D. H. (1951) *Utility and All That*. London.

Robertson, R. M. (1951) Jevons and his precursors, *Ecta* **19**, 229–49.

Robinson, J. (1932) Imperfect competition and falling supply price, *EJ* **42**, 544–54.

Robinson, J. (1933a) *Economics of Imperfect Competition*. London: Macmillan.

Robinson, J. (1933b) Imperfection of the market – comment, *EJ* **43**, 124–5.

Robinson, J. (1933c) A parable on savings and investment, *Eca*, 75–84.

Robinson, J. (1937) *Essays in the Theory of Employment*. In Robinson (1973a).

Robinson, J. (1942) *An Essay on Marxian Economics*. London.

Robinson, J. (1953) The production function and the theory of capital, *RES* **21**, 81–106.

Robinson, J. (1956) *The Accumulation of Capital*. London: Macmillan.

Robinson, J. (1962a) *Economic Philosophy*. Harmondsworth: Penguin.

Robinson, J. (1962b) *Essays in The Theory of Economic Growth*. London: Macmillan.

Robinson, J. (1973a) *Collected Economic Papers*, vol. IV. Oxford: Basil Blackwell.

Robinson, J. (1973b) Foreword to Kregel (1973).

Rogers, J. E. T. (1866–1902) *History of Agriculture and Prices in England*. Oxford.

Rogers, J. E. T. (1884) *Six Centuries of Work and Wages*. London.

Rogin, L. (1956) *The Meaning and Validity of Economic Theory*. New York.

Roll, E. (1973) *A History of Economic Thought*. London: Faber.

Roncaglia, A. (1977) The Sraffian revolution. In Weintraub (1977).

Roncaglia, A. (1978) *Sraffa and the Theory of Prices*. New York: Wiley.

Rose, H. (1973) Effective demand in the long run. In Mirrlees and Stern (1973).

Rosenstein-Rodan, P. N. (1943) Problems of industrialization in eastern and south eastern Europe, *EJ* **53**. In Agarwala and Singh (1958).

Rosenstein-Rodan, P. N. (1961) Notes on the theory of the 'big push', in *Economic Development for Latin America*, ed. H. S. Ellis. Reprinted in Meier (1970).

Rostow, W. W. (1960) *The Stages of Economic Growth, a non-Communist Manifesto*. Cambridge.

Rothbard, M. N. (1976) Praxeology: the methodology of Austrian economics. In Dolan (1976).

Rothschild, M. and Stiglitz, J. E. (1976) Equilibrium in competitive insurance markets: and essay on the economics of imperfect information, *QJE* **90**, 629–49.

Ruggles, N. (1949a) The welfare basis of the marginal cost pricing principle, *RES* **17**, 29–46.

Ruggles, N. (1949b) Recent developments in the theory of marginal cost pricing, *RES* **17**, 107–26.

Rutherford, M. (1983) J. R. Commons's institutional economics, *JEI* **17**, 721–44.

Rutherford, M. (1984) Thorstein Veblen and the processes of institutional change, *HOPE* **16**, 331–48.

Sabine, B. E. V. (1970) *British Budgets in Peace and War, 1937–45*. London.

Samuels, W. J. (1976) The Chicago school of political economy: a constructive critique, in *The Chicago School of Political Economy*, ed. Samuels. Association for Evolutionary Economics/Michigan State University.

Samuels, W. J. (1977) Technology vis à vis institutions in the *JEI*: a suggested interpretation, *JEI* **11**, 871–95.

Samuels, W. J. (1978) Information systems, preferences, and the economy in the *JEI*, *JEI* **12**, 1–41.

Samuelson, P. A. (1938a) A note on the pure theory of consumers' behaviour, *Eca* **5**, 61ff.

Samuelson, P. A. (1938b) Welfare economics and international trade, *AER* **28**, 261–6. In Samuelson (1966a).

Samuelson (1939a) The gains from international trade, CJEPS **5**, 195–205. In Samuelson (1966a).

Samuelson, P. A. (1939b) Interaction between the multiplier analysis and the principle of acceleration, *REStats* **21**, 75ff.

Samuelson, P. A. (1946) Lord Keynes and the General Theory, *Ecta* **14**, 187–200.

Samuelson, P. A. (1947) *Foundations of Economic Analysis*. Cambridge, Mass.: Harvard University Press.

Samuelson, P. A. (1948a) *Economics*, 10th edn, 1976. London: McGraw-Hill.

Samuelson, P. A. (1948b) International trade and the equalization of factor prices, *EJ* **58**, 163–84. In Samuelson (1966a).

Samuelson, P. A. (1949) International factor price equalization once again, *EJ* **59**, 181–97. In Samuelson (1966a).

Samuelson, P. A. (1950) Evaluation of real national income, *OEP* **2**, 1–29. In AEA (1969).

Samuelson, P. A. (1952) The transfer problem and transport costs: the terms of trade when impediments are absent, *EJ* **62**, 278–304. In Samuelson (1966a).

Samuelson, P. A. (1953) Prices of factors and goods in general equilibrium, *RES* **21**, 1–20. In Samuelson (1966a).

Samuelson, P. A. (1954a) The pure theory of public expenditure, *REStats* **36**, 387–9. In R. W. Houghton (ed.), *Public Finance*, Harmondsworth: Penguin. 1970.

Samuelson, P. A. (1954b) The transfer problem and transfer costs II: analysis of the effects of trade impediments, *EJ* **64**, 264–89. In Samuelson (1966a).

Samuelson, P. A. (1955) Diagramatic exposition of a theory of public expenditure, *REStats* **37**, 350–6. In R. W. Houghton (ed.), *Public Finance*, 1970. Harmondsworth: Penguin.

Samuelson, P. A. (1962) Economists and the history of ideas, *AEA* **52**, 1–18.

Samuelson, P. A. (1963) Problems of methodology – discussion, *AER* **53**, 231–6.

Samuelson, P. A. (1966a) *The Collected Scientific Papers of Paul A. Samuelson*, vol. II. Cambridge, Mass.: MIT Press.

Samuelson, P. A. (1966b) A summing up, *QJE* **80**, 568–83. In Harcourt and Laing (1971).

Samuelson, P. A. (1967a) The monopolistic competition revolution. In R. E. Kuenne (ed.), *Monopolistic Competition Theory, Studies in Impact*. New York.

Samuelson, P. A. (1967b) Marxian economics as economics, *AER* **57**, 884ff.

Samuelson, P. A. (1968) What classical and neo-classical monetary theory really was, *CJEPS* **1**, 1–15. In Clower (1970).

Samuelson, P. A. (1971) Ohlin was right, *SJE* **73**, 365–84. In Samuelson (1977).

Samuelson, P. A. (1974) Marx as a mathematical economist. In G. Horwich and P. A. Samuelson (eds), *Trade Stability and Macroeconomics, Essays in Honour of L. A. Metzler*. New York: Academic Press.

Samuelson, P. A. (1977) *The Collected Scientific Papers of Paul A. Samuelson*, vol. 4. Cambridge, Mass.: MIT Press.

Samuelson, P. A. (1978) The canonical classical model of political economy, *JEL* **16**, 1415–34.

Samuelson, P. A. (1980) Noise and signal in debates among classical economists: a reply, *JEL* **18**, 575–8.

Samuelson, P. A. and Solow, R. M. (1960) Analytical aspects of anti-inflation policy, *AER* **50**, 177–94. In Mueller (1971).

Sandmo, A. (1976) Optimal taxation – an introduction to the literature, *JPubE* **6**, 37–54.

Santos, T. dos (1970) The structure of dependence, *AER* **60**, 231–6. In Livingstone (1981b).

Sargent, T. J. and Wallace, N. (1975) Rational expectations, the optimal monetary instrument and the optimal money supply rule, *JPE* **83**, 241–54.

Sargent, T. J. and Wallace, N. (1976) Rational expectations and the theory of economic policy, *JME* **2**, 169ff. Reprinted in Korliras and Thorn (1979).

Sargent, T. J. and Wallace, N. (1982) The real bills doctrine versus the quantity theory: a reconsideration, *JPE* **90**, 1212–36.

Satterthwaite, M. (1975) Strategy-proofness and Arrow's conditions: existence and correspondence theorems for voting procedures and social welfare functions, *JET* **10**, 187–217.

Savage, L. J. (1954) *The Foundations of Statistics*. New York: Wiley.

Say, J. B. (1803) *A Treatise on Political Economy*. Translated by C. R. Prinsep, 1821. London.

Scarf, H. (1960) Some examples of global instability of competitive equilibrium, *IER* **1**, 157–72.

Scarf, H. (1962) An analysis of markets with a large number of participants. In *Recent Advances in Game Theory*. Princeton: Princeton University Press.

Scheiber, H. N., Vatter, H. G. and Faulkner, H. U. (1976) *American Economic History*. London: Harper and Row.

Schlesinger, K. (1933) On the production equations of economic value theory. Translated in Baumol and Goldfield (1968).

Schmoller, G. (1900) *Grundriss der Volkswirtschaftslehre*.

Schultz, T. W. (1964) *Transforming Traditional Agriculture*. New Haven: Yale University Press.

Schumpeter, J. A. (1908) *Das Wesen und der Hauptinhalt der theoretischen Nationalokonomie*.

Schumpeter, J. A. (1910) Über das Wesen der Wirtschaftkrisen, *Zeitschrift für Volkswirtschaft*, 271–325.

Schumpeter, J. A. (1912) *The Theory of Economic Development*. Translated by R. Opie, 1934. Cambridge, Mass.

Schumpeter, J. A. (1939) *Business Cycles*. New York.

Schumpeter, J. A. (1942) *Capitalism, Socialism and Democracy*. London.

Schumpeter, J. A. (1954) *History of Economic Analysis*. New York: Oxford University Press.

Schumpeter, J. A. (1982) The 'crisis' in economics – fifty years ago, *JEL* **20**, 1049–59.
Schwarz, P. (1972) *The New Political Economy of J. S. Mill*.
Scitovsky, T. (1941) A note on welfare propositions in economics, *RES* **9**, 77–88. In AEA (1969).
Scitovsky, T. (1954) Two concepts of external economies, *JPE* **62**. In Agarwala and Singh (1958).
Seers, D. (1979) The birth, life and death of development economics, *Development and Change* **10**, 707–19.
Seligman, B. B. (1962) *Main Currents in Modern Economics*. New York: Free Press.
Sen, A. K. (1970a) *Collective Choice and Social Welfare*. Cambridge: Holden Day.
Sen, A. K. (1970b) The impossibility of a Paretian liberal, *JPE* **78**. In Sen (1982).
Sen, A. K. (1974) On some debates in capital theory, *Eca* **41**, 328–335.
Sen, A. K. (1982) *Social Choice and Welfare*. Oxford: Basil Blackwell.
Senk, A. K. (1983) Development: which way now? *EJ* **93**, 745–62.
Sen, A. K. (1985) Social choice theory. In K. J. Arrow and M. J. Intriligator (eds), *Handbook of Mathematical Economics*, vol. 3. Amsterdam: North Holland.
Sen, A. K. (ed.) (1970c) *Growth Economics*. Harmondsworth: Penguin.
Senior, N. (1836) *An Outline of the Science of Political Economy*. LSE series of reprints. London: LSE.
Seton, F. (1957) The 'transformation problem', *RES* **25**, 149–60.
Shackle, G. L. S. (1949) *Expectation in Economics*, 2nd edn, 1952. Cambridge: Cambridge University Press.
Shackle, G. L. S. (1961) *Decision Order and Time in Human Affairs*, 2nd edn, 1969. Cambridge: Cambridge University Press.
Shackle, G. L. S. (1967) *The Years of High Theory*. Cambridge: Cambridge University Press.
Shackle, G. L. S. (1972) *Epistemics and Economics*. Cambridge: Cambridge University Press.
Shand, A. H. (1984) *The Capitalist Alternative*. Brighton: Wheatsheaf.
Shaw, A. G. L. (ed.) (1970) *Great Britain and the Colonies*. London.
Sheffrin, S. M. (1983) *Rational Expectations*. Cambridge: Cambridge University Press.
Shell, K. (1971) Notes on the economics of infinity, *JPE* **79**, 1002–11.
Shove, G. F. (1933) The imperfection of the market, *EJ* **43**, 113–24.
Shove, G. F. (1942) The place of Marshall's Principles in the development of economic theory, *EJ* **52**, 294ff.
Shubik, M. (1959) Edgeworth market processes, in *Contributions to the Theory of Games*, vol. IV, ed. A. W. Tucker and R. O. Luce. Princeton.
Shubik, M. (1981) Game theory models and methods in political economy. In Arrow and Intriligator (1981).
Sidgwick, H. (1874) *Methods of Ethics*, 2nd edn, 1884. London.
Sidgwick, H. (1879) The wage fund theory, *FR*, 1 September.
Sidgwick, H. (1883) *The Principles of Political Economy*, 2nd edn, 1887. London.
Sidrauski, M. (1967) Inflation and unemployment, *JPE* **75**, 796ff.
Simon, H. (1956) *Administrative Behaviour*. New York.
Simon, H. (1957) *Models of Man*. New York.
Simon, H. (1976) From substantive to procedural rationality. In Latsis (1976).
Simon, H. (1978) Rationality as process and as product of thought, *AER* **68**, suppl., 1–16.

Simons, H. C. (1942) Hansen on fiscal policy, *JPE* **54**, 161–96. In Hansen and Clemence (1953).

Singer, H. W. (1949) Economic progress in underdeveloped countries, *Social Research* **16**, 1–11.

Singer, H. W. (1950) The distribution of gains between investing and borrowing countries, *AER* **11**, suppl. In Singer (1964).

Singer, H. W. (1952) The mechanics of economic development, *Indian Economic Review*. In Agarwala and Singh (1958).

Singer, H. W. (1964a) Recent trends in economic thought on underdeveloped countries. In Singer (1964b) and in Singer (1975).

Singer, H. W. (1964b) *International Development: Growth and Change*. New York.

Singer, H. W. (1975) *The Strategy of International Development*. London: Macmillan.

Skidelsky, R. (1983) *John Maynard Keynes*. London: Macmillan.

Skinner, A. (1979) *A System of Social Science*. Oxford: Oxford University Press.

Slutsky, E. (1915) On the theory of the budget of the consumer. *GdE*. Translated in AEA (1953).

Smith, A. (1759) *The Theory of Moral Sentiments*. Glasgow ed. 1976. Oxford: Clarendon Press.

Smith, A. (1776) *An Inquiry into the Nature and Causes of the Wealth of Nations*. Chicago: University of Chicago Press, 1976.

Smithies, A. (1942) The stability of competitive equilibrium, *Ecta* **10**, 258–74.

Smyth, L. (ed.) (1962) *Essays in Economic Method*. London: Duckworth.

Solow, R. M. (1956) A contribution to the theory of economic growth, *QJE* **70**, 65–94. In Sen (1970c).

Solow, R. M. (1957) Technical progress and the aggregate production function, *REStats* **39**, 312–20. In Sen (1970c).

Solow, R. M. (1961) Note on Uzawa's two sector model of economic growth, *RES* **29**, 48–50.

Solow, R. M. (1963) *Capital Theory and the Rate of Return*. Part reprinted in Harcourt and Laing (1971).

Solow, R. M. (1980) On theories of unemployment, *AER* **70**, 1–11.

Solow, R. M. and Stiglitz, J. E. (1968) Output, employment and wages in the short run, *QJE* **82**, 537–60.

Sombart, W. (1922) *Der moderne Capitalismus*. Berlin.

Sonnenfels, J. v (1765) *Grundsatze der Polizey, Handlung und Finanzwissenschaft*.

Sonnenschein, H. (1983) The economics of incentives: an introductory account, 1983 Nancy Schwarz Lecture, Northwestern University. In R. Sato and M. J. Beckman (eds), *Technology, Organization and Economic Structure*. Springer.

Spence, M. (1974) *Market Signalling*. Cambridge, Mass.: Harvard University Press.

Spence, M. (1976) Informational aspects of market structures: an introduction, *QJE* **90**, 591–7.

Spengler, J. J. (1968) Exogenous and endogenous influences in the formation of post 1870 economic thought. In R. V. Eagly (ed.), *Events, Ideology and Economic Theory*.

Spiegel, H. W. (1983) *The Growth of Economic Thought*, 2nd edn. Durham, N.C.: Duke University Press.

Spiegel, H. W. (ed.) (1952) *The Development of Economic Thought*. New York.

Spiegel, H. W. and Samuels, W. J. (eds) (1984) *Contemporary Economists in Perspective*, 2 vols. Greenwich, Conn.: JAI Press.

Spiethoff, A. (1932) Die allgemeine Volkswirthschaftslehre als geschichtliche Theorie: die Wirtschaftsstile, *Schmoller's Jahrbuch*. **56**, 891–924.

Sraffa, P. (1926) The laws of returns under competitive conditions, _EJ_ **36**, 535–50. In AEA (1952).

Sraffa, P. (1960) _Production of Commodities by Means of Commodities_. Cambridge: Cambridge University Press.

Stackelberg, H. v (1933) _Zwei kritische Bemerkungen zur Preistheorie Gustav Cassels_, _ZN_ **4**, 456–72.

Stackelberg, H. v (1934) _Marktform und Gleichgewicht_.

Stark, W. (1944) _History of Economics in Relation to its Social Development_. London.

Starratt, D. (1973) Inefficiency and the demand for "money" in a sequence economy, _RES_ **40**, 437–48.

Steedman, I. (1977) _Marx after Sraffa_. London: New Left Books.

Steiger, O. (1978) Prelude to the theory of a monetary economy: origins and significance of Ohlin's 1933 approach, _HOPE_ **10**, 420–46.

Stein, J. L. (1971) _Money and Capacity Growth_. Columbia.

Stewart, I. (1977) _Reasoning and Method in Economics_. London: McGraw-Hill.

Stewart, M. J. (1972) _Keynes and After_, 2nd edn. Harmondsworth: Penguin.

Stewart, M. J. (1977) _The Jeckyll and Hyde Years: Politics and Economic Policy since 1964_. London: Dent.

Stigler, G. J. (1941) _Production and Distribution Theories, the Formative Period_. New York.

Stigler, G. J. (1943) The kinky oligopoly demand curve and rigid prices, _JPE_ **55**, 432–49.

Stigler, G. J. (1947) _The Theory of Price_. New York.

Stigler, G. J. (1950) The development of utility theory, _JPE_ **58**. In Stigler (1965).

Stigler, G. J. (1954) The early history of empirical studies of consumer behaviour, _JPE_ **42**. In Stigler (1965).

Stigler, G. J. (1960) The influence of events and policies on economic theory, _AER_ **50**, 36–45. In Stigler (1965a).

Stigler, G. J. (1961) The economics of information, _JPE_ **69**, 213–25.

Stigler, G. J. (1962) Information in the labour market, _JPE_ **70**, 94–105.

Stigler, G. J. (1965) _Essays in the History of Economics_. Chicago: University of Chicago Press.

Stigler, G. J. (1965b) Textual exegesis as a scientific problem, _Eca_ **32**. In Stigler (1982).

Stigler, G. J. (1976) The successes and failures of Professor Smith, _JPE_ **84**. In Stigler (1982).

Stigler, G. J. (1982) _The Economist as Preacher_. Oxford: Basil Blackwell.

Stigler, G. J. (1984) Economics – the imperial science? _SJE_ **86**, 301–13.

Stiglitz, J. E. (1974) Incentives and risk-sharing in share-cropping, _RES_ **41**, 219–55.

Stiglitz, J. E. (1977) Symposium on economics of information: introduction, _RES_ **44**, 389–92.

Stolper, W. F. and Samuelson, P. A. (1941) Protection and real wages, _RES_ **9**, 58–73. In Samuelson (1966a).

Suppe, F. (1977) _The Structure of Scientific Theories_. University of Illinois Press.

Swan, T. (1956) Economic growth and capital accumulation, _Economic Record_ **32**, 334–61. Part in Harcourt and Laing (1971).

Sweezy, P. (1939) Demand under conditions of oligopoly, _JPE_ **47**, 568–73.

Sweezy, P. (1942) _The Theory of Capitalist Development_. London.

Sweezy, P. (1949) Introduction to 1949 edn of Böhm-Bawerk (1896).

Sylos-Labini, P. (1962) _Oligopoly and Technical Progress_. Cambridge, Mass.

Tarshis, L. (1939) Changes in real and money wages, *EJ* **49**, 150ff.

Taussig, F. W. (1892) Reciprocity, *QJE* **7**, 26–39.

Taussig, F. W. (1911) *Principles of Economics*. New York.

Taussig, F. W. (1917) International trade under depreciated paper. A contribution to theory, *QJE* **31**, 380ff.

Taussig, F. W. (1927) *International Trade*. New York.

Taussig, F. W. (1924) Alfred Marshall, *QJE* **39**, 1–14.

Taylor, A. J. (1972) *Laissez-faire and State Intervention in Nineteenth Century Britain*. London: Macmillan.

Thornton, H. (1802) *An Essay on the Nature of the Paper Credit of Great Britain*, ed. F. A. Hayek, 1939. London.

Thünen, J. H. v (1826) *Die Isolierte Staat*.

Thurow, L. C. (1983) *Dangerous Currents: the State of Economics*. Oxford: Oxford University Press.

Tinbergen, J. (1935) Quantitative Fragen der Konjunkturpolitik, *WA* **42**, 316–99.

Tinbergen, J. (1939) *Business Cycles in the United States of America, 1919–32*.

Tinbergen, J. (1952) *On the Theory of Economic Policy*. Amsterdam.

Tobin, J. (1952) A survey of the theory of rationing, *Ecta* **20**, 521–53.

Tobin, J. (1958) Liquidity preference as behaviour towards risk, *RES* **25**, 65–86.

Tobin, J. (1960) Towards a general Kaldorian theory of distribution: a note, *RES* **27**, 119–20.

Tobin, J. (1963) Commercial banks as creators of money, in D. Carson (ed.) *Banking and Monetary Studies*. Homewood, Ill.

Tobin, J. (1965) Money and Economic Growth, *Ecta* **33**, 671–84.

Tobin, J. (1969) A general equilibrium approach to monetary theory, *JMCB* **1**, 15–29.

Tobin, J. (1970) Money and Income: post hoc ergo propter hoc? *QJE* **84**, 301–17.

Tobin, J. and Houthaker, H. (1951) The effects of rationing on demand elasticities, *RES* **18**, 1–14.

Tomlinson, J. (1981) *Problems of British Economic Policy, 1870–1945*. London: Methuen.

Tooke, T. (1838) *A History of Prices*. London.

Tooke, T. (1844) *An Inquiry into the Currency Principle*. London.

Torrens, R. (1821) *An Essay on the Production of Wealth*. London.

Toulmin, S. (1972) *Human Understanding*. Oxford: Clarendon Press.

Toynbee, A. (1908) *Lectures on the Industrial Revolution of the Eighteenth Century in England*.

Triffin, R. (1940) *Monopolistic Competition and General Equilibrium Theory*. Cambridge, Mass.

Tugan-Baranovsky, M. (1894) *Industrial Crises in England* (in Russian). German translation 1901; French translation 1913.

Uzawa, H. (1961) On a two-sector model of economic growth, *RES* **29**, 40–7.

Uzawa, H. (1962) On the stability of Edgeworth's barter process, *IER* **3**, 218ff.

Uzawa, H. (1973) Towards a Keynesian model of monetary growth. In Mirrlees and Stern (1973).

Veblen, T. B. (1898) Why is economics not an evolutionary science? *QJE* **12**, 373–97. In Veblen (1919).

Veblen, T. B. (1899) *The Theory of the Leisure Class*. New York.

Veblen, T. B. (1899–1900) The preconceptions of economic science, *QJE* **13**, 121–50, 396–426; **14**, 240–69. In Veblen (1919).

Veblen, T. B. (1904) *Theory of Business Enterprise*. New York.

Veblen, T. B. (1906) Professor Clark's economics, *QJE* **22**, 147–95. In Veblen (1919).

Veblen, T. B. (1906–7) Socialist economics of Karl Marx and his followers, *QJE* **20**, 575–95; **21**, 299–322.

Veblen, T. B. (1914) *The Insight of Workmanship and the State of the Industrial Arts.*

Veblen, T. B. (1915) *Imperial Germany and the Industrial Revolution.* London.

Veblen, T. B. (1919) *The Place of Science in Modern Civilization and Other Essays.* New York.

Veblen, T. B. (1921) *Engineers and the Price System.* New York.

Vernon, R. (1966) International investment and international trade in the product cycle, *QJE* **80**, 190–207.

Villard, D. (1948) Monetary theory. In Ellis (1948).

Viner, J. (1924a) *Canada's Balance of International Indebtedness.* Cambridge, Mass.

Viner, J. (1924b) The most-favoured nation clause in American commercial treaties, *JPE* **32**, 101–29.

Viner, J. (1931) The most-favoured nation clause, *Index* **6**, 2–17.

Viner, J. (1937) *Studies in the Theory of International Trade.* London.

Viner, J. (1941) Marshall's economics in relation to the man and to his times, *AER* **31**, 223–35.

Viner, J. (1950) *The Customs Union Issue.* London.

Viner, J. (1958) Modest proposal for some stress on scholarship in graduate training, in *The Long View and the Short.* Glencoe, Ill.

Wakefield, E. G. (1833) *England and America*, in *Collected Works of Edward Gibbon Wakefield*, ed. M. F. Lloyd Pritchard, 1968. Glasgow.

Wald, A. (1933–4) On the unique non-negative solvability of the new production equations. Translated in Baumol and Goldfield (1968).

Walker, F. A. (1876) *The Wages Question.* London.

Walras, L. (1874) *Elements of Pure Economics.* Translated by W. Jaffe, 1954. London: George Allen and Unwin.

Walras, L. (1896) *Etudes d'Economie Politique Appliquée.* Paris.

Walras, L. (1898) *Etudes d'Economie Sociale.* Paris.

Walras, L. (1965) *Correspondence of Leon Walras and Related Papers*, ed. W. Jaffe. Amsterdam: North Holland.

Wan, H. Y. (1971) *Economic Growth.* New York: Harcourt Brace Jouanovitch.

Ward, B. (1972) *What's Wrong with Economics?.* New York: Basic Books.

Weber, M. (1904) *The Protestant Ethic and the Spirit of Capitalism.* Translated by T. Parsons, 1930. London: Allen and Unwin.

Weintraub, E. R. (1979) *Microfoundations.* Cambridge: Cambridge University Press.

Weintraub, E. R. (1982) Substantive mountains and methodological molehills, *JPKE* **5**, 295–303. In Caldwell (1984).

Weintraub, S. (ed.) (1977) *Modern Economic Thought*, Oxford: Basil Blackwell.

West, E. (1815) *Essay on the Application of Capital to Land.*

Wheatley, J. (1807) *An Essay on the Theory of Money*, vol. 1.

Whitaker, J. K. (1974) The Marshallian system in 1881: distribution and growth, *EJ* **84**, 1ff.

Whitaker, J. K. (ed.) (1975) *The Early Writings of Alfred Marshall, 1867–1890*, with introduction by editor. London: Macmillan.

Whitaker, J. K. (1977) Some neglected aspects of Alfred Marshall's economics and social thought, *HOPE* **9**, 161–97.

Whitman, M. v N. (1975) Global monetarism and the monetary approach to the balance of payments, *Brookings Papers on Economic Activity* 491ff.

Wicksell, K. (1893) *Value, Capital and Rent.* Translated by E. Frowein, 1954. London.
Wicksell, K. (1898) *Interest and Prices.* Translated by R. F. Kahn, 1936. London.
Wicksell, K. (1906) *Lectures on Political Economy,* 2 vols. Translated by E. Cassen, 1934. London.
Wicksell, K. (1918) International freights and prices, *QJE* **32**.
Wicksteed, P. (1894) *Essay on the Coordination of the Laws of Distribution.* LSE series of reprints. London: LSE.
Wieser, F. v (1893) *Natural Value,* translated 1893. New York: A. M. Kelley, 1971.
Wieser, F. v (1913) *Social Economics.* Translated by A. F. Hinrichs, 1927. London.
Wieser, F. v (1929) *Gesammelte Abhandlungen.*
Wilber, C. K. and Harrison, R. S. (1978) The methodological basis of institutional economics: pattern modelling, storytelling, and holism, *JEI* **12**, 61–89.
Wilber, C. K. and Jemeson, K. P. (1983) *An Inquiry into the Poverty of Economics.* London: University of Notre Dame Press.
Williams, J. H. (1920) *Argentine International Trade under Inconvertible Currency.* Cambridge, Mass.
Williamson, O. E. (1977) Firms and markets. In Weintraub (1977).
Winch, D. (1963) Classical economics and the case for colonization, *Eca* **30**. In Shaw (1970).
Winch, D. (1965) *Classical Political Economy and the Colonies.* London.
Winch, D. (1969) *Economics and Policy.* London.
Winch, D. (1973) The emergence of economics as a science, 1750–1870. In C. M. Cipolla (ed.) *The Fontana Economic History of Europe,* vol. 3. London: Fontana.
Winch, D. (1983) Science and the legislator: Adam Smith and after, *EJ* **93**, 501ff.
Wiseman, J. (1983) *Beyond Positive Economics,* Proceedings of BA 1981. London: Macmillan.
Wood, J. C. (1983) *British Economists and the Empire.* London: Croom Helm.
Wood, S. (1888) A new view of the theory of wages: 1, *QJE* **3**, 60–86.
Wood, S. (1889) A new view of wages: 2, *QJE* **3**, 462–80.
Young, A. A. (1925) The Trend of Economics, as seen by some younger American economists, *QJE* **39**, 155–83.
Zeuthen, (1933) Das Prinzip der Knappheit, technische Kombination und okonomische Qualität, *ZN* **7**, 1–24.

# Index